AUSTRALIA
Where the Fun Is

Lauren Goodyear & Thalassa Skinner

Mustang Publishing Co.
Memphis, TN

Disclaimer

As you plan your trip with this guide, please remember that some things probably have changed. Though the book was as accurate as possible at publication, it's inevitable that pubs will close, restaurants will move, hours will vary, and prices will rise. We urge you to use this book as a general reference and always call ahead to confirm specific details. We accept no responsibility for any problems you encounter as a result of an inaccuracy in this book.

Of course, if you do find an error—or if you'd like to criticize or praise our effort—we'd love to hear from you. Write us in care of Mustang Publishing, P.O. Box 3004, Memphis, TN 38173.

Library of Congress Cataloging-in-Publication Data

Goodyear, Lauren
    Australia : where the fun is / Lauren Goodyear, Thalassa Skinner.
      p. cm.
    ISBN 0-914457-20-9 (paper : acid-free paper) : $12.95
    1. Australia–Description and travel–1981- –Guide-books.
2. Amusements–Australia–Guide-books.   I. Skinner, Thalassa.
II. Title.
DU105.2.G66 1991
919.404'63–dc20   88-60465
                                             CIP

Printed on acid-free paper.

10 9 8 7 6 5 4 3 2 1

Acknowledgments

Without the support and infinite patience of friends and family, this book would not exist. So, with all our gratitude and love, we thank our Moms, Toby and Cathy; our Dads, Rummy and Brian; Nanny, Bob, and Bev; Sandy and Lesley; Mark and Didy; and all of the Aussie Skinners who gave us a home, advice, and Jacob's Creek when we most needed it.

Also: Alison, Greg, Annie, Paula Luv, George Packard, Neil and Margaret Williams, Mark Gummer and Michelle Mearns, Tony Horan, Kelly Talbot, Charlie Lord, Noah Emmerich, Winifred and Stuart Barrett, and everyone else who selflessly contributed time and energy to our cause.

Plus: Diane Anderson at Air New Zealand, Peggy Bendel at the Australian Tourist Commission, Allan Williams at Australian Airlines, Deluxe Coachlines, Railways of Australia, Joanie Williams at World Expeditions, Contiki Holidays, and the many wonderful people who helped us at the Australian Youth Hostel Association.

Finally, our biggest thank you to Merv Godfrey, who supplied many of the maps in this book. Merv's generous assistance exemplifies all the best traits of Australians.

Lauren Goodyear & Lassa Skinner

Preface

The idea for this book originated in Adelaide, in a coin laundromat, in a hailstorm. Our trip was almost over, and we were looking for a way to return to Australia. Researching a guidebook seemed like the ideal excuse—a guide, we decided, that would be for travelers like ourselves, who want to see the real Australia beyond the "checklist" sights, without spending an arm and a leg.

To the great surprise of our families and friends, we did it. Assisted by those who believed in our mission—our parents, our publisher Rollin Riggs, the Australian Tourist Commission, the Australian Youth Hostel Association, Air New Zealand, and, most important, dozens of generous Aussies who fed and housed and loved us—we circumnavigated the Australian continent, exploring, talking, probing, having fun, and recording most everything we found.

So, here is our "excuse." We've included all the secrets we discovered, plus every bit of practical information we could possibly dig up. We hope our readers will love Australia as much as these two Yanks did.

Editor's Note

At press time, we learned that **Deluxe Coachlines**, one of the main bus companies in Australia, was having severe financial difficulty and was attempting a re-organization. We urge you to check carefully with your travel agent and the Australian bus companies before planning to travel by bus.

Contents

Australia's Vital Statistics

Population: just over 16 million

Sheep population: 160 million

Area: 2,966,144 square miles (roughly the size of the continental U.S.)

Rate of literacy: nearly 100%

Australia is one of the most urbanized nations in the world—80% of the population lives along the eastern seaboard between Brisbane and Adelaide. Almost everyone else lives on the fertile edges of the continent, leaving a vast inland region populated mostly by cattle, sheep, and, in the most arid areas, only desert plants and animals.

Australia is comprised of six states and two territories:

State/Territory	Population	Capital
New South Wales (NSW)	5.5 million	Sydney
Queensland (QLD)	2.6 million	Brisbane
South Australia (SA)	1.4 million	Adelaide
Tasmania (Tas.)	500,000	Hobart
Victoria (Vic.)	4 million	Melbourne
Western Australia (WA)	1.5 million	Perth
Northern Territory (NT)	150,000	Darwin
Australian Capital Territory (ACT)	250,000	Canberra

Timor Sea Melville Island Cobourg Peninsu

Bathurst Is

DARWIN ★

Christmas Is

Adelaide River 354

Joseph Bonaparte Gulf

Kalumburu

Wyndham Kununurra Timber Creek

Dal Wate

Lake Argyle 626

KIMBERLEY Ord R 910

Top Springs

Cockatoo Island Kalkarindji L.We

Derby Geikie Gorge Halls Creek

Indian Ocean Fitzroy 696 Victoria NORTHE

Broome Fitzroy Crossing 1 Tennan

TERRITO

616 Wolf Creek Meteorite Crater TANAMI DESERT

GREAT SANDY DESERT

N

Port Hedland +Mt.Goldsworthy L.White

Dampier Marble Bar Telfer L.Mackay

Barrow Is Karratha

Onslow 95 MACDONNELL RANGES

North West Cape Wittenoom Roy Hill

Exmouth Tom Price Tropic of Capricorn T

Mt.Meharry Palm Valley

Paraburdoo Newman L.Disappointment Docker River Mt. Olga 242

907 Ashburton 912 GIBSON DESERT + Ayers Rock Yulara

PILBARA

L.Macleod Gascoyne R WESTERN

Carnarvon ★ R L.Carnegie Warburton

Shark Bay Murchison AUSTRALIA GREAT VICTORIA DESERT

Denham 483

Meekatharra Serpentine Lakes SO

Kalbarri Co

Mt. Magnet 762 Laverton L.Maurice Mar

Geraldton ★ L.Barlee Leonora

L.Moore NULLARBOR PLAIN

95 AUSTRALIAN RAILWAY

478 DARLING Coolgardie Kalgoorlie TRANS Eucla

New Norcia 94 Boulder Madura

1 Northam 723 Kambalda 725

PERTH ★ Hyden Norseman

Rottnest Island Balladonia

Fremantle Narrogin Great Australian Bight

Bunbury RANGE 401

Busselton 682

Manjimup Esperance

Augusta Pemberton

Albany Southern Ocean

Scale 0 500 1000 kilometres

0 500 miles

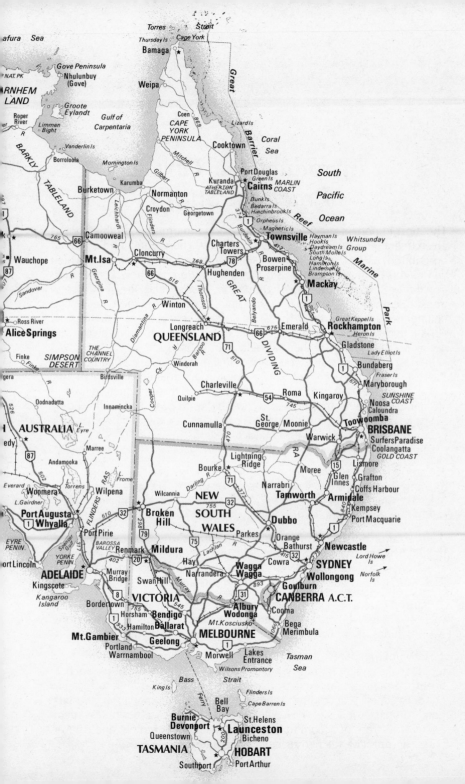

Introduction, Part I: Practical Stuff

The most important practical and background information in this book is given in the introduction to each state chapter. There, you'll find a general description of *When to Go, Itinerary* (highlights and a logical order in which you might see them), *Getting Around, Information* (i.e., how to find additional travel information), *Accommodation, History,* and one or more sections on something particular to that state. For instance, the Queensland chapter includes sections on the Great Barrier Reef, rainforests, diving, and "Box Jellyfish and Other Nasties." Read the state introductions before you get to Australia, and use them to help plan your trip.

In most Australian states, you'll arrive first in the capital city and explore the rest of the state from there. State chapters are organized to reflect this; a section on the state capital immediately follows the introduction (except Tasmania, where most visitors arrive on the north coast first), followed by "Trips From" the capital. Other parts of the state are divided into sections according to geographical and political regions.

Each major city is divided as follows:

1. Getting There: Includes bus and train options, general flight information, and how to reach the city from the airport on arrival. This gives you a general idea of your options—always check with travel agents and individual transport companies for their latest offerings.

2. Orientation and Practical Information: Includes a description of the city's major areas of activity, general practical information, and a list of important telephone numbers and addresses. You'll probably flip back to the list over and over again as you plan travel around the state.

3. Transportation: Describes the public transportation system with details such as where to buy tickets, where to get maps, and special fare options. Also includes, if applicable, bike and car rental and driving tips.

4. Accommodation: Starts with the best budget options, follows with good to adequate budget options, ends with more expensive options (such as licensed hotels). In large cities, listings are divided according to location or, occasionally, according to the type of accommodation (hostels; hotels/motels). All hostels have kitchen and laundry facilities unless specified. Other types of accommodation, such as hotels, motels, and caravan parks, do not have kitchen or laundry facilities unless specified.

5. *Things to See and Do:* This section directs you to the most distinctive and important places to visit first, with descriptions organized in the order in which you'd most logically and efficiently see them by walking or public transport. Be prepared for opening hours that shift unpredictably, especially in the city's non-tourist season.

6. *Food:* Use this section primarily to find good meals at cheap prices. The specific listings will give you an idea of what's available, but **beware**! Restaurants are here one day, gone the next. Off-season hours are often reduced and, in summer, some proprietors just disappear. Don't make the extra effort to get to a place until you've called to confirm hours, prices, and existence. The restaurant listing starts with the best inexpensive meals in town, with an attempt at variety and emphasis on the regional specialty. More expensive restaurants are at the end of the listing; these are always worth the splurge if you have extra cash. We sometimes use Aussie terms: a "main"=an entree, and an "entree"=an appetizer. Cheap=up to $6/main, moderate=$6-$12/main, expensive=above $12/main.

7. *Nightlife:* As with restaurants, the hours, ambiance, and existence of nightclubs are unpredictable at best. Open until "late" means an establishment closes at 2:00am or later, depending on the amount of business on a particular night. For nightlife ideas, check the "Entertainment" listings as well.

8. *Entertainment:* Describes all variety of performances and activities. The section starts with a rundown of performing arts (theater, dance, music), and includes also movie theaters, spectator sports, and sometimes open-air markets and river cruises. We've tried hard to include free entertainment and special discounts.

Chapters on important small cities parallel the format for major cities, though descriptions are less extensive. Chapters on rural areas begin with a general description which, with a quick read, should help you decide whether you're interested in visiting.

Planning an Itinerary

There are a few important things to be aware of before planning your travel around Australia. In Australia, there are no equivalents to the Louvre, the Taj Mahal, or St. Peter's. Its wonders are mostly natural, not cultural, and therefore it's a country best experienced by doing, not just observing. You can't fully appreciate Ayers Rock until you've climbed it, or the Great Barrier Reef until you've dived it, or Kakadu National Park until you've swum in its freshwater lagoons and chased a wombat from the campfire.

One of Australia's most unique characteristics is the outback. Outback territory covers most of the country and yet, amazingly, it's quite possible to visit Australia and never see it. But make sure you don't miss out!

The Australian people are the country's greatest asset. They certainly live up to their reputation of warmth, openness, and easy-going charm, and you'll want to meet and get to know them. Because they are so friendly, this isn't too difficult—but it does require making an effort to get off the beaten track of other international travelers, and out of cities. It also requires spontaneity, which is why before making an itinerary, you should consider **not** planning every move. Take it from the Aussies themselves, and go with the flow.

How Much Time?

One of the most common misconceptions about traveling in Australia is that it can be seen in just a few weeks. On the contrary, Australia is gigantic. The state of Western Australia alone is the size of Europe and the British Isles combined. If you have just a few weeks, we suggest limiting yourself to one or two regions, unless you have the money to fly. For most travelers, those two regions will be northern Queensland and New South Wales, and possibly Central Australia (i.e. Alice Springs and Ayers Rock). If you're only in Australia for a few weeks, keep in mind that your travels don't have to start in Sydney or Melbourne. International flights fly directly into Cairns (driving Sydney-Cairns takes 40 hours), and you can also get connecting flights into Rockhampton, Airlie Beach, Townsville (all in Queensland), and all state capitals.

We think you need at least two months to truly soak the place in, and you could easily spend an entire year (if you can convince immigration authorities to renew your visa). This is especially the case for those determined to see Australia's outback and discover its frontiers. Seeing Western Australia, South Australia, and the Northern Territory will give you an entirely different perspective on the country than a visit to just the eastern states.

Highlights

We also think it's important to get off the beaten path, especially because there are so many incredible places that aren't besieged by tourists. But most of the well-known attractions are popular with good reason, and there are a few which you shouldn't miss:

Sydney (New South Wales)
The Great Barrier Reef (Queensland)
The Whitsunday Islands (Queensland)
Kakadu National Park (Northern Territory)
Ayers Rock and the Olgas (Northern Territory)
Wine Valleys (see "Drink" in *Australia: An Overview*)

Highlights unknown to most international travelers include:

The Bungle Bungle Range and the Hamersley Gorges (Western Australia)
Tropical rainforests of far northern Queensland
The Great Ocean Road (Victoria)
Kangaroo Island and Coober Pedy (South Australia)
Tasmania (especially if you haven't been to New Zealand)
An outback experience

Getting to the Outback

Exactly what is the "outback"? To most foreigners, the term conjures up images of ranch country (in Aussie lingo, "station country"), but the meaning is actually more general: outback is back country or, simply, the bush. Outback is also an adjective and an adverb: An outback town is a remote town. One can go outback, meaning head for the bush.

The concept of "outback" is integral to Australia's history and Australians' concept of their place in the environment. Traditionally, "outback" referred to any area outside of the city, because not too long ago Australia consisted only of cities and harsh, uninviting inland. Now, civilized countryside buffers the cities from the outback, but the city/country dichotomy is still quite pronounced.

Ancient, rust-red mountain ranges, weird rock formations, and desert moonscapes weathered to virtual flatness—all are features of the outback that possess an almost mystical quality for travelers who have never known its desolation. The largest privately-owned properties in the world, some stretching 12,000 square miles, spread across much of this land.

With some planning, it's perfectly feasible to get into the outback. If you can, go to Australia's remote northwest corner, a region known as the Kimberley (also called "the Kimberleys," a reference to the ancient mountains that spread across the area). The Kimberley coast is literally Australia's last frontier, with areas so rugged that they are as yet unexplored, except from the air. Intense heat, winter drought, and monsoons kept it almost uninhabited until the discovery of rich mineral deposits in the 1980's. The road through was finally paved in 1986. There are other reasons to get up to the Kimberley, most notably the Bungle Bungle Range, where fantastic, beehive-shaped domes and plunging gorges are just now being explored.

If you can't get to Western Australia, go to Lightning Ridge or Broken Hill (New South Wales), Carnarvon Gorge (Queensland), Coober Pedy or the Flinders Ranges (South Australia). Ayers Rock and the Olgas, in the Northern Territory, are certainly worth visiting, but their commercialism keeps them from being truly outback. The remainder of the Northern Territory, however, is sparsely populated and seldom seen. If you can, take the Stuart Highway from South Australia through Alice Springs and up to Darwin (or vice versa). Other remote, paved routes are the Eyre Highway from Adelaide to Perth, across the Nullarbor Plain (which also can be done by rail); and Western Australia's North West Coastal Highway, from Perth to Broome. There are several four-wheel drive tracks through central desert lands, including the Gunbarrel Highway (Ayers Rock to Western Australia) and the Birdsville track (Birdsville, QLD to Maree, S.A.). See the introduction to South Australia for other outback routes.

Visiting a ranch ("station") takes some leg-work and a bit of ingenuity. Travelers who get out to stations usually either make the right friends and/or get a job on one (see *Appendix*).

Note: If you're planning to camp and drive in extreme remote regions, you need to understand how to take care of yourself out there. Always get plenty of advice before venturing into the bush. Bush survival courses are available in some cities.

Finding Your Favorite Activities

Sailing: Sailing fanaticism among the Aussies crosses all class and regional lines; it's a national obsession that the 1987 America's Cup triumph only inflated. The Sydney-Hobart Yacht Race, Australia's most famous annual regatta, begins in Sydney on Boxing Day (December 26) and finishes in Hobart, Tasmania on New Year's Day. It's worth making it to either end for the festivities, especially if sailing is your thing.

Fremantle, just south of Perth, hosted the America's Cup and is the yachting mecca of the nation. Lancelin Beach, north of Perth, is also known for its world-class windsurfing and sailing. The *Leeuwin* offers an education in sailing on its cruises from Perth to Carnarvon and back (call the Sail Training Association in Fremantle at 09-430-4105). Sailing around the Whitsunday Islands (QLD) is spectacular, and any number of highly-recommended day and overnight sails are available from nearby Airlie Beach. There's opportunity for sailing in the Top End (Darwin area) as well—expensive, but well worth it. Contact World Expeditions or Cobourg Marine (see *The Cobourg Peninsula, Northern Territory*).

You can rent sailboats and windsurfers in most Australian cities and coastal communities.

Diving: It hardly needs to be mentioned that the Great Barrier Reef is one of the best places in the world to scuba dive. Details on diving are in the introduction to Queensland under "Great Barrier Reef" and "Diving." Western Australia also offers some fantastic diving, including the waters surrounding Rottnest Island, the Abrolhos Islands, the Monte Bello Islands, and Ningaloo Reef (off Exmouth). See *Trips from Perth* for general diving information in W.A. The underwater limestone caverns at Piccaninnie Ponds, S.A. (near Mt. Gambier) are known by expert divers, while Kangaroo Island and the coast of the Eyre Peninsula, also in S.A., offer more diving for the experienced.

Australia is a fantastic place to learn to dive. There are scores of certification courses to choose from in Queensland, the cheapest being in Cairns. Divers must have a C- card, as proof of certification is required by any reputable outfit.

Surfing: Surfers ("surfies") are a visible and distinct subculture in seaside towns of northern New South Wales and southern Queensland, particularly Surfers Paradise and Coolangatta on Queensland's Gold Coast; Noosa Heads and the Sunshine Coast (QLD); and Byron Bay and Lennox Head (northern N.S.W.). Surf boards are available for hire at most hostels and hotels in these places. If you'd like to watch, get to Sydney for the January surf carnivals (in true Aussie fashion, the festivities dominate the actual surfing at these events). Most people don't know that Australia's southwest coast offers fantastic surfing as well (waves are rumored to reach 5 meters!). Margaret River holds international competitions in November, and beaches around Perth are also very good.

Hiking: Australia's hiking spots are far too numerous to mention here specifically. Information on hiking ("bushwalking") near metropolitan areas can be found at the beginning of "Trips From" sections. There is also extensive information on hiking in the introductions to Tasmania and Victoria, where hiking is especially popular. Chapters on particular national parks include relevant hiking information, and worthwhile walks and hikes are mentioned throughout the text. Keep in mind that in arid regions, trails are sometimes closed during summer because of fire bans, just as monsoonal flooding can wash away hiking plans in the tropics. You can rent camping equipment in major cities.

Biking: You can't go wrong biking the flattest continent in the world. However, the isolation of many roads and the problem of water supply are very real; anyone undertaking a bike trip in remote or arid regions needs to consult local experts first. Australia's most popular bike trip is around Tasmania; the southwest corner of Western Australia is also popular.

You can hire good bicycles equipped for cycle-touring once you're in Australia, but serious bikers usually bring their own. Bikes can be brought over with no extra charge on some airlines; some charge up to $50.

Horseriding: The high plains of Australia's Great Dividing Range offer some of the world's most romantic and scenic riding country. Horse ranches in the Blue Mountains, Snowy Mountains (both in NSW), and Victorian Alps offer guided or unguided pack trips, ranging from one to several days. Riding is also popular in the Darling Ranges, just east of Perth.

Skiing: Skiing is the best way to enjoy Australia's rare snow, and it can be done downhill or cross-country in the Snowies (NSW), the Victorian Alps, and Tasmania. Tasmanian skiing is cheaper than elsewhere, but not as good. High ski season is June-September, with the most reliable snow in August. Cross-country and downhill equipment is available in major cities and at ski resorts. The only hitch is a shortage of lodging; reservations should be made several months in advance.

Fishing: Serious anglers should bring their own equipment, as the opportunity to rent tackle is pretty rare. However, charters for deep-sea fishing are offered from most big ports. Fishing in the ocean is possible almost anywhere along Australia's endless coasts—Cairns on the east coast and Exmouth on the west coast are the best-known spots. Fly-fishing is best in Tasmania's central plateau, the Victorian Alps, the Snowy Mountains, and Western Australia's southwestern corner around Pemberton.

When to Go
We can't overemphasize the importance of planning your travel to follow the good weather. When Australian weather is bad (which, incidentally, isn't all that often), it's really bad. Summer monsoons are the main culprit. Keep these general rules in mind:

1. Don't plan on seeing the northerly tropics (i.e. Queensland, north of Cairns; Darwin and Kakadu National Park in the Northern Territory; and north of Exmouth, Western Australia) from December until the beginning or middle of April. During this time, monsoonal rains of "the wet" render

the tropics virtually unnavigable. Even if you did get there, it wouldn't be much fun. Summer is also prohibitively hot in Central Australia and all inland areas, except to the most determined travelers. Stick to the southeastern, southwestern, and southern coasts during summer, or visit Tasmania.

2. Winter (June-August) is chilly and rainy in southern coastal areas. This is the best season to visit Central Australia (Alice Springs, Ayers Rock, etc.) and the Top End (Darwin and Kakadu National Park).

3. Transition seasons (September-November; March-June) are the best times to travel.

4. For more specifics on prime times (or awful times) to visit a given area, see "When to Go" in each state's introduction.

Getting There

Airfares to the South Pacific aren't cheap. However, flights to Australia are cheaper now than ever, and it looks like this trend will continue. To find the best deal, research your options with a good travel agent who has your best interests in mind, like CIEE and STA Travel, both of which cater to budget-conscious travelers (explained later in this section). Keep in mind that the least expensive time to head Down Under is April-September; avoid peak season, December-February.

Currently, the main carriers to Australia and New Zealand from continental North America are Air New Zealand, Qantas, United, Continental, Canadian Pacific, and U.T.A. French Airlines (which goes via Asia). Hawaiian Airlines, which leaves from Hawaii, offers some terrific deals. If you have a choice, fly Air New Zealand. Every year they win awards for the best international services, and deservedly so. Air New Zealand has some of the best prices, and they offer special discounts to students through STA Travel.

Most U.S.-Australia flights leave from the west coast of the U.S. Non-stop Los Angeles-Sydney takes 14 hours, Los Angeles-Auckland 12-13 hours, but with stops in Hawaii, Tahiti, Fiji, and/or New Zealand, the trip takes closer to 18-20 hours (and most flights make a stop to refuel).

Budget travelers have a few fare options on the major airlines, though discount travel agents deal mainly with APEX fares—invariably cheaper than economy tickets but with more restrictions: minimum and maximum stay lengths, limited stopovers, and hefty cancellation fees. "Standby" tickets are generally cheaper than APEX fares, but more risky. Your seat is unconfirmed until just before departure, and you may be bumped off the flight if the space is filled by a better-paying customer (in offseason, this is unlikely).

Keep in mind that there are plenty of package deals available, such an APEX ticket offered by Air New Zealand that originates in the U.S. and allows four stopovers in South Pacific countries (including New Zealand), good for 6-12 months. Those traveling more extensively should consider an Around-the-World ticket, a package offered by most major airlines. For a set price (starting at about $2,200), the ticket is good for travel around the globe in one direction on a specific network of airlines.

Be sure to ask your travel agent about discounts on domestic travel within Australia and New Zealand that come with the purchase of certain international flights. For example, Air New Zealand offers special fares around New Zealand on Mt. Cook Airlines, if you travel with them from North America. Also, traveling within Australia on international carriers can be cheaper than using the national airlines.

Those who aren't coming from North America can find especially good ticket prices to the South Pacific from London, Singapore, and Hong Kong. London's "bucket shops" and discount travel agents in Singapore and Hong Kong are easy to find. Darwin (Northern Territory) is Australia's cheapest gateway from Southeast Asia.

Finally, be sure to join any frequent flyer/bonus mileage program offered before you take off. There are many miles (sorry, kilometers) to accumulate between North America and the South Pacific.

Where to Buy Tickets

For the best deals and advice, go to the experts—STA Travel or CIEE's Council Travel. Though each specializes in discount fares for students, people under 26, and teachers, they'll find the best fares for anyone, regardless of age or profession. They are the only main competitors for discount travel between the U.S. and Australia or New Zealand.

STA Travel is an Australia-based student and budget travelers' travel agency. They specialize in deals to the South Pacific, offering flights to Australia and New Zealand (sometimes through Asia) for as little as $850, and all their fares include free stopovers in Honolulu, Fiji, Tahiti, or New Zealand. STA Travel can also book discounted domestic flights in Canada and the U.S. (if added onto an international flight) and discounts for domestic air travel within Australia and New Zealand. International Student IDs are also available from them. Call their U.S. toll-free number to locate the office nearest to you (800-777-0112). In Canada, contact CUTS at (416) 979-2406.

Council Travel is the travel division of Council on International Educational Exchange (CIEE). Like STA Travel, they offer special deals on airfare to the South Pacific, as well as discount transportation within Australia and New Zealand. In addition, their offices issue on-the-spot YHA cards and International Student IDs. CIEE is also the primary source for student work abroad (see *Appendix*). Contact their New York headquarters at 205 East 42nd St. (phone 212-661-1450) for location details.

Entry and Departure Regulations

There is strict control over the importation of any fruits, vegetables, seeds, plants, and animals into Australia. They'll even spray the airplane cabin with a disinfectant before you're allowed to disembark.

Keep $10 (Australian) with your plane ticket. When you wave your final goodbye, you'll have to hand it over for departure tax. (Count your blessings— it used to be $20!)

One person can lawfully carry out of Australia free of duty: $400 of purchases (retail value) and a liter of alcohol (you can get away with two regular-sized bottles of wine). If you want to take more, you'll have to pay Australian duty tax on it. The amount of tax levied is up to the individual customs officials. If you foresee running into problems with the $400 limit you can mail things home, but single mailings can't contain more than $50 worth of goods or they'll be taxed.

Documents: All visitors to Australia and/or New Zealand must have a valid passport and visa (for Australia), proof of funds to support them through their stay, a plane ticket proving on-going travel with a confirmed departure date, and the necessary documents (like visas) for their next destination. Also, anyone entering Australia from a yellow fever-infested country must have a valid vaccination.

Those are the only vital documents you'll need. Otherwise, an International Youth Hostel Card may save a bit of time on the other end (you'll need a membership before you can stay in a YHA hostel), but it's not necessary. You can join YHA while you're in Australia. An international driver's license isn't required for renting or driving a car in Australia. All you need is a valid driver's license from home. Most travel passes for transportation within Australia can be bought once there, except the Austrailpass (rail) and air passes.

If you're a student, get an International Student Identification Card (ISIC). It is only occasionally needed for entrance to sights (a regular school ID almost always suffices to get student discounts). However, becoming an ISIC holder makes you eligible for special discounts on travel to and around Australia and New Zealand (for example, it gives you a 25% discount on Australian Airlines flights and a 10% discount on Deluxe Coachlines' Koala Pass). Also, purchase of an ISIC includes limited accident/medical travel insurance. For more information, contact the Council on International Education Exchange (CIEE).

Visas: Everyone, except holders of a valid Australian or New Zealand passport, must have a visa to enter Australia. The maximum stay for visitors to both countries is six months, and the visa is good for ten years (meaning you could potentially spend six months of every year in Australia for up to ten years on the same visa). You can apply (and pay) for an extension while in Australia, but it's not always granted.

To get a visa (which is free), contact the appropriate Australian consulate for your state or area (see *Appendix*) and complete the following checklist:

1. Completed visa application form (issued by consulate).
2. Valid passport with at least two blank pages.
3. One recent passport-type photograph.
4. If under 18 and unaccompanied by parents, a notarized letter of permission from your parent(s).
5. If applying by mail, enclose a self-addressed, stamped envelope.

If you apply for your visa in person, the process will be much quicker (48 hours) and safer. If applying by mail, make sure to use registered or certified mail on both legs of the trip.

For New Zealand, no visa is required for US or Canadian citizens staying fewer than three months. If you want to stay longer, you can apply for permission while you're there.

Helpful Addresses:

Bureau of Consular Affairs/
Passport Services
Dept. of State
Washington, DC 20524
(202) 647-0518

U.S. Customs Service
PO Box 7407
Washington, DC 20044
(202) 566-8195

Australian Embassy
1601 Massachusetts Ave. NW
Washington, DC 20036
(202) 797-3000

New Zealand Embassy
37 Observation Circle NW
Washington, DC 20008
(202) 328-4800

Australian High Commission (Canada)
50 O'Conner St., Suite 170
Ottawa, Ontario K1P 5MP
(613) 236- 0841

New Zealand High Commission
(Canada)
Suite 801, Metropolitan House
99 Bank St.
Ottawa, Ontario K1P CG3
(613) 238-5991

Health Insurance

Before you travel anywhere, make sure your medical insurance will cover you overseas.

If your stay in Australia is for more than six months, you can enroll in Australian Medicare upon arrival in Australia. For more information, contact the Australian Embassy or write "Medicare, GPO 9822" in any Australian capital city.

Money

Investing in travelers checks saved our necks on one memorable occasion, and we highly recommend carrying them whenever you travel. You'll usually pay a 1% commission when you buy them, and banks often charge a small transaction fee when they're cashed, but the extra charges are worth it. Travelers checks are refunded if stolen, can be cashed almost anywhere, and get a higher trade-in value than cash. They are also useful in remote areas of Australia, where banks are scarce. It doesn't really matter what kind of travelers checks you buy, and you won't need to have them in Australian dollars. Owning American Express travelers checks (or credit card) will allow you to receive mail through their offices.

Most hotels, larger restaurants, and stores in Australia accept at least one of the major American credit cards (Visa, Mastercard, American Express).

It is possible to get cash advances through a major credit card at most Australian banks. However, the banks vary as to which card they'll accept, so you'll have to shop around to find the one that takes yours (for example, Westpac takes Mastercard, and ANZ takes Visa).

There are several ways to prepare for money emergencies. A credit card will get you money on the spot. You can also have money wired for a fee of $10-$15, depending on the home bank. With the time difference, the transaction takes at least a day and could take longer, depending on the size of your home bank and your location in Australia. A lesser-known but far more convenient approach is to obtain a "traveler's letter of credit" from your bank before leaving home, guaranteeing that you have a given amount of credit with that bank. Australian banks will honor this as long as you can prove your identity.

The major Australian banks are Australia and New Zealand Bank (ANZ), Westpac Banking Corporation, National Australia Bank, and Commonwealth Banking Corporation of Australia.

U.S. banks in Australia include Bankers Trust, Bank of America, Chase A.M.P. Bank, and Citibank. British banks are Barclay's Bank (Australia) PLC, and Lloyd's Bank NZA PLC.

Budgeting

Everyone has different interests and budgeting priorities. Someone with lots of gift-demanding relatives will need to bring more money than someone who plans to send a postcard each to Grandma and Aunt Edith and a couple of aerograms to Mom and Dad. The same holds for daily travel expenses. Some are willing to live on next to nothing by camping, cooking for themselves, and hitchhiking; others allow themselves a few luxuries.

The following quoted prices are in Australian dollars. (One Australian dollar equals approximately $.75 U.S.) Don't be scared off by the prices; there are many ways to cut back on costs, and most hostellers pick up a few odd jobs to help with the bills.

Transportation will be your greatest expense. Six-month bus passes cost anywhere from $400 to well over $1,000, depending on how much freedom the pass allows. Expect to spend at least $200 on rental cars or tours, where local transportation is limited. However, you could potentially travel for nothing if you hitchhike. See "Buying a Car" in the *Appendix* for an idea of what to expect in that regard. If you're planning on internal air travel, your transport costs will rise fast.

Set aside between $10-$15 per night for accommodation. This assumes you'll be staying mainly in hostels, doing some camping, and spending occasional nights in licensed hotels or budget motels. Accommodation is most expensive in cities. Country hostels are generally below $10/night, while city hostels can reach $15/night. Of course, the more you camp, the less you'll spend. If you plan to stay in cheap hotels, expect to spend an average of $25/night.

If you buy your own groceries and cook for yourself most of the time, budget $10/day for food, extra for alcohol. However, if you like eating out and would rather drink cognac in the Hilton than beer in the local pub, you'll need to bring substantially more.

Personal items are generally expensive in Australia, costing up to twice as much as at home. Film for your camera, film developing, and postage fees are expensive, too—it costs about $.80 (and rising) to send an airmail postcard to the U.S.

Most importantly, don't deprive yourself of special and unique Australian experiences like diving on the Great Barrier Reef, going in with a group on a four-wheel drive rental to explore the outback, or riding a balloon over the red plains of Central Australia. These extras don't have to completely drain the coffers: allow $300-$600 for one or two splurges.

What to Bring

On most international flights, you're allowed only two pieces of luggage, and neither should weigh more than 70 lbs. Carrying belongings on your back is the only way to travel efficiently and easily. Use a waterproof knapsack (preferably with interior frame and straps that can be zippered under fabric for long-distance travel), and bring a small backpack for the day. A sleeping bag, towel, and flashlight come in handy for hostelling and camping. Many hostels (especially YHA hostels) require that you use a YHA sleeping sheet (or 2 sheets and a pillowcase). We recommend a small tent as well.

Sunglasses and a hat are vital. Carry suntan lotion and insect repellent at all times. Toiletries tend to be expensive, so try to bring what you need. A water bottle is needed for hiking, and a knife, fork, spoon, bowl, and cup are essential for camping (and come in handy for hostelling, too). Binoculars are helpful for animal- and bird-watching. You may want to invest in a telephoto lens for your camera to capture that unique, and often evasive, Aussie fauna on film, and divers may want an underwater camera. A sturdy waterproof jacket is smart, especially if you're going to Tasmania or New Zealand or hitting the monsoon season. Though crime in Australia is not a big worry, a money belt will help you keep track of vital documents and is useful in big cities. Try to do without electrical stuff (i.e. electric razors and blowdryers) unless you want to deal with buying a converter for Australia's 240/250 voltage.

Australians are "casual" dressers, but casual doesn't mean sloppy. Aussie clothing is neat and trendy, especially in the cities, so try to be comfortable but presentable. Sneakers, jeans, and uncollared shirts (for men) are not allowed in nightclubs or casinos. Also, shorts are sometimes barred from restaurants. With regard to clothing and climate, always wear layers. Certainly bring shorts, t-shirts, and a long-sleeve shirt. Bring a turtleneck, heavy sweater, and long underwear for the winter months anywhere south of Brisbane (there's practically no central heating). A sweatsuit is highly recommended (for comfort, exercising, and extremely cold hostels where you're not allowed to use your sleeping bag). Avoid wearing white: Australia's red soil and dust won't leave it white for long.

For your feet, bring sandals, sneakers (or comfortable walking shoes), and a pair of dressier shoes.

Travel and Information Resources

Australian Tourist Commission
489 Fifth Ave., 31st floor
New York, NY 10022
(212) 687-6368

The Australian Tourist Commission is the official government tourist bureau. They are extremely helpful and will do everything in their power to answer your questions or refer you to someone who can. Direct your specific questions to the state commissions, each of which has one or two U.S. offices (see Appendix).

New Zealand Tourist and Publicity Office
10960 Wilshire Blvd., Suite 1530
Los Angeles, CA 90024
(213) 477-8241
*Like its Aussie counterpart, the people in this office couldn't be more help-
ful. Don't hesitate to call them if you have questions.*

American Youth Hostels, Head Office
1017 K Street, N.W.
Washington, DC 20001
(202) 783-4943

American Youth Hostels
75 Spring St.
New York, NY 10012
(212) 431-7100

Canadian Hostelling Association, National Office
333 River Rd., Place Vanier
Tower A Vanier City
Ottawa, Ontario KIL 8H4
(613) 748-5638

STA Travel Head Office
7204 1/2 Melrose Ave.
Los Angeles, CA 90046
(213) 937-5714; (800) 777-0112

Council on International Educational Exchange (CIEE)
205 East 42nd St.
New York, NY 10017
(212) 661-1450 (travel information), (212) 661-1414 (work abroad information)

Canadian Universities Travel Service (CUTS)
187 College St.
Toronto, Ontario M5T 1P7
(416) 979-2406

Introduction, Part II:
Practical Orientation

Getting Around

Getting around Australia is expensive and difficult. Unlike Europe, where distances between destinations are relatively short and efficient transportation systems take you virtually anywhere, Australia is an enormous country with little to see along its vast stretches of road. No matter how you decide to travel, it's costly and often tedious.

The major sights in Australia are primarily natural rather than cultural, so being able to get off the beaten track into scenic and remote territory is crucial. Public transport to such places is limited (some buses run just once a week) or non-existent. And getting around once you reach your destination is almost always difficult, except in major cities. You'll end up taking a tour or renting a car, "moke" (like a golfcart, with a canopy roof), motorcycle, or bicycle.

Keeping these essentials in mind, how you choose to get around will depend on how much time you have, how much money you're willing to spend, and where you plan to travel. It will also depend on your individual style: whether you prefer independence to a group, what your pace is, and whether you value the ability to take back-road diversions or change plans on an impulse.

Backpacking travelers generally use buses, hitchhike, or buy a motorcycle or car; some choose a mish-mash of all three. (Motorcycling has become quite popular, ideally suited to Australia's flat terrain and good weather.) In addition, train is the prevalent mode of transport in some states and can be cheaper than the bus. Those who need to get around speedily should, of course, fly. Finally, some excellent, inexpensive tours are offered in Australia in areas you wouldn't otherwise be able to get to. Don't reject the idea of taking a tour without looking into it first.

For cheap deals and general advice on getting around the country, head for Youth Hostel Association (YHA) travel agencies or STA Travel offices when you arrive in Australia. YHA and STA Travel addresses are listed in major city chapters.

Bus

While taking buses often requires traveling at strange hours and isn't the most comfortable mode of travel, it's a great way to get a feel for Australia's countryside. The bus network is far more comprehensive than any of the other public transportation options, and it's usually cheaper. For travel in the west (Northern Territory and Western Australia), the bus is the safest way to go (your other option is driving), though pick-up and drop-off times are often horrendous and you'll need to take tours or rent a car locally in order to see anything.

Buses in Australia are luxurious compared to what you may be used to in North America, with video and stereo systems, plush seats, and sometimes a second level. It's a good thing, too, because some trips are long and boring. The Perth-Darwin run is the longest bus route in the world: about 57 hours, with not much in between. If you plan to travel in buses, you'll have to get used to sleeping on them. It helps to bring your sleeping bag or a blanket on board, and a soft jacket or sweater to use as a pillow. Air-conditioning is usually more than ample, so be prepared for a chilly ride regardless of the outside temperature.

You should be aware of special laws that affect bus travel with interstate bus companies. In Victoria, you must be traveling from another state to be dropped off in destinations that are also serviced by train. (This rule does not apply to bus pass holders.) In New South Wales, you can be dropped off from within the state, but you usually must travel a minimum of 200 km. In Western Australia's southwest, some companies can make drop-offs from within the state, again provided a minimum distance is traveled. These laws are always in flux and influence individual bus companies differently, so ask each bus line specifically about your destination.

There are four major interstate bus companies in Australia: **Deluxe**, **Greyhound**, **Pioneer Express**, and **Bus Australia**. Bus Australia is run by McCafferty's on services from Melbourne and Sydney to Queensland, and within Queensland. Deluxe is the best all-around bus line, with dependable, comprehensive services, well-serviced coaches, and good prices. Deluxe offers discounts to foreigners and YHA members, as do Greyhound and Bus Australia.

Bus Passes: If you plan on seeing more than just the east coast, look into buying a bus pass to use during some, or all, of your travels. Prices seem steep, but not when you consider the high cost of individual sector fares. Some bus passes include significant discounts on other things such as travel with local bus companies, rental cars, and tours. Foreigners get a big discount on some bus passes, as do YHA members and students.

Your bus pass options are many and varied. Take a look at what each company has to offer before buying. We recommend Deluxe, but Greyhound is very good too, and deals are ever-changing. Deluxe and Greyhound both offer passes that require you to travel in a certain direction and follow a designated route, at a cheaper price than their regular, unrestricted passes. Deluxe's is the best deal for long-term travel: $800-$900 for a 12-month pass that gets you around Australia's periphery and into Alice Springs and Ayers Rock. Greyhound offers a six-month pass on the same route, for slightly more; they also offer more restricted routes for $400-$500. Deluxe's Koala Pass, which allows you to go anywhere you want within a certain time-frame, is about $500 for 21 days, $650/30 days, etc. (up to 90 days). Greyhound's prices are comparable.

The cheapest unrestricted pass option is Deluxe's Space Pass, which gives you the same unlimited travel as the Koala Pass, but on a space-available basis. You can reserve four hours ahead of time, which is fine when you're not traveling during school or public holidays. Space Pass prices are about $350/21 days, $475/30 days, etc. (Above prices are in Australian dollars and include the discount for foreigners.)

You can buy most bus passes once you get to Australia. Bring along your passport to get an international travelers discount. While it's not necessary (except for Pioneer passes), you have the option of buying your pass in North America through your travel agent (at least two weeks ahead of time). Before doing so, get information from the company agents (who sometimes don't sell passes directly). For Deluxe, contact ATS/Sprint at 800-423-2880 or 818-244-1328 (California); 416-863-0799 (Toronto) or 604-687-4004 (Vancouver). For Greyhound and Pioneer, contact Greyhound International Travel in San Francisco at 800-828-1985 or 415-882-4900; or Goway Travel in Toronto at 416-322-0134.

Train

Consider traveling by train some of the time. In fact, in Victoria and many areas of New South Wales you will have no choice but the train because laws limit services of bus companies. Some sectors are cheaper by rail than bus when you get special discounts.

The government-run railway system (including rail-operated buses) covers most places you'd care to go in New South Wales, Victoria, and Queensland. South Australia, the Northern Territory, and Western Australia don't offer many in-state services, but interstate trains run through. Tasmania, and most of the middle and western parts of the continent, have no trains.

There are some classic train trips in Australia, in themselves a unique experience. The most famous is the *Indian-Pacific* between Perth and Sydney. It crosses the Nullarbor Plain, some of the most desolate outback country in Australia, and runs perfectly straight for 478 km, the longest straight stretch of railway track in the world. Another famous train route, the *Ghan* (Adelaide-Alice Springs), follows the original path of north Indian and Afghan cameleers, who brought supplies to Alice from the end of the railway at Oodnadatta.

The *Ghan* and the *Indian-Pacific* routes are vastly better by train than bus because of the great distances involved. Each runs two-three times a week (sometimes just First Class). A warning: June and July bookings for Perth and Alice trains are booked up six months in advance, and Perth trains also fill up way in advance during September and October.

With Caper and Standby Fares, taking the train can be cheaper than the bus. Caper Fares give you up to 30% off certain services. All you have to do is request a Caper Fare at least seven days in advance, but reserve early because seats are limited. Standby fares are available for Melbourne-Sydney and Melbourne-Adelaide services.

Of the great train trips of the world Australia has more than its share.

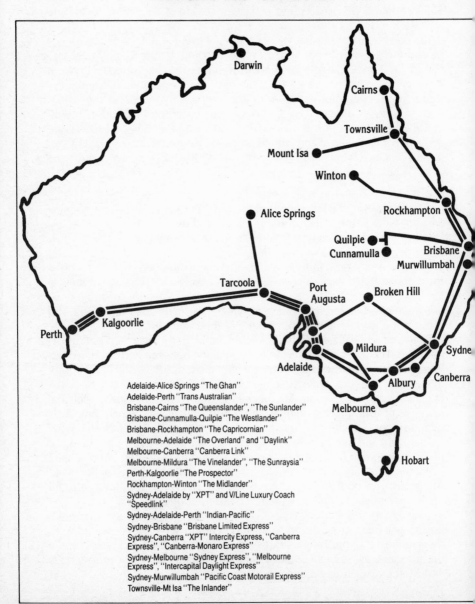

Adelaide-Alice Springs "The Ghan"
Adelaide-Perth "Trans Australian"
Brisbane-Cairns "The Queenslander", "The Sunlander"
Brisbane-Cunnamulla-Quilpie "The Westlander"
Brisbane-Rockhampton "The Capricornian"
Melbourne-Adelaide "The Overland" and "Daylink"
Melbourne-Canberra "Canberra Link"
Melbourne-Mildura "The Vinelander", "The Sunraysia"
Perth-Kalgoorlie "The Prospector"
Rockhampton-Winton "The Midlander"
Sydney-Adelaide by "XPT" and V/Line Luxury Coach "Speedlink"
Sydney-Adelaide-Perth "Indian-Pacific"
Sydney-Brisbane "Brisbane Limited Express"
Sydney-Canberra "XPT" Intercity Express, "Canberra Express", "Canberra-Monaro Express"
Sydney-Melbourne "Sydney Express", "Melbourne Express", "Intercapital Daylight Express"
Sydney-Murwillumbah "Pacific Coast Motorail Express"
Townsville-Mt Isa "The Inlander"

The four options for train travel are Economy and First Class seats, and Economy and First Class berths, but not all are offered on every train. An economy seat is by far the cheapest; however, a sleeping berth is crucial for rides like the Indian-Pacific, which spans three nights. Most of the long-distance trains have special entertainment, dining cars, and lounges.

Booking trains: Book as far ahead as you can for interstate travel, which is particularly popular during school holidays. Bookings in Australia can be made through any state rail offices (listed in each major city chapter), or from overseas through travel agents. Each state's train system is run by a separate government authority: New South Wales=State Rail; Victoria=V/line; Queensland=Queensland Railways; South Australia=State Transport Authority; Western Australia=Westrail.

The Austrailpass: Austrailpasses are only available to foreigners and must be bought before leaving home. The Austrailpass gives you unlimited travel within 14-90 days. It includes suburban, intra- and interstate train travel, and rail-operated coaches. The pass can be activated any time within 12 months of purchase. A Budget Austrailpass gives you an economy seat (you pay extra if you want a berth and meals). Some trains only have First Class seating, in which case you pay the difference.

The pass is worth buying if you plan to cover lots of territory in a short span of time, for instance Sydney/Alice Springs/Perth in two or three weeks. See "Getting There" in each chapter to compare individual sector fares with Austrailpass prices. Keep in mind that a Budget Austrailpass doesn't cover meals or berths (meals are compulsory for berth-holders on some extended trips). Austrailpasses get you a 20% discount on Hertz rental cars, too.

The Austrailpass is available in North America through travel agents. To obtain information on your own, call ATS/Sprint at 800-423-2880 or 818-244-1328 (California), 604-687-4004 (Vancouver), or 416-863-0799 (Toronto). Approximate prices are $400 for 14 days, $520/21 days, etc., up to 90 days (all in Australian dollars).

Plane

Domestic air travel in Australia is similar to North America. The food's not as good, but the wine's better. And be warned: they're very strict about carry-on luggage; bring just one item. Some deals are available only from outside Australia, so look into plane travel before leaving home.

There are essentially two major airlines—**Australian Airlines** and **Ansett**—but the deregulation of late 1990 will no doubt change that. Australian Airlines is smaller and has more personalized service; they also offer a 25% discount to students (with an International Student ID Card), and tickets are fully refundable. Australian Airlines and Ansett have subsidiaries in each state, the larger carriers being East-West Airlines, Air New South Wales, Air Queensland, and Kendell Airlines.

Foreigners can buy sector fares at a 25% discount on all Australian Airlines and Ansett flights, provided

1. You fly to Australia on a discounted fare or a frequent flyer ticket.

2. You are flying more than 1,000 km total with the airline.

3. You buy your ticket within 30 days of arrival (Ansett only).

4. You are staying in Australia 30 days or less (Australian Airlines only).

East-West, which covers Queensland, New South Wales, Victoria, Hobart, and Alice Springs/Ayers Rock, offers a special pass that's a great deal if your time is limited and you want to stay on the east coast. Call 800-366-1300 for more information.

For current information on fares and special deals for Australian Airlines, call 800-922-5122 or 213-626-2352. For Ansett and East-West call 800-366-1300.

Car

If you're adventurous and can afford it, driving is the best way to see the country for all it's worth. However, driving involves much more preparation and work than you might think, especially in the outback, where driving alone is monotonous (though certainly a once-in-a-lifetime experience!), and the possibility of a breakdown is real and unattractive.

Those planning an extended stay in Australia should consider purchasing a car (see *Appendix*). If that's out of the question, rideboards in hostels often advertise rides. You may also end up renting a car or four-wheel drive vehicle where it's impossible to enjoy a place without the freedom of your own wheels.

Overseas driver's licenses are recognized for up to a year in Australia. An International Driver's License is not necessary but may help if you have to buy insurance.

Whether you're driving your own car or a rental, be sure the car is in good condition. In Australia, you can't always count on a nearby mechanic—the closest might be hundreds of kilometers from a breakdown. Also, roads that look like major thruways on a map sometimes aren't even paved. Good tires and shocks are essential. Kangaroos become a major hazard at night, so much so that in areas with high 'roo populations, many people don't drive after dusk. Most cars that frequent the outback have "roo bars" protecting the front end. Also beware of cattle. See Stuart Highway (Northern Territory) for pointers on long-distance outback driving. When driving on unpaved outback roads, always ask for local advice before taking off.

A few driving conventions to keep in mind: Australians drive on the left, so the steering wheel is on the right and everything on the dashboard is reversed from U.S. standards. You'll turn on the windshield wipers instead of the blinker on your first few turns, but you'll soon get used to it. The speed limit is an understood 100-110 km/hr (depending on the state) outside of residential or commercial areas, and 60 km/hr in built-up areas. Traffic police exist, but speed traps are mainly in residential areas. Pedestrians have right-of-way on white striped pedestrian crossings. Be prepared to stop, because Aussie walkers are used to their privilege and will step right in front of you. Seat belts are compulsory. See "Driving" in the introduction to Victoria for Victoria's unique driving laws.

Gasoline ("petrol"), sold by the liter, is astronomically expensive by U.S.

standards. You have to be conscious of your fuel level in isolated areas because of great distances between service stations. During weekends, petrol stations on remote roads open and close according to a roster system.

We strongly recommend joining an Automobile Association if you plan to drive. They provide excellent free maps, the best national accommodation directory, towing and break-down services, and advice to car buyers, among other things. AAA (American Automobile Association) has reciprocal membership with each Australian state's Automobile Association (cost to join in Australia is about $60), and you can join or claim reciprocal membership in any branch office. Membership in one state gets you membership in all other states.

Car Rental: You'll probably rent a car at least once. Often people in hostels get together on a rental car to get to a remote site, and this is sometimes cheaper than public transport alternatives. Four-wheel driving is popular in Queensland, the Northern Territory, and Western Australia, and 4WD rentals start around $60/day. It's worth saving for, and not too expensive if you gather a group.

Rental cost ($30-$50/day) in major cities is considerably less than in rural areas, so always consider renting before you leave a metropolitan area. Some companies charge extra if you exceed a certain number of kilometers, and others place restrictions on where you can go; be sure to ask when you call. Stamp duty is not included in the stated rental price.

In some cases, you must be 21 or older to rent. However, written proof of liability insurance from a company back home should enable you to rent if you're under 21.

Hitchhiking
Hitchhiking is possible on parts of east coast Australia (New South Wales and Queensland are the best) and Tasmania, and virtually impossible in most of the middle and western part of the country. The big problem is not so much fear of getting picked up by a weirdo (though we did hear a few horror stories in Queensland), but not getting picked up at all. Many roads simply aren't frequented. Hitching in Australia is safer than in most countries, but there are always exceptions, and women should take extra care to travel in pairs.

Tours
Whether you want to get to challenging wilderness areas or need a way to get around remote destinations, taking a guided tour will solve the problem. National and international tour companies, as well as smaller, locally-run operations, offer a variety of excellent tour options in Australia. There are two basic kinds of tours within the means of budget travelers: coach tours that include bunk-style accommodations or camping, and 4WD camping tours. The former are designed to get you to as many points as possible while still getting a feel for the places you see. The latter are generally smaller, more expensive, and concentrated within a smaller area.

Most tours can be booked once you get to Australia. However, for the international tour companies like **Contiki Holidays** and **World Expeditions**, you should get brochures and make reservations before departure.

In deciding where to tour, take a look at the "Getting Around" section in the state chapter introductions. Information about good local tours is in individual "Getting There" or "Getting Around" sections. We especially recommend tours in the far north of Australia (Cape York, Queensland; the Top End, including Kakadu National Park; and the Kimberley region of Western Australia), the Whitsunday Islands, the Gunbarrel Route across the Western Australian desert to Ayers Rock, and any other outback areas, especially in Western Australia and the Northern Territory.

Tours that require at least a one month advance booking include the following:

Cape York Frontier Adventures
P.O. Box 6883
Cairns Mail Centre, QLD 4871
phone 070-57-7366
A budget four-wheel drive tour of Cape York—the least expensive tour offered in the area and reputed to be excellent.

Contiki Holidays
1432 East Katella Ave.
Anaheim, CA 92805
phone 800-626-0611
In Canada:
415 Yonge St., Suite 1616
Toronto, Ontario M5B 2E7
phone 800-268-9140 (or 800-387-2699 in Ontario)
In Sydney, phone (02) 264-3366, reservations (02) 290-3977
In Auckland, phone (09) 39-8824
Contiki offers budget coach tours all over Australia and New Zealand, including Tasmania. Their tours are geared specifically to an 18-35 crowd, with lots of partying and late nights and full days of activities and sightseeing. Contiki's tours provide a great opportunity to get to know Australians, who will comprise most of your comrades. (If you take a Contiki tour at the beginning of your trip, you'll have people to stay with all around the country for the remainder of your travels.) Their Red Centre tours to Alice Springs, Ayers Rock, King's Canyon, and up the Stuart Highway to Darwin and Kakadu National Park are particularly worthwhile. Contiki also has tours along Queensland's coast, including a stay at their Whitsunday Island Resort and excursions to the Great Barrier Reef. Be sure to ask about special deals on Air New Zealand flights.

Sam Lovell
34 Knowsley St.
Derby, W.A. 6728
phone (091) 91-1084

Sam Lovell's four-wheel drive tours are famous because he's one of a hand-

ful of people in the world who knows the Kimberley coast. His tours originate in Derby and go to the Prince Regent River, the Bungle Bungles, and the Mitchell Plateau. The tours aren't cheap, but if you can afford it, they're worth the money.

World Expeditions
690 Market St., Suite 1206
San Francisco, CA 94102
phone 415-362-1046 or 800-541-3600
In Canada:
c/o Worldwide Adventures
920 Yonge St., Suite 747
Toronto, Ontario M4W 3C7
phone 416-963-9163 or 800-387-1483
In Sydney, phone (02) 290-3622, reservations (02) 290-3977
In Melbourne, phone (03) 419-2333
This Australian outfit is the largest outdoor adventuring tour company in the world. If you're looking for rugged, off-the-beaten-track adventure, their tours are the best available. Tours are usually devoted to a certain activity (like sailing, hiking, or rafting), and through that activity you see a unique wilderness area.

World Expeditions' tour options in Australia are numerous. Among them are rafting in northern Queensland or Tasmania, horse-riding in the Snowy Mountains, sailing in Queensland or off the northern coast of the Northern Territory, and four-wheeling up Cape York or through Kakadu National Park.

Youth Hostel Association of Western Australia Tours
257 Adelaide Tce.
Perth, W.A. 6000
phone (09) 325-5844
Outback tours run by YHA of Western Australia are the best YHA-sponsored tours in the country, better than any others offered in Western Australia, and by far the cheapest. We especially recommend the 4WD Gunbarrel Highway trek.

Accommodation

Hostellers ("backpackers") will find a comprehensive, competitive hostel network in heavily populated areas of Australia. There are also hostels in the semi-remote regions of the eastern states (Queensland, New South Wales, Victoria, and Tasmania). While hostels are cheap and an invaluable source of travel information, they're generally not the best places to get to know Aussies or to take in the essence of Australia.

If you plan to get off the beaten track, especially in the Northern Territory and Western Australia, camping is the way to go. The more remote the area, the higher hotel and on-site caravan rates. In very remote areas, you may find nowhere to stay at all. Though most places you'll travel aren't quite so uncivilized, a tent is nonetheless handy.

Aside from hostels and camping, other budget options include on-site caravans, licensed hotels, YMCA's, and occasional motels. Bed & Breakfasts (B&B's) and Farmstays also sometimes fall into the inexpensive category and are a great way to meet the locals.

If you're traveling on a tight budget but not staying in hostels, get your hands on an RAA (Royal Automobile Association) *Australian National Tourguide*, an exhaustive list of accommodations (except hostels) throughout the country, including caravan parks. It's updated annually and is incredibly useful. It's free to Auto Association members, but unfortunately isn't for sale otherwise.

Hostels

The Youth Hostel Association (YHA) of Australia has well over 100 hostels around the country. In addition, scores of privately-owned hostels, generally known as "Backpackers" hostels, populate the coast of New South Wales, Queensland, and all major cities. Hostellers are a visable subculture in cities like Cairns and some eastern beach communities.

The hostel network is a tremendous source of information and companionship. Hostel log books and bulletin boards, hostel managers, and fellow hostellers can give you insider's information that no travel agent or tourist officer would have a clue about. Carpooling is organized through hostel rideboards. Swedes, Germans, English, Irish, New Zealanders, and Canadians are the most dominant nationalities, but people from all corners of the earth stay in Australian hostels. In hostels, as in no other type of lodging situation, you get to know your fellow travelers.

Many YHA hostels close during the day and require that you perform a daily cleaning duty. (Note, however, that Australian YHA hostels rarely have the curfews and early wake-up hours of European hostels.) Backpackers hostels are generally more relaxed than YHA hostels, but this sometimes translates into unkempt, even unsanitary, conditions. Other variables also come with the Backpackers option, like the possibility (albeit remote) of co-ed bunkrooms or an undefined "lights out" time. On the other hand, the highly competitive hostel market (especially in New South Wales and Queensland) means that many hostels are of resort caliber (as are some YHA hostels), with private rooms, swimming pools, and modern facilities. All hostels have kitchens, and most have laundry facilities.

There are at least five hostel networks in Australia. Like warring fiefdoms, each tries to depict itself as the definitive organization for budget travelers. It's all extremely confusing, since everyone but YHA (and a few small networks like "Cotels") calls themselves "Backpackers." Keep in mind that each hostel network (aside from YHA) is formed for the purpose of publicity, so standards vary enormously within each. Except for YHA, membership is not required.

Practically speaking, it's unnecessary to carry around the separate accommodation directories. All the decent places are listed and evaluated in this book. New hostels are starting up all the time, but if they're good (or bad), you're bound to hear about them from fellow travelers or read about them in hostel comment books. The various directories are available in hostels (excepting the YHA booklet, which comes with membership). Backpackers Travel Company's magazine is also available at some newsstands in New South Wales and Queensland, for about $4.

There are three major Backpackers organizations:

Backpackers Resorts of Australia Pty. Ltd.
3 Newman St.
Nambucca Heads, N.S.W. 2448
phone 065-68-6360
Hostels are all good.

Backpackers Travel Co.
PO Box 117
Sydney, N.S.W. 2001
phone 070-31-1266
Though the information in their attractive magazine isn't always reliable, the hostels included are high quality.

Hostel Resorts of Australia (HRA)
148 The Esplanade
Cairns, QLD 4870
phone 070-51-2431 or after hours 53-5414
Some of the best and some of the worst hostels are listed in their directory.

Reserving Hostels: Sometimes calling ahead will secure a place and sometimes it won't, but it's always worth trying, especially in larger cities and along the east coast during summer holidays. In some states YHA has a system allowing you to book and pay for a hostel in advance through your current hostel.

At crunch times (January in Sydney, for instance), try to arrive at hostels before 10:00am to get a place for the night (most hostel offices close after that). Of course, you won't always make that morning deadline, in which case there's sometimes a posted list where you can leave your name and come back when the office opens.

It's rare that all the hostels in town are filled up. Exceptions are Sydney in summer (late Dec.-Feb.), ski resort hostels in July-August, any coastal area during school holidays, and during annual festivals that are held in many cities.

YHA Membership: If you plan to stay in hostels at all, get YHA membership. YHA has by far the most comprehensive network, so you'll almost certainly stay in YHA hostels some of the time.

Membership is required to stay. If you buy your membership before October 1, it will expire on December 31 of the same year (otherwise, it expires on December 31 of the following year). With membership comes a handbook and lots of valuable discounts, such as a 10% discount on Deluxe Coachlines' Koala Pass. YHA head offices (one in each Australian state) are a rich source of travel information, and most have a travel agency where you can book everything from local tours to international flights.

You can join YHA in Australia at some hostels and at any state head office. You can also join before departure, by mail or in person (cost is a bit more than in Australia—about $20 U.S. as opposed to $20 AUS).

In the U.S., call the American Youth Hostels (AYH) Head Office in Washington, DC at 202-783-6161. They'll give you a membership sales agency near you for applying in person, or they'll tell you exactly what information and money they need for a mail application. Their address is American Youth Hostels, Travel Store, P.O. Box 37613, Washington, DC 20013-7613. Allow three weeks by mail. You can purchase sleeping sheets, hostel handbooks, and advance booking vouchers at the AYH Travel Store or by mail. YHA's New York office has similar services (75 Spring St., New York, NY 10012, phone 212-431-7100), as does the Canadian Hostelling Association (National Office is at 333 River Rd., Place Vanier, Tower A Vanier City, Ottawa, Ontario, KIL 8H4, phone 613-748-5638). You can also join YHA through any CIEE office.

YHA Customs: Each state YHA organization operates a little bit differently, but there are some general YHA customs you should know about.

First and foremost, sleeping sheets are always required. A sleeping sheet is basically a sleeping bag made out of sheets, which gets supplemented by blankets and a pillow (provided by the hostels). Sleeping sheets are also required at some Backpackers hostels. You can rent sleeping sheets for about $2 at most hostels, but the more practical route is to buy an official sheet from YHA state offices or make your own (guidelines for making them are in the YHA handbook).

Most YHA hostels have three- or five-night limits (depending on the state), though some, especially those in remote areas, will let you stay as long as you like. Lodgers are often required to perform a duty in the morning, like sweeping the kitchen floor or cleaning the sinks. Lights are out sometime between 11:00pm and midnight, but you can usually come in later without a hassle. Many hostels are closed from 10:00am-5:00pm, during which time you can't go in the bedrooms but often can hang out in the common room (and store your luggage). You can check in from 5:00pm-7:00pm, and check out between 8:00am-10:00am. Be ready to pay on arrival.

Camping
If you're really looking to travel cheaply, camping is the way to do it. Many travelers combine camping and hostelling, staying in hostels where they exist, and camping in remote areas where there are no hostels. Though not strictly legal, camping on the side of the road in the outback or even near civilization is rarely a problem.

Renting equipment is a good idea if you're only going to use a tent once or twice, and rentals are available in the major cities. Rates are about $65/week for a tent. Tents can sometimes be hired at caravan parks for use in the park's campground.

Local weather will greatly influence your ability to camp, and Australia has a variety of seasonal quirks, including monsoons, intense heat, and brutal cold. The most important (and least publicized) condition to fear is flash floods that occur in outback areas during winter/spring. Camp well away from water sources, and listen to weather reports. Flash floods drown campers every year, but if you take simple precautions you have no reason to worry.

Where to Camp: Aussies are pretty mellow about discreet roadside camping (except near metropolitan areas). Caravan parks usually have a camping area. While camping in a caravan park isn't always aesthetically pleasing, it normally costs only $3-$5 and gives you the luxury of bathrooms, showers, a supply store, and sometimes barbecue grills. Near cities, caravan parks are the best place to pitch a tent.

Though private campgrounds do exist in Australia, most adjoin national parks and are run by the National Parks Service. Their overnight cost is also low and often includes showers and toilets. Often, national parks require you to camp in designated areas, and sometimes these must be booked ahead. Popular national parks get booked up in high season. Details on reserving ahead are included in this book, when applicable.

Supplies for Camping: Bring all the obvious items, plus a mosquito net, insect repellent, and large water containers. A gas stove or disposable heating flame is needed for national park camping, where no fires are allowed. Most caravan parks and national park campgrounds provide barbecue grills but no utensils. Water supply, it should be emphasized, is often an issue in the outback. Large, crushable water bottles should do the trick for those camping near civilized roads. But if you plan to go on unpaved roads without service centers, you must be able to carry several gallons. Check locally for advice.

Hotels

Hotels in Australia fall into two categories: *licensed* and *private*. A private hotel has only accommodation and is generally expensive; a licensed hotel is primarily a drinking establishment but, by law, must provide some sort of accommodation. Most licensed hotel lodgings fall into the budget category (about $20/night per person), with simple rooms and communal bathrooms. Some are pretty rough. There's often a refrigerator and tea/coffee-making facilities in the room, but the niceties stop there. Expect noise, because the downstairs goings-on often reverberate throughout.

One rule of thumb is to check closing times of the downstairs bars before deciding where to stay. Normally, you check in with the bartender.

A note for women: Obtaining keys in a pub can be one of the more uncomfortable experiences you'll have in Australia, especially in rural areas. If you can ignore the sudden hush and ogling, fine. If not, choose your hotels carefully.

Motels

Motels in Australia are just what they are in North America: mid-priced accommodations with individual, outdoor access to rooms. Usually more expensive than licensed hotels, motels are rarely listed in this book.

Caravan Parks

We assume you won't be caravaning. Nonetheless, it's likely you'll stay in a caravan park at least a few times during your travels, because caravan parks are everywhere, including where hostels and hotels are not.

On-site caravans, which sleep 2-3 people, are available at the majority of caravan parks and cost about $20/night. Many have a sink and cooking utensils; all include access to the park's supply store and "amenities block" (toilets and showers). Campgrounds often adjoin caravan parks, and tents can sometimes be rented from the park.

We include caravan park listings where less expensive accommodations are not available, mostly in rural areas.

B&B's and Farmstays

Bed & Breakfasts aren't as common in Australia as they are, for example, in Great Britain. But they can be found in pockets throughout the country: in Tasmania, southeastern South Australia, Canberra, Albany, the New England region of New South Wales, and throughout Victoria.

B&B's can be surprisingly cheap and are a wonderful way to take in the charm of an area. They're worth the extra money for one or two nights, especially if you're sick of hostel bunkrooms.

Farmstays are a slightly different concept, but often incorporate the B&B idea. Some Farmstays are commercialized; others are on a genuine farm or station (ranch), where you are treated as a guest of the family. Farmstays are $25/night per person and up, with some exceptions (cost per person is generally less if you're traveling in a group).

Times to Book Ahead

School summer holidays in Australia last from just before Christmas through February. The popular spots at this time are the coasts of southern Queensland, New South Wales (especially Sydney), Victoria, and South Australia, southwestern Western Australia, and Tasmania. No matter what kind of accommodation you're counting on, you need to reserve ahead in these places.

At any time of year, you should book at least a week ahead for Ayers Rock accommodations. If you plan to ski, make reservations as far ahead as possible. Finally, festival crowds in major cities are apt to surprise travelers. For specific festival times, see "Major Annual Events and Festivals" below.

Long-Term Accommodation

A number of privately-owned hostels offer special rates for long-term boarders, and some even have a separate living space for "semi-permanents."

Another option is university housing, available mainly in summer (Dec.-Feb.). Rates are about $20/night with breakfast, sometimes less.

Finally, you might want to rent an apartment ("flat"), in which case universities are again an excellent resource. Student Housing Offices have apartment listings and bulletin boards covered with ads. The Housing Office is usually in the Student Union building. Also, check the classifieds of a local newspaper.

Your First Night in Australia

Many of you will fly into Sydney, where finding room in a hostel can be difficult (especially in summer). Regardless of where you arrive, find a private room for a few nights to recover from jet lag, and save stress by booking ahead. You can also book a YHA hostel (some of which have private rooms) from abroad. And there's always the airport information booth, where tourist officers will help you find a place.

Hostels giving free transport from the Sydney airport are listed in the Sydney "Accommodation" section.

Getting Information

Each state in Australia has its own tourist commission, with offices in the capital city and in smaller cities as well. They also have offices in the capital cities of other states.

The tourist commissions vary in quality: Tasbureau (Tasmania), for instance, has great maps, honest promotional material, and good information on budget travel. New South Wales, South Australia, Western Australia, and the Northern Territory also have informative tourist officers and good information. Queensland's organization seems geared towards high-paying customers, while Victoria's is a bit disorganized, though they put out some useful literature.

There are also local tourist bureaus, which may or may not be part of the state organization.

Weather

Two rules of thumb on the Australian weather:

1. Australia's seasons are opposite to the Northern Hemisphere's. Summer is December-February, autumn (not "fall") is March-May, winter is June-August, and spring is September-November. Be prepared to spend Christmas and New Year's at the beach.

2. As you move south, temperatures get colder. Head north, and the temperature rises.

The weather in Australia is generally warmer and seasons are less defined than in North America. The sunshine can be brutal (105 °F is typical in arid inland regions during summer), and the general dryness means you don't always feel the heat in time. It's no wonder Australians have the highest rate of skin cancer in the world.

Winter can be quite chilly, especially along the southeastern, southern, and extreme southwestern coasts, and in Tasmania. Winter days occasionally get below freezing (though they average 40-60 °F), and plenty of snow falls in the southeastern mountains. While winter is better than summer for travel in the tropics and central Australia, it gets chilly there, too. Alice Springs, in the center of the country, has nightly frosts in winter (though it's usually warm and sunny during the day), and even southern Queensland (south of Townsville) gets an occasional winter freeze.

In the tropical north, monsoonal rains of the "wet" begin in December and last through March or early April, making travel impossible. Large-scale cyclones hit northern coasts five or six times a summer. Intense heat also comes with the wet. (The wet is preceded by an incredibly hot and humid period called the "silly season," so named because the weather is said to cause temporary insanity.) Central Australia occasionally gets floods that stop all travel for 3-4 days. These come in any season, unpredictably. "Beautiful one day, pissing down the next," disgruntled locals say.

Cut off from the mainland by the turbulent Bass Strait, Tasmania's wind currents and weather patterns create a unique climate. Tassie's weather tends to be more extreme, with high rainfall on the western side and colder temperatures on average. Winter can be extremely cold, especially in the mountains.

Business Hours

In general, shops are open Monday-Friday 9:00am-5:30pm, 9:00am-noon on Saturday, and closed Sunday. Late night shopping (until 9:00pm) is usually available Friday in the cities, Thursday in the suburbs.

Bank hours are generally Monday-Thursday 10:00am-3:00pm, and Friday 10:00am-5:00pm.

Post offices are open Monday-Friday 9:00am-5:00pm.

Typical hotel (pub) hours are Monday-Saturday 10:00am-10:00pm, and until 8:00pm on Sunday. However, these times vary according to state and, often, according to pub. In the larger cities, pubs tend to stay open until 11:00pm or midnight on Friday and Saturday nights. Hotel counter meals are usually served from noon-2:00pm and 6:00pm-8:00pm.

Sightseeing Hours

Museums, historic buildings, and tour operators have quirky hours, to put it mildly. In some regions, sights are open only on weekends, Wednesdays, and public holidays. In others, sights and tours operate only on weekdays, except public holidays. During holidays, some places extend their hours, while others close or limit their hours so they can go on vacation, too. It's not uncommon for museum proprietors to decide suddenly it's a good afternoon for the beach, or a terrific *month* to go on holiday!

The best approach to all this unpredictability is to be as easy-going as the Aussies themselves. Figure that last-minute plan alterations are inevitable, and roll with the punches.

Mail

There's nothing better than a letter from home after many months on the road. Unless you've got Aussie friends, your options are post offices, American Express offices, and hostels or other accommodation. Don't leave mail unclaimed for more than a month, or it'll go back to the senders.

Airmail letters between Australia and North America can take as little as four days and as long as three weeks (either direction), and Australian postage fees are pretty steep.

To get mail through the GPO (General Post Office) in the main Australian cities, use this address: Your Name, c/o (CITY) G.P.O., [state and state's zip code], AUSTRALIA. The capital cities and their zip codes are as follows: Sydney, N.S.W. (2000), Melbourne, Vic. (3000), Brisbane, QLD. (4000), Adelaide, S.A. (5000), Perth, W.A. (6000), Hobart, Tas. (7000), Canberra, A.C.T. (2601), and Darwin, N.T. (0800).

If you use American Express traveler's checks or credit card, you get free access to the best way to receive mail. All the main Australian cities have American Express offices. To get your mail, present an American Express traveler's check (or credit card) and your passport as identification. For a small fee, you can have mail forwarded to another American Express office.

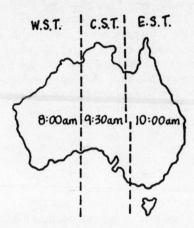

Time Zones

The above map shows Australia's three time zones: Western Standard Time (WST) which includes Western Australia; Central Standard Time (CST) which includes South Australia and the Northern Territory; and Eastern Standard Time (EST) which includes New South Wales, Queensland, Victoria, the Australian Capital Territory, and Tasmania. EST is a half-hour ahead of CST, and two hours ahead of WST. To confuse matters, Queensland and Western Australia don't observe Daylight Savings time.

When neither Australia nor the U.S. is in Daylight Savings, New York is 15 hours behind Sydney, and Los Angeles is 18 hours behind. (Even if you think you've worked this mess out, double-check with the operator before you call and wake up everyone back home.)

The National Trust

The National Trust is a non-profit organization that restores historic buildings and grounds (sometimes even whole towns). You can become a member anywhere and have reciprocal rights at any National Trust-owned property in Australia, New Zealand, the U.S., and the U.K.

We recommend joining if you're interested in visiting more than a couple of the museums (there are hundreds across Australia). Entrance fees are usually between $2-$4, but free or discounted if you're a member. An annual membership costs about $30 ($20 for students under 25).

Each Australian state has a National Trust headquarters in its capital city, where you can join. You can also join on the spot at most National Trust properties. For information in the U.S., contact National Trust for Historic Preservation, 1785 Massachusetts Ave. N.W., Washington, D.C. 20036 (phone 202-673-4000).

Telephones

In Australia, you don't call, you "ring." There is a 30-cents charge for ringing locally (even on a private phone). For long distance calls, those weighty Australian coins you'll curse finally find a purpose. Use a "Gold Phone" (they are bright orange and easy to spot). They aren't cheaper than regular phones, but they accept many dollars' worth of coins and display your ongoing tally.

If you don't want to deal with pay phones, head to the nearest post office, where you'll get an assigned phone box and pay when the call is over.

There's no cheap time to make an overseas call. You pay a steep minute-by-minute rate regardless of the time. (A beep sounds every three minutes to make you aware how long you've been talking). International calling cards can be used only for calling the country from which the card is issued (i.e., you can't call from Australia to Singapore on a U.S. calling card).

Currency

Australian bills ("notes") are rainbow-colored. Each denomination ($5, $10, $20, $50, $100) is a different bright color and a slightly different size. There are 100 cents in one dollar. One- and two-cent pieces are copper, five- to 50-cent pieces are silver-colored, and the $1 and $2 coins are gold-colored.

Australia's economic fluctuations generally follow the United States'. Australia's inflation rate is 8%-10% per year. At this writing, $1 Australian=$.75 US.

Tipping

Much to the delight of all budget travelers, tipping isn't customary in Australia. In fact, it can be insulting, so resist the urge to tip waiters, waitresses, taxi drivers, and porters at airports. However, if you're dining in an elegant restaurant where the service is especially good, you should leave about a 10% tip.

Metric Conversions

Temperature: 0° Celsius (32° Fahrenheit)=freezing point of water. 100° C (212°F)=boiling point of water. Fahrenheit=(C x 1.8) + 32.

Volume: 1 liter=1 quart or 4 cups (approximately)=0.26 gallons

Weight: 1 kilogram (kg)=2.2 lbs.; 1 gram=0.035 ounces; 1 stone=14 lbs. (an old British measure, not metric, but still used).

Length: 1 centimeter (cm)=0.4 inches; 1 meter=3.3 feet; 1 kilometer (km)=0.62 miles; 1 hectare=2.5 acres.

Electricity

Australia uses 240/250 voltage (as opposed to 110/120 in the U.S.), and AC 50HZ. Unless your appliance has a built-in converter, you'll need an adaptor. In addition, Australian electrical outlets ("power points") often have three prongs, so an attachment may be needed as well.

Clothing

Women's clothing: Australian 10=U.S. 8; Australian 12=U.S. 10; Australian 14=U.S. 12; and so on.

Men's pants: Australian 92=U.S. 36; Australian 97=U.S. 38; Australian 102=U.S. 40; and so on.

Men's shirts: Australian 36=U.S. 14; Australian 37=U.S. 14 1/2; Australian 38=U.S. 15; and so on.

School Holidays
Be aware of school vacations and plan accordingly, because accommodation and transportation are tight at these times, especially during the long summer break from Christmas through the beginning of February.

The schools in all states have a four-term system (except Tasmania, which has three terms). New South Wales, Victoria, and the A.C.T. follow practically the same schedule, while Queensland, South Australia, and Tassie do their own thing. The 1989-90 school holiday schedule was as follows, and school holidays always fall near these dates:

New South Wales and A.C.T.: March 24-April 2, June 24-July 9, Sept. 24-Oct. 8, Dec. 16-Jan. 28

Victoria: March 24-April 2, June 24-July 9, Sept. 23-Oct. 8, Dec. 23-Feb. 7

South Australia: April 15-April 23, July 1-July 16, Sept. 23-Oct. 9, Dec. 16-Jan. 29

Queensland: March 18-March 27, June 17-July 2, Sept. 9-Sept. 24, Dec. 16-Jan. 29

Tasmania: May 27-June 11, Aug. 26-Sept. 10, Dec. 21-Feb. 19

Public Holidays
During Australia's numerous public holidays, banks, stores, and sometimes public transportation systems close for the day. The nation-wide holidays are New Years Day, January 2, Good Friday and Easter Monday, Anzac Day (April 25), Christmas, and Boxing Day (Dec. 26). The Queen's Birthday on June 14 is observed by every state except W.A., and Australia Day is in January but the day varies according to the state. Labour Days, Bank Holidays, and special sporting events (Melbourne and Adelaide Cup Days, N.T.'s Show Days) are observed at different times by individual states.

Major Annual Events and Festivals
January: Sydney Festival

Feb-March: Festival of Perth

March: Adelaide Festival of the Arts (biannual)

September: Victorian Football League Final, Melbourne; Henley-on-Todd Regatta, Alice Springs (or early October)

October: Grand Prix, Adelaide

November: Melbourne Cup (first Tuesday)

December: Sydney-Hobart Regatta (Boxing Day-New Years Day)

Introduction, Part III:
Australian History and Culture

Prehistory

Today the Australian continent is an isolated island. But 45 million years ago it was linked to Antarctica and South America. 90 million years before that, New Zealand, Africa, and India were also part of the giant landmass that scientists call Gondwana.

When Australia was connected to Gondwana, it shared common environments, plants, and animals. Once it drifted, winds and sea currents around the new island created new climates, forcing life there to adapt or perish. Australia's long isolation is the key to its unique flora and fauna.

Excluding Antarctica, Australia is the driest continent in the world. Once, however, great seas covered its arid center, the climate was warm and moist, and rainforests prevailed. About 15 million years ago, a drying-out began which transformed the tropical flora into the woodlands and grassy plains that exist today. A few small patches of ancient rainforest still exist, scattered down the eastern coast in protected niches of the Great Dividing Range and on the northwestern side of Tasmania.

The original fauna, primarily rainforest dwellers, also adapted to the drying climate and expanding grasslands. Characteristics from rainforest ancestors are still apparent in modern Australian animals. With a few exceptions, related species have become extinct on the other Gondwana fragments.

The first humans arrived from Southeast Asia sometime within the past 100,000 years, probably during extreme glacial periods when low sea levels made crossings from Asia shorter and easier. Though the precise location and date of their first footprints is yet unknown, archaeologists have discovered fragmentary evidence of human occupation on the mainland from 40,000 years ago.

Physical Features

Australia is 2,966,144 square miles, roughly the same size as the continental United States, and is both the flattest and the driest inhabited continent on earth. An island and a continent, Australia is bounded to the west by the Indian Ocean, to the south by the Southern Ocean (which also circles Antarctica), to the north by the Timor and Arafura seas, and to the east by the Pacific Ocean (including the Tasman and Coral Seas).

Tasmania, one of the states of Australia, is an island 150 miles south of the southeastern corner of the continent across the Bass Strait.

Roughly two-thirds of the continent is desert or near-desert. The most striking feature of this arid landscape is the soil color, which ranges from rusty-brown to vibrant brick-red and orange, depending on the iron content. Everything that comes in contact with it eventually acquires a reddish tinge, including humans and their clothing. Amidst the redness, many weird and wonderful formations have been created by wind and water erosion— from deep ravines to rounded domes to jagged outcrops. Ayers Rock ("Uluru") is one of the most famous weathering phenomena, an enormous outcrop of sandstone that rises from the desolate plains of Central Australia.

Only a small portion of the country is truly uninhabitable by humans. Even the most desolate areas, including the Simpson, Great Sandy, and Great Victoria deserts, support a few nomadic Aborigines. The deserts in central Australia, such as Sturt's Stony Desert, are covered by small, sharp stones ("gibbers"), the remains of ancient landforms after thousands of years of weathering.

The true deserts, whether stony or sandy, receive under 10" of rain per year and cover one-third of the country. Another third is arid land that receives between 10"-15" rainfall, enough to support sheep and sparse human life. Almost two-thirds of the country has no continuously flowing rivers or streams. Those who live there know where to find "soaks" or "waterholes," part of an ancient drainage system just beneath the surface.

Giant salt lakes cover large areas of the central plains, occasionally filling when the rains are generous (about three times a century). Lake Eyre, located in northern South Australia, is the largest dry salt lake in the world.

The Great Dividing Range, which runs north-south down the eastern coast, was formed before Australia broke away from Gondwanaland. Although small in comparison to other mountain ranges in the world, the Great Dividing Range serves the important purpose of fending off winds from the ocean, trapping moisture to create tropical pockets in the north, the snowy region in the south, and dense vegetation growth along the east coast. About 18% of Australia's forest land lies along the ranges. The range also stops moisture from traveling inland, forming a distinct boundary between the lush, mountainous eastern seaboard and the dry land to its west.

Australia's highest peak, Mt. Kosciusko, is in New South Wales and rises 2,228 meters. Other notable ranges across the country include the Flinders Ranges in South Australia, the Macdonnells in the Northern Territory, and the weather-eroded Kimberleys (which include the rounded domes of the Bungle Bungle Range) in northern Western Australia.

Australia's largest river, the Murray, originates in New South Wales and flows west for 2,000 twisting kilometers to meet the Southern Ocean southeast of Adelaide, South Australia. Many small rivers and streams flow from the Great Dividing Range to the sea, but the land's dryness rapidly increases as you head west, where permanently flowing waters are few.

The Great Barrier Reef has been growing for over 15 million years, with intermingled periods of growth and stagnation. Continental drift created the space, ocean currents brought a favorable temperature, and the warm northern waters became a nurturing home for corals. Today the famous reef, which parallels the Queensland coast for 2,300 km, is home to thousands of varieties of tropical fish, coral, and other sea-dwelling species, and entices snorkelers, scuba divers, and sun-worshippers.

Fauna

It's difficult to conjure an image of Australia that doesn't include the kangaroo or the cuddly koala. There are 182 species of marsupials found only in Australia, far more than in any other continent in the world. Marsupials are a distinct group of mammals because of their reproductive system: At an early period in its development, the embryo struggles to its mother's pouch, where it remains until fully developed. Among the hundreds of unique Australian marsupials are the kangaroo, wombat, possum, bandicoot, wallaby, koala, and Tasmanian Devil.

The original kangaroo was a small, tree-dwelling marsupial, similar to the possum, who lived in the ancient Gondwana rainforests. As the rainforests became woodlands and open plains, these creatures moved onto the ground and evolved into the animal we now know. Its hind legs, made powerful by tree-climbing muscles, were perfectly suited for bounding across the vast plains, and gradually its teeth and digestive system adjusted to the tough grasses and scrub.

The most primitive living kangaroo, the musky rat kangaroo, exists in a few pockets of Queensland's rainforests. Tree kangaroos, more closely reminiscent of past ages, live in the tropical forests of Papua New Guinea. Today's ground-dwelling, hopping kangaroos are ubiquitous on the continent and come in all shapes and sizes, including the miniature quokka (found only in the southwest corner of the country) and a variety of wallabies.

The koala isn't a bear at all. Descendants of an ancient burrowing animal similar to the wombat, koalas at some point left their burrows and took to the trees. Today the koala lives in the branches of a few species of eucalyptus trees and feeds solely on their strong-scented leaves.

For many years, koalas were killed for their soft fur pelts. Though they are now on the endangered list, they're still in trouble due to loss of habitat, road kills, and a reproductive disease that leaves females infertile. Koala-cuddling is possible in some wildlife parks, and they are fun to hold (though their sharp claws don't exactly put you at ease).

The Tasmanian Devil bears no resemblance to the cartoon character and couldn't possibly spin like a tornado even if it wanted to. Looking more like a small rodent with wolf-like jaws, the nocturnal creature is found only in Tasmania, though it once inhabited the rest of the continent. It's quite rare to see a Devil in the wild, and even in zoos it is elusive (or often asleep).

Australasia (Papua New Guinea and Australia) is home to the earth's most primitive mammals, the monotremes, only three species of which survive today: the platypus and two species of echidna. Monotremes maintain both mammalian and reptilian characteristics. They lay eggs like reptiles but suckle their young like mammals, nurturing them either in a pouch (echidna) or in a similarly protected spot between the belly and tail (platypus). Although liberally distributed across the eastern coast and in Tasmania (the platypus in streams and the echidna in burrows), they are shy, and wildlife sanctuaries are the best places to see them.

It's impossible not to appreciate Australia's varied bird life. Dozens of brightly-colored parrots (such as the rosella) and other flamboyant birds are everywhere. Cockatoos, among the most common of all Australian birds, include the famous pink-headed galah and both sulphur-crested and pink cockatoos. The flightless emu's gangly yet powerful legs can reach extraordinary speeds on Australia's open plains. Elusive and at home in dense forests, the lyrebird is best known for its magnificent tail plumage and the male's courtship song, which imitates other noises in the bush.

By far the most famous Australian birdsong is the infectious laugh of the kookaburra. When one starts up, others join in until there's such a cacophony that it's hard not to crack a smile. You'll hear their guffaws in most parts of the country, wherever there are comfortable perches and plenty of grubs.

Introduced Fauna

Sheep, rabbits, buffalo, camels, and horses were among the animals brought by Europeans after their arrival in 1788. Today, wild horses ("brumbies") and camels roam the outback without much problem, while other introduced species, such as rabbits and buffalo, have wreaked havoc with the environment.

Sheep were brought by the first white settlers and have adapted so well to Australia's open grazing land that they outnumber the human population 10 to 1. Though cattle and sheep damage the landscape with their hoofs and deplete native animals' food supply, they have been crucial to the economy.

Another introduced animal makes even more trouble and has far fewer assets. Brought over for sport by a British landowner in 1859, the rabbit's extensive burrowing immediately disturbed Australia's natural environment. Its phenomenal reproductive ability quickly brought the population to plague proportions. Finally, in the 1950's, the rabbit-eradicating myxomatosis virus was released, bringing the problem under control. However, rabbits are still a big environmental problem.

Though considered intrinsically Australian, the dingo (a variety of dog) is yet another introduced animal. Thought to have been brought either by early Asian fishermen or Aboriginal immigrants, fossil records show that the dingo has been on the continent under 12,000 years. Dingoes, Australia's main faunal predator, are a constant threat to sheep and cattle. In an effort to keep dingoes from livestock, fences thousands of miles long have been erected across Australia's plains.

"Nasty Beasts"

Well known for its "nasties," Australia boasts seven of the world's ten deadliest snakes, plus a multitude of other poisonous and non-poisonous varieties. Hundreds of lizard species (including the gigantic lace-monitor and flamboyant frill-neck lizard) live throughout the continent, a few of which are also venomous.

Few people are ever injured by these creatures, and most likely you won't see any. Just remember to be on guard when camping or hiking.

The best-known poisonous spiders are the black widow ("red-back") and the funnel-web, whose gradual movement down the eastern coast is creating a lot of commotion. The huntsman spider's hairy body, which can grow as large as the palm of your hand, may give you momentary heart failure, but it's harmless.

Crocodile Dundee publicized the terrible, flesh-eating saltwater crocodile. Crocodiles *are* a serious threat, but only if you annoy them by trespassing in their territory. Fatalities caused by crocs are rare and occur mainly when people refuse to heed blatant warnings. The trick is to remember that a crocodile's territory includes riverbanks and coastal mouths of tropical northern regions. Don't swim or wade in these spots unless you're told it's safe.

Everyone has heard gruesome stories about the man-eating sharks in the warm Australian waters. However, for a country that spends a huge percentage of its leisure time at the beach, the number of shark attacks is so tiny that it's not worth worrying about. Far more threatening are box jellyfish ("stingers") in tropical northern waters. Their venomous sting can be fatal. When the stingers are out (approximately October-May) stick to designated swimming areas protected by nets. For more information on sea-dwelling nasties, see Queensland's introductory section.

Last, but far from least, is the Australian fly, one of the most annoying creatures on earth. Particularly thick in arid regions during the driest months, unfathomable numbers of these pests will descend on any exposed part of your anatomy (especially the eyes and mouth) in search of moisture. Natives have lived with their crawling and buzzing for so long that they don't seem to notice it anymore, but visitors may find it maddening. Wear a hat and try to construct some kind of veil. While the flies are persistent, they are also lethargic, and you can get vengeance by squashing several in a single blow.

At least those flies don't bite, which is more than can be said for the sandflies on many of the country's beaches. Aussies have developed an effective repellent for sandflies and marchflies that they've appropriately named Rid. We suggest you keep it handy at all times. Unfortunately, regular flies seem to disregard all repellents.

Flora

Much of the periphery of the Australian continent is forested. Dominating the vegetation are eucalypts, majestic trees whose branches and leaves are home and dinner for the koala. There are more than 500 eucalypt species across the country, many of which exist only in Australia. They include the world's tallest hardwood, the mountain ash (found in Tasmania and Victoria), which grows to over 100 meters. Eucalypts are found in all climates and terrains across the continent, from near-desert regions to tropical rainforests.

Like most of Australia's native plants, eucalypts descended from the ancient Gondwana rainforest. Their ancestors grew on the outskirts of the rainforest and, as the climate became drier, eucalypts (and any other plants that could cope with the aridity) survived.

Besides being able to draw nutrients from extremely poor soil, eucalypts can handle fire, a common and serious threat in dry environments. Their leaves contain a flammable oil (with a strong, peppermint scent) that burns hot and fast, charring the outside trunk but saving the inside. After a fire, new buds quickly emerge and the tree begins rejuvenation almost immediately. Indeed, many native plants have adapted so well to fire that it has become vital to their reproduction: the heat causes seeds and pods to burst open and release their life-bearing contents. This phenomenon is so important that many parts of the country practice controlled burning.

Confined to sheltered niches down the eastern coast of the continent and western Tasmania, Australia's modern rainforests are as lush as those found in any part of the world. Approximately 1,200 plant species compose the rainforests' dense, tropical vegetation, much of which is unique. Survival in the rainforest is contingent upon accessibility to sunlight (or adjusting to life within the gloom) and parasitic relationships. Most of the plants depend on their neighbors in some way.

The growth cycle of a fig tree, whose thick mass of airborne roots form a distinctive, spaghetti-like trunk, is a perfect example of this dependency. Seeds from other trees are dropped (often by birds) in a fork of the fig-branch and gradually send roots toward the ground in search of nutrients. The enormous canopy of the fig's branches cuts off much of the seedling's light source and it eventually dies, its roots then becoming part of the fig's massive trunk.

Much of Australia's arid lands are covered by a variety of dry, spiny grasses (spinifex) and spindly trees and bushes called acacias (wattles), but there is a vast array of desert flora that often goes unnoticed. Western Australia, separated from the rest of the country by deserts, is covered with a low-lying vegetation called heath, whose origin also lies within the ancient rainforest. Amongst the heath are over 3,600 wildflower species, 2,450 of which occur only in Australia. Spring rains (Sept-Oct) bring a burst of vibrant wildflowers which people travel great distances to see.

Other remnants of the Gondwana rainforest can be found even within the harshest of Australia's desert lands. Oases of palms, ferns, and cycads, one of the world's oldest plants, lie hidden in protected chasms and gorges of weather-worn mountain ranges.

The Australian Aborigines

Since traditional Aboriginal way of life ended when Europeans colonized Australia in 1788, the Aborigines did not join the country's bicentennial celebrations. Instead, Aborigines boycotted the events and arranged public displays, raising public consciousness and gaining international attention on their plight.

There is an increasing desire to preserve what is left of Aboriginal traditions and reacquaint the dwindling native population with its heritage before it is completely lost. Those interested in learning about the Aborigines should make sure to visit Kakadu National Park and Uluru National Park (Ayers Rock and The Olgas), both in the Northern Territory. You'll have the most first-hand contact with Aborigines if you travel in the N.T. and Western Australia.

Visitors with a specific interest in the Aborigines may visit Aboriginal reserves if they write at least a month ahead with a stated purpose and specific dates. (See *Appendix* for Land Council addresses and specific reserves.)

Arrival in Australia

Scientists believe the first humans crossed the channels between Australia and southeast Asia within the last 100,000 years, probably during two small ice ages 60,000 and 18,000 years ago, when sea levels were very low. Whether they came by choice or accident is unknown, and all record of initial contact probably washed away when the sea rose. The earliest evidence of human occupation in Australia is currently at Lake Mungo, New South Wales, and dates to 38,000 years ago.

The Aborigines' first contacts probably were with Melanesian and Indonesian fishermen, who brought pottery, canoes, and their cultural traditions. The first European visitors were the Dutch explorers in the 1600's, but they were just passing through. It wasn't until the British arrived in 1788 that real conflicts were posed to traditional Aboriginal life.

Aboriginal Philosophy and Way of Life

The theme underlying Aboriginal heritage is that of oneness with nature. Nature is respected, not conquered, because the Aborigines' health and well-being are inextricably connected to that of the environment (including the earth, plants, and animals).

This concept of the world is seen through Aboriginal creation myths, which

Drop Us a Line!

Please send us a postcard to let us know if we got something wrong—or something right. And tell us how we can improve the book in future editions. If we use your contribution, we'll send you a free copy of the next edition.

Mail postcards to us at Mustang Publishing, P.O. Box 3004, Memphis, TN 38173 U.S.A.

take place during the "dreamtime." Dreamtime Ancestors (or creators) took the form of large animals, birds, and plants. The Ancestors traveled across the vast, flat landscape, their movements and songs creating geologic features and their offspring generating the floral and faunal communities. At the same time, the Ancestors created the "rules" of the world, which can be read and remembered through the land features they created.

Thus, Aboriginal myths are "written" in the land, their symbolic importance rendered mostly through sung stories. These songs teach practical lessons about the land, explain creation, delineate tribal boundaries, and define social structure.

The Elders, a small group of highly-respected men who serve as the tribe's governing body, are the guardians of myths. Most members of a tribe know the general stories behind the myths, but the detailed sacred versions are reserved for initiated men.

The intensity and content of myths varies from one tribe to the next. If one tribe's territory contains many landforms, for example, it may have many more myths (to "explain" these features) than another tribe of a less diverse landscape. A tribe may "own" a section of a myth, and when a number of tribes meet, the group can piece together the whole myth by each performing its part. Thus there is a distinction between the sacred beliefs of individual tribes, yet an underlying unification amongst all tribes.

Although Westerners have perceived Aborigines as an unstructured, undisciplined people, Aboriginal life is highly regimented. Each tribal community is broken into smaller units, from clans, to bands, to the smallest unit, the family, and every individual has specific duties. Women provide the food staples that form the bulk of the diet (seeds, roots, nuts, grasses, insects, snakes, lizards, and fish, if available). They are also the food preparers and home builders. The men don't have familial duties because they must hunt large animals. More importantly, men must be free to participate in tribal rituals and ceremonies. It is the man's primary obligation to pass on the sacred traditions, care for the community at large, and uphold social order. To do so, he must learn the sacred myths, a life-long process taught through ritual and ceremony.

Although each tribe has a special affiliation to a specific area and tribal boundaries do exist (marked by natural features), there is no land ownership. An unspoken cooperation allows one tribe to wander into another's lands in search of food. Yet they are conscious of the boundaries and, in general, tribes keep to themselves.

Living on the Land

Aborigines live nomadically, moving in response to seasonal changes and resource availability. Instead of depleting food sources, they move on, letting the supply regenerate. Tribes vary in migrational habit: desert tribes are constantly mobile, while the better-endowed coastal tribes move between a selection of camps. In this manner, the Aborigines lived in peaceful equilibrium with the land for thousands of years.

The Aborigines do not cultivate land in the traditional sense but employ various methods to reap the greatest benefit from the environment. The most important, fire, is the central focus of camp, providing warmth, light, and a place to cook. In addition, setting fire to the bush makes hunting easier.

There is heated debate over the extent to which the Aborigines have manipulated and influenced long-term environmental changes. Fire is a constant threat to the native flora and fauna, but it has also become an important part of the natural cycle. (Many Australian plants, such as the eucalypt, need fire to procreate.) Controlled burning also helps keep natural fires (common in arid Australia) in check by clearing the dry, flammable undergrowth. Supervised bushfires are set in most of the country's national parks, but unregulated burning can be dangerous and is strictly prohibited—thus affecting an integral facet of Aboriginal life.

Aboriginal Art

Because the Aborigines have no written tradition, art is a vital means of communication and is often highly symbolic. Their art forms include story-telling, singing, music, dance, and visual art.

To most, Aboriginal art means rock paintings and carvings. Paintings are also often on bark and, for ceremonies, the human body. Intersecting circles, spirals, and dots create highly-stylized designs that explain myths, tell stories, and deliver messages (such as where a waterhole is located or what happened in the recent hunt). The colors, too, have specific meanings. The paintings are only really understood by the tribal members who have learned their meanings and intricately know the land.

Some of the best known examples of Aboriginal rock paintings, both modern and ancient, are found in Kakadu National Park (some of the oldest art in the world is at Ubirr, in Kakadu) and in the Kimberleys.

In tribal ceremonies, music, dance, and body-painting are used to dramatize sacred myths. Aborigines also enjoy music and dance in daily life. The term corroboree means a singing and dancing event, often non-sacred, which focuses on daily experiences. Tour operators in the Northern Territory offer visitors the opportunity to see contrived corroborees, but chances of seeing a real one are slim.

Among the unique Aboriginal musical instruments is the didjeridu, a hollowed-out branch that produces a mournful, droning sound. Some modern Australian bands ("Galapagos Duck," for example) use Aboriginal instruments and are definitely worth hearing.

European Contact and Assimilation

Once the British arrived on Australian shores, traditional Aboriginal lifestyles could no longer exist. Europeans believed in land-ownership, a concept so foreign to the Aborigines that they formed no defense against it. There was little understanding between the two cultures and little question over who would dominate. European weapons and desire for "law and order" quickly took control.

Many bloody clashes occurred as the Europeans cleared Aborigines off the land to make way for farming and livestock. The Aboriginal population, estimated at 300,000 by the first Europeans, rapidly dropped as they fell prey to European guns and diseases. In Tasmania, the slaughter was so complete that the last surviving Tasmanian Aborigine, Truganini (also known as Fannie Cochrane Smith), died in 1876.

Soon after Europeans came in contact with Aborigines, religious missions were set up to house, clothe, and educate them in "civilized" ways. Gradually the Aborigines were allowed to participate in political and social areas, though some states were far more progressive than others.

In 1966, South Australia led the way with the first anti-discrimination legislation, banning all types of race and color discrimination. In the mid-1960's, Aboriginal land reserves were created, and Aborigines got the right to vote in Federal elections at the end of the '60s. They received full Australian citizenship in 1968, the same year the Commonwealth Office of Aboriginal Affairs was formed. Neville Bonner was the first Aboriginal Member of Parliament, elected on the Liberal Party ticket to represent Queensland in 1972. There have since been other Aboriginal statesmen and members of the Federal government, though relatively few.

The Current Aboriginal Situation

All Australian Aborigines have now been exposed to white Australia. Some live on reserves, maintaining tribal traditions but still influenced by European culture. They drive cars, depend on Western medicine (mostly to cure Western-borne diseases), and eat European foods. Others live on the fringes of towns, like Alice Springs, alienated from both white society and their own tribe. Others live in city slums.

Most Aborigines are dependent on European goods and services but can't fully embrace the European culture. Their non-materialistic, non-individualistic world view has kept them from progressing economically, as has lack of European education. The current unemployment rate for Aborigines is six times the national rate.

Alcohol has done serious damage to individuals and the image of Aborigines as a whole. Tribal elders have banned alcohol from Aboriginal reserves in an effort to control it, but large numbers of addicted Aborigines leave their tribes for the pubs and end up alone, unacceptable to any community.

The current Aborigine population is between 200,000 and 300,000, very few of whom are full-blooded. Life expectancy for an Aborigine is 56 years (as opposed to 76 for an average European Australian), and Aboriginal infant mortality is three times the national rate.

The Aboriginal Lands Trust Act, passed in 1966, gave 18 million acres of land (most of it undesirable to white Australians) to the Aborigines to be managed by elected Aboriginal leaders and used for the benefit of their people as a group. However, land rights have been, and continue to be, responsible for many bitter disputes. Mining companies are currently uncovering rich deposits in land designated as Aboriginal territory, and the ensuing battle between money and property is never-ending.

History of Europeans in Australia

The existence of a great southern continent had been suspected by Westerners since at least 150 A.D. Sixteenth century charts show the Portuguese and Spanish believed *Terra Australis* existed, and they may have seen it; other records reveal that a Chinese vessel visited Australia's north coast in the 1400's.

But it was the Dutch who made the first official landings. Beginning with Willem Jansz in 1606, Dutch East India Company captains discovered and charted the western and far northeastern coasts of the continent. In 1642, Abel Tasman found Tasmania (he called it *Van Dieman's Land*), and two years later he charted most of the north coast of the mainland, calling it "New Holland." The Netherlands had every opportunity to claim New Holland as their own (and continued to land on the west coast from time to time) but abandoned thoughts of colonization, probably because the Dutch East India Company believed it would interfere with its trading activities.

Australia was thus open for the British to explore and colonize, starting with William Dampier's 1688 and 1699 voyages along the western and northern coasts. Seventy years later, Captain James Cook anchored the *Endeavour* at Botany Bay (south of modern Sydney). From there he sailed north and charted the entire east coast, officially claiming the land in the name of King James III. He named his discovery "New South Wales."

Settlement

A dire problem in England prompted the first colonization of Australia: the English criminal system was not functioning in slums, where petty crime was rampant. Most crimes went unpunished, because the police couldn't cope and jails had no room. But those who were caught and convicted got punished severely. Theft of more than one shilling, for instance, was punished by death.

A partial solution was to send convicts to America. When the American colonies became independent, the British decided to try Australia.

Preparations for that famous First Fleet, carrying Australia's first European settlers, were hasty and haphazard. Nonetheless, in May 1787, the First Fleet left Portsmouth, arriving at Botany Bay on January 18, 1788. They quickly moved to Port Jackson and founded a colony (now Sydney). There were 1,030 settlers, 736 of them convicts and the remainder mostly military personnel. Thus began the New South Wales colony.

Australia's second permanent settlement, Hobart, was founded in 1803, and several other penal settlements in Van Dieman's Land followed. Penal colonies at Moreton Bay (present-day Brisbane) in 1824, and Albany (south coast of Western Australia) in 1826 consolidated Britain's rule over the continent.

Free settlers had also begun to trickle over to Australia, fleeing depressed England and seeking new opportunities. In 1829, a group of investors put together a company that established Australia's first free settlement, at the mouth of the Swan River (now Perth). The second free settlement began in 1834 when pastoralists from Van Dieman's Land settled in Portland Bay, on the south coast of present-day Victoria. In 1836, a group of middle-class citizens seeking individual liberties settled Adelaide. The British parliament created an immigration plan in 1832, encouraging people who couldn't otherwise afford it to settle.

Convict Transportation

Convict labor was crucial to the survival and growth of the colonies. In fact, the Swan River Colony nearly failed without the cheap labor of convicts, and in 1850 convict transportation to Western Australia began out of economic necessity.

But as free settlers began to outnumber convicts, convicts came to be seen as a societal burden. Many settlers felt they were getting the dregs of English society. Furthermore, stories of misery in the penal settlements (sometimes leaked in Britain as a crime deterrent) and rumors of amorality in the larger society prevented more "upstanding" immigrants from settling. There was also a growing uneasiness about using convicts as semi-slave labor.

Meanwhile, liberals in Britain began to object to the conditions of penal camps. Men in power, most importantly the Home Secretary, sought to overhaul the British criminal system. Furthermore, England wanted enterprising, monied individuals to buy Crown Lands in Australia, and the convict system wasn't helping their promotional efforts.

In the end, the decision to slow down convict transportation was agreeable to decision-makers in both Britain and the colonies. It ended in New South Wales in 1840, and by 1853 it had ceased altogether on the east coast (Western Australia took convicts until 1868). In the final count, 163,663 convicts came to Australia from England, most of them to New South Wales or Tasmania.

Contrary to some expectations that freed convicts would become a permanently sullied class of people, many of them built successful lives and eventually assimilated into the general population.

Self-Government

England granted self-government to New South Wales, Victoria, Tasmania, and South Australia in 1855-1856, to Queensland in 1859, and to Western Australia in 1890. The next step, to nationhood, was taken reluctantly. As early as 1852, there was discussion of the need for a general colonial legislative authority.

But it wasn't until 1891 that the first federal convention began to write an Australian national constitution, which was accepted several drafts later by each colony. Australia retained strong ties to England, leaving the Queen as sovereign, the British parliament with authority to overrule Australian parliamentary legislation, and the Queen's Privy Council as highest appellate court. Federation came to the colonies in 1901, by an act of the British Parliament.

Gold and Immigration

The discovery of gold in 1851 near Bathurst, New South Wales, and much larger finds in Victoria (Ballarat and Bendigo) began a flurry of immigration, exploration, and economic activity in the Australian colonies. Subsequently, gold was found in Gympie, Queensland (1867), Mt. Morgan, Queensland (1882), and Coolgardie and Kalgoorlie, Western Australia (1892-93).

The waves of gold-seekers brought new faces to the country. Chinese came in large numbers, causing xenophobic riots on some gold fields. The bottom line, it seems, was that Chinese success threatened the status-quo.

Almost all the Chinese fortune-seekers returned home when the rushes were over, but a general resentment against Asians has remained in Australian history. Its twentieth century outgrowth, known as the "White Australia" policy, was a set of immigration laws that heavily favored Europeans (over 85% of immigrants to Australia until the early 1960's were European). One such law lasting until 1958 required entrants to pass a dictation test in a "European language" chosen by the immigration official—thus allowing Europeans and non-European British subjects (mostly Indians) to enter, while eliminating most Asians. All discriminatory laws were removed in 1973, and now more than a third of immigrants to Australia are Asian.

Non-British Europeans, too, were subject to narrow immigration quotas until after World War II, when Australia realized it needed bodies to help defend itself militarily and economically. Greeks, Italians, Yugoslavs, and Germans, among others, came in large numbers as part of an assisted immigration plan in the late 1940's.

Wars

Australia's twentieth-century history is inextricably linked to events in England and the United States. The Great Depression and the wars of this century were not just European and American worries. Australia sent troops to Korea and Vietnam, and, as part of the British Empire, Australia had to supply troops for both World Wars.

About 330,000 Australians (from a population under six million) fought in World War I. Their casualties were a staggering 226,073 (59,258 of whom were killed or missing). The landing at Gallipoli Peninsula on April 25, 1915 by ANZAC (Australia and New Zealand Army Corps) forces, and the ensuing eight-month battle that was eventually lost to the Turks, remains one the nation's most heroic and tragic events.

Australia suffered again in World War II, when the threat was more immediate. In 1942, the Japanese bombed the entire north coast, from Exmouth to Cape York. Darwin was bombed 64 times, killing 261 civilians. Nearly 34,000 Australians died in combat or in Japanese prison camps in World War II.

Government

When the Commonwealth of Australia was born in 1901, it was envisioned as a constitutional monarchy, with the English monarch as ceremonial head and a bicameral parliament, lead by a Prime Minister, as the main governing body. There were six states: New South Wales, Victoria, Queensland, Western Australia, South Australia, and Tasmania. The Northern Territory and Australian Capital Territory, or A.C.T. (a small region surrounding Australia's capital, Canberra) were added as territories in 1911.

The system remains essentially the same, though ties to Britain have loosened. The British crown still appoints a Governor General, whose position is largely ceremonial. There are 12 senators from each state and two from each territory. The House is roughly twice the size of the Senate and members are elected according to population, though no state can have fewer than five representatives.

Voting in Australia is compulsory for all adults. The law is strictly enforced, and if you don't vote, you get fined.

State government mirrors the federal system: the state premier is the head of the majority party in parliament; state parliaments have an upper and lower house (except for Queensland, which is unicameral); and the crown appoints a governor.

In 1986 the final judicial ties to Britain were severed by the Australian Act, which made Australia's highest court of appeals the Australian High Court, rather than Britain's Privy Council. The High Court consists of seven justices and is responsible for interpreting the Constitution and federal law, as well as for taking cases appealed from lower courts.

Australia's major political parties are the Australian Labor Party and the more conservative Australian Liberal Party, in coalition with the National Party.

There is a strong tradition in Australia of government social programs, including fully socialized health services. Utilities and transportation are generally government-run, and university education is virtually free. (A recent university fee of about $300 a year caused a nationwide uproar.) Unions have enormous power; they work hand in hand with the ruling Labor Party, and workers do well in Australia by world standards. 55% of the workforce is unionized, topping Great Britain by more than 10%, and workers average 4-6 weeks of vacation per year.

A new right wing has recently gained momentum in state and federal politics, and in the last decade unions and the socialized state have been under increasing scrutiny, largely due to a faltering economy.

Economy and Resources

Australia's per capita income is one of the highest in the world. That's the good news. The bad news is that unemployment is high, the country has accrued a huge foreign debt, the currency is declining, and, despite enormous natural resources and protective tariffs, many manufacturing businesses can't make a profit.

Australia's mineral and energy resources are large and rich, comprising 40% of the country's export revenue. Mt. Isa (Queensland) and Broken Hill (New South Wales) have some of the richest silver, lead, and zinc deposits in the world. Gold and copper, which first energized Australian colonial economies in the 19th century, are still mined extensively, as are iron and zinc. Australia provides about 28% of the free world's uranium (especially near Darwin), and the world's largest bauxite deposit is at Weipa on Cape York

Peninsula. About 90% of the world's opal supply comes from Coober Pedy (South Australia) and Lightning Ridge (New South Wales), and the earth's only black opals are mined at Lightning Ridge. The largest industrial diamond mine in the world is just outside Kununurra, Western Australia. Coal (the nation's leading source of export revenues), petroleum, and natural gas are other major resources.

Traditionally the backbone of the Australian economy, agriculture is still enormously important. It's probably not a surprise that Australia is the world's top wool producer and second largest lamb exporter (behind New Zealand). Australia is also the world's leading exporter of beef and veal. Dairy products are also important. The nation's top two crops are sugarcane and wheat, with barley close behind. Among the most prominent fruits grown are apricots, apples, pineapples, and grapes, and Australia's wines have received international praise.

The Language

Before arriving Down Under, most people have heard Paul Hogan's endearing "G'day" (pronounced "gidd-AY," not "gidd-EYE") and a few other Australian-isms like "mate" and "no worries." But once there, the English language takes on new meaning. "Strine," or Australian English, has a vocabulary unto itself, and the cockney-esque accent, while charming, is difficult to interpret. Aussies—"ozzies"—love it that way.

In Strine, minimizing the spoken word is vital. Why bother with "Good day" when "g'day" is so much easier? Or waste breath asking for tea or coffee when "'ave a cuppa?" brings out the steaming mugs just as fast? Simply drop all unnecessary words and stick to the essentials. Aussies don't care much for frills.

Abbreviate whenever possible. When in doubt, drop the last syllable and tack on "ie," "y," or "o." In the morning, you'll awake and eat *brekkie,* then in the *arvo* (afternoon) you can enjoy a *footy* match (Australian-rules football) or play the part of a *touro* and see the sights.

Everything gets a nickname. While researching our way across the country, we learned to accept the title of *journo* after realizing that most professions are similarly abbreviated (postmen are *posties,* trash collectors *garbos,* etc.). Nicknames are rarely offensive (though doctors are commonly called "quacks")—it's all part of the Australian disregard for pretension.

Before tackling Strine, you'll need a basic vocabulary toolkit. *Bloody* is a ubiquitous adjective, used for emphasis whenever the spirit moves. Try not to get in the habit of using it, because it's bloody hard to stop once you've bloody started (and it's not particularly polite, either). Other true blue Aussie words are *beaut* (short for beautiful, used when things are great or going well), *fair dinkum* (true or honest), *loo* (bathroom, a.k.a. *dunny*) and *tucker* (food). We've adopted a few more which are used in the text: *uni* (university), *grotty* (dismal; also dirty or unkempt), *petrol* (gasoline), and *nasty* (dangerous animal, insect, reptile, or sea-dwelling creature).

Boozing (or *swilling*) is a favorite Australian pastime. No doubt you'll visit at least one bar (*pub, hotel*) during your stay. The general term for alcohol is *grog*. Cheap wine is *plonk*, and each state has its own set of names for beer sizes, including *pony, middy*, and *schooner* (see below for details). But beware: Heavy *raging* may make you *blotto* (a.k.a. *blind*) and leave you feeling *crook*.

Aussies have nicknames for all nationalities and use them unabashedly. New Zealanders are *kiwis*, Brits are *poms* (from P.O.H.M., which stands for "Prisoner Of Her Majesty"), and Americans are *yanks* (usually preceded by "bloody"). As long as the tone of voice is friendly, these aren't meant to insult. However, if you're called a *bugger, drongo*, or *galah* (an Australian parrot), you're not being complimented.

Women are sometimes referred to as *sheilas*. This is an old Australian term meaning "young ladies" that harkens back to the heyday of Aussie male chauvinism. It is rarely used nowadays but when it is, it's not taken politely. (A synonym for *sheila* is *skirt*, similarly unappealing.)

When you see a sign saying "No Sandshoes," you'll need to change out of your sneakers. Yes, even clothing (*togs*) has its own vocabulary. A *windcheater* is a sweatshirt, sweaters are *jumpers*, and a *skivvy* is a turtleneck. And don't forget your *bathers* (swimsuit) and *thongs* (flip-flops) when you head to the beach.

If you've ever heard *Waltzing Matilda*, you've probably wondered what it all means. The song is quintessential Strine. A *swagman* goes *waltzing Matilda*, meaning a wanderer carrying a *swag* (a bag of possessions) goes wandering. A *billy* is a tin can used to make tea on an open fire. *Jumbucks* are sheep, and sheep live on *stations* (ranches). Stations are worked by male *jackaroos* and female *jillaroos* (ranch hands, often apprentices), *stockmen, drovers*, and *ringers* (the station's best horseman or shearer). The farther you go into the *bush* (anything that's not city), the more these words will come in handy.

Every now and then you'll hear someone say something that makes absolutely no sense. Don't worry: it's just rhyming slang (or else someone who's been in the pub too long). An Irish-born phenomenon, rhyming slang is an intricate language of riddles in which obscure rhyming words or phrases are substituted for the proper words. (For instance, "pass the dead 'orse" is a request for the tomato sauce.) If you can unveil a single riddle, consider yourself fair dinkum Aussie.

Although you probably won't hear Aboriginal spoken, you'll notice many towns and geographic features with incredibly long names and lots of vowels, like Coonabarabran and Wooloomooloo. These are Aboriginal words with meanings that often relate to the town's geological setting or other interesting characteristics. They're far too long for Australians, who usually abbreviate them (e.g. "Coona" and, unfortunately, " 'loo").

One final word of warning: If you go to a footy match, avoid asking the person next to you whom they're "rooting" for. The Strine definition is unprintable—try "barracking" instead.

Australian Sports

Australians may be the most sport-crazed people in the world. The country stops in its tracks for events like the V.F.L. (Victorian Football League) final and Melbourne Cup day (horse race). School teachers turn on the radio, and office workers gather for chicken and champagne before taking the rest of the day off. When Australia won the America's Cup in 1987, the entire country closed for the day and headed to the nearest pub.

Blame it on the Southern Hemisphere's beautiful weather. Most Australians live on the coast, and everybody enjoys swimming, sailing, windsurfing, snorkeling, and scuba-diving. Among the most distinctive Aussie sports are footy (Australian-rules football), cricket, rugby, and horse racing. Golf is also popular. There are hundreds of golf courses across the country, even in the arid regions (where the greens are more like "reds"). If you've never played tennis on finely-cropped grass, try it Down Under.

Cricket has been a national passion since it was first played in Australia in 1838. Though we really tried, comprehending the game evaded us. There is a man wearing huge shin guards and carrying a big bat. Some other man hurls the ball very hard at him, and he swings at it from somewhere around his ankles. If the batsman hits it, he runs back and forth between two posts and scores runs. Other than that, there's not much action nor is there a time-limit (unless it's a one-day match). Everyone looks very nice on the field, all dressed in white, and it's fun to sit on the lawn, sip sherry, and enjoy a match on a sunny day. Cricket season is October-February.

Horse racing is another favorite Aussie pastime. Modelled after Ascot in England, the Melbourne Cup was first established in 1861 and is held on the first Tuesday in November. Everyone who's anyone in Melbourne attends, but there's always a big crowd of irreverent viewers, sipping stubbies and doing their own, undeniably Aussie, thing.

As for Australian-rules football: Invented in Melbourne in 1858 to keep cricketers fit, *footy* must be one of the world's most physically demanding sports. It's a game of incessant running and no substitutions (unless there's an injury—which isn't unusual since no padding is worn—and even then only two substitutions are allowed). The leather ball is heavier and rounder than the American football, and the game is reminiscent of rugby.

A footy field is a grass-covered oval approximately 200 yards long by 130 yards wide. At each end are four posts. The object of the game is to get the ball through the central goal posts (6 points) or, less ideally, through the outer "behind" posts (1 point). The ball must be kicked through the posts for a full score; if it's punched or run through, only one point is scored. In order to accomplish this, the 18 players can kick, punch, or run with the ball, and it must touch the ground every five yards.

At the start of the game, at the half, or after a goal has been scored, a referee takes the ball to a circle in the center of the oval and bounces it on the ground as hard as he can between the two opposing ruckmen. The *rucks*, often the tallest men on the field, run at full speed towards the airborne ball and take a flying leap with an outstretched arm in an attempt to knock it to one of their teammates waiting outside the circle's edge. They then try to move the ball down to the goal posts as fast as possible. If a player catches a kicked ball before it hits the ground (a "mark"), he is given a free kick. This often results in a goal if it's close enough to the posts.

Victoria dominates the footy scene (though other states would object vehemently to this statement); the Victorian Football League (V.F.L.) is the biggest league in the country. Its players (always men) used to have another profession and played football on the side, practicing a few times a week for Saturday matches. Now the players are getting paid enough to make footy a full-time career, though their salaries are nothing like those of American football players.

Footy season starts in March and ends in September with the V.F.L. final. Melbourne and Adelaide are the best places to see league footy. To do it in true Aussie fashion, be sure to have a meat pie and beer while you watch.

Food

Though perhaps not what you'd call gourmet, Aussie *tucker* has a charm of its own. You don't have to look far to find it: meat pies, sausage rolls, and *pasties* are sold in every little food shop, and there's a hotel *counter meal* on practically every corner.

Australia's recent immigrants have begun to re-define the food scene. Among the more visible ethnic groups are Chinese, Middle Easterners, Vietnamese, Italians, and Greeks. (Melbourne supposedly has the largest Greek community outside Athens.) Some of the best and cheapest meals are in the ethnic restaurants. A large bowl of Vietnamese noodles, a few Lebanese "dips" with homemade flat bread, or an array of Chinese *dim sum* (or *yum cha*) will fill you up for nearly nothing.

But traditional Aussie fare does have its merits—so don't leave the country without braving the Vegemite jar!

Of course, true Australian food is Aboriginal bush food. However, unless you want to search for roast goanna (lizard), witchetty grubs (larvae), and honey ants, you'll probably have to give it a miss.

Before embarking on your first Australian meal, take note of a few terms that could lead you astray. Australians call the main course a *main*, the appetizer an *entree*, and desserts *sweets*. The term *tea* doesn't necessarily mean an afternoon affair with coffee, tea, and cakes (though Devonshire teas do exist). *Tea* (a.k.a. *supper*) generally refers to the evening meal, and *dinner* means the midday meal, but often these terms are used interchangeably.

By the way, "water" said with an American accent is one of the most difficult words for Australians to interpret. Restaurants don't serve water automatically, so you'll have to request it. Despite the language barrier, H_2O will eventually appear if you persist.

For the quintessential Australian dining experience, pack an *eski* (cooler) with plenty of beer, wine, and ice and head to the bush or beach for a *barbie* (barbecue). Build a fire, throw on some chops and *snags* (sausages), and if you can find an Aussie to show you what to do, make *damper* (unleavened, fire-baked bread) and *billy tea* (tea made in a well-seasoned tin can which must have a handle so it can be swung overhead to "settle the tea leaves"). For real authenticity, be sure to notify the fly population of your locale. The next best thing to a barbecue is a hotel (pub) *counter meal*. By law, all hotels are required to serve meals, but food quality varies drastically. Menus are usually written on a chalkboard in front of the entrance. You choose a *main* (typically roast beef, lamb, chicken, deep-fried fish, or veal patties), and it comes on a plate heaped with carbohydrates: a roll, chips (french fries) or another form of potato, and salad (usually coleslaw, beets, and potato salad—maybe a lettuce leaf). Of course, a glass of beer helps wash those carbos down.

Australians eat lots of fast food, but it's not the same as in the United States (though McDonald's, Kentucky Fried Chicken, and Burger King—which they call "Hungry Jack's"—are very popular). Australian *takeaways* include meat pies, *pasties* (a meat and vegetable turnover), sausage rolls, and fish 'n chips. (*Chips* are french fries, *crisps* are potato chips, and you'll need to request "tomato sauce" if you want ketchup.) There's plenty of pizza, but it's topped with novelties like chopped pineapple and chicken.

Don't let confusing names stop you from trying the many fresh- and saltwater-dwelling delicacies across the country. *Prawns* are shrimp, and lobster is also called *marron* (saltwater relatives are "crayfish" and "Moreton Bay bug"). There are dozens of new fishes to taste, including John Dory, barramundi, and trevally. Whiting is the best choice in a fish 'n chips shop. If you can afford them, fresh Sydney rock oysters are worth a splurge.

Australian breakfasts are expensive and not very good by U.S. standards. Instant coffee is the norm, and a small cup costs about $1.20. Weetbix cereal, rectangles of compressed wheat flakes, instantly become mush when milk is administered. "Cooked breakfasts" are typical English-style fare (eggs, bacon, and grilled tomatoes) but also feature spaghetti or baked beans on toast and other intriguing fare.

However, far and away the most important Australian breakfast food is Vegemite, a dark brown, shoe-polish-like goop with an alarmingly long shelf life. Aussies are hooked on this salty, beef-flavored yeast extract (rumored to be the scum off fermenting vats of beer). To eat Vegemite properly, scrape a thin layer on hot, buttered toast.

The typical Australian has an big sweet tooth. Cadbury's chocolates are everywhere, but the authentic Australian *lollies* (candies) are "Violet Crumble" and "Cherry Ripe" (chocolate bars filled with spun-sugar "honeycomb" and mashed cherries, respectively). For dessert, try a slice of *pavlova* (meringue cake with whipped cream and fresh fruit), a *lamington* (sponge cake covered with icing and coconut), or *Peach Melba* (a peach poached in syrup, topped with vanilla ice cream and set amidst raspberry puree). If you're craving a late afternoon snack, dive into a plate of hot scones, whipped cream, and homemade jam—otherwise known as *Devonshire tea*. This investment is often so good that you'll be sated until the next morning.

Where to Eat

B.Y.O. restaurants, a blessing for budget travelers, allow diners to buy wine or beer at the local liquor store and bring it to the restaurant, thus avoiding inflated restaurant alcohol prices. Generally, B.Y.O.s have the cheapest meal prices (though not always, and sometimes there's a small corkage fee).

Hotel counter meals are a great way to fill up cheaply. Counter lunches are usually served from noon-2:00pm, dinners from 5:00pm-7:00pm, and cost between $6-$10.

For a cheap meal and a uniquely Australian cultural experience, try a service or sports club. These establishments always have some sort of restaurant (inexpensive, pub-quality food), in addition to bars, game rooms, and a crowd of friendly Aussies. Foreigners can sign in as guests without a sponsoring member and usually at no additional cost.

The Hare Krishnas have made it to practically every major city in the world, and they've definitely found Australia. Though you may not agree with their philosophies, there is no denying that their food is good and the prices unbeatable. If you can stand the proselytizing (which isn't usually too pushy), you can stuff yourself with all kinds of vegetarian food for under $4.

Budget travelers can really save by cooking for themselves. Most hostels provide cooking facilities and a refrigerator. The larger cities have open-air markets and supermarkets that sell fresh produce and meat, and even small country towns have a bakery with irresistible fresh bread.

Remember that tipping is not customary. Another blessing for penny-counters is that there's no additional tax: whatever price you see on the menu is the price you'll see on the bill.

Drink

Alcohol is an integral part of Australian life. A *barbie* just wouldn't be the same without a cooler full of *grog*, and nothing goes better with footy than ice cold beer. The legal drinking age is 18, but no one cares much. There has been an attempt to clamp down on drunken drivers, but with the popularity of drive-through liquor stores, habits probably won't change much.

Australian beer and wine are both cheap and good. A glass of beer in a pub costs about $1, wine about $1.20. Large discount liquor stores or Coles' Liquorland are the best places to find a wide selection of good, inexpensive wines. Beer's easy to find anywhere. If you like a particular bottle of wine while visiting a vineyard, buy it; chances are you won't find it in a store.

A *hotel* in Australia is primarily a drinking establishment. It has one or more public bars (hence the name "pub") and is required to provide food and lodging (though standards vary enormously). Even the smallest outback towns have a hotel. In fact, some "towns" are only a hotel and a petrol station. Usually made of wood with a roof of corrugated iron, outback pubs are a cultural experience in themselves—especially for single women.

When you go into an old Australian hotel, you'll notice both the "public bar" and a "ladies lounge." Not so long ago, women were not allowed in the main bar area, and they quietly drank in the ladies lounge while the men boisterously swilled in the public bar. The lounge area tends to be the plusher of the two bars and is often still more welcoming for women.

As a conservation measure during World War I, Australian pubs closed at 6:00pm, giving birth to the "five o'clock swill." As soon as the 5:00pm workday ended, everyone headed to the nearest hotel and lined up a row of beers to guzzle before the 6:00pm whistle. (You can witness a similar event by walking the streets in "The Rocks" section of Sydney at 11:00pm on Friday or Saturday.) Pub owners were delighted to complete their nightly duties in one frenzied hour, and the 6:00pm closing continued through to the 1950's.

Today, hotels are generally open 10:00am-11:00pm on weekdays, 11:00am-midnight Friday and Saturday, and 11:00am-8:00pm Sunday (after which hearty partiers migrate to nightclubs).

Beer

Aussie beer is world famous, not only because enormous quantities are consumed each night in hotels throughout the country, but also because it's good. Overseas, most people have heard of Fosters (of the renowned "oil cans"), and other brands are breaking into the international market. So if you get hooked on Australian beer, you should be able to relieve the craving back home.

Australian brew comes in a variety of styles, including pale ale, bitter ale, and light lager, and its alcohol percentage hovers around 6%. Bottles of beer are called *stubbies* (because of their stumpy necks), cans are *tinnies* or *tubes*.

However, when you order in a pub, the name game becomes complicated. A "glass of beer" means something different in each state: in Western Australia you'll get 5 oz., in Tasmania 6 oz., and in Victoria 7 oz. The chart should help you through the maze of Aussie pubs. It isn't comprehensive (especially with regard to beer brands) nor definitive, but it should provide insight into the vast Australian beer world.

Wine

Australian wines are gaining international fame. The recent introduction of *cask wine* (cardboard boxes holding wine-filled plastic bags) has made bulk wine cheaper than bottled beer. They also sell two liter, headache-promoting flagons of cheap port and sherry. However, Australia has plenty of good, reasonably priced bottled wines.

Most exported wines are mass-produced table wines from Australia's wine giants which, though good, aren't representative of the quality available in the country. You're allowed to bring back only two bottles duty-free, so you'll either have to take another trip Down Under or pay extra export tax.

If you're interested in learning about wine, Australia is a great place to start because its total production is small, and its vineyards are unpretentious and welcoming. The best way to learn is by going to any of Australia's wine-growing areas and tasting at vineyard cellars. The best known wine regions (and the most tourist-oriented) are the Hunter Valley, north of Sydney, and the Barossa Valley, north of Adelaide, but there are many others. South Australia's Southern Vales, the Margaret River area in southeastern

Australian Beer Brands and Sizes

State	Brands	Sizes
South Australia	Cooper's Ale, West End, Southwark Bitter	6 oz. "butcher" 9 oz. "schooner" 15 oz. "pint"
Western Australia	Swan, Emu	5 oz. "glass" 7 oz. "middy" 10 oz. "pot"
Victoria	V.B. (Victoria Bitter), Carlton, Foster's	7 oz. "glass" 10 oz. "pot"
New South Wales	Tooey's, K.B., Tooth's	7 oz. "seven" 10 oz. "middy" 15 oz. "schooner" 20 oz. "pint"
Tasmania	Cascade, Boag's	6 oz. "six" 8 oz. "eight" 10 oz. "ten"
Queensland	4X, Bulimba, Mac's, Cairns, Powers	8 oz. "beer" 10 oz. "pot"
Northern Territory	Swan and Carlton breweries in Darwin	7 oz. "glass" multi-oz. "Darwin Stubby"

Western Australia, and Mudgee, east of the Hunter Valley, are our favorites.

The original colonists planted the first vines near Sydney in 1788. As the colonists spread, so did the vines. Though most of those early growers were untrained, they knew what they wanted and wrestled with the environment to get it. It was a hard battle; whole regions were wiped out by insects and drought. As a result, Australia's wine industry grew haphazardly, and its wine-growing regions are not unified.

Only a few areas in Australia have a climate mild and dependable enough to grow grapes. All of the notable wine-growing areas are between the latitudes 32° and 38°S (except for those in Tasmania)—latitudes comparable to the most famous wine districts in France. South Australia produces most of the country's wine. The biggest companies include Hardy's, Orlando,

Lindeman's, Penfolds, and Seppelts, bit it's hard to keep straight who owns what and where. Larger wineries are constantly expanding by buying smaller wineries, and table wines are often blends from grapes of a few regions.

Most Australian wineries make a number of wines, all of which are available for tasting at their cellars. The wine styles and grape names are confusing, borrowed from Europe and often misspelled in the process. The red wine grapes are usually Cabernet Sauvignon blended with either Shiraz (Sirah, Syrah, Hermitage), Merlot, Malbec, or Grenache, and the result is called "Claret" or "Burgundy." Grapes used for white wines are mainly Reisling and Chardonnay. True to their British heritage, Australians love port. The Grenache grape is predominantly used to make this after-dinner drink (but Australian Shiraz ports are also addictive).

When vineyard-hopping, bring along a loaf of bread and some cheese; it'll help clear your tastebuds as well as your head. If you're serious about wine, there are a number of books available that will help unravel the mysteries of the Australian wine industry and lead you to the vineyards.

Books, Films, Bands
Here are some of the best books (ranging from fiction to scientific) we've found about Australia. Some are available only in Australia. However, if you're eager to get a book before leaving home or after you're back and have trouble locating a copy, contact **The Australian Book Source, 1309 Redwood Lane, Davis, CA 95616 (phone 916-753-1519).**

The Fatal Shore, by Robert Hughes
A Fortunate Life, by A.B. Facey
The First Australians, by R.M. and C.H. Berndt
Insight Guides: Australia, APA Productions
Kings in Grass Castles, by Mary Durack
The Magic Pudding, by Norman Lindsay
Nature of Australia, by John Vandenbeld
The Songlines, by Bruce Chatwin
The Thorn Birds, by Colleen McCullough
Tracks, by Robyn Davidson
We of the Never Never, by Jeannie Gunn (Mrs. Aeneas)
Australia's Kakadu Man, by Bill Neidjie, Stephen Davis, & Allan Fox

Aussie-oriented films include A Man from Snowy River, and its sequel, Return From Snowy River, Crocodile Dundee, and its sequel, Crocodile Dundee II, Breaker Morant, Gallipoli, Mad Max, A Town Like Alice, My Brilliant Career, The Last Wave, Walkabout, Picnic at Hanging Rock, The Coca Cola Kid, and The Thorn Birds.

For a slice of Australian humor, see if Barry Humphries is in town. Humphries plays a few outrageous characters, the most popular of which is the garish, ultra-flamboyant Dame Edna, who's sure to offend at least 90% of her (his?) audience. (Word of warning: don't arrive late to a Barry Humphries show.)

Musicians and bands with an Australian flavor include INXS, Air Supply,

Crowded House, Men at Work, AC/DC, Midnight Oil (in particular *Beds Are Burning*, a political song about the Aboriginal situation), Olivia Newton-John, and The Bee Gees.

Shopping

Australia's tourist industry has soared lately, and so has the number of Australiana shops. Their shelves are crammed with stuffed koala bears, tea towels and coasters with Australian wildflower designs, *stubby holders* (beer can holders), boomerangs—anything "Australian" that will sell. Ken Done's colorful cartoon-like sketches of Sydney's harbor, koalas, and other Australian symbols are practically a national emblem and boldly emblazon t-shirts, mugs, stickers, cards, and any marketable surface. Often, though not always, the prices are outrageously high, and the quality is poor. Our advice: stick to postcards and save your money.

Most people want to bring home "outback" gear, the hats and clothes worn by REAL Australians on the sheep stations. Well, they really do wear those things, and you can actually buy the same ones—but they're expensive. Felt Akubra hats cost at least $80AUS. *Driza-bone* coats (or *oilskins*) are around $200AUS. However, they're made to withstand the Australian climate and should last at least a lifetime.

The biggest name in outdoor wear is currently R.M. Williams. Their stores, found in every major Australian city, stock every style Akubra hat and oilskin made, as well as moleskin pants, wool sweaters, and leather boots. The cheapest place to buy an Akubra is through a stockman's supply company, if you can find one; ask a local for help.

Aboriginal art—mainly bark paintings, musical instruments (like the *didjeridu*), wooden bowls, and spears—are sold in galleries throughout Australia for phenomenal prices. If you can make the trip, the best prices are at the reserves, where you're also assured that most of your money goes to the artist. Otherwise, the next best place to buy Aboriginal art is in Alice Springs, Darwin, or at Ayers Rock.

With all those sheep, it's no surprise to find a bit of wool around. Hand-knit sweaters (*jumpers*) aren't cheap, but they're well-made and often have colorful, inventive designs. Knitters looking for skeins to make their own sweaters will be in seventh heaven, though they too will pay for quality. Other sheep-related products are rugs, car seats, and "Ugg" boots (rubber-soled sheepskin boots that are a necessity for winter days in Adelaide, Melbourne, and Tasmania—also perfect for North American winters.)

The only place in the world that produces black opals is Lightning Ridge in northwestern New South Wales. (Black opals have the same iridescent play of colors as white opals, but the background is dark rather than white). Most of the world's opals come from Lightning Ridge and Coober Pedy, S.A.

You can buy opals in three forms: solid (which, unless you're willing to spend large sums of money, you'll have to skip), "doublets," and "triplets." The latter two are actually thin slices of opal glued to a glass or quartz backing, and a triplet has an additional convex glass or quartz covering. Solid opals eventually dry out and crack (wipe them with mineral oil periodically to help prevent this), so the protective layering of a triplet can be more appealing than it sounds.

T-shirts and sweatshirts (*windcheaters*), for some unknown reason, are incredibly overpriced, but there's plenty of affordable clothing if you stay out of the chic boutiques. Petrol and cars, anything electronic, film and photo processing, books, and cigarettes are other wallet-damaging items you'll find Down Under. We suggest you stick to the large department stores (like Coles), and avoid buying toiletries at *chemists* (pharmacies) or groceries at *milkbars* (small convenience stores).

Scattered throughout the country, open-air markets offer inexpensive shopping, eating, and entertainment. In northern New South Wales and Queensland, "roving" Sunday markets are laid-back affairs that move between towns selling jewelry from Bali, tie-dyed clothing, and Indonesian food. Paddy's market in Sydney has a huge assortment of handmade crafts, jewelry, and clothing. One of the best markets in the country is in Darwin, where hundreds flock to spend the evening on Mindil Beach to buy dinner from a huge selection of international foods, wander about surveying the array of Balinesian jewelry, then relax on blankets with bottles of wine and listen to music. There are also fresh produce markets in every big city which usually have the best (and cheapest) fruit and veggies around. Melbourne's Queen Victoria Market is, deservedly, the most famous.

About the Maps

There are two kinds of maps in this book: professional maps (many by Merv Godfrey, and some from the Australian Tourist Commission) and "homemade" maps, which you should use for orientation only. If you're driving, get a detailed road map. On the homemade maps, note the following:

1. North is always at the top (approximately).

2. Solid lines=coastline

   Dotted lines=roads

   Dashed lines=state borders

   Black areas (solid)=national parks/reserves

3. Distances are rounded to the nearest multiple of 5 km.

New South Wales

Australia's oldest, most populated, and most industrial state isn't all that old (founded in 1788), or populated (six million), or industrial (manufacturing is limited to the urban sprawl from Newcastle—120 km north of Sydney—to Wollongong, 70 km south of Sydney; wool and wheat production are still a significant sector of the economy). While the state is urban and sophisticated by Australian standards, N.S.W. has plenty of outback.

About 60% of the state's population lives in greater Sydney, and almost all the remainder lives east of the Great Dividing Range.

New South Wales has no spell-binding or unique natural attractions—at least, nothing equal to the Great Barrier Reef, Ayers Rock, or Kakadu National Park. For the traveler, N.S.W. is a place to meet Aussies and observe their everyday lives.

To be sure, there's much to enjoy—Sydney, first and foremost, the dramatic Blue Mountains, numerous gorges and waterfalls on the eastern scarp of the Great Dividing Range, wine valleys, and beautiful coastal areas.

New South Wales is a popular place to travel. Always book ahead for coastal destinations, especially in December and January for accommodations on the coast between Sydney and Brisbane, Queensland. If you're considering a trip to the Snowies in winter, you need to book accommodation as far ahead as possible, since local skiers make their plans months ahead of time.

When to Go
The climate is generally moderate, with coastal-zone summer temperatures rarely above 32 °C (90 °F) and winter temperatures around 12 °C (55 °F), though it occasionally freezes at night.

The only special consideration is outback regions west of the Great Dividing Range, where summer temperatures can reach 50 °C (120 °F). In the heat of summer, you might be more comfortable traveling by public transport rather than using your own car to reach places like Lightning Ridge and Broken Hill.

Itinerary
Allow plenty of time for Sydney and the area (Hunter Valley, Blue Mountains), and see the rest of the state on your way elsewhere.

For instance, get to Queensland via the northern coastal route from Sydney, or via New England. Go to Lightning Ridge and Queensland's Darling

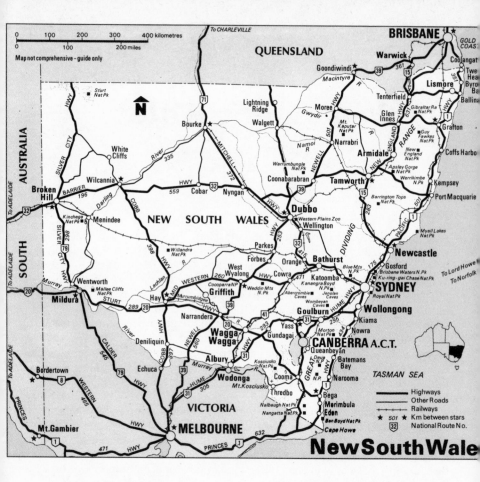

Downs via the midnorth region (Mudgee, Dubbo, and Coonabarabran). Visit the Illawarra (Bundanoon and Gerringong) en route to Canberra, and see the Snowies from Canberra. See the south coast or the Snowies, or both, on the way to Victoria. Visit Broken Hill on the way to South Australia.

Sydney is really the only "must see."

Getting Around

N.S.W. is well-serviced by public transport, but there's a catch. Licensing laws protecting the government-run State Rail (which operates both train and coach services) limit the scope of commercial interstate buslines.

For the most part, you must be traveling interstate or a minimum of 200 km to use the big buslines, such as Deluxe, Greyhound, Pioneer, and Bus Australia. Exceptions are made for bus pass holders, and each bus company has different restrictions, so get specifics in Sydney before taking off. (YHA's travel agency, at 176 Day St. in Sydney, is a good place to ask. Otherwise, individual bus companies will tell you.) Take heart in the fact that those places which can't be serviced by the major buslines are serviced by State Rail or local bus companies.

State Rail offers a 14-day, unlimited travel **Nurail Pass**. Get details on this and all State Rail service in Sydney at Transport House, Wynyard Station, 11-31 York St. (phone 02-29-7614).

Airlines service most country areas, all from Sydney. East-West and Air New South Wales are the major companies; check with a travel agent for updated information.

Finally, budget tours and activity groups are a great way to see places you wouldn't otherwise be able to get to. **Rob's Outback Tours**, based in Sydney, are low budget and highly recommended. **YHA of N.S.W.** has an activity group that offers trips of all sorts, from small outings to extended hikes. The trips are open to anyone and free, except for direct costs such as food, gas, and entrance fees. The program schedule is available at YHA and weekly meetings are in the Sir Thomas Mitchell Room, Sydney School of Arts, 275c Pitt St. in Sydney.

Information

The Tourism Commission of N.S.W., well-organized and helpful, publishes a series of pamphlets on each of 10 designated tourist areas of the state. Inside each pamphlet is a separate listing entitled *Good Stuff to Know About...*, a useful list of attractions and accommodations. Get a pamphlet at the Commission's Sydney office (corner Pitt and Spring St.; phone 231-4444).

Most N.S.W. towns have a local tourist office, open weekdays and usually one day on the weekend.

YHA of N.S.W. has an excellent travel service in its Sydney offices. You can plan travel around N.S.W. there, plus book domestic and international flights. They are well-informed of the least expensive means of getting around.

Accommodation

N.S.W. has about 30 YHA or YHA-Associate hostels, plus several Backpackers hostels. On the north coast, where YHA has stiff competition, some of the usual YHA rules (daily duties, curfews, daytime closings) are lifted. Competition in this region also keeps hostel quality high, and modern facilities, double rooms, and swimming pools are the norm.

YHA of N.S.W. is located at 176 Day St., GPO Box 5276, Sydney, 2001. For YHA hostel information and travel agency services, call 02-267-3044 or toll free 008-45-1204 in N.S.W. outside the 02 area code. Office hours are M-F 9:00am-4:30pm, Th until 7:00pm.

For information on other traveler's hostels in the state, go to the **Backpackers** hostel at 162 Victoria St. (office open all day). While they don't always have the relevant directories (of which there are three!), they will be able give you information on all hostels. The *Backpackers Travel and Accommodation* magazine is available at newsstands for $4.

Most places you'll want to visit have hostels, but in the absence of a hostel, on-site vans in caravan parks or inexpensive hotels are usually available. In contrast to many other areas of Australia, in N.S.W. you won't find yourself in the middle of nowhere with nowhere to stay. The N.S.W. Tourism Commission's pamphlets include local caravan parks and hotels, with phone numbers and addresses (but no prices). In New England and the midnorth, farm accommodation is quite reasonable. Look into this at local tourist bureaus or in the Tourism Commission's Sydney office, where "Farm Holiday" pamphlets are available.

At certain times of year, you need to be sure to book ahead. For coastal areas, book ahead in summer holiday season (late Dec. through Jan.). Sydney hostels will also need to be booked ahead for summer. In August, the height of ski season, the Snowy Mountains accommodations get booked way in advance.

History

When the U.S. War of Independence interfered with convict transportation to the American colonies, Britain needed a new place to dispose of criminals. This, and the desire for an outpost in the South Seas, prompted Britain to designate a new colony site at Botany Bay (which had been discovered and named by Captain Cook eight years before).

Capt. Arthur Phillip arrived with the famed First Fleet, consisting of convicts and a few troops, on January 26, 1788. He quickly moved from Botany Bay to present-day Sydney, a few kilometers north in Port Jackson.

The mother country all but ignored the new colony, allowing three years to lapse between Governor Phillip's departure and the arrival of the colony's second governor. Military officers filled the power vacuum, and for several years a struggle ensued between the official government and military. It wasn't until Colonel Lachlan Macquarie arrived in 1809 and disbanded the N.S.W. Corps that the colony ran smoothly.

The 1820's and '30's saw exploration and expansion by wool producers, along with near decimation of the resident Aborigines, with whom no official agreements or treaties were ever made. Starting in the 1830's, free settlers began to arrive in large numbers under an assisted immigration scheme. The N.S.W. colony spread to parts of present-day Tasmania, South Australia, Victoria, and Queensland, but by the end of the 1850's, the separate colonies had firmed up borders, and N.S.W. had achieved self-government.

Sydney

Sydney is to Australia as Paris is to France or New York is to the United States. It is utterly distinct from the rest of the nation (you could never claim to have seen Australia if you'd only been to Sydney), yet it is the heart from which all trends and transactions circulate. It is a total (and welcome) contrast to a continent that seems incredibly remote and isolated to the average urbanized traveler.

Sydney is alive with the very best and the very worst that cities have to offer: big business deals and marketplace haggling, street fairs and arts festivals, construction, manufacturing, drug trafficking, and crime. Despite the rat-race, Sydney is a friendly and open place. "Sydneysiders" are a smiling bunch, the weather is almost always sunny, and the physical setting, with rambling lawns and the glimmering Sydney Harbour, makes it one of the world's most beautiful cities.

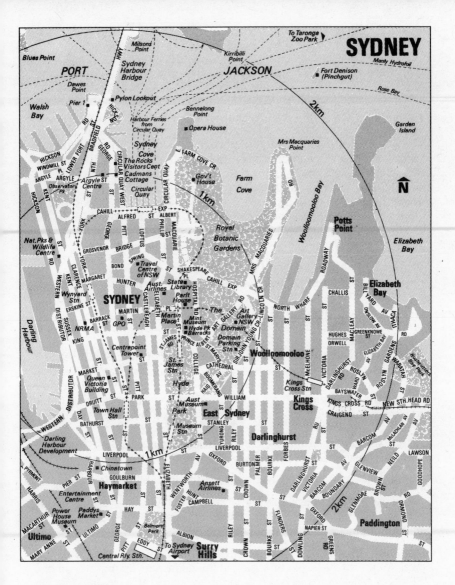

SYDNEY

Getting There

The major buslines (Deluxe, Bus Australia/McCafferty's, Greyhound, and Pioneer) each have at least one daily service from all major cities. A few smaller lines service Sydney from other N.S.W. destinations and Queensland, including Murray's and Skennars.

From Melbourne, a bus costs $50 and takes 14 hours. The trip from Brisbane is 14 hours via the Pacific Hwy. and 15 hours via the New England Hwy., and also costs about $50. From Adelaide, the trip is 21 hours and $95.

The train option is particularly reasonable from Melbourne. You pay $75 economy sit-up ($35 stand-by) or about $50 with the special Caper Fare. A berth is $140 (first-class only) or $100 Caper. The Brisbane trip is $75 economy sit-up or $50 Caper; $145 berth (first-class only) or $98 Caper. The trip from Adelaide costs $125 economy sit-up or $250 for a berth (first-class only).

Planes from all over the world fly into Sydney. If you're arriving by air, there's both a public bus and a private shuttle service available to the city.

The public bus services both domestic and international terminals every 20 or 30 minutes, from 6:15am-10:15pm daily (Route 300 "Airport Express"). It stops at the Central Railway Station, Town Hall, the Regent Hotel in Market St., and No. 2 Jetty Circular Quay. For further information, call the Urban Transport Authority at 29-2622.

The private shuttle bus also departs from all terminals and goes to most hotels and even some hostels, for about $3. Call the **Kingsford Smith Airport Bus Service** at 667-3221 or 667-0663 to book trips from the city to the airport.

Orientation and Practical Information

Sydney and its suburbs are built around Port Jackson, better known as Sydney Harbour. The city center surrounds two coves in the harbor, and, because of the curvature of the waterfront, the hilly topography, and the haphazard growth of the city, Sydney streets aren't organized in the most logical of patterns.

Still, it's not difficult to make your way around. You can usually see Sydney Tower, in the middle of the business district, and use it as a directional reference, and the Sydney Opera House juts so far into water that it's visible from almost anywhere on the harbor. Odd and even street numbers run in the same direction on opposite sides of the street, but sometimes they're off-sync by a few blocks.

When you get a map, be sure it includes detail of inner suburbs like King's Cross, Paddington, Glebe, and Newtown. Drivers should pick up a *Gregory's Street Directory* or N.R.M.A.'s (National Roads and Motorists' Association) Sydney and district map.

Business hours are generally M-W 9:00am-5:30pm, Th-F until 9:00pm, and Sat 8:00am-noon or 1:00pm. Banks are open M-Th 9:30am-4:00pm, F until 5:00pm.

Important Addresses and Telephone Numbers (area code 02)

Travel Centre of New South Wales, corner Pitt and Spring Sts. (phone 231-4444). State-wide reservations and information, also city information. Their pamphlet called *Good Stuff to Know about Sydney* has an encyclopedic listing of things to see and do. M-F 8:30am-5:00pm.

Martin Place Kiosk, Martin Place (phone 235-2424). M-F 9:00am-5:00pm. City tourist information.

Phone information for visitors: 669-5111. Available daily 8:00am-6:00pm.

General Post Office, corner Martin Place and George St. (phone 230-7033). M-F 8:15am- 5:30pm; limited service Sat 8:30am-noon. Suburban post offices open M-F 8:30am-5:00pm.

U.S. Consulate, T&G Towers, corner Park and Elizabeth Sts. (phone 264-7044).

Canadian Consulate, 50 Bridge St. (phone 231-6522).

American Express, American Express Tower, 388 George St., Sydney, N.S.W., 2000 (phone 239-0666).

Youth Hostel Association of N.S.W., 176 Day St. (phone 267-3044; toll free travel agency number is 008-45-1204 and can be dialed outside 02 area code in N.S.W.). Memberships and bookings. Best budget travel agency in the city for travel within Australia. M-F 9:00am-4:30pm, Th until 7:00pm.

National Parks and Wildlife Service, 189-193 Kent St. (phone 237-6500). Information on national parks and topographical maps.

STA Travel, 1A Lee St., Railway Square (phone 212-1255). Or Holme Building, University of Sydney.

N.R.M.A. (National Roads and Motorists' Association), 151 Clarence St. (phone 260-9222). A.A.A. members have reciprocal membership. Free maps and travel info to members.

Transport House, Wynyard Station (ground floor), 11-31 York St. Information on all metropolitan transportation. Information and bookings for all state-wide and interstate trains. Open M-F 8:00am-5:30pm. Call 29-2622 for city transport info; 217-8812 (7:00am-10:00pm daily) for train info.

Deluxe, Sydney Coach Terminal, corner Castlereagh and Hay Sts. (phone 212-4888).

Greyhound, Oxford Square, corner Oxford and Riley Sts. (phone 268-1494).

Pioneer, Oxford Square, corner Oxford and Riley Sts. (phone 268-1881).

Bus Australia/McCafferty's, McKell Bldg., corner George St. and Rawson Pl. (phone 281-2266).

Murray's and Skennars, pick-up is outside Central Station on Eddy St.

Air New South Wales, phone 268-1242.

East-West Airlines, phone 20-940.

Australian Airlines, 70 Hunter St. (phone 693-3333).

Ansett Airlines, corner Oxford and Riley Sts. (phone 268-1111).

Air New Zealand, phone 234-4111.

Qantas, phone 436-6111.

United Airlines, phone 233-1111.

Working Holiday Office, YMCA, 325 Pitt St. Referrals for those seeking casual work.

C.E.S. (casual work section), 818 George St. (phone 219-7200), M-F 6:30am-3:30pm. Also, 110 Darlinghurst Rd., King's Cross (phone 332-1122), M-F 8:45am-5:00pm. Government employment agency; services for those with working visas.

Taxis, phone 699-0144 or 399-0488.

Sydney Hospital (Emergency Medical), phone 230-0111.

Wayside Chapel Crisis Centre, corner Hughes St. and Orwell Lane, King's Cross (phone 358-6577). Open 24 hours.

Transportation

Sydney's public transportation system is comprehensive and reliable. Most trains and buses operate 7:00am-11:30pm or midnight. It's worth buying an Urban Transit Authority *Travelmap*, which outlines all public transport routes (train/bus/ferry) for Sydney and suburbs and includes all bus stops and bus numbers. Bus, train, and ferry information and schedules are all available in the Transport House on the ground floor of Wynyard Station.

There's an informational phone service from 7:00am-10:00pm daily that covers all transport questions, at 29-2622. Information for trains: phone 20-942; for buses, phone 20-543 (7:00am-7:00pm weekdays).

Bus: Most buses depart from Circular Quay, Railway Square, Central Station, or along George St. Fares vary according to the number of zones traveled, and you pay as you get on.

There are two free buses: #777, the shopping route, which does a circuit of the city and departs every 10 minutes from Hunter St. between George and Pitt Sts., terminating at Wynyard Park (M-F 9:15am-4:00pm); and the Art Gallery bus (#666), which runs every 30 minutes from the same place and goes to the Art Gallery in the Domain (M-Sat 10:10am-4:30pm, Sun 12:10pm-4:30pm).

The **Sydney Explorer Bus** runs an 18 km circuit to 20 points of interest around the city, and you can get on and off wherever you like. You wait at the red signpost in front of any major attraction and buy a ticket from the driver. The bus runs every day from 9:30am-5:00pm, and it's about $12 for the day. You can also use the ticket until midnight on any regular bus operating between Central Railway Station and the Rocks.

Train: The "Sydney System," both under- and above-ground, includes six suburban lines, four of which link with country trains to the Blue Mountains, southern coast, and regions north of the Hawkesbury River. Central and Redfern stations, south of the city center, provide access to all the lines. Purchase tickets at the booths before you get to the train platforms, and even though a ticket isn't always needed to board, you must have a valid ticket to exit.

Make reservations for country and interstate trains (State Rail) through the **Rail Travel Centre** at Wynyard Station (phone 217- 8812).

Ferry: All ferries board at **Circular Quay**, located between the Opera House and the Harbour Bridge. This is the best mode of transport for getting to northern suburbs and other harbor destinations.

Taxis: Never get one if you're in a rush! Taxi drivers are paid by the minute, not by the mile—and are a welcome and sane relief from the aggressive driving of other Sydney-dwellers.

Driving: Sydney suburbs are hilly and the streets are narrow and winding. Driving is as hazardous as in any city, and traffic can get heavy. *Gregory's Guide* is Sydney's best street directory. If you've got your own car, don't try to navigate without it. The city center is full of one-way streets and construction. You'd do best to park on the outskirts and use public transport or walk in the downtown area.

Accommodation

The majority of Sydney hostels and budget hotels are in King's Cross, a seedy part of town plagued by drug trafficking and prostitution. We strongly advise you to look elsewhere first. Go first for the City Backpackers, and next look to Glebe and Forest Lodge, pleasant suburbs not too far from the downtown action (all listed below in the *Choice Hostels* section).

Despite the plethora of hostels and budget hotels in Sydney, cheap accommodation is a crisis situation during the summer season. If you're coming from overseas, write ahead if possible (though note that many budget accommodations won't take reservations). Otherwise, make arrangements at a budget hotel, where at least you'll be assured of a place to recover from travel for a day or two.

YHA opens extra hostels in the summer to deal with the crowds. For information, inquire at any of the three YHA hostels listed below or the Head Office at 176 Day St., phone 02-267-3044. If you're planning an extended stay, several hostels offer weekly and monthly rates. Make sure to arrive before 10:00am on the day you need a room, because many hostels close during the day until around 5:00pm, by which time places are often filled.

During university holidays (Dec.-March), lodging is sometimes available at International House (phone 02-660-5364) and Women's College (phone 02-51-1195) at Sydney University. The "Uni" Housing Office may be able to help you find a temporary flat. They're on the 2nd floor of the Student Union (Holme Building).

We've listed Sydney's hostels according to the following categories: *Choice Hostels* (go for these first, but they are often booked), *King's Cross* (you're more likely to get a spot here, but the area isn't great), *Suburban Hostels* (some of these are fantastic, if you're willing to be a little out of town—some people prefer the peace and quiet), and *Private Hotels* (more expensive than hostels, but still cheap).

Choice Hostels

City Centre Backpackers, 7 Elizabeth St. (phone 02-59-2850). Airport shuttle stops here. $12/4-6 per room. The ultimate location. Most units have private kitchen, bathroom, color TV, and washing machine. The owners, Orm and Maureen, are in the business for love, not money, and are always ready to help. Office (6th floor) open 8:30am-10:30am, 4:30pm-6:30pm.

Forest Lodge YHA, 28 Ross St., corner St. John's Rd. (phone 02-692-0747). $12/4-6 per room. Beautifully restored 1873 mansion, clean, and comfortably furnished. Smoking and non-smoking lounges, laundry, nice managers. However: loud street noises, and closed during the day (10:00am-4:00pm).

Wattle House Hostel, 44 Hereford St., Glebe (phone 02-692-9879 or 02-337-1689). $12/3-4 per room; $28/double. Linen deposit. Quiet street in good suburb. Nicely renovated and furnished like a home. Friendly crowd. Can book without deposit.

Glebe Point YHA Hostel, 262-64 Glebe Point Rd., Glebe (phone 02-692-8418). Open all day. $14/double. Terrific location near nightlife and restaurants. Clean and friendly. Drab building but worth the price.

Hereford Lodge YHA Hostel, 51 Hereford St., Glebe (phone 02-660-5577). $14/4-person room; $16/double. All rooms have bathrooms. Rooftop pool, sauna, and BBQ. Cafeteria serves breakfast and dinner. (Also offers motel-style accommodation at $45/single, $56/double.)

Billabong Hostel, 11 Egan St., Newtown (phone 02-519-8940). $12/4-6 per room. Homey setting, friendly and clean. Dart board. Pool table. TV. Good parties—manager joins in.

King's Cross

Victoria St. in King's Cross is the hub of Sydney's hostel scene, with several hostels, laundromats, bulletin boards, and tons of people. Non-Australians carrying backpacks are the norm, rather than the exception. Shaded by gums and lined on both sides by pretty Victorian townhouses, the street is a contrast to the neon lights of central King's Cross.

However, security is a big problem in many hostels, and local junkies know well how to rip-off travelers. Make sure to lock your stuff up. Several cars have been stolen from travelers in the area, so if you own a vehicle it may be worth finding a garage.

Real estate is booming in this part of town, which will probably cause an upheaval with the hostels. Use the prices below only for comparison.

To get to King's Cross from downtown, take bus 312 or the train from Central Station; or buses 324, 325, or 369 from Circular Quay.

Budget Young Travelers Hostel, 25 Hughes St. (phone 02-358-1143). $12/3-person room. Set up like an apartment building, and very secure. Common room with TV. Rooftop outdoor area with BBQ and picnic tables. Small kitchen.

Rucksack Rest, 9 MacDonald St., Pott's Point (phone 02-358-2348). $12/night; $65/week; $26/double. Singles available. Linen included. Quiet street away from the Victoria St. rat race, and very secure and clean. Cooking and TV in room. No laundry.

l'Annexe Hostel, 19 Hughes St. (phone 02-357-2273). $12/3-6 per room; $26/double. Office 8:00am-11:00am, 5:00pm-8:00pm. Never overcrowded. Very secure. Quiet, older clientele. All rooms have private 'fridge, stove, TV, and some have fireplaces. Alain, the manager, is a nice guy and runs a tight ship. He'll take bookings without deposit.

Young Travelers Hostel, 15 Roslyn Gardens, Elizabeth Bay (phone 02-357-3509). $12/dorm room. One night free per week. Linen provided. Nice neighborhood, but not terribly clean and often crowded. No TV. Storage lockers. Office open 8:00am-11:00am, 4:00pm-7:30pm, and all day Sunday.

International Cotel, 170 Victoria St. (phone 356-3844). $12/night or $50/week, average 6 per room. Nice Victorian building with fireplaces. Not terribly secure, though friendly. No laundry. Storage lockers. Summertime BBQ's and parties. Open before 10:00am, after 5:00pm.

Cotel Annex, 1a Roslyn St., go first to above address. $34/double, $12/extra person; $220/week. Light and attractive. Kitchen and bathroom in suite. Some rooms have large picture windows.

Backpacker's Hostel, 162 Victoria St. (phone 02-356-3232). $12/night, $24/double. 250 capacity in seven buildings, all Victorian townhouses. Some rooms have private kitchen, bathroom, washing tub; otherwise there are communal facilities. Crowded and chaotic, but the best place for information of all sorts. Long term storage available. To book, write in advance then call morning of arrival—no guaranteed place. Office open 8:00am-8:00pm.

Plane Tree Lodge, 172 Victoria St. (phone 02-356-4551). $12/night, $30/double. Cooking facilities, bathrooms, and TV all in suite. No common room. People keep to themselves.

Travellers Rest, 156 Victoria St. (phone 02-358-4606). $12/night, 5-share rooms. Crowded but friendly. TV and 'fridge in rooms. Outdoor common area. Office open M-F 8:00am-1:00pm, 5:00pm-7:00pm; Sat-Sun 8:00am-noon.

The Jolly Swagman, 144 Victoria St. (phone 02-358-6400). $12/night, $60/week in 3-4 person room; $26/double, $155/week in double room. 'Fridge and cooking facilities in room. No common room. Reclusive people.

Suburban Hostels
A couple of the hostels listed below are excellent but didn't get on our "choice" list because of non-central locations.

Coogee Beach Backpackers, 94 Beach St., Coogee (phone 02-665-7735 or 02-665-8514). $12/night, 6 per room. A few doubles available. Key deposit $10. Day rate $5 after 10:00am. Great location overlooking the beach. Not overcrowded, not overwhelmingly clean. Office open 8:30am-10:30am, 7:00pm-8:00pm.

Airport Backpackers, 46-48 Cameron St., Rockdale (phone 02-597-1250 or 02-599-1963). Free pick-up from airport; or take train to Rockdale from city then make 10 min. walk from stop. $9/night, 4-6 per room. One house for semi-permanents, one for those passing through. Very friendly, clean, and well-managed. Regular BBQs. Free trips to the country with the owners (same ownership as City Backpackers).

Dulwich Hill YHA Hostel, 407 Marrickville Rd., Dulwich Hill (phone 02-569-0272). 15 min. train ride from city to Dulwich Hill and signs from there. Open all day. $12/night, 2-4 per room. Huge, cement-block building. Rooms have closets, shelves, and privacy. Very clean, large kitchen. School groups often stay.

Kangaroo Bakpak, 635 South Dowling St., Surry Hills (phone 02-699-5915). Airport shuttle stops. 10 min. walk from Central Station. $10/night, $62/week, 4-6 per room. $5 key deposit. Unkempt exterior, but nice inside. Noisy road in deserted part of town. Many permanents but friendly, with regular parties. TV. Daily duties required.

Beethoven Lodge, 663 South Dowling St., Surry Hills (phone 02-698-4203). $10/night, mostly 6 per room. Unkempt outside, okay inside. No outdoor area. Daily duties required. Office open 9:00am-10:00am, 7:00pm- 8:00pm.

Private Hotels
YWCA, 5-11 Wentworth Ave., Darlinghurst (phone 02-264-2451). Central location on the corner of Hyde Park. Women and married couples only. $14/night, 4 per room (max. stay in dorm 3 nights). Singles and twins also available. Linen provided. Fully carpeted. Very clean. No kitchen. Cafeteria and gym facilities. Must book ahead.

C.B. Hotel, 417 Pitt St., City (phone 02-211-5115). $24/single, $36/twin or double. Central location. Spartan but very clean. TV lounge. No kitchen. Open 24 hours.

Sydney Tourist Hotel, 400 Pitt St., City (phone 02-211-5777). $24-$26/single, $32/double. Huge and impersonal but clean. TV lounge. Dining room. No kitchen facilities.

The Budget Inn, 358 Victoria St., Darlinghurst (phone 02-33-3772). $35/single, $145/week; $45/double, $165/week. Rooms have private 'fridge, table, sink, tea pot, and toaster. Quiet, safe, secure, and clean. Can rent TV.

Springfield Lodge, 9 Springfield Ave., King's Cross (phone 02-358-3222). $26-$28/single; $30-$34/double. Weekly rate available. Rooms have private 'fridge, toaster, electric frying pan (on request), tea pot, basin, and TV.

Things to See and Do
There's tons to see in Sydney—so much that it's hard to know where to start. There are a few must sees: the Opera House, The Rocks, Darling Harbour Complex, Taronga Zoo, and Hyde Park Barracks. But some of the best things aren't so obvious. It's by wandering around the less prominent downtown areas and in the suburbs that you really get to know Sydney. Where you end up exploring is a matter of taste and coincidence.
    We've divided the city into categories by location: *The Opera House and the Rocks*, *The Domain Area* (where most of Sydney's museums reside), *Downtown* (including Chinatown and the Darling Harbour complex), *Sydney Harbour*, *Suburbs* (King's Cross, Paddington, the Univ. of Sydney, the

eastern suburbs, Manly, Parramatta, Botany Bay, and wildlife parks), and *City Beaches.*

Sydney's city center is compact enough to see on foot, if you're up for some brisk walking. Or take the Explorer Bus, which covers all the major sights including those in King's Cross, or either of the two free buses, #666 and #777. Or, Sydney Hostel Tours runs an inexpensive "Sydney Orientation" all day Sunday. Call 212- 6328 from 9:00am-5:00pm weekdays, or 360-1665 after hours.

Almost all city museums are free, except where indicated.

The Opera House and The Rocks
Probably every brochure you've ever seen for Australia has a photo of the **Sydney Opera House**. Completed in 1975, the structure was designed by a Dane named Joern Utzon, who left midway through construction after sharp clashes with others in the project. He apparently never returned to see the finished product.

You can take an hour-long guided tour into the complex's five theatres (M-Sat 9:00am-4:00pm; $4, student discount available) or a longer, more extensive backstage tour on Sunday ($6). Or have lunch on the terrace, with gorgeous views of the harbor. Student discounts are available for most performances (see *Entertainment* below).

Across Sydney Cove from the Opera House is **The Rocks**, site of Australia's first European settlement. Built by the earliest convicts back in 1788, The Rocks became the worst part of the city during the 1800's. But no longer: The oldest buildings have been restored and the area is now tourist-infested and filled with pricey shops and restaurants. Ken Done's colorful designs and other Australiana are everywhere, which makes for fun browsing even if you can't buy.

Don't let the commercialization turn you off to the history in the renovated buildings. Wander down George St., the main thoroughfare, and visit **The Rocks Visitors Centre** first (104 George St., open M-F 8:30am-4:30pm, Sat-Sun 10:00am- 5:00pm.) for historical information and detailed maps.

Cadman's Cottage (110 George St.) and Colonial House Museum (53 Lower Fort St.) are two museums to check out. **Cadman's Cottage**, a maritime museum, is the oldest dwelling in Sydney, dating to 1816 (open M-F 9:15am-4:30pm, and 9:45am-4:30pm weekends). **Colonial House Museum** is a restored terrace house, decorated in 1880's fashion (open 10:00am-5:00pm daily). Nearby, along Lower Fort St., there are several old cottages and a hotel built in the 1830's.

Fans of Aussie wine should visit the **Australian Wine Center** in Campbell's Storehouse (17-21 Circular Quay West). The wines come from all wine valleys in the country, and you can taste many of them there. The center will ship wine home for you, too.

Keen shoppers should go to the Rocks during the weekend, when there's an all-day sidewalk gallery of artisans and craftspeople on **Kendall Lane** (off Argyle St.).

Following George St. to the end, you'll find yourself in **Dawes Point Park**, underneath the Sydney Harbour Bridge. A pedestrian walkway (off Cumberland St. in the Rocks) runs along its eastern side, and Sat-Mon from 9:30am-5:00pm you can climb inside one of its pylons for $1.

Up Argyle St. to the western side of the bridge is a group of colonial sandstone buildings known as **Observatory Hill**. The astronomy museum there is free and open M, T, Th, F 10:00am-noon, Wed. 10:00am-5:00pm, Sat-Sun 1:00pm-5:00pm. Call 241-2478 to find out about star-gazing. Next door at the N.S.W. headquarters of the **National Trust**, there's a good bookshop and tea room with an art exhibition hall.

A bit further north, next to the southern pylon of Sydney Harbour Bridge, is the much-publicized **Pier 1 Shopping Centre**, a redeveloped shipping terminal that houses a bunch of tacky stores, mediocre food stalls, and an amusement center. The one redeeming feature is the Harbour Watch restaurant, a great place to order a drink at dusk and watch the sunset.

The Domain Area
Farm Cove is entirely surrounded by the Domain parklands, which extend south to the inner suburbs of East Sydney and Wooloomooloo. The Domain's expansive lawns and large shade trees make it a great place to wander, picnic, or just hang out. There's also lots to see in the Domain, including the Botanic Gardens, Government House, and the Art Gallery of New South Wales.

The Botanic Gardens are open daily from 8:00am-sunset. **Government House**, a Gothic Revival building at the northern tip of the Botanic Gardens, houses the Queen's appointed Governor of New South Wales. Call 635-8149 for information on visiting. The most impressive display in the **Art Gallery** is a modern Australian painting exhibition, and there are several permanent collections of Australian and European art. (Open M-Sat 10:00am-5:00pm, Sun noon-5:00pm.)

The State Library, Parliament House, Mint, and the Hyde Park Barracks border the Domain along Macquarie St. **Hyde Park Barracks**, built in 1819 to house convicts, is the best historical museum in Sydney and an excellent place to learn about the beginnings of the nation. The Barracks museum outlines early colonial and convict history and the development and history of Sydney, including an exhibition on Sydney's immigrants (open daily 10:00am-5:00pm, except Tue noon-5:00pm). Next door is the former **Mint**, one of the oldest city buildings (1817), now a small museum with various state memorabilia. (Open daily 10:00am-5:00pm, Wed noon-5:00pm.)

Parliament House has free guided tours when the State Parliament is in recess, and when it's in session you can watch from the gallery (call 230-2111 for tour times). The **State Library** houses the most important set of Australiana, prints, and maps in the country, and you can use its VCR's to while away a rainy afternoon (open M-Sat 9:00am-9:00pm, Sun 2:00pm-6:00pm.)

Hyde Park, adjacent to the Barracks, is a lovely shaded spot frequented by locals and tourists, especially at lunch. At its northern end is Archibald Memorial Fountain, the center is lined by a magnificent row of large trees, and at the Liverpool St. end is an **Anzac War Memorial**. A basement area in the memorial has memorabilia and a display on Australian wartime participation (open M-Sat 10:00am-4:00pm, Sun 1:00pm- 4:00pm). Across College St. from the park, the **Australian Museum**, with a large natural history collection, is set in somewhat shabby surroundings and flooded with school groups (open T-Sun 10:00am-5:00pm, Mon noon-5:00pm.) You can't miss the massive and graceful **St. Mary's Cathedral**, also across College St. from Hyde Park.

Downtown
Downtown is flanked by George St. to the west and the Domain area to the east, with Martin Place at its heart.

Built on an incline between George and Macquarie Sts., **Martin Place** is a brick pedestrian area bustling with activity and entertainment, everything from buskers to lunchtime performances in the outdoor amphitheater. North of Martin Place along Pitt St. is Sydney's financial center, with the **Stock Exchange** at 20 Bond St. Sydney also finally got its **pedestrian mall**, the last major Australian city to surrender to the trend. The section of Pitt St. between King and Market was bricked over in 1987 and is now lined by franchises and department stores.

The **Sydney Tower**, rising above the gargantuan Centerpoint Shopping Complex (corner Market and Castlereagh Sts.), is the highest structure in the country at 305.4 meters. Go in the late afternoon and watch the sunset. (Open M-Sat 9:30am-9:30pm, Sun 10:30am-6:30pm, admission $4.) Dinner in the revolving restaurant will set you back at least $20.

South of the mall on George St. and covering an entire city block is the imposing **Queen Victoria building** ("Queen Vic"), built in 1893 as the city's marketplace. Recent restoration has transformed the structure into an expensive shopping complex. Have a look at the **Town Hall** (corner of George and Druitt Sts.), another impressive Victorian building, which hosts musical performances throughout the year, many free. Call 265-9333 for concert information.

Continuing south on George St., you hit the Chinatown/Haymarket area, full of cinemas and restaurants. **Chinatown** is centered on Dixon St., a pedestrian area marked at each end by a traditional ornate archway. Don't miss the **Burlington Center** (102 Hay St.), a Chinese market with t-shirts, shoes, crafts, and food. And **Paddy's Market** on Hay St. is a Sydney institution. Since the 1850's, the market has been a weekend commercial center, and thousands still come to bargain for the best of Asian and European edibles, clothes, jewelry, and crafts (open Sat-Sun 9:30am-4:30pm).

Across Hay St. from Paddy's Market is Sydney's new **Darling Harbour Complex**, encircled by a monorail and containing parks, a Chinese Garden, a Maritime Museum, an aquarium, shops, restaurants, a huge Entertainment Center, a casino, theater, transport museum, and planetarium.

Sydney Harbour
The harbor is Sydney's most famous and most beautiful feature, and the best way to get a good look is from the water. For the cheapest boat ride around, hop on a **UTA ferry** to Manly (see *Suburbs*) or Taronga Zoo. UTA also pro-

vides a harbor cruise for $7 for a 2 1/2-hour ride with commentary. Numerous private companies offer Harbour and Hawkesbury River cruises at all hours, with morning tea, gourmet "Harbourlight" dinners, etc. ($8-$50). All of them leave from Circular Quay.

The **Taronga Zoo and Aquarium**, across the harbor in Mosman, is built on a steep incline to give viewers a look at the animals from above and at eye level. It's one of the best zoos in the country—with a great view of the city—and the boat ride there ($2) is great (open daily 9:00am-5:00pm, admission $8.50).

The Maritime Services Board runs tours to **Fort Denison**, on a tiny island in the middle of the harbor. Built by settlers in 1857 out of quarried sandstone, the island was originally a military installation and not, as some claim, another Alcatraz. Completely intact, the fort now serves as a tidal reading station, and the family living there conducts the 1.5-hour tour T-Sat. The Maritime Board also runs a tour to **Goat Island**, where a shipyard operates. (Tour runs Wed-Sun.) Both tours are interesting, though slow-moving relative to other tourist attractions. Both cost $6 (discount with student ID) and must be pre-booked by calling the Board at 240-2111, ext. 2036.

A ferry to **Birkenhead Point** shopping complex in Drummoyne takes you to a giant city of Legos, supposedly the best such display in the world. Experts can gauge their childhood efforts against the display, which has hundreds of models in all shapes and sizes and is quite impressive.

Suburbs

King's Cross
The King's Cross area, including Pott's Point and Elizabeth Bay, is a study in contrasts. The red light district centers on Darlinghurst Rd., which runs right through the heart of "The Cross." By day it's pretty normal, albeit a bit seedy; at night drug dealers and prostitutes push their wares, and you'll have a well-founded urge to grip your wallet.

Just a few blocks away, the streets are quiet and pleasant. Victoria St., the hostellers' "ghetto," is lined by gum trees and renovated terrace houses, and Kellett St. draws fashionable people to its all-night cafes. A stone's throw from King's Cross are the elegant neighborhoods of Pott's Point and Elizabeth Bay, where you can visit a beautiful National Trust home, **Elizabeth Bay House** on Onslow Ave., a five-minute walk from King's Cross Station (open T-Sun 10:00am-4:30pm, admission $3).

Paddington
A walk southeast of the city on Oxford St. will take you through Darlinghurst to Paddington, 2 km from downtown. This artsy neighborhood is well-worth seeing for the building restorations, art galleries, and tempting jewelry and clothing. Frequented by young people and artists, there are myriad cafes and chic pubs. Go first to the **New Edition Bookshop** (328a Oxford St., open daily) for a free guide to all the galleries and shopping, plus a historical walk through Paddington.

The most obvious architectural highlights of Paddington are the **Town Hall** and the **Victoria Barracks**. Built for the army in the 1840's, the Barracks remains a headquarters for all branches of the Australian military. You can visit only on Tuesdays, February-November, when there's a changing of the guard ceremony at 10:00am and a guided tour of the installation immediately after.

The **Paddington Markets** on Oxford St. are open 9:00am-4:00pm Saturdays, with jewelry, crafts, clothes, and a bohemian flair.

The University of Sydney

Sydney's "Uni" is the most scenic campus in Australia, with neatly clipped lawns and gothic buildings reminiscent of Oxford. Walk up the drive to the Great Hall (it's unmistakable), go through the archway, and in the opposite right-hand corner of the courtyard is the Student Office, which has campus maps and a self-guided tour called "A Two-Foot Tour of Grose Farm."

For a taste of student life, check out the **Student Union** in the Holmes Building. The Uni housing office is on the second floor of this building, and the Student Union reading room is a nice hideaway with high cathedral ceilings. Residential colleges to take a look at are St. Paul's, founded in 1854 (the oldest in Australia), St. Andrews, and Women's College, which began offering university education to women in 1892. Two museums on campus, the Nicholson Collection (archeology, mainly Egyptian) and the Macleay Collection (natural history) are extensive but mostly for experts.

Students hang out in the nearby suburb of **Newtown**, where there are excellent cheap eats and cafes, plus pottery, second hand clothes, and the like.

The Eastern Suburbs

The fashionable eastern suburbs (Double Bay, Bellevue Hill, Woollahra, Vaucluse, and Rose Bay) have traditionally been the home of Sydney's upper crust. Aside from Double Bay's expensive boutiques (it looks like a transplanted Beverly Hills), there are some gorgeous old homes.

Vaucluse House on Olola Ave. in Vaucluse is a gracious neo-gothic estate built in 1803 for William Charles Wentworth, one of Australia's most prominent early colonists. Most of the original furniture remains, and the gardens are spectacular. There's also a display on Wentworth's Blue Mountains exploration in one of the out-buildings. The house is one of the most impressive and well-preserved in the country, though it's more European than Australian. Bus 325 from Circular Quay or Pitt St. stops at the front gate. (Open Tue-Sun 10:00am-4:30pm, admission $3, discount with student ID. Free first Thursday of every month.)

Manly

Ferries run frequently from Circular Quay to Manly, a touristy but relaxed beachside suburb of Sydney. A quick get-away from the city, it's a popular day trip for travelers. Make sure to go if you're in Sydney during one of Manly's summer surfing carnivals.

The half-hour ferry ride takes you to the mouth of Port Jackson for about $3 roundtrip. The hydrofoil takes 20 minutes and costs about the same, but you can't ride outside in the sea air like you can on the ferry. Ferries run until midnight.

When you get off the Manly ferry, cross the street and head diagonally to your right, where you'll be at one end of the **Corso**, the main pedestrian mall, where you'll find the country's best ice cream (try a homemade waffle cone from Royal Copenhagen). At the opposite end of the mall is **Manly Beach**, distinguished by a magnificent row of Norfolk Island pine trees. Tourist Information is located on the beachfront to the left, in case you're interested in activities besides beach-bumming.

A walk to the right of the beach takes you around Shelly Beach and to a rocky point overlooking Manly Beach and the coast beyond. Other recommended walks are posted on a large kiosk in the center of the jetty where the Sydney ferries dock. You can also try one of the water slides at **Manly Waterworks** on the West Esplanade (open daily 9:00am-9:00pm, closed May-August), and there's a museum, art gallery, and marine park as well.

Manly's nightlife is hopping, especially on weekends. Both **Hotel Manly**, before you as you leave the ferry (phone 977-5599) and the **Steyne Hotel** in the Corso (phone 977-4977) have bands Th-Sat nights. **Manly Pacific Hotel** at 55 N. Steyne Rd. (phone 977-7666) has a piano bar (Tue-Sat from 8:30pm). **Sweet Emma's** and **Tango's** have various jazz venues; both are on Pittwater Rd.

Parramatta

Founded in 1788 by Governor Phillip as a center for crop cultivation and the wool industry, Parramatta was Australia's second settlement. Parramatta may be an integral part of Sydney's history, but the charm and beauty you'll expect after reading its promotional literature are hard to find.

All attractions are closed on Monday. The Western train-line stops in Parramatta, and Tourist Information is next to the Cultural Center on Church St. (open M-F 10:00am-4:00pm, Sat 9:00am-1:00pm, Sun 10:30am-3:00pm.), and they have a guide to historic buildings in the area.

If you make it to Parramatta, be sure to see Elizabeth Farm (70 Alice St.) and the Old Government House by the Parramatta River. **Elizabeth Farm**, built in 1793, is the oldest standing house in Australia. While there are very few original furnishings, the house is interesting because it combines the style of an English country house with an Australian homestead (open T-Sun 10:00am-4:30pm, admission $3, discount with student ID).

The Government House, built for Governor Hunter in 1799, is restored and furnished in its original style (open 10:00am-4:00pm T-Th & Sun, closed February, admission $5).

Botany Bay

On April 29, 1770, Captain Cook sailed the *Endeavour* into Botany Bay and anchored at what is now **Captain Cook's Landing Place** (clever name, eh?) on the southern cape of the bay entrance—now a reserve with monuments and a good little museum that details the whole event and has relics from the *Endeavour* (open M-F 10:30am-4:30pm, Sat-Sun 10:30am-5:00pm).The park is free unless you enter in a car, and firewood is provided for barbecues. Captain Cook's Landing Place is a 40 km hike from the city. Take the train to Cronulla, then bus 67.

The northern cape that forms Botany Bay is where French Captain La Perouse landed, just a few days after the First Fleet arrived in 1788. There's a monument to the event, as well as an old military fort on **Bare Island**, built in 1885 as protection against a feared Russian or French invasion. It's completely intact and visitors are allowed to wander through (open daily 9:00am-5:00pm). The area is pretty, and there's a small beach with windsurfers for rent and a seafood restaurant at the point. La Perouse is 15 km south of the city.

Wildlife Parks
There are two places where you can pet kangaroos and koalas, each a good 45 minutes from the city. The first is **Waratah Wildlife Park** on Namba Rd., Terrey Hills. Take the train to Chatswood, then bus 56. (Open daily 10:00am-5:00pm.) The larger one is **Featherdale Wildlife Park** on Kildare Rd., Doonside, and a train goes directly to Doonside. (Open daily 9:00am-5:00pm.)

City Beaches
Sydneysiders flaunt the fact that dozens of beaches lie just minutes from downtown. However, while there are some pleasant spots, most city beaches are crowded and polluted. If you have the time and resources, head to the northern suburban beaches (see *Trips from Sydney*).

The best harbor beaches are **Nielson Park** (at Shark Point), and **Watson's Bay**, **Campcove**, and **Lady Bay** (on South Head). Nielson Park has a large grassy area and nice views to Manly. The South Head beaches are adjacent to a military reserve that keeps the place free of commercialism and protects the shoreline from crowds. There are lovely views all along the South Head coast. Watson's Bay has shower facilities.

The nearby ocean beaches are Bondi, Bronte, Clovelly, and Coogee. There's also Manly Beach, to the north. Manly and Bondi are the best of the lot for surfing.

Once fashionable, **Bondi Beach** (pronounced "bond-eye") no longer has much glamour. Far too crowded and commercialized to be exclusive, it has become touristy, if not a bit sleazy. However, there are some fun, expensive cafes along the waterfront, and it's lively at night. You can take a beautiful cliff-walk from Bondi to Tamarama Bay and Bronte Beach.

Clovelly is a secluded beach on a little inlet. A short stroll to its mouth takes you to ocean cliffs eroded by relentless surf. **Coogee** is a small, beachy suburb with seafood shacks and the like. There's a hostel overlooking the beach (see *Accommodation*).

Bondi, Bronte, and Coogee have showers and toilets.

Food
Sydney is most famous in the restaurant world for its spectacular variety of seafood. Don't leave without tasting a Sydney rock oyster, though it may leave a dent in your wallet. To do it in style, go to **Doyle's Restaurant** (phone 337-1572) in Watson's Bay, owned and run by a family of fourth generation fishmongers. It's expensive ($20 and up), but the harbor view is fantastic

and the quality excellent. They also have moderately-priced takeaways. A cheaper option: buy seafood at the fish market in **Pyrmont** on Blackwattle Bay (along Bank St., near city center). It's a seafood lover's dream. Ethnic food is plentiful and excellent, particularly Italian, Chinese, Vietnamese, and Thai. Vegetarian and standard Aussie fare can be found cheaply, most often in a cafe setting. The best value for money, with a traveler's budget, is in Newtown. For the most current information, see *Cheap Eats in Sydney*, available at most newsstands and bookstores.

Since several of our recommendations are popular and always crowded, call ahead. Confirm hours of business, especially Sunday and Monday nights, when restaurants sometimes just close without warning. Watch for holiday and Sunday surcharges and minimum charges.

Chinatown, The Rocks, Business District

Most downtown restaurants serve only breakfast and lunch, and almost none of them classifies as "budget." It's easy to get stuck in the business district with an empty stomach and nothing affordable in sight. The solution is a short walk to either Chinatown or East Sydney, just east of Hyde Park. The Rocks also has several restaurants, but almost all of them are pricey.

Chinatown is full of little Chinese and Vietnamese eateries that don't attempt to draw you in with a cozy or inviting atmosphere— fluorescent lights and plastic tabletops are standard. But they are a great value. The best way to fill yourself cheaply is a *yum cha* (*dim sum*) lunch: a waiter comes by with a cart of goodies (spring rolls, dumplings, etc.), and you point to your choice.

Sir John Young Hotel, 557 George St., City (phone 267-3608). Fish dishes with a Spanish flair, around $10. Dark wood pub room. Lunch and dinner M-Sat.

Enzuccio, 115a Sussex St., City (phone 29-2956). Great old pub with courtyard dining. $5/person for Monday night barbecue and Tuesday night pasta. Other options are more expensive.

Roma Coffee Lounge (BYO), 189 Hay St., City (phone 211-3909). One of the city's best cafes, a local favorite. Great coffee and huge assortment of Italian pastries. Homemade pasta dishes ($4). M-F 7:30am-5:30pm, Sat til 3:30pm.

Minh Hai (BYO), 734 George St., Haymarket (phone 281-1875). Vietnamese. Very cheap. Menu is written on the walls in both Vietnamese and English. Noodle, soup, and rice dishes all $6 and less. Open daily 10:00am-10:00pm.

Old Spaghetti Factory, 80 George St. N., The Rocks (phone 241-2801). Pasta and meats $9, including salad and bread. M-Th noon-2:30pm, 5:30pm-9:00pm; F til 10:30pm; Sat noon-11:00pm; Sun 11:30am-9:00pm.

Philips Foote, 101 George St., The Rocks (phone 27-2585). Grill your own steak for $12, including a glass of wine. Lunch and dinner daily.

King's Cross, East Sydney, Wooloomooloo, Darlinghurst

Crown and Stanley Streets in East Sydney may look a bit rundown, but behind the faded exteriors you'll find the best Italian food in the city. King's Cross and Darlinghurst offer several cafe-style eateries and late-night dessert and coffee joints, but watch for changes in both suburbs because increasing rents are inflating food prices and putting many places out of business.

No Names (BYO), 2 Chapel St., East Sydney (phone 357-4711). No frills and great value, it's the ultimate traveler's meal. Share tables. $5 huge pasta entree, salad $2, bin of bread on the table comes with the meal. Lunch and dinner daily.

Nido, 7 Stanley Lane, East Sydney (phone 332-2835). In a little alley off Riley St., sign says "Trattoria." Tiny and simple decor, traditional Italian. Pasta and pizza around $8; veal and chicken up to $12. Dinner daily, lunch M-F.

Forbes Restaurante Italiano (BYO & L), 155 Forbes St., Wooloomooloo (phone 357-3652). Popular and frequented by uni-aged crowd. Three course meal for $11, a la carte also available. Lunch M-F, dinner M-Sat.

Watermelon, 13 Kellett Way, King's Cross (phone 357-3824). Delicious, inexpensive gourmet vegetarian fare. Best tropical cocktails in the city. Under $10. Dinner T-Sun.

Gado Gado (BYO), 57 Bayswater Rd., King's Cross (phone 331-1577). Indonesian chicken, beef, and lamb satays, all $7; seafood specials range around $8. Small corkage fee. 6:00pm-11:00pm daily.

New York Restaurant (BYO), 23 Bayswater Rd., King's Cross (phone 357-2772). Not elegant, but serves the cheapest cooked meals in the city: grills, roasts, and steaks; fish, salads and omelettes (all below $7). Minimum charge $3. Lunch and dinner M-Sat.

KK Restaurant, corner Hughes and Macleay Sts., King's Cross (phone 358-4412). Fresh Vietnamese and Chinese fare in pleasant setting. $5-$10. M-Sat noon-3:00pm, 5:00pm-11:30pm; Sun 5:00pm-10:30pm.

Dean's Cafe (BYO), 1/7 Kellett St., King's Cross (phone 358-2174). Leafy terrace setting. Light meals, coffee and cakes. Sun-Th noon-3:30am, all night Fri-Sat.

Metro Cafe (BYO), 26 Burton St., Darlinghurst (phone 33-5356). 1950's diner style, with wooden seats and ceiling fans. Cheap and great vegetarian food. Very popular. $7/main, $3/desserts. Dinner Th-Sun. Closed three months of the year, so call first.

Oxford Street

Oxford Street, which runs along the southern edge of Darlinghurst and straight through Paddington, offers Thai, Balkan, Greek, French, and other food, most of it not quite within the budget traveler's price range. Main courses cost around $10-$15. If you can't splurge, go to one of Oxford Street's many cafes for dessert or coffee. Below are a few on the cheaper end of the scale that also happen to be good.

Thai Silver Spoon (BYO), 203 Oxford St., Darlinghurst (phone 357-4669). Delicious and beautifully presented Thai food, not for huge eaters unless you order two courses. $8 minimum per table, and $1 surcharge on holidays. Dinner T-Sun from 6:00pm; lunch W-F noon-2:30pm.

Green Park Diner (BYO), 209 Oxford St., Darlinghurst (phone 357-5391). American-style, including hamburgers, tuna melts, and other sandwiches, all served with salad and fries. Around $7. M-Th 11:30am-11:00pm, Fri-Sat 11:30am-midnight, Sun 11:30am- 10:00pm.

Paris Express, 179 Oxford St., Darlinghurst (phone 331-3229). Croissants and other pastries. Quiche, rump steak, and other mains $4-$8. A nice place to linger, outdoor tables in summer. 8:00am-midnight daily.

Cafe Schubert, 122 Oxford St., Darlinghurst (phone 357-5610). Viennese cakes, pastries, scones, bread. Mostly takeaway. Open 24 hours, 7 days.

Spago (BYO), 16 Glenmore Rd., Paddington (phone 33-5607). Chic, tiny Italian cafe off the main drag. $12 for three courses. Lunch and dinner daily.

Tickle Your Ribs (BYO), 462 Oxford St., Paddington (phone 332-1019). American baked goods, such as innovative quiche and giant chocolate chip cookies. Mostly takeaway. 11:00am-midnight daily.

Newtown, Glebe, Surrey Hills
King St. in Newtown has the best value in Sydney, thanks to the University of Sydney around the corner. There are several takeaways and bakeries here, in addition to a variety of affordable restaurants. Glebe Point Rd. in Glebe, west of the Uni, is quieter and best for takeaways and cafes, while Cleveland St. in Surrey Hills is lined with Lebanese restaurants.

Bali Restaurant (BYO & L), 137 King St., Newtown (phone 51-3441). Good and filling Indonesian and Malaysian food, about $7. Lunch and dinner daily.

Cafe Zambezi (BYO), 182 King St., Newtown (phone 51-3462). Walls are painted with tropical jungle scenes, but the decor is 1950's and there's a mish-mash of people. Roasts, vegetarian dishes, curries ($7-$12), desserts about $3. Live jazz nightly. Buskers and taro card readings. T-F 11:00am-late, Sat-Sun noon-late.

Mamma Maria's Upstairs Restaurant (BYO), 239a King St., Newtown (phone 516-4428), entrance off King on Church St. Huge variety of Italian meals, all $8. $1 corkage fee. Casual and noisy atmosphere, with yelling waiters. Perfect for a group. 6:00pm-midnight daily, M-F noon-3:00pm.

Thai Tanic (BYO), 127 King St., Newtown (phone 517-1350). Good Thai food at excellent prices. Mains around $8. Seafood is more expensive, but worth it. Dinner T-Sun.

No Names 2, 58 Cowper St., Glebe (phone 660-2326). Great value, but go early to get a place. Simple Italian fare. High ceilings and pub atmosphere. Bustling and crazy. About $7. Lunch and dinner M-Sat.

Cafe Troppo, 175 Glebe Point Rd., Glebe (phone 660-7332). Go for the huge and scrumptious desserts ($5). Meals are around $12. Open 11:00am-1:00am daily.

Badde Manors (BYO), 37 Glebe Point Rd., Glebe (phone 660-3797). Wholesome vegetarian fare, salads, desserts, and coffee. Nothing above $8. Light and pleasant atmosphere. Very popular. 8:00am-2:00am daily (opens 9:30am weekends).

Johnie's Fish Cafe (BYO), 57a Fitzroy St., Surry Hills (phone 331-1623). No frills—probably the cheapest place for decent seafood in Sydney. $8-$12. Everything comes with salad and chips. Open 10:00am-8:30pm M-Sat.

The Prophet (BYO), 274 Cleveland St., Surry Hills (phone 698-7025). Greek fare: shish kebab, lamb, etc. $9/combo plate. Fill yourself and sit as long as you like. 5:30pm-11:00pm daily.

Nightlife

Sydney nightlife has two major themes: cafes (with all variety of food, entertainment, and crowds) and pubs, where most of the local bands play. There are plenty of spots to party into the wee hours, if you're so inclined. Check Friday's Metro section of the *Sydney Morning Herald* for local bands and for unusual events, such as the occasional African dancing night at the Paddington Town Hall or Bondi Pavilion (a great time!).

Nighttime activity doesn't happen only downtown. King's Cross, Bondi, and Manly are all hopping, while Glebe and Newtown have busy cafes of a quieter variety. The popular pubs are spread all over the city.

Pubs

With a few exceptions, pubs are licensed for business until midnight on weekends and 11:00pm on weekdays.

Many travelers automatically head for pubs in **The Rocks** to find a good time. The Rocks may be placid by day, but the area is surprisingly rough by night. Still, pub-hopping there is a lot of fun, and places are always full until everyone gets kicked out and the area becomes awash with drunken, singing people with nowhere to go.

Paddington has some quiet, nicely restored pubs for a low-key night out; it's also the nighttime hangout for Sydney's large gay population. Try **The Royal** (237 Glenmore Rd.) for a cozy conversation setting. **The Exchange** (34 Oxford St., phone 331-1936) hosts a fashionable gay crowd and stays open past normal pub hours.

King's Cross, mostly a nightclub and cafe scene, also has some good pubs. **The Rex** (58 Macleay Rd.) always has a bunch of travelers in the "Bottoms Up Bar." Go to the **Bourbon and Beefsteak** (24 Darlinghurst Rd.) for free munchies, chicken, and 2-for-1 drinks during happy hour (5:00pm-7:00pm).

One of the most popular ways to spend a sunny Sunday afternoon is at the **Watson's Bay Hotel** (Military Rd., Watson's Bay, phone 337-4299). Sit out on the terrace overlooking the harbor, and have some calamari and hot chips. It often turns into a roaring party.

Downtown pub crowds vary according to the day of the week, but we have a few suggestions:

The Metropolitan, George and Bridge Sts., The Rocks (phone 27- 2132). Rock 'n roll bands Th-Sat. Crowded and fun.

The Mercantile, 25 George St. N., The Rocks (phone 27-3570). Irish pub with all kinds of live and recorded music. Sunday night is the best time.

Harbour View, 18 Lower Fort St., The Rocks (phone 27-3292). There's no view, despite it's name. Go on Sunday for the "Reel Matilda" from 4:00pm-7:00pm, when there's bush music and sometimes bush dancing.

Jackson's on George Hotel, 176 George St., Circular Quay just as you enter The Rocks (phone 27-2727). More of a yuppie scene than the others. Live background music, W-Sat. Open 10:00am-midnight M-Sat, til 10:00pm Sunday.

To hear some of Sydney's excellent local bands, go to Surry Hills or suburbs further east, and check the Metro section first.

Hopetoun Hotel, 416 Bourke St., Surry Hills (phone 33-5257). No cover charge for live Sydney bands. Exposed brick and dark inside. Pool table. Mixed crowd, many students. Popular, but not raging.

Strawberry Hill Hotel, 453 Elizabeth St., Surry Hills (phone 698-2997). Depending on the night, this place is either dead or filled. Pleasant and comfy. Older crowd. Live jazz Friday nights.

Herald Park Hotel, 115 Wigram Rd., Glebe (phone 692-0564). Artsy university crowd. Good local bands, occasional poetry readings.

The Stand, main football oval at the Uni, under the grandstand. Dirt-cheap drinks, tons of students, and rowdy. Live bands Th & Fri.

The Oaks, 118 Military Rd., Neutral Bay (phone 90-5515). Jam-packed with all ages. Live bands. Good place to meet people. Thursday night is the best.

The Bayswater, 100 Bayswater Rd., Rushcutter's Bay (phone 331-2941). Not far from King's Cross. Clean-cut uni crowd. Place to head after the rest of the pubs close. Last call 1:00am.

Cafes

Kellett St. in King's Cross is a leafy hideaway from the rough scene around Darlinghurst Rd. There are a few outdoor cafes in restored terrace houses on this little street, most of them open all night. They serve light meals and aren't licensed to serve alcohol. Glebe, Newtown, and Paddington also have plenty of cafes (see also *Food* section).

Tzers (BYO), Kellett St., King's Cross (phone 358-3381). Live jazz and cabarets on weekends. Downstairs jukebox, sometimes dancing. Open M-Th 6:00pm-4:00am, F-Sat til 5:00am.

Lolita's, 29 Glebe Point Rd., Glebe (phone 692-0493). Quiet, artsy crowd. Snacks. Open noon-1:00am, except Sun-M til 9:30pm.

Nightclubs and Bars

Most of the city's nightclubs are in King's Cross or the city center in the George St./Circular Quay area.

The Basement, 29 Rigby Place, Circular Quay (phone 27-9727). *The* place to hear jazz, with the best musicians and dancing. People generally dress up. Cover varies from $3-$15.

The Tivoli Tavern, 256 George St., City (phone 267-5499). The best visiting bands play here. Huge floor area. Can be rough—go for the music, not the atmosphere.

Jamison Street Nightclub, 11 Jamison St., City (phone 251-1480). Mingle with designers and dress accordingly for "The Berlin Club" Tue night. $12 cover, open T-Sat 9:00pm-3:00am.

Marble Bar, Hilton Hotel on George St. between Market and Druitt Sts., City. Art Deco decor. Mixed crowd, lots of students. Pricey drinks.

Hip Hop Club, 11 Oxford St., Paddington (phone 332-2568). Popular city bands. Dancing, also disco downstairs. Sometimes cabaret-style entertainment. Dinner available. Dress up.

All Nation's Club, 50 Bayswater Rd., King's Cross (phone 33-0954). Live music nightly: rock, jazz, vocalists. Cheap drinks. Video room. Casual dress. $5 cover. Open until 2:45am M-Th, 5:00am Sat-Sun.

Kardomah Cafe, 22 Bayswater Rd., King's Cross (phone 358-5228). Classy building. Australia's top bands. Live music nightly. Cover around $7 depending on band. Open til 4:00am.

Blue Moon, 39 Darlinghurst Rd., King's Cross (phone 358-6368). Cozy setting for live jazz and blues.

Entertainment

If you find the rest of Australia a bit lacking in high culture and innovative entertainment, Sydney will make up for it. Its greatest performance center, the **Opera House**, houses not only the Sydney Opera Company (training ground for Joan Sutherland, among others), but the Sydney Dance Company, Sydney Ballet, and Sydney Theater Company. (The Dance and Theater Company also play at the **Wharf** Theatre, Hickson Rd. in Miller's Point, phone 250-1761.)

There's always a big-name band at the **Sydney Entertainment Centre**, and several local rock and jazz bands are first-rate. If you can't spend much money, there are free concerts, interesting films, and top-notch sporting events to keep you busy. Student discounts are available for most everything.

The *Sydney Morning Herald*'s Friday Metro section and Saturday advertisements provide a guide to the entertainment scene, or phone 11-688 for a complete list of current offerings.

For information and bookings, go to **Halftix** in the kiosk at Martin Place, near the Elizabeth St. intersection. They're open noon-6:00pm M-Sat and sell half-price tickets on the day of performance for all shows and concerts (depending, of course, on availability). Tickets are sold on a first-come, first-served basis (no phone bookings), and they accept *only* cash. Make credit card bookings for most events on the telephone through Bass at 266-4800, 9:00am-9:00pm M-F or 9:00am-5:00pm Sat. Bass has outlets at the Sydney Entertainment Centre and at Grace Brothers on Market St. in the city.

The Opera house has a theater, concert hall, cinema, and exhibition hall. Pick up an "Opera House Diary" for what's up, or call their information line on 250-7111.

The Sydney Opera and the **Sydney Dance Company** (modern dance) are both world-renowned. Whatever you see there is worth the visit just to experience the building from the inside. You can even go for free—there's often entertainment on the terraces facing the harbor, and most Sundays there's chamber music in the Recording Hall.

Students with ID get the best deal in town: At 7:00pm, extra tickets are sold as "student rush" seats. Opera tickets are reduced to about $12, symphony tickets reduced to $8-$13, and for M-Th & Sun afternoon performances, plays are reduced from the regular $32 to about $24.

Sydney offers numerous opportunities for free entertainment. There are lunchtime performances almost every weekday in the **Martin Place Amphitheatre**. The **Conservatorium of Music** (next to Government House, phone 27-4206) holds a free concert every Wednesday during the school term at 1:00pm, plus evening concerts. The **University of Sydney** has a long tradition of "reviews" staged by students. Their season is June and July; check the Uni bulletin boards for what's on and where.

Jazz fans should get to Sydney in October for the annual **Manly Jazz Festival**, and the **Sydney Festival** occurs each January. Part of the celebration includes free performances on the Domain grounds every weekend by the opera company, symphony, and rock and jazz bands. Get to these performances at least an hour early.

George Street between Bathurst and Liverpool Sts. has an impressive collection of movie theaters. There are about six different complexes, each showing 3-10 films. Movies are expensive ($8), but Tuesday night is half-price at most theaters.

For non-blockbuster and less expensive films, you have a few choices. **Valhalla** at 166b Glebe Point Rd. (phone 660-8050) is an alternative-type theatre with old flicks and artsy films. The **Academy Twin Cinema** (Oxford St., Paddington, phone 33-4453) shows foreign movies. Go to a great little cafe called **Cappuccino City**, across the street, for coffee after the show. The Australian Film Institute screens at the **Chauvel**, behind the Paddington Town Hall (corner Oxford St. and Oatley Rd.; phone 33-5398). For golden oldies, try the **Opera House Cinema** (phone 250-7111).

Call the Dept. of Sport and Recreation for what's going on in sports (phone 231- 7100). Cricket and horse racing are big, with some major cricket matches at the **Sydney Cricket Ground** and spring horse races at the **Royal Randwick Racecourse**. Sailing is another favorite. The start of the Sydney to Hobart Regatta takes place in Sydney Harbour on Boxing Day—an event not to be missed if you're anywhere in the vicinity.

The **January Surf Carnivals**, a unique slice of Aussie culture, are all-day beach events, with water sports, competitions, and a festival atmosphere. Check the *Sydney Morning Herald* or call 599-4500 for info.

Trips from Sydney

Sydney lies minutes from the ocean, where enormous waves pound a coast swarming with surfers and sunbathers. It's just two hours by train from the Blue Mountains, where elegant estates and resorts overlook the rugged, distinctly Australian mountain range. Wine drinkers are 1.5 hours from the Hunter Valley, Australia's oldest wine valley. And Sydney offers nearby hiking in the Blue Mountains, Ku-Ring-Gai Chase National Park (an hour north), and Royal National Park (an hour south).

Public transport is extensive and covers most places you'd want to go—the big exception being the Hunter Valley, where shuttling from winery to winery requires your own steam. Organized trips to the Hunter Valley and the Blue Mountains, among other places, are offered by **Sydney Hostel Tours** (call 212-6328 for information).

There are YHA and Backpackers hostels in Katoomba (Blue Mountains), Cessnock (Lower Hunter Valley), Scone (Upper Hunter), Pittwater (Ku-Ring-Gai Chase National Park), Royal National Park, and Avalon Beach.

Hiking

Ask at YHA of N.S.W.'s Head Office about organized hikes to nearby national parks. For a $14 membership fee, you can join any of the treks of the **National Parks Association** (275 Pitt St., phone 264-7994). There are a few excursions each week to nearby parks. Call for a current listing.

For camping equipment, **Paddy Pallins** (507 Kent St., phone 264-2685) rents gear. Other rental companies are listed in the Yellow Pages. **Army Disposals** on Pitt St. has good deals on tents, and **Southern Cross** (293 Kent St.) gives a discount to YHA members on all purchases. They also rent knapsacks. Topographic maps and information on all N.S.W. national parks are available at the **National Parks and Wildlife** headquarters (189-193 Kent St., phone 237-6500).

Northern Beaches

Sydney's beaches were once a topic of fiery debate: which are better, city beaches or northern beaches? With the population explosion of the last 20 years, the winner is the north, hands down. Though harder to reach than city beaches, northern beaches are far more scenic and have better surfing.

Scores of public beaches border the northern suburbs, and any map of greater Sydney will show beaches at Harbord, Curl Curl, Dee Why, Narrabeen, Warriewood, Bilgola, Avalon, Whale, and Palm. The coastal settlements become increasingly posh as you head north, **Palm Beach** (at the northern end) being the traditional meeting spot of Sydney's elite. **Whale Beach**, just south, is as nice and less crowded—our favorite of the lot.

Most of the beaches provide free shower facilities, and a few have seawater swimming pools adjacent to the beach, including Dee Why and Warriewood. A walker's trail, built for the Bicentennial, runs the length of the coast from Manly to Palm Beach. Sydney's popular music stations give regular surf reports.

There's a new **Backpackers hostel** in Avalon, a short walk from the beach. It wasn't completed at the time of our visit, but if the exterior was any indication, it's worth checking out. The address is 59 Avalon Rd., Avalon Beach (phone 02-918-9709). See below for YHA's Pittwater hostel, also on the water.

Getting There: You can reach almost all beaches by buses 185, 186, or 190 from the city. You can also take a ferry to Manly and catch a beach-bound bus from there.

Ku-Ring-Gai Chase National Park and the Hawkesbury Mouth

If good surf is your pursuit, stick to the ocean beaches. But those seeking a peaceful bush retreat and a waterfront setting should head for the western shore of Pittwater, where Ku-Ring-Gai Chase National Park and a fabulous YHA hostel overlook the mouth of the Hawkesbury River.

The **Pittwater YHA hostel**, or "Bensuta Lodge," is on Towler Bay, surrounded by the rough, hilly bush of Ku-Ring-Gai. It's a gorgeous, newly-renovated hostel set atop a hill, with a wide veranda that looks to the shore and far beyond. Lorikeets and kookaburras will wake you, and other wild animals make their homes nearby, including koalas and wallabies. Fishing, sailing, canoeing, and hiking are all available. Ask about seeing stone engravings by local Guringai Aborigines. The overnight cost is $10 ($15 on Saturday nights). Call ahead to make sure there's room (phone 02-99-2196), and be sure to bring food. There's a supermarket at Church Point.

Since the hostel is surrounded by national parklands, you must take a ferry to get there. The ferry leaves hourly on weekdays and half-hourly on weekends from the little port of Church Point (ferry phone is 02-99-3492). The last ferry is at 6:30pm. It takes you to Hall's Wharf, where directions to the YHA hostel are posted (about a five-minute walk). To reach Church Point, take buses 185, 186, or 190 to Narrabeen and change to 155. Or take the ferry to Manly and catch the 155 from there.

Though the **Hawkesbury Mouth** is best viewed from Ku-Ring-Gai Chase National Park, there are other ways to see it. River cruises—from day trips to weekend luxury bashes—leave from Brooklyn, about 50 km north of Sydney (off the Pacific Hwy.). **Hawkesbury River Ferries** (Dangar Rd., Brooklyn, phone 455-1566) offers the least expensive day cruises. Book through the N.S.W. Travel Center in Sydney. A State Rail train runs between Sydney and Brooklyn.

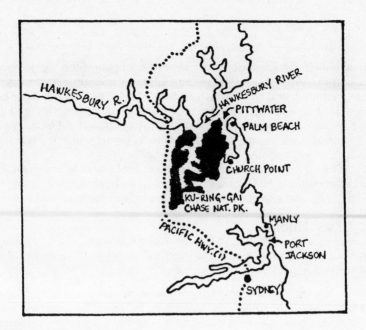

Royal National Park

Royal National Park, the second oldest national park in the world, is an easy day trip from Sydney or a pleasant stop en route to Bundanoon or the southern coast of N.S.W.

A network of walking tracks crosses rainforests and eucalypt woodlands to reach impressive sandstone escarpment, steep cliffs, and swimming beaches. Garie Beach, on the southern edge of the park, is known for great surf and swimming. The Visitors Center, at the park's northern entrance, is open daily 8:30am-4:30pm (phone 02-521-6467). You can rent canoes and rowboats there, and the farther you can row away from Audley, the fewer people you'll see.

Camping is allowed throughout the park, but a permit for each camper must be obtained from the Visitors Center or a ranger. Car or caravan camping is allowed only in Bonnie Vale. Weekends and holidays are heavily booked. A small, unpowered YHA hostel is 1 km from Garie Beach, or a 15 km walk from the ferry's drop-off point in Bundeena. A key to the hostel and the $5 nightly fee must be arranged at YHA's N.S.W. head office in Sydney (176 Day St., phone 02-267-3044). Get specific directions for finding the hostel when you book, and bring a flashlight ("torch").

Getting There: The train from Sydney goes down the Park's western boundary to Cronulla. A ferry service (phone 523-2990) runs between Cronulla and Bundeena.

The Hunter Valley

The Hunter Valley is the oldest commercial wine-producing district in Australia, and probably its most famous. Although vines came with the First Fleet, it wasn't until 1832 that wine making became a significant industry.

Local wine production occurs in two distinct regions: the Lower Hunter (centered in Cessnock) and the Upper Hunter (surrounding the townships of Muswellbrook and Denham). The Lower Hunter is by far the more convenient for travelers and the more commercialized. Its wineries are close together and can accommodate busloads. By contrast, the Upper Hunter has just a few large, less-frequented wineries (of comparable quality) in very scenic, "horsey" country.

We advise those taking only a day to head for **Cessnock**. Those on their way to the northern N.S.W. coast (if you have a car) should stay a night or two in Scone and explore the Upper Hunter from there.

The Lower Hunter

Cessnock City Tourist Board, Wollombi and Mt. View Rds., Cessnock (phone 049-90-4477. Summer: daily 10:00am-6:00pm; winter: daily 10:00am-4:00pm.

Many of Australia's best-known wineries are in this area, including Hungerford Hill, Tyrells, and Lindemans. Wyndham Estate, at Dalwood, was established in 1828 and is the oldest operating winery in the country. We suggest avoiding a winery that has tour buses in its driveway. Wineries are generally open 9:00am-5:00pm daily.

Your first stop should be the Cessnock City Tourist Board, where a local map and winery information is free.

Getting There and Getting Around: Lower Hunter wineries are close enough to one another to visit on bike and even by foot (a few, at least). However, we strongly suggest that day trippers rent a car from Sydney. Drivers should follow the Pacific Hwy. to the New England Hwy. (Rte. 15) and expect about a 2.5 hour trip.

Those taking public transport can take a State Rail train from Sydney to Maitland then catch the local **Rover Motor Bus Service** to Cessnock (for Rover schedule information, call 049-90-1175). Or, **Batterham's Bus Lines** offers a daily Sydney-Cessnock service (181 Vincent St., Cessnock; phone 049-90-5000 in Cessnock or 02-27-2672 in Sydney). If you're traveling from interstate, Pioneer stops in Cessnock along its Brisbane-Sydney route. You can also take Deluxe, Greyhound, or Bus Australia, all of which make stops in Maitland on their Sydney-Brisbane services.

Accommodation: The **Black Opal Hotel**, located at 216 Vincent St. (phone 049-97-3075) sets aside 16 beds for hostellers. If it's booked up, try bed & breakfast at the **Wentworth Hotel** (36 Vincent St., phone 049-90-1364; open Th-Sat only). **Valley View Cessnock Carapark** (phone 049-90-2573) is 2 km from town on Mt. View Rd. and has on-site vans and cabins. The local tourist office can help with reservations.

The Upper Hunter

Genteel traditions and lush, rolling hills of the Upper Hunter contradict any preconceived ideas you may have had about a rugged and uncivilized Australia. Fox-hunting and steeple-chasing are regular leisure activities of the local people, many of whom own or work on regional horse farms.

The wine centers are Muswellbrook and Denman, while 25 km north is the picturesque town of Scone, which has a YHA hostel. All three towns are interesting to poke around, with antique shops, craft galleries, and tea rooms. There are several bed & breakfast accommodations on farms in the region—ask at the local tourist bureau for locations and prices.

Set on a country road in the heart of horse country and 10 km from town, the YHA hostel at Scone is an excellent place from which to bike, hike, and taste wines (if you have your own transport). You are welcome to wander around next door at Taranga Stud farm. The little-used hostel is attractive and well-equipped, certainly worth your while if you've got a car to get places. The hostel rents bikes, and within biking distance are **Glenbawn Dam** (6 km east) and **Burning Mountain Nature Reserve** (22 km north). The overnight cost is $9, and the hostel is on Segenhoe Rd. (phone 065-45-2072).

Getting There: Deluxe, Bus Australia, and Greyhound stop in Muswellbrook and Scone on the way to and from Queensland. From Sydney, trains make the 5 hour trip to Scone several times daily, Mon-Sat. There's no local public transport, but getting to the Scone hostel isn't too hard. Rides are easy to get during the day, or you can catch the local school bus from Scone Primary School at 3:30pm (M-F during the school year). The bus driver will give you a free tour of the area if you ask. If all else fails, ring the hostel managers, who'll do what they can to help.

The Blue Mountains
The Blue Mountains Tourist Information Centre, Echo Point, Katoomba (phone 047-82-1833). Open daily 9:00am-5:00pm.

Plunging valleys and canyons, rather than peaks, characterize the formidable landscape of the Blue Mountains. The dramatic scenery is shrouded by a blue veil when seen from afar, an effect created as the oil from eucalyptus leaves evaporates in the sun.

The Blue Mountains are a magnet for hikers, photographers, and nature lovers from all over. You can get there and back from Sydney in one day, but it's better to spend a few days hiking, soaking in the scenery and mountain air, and wandering about the towns.

The Blue Mountains presented an impenetrable barrier to the first European settlers, but severe droughts in the early 1800's and the need for new grazing land eventually made westward expansion a necessity. In 1813, the exploration team of Gregory Blaxland, William Lawson, and William Charles Wentworth made the first successful crossing, ending at Mt. Blaxland. By the 1920's, a number of splendid hotels and spas drew hoards of wealthy holidayers to the Katoomba region. The oldest and most palatial is the **Carrington Hotel** on Katoomba St. in the center of Katoomba. It was built in 1882 and is currently undergoing massive restoration.

Getting There: N.S.W.'s State Rail operates a "Blue Mountains Line" train service between Sydney and Lithgow that stops in Wentworth Falls, Leura, Katoomba, Medlow Bath, Blackheath, and Mt. Victoria. The trip from Sydney to Katoomba takes about two hours.

Orientation and Practical Information: Katoomba, 105 km west of Sydney, is the focal point for visitors. Wentworth Falls, Leura (east of Katoomba), Blackheath, and Mt. Victoria (west of Katoomba) are other mountain towns you'll likely pass through. The Jenolan Caves are about 75 km southeast of Katoomba (see below). The Blue Mountains range is protected by **Blue Mountains National Park** and **Wollemi National Park**, with dozens of hiking trails and scenic lookouts.

The Blue Mountains Tourist Information Centre is just south of Katoomba at Echo Point. Centre displays give background on geology and flora of the mountains, and the tourist officers have information on area hiking. Pick up the Blue Mountains Tourism Authority's *Visitor's Guide*, which has a useful map (not to scale!) of attractions. The YHA hostel sells more detailed maps of townships and walking tracks.

As in any mountain region, the weather can suddenly turn nasty. Bring warm clothes, even in summer, and raingear. Fog sometimes obliterates the view, but it often burns off by afternoon. Restaurants and sights are open all weekend, but watch out on Mondays and Tuesdays, when sights and even some accommodations often close.

Transportation: The State Rail train from Sydney runs between the local townships several times daily and is the best mode of local transportation.

There are two bus services. The Katoomba-Woodford bus (phone 82-4213) runs between Wentworth Falls, Leura, and Katoomba (Katoomba stops are Goyder Ave., The Skyway, and the Golf Links). Hours of operation are M-F til 4:15pm, Sat til 5:15pm, and Sun until 3:25pm. The other bus company is the Katoomba-Leura Bus Service (phone 82-3333), which makes a loop from Leura Golf Links, stopping in the center of Leura, Echo Point in Katoomba, the Carrington Hotel in Katoomba, the Ritz in Leura, and Gordon Falls. It runs M-F til 4:15pm and Sat til 12:25pm (except public holidays). Call the bus companies for schedule information or ask at the YHA hostel.

On weekends and public holidays, an "Explorer Bus" for tourists makes a large loop including downtown Katoomba, Echo Point, the Scenic Railroad and Skyway, and Leura.

The only key destination not serviced by public transport is Jenolan Caves. You can hitch there successfully on weekends; otherwise, tours are expensive. Hostellers often get together and rent a car for the jaunt. **Cales Rent-A-Car** (60 Wilson St., Katoomba) charges about $60/day, plus $100 deposit for a mini-bus or a truck. Call 82-2917 or 82-3999 between 7:00am-9:00pm M-F or until noon on Sat.

The extremely fit can rent bicycles at the corner of Warwick and Lurline Sts. in Katoomba (phone 82-2281). **Bush Experiences** (phone 84-2361) has guided bike tours that let you cycle downhill (they'll bring you and the bikes back by car).

Accommodation: Because the weekends are so popular, many guesthouses offer reduced rates during the week for bed & breakfast packages. These offers vary with the seasons, so check with the tourist bureau for updated information.

Katoomba YHA Hostel, 1 Wellington Rd., Katoomba (phone 047-82-1416). A hilly 1.2 km walk from the center of town. $10/night. A small, pleasant, cabin-type hostel. Lots of local information and area maps available. Definitely call ahead, especially on the weekends. Closed until 5:00pm.

Rayton House, corner Lurline and Waratah Sts. (phone 047-82-1329). Renovated 1870 guesthouse with a few rooms set aside for backpackers. $20/night each, in a 4-person share room. Bathroom en-suite, and some rooms have TV. Great lounge with fireplace. Gourmet (and expensive) restaurant, and terrific bar.

Hiking: If you only have a day, plan to hike from Katoomba. The principle walking tracks in Katoomba are **Prince Henry Cliff Walk** and the **Federal Pass**, both of which start at the Scenic Railway and Skyway (about a mile west of Echo Point on Cliff Dr.) and end up in Leura. Both trails are accessible from Echo Point.

Travelers with more than a day in the area should hike from Blackheath, where walks are longer, equally scenic, and not as crowded. There are also long trails for extended overnight hiking throughout the national parks.

Hiking maps and information are available at the Echo Point Information Centre. The **National Parks and Wildlife Service** in Blackheath (65 Leichardt St., phone 87-8877) is another useful information source. For those planning extended walks, the best guidebook is called *Exploring the Blue Mountains* by Hungerford & Donald. It includes all trail information plus historical background and is available at Echo Point.

The **Upper Blue Mountains Bushwalking Club** (phone 82-3287) posts various walks in Tourist Information. There's a small fee to join. Discounts are available to YHA members on all guided climbs and private instruction at the **Blue Mountains Climbing School** (285 Main St.).

Note: You can't drink from the mountain creeks, so be sure to bring plenty of water with you on hikes.

Things to See and Do: The most famous spot in the Blue Mountains, **Echo Point** gives you a view of the **Three Sisters**, a series of giant, craggy, pillar-like rock formations—a truly awesome feat of erosion. The Sisters rise from Jamison Valley, a deep canyon where changing blues of eucalyptus forest render a gorgeous panorama. You can walk from the lookout into the valley, and those who want to avoid climbing back up can walk westward along Federal Pass to the Scenic Railway.

Those who don't plan to hike (but even those who do) shouldn't miss Katoomba's **Railway and Skyway**. The train has a 250-meter vertical drop and passes through a natural tunnel. Built in 1872 to haul coal, the railway descends at a 52° angle, the steepest in the Southern Hemisphere. The Skyway is a gondola, and on a clear day the views are fantastic, especially of Katoomba Falls. Both the train and Skyway cost about $4, or you can take the train one-way for $2. Hours are 9:00am-4:45pm daily.

The other major scenic lookout area in the Blue Mountains is just north of Blackheath: **Govett's Leap**, **Evan's Lookout**, and **Anvil Rock** all offer tremendous views of the Grose Valley. You can get to Blackheath by local bus or State Rail train. The bus goes as far as McLaren's Crescent on Govett's Leap Rd. and doesn't go to Evan's Lookout Rd. or Hat Hill Rd. (for Anvil Rock), so those relying on public transport will have to do some walking.

There's more than. enough in the way of historic estates, museums, and quaint towns to keep you entertained in rainy weather. East of Katoomba in Wentworth Falls is an 1880's estate known as **Yester Grange**, formerly owned by a Premier of N.S.W., John See. The current owner, a friendly fellow named Gil Clarke, bought it to live in but later opened it to the public. Even more impressive than the house are the grounds, which extend down to the Jamison Valley floor. There's a path from the house to the top of **Wentworth Falls**. Mr. Clarke serves a generous Devonshire tea in the mansion tearoom, much welcomed on a chilly day. Entrance to both house and grounds is about $5. (Open W, Th 10:00am-3:30pm, F-Sun and holidays 10:00am-5:00pm.) Yester Grange is on the "Explorer Bus" route, or you can take a local bus to Tableland Rd., walk down Tableland Rd., and take your first right onto Yester Rd.

Leuralla, easier to get to than Yester Grange but not as worthwhile, is an Art Deco mansion at the corner of Olympian Pde. and Balmoral Rd. in Leura. Leuralla is a memorial to the highly-touted Australian statesman, Dr. H.V. Evatt. Admission to the house and gardens is $4, and it's open F-Sun 10:00am-5:00pm.

West of Katoomba, on the road to Blackheath and Mt. Victoria, there's an enormous hotel called the **Hydro-Majestic**, established in 1904 as a health resort. Three grand buildings, only one of which has been refurbished, sit on 300 acres overlooking the Megalong Valley. Huge picture windows show off the magnificent view and make a great place to stop for a drink or snack. The coffee shop is open daily from 11:00am-5:00pm and serves light lunches between noon-2:30pm. Catch either the bus or train to Medlow Bath. The hotel is on the Great Western Hwy.

Blackheath is a quaint town filled with tearooms and antique shops. **Mt. Victoria**, just west of Blackheath, has a smaller array of the same. The historic **Victoria and Albert Guesthouse** in Mt. Victoria is a renovated Victorian-style hotel. Although the restaurant may surpass your means, there's a cafe open W-Sun 10:00am-5:00pm, and a bar area. The Victoria and Albert is at 19 Station St. (phone 87-1241). Housed in the old refreshment rooms of the historic railway station, the **Mt. Victoria Historical Museum** has photos and artifacts from the area and is open Sat-Sun 2:00pm-5:00pm ($3 admission). Mr. McDonald, overseeing the front door, spent his life working the local soil and donated his father's plow and other farming tools.

From Blackheath, those with a car can drive south (and down) into the Megalong Valley for horse riding with **Werriberri Trail Rides** (for more information, call 87-9171).

In the spring months of October and November, the Blue Mountains overflow with flowering plants and rhododendron bushes of gigantic proportions. If you're lucky enough to be there at this time, rent a car and drive up to **Mount Wilson**, where several stately homes maintain acres of azaleas, rhododendrons, and fruit trees. Many gardens open to the public during peak season. You can also enjoy the spring closer to Katoomba. Private gardens in Leura and Blackheath also open for viewing at this time. Purchase admission, usually $3/garden or $8/day, at garden entrances.

The **Rhododendron Gardens** in Blackheath (open daily 9:00am-5:00pm, free) label the many species, and in early November the town holds a Rhododendron Festival. Leura also has beautiful public gardens on Denison St. called **The Everglades**, nice at any time.

Finally, those traveling west towards Lithgow will pass by the **Zig-Zag Railway**, constructed in 1869 and used until 1910 to descend the western escarpment into Lithgow. Rides on the original railway run between 10:00am-4:00pm every 72 minutes on weekends and public holidays ($8/person). It makes six stops along the way, and you can get out, have a picnic, and rejoin later. The round trip is one hour with no stops. The closest public transport to the Zig-Zag is by train to Lithgow, where you'll have to catch a taxi out to the railway (about $12).

Food: Restaurants in Katoomba are fairly expensive, with dinners ranging from $10-$15. We managed to find a few exceptions: The **Katoomba Hotel** (on Park St.), and **Memsahib's Kitchen**, which serves large Indian meals (94 Waratah St., open F-Sun only; BYO). **Papadino's** on Katoomba St. is a family-style, BYO Italian restaurant. Their pizza and a few of the pasta options will fill you up cheaply. It's open all week.

For afternoon tea, try the **Paragon Cafe** (Katoomba St., open daily from 9:00am-6:00pm), a perfect example of the locally-favored Art Deco style. A large assortment of handmade chocolates and other goodies are up front, and a small cafe is at the back.

Jenolan Caves

The drive to Jenolan Caves, about 75 km southeast of Katoomba, is exciting in itself. A narrow road winds its way to the caves, with breathtaking (if not hair-raising) views of the valley far below. We quite seriously warn drivers to get to the caves before noon and leave after lunchtime to avoid meeting tour buses head on. Since there's no public transport to the caves, you'll need to rent a car and test your dexterity at the wheel or hop on a tour leaving from either Katoomba or Sydney.

According to the legend, the first of the Jenolan Caves was discovered in 1838 by Charles Whalan while searching for an outlaw. Later, groups found numerous caves in the huge, limestone complex. A Tudor-style **Caves House** was built for visitors in 1898, and an old-world German flavor still pervades (especially during Oktoberfest). Rooms in the House are not for the budget-conscious, but self-contained cabins accommodating up to six are available at about $50/night. Bring your own supplies.

There are nine caves to visit, ranging in admission price from $7-$14 (the higher price means fewer people, not better formations), and you must go on a tour to view them. All are impressive, so our only suggestion for choosing among them is that **Lucas Cave** has the best formation variety. Tour times change daily and are decided the afternoon before. The first tour is around 9:00am, the last at 5:30pm. Those wanting precise times should call 063-59-3304 and ask for the ticket office. Make tour bookings as soon as you arrive, as busloads quickly fill them up. The caves are open 365 days a year.

Extensive walks lead through the grounds to Blue Lake (colored by calcium carbonate), a dam (which was once used to generate power for cave lights), and into adjacent **Kanangra Boyd National Park**. The whole area is most picturesque, and you can easily amuse yourself here for one or two days.

The Northern Coast

Most travelers heading north go directly to Queensland, maybe stopping once along the way. But coastal N.S.W. is actually worth a few stops, particularly far northern spots such as Byron Bay and Lennox Head, with great surfing, or Nimbin and Murwillumbah, with subtropical rainforests. Plus, unlike Queensland, N.S.W. isn't swamped by other backpackers. You tend to get lots of personal attention in the hostels, and many of the hostel managers arrange trips for at-cost fees.

One unique sight on a trip through northern N.S.W. is the "alternative lifestyle" communities, where there appear to be at least three kinds of escapees from the mainstream:

First, there are upscale hippies—former city dwellers who traded their offices for the fertile northern soils, drive Volvos, dabble in their gardens, and eat expensive health food. Bellingen, a small, historic town, is their hub.

Then there are the commune-dwellers, who wear long hair and live off the land. Nimbin, west of Byron Bay, is the home of the largest commune in Australia.

Finally, the most publicized and disdained class of alternatives are those living off unemployment compensation ("the dole"). Their ranks get thicker as you move north into Queensland.

There are YHA and Backpackers hostels at Port Stephens, Girvan, Wauchope, Port Macquarie, Nambucca Heads, Coff's Harbor, Lennox Head, Byron Bay, Nimbin, and Murwillumbah. A new hostel in Ballina, just south of Byron Bay, opened after our visit. According to hearsay, it's worth checking out (information is in the YHA handbook).

Getting There and Getting Around

State Rail runs a coastal rail and bus service, the relevant stops being Wauchope (where you change from train to bus for Port Macquarie), Nambucca Heads, Coff's Harbour, Lismore (where you change to a Kirklands bus for Lennox Head or Ballina), Byron Bay, and Murwillumbah. It's about 8 hours

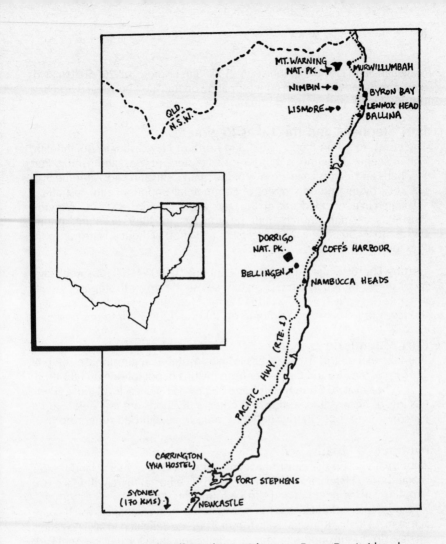

to Nambucca Heads and Coff's Harbour, 13 hours to Byron Bay (with a change on most services in either Grafton or Casino), and 17 hours to Murwillumbah, with a change in Grafton on some services. For State Rail train information, call 02-20942 in Sydney, 066-52-2312 in Coff's Harbour, or 066-72-1752 in Murwillumbah.

Kirklands runs a direct Sydney-Ballina bus service, which connects with other local buses to small towns further north. For schedules and bookings, call 02-267-5030 in Sydney or 066-21-2755 in Lismore.

Deluxe, Greyhound, Bus Australia, and Pioneer run daily services along the Pacific Hwy. between Sydney and Brisbane, stopping in most sizeable towns along the way. You must be traveling at least 200 km to use them unless you're a bus pass holder.

Kirklands has several services from Lismore to Lennox Head, Ballina, and up to the Gold Coast and Brisbane (Queensland). Their main office is 4

Magellan St. in Lismore (phone 066-21-2755 in Lismore, 02-267-5030 in Sydney). See *Byron Bay* section for information on transport between Byron Bay, Lennox Head, and inland destinations.

Port Stephens and the Lakes Region

The coast from Port Stephens (32 km north of Newcastle) to Bulahdelah, rich in scenic shoreline, is famous for its oysters, prawns, and fishing. Port Stephens and Wallis Lake are two of the main cultivating areas for the Sydney rock oyster, the only oyster of commercial importance in Australia.

Located in a secluded area on the bay's western side, the **YHA Carrington Hostel** is a small church built by convicts in 1849 ($7/night, phone 049-97-3075). Reaching the hostel takes real effort without private transport. Buy food before going.

Getting There: White & Leary Busline (phone 049-97-4287) runs weekdays. It doesn't go right through Carrington, so ask the driver to stop as close as possible. If you're driving, exit the Pacific Hwy. at the sign to Tahlee (after the town of Karuah) and continue on that road for 5 km to the hostel.

Port Macquarie

The Port Macquarie Backpacker's (**Mayes Motel**) is a guesthouse setup at 135 Horton St., around the corner from the bus depot (phone 065-83-1913). A YHA hostel at 40 Church St. (phone 065-83-5512) offers local tours. "Port" has lots of history, and surfing and other watersports are available. Stop if it's convenient, but otherwise there's more to see and do further north.

Nambucca Heads

About halfway up the coast between Sydney and the Queensland border is Nambucca Heads, a small seaside town. The hostel there will make you happy if you enjoy quiet and dislike tourist hype.

Nambucca Backpackers is run by two of the nicest managers you'll come across in Australia, Knut and Sally Meyer. They are delighted to take hostellers on day trips to surrounding sights, like Bellingen and Dorrigo National Park for a nominal fee. The Meyers have barbecues two nights a week, plus snorkeling gear, boogie boards, and droplines. The hostel is at 3 Newman St., a short walk from the town center. Doubles are available. Call when you arrive for free pick-up (phone 065-68-6360). Be sure to book ahead.

Coff's Harbour

Coff's Harbour, a.k.a. the capital of the "Banana Republic," is brazenly announced by a giant banana marking the entrance to **Big Banana Plantation**, 3 km north of town on the Pacific Hwy. The plantation has guided tours and a restaurant which serves bananas in many disguises (open daily 8:30am-5:30pm).

Coff's Harbour's tourist population is high, hence the $30 million shopping complex and a computerized Tourist Information kiosk (in High St. Mall). Most attention is focused on the water, where there's windsurfing, sailing, and deep-sea fishing, and a fishermen's co-op on the main jetty. You'll need a car to reach the good beaches.

Coff's Harbour is convenient to several state forests and national parks, which make for good day trips and hiking. Both hostels offer trips inland to Dorrigo National Park, the Bellinger River, and other area attractions.

Accommodation: We recommend the **Aussitel Backpackers** at 312 High St. (phone 066-37-1871), about 2 km from town. It's a modern building with immaculate facilities and a huge kitchen/dining area. Most important, it has a very friendly atmosphere, and the managers arrange beach parties and barbecues.

The YHA hostel **Albany Lodge** is comfortable, but not as spacious as Aussitel (110 Albany St., phone 066-52-6462).

Lennox Head

A tiny, low-key town 27 km south of Byron Bay, Lennox Head is often skipped because it's not on the main thoroughfare. But here, at long last, you'll find a stretch of beautiful beach without industrialization and tacky tourist gimmicks.

The **Lennox Beach House Hostel** is at Lot 2 & 3, Ross St. (phone 066-87-7636). Bunkrooms are clean and comfortable, and the hostel is next to a long, white beach and a lake. The surfing is supreme. Bikes, boogie boards, and a windsurfer are available from the hostel, free.

Getting There: The only major busline to service Lennox Head is Deluxe, from the Gold Coast. State Rail goes to Lismore (catch a Kirklands bus from there) or Byron Bay (local buses run from there as well). Call Byron Bay Travel at 066-85-6552 for all local bus information.

Byron Bay

Tourist Information, Community Centre, Jonson St. (phone 066-85-6807). Open daily 9:00am-4:30pm.

Don't miss Cape Byron, the most eastern point of Australia. Byron Bay is a backpacker's haven, with a good selection of hostels, beautiful beaches, and tons of young people.

The local populace is a mix of surfing fanatics and hippies (many of whom came in the '60s and never left), while the visiting population consists of backpackers and young, affluent families. The best place to meet locals is the Sunday outdoor market, where you'll find bohemian clothing, jewelry, and stuff from Bali. The market, in Byron Bay the first Sunday of each month, moves to nearby towns other Sundays.

Getting There and Getting Around: State Rail runs both bus and train services to Byron Bay. Of the major buslines, only Deluxe and Pioneer go to Byron Bay, from the Gold Coast. For buses to nearby Lismore, Lennox Head, and the Gold Coast, call **Byron Bay Travel** (phone 85-6552) or see Tourist Information for schedules and directions. Buses run frequently on weekends.

Rag Top at 87 Jonson St. (phone 85-8175) rents cars. **Ride On**, also on Jonson St., hires out motorcycles (phone 85-6304). Bicycles are available at most of the hostels.

Accommodation: Byron Bay's hostels are uniformly great, with modern facilities, swimming pools, and double rooms. You can't go wrong.

Belongil Beachhouse, Childe St. (phone 066-85-7868). Modern, wooden structure with fabulous common area. Laid-back and friendly. Very clean. Just off an excellent beach. Horse riding available from nearby beach resort.

The New Arts Factory Hostel, Skinners Shoot Rd. (phone 066-85-7709). All wood, very attractive hostel with a partying atmosphere. Great location near the beach and away from town. Pool and spa. Trampoline. The Piggery and Oz Dive are also here. Office hours 8:30am-11:00am, 4:00pm-7:00pm.

Backpackers Holiday Village, 116 Jonson St. (phone 066-85-7660). Free bicycles and surfboards. Pool and spa. Scuba instruction. Office hours: 7:30am-1:30pm, 4:30pm- 7:00pm.

YHA Byron Bay, 78 Bungalow Rd. (phone 066-85-6445). 6-12 per room, doubles available. Clean, orderly building. Nice managers. Pool. Free bikes and surfboards. Next to Tallows beach. Spaghetti Nights, BBQs, and beach parties. Shuttle bus to town twice daily. Office open 8:00am-9:00pm.

Things to See and Do: Almost everything in Byron Bay is on one main drag, Jonson St. The Community Centre on Jonson St., recognizable by its colorful facade, houses Tourist Information. Byron Bay's Main Beach is at the northern end of town, but there are several beautiful beaches, including one for nudists. You can often see dolphins and whales playing in the waves, along with surfers.

At the eastern end of Main Beach, just before Cape Byron and the Lighthouse, is **The Pass**, the Bay's most famous surfing spot. 2.5 km offshore is the **Julian Rocks Marine Reserve**, where fish and turtles take refuge. **Oz Dive**, based at the Arts Factory Hostel on Skinners Shoot Rd., offers snorkeling and diving trips there and elsewhere. They also have a shop on Jonson St. (phone 85-6197).

The path along the perimeter of the cape and up to the Cape Byron lighthouse has sweeping coastal views and rocky descents to a turbulent sea. Trips from town to nearby rainforests are available through hostels or at Tourist Information.

Food and Nightlife: Earth 'n Sea (Jonson St.; BYO and L) is a local institution featuring homemade pizzas with a variety of toppings, homemade pasta, and ice cream. There are plenty of other restaurants on Jonson St. if it's too crowded.

For nightlife, the most famous of the local nightspots is **The Piggery** (phone 85-7276), with live bands and even some international groups. Check Friday's paper for what's up. The Piggery's restaurant/cabaret is open Saturdays from 6:00pm-midnight, Sundays 6:00pm-10:00pm. It's part of the Arts Factory complex on Skinners Shoot Rd.

There's also a nice bar in the refreshment room of the **Byron Bay Railway Station** on Jonson St., which has a diverse mix of people, live music, and a fun, casual atmosphere.

Nimbin
Cosmic swirls and rainbows painted on the storefronts of Nimbin's only commercial street will immediately send you into a 1960's time warp.

There are at least two classes of Nimbin "alternatives." The prevalent group (who make Nimbin famous) are the communal farmers, like those living near Tuntable Falls in the country's largest commune, run as a pure democracy, with no leaders. A smaller group of alternatives is best described by a local jingle:

> Dole days, dole days, days of unemployment
> Dole days, dole days, subsidized enjoyment!

If you want a first-hand glimpse of Nimbin life, try a healthy meal at the **Rainbow Restaurant**, where locals come to get communal, listen to live music, and smoke home-grown dope.

Although the **Tuntable Falls commune** is closed to the public, a public trail leading to the top of Tuntable Falls passes through the commune gate. Commune members are sometimes open to conversation, though wary of nosy outsiders. To reach the falls, go through the commune gate and follow the trail above the creek (about an hour's walk). The road to the commune turns off to the right from Newtown a few kilometers before Mt. Nardi, and we suggest you get specific directions before going because it's tough to find. There's no public transport.

The subtropical rainforests of the region are some of Australia's most substantial, the most beautiful being **Terania Creek** in Nightcap National Park. Protected in 1973 after a bitter struggle over logging, Terania has dense vegetation, including palm, strangler, fig, and yellow carabeen.

Other highlights of **Nightcap National Park** are Tuntable Falls and the Mt. Nardi lookout. A pamphlet from the National Parks and Wildlife Service includes directions, a map, and trail information. Get it in Lismore or at the general store in Channon (a tiny town southeast of Nimbin). For more information on Nightcap National Park, call 066-28-1177 in Lismore.

Getting There: Getting to Nimbin without a car is tough, but not impossible. Kirkland's stops daily; otherwise, catch a local bus to Nimbin from Lismore (M-Sat, and only one time Sat), Murwillumbah (M-F once daily), or Ballina. Both Murwillumbah and Lismore are serviced by State Rail. All interstate buses pass through Murwillumbah from the Gold Coast. Only Pioneer, Deluxe, and Kirklands service Lismore to and from Queensland.

Accommodation: The Nimbin YHA-Associate hostel, **Granny's Farm on the Creek** (phone 066-89-1333), is a 5-minute walk from town on the main road.

Munching cows fill the surrounding pastures, a creek with elusive platypuses and tortoises runs along the edge of the property, and peaceful quiet rules. There's a swimming hole and trampoline, and you can even play tennis (they have racquets). The hostel bulletin board details everything there is to do around Nimbin, and the manager will give you directions, if needed. Cost is $9/night.

Murwillumbah

10 km west of Murwillumbah, **Mt. Warning** at sunrise is something you shouldn't miss if you can drag yourself awake in time. Its angular, 22-million-year-old bulk, once the central plug of Australia's largest volcano, dominates the entire Tweed Valley and was even noted by Captain Cook as he sailed past Cape Byron. A 4.5 km hike to its summit takes about four hours round trip, and from there you can see the Cape Byron Lighthouse and north to Surfers Paradise.

The YHA-Associate **Riverside Hostel** is on the Tweed River in Murwillumbah (1 Tumbulgum Rd., phone 066-72-3763). The town isn't too exciting but Tassie, the hostel manager, has created a number of day trips for hostellers, including treks to Mt. Warning and rainforests. A homemade riverboat takes hostellers on night cruises if there's interest, and canoes are free. The hostel itself tends to be crowded and not too clean. Cost is $9.50/night.

The Midnorth

Wedged between the tablelands of New England and arid plains of the N.S.W. outback, the "midnorth" region is a diverse landscape ranging from fertile, gentrified properties of Mudgee, to cattle country around Dubbo, to the ancient Warrumbungles Range near Coonabarabran. All three towns are convenient stops en route to Lightning Ridge from Sydney or between Queensland and Melbourne or Adelaide. Without a car, though, the trip takes perseverance. While most destinations are easy to reach, getting around once there (especially Coonabarabran) is either expensive or impossible. Hitching isn't dependable, either.

On a more encouraging note, travelers will be astounded by local friendliness and hospitality, partly because foreigners don't often make it there. Mudgee in particular will welcome you with open arms. If you're going to the Blue Mountains, go that extra mile to visit Mudgee.

There is hostel accommodation in Dubbo and Coonabarabran. Regional caravan parks are numerous and most have a few on-site vans.

Getting There

State Rail's Sydney-Dubbo train/bus services go to Mudgee, Coonabarabran, and Dubbo. Mudgee services run several times daily (6 hours). Dubbo services are less frequent but run daily also (12 hours). Coonabarabran services run Tues, Thurs, & Sat (9 hours). For information, call 063-72-1188 in Mudgee, 068-82-4053 in Dubbo, and 068-42-1024 in Coonabarabran. There's also a direct Canberra-Dubbo bus service 4 times a week on Hunt's Capital

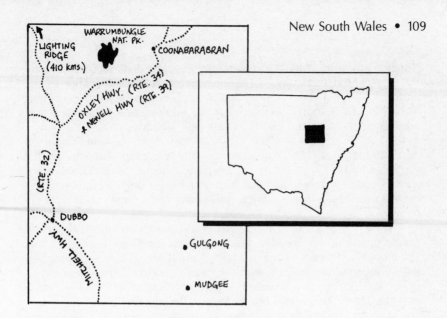

Coachlines (phone 062-88-6370 in Canberra).

Dubbo and Coonabarabran are also serviced by Deluxe, Greyhound, Pioneer, and Bus Australia. Pioneer also offers a direct Canberra-Dubbo service twice a week (operated by Capital Coachlines).

Mudgee
Mudgee Tourist Office (and Town Hall), 64 Market St. (phone 063-72-1944).

Mudgee, an Aboriginal word meaning "nest in the hills," is a wealthy country town producing wool, thoroughbred horses, wine, honey, and pottery. It's the oldest town west of the Blue Mountains, established and cultivated mainly by Germans. Australian author Henry Lawson was born and raised in the district, and many of his writings are set in the area.

Mudgee's sights are fairly spread out. Biking is viable because the area is flat, but we found no rental outlets. The local car rental is **Country Car Rentals** on Church St. (phone 72-2364).

Mudgee Personalized Tours (phone 72-3347) offers winery tours, and vineyard-visiting is a great activity in this region of green pastures and soothing countryside. Local wine-makers founded their own Appellation Society in 1978, the only self-regulated certification system in any Australian wine-growing region. (Look for the mark on local bottles.)

The 18 wineries are small, friendly, and easy-going. Most are north of town, along either Henry Lawson Dr. or Cassilis Rd., and open daily 9:00am-5:00pm (hours do vary, so check). **Craigmoor Winery** (on Craigmoor Rd.) is the largest and oldest, established in 1858. Among the best are **Miramar** and **Montrose** (both on Henry Lawson Dr.) and **Huntington Estate Winery** (Cassilis Rd.). For a different twist, taste the honey wine from **Mount Vincent Meadery** (in town, on The Common Rd.).

Two honey factories offer tastings of over 15 varieties of honey. **Glenrock**

Honey (Sydney Rd.), Mudgee's main factory, is open daily 9:00am-4:00pm. The smaller **Mudgee Honey Co.** (28 Robertson St.) sells a range of bee-related products. It's open M-F 9:00am-5:00pm, weekends 9:00am-4:00pm. Don't be bashful about asking to view the production process—they may be too busy to be attentive, but they'll let you look around.

About 25 km north of Mudgee is the gold rush town of **Gulgong**, preserved by a National Trust classification. As you enter Gulgong, you may feel that you've seen it before, and you probably have: its picture is on Australia's $10 note. The narrow streets are lined with over 150 historical buildings dating between 1870-1910, made of brick and stone and decorated with Victorian ironwork.

Gold was first discovered at Gulgong in 1870, and soon thousands arrived to find their fortunes. By 1872, the local population had reached 20,000. The **Pioneers Museum** (corner of Herbert and Bayley Sts.) is one of the best folk museums in the country, with a wide assortment of Australiana and insights into local history. It's open daily from 9:30am-5:00pm. The **Prince of Wales Opera House** (101 Mayne St.) was built in 1871 and is still in use. The **Henry Lawson Centre** (Mayne St.) contains the largest collection of Lawson's works outside Sydney (open daily 10:00am-noon).

There are two Mudgee-Gulgong buses a day, M-Sat (one leaves at 5:00am!), operated by State Rail. Call 72-1188 in Mudgee for times. The bus depot is at the Mudgee police station on Market Street.

Food: The best deal in town is the **Wineglass Bar & Grill** at 7 Perry St., a local favorite. They have a grill-your-own barbecue with steak, chicken, and fresh trout ($9 and up), all of which comes with hot bread, potatoes, and unlimited salad bar.

Accommodation: Riverside Caravan Park, Short St. (phone 063-72-2531). On-site vans. Very clean, right in town.

Paragon Hotel, corner Gladstone and Perry Sts. (phone 063-72-1313).

Dubbo

Visitors Information Centre, 232 Macquarie St. (phone 068-82-5359). Open M-F 8:30am-5:00pm, Sat-Sun 9:00am-5:00pm.

Dubbo is a thriving country town on the edge of the outback. Surrounded by flat plains, the district is a productive agricultural area and a major livestock center, with a variety of cattle, horse, and sheep shows between July and October.

Dubbo's greatest attraction is the **Western Plains Zoo**, where animals native and foreign roam in Australia's only open-range zoo. Tigers and cheetah are just a moat or electric wire away. 15 km of walking and biking trails wind through the enormous facility. (Bikes are available for hire.) The zoo is 6 km north of town on the Newell Hwy., and buses run frequently to and from town. (Open daily from 9:00am-4:00pm; admission $10.)

On Macquarie St. in town, early colonial history is displayed in the collection at the **Dubbo Museum**, open daily 9:00am-5:00pm. Ask at the hostel about the local rodeo, trips to the Gilgandra Observatory, and river rafting.

Accommodation: The YHA-Associate hostel is at 87 Brisbane St. (phone 063-82-0922). Its common room, complete with cathedral ceiling and pool table, is a great place to hang out, especially because the managing family is a congenial bunch. The hostel is open all day, but be sure to call ahead if you're arriving late. It costs $8.50/night, and inexpensive campsites are available. Signs point the way from the train station and bus depot.

Coonabarabran
Tourist Information Centre, Oxley and Newell Hwys., at the southern end of town (phone 068-42-1441).

Say this name 10 times fast! Coonabarabran ("Coona"), established in 1859 on what was once Coonabarabran Station, has little more than one main street. But looming behind Coona are weather-worn, jagged pinnacles of the Warrumbungles (another great name), a volcanically-formed mountain range that rises eerily from flat country. The Tourist Information Centre, along the southern highway into town, is a useful stop for information on hiking in the Warrumbungles and local Aboriginal culture.

Warrumbungle National Park is 34 km northeast of Coonabarabran on Timor Rd. The road into the park turns to gravel and dirt soon after the entrance, so beware of muddy conditions. Walking trails, ranging from short hikes to rugged overnight treks, lead through eucalypt and pine forests to a number of scenic lookouts.

You'll find trail maps and hiking information in the Park Headquarters at Canyon Camp in the park (call 25-4364 or 42-1311). Camping is permitted with permission from the Ranger. Boil all water before drinking and bring your own food.

Siding Spring Observatory, on the way to the Warrumbungles, is home to the second largest telescope in the southern hemisphere and a research center managed by the Australian National University. You can view the 260-ton telescope through a series of large windows inside the main structure, but that's as close as you'll get unless there's a special celestial event.

Adjacent to the telescope, a modern building houses "Exploring the Universe," a rather technical but excellent astronomy exhibit. The telescope and exhibition are open daily from 9:00am-4:00pm.

Accommodation: No public transport is available to Coona's YHA-Associate hostel, located 9 km from town on Timor Rd. The hostel is part of the **Warrumbungles Mountain Motel** and very small, so call ahead to make sure there's room (phone 068-42-1832; $9/night). The motel office sells supplies and food (pasta, frozen meat, milk, etc.).

It might be easier to stay in an on-site van in town. There are a few caravan parks to choose from, including the **Wayfarer** (Oxley Hwy., phone 068-42-1773) and the **John Oxley** (Chappell Ave., phone 068-42-1635). **Wagon Wheels Units** (Oxley Hwy., phone 068-42-1860) has self-contained rooms with bathrooms.

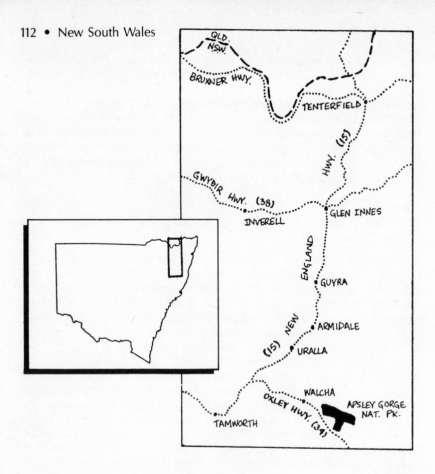

New England

Quaint, historic towns dominated by church spires in Australia's New England bear a slight resemblance to their New England counterparts in the U.S. Similar, too, are the rolling farm landscapes, bountiful streams (fly fishers take note), and autumn colors.

New England is a place to soak everything in by following your nose, which isn't easy without a car but nonetheless possible, because locals go out of their way to show travelers around. We met some Canadians who had spent the day shearing sheep on a ranch near Tenterfield because one of them had mentioned in the tourist bureau that he'd never seen a sheep-shearing. The tourist officer got a local farmer on the phone and within minutes they were in the back of a truck, headed for a sheep station.

The New England tablelands cover an area of about 27,000 square km, from the northern town of Tenterfield, to Armidale and Uralla in the south, to Inverell in the west. Those using public transport should stick to Armidale or Tenterfield, worth seeing even if you're unable to drive into the countryside. Travelers with wheels should also explore the villages of Walcha and Uralla (near Armidale), and Inverell and Glen Innes.

Accommodation

There are YHA-Associate hostels in Armidale and Tenterfield. The excellent Tenterfield facility is reason in itself to get there.

Non-hostellers will find that New England has plenty of local hotels, averaging $22/night per person. Farmstays are the best option of all (though more expensive). Local tourist bureaus can set you up.

Getting There and Getting Around

Your only transport option from Sydney is State Rail's bus and train services, which stop in Uralla, Armidale, Glen Innes, and Tenterfield (licensing laws prohibit drop-off by the interstate buses). Express services operate three times a week. The trip takes 7-12 hours, depending on the service. There's also a less frequent State Rail coach service to Inverell. For train information, call 067-72-4202 in Armidale, 067-32-3049 in Glen Innes, 067-22-3422 in Inverell, and 067-36-1832 in Tenterfield.

To reach New England from the N.S.W. coast, take a Kirklands bus from Lennox Head or Ballina (among other towns) to Lismore and change for Tenterfield. For schedule information, call 066-21-2755 in Lismore.

From Queensland, use any of the major coach companies. Or, take Border Coaches, which operates a weekday service between Inverell, Glen Innes, Tenterfield, and Brisbane. It also has a M-Sat service between Tamworth, Armidale, Guyra, Glen Innes, Tenterfield, and Brisbane (phone 07-355-0034 in Brisbane).

If you're driving, the most scenic route to New England is via the Oxley Hwy. from Port Macquarie. This road winds its way by Apsley Falls and through some of the most beautiful countryside in the region.

Armidale

Visitors Centre/Coach Centre, corner Marsh and Dumaresq Sts. (phone 067-73-8527 or 72-8666). Open M-F 9:00am-5:00pm, Sat-Sun 10:00am-2:00pm.

Armidale, 540 km northwest of Sydney, was established in 1839 by Commissioner McDonald and named after the Isle of Skye castle owned by the McDonald family.

Armidale is best known for the **University of New England**, one of Australia's few non-urban universities. Acclaimed for its arts faculty ("arts" is comparable to liberal arts in the American system), the Uni draws students from all over the country, especially Queensland.

Getting Around: Armidale Charter Coaches has regular service to the University (except on holidays) with more frequent operation during term time (approximately Feb. 1-Nov. 30). The depot is at 2 Drew St. For schedule information, call 72-3072 or 72-3116.

Check the phone book for taxi companies. **Jock Bullens** at 114 Marsh St. (phone 72-3718) rents bikes. There are a few tours of the town and area by locals, for those who want some commentary and easy transport. Ask at tourist information.

Accommodation: The **YHA-Associate hostel** is 2 km east of the town center in the Pembroke Caravan Park (Grafton Rd., phone 067-72-6470). The managers don't pay much attention to the hostel, but it's fine: large, plenty of bunks, and clean. Cost is $8.50/night. There is no public bus to the caravan park.

Armidale also has plenty of motels and inns, all costing around $30/night for a single. The **Royal Hotel** (corner of Beardy and Marsh Sts., phone 067-72-2259) has B&B accommodation. **Tattersalls** (174 Beardy St., phone 067-72-2247) is another licensed hotel offering inexpensive rooms.

Things to See and Do: Pick up the *Armidale Visitors Guide* at the Visitors Centre when you arrive in town. It's full of descriptions about various sights and gives good directions for getting around. The local **folk museum** (corner of Faulkner and Rusden Sts.) is an excellent introduction to the area's history (open daily 1:00pm-4:00pm, free).

After checking out the shops and churches around town, take a bus to the Uni. The focal point of campus is its original building, **Booloominbah**, which was built in the 1880's by one of Armidale's original settlers, Frederick Robert White. Descendants from his herd of fallow deer (imported from Indonesia in the 1890's, presumably for decoration) still graze in the enclosed area behind the grand old homestead. During working hours you can go inside Booloominbah (now an administration building) to see portraits, antiques, and late Victorian stained-glass windows. Next door is the Uni information center.

While you're touring the grounds, check the Student Union bulletin boards for student productions, local entertainment, and restaurant information.

Australia's highest waterfall, **Wollomombi Falls**, is 40 km from Armidale, and **Dangar's Falls** is 22 km south. The old gold rush town of **Uralla** and historic **Walcha** are each an hour's drive south.

Food and Entertainment: Being a university town, there are several places to eat and/or drink inexpensively. The most lively dinner spot is the "Newey" (**New England Hotel**), a student hangout on the corner of Dangar and Beardy Sts. Th-Sat nights there's live music upstairs. **Jessie's Restaurant** (113A Jessie St.) is another popular place, featuring live musicians (sometimes students). Both Jessie's and the Newey are licensed.

When school is in session, Uni movies, concerts, and plays are open to the public. A 24-hour recording, "What's on Campus" (phone 73-3100), has an updated listing.

Tenterfield

Tourist Information Centre, Council Chambers, Rouse St. (phone 067-36-1082). Open M-F 9:00am-4:00pm.

Tourist Information, Henry Parks Motor Inn, New England Hwy. (phone 067-36-1066). Open 24 hours.

Just a few km south of the Queensland border, Tenterfield is a small, friendly, historic town that offers close access to several beautiful natural phenome-na, including Bald Rock.

The YHA hostel (**Tenterfield Lodge and Caravan Park**) is one of the best-restored buildings in town. Built as a railway hotel in 1875, it's now both a hostel and guesthouse with antique furniture, bedroom fireplaces, and even a claw-foot bathtub. Cost begins at $10/night, and it's at the corner of Manners St. and Railway Ave. (phone 067-36-1477).

Tenterfield's tourist bureau will go out of its way to help you, sometimes enlisting locals to show you around. In addition to checking out some historic buildings (one, the **Tenterfield Saddler**, is made famous by a Peter Allen song), you won't want to miss two areas that lie within a half-hour's drive: **Boonoo Boonoo Falls** and **Bald Rock**. The falls, some of the highest in the area, are 35 km north of town. Bald Rock, a few kilometers further, is Australia's second-largest monolith (after Ayers Rock) and is composed of smooth granite. There's a trail up, and the summit has a fabulous view. During school holidays, rangers lead tours around Bald Rock. The tourist bureau may also find a tour for you. The hostel has bikes for getting to either place.

The South Coast

Though it's a popular holiday spot for Sydney, Canberra, and Melbourne residents, most overseas visitors don't get to the south coast of N.S.W. Too bad. The area's rich scenery—white and golden beaches, rocky headlands, green pastures, barren heath, rainforests—is magnificent, and no matter where you go the coastline is beautiful. In warm months, boats, windsurf-ers, surf and boogie boards, and fishing trips are readily available.

The fertile inland is protected by parklands that run parallel to the coast from Wollongong to the Victoria border, 540 km south of Sydney. Just about anywhere you might land in the southeast is scenic, but if you are pressed for time, head for Bundanoon and Narooma.

Southeast weather isn't consistently warm and sunny like northern N.S.W. and Queensland, but the coastline isn't ruined by highrises, either. As long as you don't go in the summer holidays (December-January) or Easter, the beaches will be semi-deserted.

There are six hostels in the southeast of N.S.W., all of them YHA or YHA-Associate hostels: at Garie Beach in Royal National Park (see *Trips from Sydney*), Bundanoon, Gerringong, Nowra, Narooma, and Bega. Call ahead for reservations on weekends and around Christmas and Easter. There are plenty of caravan parks with on-site vans and campsites along the coast, and most of the national parks provide campgrounds. The average price for caravans is $25/night.

Getting There and Getting Around

You can get most anywhere in the southeast on public transport, though services aren't always frequent. The problem is getting around once you've arrived. As is often the case, having your own car makes a big difference.

Canberra is the easiest jumping-off point for much of the southeast, since

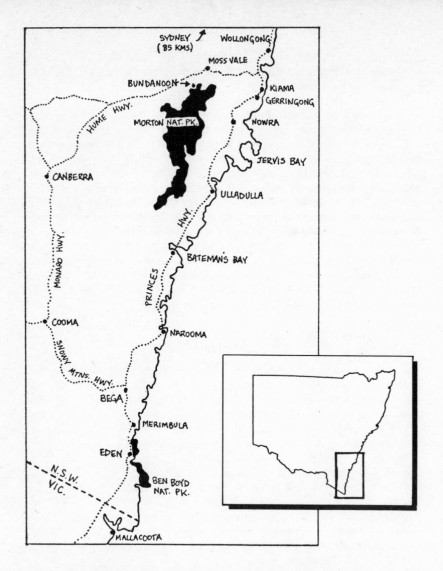

State Rail, Murray's, and Pioneer Motor Services are available there. From Sydney, State Rail is the only transport—except for extreme southern destinations where Deluxe, Pioneer Express, and Greyhound are permitted to drop off on their service between Melbourne and Sydney.

For State Rail information, call 02-217-8812 or 02-29-7614 in Sydney, 062-95-1555 in Canberra. Murray's, based in Canberra, is 062-95-3677. To call Pioneer Motor Services, dial 044-21-7722 or 044-21-7181 in Nowra.

Bundanoon

About 140 km southwest of Sydney, "Bundy" is a tiny, relaxed town. True to its Scottish name, there's a distinctly British flavor about Bundanoon, so try a Devonshire tea at one of the local tearooms.

Morton National Park, within walking distance of the town and the YHA hostel, has 16 trails through eucalypt forest to gorges, valleys, Fitzroy Falls, and the spectacular Belmore Falls. The Visitor Centre is open daily 10:00am-4:00pm. You can pitch a tent in the campground for a small fee (call 048-87-7279 for camping information).

Getting There: State Rail's Sydney-Goulburn train stops in Bundanoon several times daily (travel time is two hours). From Canberra, take the Sydney-Canberra express and change trains in Goulburn. From Melbourne, change in Goulburn as well. Deluxe, Greyhound, and Pioneer from Melbourne, and Murray's from Canberra, stop in Moss Vale. You can catch a local bus from Moss Vale to Bundanoon (schedules are opposite the courthouse in Moss Vale).

If you're driving to Bundanoon, take the Illawarra Hwy. via Macquarie National Park, a steep and winding road through dense rainforest.

Accommodation: Set amidst eucalypt woods, the **Bundanoon YHA Hostel** is a great place to relax for a few days. It's on the main road, 1 km from the railroad depot, and costs $9/night (phone 048-83- 6010). Ask the manager about hiking in Morton National Park and excursions to Glow Worm Glen. Both the local bike shop and a nearby horse riding operation give a 10% discount to hostellers. School groups often use the hostel, so call first and beware of weekends and holidays.

Trips from Bundanoon: There are several interesting places to explore from Bundanoon, for those with their own transport.

About 15 km north on the Hume Hwy. is the historic village of **Berrima**, founded in 1829 by Sir Thomas Mitchell. Most of the original sandstone buildings now house expensive shops selling crafts, antiques, and art. The courthouse, built in 1838 and open daily 10:00am-4:00pm, has tourist information and a video on the development of the district. The old **Berrima Gaol,** now a correction house for prisoners, was built by convicts in 1841 to keep the worst criminals. The building later became an internment camp for P.O.W.'s during World War I.

Built to serve wagon teams before the coming of the railway, the **Surveyor-General Inn** in Berrima is the oldest continuously licensed pub in the country and definitely worth a visit. The interior is reminiscent of an English pub, with white walls and wood panelling. It serves an inexpensive, tasty grill-your-own lunch or dinner (M-F noon-3:00pm, 6:00pm-9:00pm). On Sunday afternoons, the inn has local musicians (except during the summer).

Another unique spot you can reach from Bundanoon is **Joadja**, 60 km northwest, which once supplied the Australian Kerosene Oil and Mineral Co. with shale kerosene. But when the federal government lifted tariffs on American kerosene in the early 1900's, the competition became too great and Joadja was abandoned. An American named Pat Lee bought the ghost town 25 years ago and now lives there. Supposedly, the ghost of Robert McGregor, an old miner whose legendary task is to protect the valley, keeps her company. For a small fee, you can visit the old buildings and kilns on weekends March 1-December 1 from 10:00am-4:00pm. Call first to confirm (phone 048-71-2888).

Gerringong
Lush dairy country surrounds the small coastal town of Gerringong, 100 km south of Sydney, where Seven Mile Beach has surfing and fishing, and kayaks and aquabikes for rent. Fishing is also allowed off nearby **Werri Beach**, and neither place requires a license.

Other local sights include the blowhole at **Kiama**, 10 km north of Gerringong, where ocean spray sometimes reaches 60 meters. **Minnamurra Falls and Reserve**, a steep gorge surrounded by rainforest (call 042-36-0147 for information) is 15 km west of Kiama, and 10 km further is the hanging swamp and bird sanctuary of **Barren Grounds Nature Reserve** (phone 36-0195). A local bus operates between Gerringong and Kiama, and to Minnamurra Falls.

Getting There: State Rail's Illawarra Line from Sydney to Nowra stops in both Gerringong and Kiama daily. Deluxe, Greyhound, and Ansett Pioneer all stop in Kiama on their Princes Hwy. service from Melbourne to Sydney.

Accommodation: Gerringong's YHA-Associate hostel is in a community center on Bridges Rd., behind a church (phone 042-34-1447). It has a huge dining area and a number of small, clean bunkrooms. Watch out for school and church groups, who sometimes fill the place up. Cost is $9/night. Horse riding is available nearby.

Nowra
Shoalhaven Tourist Centre, Princes Hwy., Bombaderry (phone 044-21-0778). Open daily 9:00am-5:00pm.

Among the local sights in Nowra are the Shoalhaven River and a variety of beaches. Two-hour river cruises operate on the weekends and leave from Nowra Animal Park (Rockhill Rd.).

Most importantly, Nowra is the access point for the **Jervis Bay Nature Reserve**. Located 20 km south and 15 km east of Nowra, the reserve's rugged sandstone cliffs, sheltered bays and beaches, protected vegetation, and solitude make it one of the most beautiful areas in the southeast. A Visitor Information Centre (phone 044-43-0977) is located at the entrance (open Sun-Th 10:00am-4:00pm, F-Sat 10:00am-6:00pm). Well-mapped trails lead to rocky inlets and beaches, especially stunning along the southern coast.

The **Royal Australian Naval College** faces Jervis Bay on the northern side, and there is a missile range in the center of the reserve. The southern headland (near Murray's Beach), part of the A.C.T. (Australian Capital Territory), was the proposed site of Australia's first nuclear power station, but it was never built.

Sampson's Tours runs a bus between Nowra and Jervis Bay (call 044-21-3922 for information).

Getting There: State Rail's Illawarra Line runs between Sydney and Bombaderry (2.5-hour trip). A local Pioneer Motor Services bus connects with the train at Bombaderry Railway Station for the trip to Nowra. The driver will drop you at the hostel if you ask. Murray's offers a daily bus service to Nowra from Canberra (change in Bateman's Bay to a Pioneer bus); the trip is 5 hours. Deluxe, Greyhound, and Pioneer Express all stop on Sydney-Melbourne services.

Accommodation: The Nowra YHA-Associate hostel is in the **White House Private Hotel** (30 Junction St., phone 044-21-2084; $12).

Bateman's Bay

Bateman's Bay Tourist Centre, Princes Hwy. (phone 044-72-4225). Open daily 9:00am-5:00pm.

One of the best beaches on the south coast is **Pebbly Beach**, just north of Bateman's Bay. Part of **Murramarang National Park**, Pebbly Beach is bordered by spotted gum forest and home to docile kangaroos. A 3.5 km trail leads from the carpark to the beach.

Camping within the park is restricted to Pebbly, Pretty, and Merry Beaches, and North and South Durras. Beach cabins on Pebbly Beach can be rented for about $150/week and accommodate up to six. For reservations, call 044-21-9969 or 044-78-6006.

Getting There: Bateman's Bay is 3 hours from Canberra and 5.5 hours from Sydney. From Canberra, there's a State Rail bus (stops in Bateman's Bay are on Orient St., at the Westpac bank, or Centre Plaza). Murray's also runs from Canberra. State Rail has one service a week from Sydney (change in Bungedore), but if you get to Nowra, Pioneer Motor Services runs from there to Bateman's Bay (it connects with the State Rail service from Sydney). Pioneer Motor Services also has services to Bateman's Bay from Narooma, Bega, and Eden. Deluxe, Greyhound, and Pioneer Express stop on Princes Hwy. services between Sydney and Melbourne.

Narooma

Narooma Tourist Centre, Princes Hwy. (phone 044-76-2881). Open M-F 9:30am-5:00pm, Sat-Sun 9:30am-1:30pm.

You shouldn't miss the unforgettable **YHA-Associate hostel** in Narooma. Meg and Barry Lake own the hostel (and a leather shop) on a wooded, 15-acre property that borders Forsters Bay. Their enthusiasm is infectious, and you'll find yourself sitting around a roaring fire at night, swapping stories and feeding the opossums. The hostel is simple and geared toward group interaction.

Bring food with you, since the nearest shop is a fair distance away. If you're interested in leathercraft, ask the Lakes about lessons. They also rent canoes (for paddling on the bay) and bikes (for the 1.5 km trip to town and nearby beaches). The hostel driveway comes off "Old Highway," 1 km west of the main highway. Call 044-76-2824 to book. The cost is $10/night.

Activities in and around Narooma are fishing, boating, and walking. Local trips include beaches, rocky headlands, Wagonga Inlet (daily cruises available), and an 11 km walk up Mt. Dromedary in **Bodalla State Forest** (13 km southwest of Narooma). Try a few Narooma oysters while you're in the area. About 15 km south of Narooma, en route to Mt. Dromedary, the tiny village of **Central Tilba** is nestled amidst green, mountainous country. Established in 1895 to serve a mining community and kept alive by the local **ABC Cheese Factory**, the entire town was classified by the National Trust in 1974. A few craft shops, a general store, teahouse, small hotel, and a B&B occupy the original buildings. The cheese factory is open for purchases and tastings.

Wallaga Lake National Park, located south of Central Tilba on the western side of Wallaga Lake, is rich in Aboriginal history. Tiny **King Merrimen Island**, in the center of the lake, was the first Aboriginal sacred site to be protected under N.S.W. law and is still a ceremonial place for Aborigines of a local reserve.

Most visitors arrive in private boats and stick to the outskirts of the park, leaving most of its 3,400 acres a wilderness. Old logging tracks lead into the park from the Princes Hwy., and four-wheel drive is necessary. There are privately owned campgrounds on the opposite shore; camping is otherwise prohibited.

Getting There: Murray's offers a daily Canberra-Narooma bus, which drops you at either Tourist Information or Southfield Plaza. The trip takes 4.5 hours. Pioneer Motor Services also stops on the way from Nowra to Eden. Deluxe, Greyhound, and Pioneer all stop on the Melbourne-Sydney run. The trip from Sydney takes 7 hours.

Bega

Bega Tourist Centre, Gipps St. (phone 064-92-2045). Open M-F 10:00am-4:00pm, Sat-Sun 9:00am-noon.

About 80 km south of Narooma and 20 km west of the coast, Bega is the best access point to the Snowy Mountains from the coast. Otherwise, the town isn't too interesting. Nearby dairy farms supply the **Bega Cooperative**, one of the most modernized cheese-making plants in the country (open M-F to visitors).

Getting There: State Rail runs to Bega 3 times a week from Sydney (8 hours) and twice a week from Canberra (3 hours). Pioneer Motor Services operates local buses from Nowra, Bateman's Bay, and Eden. Deluxe, Greyhound, and Ansett Pioneer stop on the Sydney-Melbourne service.

Accommodation: The YHA hostel, 1 km from town in drab suburbia, is an attractive, modern house which closes between 10:00am-5:00pm. The manager lives elsewhere. The hostel is on Kirkland Crescent and costs $9/night (phone 064-92-3103).

Eden

Eden Tourist Centre, Princes Hwy. South (phone 064-96-1953). Open M-F 10:00am-5:00pm, Sat 10:00am-4:00pm, Sun 9:30am-4:00pm.

Eden is the most southern town on the N.S.W. coast, 500 km south of Sydney. Best known for its fishing port and fleet, Eden is also the site of a major cannery and a center for the woodchip industry. The **Harris Daishowa Chip Mill**, 24 km south of town, converts local eucalypt logs into chips and sends them to Japan. The mill is open for inspection on Wed from 3:00pm-4:00pm.

Getting There: From Sydney, State Rail's service take 9 hours and operates 3 times a week. The same service goes through Canberra, 4 hours from Eden. The State Rail bus stop in Eden is outside the Two Fold Arcade on Imlay St. You can also get to Eden from other coastal destinations on Pioneer Motor Services. Deluxe, Greyhound, and Pioneer Express stop on Melbourne-Sydney services, and most are licensed to make drop-offs from other locations within N.S.W.

Trips from Eden: 4 km north of Eden is **Twofold Bay**, the site of Benjamin Boyd's whaling station. One of the largest landowners in Australia, Boyd founded Boydtown and East Fold at Twofold Bay in 1847 and tried to create a massive whaling port. Financial ruin ended his schemes, and in 1851 he sailed for the Pacific Islands and vanished.

Boyd's Tower at Red Point, on the southern side of the bay, is a lighthouse built out of stone from Sydney. The lighthouse has never been used, but it's a great lookout point. The Eden **Killer Whale Museum** in Imlay St. (phone 96-2094) is open daily from 11:00am-4:00pm.

Ben Boyd National Park is divided into two parts which surround Eden. The northern half extends from Pambula River to Eden and includes **The Pinnacles** (not to be confused with the limestone Pinnacles formation in Western Australia), an eroded clay cliff colored by iron particles, near the entrance to a gully from Long Beach. No camping is allowed in the northern section of the park, but it is encouraged in the southern half, from Twofold Bay to Green Cape Lighthouse. Call 96-1434 for park information.

The Snowies

The gradual slopes and sweeping plains of the Snowies give way gently to Australia's highest peak, **Mt. Kosciusko** (2,228 meters). This is horse riding, trout fishing, hiking, and skiing country—not as lush or dramatic as its Victorian counterpart (the Victorian Alps), but scenic in its own right.

Spring and summer wildflowers, extensive hiking trails in Kosciusko National Park, Yarrangobilly Caves, and a series of lakes draw people during summer. Downhill and cross-country skiing in winter bring the bulk of the area's visitors, from mid-July to early September.

Of the seven ski areas, the largest and most developed is **Mt. Perisher/Smiggin Holes** resort; the most scenic is **Thredbo**. We suggest heading straight for Thredbo, with a YHA resort lodge and direct access to Mt.

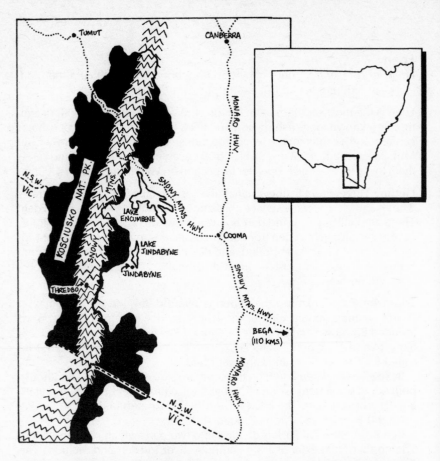

Kosciusko. Trout fishing enthusiasts might also consider **Jindabyne**, from which several lakes are accessible.

Note: Banking facilities are limited in the summer. Do your banking in Cooma, before you reach high country.

Getting There and Getting Around: Thredbo is 205 km southwest of Canberra and 519 km southwest of Sydney. Pioneer Express and Murray's have Canberra-Thredbo and Sydney-Thredbo services, which also stop in Cooma, Bullock's Flat (for the Ski Tube), The Station, and Jindabyne. The trip to Thredbo is 3 hours from Canberra and 8 hours from Sydney. (Call Ansett Pioneer in Sydney at 02-268-1881, in Canberra at 062-45-6511; Murray's in Sydney at 02-699-5775, in Canberra at 062-95-3677.)

You can also take a State Rail train to Cooma from Sydney or Canberra, and a Pioneer Express bus will meet you for the trip to Jindabyne, Perisher/Smiggins, and Thredbo. This service is infrequent but cheap. From Melbourne, Pioneer Express offers a direct Thredbo service (13 hours).

Air New South Wales (phone 02-268-1242) flies to Cooma from Sydney, Melbourne, and Queensland; Kendell Airlines (phone 03-668-2222) flies from Melbourne. Most planes are met by buses (which should be booked ahead of time through a travel agent).

A fast underground railroad called the **Ski Tube** runs to Perisher, Smiggin Holes, Guthega, and Mt. Blue Cow from Bullock's Flat. The ride takes about 15 minutes and runs all day and night. It's a particularly good way of getting around if you've got an non-winterized car or are staying in Jindabyne.

Snow chains are required for all cars in winter. You can rent them from area service stations and some ski shops.

Accommodation: Budget travelers will have trouble finding accommodation during peak ski season (August). At other times, finding a place to stay should be no problem.

YHA runs a ski lodge in Thredbo Village which offers rooms year-round. Unfortunately, during ski season you must book a few months in advance or cross your fingers and hope for cancellations. To reserve a place, write or call the head YHA office in Sydney (GPO Box 5276, Sydney 2001, phone 02-267-3044). Ski season rates (from July 1-Sept 30) are $24/night or $33 on Saturday night ($150/week). At other times, the cost is $10/night, and you can book directly at the hostel (phone 064-57-6376).

Other inexpensive accommodation is at **The Station**, a huge complex 6 km from Jindabyne on Cobbon-Beloko Rd. Pioneer runs frequent shuttles from The Station to the Ski Tube. Again, reservations may be hard to make during peak times. Call 064-56-2895 or toll free 008-02-6392.

If you have your own transportation, consider the campground or chalets at the **Sawpit Visitors Centre**, run by the Park Service. The Centre is midway between Jindabyne and Perisher/Smiggins on Kosciusko Rd. Call 064-56-2224 for reservations.

If none of these options is available, there are several booking agencies which will help you find a space. In Jindabyne, try the **Kosciusko Accommodation Centre**, Shop 15, Nuggets Crossing (phone 064-56-2022). The **Cooma Visitors Centre** also has a booking service at 119 Sharp St. in Cooma (phone 064-52-1177 or 52-1108).

Information Sources: There are National Park Visitors Centres in Sawpit Creek, Smiggin Holes, Yarrangobilly Caves, and Khancoban. Call 064-56-2102 or 069-47-0264 for National Park information. Call 069-49-5334 for information on the caves, which are open every day.

Snowy River Information Centre, Petamin Plaza, Jindabyne (phone 064-56-2444). Open M-F 9:00am-5:00pm.

Thredbo Resort Centre, Alpine Shopping Concourse (phone 064-57-6360).

The **Canberra Visitors Centre** and the **N.S.W. Tourism Commission** in Sydney also have lots of information. Also, pick up *The Complete Guide to Skiing in the Snowy Mountains,* available at all the above offices, for a rundown of the ski areas with practical information on transport, accommodation, and ski rental. Free maps of Thredbo Village are available at information centers.

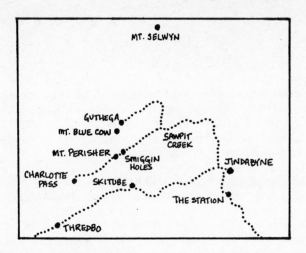

The Skiing: Skiing in the Snowies is similar to skiing in the northeastern U.S. Conditions vary widely and you can't always count on snow, but August has pretty reliable ski weather, especially with the advent of artificial snow-making at most resorts. For budget travelers, September is a good month (though it sometimes rains) because cheap accommodation is more plentiful than in peak season.

Thredbo and Perisher/Smiggins are the best-known resorts. Thredbo is considered the best mountain for experts, but there are trails for every level of skier at all the ski areas. Cross-country ski trails are extensive as well.

You can rent ski equipment at all the ski areas and at Bullock's Flat (origin of the Ski Tube). In Thredbo, try **Fleets** (phone 064-57-6383, or in Sydney at 02-799-7888).

Hiking: Many hiking trails originate in Thredbo. The **Crackenback Chairlift** up Mt. Kosciusko connects with a 13 km loop that hits every peak on the summit. The chairlift runs every day all summer, though infrequently. Call 57-6275 for times. The cost is a hefty $10.

Summer Walks on Top of Australia, a pamphlet available at the Thredbo Information Centre, outlines all trails on Mt. Kosciusko. For extended hiking and trails originating elsewhere, call the National Parks and Wildlife Service at 064-56-2102 or 069-47-0264.

Lightning Ridge

The Tourist Centre, Morilla St., opposite the Post Office (phone 068-29-0565).

Lightning Ridge, pretty much in the middle of nowhere, certainly can be classified "outback." One of the enticements in the tourist brochure: you can get there by *sealed road*!

The real draw, however, is that it's the only place in the world with **black opal**. Obviously, the thing to do in Lightning Ridge is visit an opal mine. There are a few to choose from, with underground viewings, guided tours, and opal cutting. You can buy opals at the tourist mines and at stores in town, as well as pottery made from opal clay. If you want to mine for yourself, there are designated fossicking areas, and you can get a license from the Tourist Centre.

Another nearby attraction is the **Artesian Bore Baths**, 2 km north of the Post Office (open 24 hours for free soakings).

Getting There and Getting Around: A State Rail bus service to Lightning Ridge connects with the Sydney-Dubbo train three times a week. There's a second State Rail service from Sydney via Narrabri and Werris Creek, also three times a week. Rent cars and mokes from Lightning Ridge Car Hire (phone 29-0666 or 29-0222).

Accommodation: Tram-o-Tel on Morilla St. (phone 068-29-0613) has inexpensive, self-contained units and caravans. Call ahead from November-January and around Easter. There are on-site vans and camping spaces in three other caravan parks: **Crocodile** (corner Morilla and Onyx Sts., phone 068-29-0437), **Newtown** (Onyx St., phone 068-29-0304), and **Lightning Ridge** (Pandora St., phone 068-29-0532).

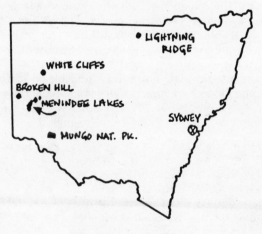

Broken Hill

Tourist and Travellers' Centre, Blende & Bromide Sts. (phone 080-88- 6077).

Broken Hill is an 8 km chain of hills that have produced over 140 million tons of silver, lead, and zinc since they were first pegged by Charles Rasp in 1883. **Broken Hill Proprietary Co.** (BHP), now one of Australia's largest industrial enterprises, originated in 1885 with the Broken Hill mines.

The town itself is still thriving, an outpost of semi-civilization in a barren land. Broken Hill is associated with South Australia rather than N.S.W. because Adelaide is much closer than Sydney, and ore from Broken Hill is shipped to other countries from Port Pirie, north of Adelaide.

Delprat's Mine conducts a daily underground tour Mon-Sat (phone 88-1604). **North Mine** (phone 97-325) runs free surface tours once a day, and you can tour **Daydream Mine** (phone 2241) by yourself. The **Gladstone Mining Museum** (corner South and Morish Sts.) has displays of mining procedures and a replica of a mine (open only in the afternoon).

Several artists find inspiration in the orange and red soil of the saltbush plains surrounding Broken Hill, and private galleries around town display their work. In fact, the **Pro Hart Gallery** houses one of the largest private art collections in the country. Most galleries are open seven days a week.

To get to outlying areas, you'll need your own transport. **Menindee Lakes**, approximately 110 km east, were dug for water storage purposes on the Darling River. The lakes offer all sorts of watersports. 260 km northeast of Broken Hill is **White Cliffs**, a well-known opal field since 1889. Several buildings in White Cliffs are underground, similar to Coober Pedy, S.A., and a few are open to the public.

The dry bed of **Lake Mungo** in **Mungo National Park** (200 km south of Broken Hill and 110 km north of Mildura) is the site of the earliest known Aboriginal occupation in Australia, and archeological excavations are still in process (no public access to the excavations).

Getting There: The *Indian Pacific* train (Sydney-Adelaide-Perth) stops in Broken Hill on its cross-continental voyage. There's also a State Rail train from Sydney that terminates in Broken Hill. The journey is about 17 hours. Most interstate buslines also have a service from Sydney. Air New South Wales flies from Sydney.

The trek from Adelaide is 6.5 hours and is available on Stateliner or Deluxe, Greyhound, and Pioneer. For direct service from Mildura, Victoria, call Wanderer Tours of Silver City at 080-88-7750 or 080-88-6956. There are also direct services from Mildura and Melbourne on Greyhound, which take 13 hours.

Accommodation: The YHA-Associate hostel is in the **Tourist Lodge** at 100 Argent St. in the center of town, next to the bus station and tourist office (phone 080-88-2086, $10/night). There is no communal kitchen, but inexpensive meals are available. **Royal Exchange Hotel** (corner Argent and Chloride Sts., phone 080-88-2308) and the **Theatre Royal Hotel** (347 Argent St., phone 080-88-3318) are two other possibilities.

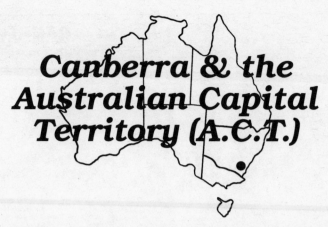

Canberra & the Australian Capital Territory (A.C.T.)

Canberra, muted and calm like suburbia, is not at all what you'd expect from a national capital. There are no traffic jams, honking horns, or big crowds. It offers scant sense of history and not much warmth.

But Canberra, like the country, is still in its infancy. Although plans for a capital began in 1912, it wasn't until the 1950's that serious development began. National buildings and monuments are still being erected. In fact, Parliament House was christened in 1988 (after 50 years in a temporary building), the Supreme Court finally moved from Sydney in 1980, and the National Museum still isn't finished.

Located in eastern New South Wales, Canberra and the A.C.T. are a small entity unto themselves, administered by a federal bureau, advised by a House of Assembly with 18 elected members. One nice thing about the place: there are no city politicians.

Set in the beautiful foothills of the Snowy Mountains, Canberra has clear, sunny weather most of the time. But bring warm clothes in winter—it gets exceedingly cold by Australian standards.

Getting There

Most people arrive in Canberra from Sydney. The cheapest service is on **Murray's**, a local company that does the trip several times daily. Their office is in the Jolimont Centre (phone 008-04-6200 in New South Wales, or 95-3677 in Canberra). Murray's has no office in Sydney, but you can book at the Central Railway Station in Sydney on Eddy Ave., where the buses depart. Murray's also has service to Canberra from most coastal towns south of Sydney, including Narooma, Nowra, Ulladulla, and Bateman's Bay.

Deluxe, Greyhound, and Pioneer also service Canberra on a regular basis, most arriving at the Jolimont Centre in the commercial center of town. (Pioneer is the exception.) The Jolimont Centre has tourist information, shops, restaurants, showers, and a TV lounge for travelers.

Canberra is also well-serviced by rail. There are direct services from Sydney, which also stop in Bundanoon. You can get to and from the Snowies by rail and railway-operated coach: trains go direct to Cooma, and there's a rail/coach service to Tumut with change in Yass. Rail-operated buses also service the N.S.W. coast, including Bateman's Bay (Friday only), Bega and Eden (M,W,F only). The Rail Information Centre is at Jolimont Centre.

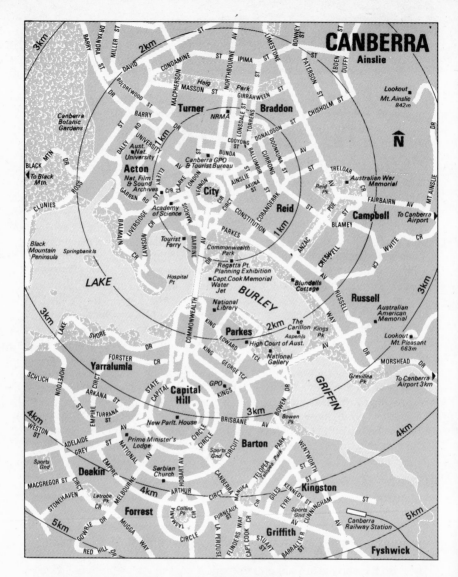

Orientation and Practical Information

Canberra is designed with a sense of space similar to Washington, D.C. or Paris. Long avenues direct the eye to the city's most important buildings, and the lack of obstructions gives the illusion that distances are short. Don't be fooled. City and Capital Hills are at least two miles apart and connected only by highway—neither a brief nor enjoyable walk.

Canberra is a completely planned city and, not surprisingly, is organized very logically. **Lake Burley Griffin** is the divider between the city's business, administrative, and commercial center (north of the lake), and the government buildings, embassies, and other buildings with national functions (south of the lake).

North of the lake, the city center (**"Civic"**) is divided down the middle by Northbourne Ave. West of Northbourne Ave. are most of the office buildings, where all administrative and legal activity takes place. East of Northbourne Ave. is the city's commercial center, much of which is for pedestrians only. You'll recognize the heart of town at the intersection of Northbourne and Alinga, where the two oldest city buildings, the Melbourne and Sydney Buildings, line Northbourne with graceful arches.

Aside from the civic and capital areas, there are several outlying towns, each of which has its own shopping and other facilities. All are entirely planned. The most distinctive town is Manuka, just southeast of the capital, an established area with older houses and some cafes and boutiques to browse.

Important Addresses and Telephone Numbers (area code 062)

Jolimont Centre, 65-67 Northbourne Ave., Civic (phone 45-6464). All tourist and transport information.

General Post Office, Alinga St., Civic (phone 48-5211), open M-F 9:00am-5:00pm

American Embassy, State Circle, Yarralumla (phone 70-5000)

Canadian High Commission, Commonwealth Ave., Yarralumla (phone 73-3844)

National Parks and Wildlife, 34 Lowe St., Queanbeyan (N.S.W.), (phone 97-6144). Information on the Snowies.

STA Travel, Arts Centre, Australian National University

National Roads and Motorists' Association (NRMA), 92-96 Northbourne Ave. (phone 43-8888)

Rail Travel Centre, Jolimont Centre (phone 39-0133)

Murray's, Jolimont Centre (phone 95-3677)

Deluxe, Jolimont Centre (phone 47-0588)

Pioneer, 150 Northbourne Ave. (phone 45-6624)

Greyhound, Jolimont Centre (phone 57-2659)

Police, phone 49-7444

Transportation

Maps make the Canberra sights look deceptively close, so keep in mind that strolling isn't always the best way to get around. Despite the comprehensive transportation system, biking is really the way to go. Bikers are everywhere, and bike paths go around and across the lake. Unlike most Australian cities, Canberra's streets are wide and have a safe shoulder for biking.

The bikes at the YHA are in good condition. Otherwise try Shop 10, City Walk, The Boulevard in the city (phone 47-5437).

The city bus system is called "Action," and though service tends to be infrequent, the network is well-organized and comprehensive. Almost all buses leave from the bus interchange at Civic (East Row/Mort St.). Bus information is available in a kiosk at the bus interchange, and the staff is helpful. For information call 51-6566 until 11:30pm Mon-Sat, and until 6:30pm Sun. Buses generally run until 11:00pm Mon-Sat, and until 6:00pm Sun. Day tickets, packets of 10 tickets, and weekly passes can be purchased at the city bus interchange, the Jolimont Tourist Information Centre, and some newsstands. The various tourist routes run only during the day and depart from Jolimont Centre. Most of these services are extremely limited.

If you plan any late night activity, a taxi probably will be necessary. **Aerial Taxi** is Canberra's only cab company (phone 46-0444).

Accommodation

YHA Canberra, Dryandra St., O'Connor (phone 48-9759). Bus 380, 360, or 390 from Civic to Miller St. $14-$18. Bush setting, near Botanic Gardens and Black Mountain. Very clean and well managed. Cathedral ceilings. Open 7:00am-10:00pm. Groups stay in a separate facility. Bike rental (and a few mountain bikes).

Canberra is the only Australian city other than Hobart that has inexpensive **bed & breakfast guesthouses**. The three least expensive are on Northbourne Ave. in Downer, a mile or so north of Civic. All three offer large cooked breakfasts and simple, full-service accommodation. Get there by bus 382 or 383 from Civic. The B&B's are as follows:

The Chelsea Lodge, 526 Northbourne Ave., Downer (phone 48-0655). $30-$40. The choicest inexpensive B&B in the city, run by a friendly French couple. Large, attractive rooms with private TV, fridge, and tea/coffee-making facilities. A member of Parliament regularly stays there, and there are many faithful clientele, so book ahead if possible. Will pick up if you're desperate.

Blue and White Lodge, 524 Northbourne Ave., Downer (phone 48-0498). $18-$40. Simple and decent. Private TV in rooms. Need deposit to ensure space.

Platon Lodge, 522 Northbourne Ave., Downer (phone 47-9139). $25. Similar to the Blue and White, but customers complain about the owners.

Another phenomenon particular to Canberra are the large hostels and private hotels for temporary Commonwealth employees. The best of these is the **Macquarie Private Hotel** (18 National Circuit, Barton, phone 068-73-2325). Many Canberra sights are within walking distance and, though huge and institutional, it's not a bad deal for about $28/night (with breakfast). Weekly rates are less expensive. Rooms are serviced three times a week, and there are game rooms and a cheap cafeteria. To get there, take bus 234 or any of the 350's.

All **Australian National University** colleges offer housing, though conferences and other functions often fill them up when the university is on break.

Occasionally there's room during term-time. Call the student accommodation office on campus to find out about vacancies (phone 068-49-3454 or 068-49-4414). Typical cost is about $24/night for a single.

Things to See and Do

As you might expect, Canberra is packed with things to see. While sights are spread out, most are either in the Capital Hill area or near the lake's northern shore between Commonwealth Ave. Bridge and Kings Ave. Bridge.

A useful first visit is **Regatta Point** in Commonwealth Park (northern lake shore, just east of Commonwealth Bridge). Its Information Centre traces Canberra's history and development, providing a context in which to understand other sights. It's open 9:00am-5:00pm daily, and if you get there at 9:00am, you'll beat the tour buses. There's a nice cafeteria with a view of the city and a 137 meter-high water jet (which operates a few hours each day). Regatta Point is on bus route 905, a very limited service.

The **Australian War Memorial** houses the best museum in the city—and our favorite museum in Australia. Don't leave Canberra without spending a few hours here, regardless of your interest in military history. The museum is a major center for research of Australian military history and the social impact of war. Imaginative, powerful exhibitions trace Australia's participation in wars from 1788 to the 1960's in Vietnam, and there's an excellent bookstore. The museum is a massive stone monument at the end of Anzac Parade (north shore), planned to give a sweeping and impressive view to Capital Hill. (Open 9:00am-4:45pm daily, free admission. Take buses 302 or 303 from Civic.)

Also in the general vicinity of the War Memorial are some of the only historic sights in the area: St. John's Church and the Schoolhouse Museum, Blundell's Farmhouse, and a bit further on, Duntroon. **St. John's Anglican Church** (Constitution Ave., Reid) is a beautiful stone church built in the 1841 for the wealthy pastoralists who first settled the area. Several of them are buried in the church graveyard. Canberra's first schoolhouse is next door (open weekends from 2:00pm-4:00pm, Wed 10:00am-noon, and every afternoon from December 26 until the end of January).

About 2 km northeast of the War Memorial off Fairbairn Drive is **Duntroon Royal Military College**, the Australian equivalent of West Point. (Take bus 303.) Duntroon is the second oldest property in the Canberra area, built in the early 1830's. The old homestead is now used as an officers' mess (only accessible to the public about twice a year on special tours), but the gardens are lovely and you can wander around. The property was converted to a national military college in 1910, and guided tours of the campus are Mon-Fri at 2:30pm from Feb-Nov (except college holidays).

The Campbells of Duntroon built a cottage for their head ploughman in 1860, now known as **Blundell's Farmhouse** (located on Wendouree Drive in Kings Park). A family with 11 kids once lived in this tiny two-bedroom cottage. It's open daily from 2:00pm-4:00pm (except Monday), but be warned that since the staff consists mostly of volunteers, you may not find it open. Admission costs about $3. Take bus 230 from Civic.

You couldn't miss the new **Australian Parliament House** if you tried. It's the focal point of the city, in view from anywhere on the south side of the lake and visually emphasized by long, wide avenues leading up to its perch on Capital Hill. Opened in 1988, the Parliament House is an architectural monument of its time. The bulk of rooms exist beneath Capital Hill, emerging from the earth in terraced concrete. An 80-meter steel needle marks its center with an Aussie flag. Construction took eight years and $1.6 billion dollars, and a glimpse inside will reveal why.

There are guided tours every day at 20-30 minute intervals, except when Parliament is in session (when you can sit in either chamber and watch the action, which often goes until 11:00pm). Exhibitions explain the Australian parliamentary system. The **Parliament Exhibition**, next door, has displays on the history and architecture of the building (open 9:00am-6:00pm daily). To get to Capital Hill take bus 350 or 353 from Civic.

A walk away from Capital Hill along the lake shore are the National Library, National Gallery, and Australian High Court. The **National Gallery** is less extensive than either Melbourne's or Sydney's State Galleries, and you can do it in an hour or so. It houses a few European and Asian masters, examples of each of the Australian masters, and specializes in 20th-century art and always has special exhibits. (Open 10:00am-5:00pm daily; no entrance after 4:00pm. $3.)

Adjacent to the National Gallery, the **High Court** is distinguished by a lengthy ramp with a waterfall running alongside it, leading to the Great Hall entrance. The building is a stunning example of modern architecture and worth a look inside. There's an explanation of the Australian court system in the entrance hall. The **National Library** lies further west, adjacent to the Commonwealth Ave. Bridge. Take bus 234 or any 350's to get to the area.

West and southwest of Capital Hill are most of the **diplomatic missions**. Eastern Yarralumla between Commonwealth Ave. and Empire Circuit has the highest concentration of them (take bus 231 to Yarralumla), and the more interesting structures—like the Indonesian and Papua New Guinean embassies—are in this area, as well as the Canadian and U.S. embassies. The tourist bureau distributes a guide to the embassies.

In the same area, on Adelaide Ave. (at the foot of Capital Hill) you can see the **Prime Minister's Lodge** (residence) behind protective walls. The architect who designed The Lodge also designed Calthorpe's House in 1927, a typical area residence that is furnished as it was originally and is open for guided tours (24 Mugga Way, Red Hill; admission $4, discount for students; take bus 350). Over in Deakin on Yarra Glen Ave. (continuation of Adelaide St.) is the **Mint**, where you can see all stages of currency production from a glassed-in gallery (open M-F 9:00am-4:00pm except noon-12:40pm; take bus 230).

The **Australian National University** (ANU) is in Acton, just west of City Hill (bus 300 from Civic). The University has only about 6,000 students but is a major national research institution. Go to the University information center on Balmain Circle for maps and information (open M-F 9:00am-5:00pm; campus maps are in a box outside for after-hours). The National Film and Sound Archive at ANU always has a worthwhile exhibition on an aspect of Australian radio, television, or film (McCoy Circuit).

Not far from the Uni, on Clunies Ross St., are the city's **Botanic Gardens**. They are extensive and thoroughly marked, and the information center there provides maps and botanical explanations—be sure to pick up a trail guide. (Gardens open 9:00am-5:00pm daily; information center open M-F 10:00am-4:00pm and weekends 9:30am-4:30pm.) The gardens border **Black Mountain**, where Telecom has a tower offering views of the city for $3. Bus 904 from Jolimont Centre will take you to both the Botanic Gardens and Black Mountain, but it runs only three times daily.

The **Australian Institute of Sport** is a short bus ride north of Civic (Leverrier Crescent, Bruce), where athletes from all over the country train for international competition. It's an excellent facility, and tours are worthwhile for those with a special interest. Tours run three times a week, for $2. Call 52-1444 to book.

For a relief from sights and museums you can always go out on the lake. Just west of Commonwealth Bridge on the north shore is an outfit that rents paddle boats, canoes, windsurfers, sail boats, etc., on an hourly basis. Windsurfing lessons are included in the rental, 10:00am-2:00pm on the hour. The calm lake is perfect for beginners.

There are several parks and picnic spots further afield. The NASA tracking station which served as a central link for Apollo moon landings is at **Tidbinbilla Nature Reserve** (open 9:00am-5:00pm daily). The reserve has very friendly kangaroos, and you'll see emus and koalas along the paths. (40 km southwest of Canberra; bus 907 from Jolimont Centre runs there three days a week.)

Another worthwhile trip from the city is **Lanyon Homestead**, 30 km south on Tharwa Dr. off the Monaro Hwy. The drive takes you through some classic Australian countryside, with beautiful stretches of golden fields bordered by enormous trees. Lanyon, a pastoral homestead built in 1859, couldn't be more picturesque or typically Australian. Also on the property is the Nolan Gallery, which houses a small but fine collection of Sidney Nolan's paintings of Australian events and people, the most famous being a series on the bushranger (outlaw) Ned Kelly. Admission to the house is $4, gallery entrance is $2 (about half-price for students).

If you go to Lanyon, stop in **Cuppacumbalong**, with its community of craftspeople, and there's a more modern homestead in a lovely spot on the banks of the Murrumbidgee River (homestead is open for viewing W-Sun and public holidays 11:00am-5:00pm). Unfortunately, there's no public transport to Lanyon or Cuppacumbalong.

Food

Travelers generally try to grab lunch during the day as they see the sights, but offerings are meager around the main attractions. You'll end up eating kiosk and cafeteria lunches. The best are at **Regatta Point** (which has a lovely outdoor terrace overlooking the lake) and the **Parliament House exhibition gallery**. Neither is over-priced. The **Botanical Gardens** has a more expensive cafe. There are buses and caravans around Civic with Asian and fast-food.

As for dinner, the cheapest area is also Civic, on **East Row**. Inexpensive ethnic restaurants line the street, especially Vietnamese and Chinese. The only place that's cheaper is the Uni. All-day restaurants include:

Gus' Coffee Shop, Bunda St., Civic (phone 48-8118). Desserts, snacks, lunches. Bagels and gourmet sandwiches. Extremely popular, and a fun place to people-watch. Open 7:00am-midnight.

Waffles, 46 Northbourne Ave. (phone 47-2913). Ice cream, burgers, pasta, waffles, pizza, and herb bread. Dinners about $8. Open seven days for all meals until late.

Corner Coffee Shop, Garema Place, Civic (phone 247-4317). Outdoors, always crowded. Cheap sandwiches and desserts. Good Italian coffee. Open M-Th until 5:00pm, Fri, Sat until 10:00pm. Closed Sunday.

Tilley's, 96 Wattle St., Lyneham (phone 49-1543). Not far from the YHA hostel. New Orleans style, with recorded jazz all day. Oozes character. Men must be escorted by a woman. Friday nights are women only. Food all day and night, breakfast all day on weekends. Pasta, quiche, fish (about $10). Breakfast about $6. Late night coffee and desserts. Open daily, 9:30am until at least midnight. See also *Nightlife* below.

K-Block Canteen, Law School, Australian National University. Super midday meal: wide variety of pastas, plus salad and bread, for about $6.

Good dinner choices include:
Stockade, 17 Lonsdale St., Braddon (phone 47- 0848). Near Civic. Wooden tables and bar. Grill your own meat, with salad and bread for about $9. Weekend sing-along after dinner. Open Mon-Sat 11:30am-12:30am, Sun 5:00pm-10:00pm.

The Acropolis Restaurant and Takeaway, 25 East Row, Civic (phone 48-6458). Casual and good value. Spaghetti, weiner schnitzel, Greek selections—all around $8. Greek wines.

Knot Holes Bar, Student Union, Australian National University. Very cheap Asian food, all under $8. Great snacks. There's an ANU student discount which they'll probably give you automatically if you look the part.

Nightlife

Workman's Club, Childers St., city (phone 48-0399). The best of the service clubs and the most popular Uni hang-out. Live local bands. Disco every Friday night. Pool table and darts in the Sportsman's Bar.

Tilley's, 96 Wattle St., Lyneham (phone 49-1543). New Orleans style, with brass and dark wood fixtures in the cafe and bar. Always hopping with all ages and types, the majority being women because men are required to have a female escort (Friday is women only from 7:30pm on). Dancing most nights. Local artists Tuesday night. Free live rhythm 'n blues or reggae on Sunday from 5:00pm-10:00pm. Food all day and night. Pauline Higginson, the owner, started it as a retreat for lonely suburban housewives. Now, travelers from all over search it out. A real find.

Dorettes, 17 Garema Place, Civic (phone 47-4946). Mostly jazz, some classical music. $4 cover if you skip dinner (which is expensive). Open Mon-Sat 5:00pm-late. Music starts at 8:00pm.

The Rex Hotel, Northbourne Ave., Braddon (phone 48-5311). The pool deck bistro is popular in summer and stays open late. Saturday afternoon jazz by the pool is a popular weekly event (3:00pm-7:00pm).

The Private Bin, 50 Northbourne Ave., Civic (phone 47-3030). Very popular nightclub and pick-up joint. Dancing upstairs (dress well). Happy hour M-F 5:00pm-7:00pm, with free food and half-price drinks.

George Harcourt Inn, Gold Creek Rd., Gungahlin (phone 30-2273). You'll need your own transport. Pseudo-English pub with mix of locals and tourists. Packed on summer weekends during the day. At night there's a sing-along in which people get increasingly (and uproariously) involved. Sing-alongs are Wed, Th until 11:00pm, Fri, Sat until 11:30pm. Closes early other days.

Entertainment

Entertainment in Canberra is low-key for a national capital city. Don't go to the Theatre Centre and expect world-acclaimed orchestral or theatrical groups. The *Canberra Times* has a page devoted to what's going on in entertainment. There's also a weekly entertainment newspaper called *Pulse*, free at ticket counters and around the University.

Most local instrumental talent belongs to a highly acclaimed amateur group, the Canberra Philharmonic. The Youth Orchestra is also well regarded. The **National Theatre** in Civic has performance information on these groups (phone 57-1077 for bookings and inquiries). For free or inexpensive (and good quality) concerts, call the **Canberra School of Music** (phone 67-1707). They hold regular lunchtime and evening concerts, sometimes including a good deal on ploughman's lunches.

For entertainment in a less formal setting, the **School of Arts Cafe** has various solo performers (mainly vocal) Th-Sat nights from 7:00pm until 10:00pm. You eat dinner (BYO), which pays for the entertainment—generally an excellent deal. There's also jazz guitar at Saturday lunch. The cafe is at 108 Monaro St., Queanbeyan (phone 97-6857) and performances are advertised in *Pulse* as well as in flyers around town.

The **Canberra Theatre Centre** in Civic regularly shows films of all genres (call 47-5060 or 43-5760). The **Boulevard Twin** on Akuna St. is another good bet for movies (phone 47-5060).

Every Sunday, there's a "community day" in **Commonwealth Park**. It's different each week, and provides a rare opportunity to watch the people of Canberra come out of the woodwork.

Queensland

Queensland marches to its own drummer. Nothing demonstrates this better than its politics, which was recently dominated by a State Premier whose enormous power and dramatic style made him the most well-known politician in Australia. Sir Joh Bjelke-Peterson stepped down (forcibly) at the end of 1987, but his legacy of business laissez-faire and fundamentalist Christian ethics lives on.

Bjelke-Peterson's reign saw a huge influx of capital for tourism, during which a floating resort hotel was built atop the Great Barrier Reef and a road was cut through one of Australia's most prized conservation areas, the Daintree Forest. "Joh's boys"—as the notoriously corrupt state police force came to be called—rip condom machines off walls and confiscate beer from Sunday strollers. Joh's consolidation of power was backed by the National Party, whose power is still almost unchallengeable because Queensland's legislature has only one parliamentary chamber, and voting districts give disproportionate weight to rural, conservative voters.

Elsewhere in Australia, Queenslanders are regarded with bemused suspicion. They are seen as being fanatically conservative and parochial in outlook, but lacking in reverence for law and order. (The latter impression is perpetuated by well-publicized scandals in various government departments.)

Queenslanders may be a bit removed from mainstream Australia, but they are certainly a friendly, fun-loving lot, striking most Americans as having a mix of characteristics from the Deep South and California. Those who consider themselves liberal or even moderate by American standards should avoid talking ethics or politics with the locals (hint: be more discreet as you move north). On the other hand, don't miss the chance to spend at least one "Sunday session" at a pub with a crew of boisterous locals.

Queensland is, of course, the favored destination for travelers to Australia. With the southern surfing beaches, the Great Barrier Reef, and the tropical rainforests of the far north, it's one of the top vacation spots in the world.

When To Go

The optimum time for travel in Queensland is June-October, especially in the region from Rockhampton north, where summer monsoons and cyclones (most years Dec-March) make travel difficult and limit outdoor activity. April and May are touch-and-go in the far north, above Cairns. Extreme heat and

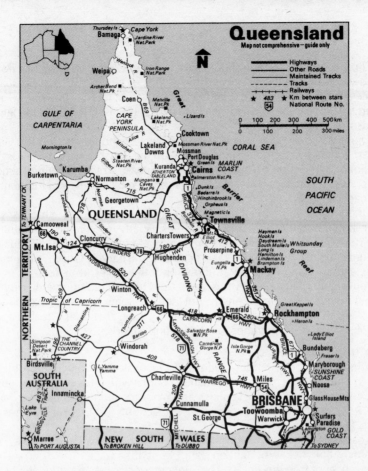

humidity are also factors during summer, as are box jellyfish in coastal waters north of Airlie Beach (mid-Oct to April). However, divers take note: summer winds are more conducive to coral viewing than those in other seasons, so if you can catch a glimpse between storms, the Barrier Reef is at its best in summer.

Those visiting in peak season (winter/spring) should remember a sweater for nights. Southern Queensland can be chilly, with average winter temperatures in Brisbane ranging from 10-20°C (50-70°F).

Itinerary

Queensland is huge, and planning a trip can be daunting to the first-time visitor. Most backpackers stick to the coast and spend the bulk of their time in the Cairns region, where Barrier Reef excursions, rainforests, and socializing entertain people for weeks (and sometimes months). The trek north of Cairns to Port Douglas, Cape Tribulation, and Cooktown is also a not-to-be-missed adventure.

The other major highlight of Queensland is the **Whitsunday Islands**, where mountainous, forested islands surrounded by clear, multi-hued waters make for some of the most scenic sailing and island-hopping in the world.

Those with limited time should start either in Cairns, heading first north then south along the coast toward Townsville, or go directly to Airlie Beach (access for the Whitsundays) and head north from there to Townsville and Cairns. This way, the only real gem you bypass is Fraser Island (off the Sugar Coast).

Those who have come to Queensland to surf should start on the Gold Coast and make sure not to miss Noosa, on the Sunshine Coast. This is not to diminish the merits of Queensland's entire coast, which is beautiful almost wherever you are, and most of which is serviced by hostels and frequented by backpackers.

Queensland pretty much has it all in terms of landscapes, which is why you should consider side trips inland—especially if you're not planning to see other regions. It's Australia's primary beef-producing state, dominated in terms of area by outback station country. **Carnarvon Gorge** is the most spectacular inland destination (though not the easiest to reach).

You will doubtless see advertisements for Queensland's numerous idyllic resort islands. Most are expensive, but there are some important exceptions, all of which are included in this text. Among them are Fraser, Great Keppel, Hook, Magnetic, Hinchinbrook, and Dunk islands.

Getting Around

Getting to most coastal destinations in Queensland poses little problem. The major buslines run from Brisbane to Cairns with numerous stops along the way (a 33-hour trip). Skennar's and other local lines fill in most gaps. On arrival to Queensland, check current discounts for students, YHA members, etc.

Coastal train service is frequent and extensive by Australian standards. Surprisingly, train tickets bought on standby or with a Caper Fare discount are often cheaper than bus tickets. The *Sunlander* and *Queenslander* offer service between Brisbane and Cairns, and the *Capricornian* runs between Brisbane and Rockhampton.

Inland destinations are more elusive and sometimes impossible to reach without your own car. McCafferty's offers the most extensive inland bus service. Inland trains go Townsville-Mt. Isa, Rockhampton-Winton, and Brisbane-Charleville-Quilpie, each twice a week.

Many backpackers hitchhike along the coast, but rides aren't always easy to get. The best stretches to catch lifts are Brisbane-Sunshine Coast and Townsville-Cairns. The section of road between Rockhampton and Mackay is reportedly dangerous. The safest and most reliable place to find rides are hostel ride-boards—there's usually room in someone's car if you're willing to wait a few days.

A final option is flying. Queensland is well-serviced by the airlines, among them Australian Airlines, Ansett, East-West, Air Queensland, and Sunstate Air. International flights go to Brisbane, Townsville, and Cairns. Domestic flights go practically everywhere along the coast, including Coolangatta (Gold Coast), Bundaberg (Sugar Coast), Rockhampton, Mackay, Prosperine (Whitsundays), Cooktown, and various resort islands.

Information

The best source of information in Queensland is the hostels, where bulletin boards are covered with tourist information and ride-shares, and many hostel managers run travel agencies that cater to backpackers. All the latest and cheapest deals on water excursions (diving, island-hopping, rafting, sailing, etc.) are available in hostel travel agencies.

Most Cairns hostels offer tourist information of some sort. If you begin your Queensland travel in Brisbane, **YHA Travel** will help you (462 Queens St., phone 07-831-2022 or 07-839-0864).

The official government tourist bureau, **Queensland Tourist and Travel Corp.**, tends to cater to visitors with big bucks and little time. They don't, for instance, include low-cost accommodation in their brochures, and they emphasize relaxation-style holidays rather than adventurous vacations. Their offices are always swamped, so go at 9:00am to beat the crowds. The **Government Travel Centre** is at 196 Adelaide St., Brisbane (phone 07-833-5300). Head Office is also in Brisbane at The Riverside Centre, 123 Eagle St. (phone 07-833-5400). Travel Centres in Melbourne, Sydney, Adelaide, Perth, and Canberra will help you with advance planning.

Some local tourist bureaus offer background information about their areas, but as far as bookings and deals are concerned, hostels usually know best.

Accommodation

Queensland reigns supreme in Australia for hostels, and the fierce competition keeps quality excellent. Some of these establishments are resort-caliber, with modern facilities and/or beautiful wilderness locations. Most have swimming pools and communal areas with BBQ facilities and the like. There are at least 50 YHA or Backpackers hostels throughout the state.

YHA of Queensland has 20 YHA or YHA-Associate hostels. With a few exceptions, they aren't as good as YHA hostels in other states or other Queensland hostels. However, because they compete with more relaxed Backpackers establishments, rules are less strict than in other states. Most are open all day, and you can stay for seven nights, if beds are available. Sheets (required) are available in most hostels for a few dollars a night, and generally you must sign in by 7:00pm. Phone bookings can be made without payment for same day or next day. **YHA of Queensland** is at 462 Queen St., Brisbane (postal address: PO Box 1128, Brisbane, QLD, 4001), phone 07-831-2022. Office hours are M-F 8:30am-5:00pm.

Camping is an excellent way to see the coast, and the only way to stay cheaply on several offshore islands—most notably Fraser, Rosslyn Bay islands (except Great Keppel), most of the Whitsunday Islands, Hinchinbrook Island, and Dunk Island. Between national parks and caravan parks, campgrounds are plentiful. Camping equipment is often available for rent in mainland access points for these islands, but you might as well bring your own if you intend to visit a few.

While those traveling the coast will rarely need hotels or other more expensive accommodation, those going inland will find almost no hostels. Only YHA operates hostels west of the Great Dividing Range. Hotels are the way to go in most inland areas, as caravan parks are also scarce.

The Great Barrier Reef

Extending 2,300 kilometers from Gladstone (just south of Rockhampton) to Papua New Guinea, the Great Barrier Reef is by far the largest reef system on earth. Its reefs and islands sustain more than 1,200 species of fish and 400 different corals, an immense diversity found nowhere else in the ocean. Fish of every conceivable color and shape swim among other mind-boggling sea creatures, such as giant clams and huge starfish. (One starfish species, the "crown-of-thorns," grows to three feet in diameter and can consume a square meter of coral in one week!)

The brilliant corals of the Great Barrier Reef are skeletons of tiny organisms called polyps and are mainly composed of carbonate of lime. Reef islands are either coral cays, formed by weathered coral deposits, or atolls, ring-shaped coral reefs with an inner lagoon.

There several ways to experience the reef. Naturally, scuba diving and snorkeling are the best way to get a firsthand look (see *Diving* below). Most day-long reef excursions include an underwater observatory visit or glass-bottomed boat trips, plus snorkeling. (The companies usually provide equipment, but always make sure equipment rental is included in the excursion price.) Most organized trips go to the "outer reef," the eastern edge of the reef where the coral is growing most actively. In some areas (especially north of Cairns), the outer reef drops suddenly to great depths, creating an awesome underworld that captivates divers.

Reef walking is another way to see the reef, though it is mostly done from islands—and most islands are expensive to reach. Bring sturdy sneakers and wear thick socks.

Finally, scenic flights allow you to comprehend the enormity of the coral system from the air, a spectacular sight if you can afford it. The best place for this is the Whitsundays, from **Prosperine Airport**.

Sunlight and wind are major factors, and they can make or break a trip to the reef. If possible, try to arrange trips on a calm, sunny day. This is especially important if you aren't diving or snorkeling.

Creation of the Great Barrier Reef Marine Park came too late to save some parts of the reef from human destruction, particularly in heavily touristed areas. This, as well as distance from the shore, are key factors when you're deciding where to see the reef.

Cairns is the least expensive and most popular access point for reef excursions. The outer reef is relatively close to the Cairns' coast and in good condition, so the only drawback is loads of tourists. Reef excursions from Port Douglas and Cape Tribulation (north of Cairns) are probably the best of all. The reef is close by and pretty much untouched, and there are few tourists. Trips cost slightly more than from Cairns, but they aren't outrageous.

You can also get to the reef from the Whitsunday coast (from either Shute Harbour or Mackay), where it is unspoiled and excursions tend to be more personalized. However, the long trip out makes tours expensive and time-consuming.

We don't recommend a trip from Townsville, because the trip takes a few hours and large sections are dying or dead. However, Townsville's fantastic new aquarium/museum is unquestionably the best place to learn about the reef ecosystem.

The Great Barrier Reef is 97% protected as a marine park, though there are varying restrictions for different areas. For instance, tourist-related construction and fishing are permitted in places. It is illegal and also dangerous to break off corals. If you get scratched on coral, wash your wound carefully and apply iodine or lime juice, then consult a doctor. Coral is toxic, and doctors usually prescribe an antibiotic to prevent illness. See also *Box Jellyfish and Other Nasties.*

The Great Barrier Reef Marine Park is jointly run from Townsville by the **Great Barrier Reef Marine Park Authority** (phone 077-81-8811) and the **Queensland National Parks and Wildlife Service** (phone 077-74-1411 or 21-2399).

Diving
Cairns is definitely the diving capital of Australia, offering diving from the beach and (more desirable) dive trips to the outer reef. The city is packed with dive shops and deals on excursions and courses for divers of all experience levels.

A no-frills certification course in Cairns runs about $60 cheaper than in Townsville or Airlie Beach. Beginners might, however, consider a course from the latter two because classes there tend to be much smaller. Safety standards are generally pretty good, though not as strict as in North America.

As for diving equipment, fitting and sizes are standard. American divers will have no problem, for example, matching their regulators to an Australian tank. In Cairns, one needn't worry about renting dive clothing. The water is usually warm, but it's not uncommon for divers to wear a suit. In the summer, jellyfish are quite a problem near the shore, and the Aussies have developed a novel "stinger suit." Made of lycra, the jumpsuits cover the entire body to protect against brushes with coral or other venomous sea creatures.

Note: Don't forget your C-card. A diving log book is often necessary on chartered excursions for the experienced.

Box Jellyfish and Other Nasties
Most foreigners are surprised to learn that Queensland's northern beaches (Airlie Beach on up) are menaced by a creature known as a "sea wasp," "stinger," or box jellyfish from mid-October to late March or early April. The long, nearly invisible tentacles of box jellyfish can be harmful and in some cases fatal, so be careful! They inhabit calm waters near the shore, particularly after rain and under overcast skies. They aren't a problem at most offshore islands or the outer reef. Check for warning signs before going in the ocean and, if in doubt, don't go in. If you get stung, vinegar soothes the wound. You can rent protective suits in major centers, and some beaches have stinger-proof enclosures.

One Queensland sea creature most foreigners *do* know about is the great white shark. In fact, sharks rarely attack people, though you might get a different idea from the popular "Shark Attack" clothing sold throughout the country.

Crocodiles inhabit muddy coastal areas and river mouths as far south as Fraser Island, but they are mainly a problem north of Cairns. Watch for warning signs.

Cone shells and stonefish are two other "nasties" you don't want to mess with. Avert an encounter by always wearing shoes or flippers in the water and never handling conical-shaped shells.

Rainforests

Most of those who visit Queensland for an extended trip will see a rainforest or two. While New South Wales, Victoria, and Tasmania also have rainforests, Queensland's northern forests are Australia's most ancient and unique. Only New Guinea, which was once attached to the Australian landmass, has similar flora.

Technically, a forest is a "rainforest" if its canopy is at least 70% closed. Some rainforests are completely shut off from unfiltered light and, consequently, they are dark and exceedingly humid. The tropical rainforests of north Queensland are sheltered by a canopy of imposing trees such as silky oak, kauri, red cedar, and Queensland teak. Underneath, a spectacular range of plant life teems with mammals, reptiles, and insects. These rainforests house the most thriving and varied array of wildlife on the continent.

Australia's most famous rainforest is the **Daintree**, subject of bitter controversy in 1984 when developers carved a road through it. The Daintree and other forests of the Cape Tribulation area offer relatively easy access to visitors. Consider also a trip to **Eungella National Park**, accessible from Mackay. Hostels often sponsor trips to these destinations.

History

The first recorded European landing in Queensland was also the first in Australia. In 1606, Dutch explorer William Jansz landed on Cape York in search of spices and precious metals. Jansz was disappointed with what he saw, so Australia's east coast was ignored for over 150 years. The next foreigners to set foot in Queensland were Captain Cook and his crew, who explored and charted the coastline in the 1770's.

European settlement was a hodgepodge affair. The first Queensland settlement, known as the Moreton Bay Colony, was an offshoot of New South Wales. Anti-convict agitation in Sydney and the necessity for more space to house arriving convicts prompted N.S.W. to create a new colony for the toughest criminals. In 1824, troops and convicts arrived at Redcliffe Point on the Brisbane River.

In 1842, the government began allotting land to free settlers. Meanwhile, free settlement of Queensland started in 1840 when an enterprising man named Patrick Leslie, with a band of squatters, followed explorer Allan Cunningham's route into the Darling Downs (inland of Brisbane). Thus began a long division in Queensland between squatters and bonafide landowners. A third group of settlers arrived further north (near present-day Gladstone) in 1847, comprised of former convicts. Despite widely divergent interests, the settlements agreed that independence from N.S.W. was the only way to administrate their territory efficiently. On June 10, 1859, Queensland was proclaimed and named at Queen Victoria's own suggestion.

At the time of statehood, Queensland's population was 23,520 and growing. Settlers came primarily to graze cattle and sheep (a substantial artesian water supply ensured healthy grazing lands) and, later, to grow cotton and sugar. The discovery of gold at Gympie in 1867 contributed to Queensland's rapid growth and triggered the first of a succession of gold rushes throughout the colony. More recently, other mineral finds (zinc, lead, silver, and bauxite) have brought considerable capital to the state, as has the tourist industry. (You will see ample, sometimes extremely overdone, evidence of the latter.)

Queensland, among the most important sugar producers in the world, is the only place where sugar is produced entirely by white labor. There is, however, an undiscussed story. One of the most bitter state conflicts in the late 19th century involved indentured labor of South Sea Islanders (or *kanakas*, as the Polynesians were called). Reports of brutality by landowners echo American slavery, while the effect on island societies was highly destructive, since men left their islands for at least three years.

The arguments by those opposed to indentured labor espoused the "Keep Australia White" theme, heard so often throughout Australia's history. Indentured kanaka labor finally was outlawed after federation in 1901, by an act of the national Parliament.

As in other states, Queensland's gold rush brought a huge influx of Chinese. During the 1870's, 17,000 Chinese worked in the Palmer River goldfields. The Chinese returned to their homeland before their presence became a controversial issue.

Brisbane

Newcomers give themselves away when they refer to Queensland's capital as "Briz-bain." The proper (and eminently smoother) pronunciation is "Briz-bun." Though there are a few worthwhile sights in the area and several recent developments (most notably the site for World Expo '88), there's no compelling reason to spend more than two or three nights in the city.

Brisbane is a thriving, semi-tropical city and seat of Queensland's notorious National Party-dominated government. While cosmopolitan compared to the rest of the state—and large by Australian standards (it's the third most populous city in the country)—Brisbane hardly exudes big city slickness.

Getting There

Deluxe, Bus Australia/McCafferty's, Pioneer Express, and Greyhound service Brisbane daily from all major Aussie cities. From Darwin the trip takes two days; Sydney, 16 hours; Cairns, 27 hours; Adelaide, 28 hours; Melbourne, 28 hours.

The overnight train from Cairns (either the *Queenslander* or *Sunlander*) runs a few times weekly, definitely an option worth considering. Caper Fares are available for the Sydney-Brisbane run. Trains service Brisbane from all states.

Australian Airlines and Ansett fly to Brisbane from all major cities. Air New

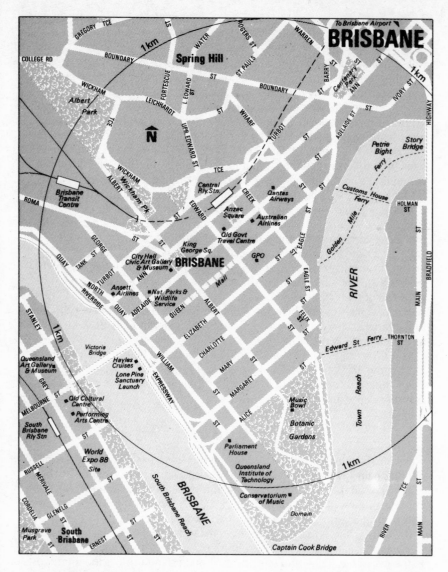

Zealand and Qantas fly from Auckland and Christchurch, and there are flights from Los Angeles, San Francisco, Honolulu, Hong Kong, Tokyo, Singapore, Thailand, and Papua New Guinea.

Orientation and Practical Information

Brisbane city is built along a large bend in the Brisbane River, 20 km from the Moreton Bay coast. The center of the city, designed in a grid pattern, spreads up and away from each side of the river. North-south streets are named for queens, east-west streets for kings. Queen Street Mall is the commercial heart of the city, with the Myer Centre as its centerpiece, featuring hundreds of stores, an indoor amusement park, restaurants, and a bus terminal. King

George Square, fronted by City Hall, is a civic center and bustling common area.

The southern front and southwest edge of the city are flanked by Botanical Gardens. Across the river (on the south side) is the Cultural Center, a comprehensive facility with an art gallery, museum, and library. Adjacent is the site of World Expo '88.

Important Addresses and Telephone Numbers (area code 07)

Queensland Government Travel Centre, corner Adelaide and Edwards Sts. (phone 31-2211 or 833-5300). Information and bookings for city and state travel. Open M-F 9:00am-4:45pm, Sat morning. There's also an information kiosk in the Queen Street Mall.

General Post Office, 285 Queen St. A historic site in itself, with the original wing completed in 1872.

American Express, 68 Queen St. (phone 229-2022). Open M-F 9:00am-5:30pm, Sat 9:00am-noon.

Youth Hostel Association of Queensland, 462 Queen St. (memberships: phone 831-2022; travel agency: phone 839-0864). Make airline, bus, and other travel arrangements here. YHA membership discounts are available for some bus lines. Open M-F 8:00am-4:45pm (opens 9:00am Wed).

National Parks and Wildlife Service, MLC Centre, 239 George St. (phone 227-4111).

STA Travel, Northern Security Building, 40 Creek St. (phone 221-9629). Or Queensland Institute of Technology, Community Building, George St.

Royal Automobile Club (RAC) of Queensland Travel Centre, 190 Edwards St. (phone 253-2444 or 221-8415).

Queensland Transit Centre, Roma St. (phone 229-7203). Info and bookings for most interstate buses. Central interchange for suburban trains and buses. Also a pick-up spot for many of the hostels.

Skennar's Coachlines, phone 832-1148.

Deluxe, Transit Centre, Roma St. (phone 844-2466). City sales office is at 40 Queen St.

Greyhound, Transit Centre (phone 844-3300).

Pioneer, Transit Centre (phone 240-9350 or 846-3633).

Bus Australia/McCafferty's, Transit Centre (phone 221-8555).

Queensland Railways, 305 Edward St. (phone 225-1122). For booking go to 208 Adelaide St.

Australian Airlines, phone 260-3311.

Air Queensland, phone 229-1311.

Sunstate Air, phone 268-5466.

Ansett Air, phone 228-8222.

East-West Airlines, phone 229-0455.

Air New Zealand, phone 229-4088.

Qantas, phone 224-3711.

Transportation

The bus network is organized like a giant wheel superimposed over Brisbane, with downtown as the hub and the buses running along the spokes
toward suburbia. The system is color- and animal-coded. Buses run
6:30am-11:15pm. For a map of the routes and special fares, stop at the information center in the underground **Queen Street Bus Station**. (Get there from
the Myer Centre, or via the "kangaroo" or "platypus" platforms). It's open
M-F 8:30am-4:45pm. Many buses depart from there, but not all do. For bus
route and timetable information, phone 225-4444.

The city is also serviced by a comprehensive train system that is clean,
reliable, and runs to key areas like Brunswick St. (near the New Farm hostels),
the Cultural Centre and Expo '88 site, and the suburbs. Trains leave from
Central Station or Roma St. Station. Some services run as late as 1:30am.
Call 225-1244 for information.

Limited ferry services operate from Edward St. and the Customs House
(Queen St.). Call the Brisbane River Ferry Service for full details (phone
399-4768).

Biking is an easy way to see the city, and there's a pleasant bike path along
the river. Call **Brisbane Rent-a-Bike** at 229-2592.

Accommodation

Lodging in Brisbane is easy to find and very affordable, with a number of
hostels and inexpensive hotels in central locations. Several hostels are in
New Farm, a 10-minute walk from the city center. Avoid wandering alone
there after dark. Paddington, where there are two more hostels, is an attractive suburb about the same distance from the city as New Farm, and a
10-minute walk from the Transit Centre.

Hostels:

Backpackers Bridge Inn, 196 Bowen Tce., New Farm (phone 358-5000). Call
for free transport. Doubles available. Quieter and cleaner than Backpackers
Downunder (below). Nice view of the river from front porch. Volleyball. BBQ.

Backpackers Downunder, 365 Bowen Tce., New Farm (phone 358-1488) and
71 Kent St., New Farm (phone 07-358-4504). Free transport to and from Roma
St. Station (call), or bus 177/178 from brown bus stops in city. Dorm beds
and doubles (difficult to get if not a couple). Often crowded. Very noisy.
Not ideal.

Brisbane International Backpacker's Hostel, 836 Brunswick St., New Farm
(phone 358-3777). Call for a ride from Transit Centre. Doubles available.
BBQ. Booking service.

Pink Galah Backpackers, 29 Barker St., New Farm (phone 358-5155). Swimming pool and sauna. Open fireplace. BBQ. Bike and canoe rental.

Brisbane YHA, Kedron, 15 Mitchell St., Kedron (phone 857-1245). 8 km from city, off Bruce Hwy. Take bus 172 to stop 27A, turn left on Broughton, then right onto Mitchell St.

Backpackers Paddington, 175 Given Tce., Paddington (phone 368-1047). 10 min. walk from bus terminal, or bus 144 to stop 5. Doubles available.

Paddington Barracks Hotel, corner Petrie Tce. and Caxton St., Paddington (phone 369-4128). Backpackers' bar and restaurant. Beer garden. Free breakfast.

Hotels:
Annie's Shandon Inn, 405 Upper Edwards St. (phone 831-8684). Quiet and friendly atmosphere. Flowers in rooms. Clean, large communal kitchen. Highly recommended.

Yale Budget Inn, 413 Upper Edwards St. (phone 832-1663). Hot breakfast included. Not outstandingly clean, but not terrible. TV room. No kitchen facilities.

Astor Motel, 1983 Whickam Tce. (phone 831- 9522). Clean, air conditioned. Some rooms with private baths. No kitchen facilities.

Dorchester Inn, 484 Upper Edwards St. (phone 831-2967). Private bath, TV, and refrigerator in all rooms. No kitchen facilities.

Things to See and Do
First, head across Victoria Bridge to South Brisbane, where the **Brisbane Cultural Centre** and the site of World Expo '88 will provide a day of entertainment. The Centre houses Queensland's official museum, art gallery, and library (on your right as you cross the bridge), with the state's **Performing Arts Complex** nearby (south of the bridge).

The art gallery, the highlight of the complex, has many worthwhile exhibits and a distinguished permanent collection. For an overview of Queensland history, the museum is also worth a look. Admission is free for both. (Art gallery is open 10:00am-5:00pm daily; museum is open 9:00am-5:00pm daily.) For guided tours of the gallery and Performing Arts Complex, call 240-7333 (gallery) or 240-7484 (Performing Arts Complex).

South of the Cultural Centre, the site of **World Expo '88** is instantly recognizable by its huge, tent-like structures and monorail. A long walk further south to the base of Captain Cook Bridge brings you to the **Maritime Museum** (Stanley St.) that has, among other displays, a dry dock ship built in 1881 (open daily).

Brisbane proper has several notable civic and historic buildings, some dating back nearly to the first settlement in 1824, when Brisbane began as a convict colony. The **Town Hall** (King George Square) is worth seeing, and there's a lift to the top where you get a nice view (open 9:00am-4:00pm weekdays). On the corner of George and Alice Sts. is the magnificent **Parliament House**, built in 1865, six years after the Brisbane colony became independent of New South Wales. It overlooks the **Botanic Gardens**, where a pretty pathway along the river is worth a saunter or a bike ride. (The nearest bike rental is at 214 Margaret St., behind the Parkroyal Hotel).

The **Old Windmill** on Wickham Tce. is the oldest surviving building in Brisbane, built in 1828. The structure was apparently an engineering blunder—the wind couldn't move the heavy sails—so it became a convict treadmill. Other areas of historic and architectural interest are **Fortitude Valley** (1 km west of the city center), an older suburb with Asian flair; **Petrie Tce.**, a pretty, residential area built in the 1880's (west of the city center); **Paddington**, a young, fashionable suburb with boutiques, galleries, and the like; and **Breakfast Creek**, with a well-known hotel (steak lovers shouldn't miss it) and **Newstead House**, the oldest standing residence in Brisbane, built in 1846 (open most days; call 52-7373 for hours).

There's a bike path along the river, and, riding toward Toowong from the city, you hit the **Regatta Hotel**, a colonial landmark that serves refreshing "frosties" (among other things) and is a local student hangout. Also out in Toowong are the **Mt. Coot-tha Botanic Gardens** (bus 39 from St. George's Square), with gorgeous views over the city and Moreton Bay. It's spectacular at night. The restaurant there serves lunch (open daily).

Mt. Coot-tha Reserve is the beginning of a string of parks known as the **D'Aguilar Range National Parks** or Brisbane Forest Park, which encompasses part of the Great Dividing Range and has several hikes through eucalypt woods and rainforest. Of the many lookouts, the most popular are at Mt. Glorious and Mt. Nebo. Further afield is **Lamington National Park** (for details, including transport from Brisbane, see the *Gold Coast* section). Contact the National Parks and Wildlife Service for more information.

Other activities include cruises and rides along the Brisbane River. The river isn't particularly clean or scenic, but cruising affords nice views of the city. Go to the Riverside Centre and city wharf area, just south of Victoria Bridge, to check out the latest cruise options. One of the best bargains is **Speranza di Capri** (phone 357-6970), where 3-hour cruises cost about $12/person (open M-Th 1:00pm-4:00pm). Or, hire your own riverboat from **Skipper Boat Hire**—affordable if you get a group of people together. Boats come fully equipped (including a stereo and food), and no license is required (phone 391-5971).

Hayles Launch goes from North Quay to **Lone Pine Koala Sanctuary** once daily (Jesmond Rd., Fig Tree Pocket—buses run from Central Station if the cruise doesn't appeal to you). The animals at Lone Pine come right up to you for food. How about eyeball to eyeball with a huge red 'roo? The sanctuary has every variety of Australian animal, including platypuses, and koala-cuddling is the highlight. Lone Pine is one of the best wildlife sanctuaries we visited in Australia. (Open daily, 9:30am-5:00pm; admission $10.)

Food

There's plenty of good, satisfying food in Brisbane, but if you're looking for gourmet cuisine and ethnic variety, you're in the wrong city. Fish 'n chips and other takeaway items are always easy to find. The **Queen St. Mall** has a variety of food for reasonable prices at its food hall, open daily 8:00am-5:30pm, and until 9:00pm on weekends. The mall is also flanked at either end by **Jimmy's**, a semi-fast-food cafe with everything from lasagna to oriental chicken salad. The prices are a bit higher, but the food is good and you eat outside, overlooking the bustle of the mall. Inexpensive food is also available on the lower levels of the **Myer Centre**.

Chinatown is just 1 km from the city center in Fortitude Valley. There are a number of Chinese takeaway stands in the Chinatown mall offering dim sum. **Given Tce.** in Paddington also has a variety of restaurants.

For hearty pub meals, try the **Embassy Hotel** (corner Edwards and Elizabeth Sts.) or the plusher **Criterion Hotel** (corner Adelaide and George Sts.). According to local fans, the **Spanish Gardens** in the Breakfast Creek Hotel, Breakfast Creek (phone 262-5988) serves the best steak in Queensland.

Note: Restaurants are often closed on Mondays, and sometimes Sundays as well.

The August Moon Cafe, in the heart of Chinatown mall, Fortitude Valley (phone 52-2718). Huge menu range (including Cantonese spring rolls, scones, tea, and sandwiches). Full-fledged Chinese meals are more expensive. Lunch and dinner daily. Moderate to expensive.

California Snack Bar, Edward St., at the end of the mall. Renowned salad sandwich. Fresh fruit drinks. Moderate.

Possums Australian Food (BYO), 681 Brunswick St., Newfarm (phone 358-1442). Sit-down or takeaway. Traditional Aussie fare (including salads, pies, chicken, lamb). Nice garden patio. Moderate.

Cubana (BYO), Wallace Bishop Arcade, 239 Albert St. (phone 221-1932). The coffee shop in Brisbane. Though the food is nothing to rave about, it's reasonably priced. Cheap.

Shingle Inn (no alcohol), 254 Edward St. (phone 221-9039). A remnant of old Brisbane. Go for the English teahouse atmosphere. Inexpensive, basic food. Cheap to moderate.

The Pancake Manor, 18 Charlotte St. (phone 221-6433). In an old church, lots of atmosphere. Everything from snacks to full-fledged feasts, all at good prices. The ideal travelers' hangout. Open 24 hours, seven days. Moderate.

Pasta Pasta (BYO), 242 Hawken Dr., Lucin (phone 371-1403). The name says it all. Popular student hangout. Moderate.

Squirrels (BYO), 190 Melbourne St., South Brisbane (phone 844-4603). Nice old Brisbane setting. Vegetarian fare. Coffee, cakes, buffet lunches—all excellent. Open M-F from 10:00am; Sat-Sun from noon. Moderate.

Mt. Coot-tha Summit Restaurant, Sir Samuel Griffith Drive, Mt. Coot-tha (phone 369-9922). Best view in town. Dinners are expensive, but stop for lunch or an afternoon tea. Open daily.

Nightlife
Pubs are the highlight of Brisbane nightlife, though there's no shortage of nightclubs.

Pubs:
Whistle Stop Pub, corner Upper Edwards and Ann Sts., above Central Station. First of a long chain of popular pubs on Edwards St. Good place to see local color.

Post Office Hotel, Another Edwards St. pub, corner Edwards and Margaret Sts. Great beer garden with big old trees, picnic tables, and jukebox. Live music F-Sun.

The Criterion and **The Stock Exchange**, opposite corners of Albert and Edwards Sts. Plusher than the average pub. Frequented by lawyers and business people of Brisbane's central district.

Stony Bridge Hotel, Kangaroo Point, across river from city center. More rustic than the other pubs. Live folk guitar.

Regatta Hotel, Toowong, 2 km from city center on river (a nice walk). Attractive colonial building at the end of the scenic river walk. Uni hangout.

Nightclubs:
Brisbane Jazz Club, Kangaroo Point. Overlooking the river. One of the best places in the city to hear live jazz. Bands F-Sun nights, cover charge. Sunday is usually the biggest night, so show up early. Plenty of dancing and drinking to accompany the jazz.

The Roxy, corner Brunswick and St. Paul Sts. Live rock every night, open until 5:00am F-Sat. Expensive cover charge. On Tuesdays, all drinks are $.20. (Yes, you read it right!)

Rosie's Tavern, Edwards St. One of Brisbane's most "raging" nightspots. Open F-Sat nights only, cover charge.

Entertainment
The **Performing Arts Complex** across the river from downtown is the main venue for musical, dramatic, and dance performances (call 240-7484 for information). The **Royal Queensland Theatre Co.** usually performs in the Suncorp Theatre (Turbot St.), and they have many worthwhile productions. There are several smaller theaters, including La Boîte Theatre and Twelfth Night Theatre. The **Queensland Youth Orchestra** is nationally acclaimed, as is the **Symphony Orchestra**. Tickets for the Symphony are somewhat difficult to obtain. Alternatively, the **Conservatorium Music School** holds frequent, inexpensive concerts ($6; student discount available).

For all performance and other entertainment information, check *The Courier-Mail*, especially on Saturday. **Ticket World**, the primary booking agency, is on Queen St. Mall, next to the Wintergarden complex, near the Hilton (their 24-hour information number is 11-644).

Most Brisbane's movie theaters are on the east side of the Queen St. Mall in Hoyt's complex and the Myer Centre, or on Albert St. in the same area. Two cinemas of note are the **Schonell** (at the Univ. of Queensland, St. Lucia, phone 371-1879), with good current movies and foreign films, and the **Crystal** (6 Le Geyt St., Windsor, phone 357-7811). At the Crystal, you're greeted by the owner and sit in canvas deck chairs. It shows a range of films.

Rugby, the dominant Brisbane sport, is played in winter. The main stadium is **Lang Park** (between the city center and Paddington). Brisbane just got its first Australian-rules football team, but the Bears haven't been too successful in the VFL (Victorian Football League). However, if you can't make it to Victoria, a footy match in Brisbane is a must.

Trips from Brisbane

The most popular trips from Brisbane are the Gold Coast and Lamington National Park (covered in *Gold Coast* section below). The islands in Moreton Bay (North Stradbroke and Moreton Isles, in particular) are other beach destinations. There are many worthwhile inland destinations, especially Carnarvon Gorge National Park—over a day's drive away but still easy to get to from Brisbane.

While public transportation to the Gold Coast and Moreton Bay islands is readily available, transport to inland areas is tricky. (See individual sections for details.) There are hostels at Jondaryan, Roma, Warwick, and North Stradbroke Island.

Aside from destinations detailed below, you should be aware that several tours from Brisbane take you to the Barrier Reef, northern Queensland rainforests, and the outback. Save Barrier Reef and rainforest excursions for operators further north, but if outback tours interest you, have a look in Brisbane. Some of the best deals come from **Aus-Trail**, which offers a variety of trips. Contact them at P.O. Box 109, Stafford 4053, Brisbane (phone 359-6651). The **YHA Travel Centre** (462 Queens St.) can recommend good tours and will help you plan any trip.

Moreton Bay

North Stradbroke Island
Close to Brisbane but still beautiful and unspoiled, North Stradbroke Island offers the chance to fish, surf, snorkel, and hike in an out-of-the-way place without the worry of fending for yourself. The hostel there offers trips and provides most equipment you'd need. Humpback whales and dolphins play along the shore, the beaches are nice, and the settlements are tiny and unimposing. Bring cash, because banking facilities are limited.

Getting There: The bus service from Brisbane takes you to the island and

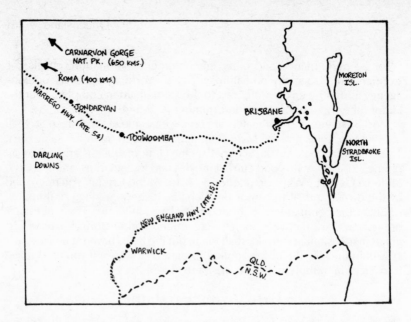

around it. It departs 190 Anne St., usually once a day. Call 376-3791 for times. There's also ferry service from Cleveland (phone 286-2666) or Redland Bay (phone 358-2122).

Accommodation: The **Point Lookout Hostel** (phone 075-49-8279), on the northeastern-most point on the island, is a pleasant place to hang out, which you may do all day. There's courtesy pick-up from Dunwich, or ask the bus driver to drop you at the hostel. The manager runs fishing and boat trips and will rent gear and surfboards.

The alternative is cabin accommodation at the **Samarinda Holiday Village**, for about the same price (phone 075-49-8279). It has a pub, and meals are available. Ask the bus driver to drop you off there.

Moreton Island
Just 40 km offshore of Brisbane, Moreton Island offers an alternative to North Stradbroke for getting easily away from city hassles to an untouched, natural setting. It's more remote than North Stradbroke, and most of the island is a national park, so there are only a few facilities and, happily, no commercialism. It's really a place for campers (with the exception of an expensive resort at Tangalooma), or for people who want to get off the beaten track. Buy all food and other supplies before arrival.

There's plenty of fishing and hiking, and the east side of the island boasts 30 km of excellent surf beach. Moreton Island also has the world's highest stable sand dune, **Mt. Tempest** (285 meters).

The island is only 38 km long and 9 km wide, and most activity takes place on the northern half, where a few lone sand roads (4WD only) provide access to coastal areas. The sheltered west coast has three settlements including **Tangalooma**, once Queensland's only whaling station.

Getting There: The most convenient access is a launch from Brisbane or Redcliffe (about 30 km north of Brisbane) to Tangalooma resort. Check with the Queensland Government Travel Centre or the National Parks office in Brisbane for details.

Accommodation: Camping is the only practical way to go. You can camp along most beaches (exceptions are outlined in the National Park Service's Visitor Information pamphlet). Three camping areas on the northern half of the island have toilet and shower facilities: **Blue Lagoon** and **Eagers Creek** (east side), and **Ben Ewa** (west side). To book a place at one of these, call the ranger at Tangalooma Resort at 075-48-2710.

Darling Downs

The Darling Downs refers to a vast, fertile area west of the Great Dividing Range, starting 120 km west of Brisbane and extending south to the N.S.W. border and north to Dalby. The area's black soil and cool temperatures (due to elevation) are a marked contrast to the subtropical coast, and those interested in scenic agricultural plains and history—or anyone tired of coastal resorts—should visit. Don't expect lots of sights; rather, it's a place to experience everyday rural life.

An option, if you're traveling south, is to head for New England (Tenterfield, Armidale, Tamworth) via Warwick, in the southern Darling Downs. There are hostels in Jondaryan, Roma, and Warwick. The large country town of Toowoomba, on the eastern edge of the Downs, can also be a base from which to explore the area. A big drawback for people without a car is that there's very little public transport.

Toowoomba

Toowoomba Tourist Information, Town Hall, 151 Ruthven St.

About 120 km west of Brisbane, Toowoomba is a pretty, thriving inland town. If you're in a car and happen to be passing through, stop at tourist information in Town Hall, where people can point you toward a tourist drive through the Downs (tourist drive #3).

There are a few worthwhile stops in the Toowoomba area, including a spectacular view from **Picnic Point** (5 km from town) and two restored buildings: the restored **Royal Bull's Head Inn**, dating to 1847, on Brisbane St. in Drayton (phone 076-30-1869 for hours and admission price), and the **Gowrie Homestead** in Kingsthorpe (phone 30-0143).

Jondaryan

If you're using public transport, head straight to Jondaryan. The YHA-Associate hostel is at the **Woolshed Museum**, the main attraction in town, just off Highway 54, three km from Jondaryan Village ($4.50/night; phone 076-92-2229, after hours 076-92-2156). Always call in advance because there's not much room.

The Woolshed is part of the old **Jondaryan Station**, built in 1859 and now set up for tourists, with demonstrations of sheep-shearing and blacksmithing. A museum houses a collection of agricultural machinery and vehicles (open daily 8:30am-5:00pm.)

The second reason to get out to Jondaryan is **Bunya Mountains National Park**, 90 km north. The park protects Australia's largest remaining stand of Bunya trees, a type of pine with edible nuts. The area was once a meeting place for Aborigines, who coveted the nuts. A rainforest, waterfalls, and gorges are other attractions in the park, which has picnic areas, three camping grounds, and a kiosk.

Getting There: The *Westlander* train goes from Brisbane to Jondaryan twice a week, and Greyhound runs a daily bus from Brisbane. The closest access to Bunya Mountains National Park is Dalby (48 km southwest of the park), where major buslines stop on their run from Brisbane to Mt. Isa. There is no public transport from Dalby.

Warwick

Warwick is a convenient stopover between Brisbane and New England, N.S.W. Tenterfield is 115 km south. The **YHA Hostel** is at 6 Palmerin St. (phone 076-61-2698). Skennar's runs buses through Warwick from Brisbane or Toowoomba daily, and their service from the Gold Coast via Beaudesert also stops there.

Roma

Roma, 300 km west of Jondaryan, is a commercial center and access point for Carnarvon Gorge. The **Red Log Caravan Park** (4 McDowall St., phone 074-22-2538) offers camping and on-site caravans. Local points of interest include a historic winery and **Meadowbank Museum**. Carnarvon National Park is 239 km northwest.

Carnarvon Gorge National Park

Carnarvon Gorge is a magnificent sandstone canyon that reaches a staggering 200 meters, with several tributary gorges and fissures. Aside from fascinating geology and scenic beauty, this large national park (encompassing much of the Carnarvon Range, an offshoot of the Great Dividing Range) has some of the best examples of Aboriginal cave painting in the country. It's a must-see, rivaling scenic wonders of Central Australia and outback Western Australia. Make a special effort to get there if you don't intend to visit these other places.

There are several hikes to points of interest, including a great half-day trek that runs the length of the gorge and crosses it 18 times. Of several caves with Aboriginal paintings, the most easily reached is the "Art Gallery."

Getting There: Carnarvon Gorge National Park is virtually impossible to get to unless you've got your own wheels. The closest bus service is to Roma. Those driving will find the park a convenient stop between Brisbane or Rockhampton and Mt. Isa.

Otherwise, 5- and 7-day tours of the park are available from Brisbane. For tour options, check with the Queensland Government Travel Centre or contact the National Parks and Wildlife Service in Brisbane.

Accommodation: Camping is the cheapest way to go, but since bookings are often made months in advance, you may have trouble getting a place. Campfires are not permitted. To make reservations, contact the National Park Service's Brisbane office or write The Park Ranger, Carnarvon National Park, via Rolleston, QLD, 4702. Include a self-addressed, stamped envelope.

The more viable accommodation option for backpackers is the **Carnarvon Gorge Oasis Lodge** with cabins and safari tents. Prepared food is available at the lodge; cooking facilities are not provided.

The Gold Coast

Visitors and Convention Bureau, on the mall between Cavill Ave. and Elkhorn St., Surfers Paradise, phone 075-38-4419. Open M-F 8:00am-4:00pm, Sat-Sun 10:00am-4:00pm.

The Gold Coast, from Coolangatta at the New South Wales-Queensland border to Surfers Paradise, is dotted with a series of beautiful beaches. That's the good news. The bad news is the entire area looks like Miami Beach. We talked to one old-timer who remembers fording streams to get to the deserted "southern" beaches. Those days are long gone, and unless you seek big surf or sparkling, expensive nightlife, you should quickly move north to equally beautiful beaches unspoiled by shadows of high rises.

Coolangatta and Surfers Paradise are the Gold Coast's main centers. Coolangatta is a quiet, friendly town with the best surf in Australia, according to local beach folk. The closer one gets to "Surfers," the noisier and more crowded the streets and beaches become. Surfers has lots of people and plenty of nighttime activity. If you want action, stay in Surfers; if you want a little peace and quiet, stay in Coolangatta.

A note on the weather: It gets quite chilly in winter, when the water is cold enough for surfers to wear wet suits.

Getting There: The Brisbane suburban train system connects with McCafferty's Bus Service at Roma St. Transit Centre five times a day, and the bus makes all town stops between Surfers and Coolangatta. Call 07-221-8555 in Brisbane for the schedule. Greyhound, Deluxe, and Pioneer Express have less frequent services.

To reach the Gold Coast from N.S.W., you have three options: 1. Take the train to Murwillumbah, where buses to Surfer's meet all trains. 2. Major buslines stop at Coolangatta and Surfers on the Sydney-Brisbane run. 3. Take a 70-minute flight from Sydney to Coolangatta on Australian Airlines.

Orientation: Surfers Paradise spreads along the coast on the Gold Coast Highway. Cavill Ave. is the main drag of Surfers, and it runs straight to the water. Centers of activity are the mall (between Cavill Ave. and Elkhorn St.) and the Esplanade, which runs along the beach. Both boast a variety of nightspots and round-the-clock chaos. The GPO is at 4217 Cavill Ave.

Coolangatta is a small town with one main street running east-west to the coast. Highway 1 goes through the west edge of town.

Transportation: The **Surfside Bus Co.** runs along the coast from Coolangatta to Surfers Paradise on the Gold Coast Highway. The Coolangatta bus stop is in front of Rockman's Department Store. In Surfers, there are a series of stops, including the casino, the Esplanade, and various places along the Gold Coast Hwy.

Gold Coast Water Taxi provides rapid water transport from Surfers to the Casino, fisherman's wharf, Seaworld, and Southport. (Main wharf in Surfers is at the end of Cavill Ave. towards Elkhorn Ave.) The whole loop takes two hours.

A taxi is the only way to get from Coolangatta to Surfers at night. It costs around $25/one-way from Coolangatta, so try to get a group together.

Renting a car or moped is pretty expensive, but it might be worth it if you plan to explore inland areas or go out in Surfers at night. **Surfers Rent-a-Car**, at 3066 Gold Coast Hwy., rents cars and mopeds (phone 92-1136).

Accommodation: We suggest you stay at one of the hostels or Backpackers inns in the area—both are as good as budget accommodation gets. If you want private accommodation, just cruise the Gold Coast Hwy. between Burleigh and Surfers Paradise. The highway is basically an unbroken string of motels with fairly uniform rates.

In Surfers Paradise, rates fluctuate wildly according to time of year and day of week. Try to hit the Gold Coast in mid-week, and avoid major school holidays. Also, be prepared to "discuss" the rate.

Accommodation in Surfers:
Backpackers Motor Inn, 2835 Gold Coast Hwy. between Wharf St. and First Ave. (phone 075-38-7250). Each unit has 2 bedrooms for 3 people each, plus a living room, kitchen, bathroom, and TV. Clean and beautifully equipped. One of the most luxurious in all of Queensland. Always full, so call ahead.

Backpacker's United, 40 Whelan St. (phone 075-38-5346). In center of Surfers next to Cavill Ave., 100 meters from bus stop. Swimming pool, squash court, pool tables.

Budget Accommodation, 48 Hanlon St. (phone 075-50-2907). Double rooms, weekly rate available. Rooms have private shower, toilet, and 'fridge. Community kitchen.

El Dorado, 2821 Gold Coast Hwy. (phone 075-31-5155). Most buses go right to the door. Licensed restaurant and bar adjoining.

Riviera Motor Inn, 2877 Gold Coast Hwy (phone 075-39-0866). 4 people share a "family unit" (3 beds and 2 sofa beds). Clean, well-equipped units with private bathroom, kitchen, and TV. Swimming pool isn't the best. Great deal if you have a group of 4 or more.

Accommodation in Coolangatta:
Backpackers Inn ("Hillside"), 45 Mclean St. (phone 075-36-2422). Alight bus at Griffith St., walk one block north to Mclean St., go left on Mclean; hostel is on right in next block. All double rooms. Pool table. TV lounge

with nightly videos. Surfboards and bikes for hire. Pub and restaurant (cheap dinner). Sean, the owner, is a lot of fun.

Coolangatta YHA, 230 Coolangatta Rd., Bilinga (phone 075-36-7644). $9/dorm bed; weekly rate available. 3 km from town, on west side of Gold Coast Hwy. near the airport. Surfside bus stop 10. Just off surfing beaches. Immaculate, new, two-storied concrete building. Swimming pool. Open all day. Can be noisy because of nearby airport, fire and ambulance depots.

Things to See and Do: The Gold Coast area boasts a huge variety of expensive themeparks and wildlife sanctuaries. Don't despair if you can't afford them: there are plenty of beaches and water sports to keep you occupied cheaply. You can rent surf- and sailboards from most motels and hostels. Also check at the Tourist Kiosk on Cavill Mall.

Aside from the out-of-town destinations mentioned below, you should have a look in Surfers at the **Fisherman's Wharf**, where shops, eateries, and a fun tavern are enlivened by street musicians and bustling crowds. Major cruises operate from the wharf. (Fisherman's Wharf is north of Surfers on The Spit, Main Beach.)

You can see native Australian wildlife at **Currumbin Sanctuary**, the **Boomerang Farm and Factory**, and **Koala Town**. Currumbin Sanctuary (Gold Coast Hwy., phone 075-34-1266) is the best value to see 'roos, wallabies, koalas, and native birds. You can feed the lorikeets at designated times. It's open daily 8:00am-5:00pm.

Sea World and **Dream World**, the major themeparks, each cost about $25 for the day. Sea World is the favored because it has dolphin, whale, and sea lion shows. There's also a free-fall waterslide, roller coasters, a monorail, and plenty of amusement park entertainment. Sea World is on The Spit (Main Beach), and it's open every day (phone 075-32-1055). You can get there by the Gold Coast Shuttle Bus, which runs every 15 minutes from major hotels, or by water taxi.

Rather than spend exorbitant amounts of money to fight the crowds at amusement parks, consider a day or overnight trip into the hinterland. The **Green Mountains**, 45 km west of the Gold Coast, are part of the Tweed volcanic basin and home to temperate and subtropical rainforests. A hike among the ferns, orchids, red cedar, and hoop pine is certainly the way to see the area, so avoid the tours offered by local companies and go on your own. There are hundreds of breathtaking views and waterfalls, and native birds frequent the area. The walking trails are extensive and well-maintained, the most popular area being at Coomera Falls and Gorge. Lamington National Park is your destination, off the Pacific Hwy. from Canungra or Beechmont.

There are two options for those without a vehicle. A Sunday-only service operates between Coolangatta airport and Binna Burra Lodge, at the park's northern end. Otherwise there's daily service from the Brisbane Transit Centre. Call **Mountain Coach Company** at 07-229-9477. There's a campground at **Binna Burra Lodge** with all facilities (call 075-33-3622), and camping in the bush is permitted. Canungra also has a hotel and motel. For further information, contact the ranger (in Beechmont: 075-33-3584; in Canungra: 075-45-1734).

Food: Along the Gold Coast Hwy. and in the numerous arcades of Surfers, there are plenty of coffee shops, cafes, and takeaways.

Vegetarians will find great value at **Healthy-Wealthy-Wise** (2995 Gold Coast Hwy.), one of a small chain of restaurants in Queensland with loose ties to Hare Krishnas. For breakfast or lunch, **Judy's Kitchen** (3045 Gold Coast Hwy.) serves quiche, pies, and deli-style sandwiches. You won't find better value (don't miss their "hummingbird" cake). A bit more expensive than the takeaway option, but worth the extra, is **Take-5 Coffee Shop** (19A Cavill Ave.), which resembles a typical '50s dive, though the decor is classier and more comfortable. It's open all day every day except Sunday, and until 1:00am F-Sat. If you're looking for a good splurge, go to **The Crab Cooker** (cnr. Thornton St. and Gold Coast Hwy., phone 38-6884), a fine seafood restaurant with a wooden, cafe-style interior.

There are fewer options for those staying in Coolangatta. **Sorrento's Pizza** on the main drag is open every night except Monday. The Italian family who owns it is very friendly and makes good pizza. Those who want to get right into the thick of local life should consider a dinner at the **Twin Towns Services Club** on the border between Tweeds Heads and Coolangatta (phone 075-336-2277). A large complex with several lounges, it's mostly a members-only club, but foreigners are welcome if they sign in. Large, basic, but excellent meals are cheap, and there's free entertainment (of dubious quality).

Nightlife: Surfers Paradise offers ample opportunity to "rage," and people come to the area for the sole purpose of doing so. Most of the nightspots are expensive nightclubs and discos catering to the young Australian vacationer. You'll be hard-pressed to find alternatives, but a night on the town is certainly one great way to meet friendly Aussies.

Most of the establishments are similar and have a $7-$12 cover charge. Remember to bring nice shoes (no sneakers), decent slacks (no jeans), and, for men, a collared shirt.

Jupiters Casino, Conrad International Hotel, Broadbeach Isle, Broadbeach. A big-time casino, 24 hours, every day of the year. Worth a look, though very touristy. Get dressed up.

Twain's, 91 Orchid Ave. A touch less posh than the Jupiters. Specials, and free admission some nights.

Club Rumours, Level 1, The Mark, Orchid Ave. Doesn't offer the specials that some clubs do, but it's one of the nicer places in town. Crowd is generally 21 and up. Variety of recorded music, all accompanied by videos on large screen TVs. Drinks are about $5; cover charge. Open until 5:00am.

Noosa and the Sunshine Coast

The Sunshine Coast is similar to the Gold Coast, but considerably, and happily, less commercialized and deluged by tourists. The area includes 150 km of semi-secluded beaches and rich, inland tropical fruit plantations. Caloundra, Maroochydore, and Noosa are the shires that form the Sunshine Coast, Noosa being the most popular destination. There are hostels in all three.

Activities include excellent surfing (some say the best on the east coast), fishing, windsurfing, and most watersports. The Sunshine Coast is a great place to kick back and enjoy the sunshine—but for those who want action, there's plenty of that as well.

The Blackall Range and Glass House Mountains are both accessible either as side-trips en route from Brisbane, or directly from the Coast. A trip to either offers the chance to get off the backpackers' beaten track and explore some unique geology and flora.

Getting There and Getting Around: All major bus companies have at least one service daily from Brisbane to Nambour and Caloundra, and Greyhound goes to Noosa as well. There's also a Brisbane-Nambour train service. A local company called Sunshine Coast Coaches operates services between towns. See below for transport to the Glass House Mountains and Blackall Range.

Caloundra

One hour north of Brisbane, Caloundra is the southern-most town on the Sunshine Coast. Beaches are the draw: you'll find excellent surf at King's, Dicky, and Kawana beaches, and Bullock's beach is best for windsurfing and fishing.

There's a **Backpackers Hostel** in Caloundra at 27-29 Leeding Tce. (phone 071-91-6278). It's got single and double rooms, a swimming pool, pool table, and BBQ. Alternately, the **Caloundra Hotel** is a good bargain (Bulcock St., phone 071-91-1382). You get a room with private bathroom, TV, and a small cooking facility.

Maroochydore

The heart and hub of the Sunshine Coast, Maroochydore is a good place from which to explore all the coast's attractions. Towns within the shire include Nambour, an administrative center and tropical fruit town; Mooloolaba, a beach resort; Alexandra Headland; and Maroochydore itself.

The Maroochydore YHA **Holiday Hostel** at 24 Schirrmann Dr. (phone 071-43-3151) is nothing to rave about, but it serves its purpose, with dorm lodging and a swimming pool. Pick-up from the bus stop is available.

Noosa Heads

Tourist Information, Tewantin Hwy., phone 071-49-7349, open seven days, 9:00am-5:00pm.

Noosa has the best of two worlds: excellent surfing in the sanctuary of a national park, plus ample opportunity for socializing and lots of entertainment. Though the area has become very stylish in the past decade, commercial development in town doesn't overshadow the beauty of the park's beaches and rocky headland.

Go first to **Noosa National Park** for some of the best surf in Australia. You can rent pedal buggies for the long, scenic beaches, or hike through a rainforest, around the headland, and up Noosa Hill (a steep ascent!). The park's brochure, available at Tourist Information, identifies trails and various flora. The Noosa River makes for pleasant boating and fishing.

Less accessible, but worth the effort, is **Cooloola National Park**, just north of Noosa. Best reached and viewed by boat, it has an everglades and is far more isolated than Noosa Heads. 4WD guided tours are the only way to gain access (inquire at Tourist Information).

Accommodation: A **YHA Hostel** is at 173 Gympie Tce. (phone 071-49-8065). Book ahead at the Brisbane YHA office. Rooms are $12 and up. Also, **Richard's Hostel** (9-11 William St., Munna Point, phone 071-49-8151) offers a basic dorm room with good facilities and a pool.

Self-contained units in Noosa are a great bargain. Try **Noosa Melaluka Units** (7 Selene St., Sunshine Beach, phone 071-47-3663), where you get a 2-bedroom, self-contained unit right on the ocean, plus a swimming pool. Call for a ride. The **Lake Cooroibah Holiday Park** offers rustic cottages, a bunkhouse, or on-site caravans (North Shore, Tewantin, phone 071-47-1225).

The motel bargains include **Takken's Top of the Hill Motel** and the **Oasis Palms**. The former, on Tewantin-Noosa Heads Rd. (phone 071-47-5377), is clean and attractive. The Oasis Palms (Noosa Drive, phone 071-47-5277) is slightly cheaper. Its location is good, all rooms have a private bath, refrigerator, and TV, and there's a swimming pool.

Glass House Mountains

About 25 million years ago, volcanic activity created the Glass House Mountain range. Rising abruptly from flat countryside, these domes and lopsided peaks are a marvel to view and a hardship to climb. Most people opt for the scenic drive, but hardcore hikers and rock climbers will love the challenge. The trails are well-marked but not well-maintained, and there are no trails for extended hikes. Non-hikers might enjoy the surrounding area, where papaya, avocado, passionfruit, banana, and pineapple grow and are sold at roadside stands.

The mountains are 65 km north of Brisbane on the Bruce Hwy., and nearby towns of Beerburrum and Glass House Mountains Township are convenient access points. There are a few national parks in the range, but since no information centers are nearby, you'll need to get info in Brisbane at the National Parks and Wildlife office or the Queensland Government Travel Centre. Information Centres on the Sunshine Coast can provide general advice. Call 071-94-6630 to contact the nearest ranger in Beerwah. Camping is not permitted.

Skennar's buses (phone 832-1148 in Brisbane) run daily from Brisbane to both mountain towns.

Blackall Range

Dense forests and scenic waterfalls are hallmarks of the Blackall Range, a series of small, popular national parks dotted with little towns featuring crafts and pottery. A visit to the range is most appropriate for day walks or picnics.

Kondalilla Falls has a 4 km trail through sections of rainforest with palms and Bunya pines, including several lookouts; **Mapleton Falls** is a favorite picnic spot; and **Obi Obi Gorge National Park** features a difficult but rewarding hike along the canyon and through rainforest. Be extremely careful after rain.

The Blackall Range is 105 km north of Brisbane and 16 km west of Nambour, slightly inland of the Sunshine Coast. For more detailed information, inquire in Brisbane before departure or call the National Parks and Wildlife office in Gympie at 071-82-4189.

Getting There: Reaching the Blackall Range without your own wheels is tough. The nearest point you can reach by public transport is Nambour, accessible from either Caloundra on the Sunshine Coast or Brisbane. From there you need to use your thumb.

The Sugar Coast

The quiet, attractive towns of the Sugar Coast are a refreshing change from the more developed Gold and Sunshine Coasts. About 275 km north of Brisbane, the Sugar Coast encompasses Hervey Bay, Bundaberg, and Maryborough. Hervey Bay, the most convenient access point for Fraser Island (one of Queensland's most beautiful spots), is the best place to stay overnight.

Getting There and Getting Around: All major bus companies stop twice daily in Hervey Bay on their Brisbane-Rockhampton run. The bus stop is in Pialba on Torquay St., in front of the Catholic church. All buslines stop in Maryborough, as does the *Sunlander* train from Brisbane. Local bus service from Maryborough to Hervey Bay departs the Maryborough City Hall twice each weekday.

Orientation: Three villages run along the Hervey Bay coast—Torquay, Scarness, and Pialba—connected by the inland Torquay Rd. and the Esplanade along the water. Across the bay, Fraser Island follows the coast. Maryborough lies 34 km south and inland of Hervey Bay; Bundaberg is 1.5 hours north by bus. The GPO is in the Pialba Shopping Center, on Main St. in Pialba.

Accommodation: Hervey Bay has a well-run Backpackers Inn, a YHA-Associate hostel, and a string of motels along the Esplanade. There are also budget caravan and camping parks with overnight vans and tent sites on the ocean.

Hervey Bay Backpackers, Centre Point Motel, 195 Torquay Tce., (phone 071-28-1458). Call for pick-up from bus station. Dorm beds and doubles. BBQ. Very attractive. John and Sally Bush, the owners, are proud of Fraser Island and will be happy to help you plan your trip. You can make all bookings through them.

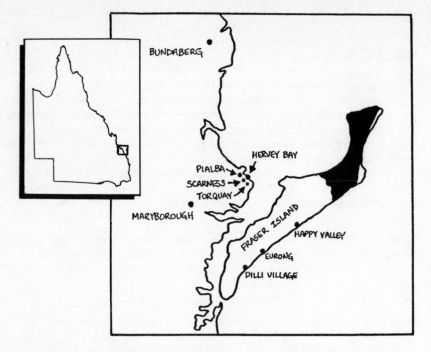

YHA-Associate Hervey Bay ("Torquay"), Torquay Youth and Conference Centre, 449 Boatharbour Dr., Torquay (phone 071-25-2506 or 071-28-1099). 5 km from Pialba bus stop, or get off the Maryborough bus at Bideford St. $7.50/dorm bed. Call ahead to ensure a place. Office hours: 7:00am-9:30am, 5:00pm-9:00pm. Hostel open all day.

The Sunseeker Motel, 354 Esplanade (phone 071-28-1942). Close to town, transport, and the beach. Standard motel room.

Scarness Caravan and Camping Park, Esplanade between Queen St. and Freshwater St., Scarness (phone 071-28-1274). On-site caravans with TV. Beautiful location, on a rise overlooking the ocean. Good tent sites.

Things to See and Do: The major attraction of the area is a trip to Fraser Island, but there are a few things to see on the mainland. A walking path along the Esplanade leads to **Gataker's Point**, a nice picnic spot. **The Pines**, a shaded rise at Beach Rd. and the Esplanade, has a pleasant ocean view. The **Hervey Bay Historic Museum** (Torquay Rd. and Zephyr St.) recounts early settlement of the area, which began in 1854. The collection consists mainly of local memorabilia and provides a good look at the growth of the small community (open F-Sun 1:00pm-5:00pm; small admission fee).

Although **Maryborough** doesn't have any place to stay for the backpacking traveler, the town makes for an interesting visit. Once the main port on the Mary River, Maryborough is 20 km upriver. Its two parks, Queens and Elizabeth, are beautiful, well-groomed, and expansive. The wharf and town center boast several homes and public buildings with intricate decorative work, retaining the feel of a colonial port.

Up the coast from Hervey Bay sits the town where **Bundaberg rum** was first invented, distilled, and distributed. Though the rum is world-famous, the town's main industry is sugar production. The distillery, in operation since 1888, is on Avenue Street. Tours through the plant and the rum museum run three times each weekday (call 071-72-1333 for times). There's also a local museum that covers the town's history and describes local heroes (open M-F only). Tourist information is on the corner of Bourbong and Mulgrave Sts. (open daily; phone 071-72-2406.) All buses that pass through Hervey Bay and Maryborough also service Bundaberg (once a day each). The trip takes about 1.5 hours.

Food and Entertainment: You won't find lots of great places to eat in Hervey Bay, beyond the standard takeaway food shops. Most people opt to do their own cooking. But you'll find the best value at **Toto's** (Fraser St. and the Esplanade, Torquay), where the pizza is great and affordable. It's open late, seven days.

Hervey Bay has a lot of pubs for a community of its size. They are generally clean and very friendly—one has a sign out front reading "Come in and join us, and if you can't, SMILE!" The pub's a good place to relax and talk, but none of them ever really hop; you may prefer spending your nights at the local cinema (corner Thomas and Watson Sts.). The **Scarborough Hotel** (Queen St. and the Esplanade), across the street from the beach, is low-key and pleasant. The **Hervey Bay Hotel** (Thomas and Watson St., Pialba) had a terrible band when we visited, but the people were friendly.

Fraser Island

You could spend a week trekking around Fraser Island. The world's largest sand island, it has a fascinating combination of habitats—mangrove shores, a rainforest, and scores of freshwater lakes. There's a resort at the north end of the beach, but neither it nor the towns are intrusive. Simply, Fraser Island is one of the jewels of Queensland. Spend as much time as you can!

Getting There and Getting Around: There are two ways to get to Fraser Island. You can either take a day tour or rent a 4WD vehicle and stay longer. We strongly suggest the latter, as there is a lot to see. Fraser Island is very spread out, and 4WD vehicles—which you must rent on the mainland—are the only means of transport.

All day-trip companies provide pick-up in Hervey Bay and Maryborough. Options include **Sid Melkshan** (phone 071-28-3411), **Fraser Islander** (phone 071-28-9370), **Fraser Flyer Adventure Safari** (phone 071-25-1655), and **Top Tours** (phone 071-28-2577).

Several 4WD rental companies operate in Hervey Bay, so check the phone book. They often rent camping equipment too, and no experience with 4WD is necessary. Rates are fairly similar. For example, **Bay 4WD Hire** (phone 071-28-2981) charges about $110/day, plus $30 for the ferry. Each vehicle holds 6-7 people, so the cost with a full group is less than a day tour.

Ferries to Fraser Island leave River Heads in the morning and return in the afternoon. There are also ferries from Urangan Boat Harbour, but the

River Heads trip is shorter and more convenient to Central Station and Eurong. The cost is $30 per vehicle and driver (small fee per additional passenger).

Orientation and Preparation: A few small communities and a ranger station exist on Fraser. **Eurong** is a small town on the east coast, built at the intersection of the main crossroad and the eastern beach. **Dilli Village**, a fitness camp, offers budget accommodation on the beach south of Eurong, and **Happy Valley** is also along the beach, 21 km north of Eurong. There are convenient general stores in both Eurong and Happy Valley.

Essential supplies are available in Eurong, Happy Valley, Cathedral Resort, and Orchid Beach Resort, but you should get food, etc., on the mainland before leaving.

If you're camping or bringing a vehicle, you must obtain a permit from Central Station when you arrive, or call *in Brisbane:* Dept. of Forestry (phone 07-224-7539); *in Maryborough:* National Parks and Wildlife (phone 071-22-2455) or Dept. of Forestry (phone 071-21-2408); *in Hervey Bay:* City Council (phone 071-25-1855).

Accommodation: Camping is by far the best way to enjoy Fraser Island. Of the numerous campsites, the best is at **Lake Mackenzie.** You can also camp at the creek mouths along the beach and in Eurong, Happy Valley, and Cathedral Beach.

There are two motels in Happy Valley and resorts in Eurong and Cathedral Beach, but you came to escape all that, right? An intermediate option is **Dilli Village Recreation Camp** (phone 071-22-4781), on the beach south of Eurong.

Things to Do: Major attractions include the dense, beautiful rainforest, freshwater lakes, and the long, wide, white Pacific coast beach. **Lake Mackenzie**, a freshwater lake in the center of the island, is two shades of "tropical paradise blue" ringed by squeaky clean sand. Equally impressive is **Lake Wabby**, hemmed in by steep rock slopes. Though the beach is unsafe for swimming due to undertow and hungry sharks, don't miss the great **beach drive**, with natural sights and a shipwreck to explore. **Cathedral Rocks, the Coloured Sands**, and the **wreck of the** *Maheno* are all between Eurong and Cathedral Beach. Four freshwater streams cut the beach, providing good camping spots; however (take notice all you hot-rodders), the camping areas are a real menace to 4WD vehicles.

Rockhampton and Surrounds

Tourist Information, Bruce Highway (next to Curtis Park), phone 079-27-2055. Open daily.

Rockhampton, a mid-sized city of 56,000, sits a few kilometers north of the Tropic of Capricorn. An important beef center, "Rocky" is surrounded by cattle country and flanked by the peculiar Berserker Range. The city is dirty and industrial—hardly an ideal vacation spot—but there are several key places nearby, including Great Keppel Island, Rosslyn Bay and the Capricorn Coast, and Mt. Morgan mine, so travelers often spend a night in Rockhampton on their way elsewhere.

If you plan to reach inland destinations like Emerald and Carnarvon Gorge, Rocky is a useful and possibly necessary stop. But if you seek an access point for Great Keppel or the Rosslyn Bay area, we suggest you stay in Yeppoon instead.

Orientation

The central city is built along the south bank of the Fitzroy River. Victoria Pde. and Quay St. run east-west along the river, and Fitzroy St. is the main north-south artery. The hub of town is the mall, located on an east-west block at the foot of Denham St. North Rockhampton, across the river, is the site of Rocky's only hostel. The GPO is on the mall, at the end of Denham St.

Getting There and Getting Around

All major bus companies stop in Rocky on the Brisbane-Cairns route, and terminals are in the center of town. The *Capricornian* and *Sunlander* trains service Rockhampton from Brisbane and Cairns at least once daily. Caper Fares are available from Brisbane. Australian Airlines and Ansett fly from all state capitals. Make travel bookings at **Duthie's Travel** on Denham St.

The town center is fairly compact, so getting around on foot is no problem. A bus runs from downtown to North Rockhampton, the airport, and suburbs. Taxis aren't too expensive and are a good way to get to the Botanical Gardens or the airport (phone 27-1111). There's a taxi stand in the mall by the GPO.

Young's Coach Lines (for trips to Mt. Morgan and Yeppoon) is at 74 George St. (phone 22-3813).

Accommodation

There is only one hostel in Rockhampton, so you may have to settle for something more pricey. The hotels in town are good and geared more towards travelers than those in Townsville or Cairns. There are at least ten motels on George St. (the Bruce Hwy.), which are a bit more expensive than hotels. All are about the same in facilities and rates. The waterfront motels are the most expensive. Most caravan parks, with on-site vans and campsites, are in North Rockhampton.

Rockhampton YHA, 60 MacFarlane St., North Rockhampton (phone 079-27-5288). $9/night, twin rooms available. Free pick-up during office hours. Clean and new, but the managers are hassled. Good kitchen and dining room. Inquire about discount on Great Keppel Cruise for YHA members, and book here for Great Keppel YHA. Office hours: M-F 7:00am-noon, 5:00pm-10:00pm. Hostel open all day.

Things to See and Do

If you're stuck in Rocky for a day, it's possible to find some pretty buildings and scenic strolls away from the industrial din. A walk west along the river on Victoria Pde. leads to the **Pilbeam Theatre** (1.4 km from town center), a regional theater that draws high-profile entertainers. Further west on Victoria Pde. is the city **art gallery**, with an interesting regional collection.

Rockhampton also has 10 acres of tropical **botanical gardens**, a pleasant place for an afternoon. The gardens are on Spencer St., 3 km south of town. Finally, the town has some impressive Victorian buildings, with a concentration on Quay St.

About 9 km west of Rockhampton, the **Gracemere Saleyards** holds a cattle auction every Monday starting at 7:30am. Gracemere is one of the biggest centers in Australia for cattle export.

Food
Rockhampton has plenty of fast-food and take-outs, but the hotels are the best place to find a good meal.

Criterion Hotel, corner Fitzroy and Quay Sts. Dinner in the Garden at the Criterion is a local favorite—and it's the best meal in town. Moderate.

Leichardt Hotel, corner Denham and Bolsover Sts. The "Brahman Bar" has counter lunches from noon-2:00pm, including very cheap steak sandwiches and hamburgers.

Texacana Burgers, corner Denham and Alma Sts. Best burgers in Rocky.

Audrey's Kitchen, The Mall. Health food. Gourmet sandwiches.

Trips from Rockhampton

Mt. Morgan
A trip to the Mt. Morgan gold and copper mine, 34 km southwest of Rockhampton on Route 17, takes you through typical Aussie cattle country and the red, dry hills of the Berserker Range. Mt. Morgan itself has been almost entirely cut away in the search for minerals, leaving a gaping pit that drops an awesome 270 meters. Tours of the mine run twice daily (phone 079-38-1551 to book). Nearby, the **Golden Mount Museum** traces the growth of 19th century mining with memorabilia that explains the life of a gold rush town. It's definitely worth a look. (Open mornings, small admission fee.)

Getting There: Young's Coach Lines runs three times daily on weekdays and leaves from 74 George St. in Rockhampton (phone 22-3813).

Yeppoon
Yeppoon is a quiet beach town 40 km northeast of Rockhampton. Its main drag, James St., runs down to a wide, clean beach that looks out to Great Keppel Island. Locals swear that even in midsummer the town enjoys cool sea breezes. Regardless, Yeppoon is a more desirable place to stay than Rockhampton.

Getting There: Young's Coach Lines departs from 74 George St., Rockhampton (phone 079-22-3813) and drops off on Normandy St., Yeppoon. Services run every two hours throughout the day, M-F. Otherwise, the Backpackers hostel will pick you up in Rocky between 6:00pm-9:00pm if you call.

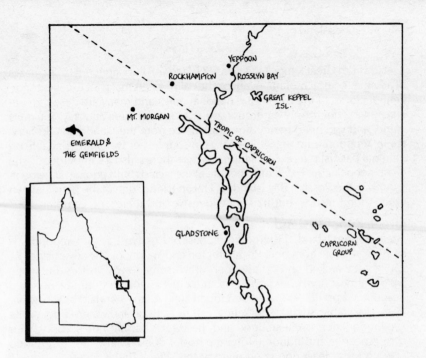

Accommodation: Barrier Reef Backpackers (phone 079-39-4702) is the best choice for Yeppoon—and one of the friendliest hostels in Australia. The three guys who run the place devote all their energy to their guests, offering home-cooked meals, trips around the area, advice on scuba diving, and much more. Linen is included and there's a TV, VCR, and pool table. Call Sean, Calvin, or John for a free ride from Rockhampton or find them at 30 Queen St. Four-bunk rooms and doubles.

The **Yeppoon Backpackers Hostel** (phone 079-39-2122) is at 12 Anzac Pde., across the street from the beach. It's clean, new, and has a pool. 4-bed dorm rooms and twins. **Tony's Restaurant**, attached to the hostel, offers a discount to hostellers. The managers can book all Great Keppel transport and lodging.

The least expensive of the Yeppoon motels is the **Tidewater** (7 Normandy St., phone 079-39-1632).

Rosslyn Bay and Capricorn Coast
Rosslyn Bay, on the coastline about 40 km east of Rockhampton, is where you catch the ferry to Great Keppel. There's a scenic harbor, and seafood lovers should stop at the fisherman's co-op. There are three short hikes at the head of Rosslyn Bay Harbour in **Double Head National Park**, the longest being a half mile—a perfect way to occupy yourself while awaiting the ferry. All the trails offer great views.

If you're driving, stay along the unspoiled stretch of coast from Rosslyn Bay south to Emu Park. Just south of Double Head, **Kemp Beach** is a deserted, 1 km-long stretch of sand flanked by national park headlands. Equally beautiful is **Mullambin Beach**, 2 km further south. There is a campground just above the beach and campsites on other beaches further south as well.

Aside from Great Keppel, there are 17 islands off the Capricorn Coast, peaks of a former coastal mountain range. The calm waters make for excellent snorkeling. Eleven of the islands are national parks and many are deserted, but it is possible for the adventurous traveler to get out there and stay. You must camp, and you need permission and advice from the National Parks Service in Yeppoon (phone 079-27-6511). No supplies or water are available on national park islands except Humpy, where there's also a campground. The Great Keppel launch will drop people at the islands with prior arrangement.

Among the Rosslyn Bay islands is **Heron Island**, one of the better-known Queensland resorts, but it's very expensive and there's no camping.

Great Keppel Island

Great Keppel Island, 13 km off the coast of Rosslyn Bay and Yeppoon, is easily accessible from both Rockhampton and Yeppoon. The advertising slogan "I got wrecked on Great Keppel" draws some rowdy visitors, but while a party atmosphere does grip the island, don't forget the stunning, deserted beaches a short hike from the developed area. All the standard beach activities are available, such as snorkeling, fishing, sailing, and waterskiing. While accommodation is cheap, food and the Wreck Bar are not, so bring your own groceries and liquor. (Note: the hostel doesn't allow booze.) But do save up for at least one good night at the Wreck Bar!

Getting There: The *Victory* runs to Great Keppel from Rosslyn Bay every morning. Most people book a bus/ferry link from the Rockhampton or Yeppoon hostels. You can also make bookings at most motels. The cost for a round-trip ticket is about $35.

Accommodation: Wapparaburra Haven (phone 079-39-1907) offers cabins and campsites. If you don't have a tent, they'll rent one. Cabins cost $60 (and hold 3 people) with all facilities, including a kitchen. If the weather is clear we suggest you camp. Everyone showers at the waterfront by the Wreck anyway because the hostel's showers are awful. But if the weather is dubious, don't camp! People sometimes get completely washed out of their tents.

The **Great Keppel YHA** (no phone) must be booked ahead of time at either the Rockhampton hostel or the Yeppoon Backpackers. It's $9/night for dorm rooms (ask for rooms #1 or #2, quieter and smaller than the rest), $10/night for cabins. The hostel is shabby and not real clean.

Things to Do and See: Visit the **Wreck Bar** (open 9:00pm-3:00am; cover charge). It's just a basic disco, but everyone goes there determined to have fun. The drinks are small and expensive, but it's worth a splurge. (Order white wine. For some reason they give you a huge amount for practically nothing.)

Don't make the common mistake of sitting on the beach by the resort and the hostel. Instead, make the short hikes to **Long Beach** or **Monkey Bay**, and you'll be rewarded with deserted stretches of first-rate beach. You can rent windsurfers, catamarans, jet skis, motor boats, air mattresses, and scuba and fishing equipment from **Wapparaburra Haven**.

Emerald and the Gemfields

Despite the town's name, sapphires are the hottest commodity in Emerald and the area. In fact, emeralds are not even among the six gems mined in the area. You can get a license and instruments to search for treasure yourself, and authorities claim that many tourists get lucky. An equally compelling draw to the area is the trip from the coast, which gives you a chance to experience remote outback.

The town of Sapphire has a hostel, so the only difficulty in making the trip is infrequent bus services. The "gemfields" include the towns of Emerald, Sapphire, Rubyvale, Anakie, and Willows.

Obtain a "Miner's Right" from the Emerald Courthouse, the Anakie Police Station, or any Dept. of Mines office. The hostel rents equipment; otherwise rent it in Anakie or Rubyvale. There are two mine tours in Rubyvale— inquire either at the hostel or tourist information in Emerald.

Getting There: Greyhound goes to Anakie three times a week on its Rockhampton-Longreach service. Having your own transport is particularly useful out there in the boondocks, especially since Emerald is en route to one of Queensland's best natural wonders, Carnarvon Gorge. **Thrifty** in Rockhampton offers discounts on cars for hostellers over 23 traveling to the gemfields (phone 079-27-8755).

Accommodation: The YHA-Associate hostel is at **Sunrise Cabins**, Sapphire, and it's $8/night (phone 079-85-4281). Sapphire is 11 km north of Anakie, where the bus comes in, and the managers will pick you up for a small fee. The hostel is in walking distance of a mining area, and the managers give personal tours of the gemfields.

An alternative to the hostel is the **Emerald Caravan Park** at 64 Opal St., Emerald (phone 079-82-1300), with on-site vans.

Mackay

Mackay, the most southern access for the Great Barrier Reef, also gives access to Brampton Island, just below the Whitsunday Islands. The best reason to stop is Eungella National Park, which encompasses the Clarke Range and is home to scores of unique creatures. Somewhere between a town and a small city in size and atmosphere, Mackay is Australia's largest sugar-producing area.

Getting There: All major buslines include Mackay on their coastal Brisbane-Cairns route. The train also services Mackay from both Cairns and Brisbane, as do Australian Airlines and Ansett. If you're coming by car, stop at the information center as you approach town on the Bruce Hwy., as there's little information available in town.

Accommodation:
Backpackers Mackay Hostel/YHA Associate, 32 Peel St. (phone 079-51-3728). $10/dorm bed. 10-minute walk from bus/train. Traditional home built in 1930. Clean, crowded. Friendly management. Swimming pool. Convenient to everything. Trips to Eungella National Park. Office hours 8:00am-10:00am, 5:00pm-9:00pm. Hostel open all day.

Central Lodge, 231 Alfred St. (phone 079-57-3654). Single and double rooms with private 'fridge, fan, and cooking facilities. Residents are cliquey because most are semi-permanents.

Things to Do and See: About 80 km up the Pioneer Valley from Mackay is **Eungella Rainforest**, situated in the Clarke Range. Walks through the area are short (2-8 km) and lead through forests with lookouts and swimming. **Broken River Campground**, the origin of several trails, gives access to platypus domain. You walk through pockets of red cedar on the **Forest Glen Nature Walk** (from Broken River) or along the **Valley View Track** (above Eungella Township).

Among the creatures the park protects is the gastric brooding frog, found nowhere else in the world. This creature is named for its unique reproductive process, in which the female frog swallows fertilized eggs. During her "pregnancy," her stomach stops producing acids. Eungella Rainforest is a worthwhile trip, and the best way to get there is by tours from the Mackay hostel.

While the Barrier Reef is far offshore, **McLean's Cruises** offers trips to the reef and to southerly Whitsunday Islands (phone 079-55-3066). **Barnes Reefdiving** (same phone) has diving courses and trips.

Brampton Island, part resort island, part national park, is the closest offshore trip. Unfortunately, the resort is expensive and there's no camping, but you can take a launch out for the day. The hostel has information on current deals.

Airlie Beach

Whitsunday Tourism Association, phone 079-46-6673.

The highest concentration of travel agents must exist per block in Airlie Beach than in any resort town in the South Pacific—mainly because the only purpose for Airlie Beach is to provide access to the **Whitsunday Islands**. Most of the activity at Airlie occurs at night, when people return from their day trips to the Whitsundays. There's a good selection of pubs and restaurants, and even a respectable nightclub. The only beach at Airlie is artificial, and most of the time it's just a big mud flat—not great, but you can swim (at high tide only).

Airlie Beach is far enough north to have a defined wet season, from Jan-March. High tourist season is April-Oct.

Getting There and Getting Around: All the major bus routes include a stop in Airlie between Brisbane and Cairns. To arrive by train, take the *Sunlander* to Prosperine, where a bus to Shute Harbor and Airlie Beach meets all trains. Australian Airlines, Ansett, and Air Queensland fly into Prosperine.

Buses connect Shute Harbour with Prosperine, Cannonvale, and Airlie Beach (stops are indicated all along Shute Harbour Rd.). For schedule information, call **Sampson's Bus Service** at 45-2377. Some of the hostels have shuttles in the morning to Shute Harbour. To order a taxi, call 46-6289 in Airlie, Cannonvale, and Shute, or 45-1235 in Prosperine. Getting around Airlie itself is simple—the entire town is only 4 blocks wide by 10 blocks long.

Accommodation: The first two hostels in this list are slightly out of town on opposite ends, while the Hibiscus Lodge is on Airlie's main strip. The first choice for anyone planning to stay a while should be Reef Oceana Village in Cannonvale.

Bush Village Backpacker's Haven, Cannonvale, near the beach (phone 079-46-6158 or 46-6177 after hours). 1.6 km from town, managers will provide transport if you call. 4-person, self-contained cabins with stove, 'fridge, TV, and bathroom. Swimming pool. Owners are very friendly and have good travel tips.

Backpackers By the Bay, Lot 5, Hermitage Dr. (phone 079-46-7267). Just south of town towards Shute Harbour. 4 per room. Very clean. Nice atmosphere and friendly owners. Ceiling fans. Big TV lounge. Pool table. Excellent kitchen. Swimming pool.

Hibiscus Lodge, 32 Shute Harbour Rd. (phone 079-46-6105). 4-person, spacious units. Barbara, the manager, will give you lots of advice on Airlie Beach and surroundings.

Reef Oceana Village, Shute Harbour Rd., Cannonvale (phone 079-46-6137). Bus shuttles daily to Airlie; call for ride. Cabins of 4-8 people. For a bit more money you can get a private kitchen. More institutional than the others, but in very good taste. Lush, expansive grounds. Swimming pool. BBQ. Scuba lessons. Will make reservations for excursions. Restaurant with excellent, inexpensive dinner.

Food: Airlie's restauranteurs know they've got a monopoly on travelers to the Whitsundays, so eating establishments tend to be rather pricey and not so great. The following are some exceptions:

Pinky's Coffee Shop, Picaninni St. Large, hearty breakfasts, the perfect way to prepare for a day in the Whitsundays. Budget dinners until 7:30pm include crepes, pasta, and casseroles for under $10 (the cheapest in town). Open 6:30am-7:30pm. Moderate.

K.C. Steak House, Shute Harbor Rd. Their specialty is meats, as the name suggests. Mains come with all-you-can-eat salads and vegetables. Moderate.

Coconut Palms Chinese Food, Shute Harbor Rd. All-you-can-eat smorgasbord on Sunday nights (about $14).

Nightlife: The Bar (end of Shute Harbour Rd.) is one of the most hopping nightspots in Airlie Beach. Every Tuesday and Thursday night, the special attraction is toad racing: you "sponsor" a toad for $5 and get the chance to win a free cruise in the Whitsundays. It's a hilarious, noisy evening, with screaming fans and an emcee who provides commentary. Odd as this event may sound, it's a must.

Another good spot for an evening out is the **Rendezvous**, located in the center of town on Shute Harbor Rd. Torches light the patio and a live band plays good dance music. It's usually crowded and fun.

The only nightclub in town is at the **Red Hotel**, directly across from The Bar. It's open until 2:00am and has a good dance floor but expensive drinks. Since almost everything else closes by 11:00pm, it's the only spot for late-night partying.

The Whitsundays

About 8,000 years ago, rising sea levels transformed a mountain range into an island group now called the Whitsundays, named by Capt. Cook when he sailed through on Whitsunday (a.k.a. Pentecost) in 1770. The islands are rough and hilly, rising abruptly from the sea. Most are covered by forests and encircled by beautiful white beaches. The clear waters of the Whitsunday Passage reveal colorful coral reefs and other sea life.

Forty km east, the Great Barrier Reef provides protection from rough seas, making the area one of the best and most scenic places in the world for sailing. Of the 74 islands, only seven have tourist resorts; most of the others are national parks.

Jobs are easy to get in the Whitsundays because of a booming tourist trade and high turnover. Also, there's some fantastic fishing in the area, mostly available by chartering a boat.

Getting There and Getting Around

Almost all sailing charters, reef trips, and launches leave Shute Harbour and can be booked on the main strip in Airlie Beach. Some cruises have courtesy pick-up, and a few leave from Airlie Beach. Launches generally leave Shute Harbour at 9:00am and there are no afternoon cruises, so if you plan a day of exploring the Whitsundays, don't sleep late! See below in *Things to See and Do* for launch details.

Campers who want more than a day to see the islands can hop on a boat, get off wherever there's a nice spot, and ask to be picked up in a day or two. You can usually work out such a deal with charter boats and sometimes with water taxis. See below for information on extended trips.

Air Whitsunday offers scenic flights from the Airlie Beach Airport (phone 079-46-9133). Costs range from $30-$150.

Accommodation

Budget accommodation on most of the islands is non-existent. The only island that offers true hostel-priced accommodation is Hook Island, while a few others have specials for about $40/night. (For specifics, see below.)

For budget travelers, camping is the best option, and it's free on many islands with a permit from the National Parks office in Airlie (phone 079-46-9430). Rent camping gear at **Airlie Camping and Gas Centre** (phone 46-6145). Established campgrounds are on Thomas, Henning, Whitsunday, North Molle, Outer Newry, Rabbit, and Shute islands. Other islands have no facilities, but camping is permitted. The only places where pitching a

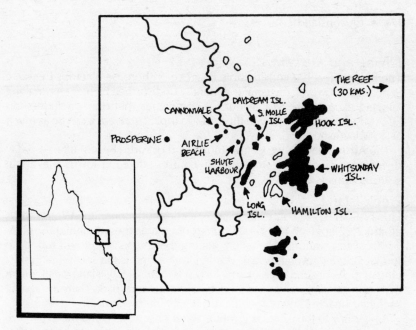

tent is forbidden are the resort islands of Long, Newry, South Molle, and Lindeman.

Things to See and Do

Sailing

Sailing is the definitive way to see the Whitsundays. Scores of companies offer tours on sailboats and catamarans, most of them day trips. Information kiosks along the main strip in Airlie Beach advertise the latest deals. For day sails, the best bargain comes from the yacht *Thekla*, an 18 meter steel cutter that competed three times in the Sydney-Hobart Regatta. For about $30 you get a full day of island hopping, snorkeling, reef viewing, sun soaking, and fishing, plus lunch. Not only is *Thekla* cheaper than the others, its itinerary is more extensive. Call 079-46-9510 or 079-46-6105.

Serious sailors should note that all the day charters take 30-40 people, so to participate in any of the sailing and enjoy extra deck space, an overnight cruise is the way to go. While this option is costly, it's a worthwhile splurge. *Apollo III* is the best sail-cruising choice (PO Box 598, Airlie Beach, 4802; phone 079-46-9334). She's a 17 meter racing sloop (designed by Ben Lexcen of America's Cup fame) that sails the Whitsundays on week-long charters—a ship that any knowledgeable sailor will appreciate. They take a maximum of 12, so you're guaranteed personal attention, sailing participation, and deck space; plus the crew is terrific. You can also join the cruise during the week at designated points, for a minimum of two days. (For instance, if you go to Hook Island, *Apollo III* will pick you up Thursday morning and drop you in Airlie Beach Saturday afternoon.) The weekly rate works out to about $100/night, which isn't bad considering you get three meals a day, accommodation, and unbeatable sailing. *Apollo III* leaves Shute Harbour every Sunday.

Diving and Reef Trips

The Barrier Reef is a considerable distance offshore, so day trips there are expensive. However, the coral is generally undisturbed by humans, making viewing exceptional. Watch out for companies that don't include snorkeling/diving equipment with the cost of a trip! Scuba rental can be as much as $50/day extra.

The **Airlie Beach Dive Centre** (north end of Airlie Beach) offers a 6-day dive course for a price comparable to courses offered in Townsville, about $300. (Cairns is cheaper.)

Hook Island

Hook Island has the only hostel-style accommodation in the Whitsundays at about $22/person in a 6-bed bunkroom (campsites available). Call 46-6900 for reservations. The catch: getting there costs about $45 roundtrip (price includes several extras). While Hook Island is the second largest island in the Whitsunday group (the largest is Whitsunday Island itself), much of it is inaccessible, forested mountains of the national park. There are several secluded beaches, two of which are reachable by land.

A big draw to the island is its underwater observatory, and the expensive admission fee is included in most roundtrip tickets. The observatory offers non-scuba divers a look at coral and other sea life, but be forewarned that the water is sometimes murky. We recommend going only if your entrance fee is part of the package deal.

The only outpost of civilization on the island, the **Hook Island Resort**, consists of dormitories, a gift shop, a coffee shop that sells canned and dry food, and a bar. There isn't much to do on Hook, but that's its virtue. Volleyball, paddle board, and snorkeling are all available. The presence of a bar can transform the peaceful daytime setting into an outrageous evening.

Getting There: The launch to Hook aboard **South Molle Island Cruises** leaves from Shute Harbour every morning (phone 46-6900 for reservations). The trip includes a stop at Daydream Island, coral viewing in a "coral sub" and underwater observatory (both on Hook), and a stop at South Molle Island on return.

Food: There are several BBQ grills for communal use, but no utensils are provided and no meat is sold on the island. No other cooking facilities exist, but there is a community 'fridge. If you plan to cook for yourself, come prepared. Otherwise, the resort serves moderately-priced meals.

Long Island (Contiki Resort)

A more expensive, but still a reasonable option for backpackers in the Whitsundays, is Contiki's resort on Long Island. **Contiki Holidays**, the largest tour operator in Australia for the 18-35 age group, completed the resort in 1988. It's a huge complex including tennis courts, a swimming pool, sauna, gym, restaurants, bar, and disco. Waterskiing, windsurfing, scuba and snorkeling lessons, and sailing are all available. You'll love this place if you want to meet young Aussies and have a good, rollicking party.

Call 079-46-9400 for prices, which was $32/night (and rising) when we were there. You may have to stay several days to get a budget rate.

Getting There: The launch from Shute Harbour costs about $25/roundtrip, or $60/roundtrip from Hamilton Island.

Daydream Island

One of the smallest Whitsunday resorts is on Daydream Island. The stand-by rate is about $80/night for a twin room, including transport, meals, and watersports—not a bad price considering the excellent facilities. To get that price, you have to book 24 hours or less in advance, and on a day-to-day basis. Otherwise, the cost is about $120/night.

Daydream is a popular honeymoon-type resort, with romantic beaches and a relaxed atmosphere. For information and reservations, call the **Daydream Island Resort** at 079-46-9200 or toll-free 008-07-5040.

Getting There: The launch leaves three times a day from Shute Harbour. Call resort for times and price.

South Molle Island

Like Daydream, South Molle is a casual island, with long, empty beaches. The stand-by cost of $80/night includes transport, meals, and watersports, and must be booked under the same conditions as Daydream. Book directly at 079-46-9433, or through the **South Molle Island Booking Office**, 43 Shute Harbour Rd., Airlie Beach (phone 079-46-6900 or 008-07-5080).

Hamilton Island

Hamilton Island is the most expensive, posh, and commercialized of the Whitsunday group. The only reason for a budget traveler to go is that resort-related jobs are easy to find and pay pretty well. If you want to visit but don't want to pay for the *Quickcat*, you may be able to talk your way onto the employee barge that runs from the mainland daily. For general information on the island, including transport, call 079-46-9144.

Townsville

Magnetic North Tourism Authority, Flinders Mall (in the "Coppertop"), phone 077-71-2724. Open M-F 9:00am-5:00pm, weekends 9:00am-noon.

Founded in 1866, Townsville is Queensland's third largest city, with a population over 100,000. The inland mining towns of Mt. Isa and Charters Towers export minerals through Townsville, while cattle stations of the Gulf Country, sheep properties of the Western Downs, and the state's sugar industry all depend on the port. Meat processing, sugar milling, vegetable canning, and copper refining are among the local industries.

Townsville is also a center for marine biology research, and there's no better place to find out about the Great Barrier Reef. James Cook University, the Australian Institute of Marine Science, a CSIRO Tropical Agriculture research station, and the headquarters of the Great Barrier Reef Marine Park Authority are all in town.

For the traveler, Townsville and the area has much to offer. It's an easy-going city with access to one of the nicest island destinations for hostellers in Queensland: **Magnetic Island**. Despite the fact that commercial launches take you to a poor location on the reef, Townsville is a good place to get diving certification.

While Townsville is in a weather district known as the "dry tropics," there is a wet season Dec-March, when cyclones and rainfall are likely.

Getting There

All major bus companies stop in Townsville on their Brisbane-Cairns route, and the train stops as well. The bus trip is 20 hours from Brisbane and 5 hours from Cairns. Trains service Townsville from Brisbane, Cairns, and Mt. Isa. Qantas and Air Nuigini fly into Townsville's international airport, and you can also fly on Australian Airlines or Ansett from most major Australian cities.

Orientation and Practical Information

Bordered by Ross Creek, Rowes Bay, and Castle Hill, the city is contained within unyielding natural boundaries. Most activity takes place on Flinders Mall and its continuation, Flinders St. East, and the Breakwater Marina, where ocean and river meet, is a new tourist hub. The marina has shops and cafes and serves as a departure point for cruises and ferries. Other boats leave from various points along Flinders St. East, which runs beside Ross Creek. The Strand goes along the ocean shore and borders a marina, and, though there's no beach, it's a pleasant walk. Downtown is compact enough for walking. Limited transportation is available to suburbs.

For cruises and travel bookings, go to the **Reef Travel Centre** (181 Flinders St. E., opposite the Magnetic Island Terminal; phone 72-4688), open daily, with limited weekend hours.

Accommodation

Civic House, 272 Walker St. (phone 077-71-5381). Call for transport from bus, train, or ferry. Deluxe will drop off. Walking distance from town. Friendly, clean, homey atmosphere. Good kitchen, TV, BBQ. Fans in all rooms. Nicest hostel in town. Open 24 hours.

Adventurer's Resort, Palmer Street, S. Townsville, next to Crown Hotel (phone 077-21-1522). A $5 million, 300 bed resort for backpackers! All types of accommodation. Institutional, cement-block rooms but amazing facilities—and immaculate. Restaurant, beer garden (with tropical atmosphere), and grocery store. Pool. Sundecks. Laundry on each floor. Dive school and booking agency. Call for free bus service.

Other hostels of comparable quality to one another are **Globetrotters** on Palmer Street (phone 077-71-3242), **Wills Street Hostel** (23 Wills St.; phone 077-72-2820), and **Robin's Nest** (8 Moorehead St., S. Townsville; phone 077-71-5849). All but the Wills Street hostel offer free pick-up from town. The Wills Street hostel is centrally located, opposite the law courts.

The **International Backpackers Hostel**, at 205 Flinders St. East, has a terrible reputation for rude management and their check-out time is 9:00am, but if you're desperate, their number is 077-72-4340. YHA operates the **Reef Lodge Hostel** at 4-6 Wickham St. (phone 077-21-1112)—$10/night, twins and doubles available.

Sunseeker Motel, 10 Blackwood St. (phone 077-71-3409). Very nice rooms with fans. Communal bathrooms. Comfortable TV lounge and sitting room.

Downtown Motel, 121 Flinders St. (phone 077-75-5022). All rooms have private bath, TV, and air conditioning. Swimming pool.

Things to See and Do

A trip to Magnetic Island (see below) and diving are the two major activities for travelers to the area.

There are certainly more scenic places to dive than the Townsville coast, but few better places to learn. **Mike Ball Dive Expeditions** (252 Walker St., next to Civic House hostel) is the only dive school with a five-star rating in Northern Queensland—super facilities and small classes. The diver training course consists of three days in the classroom pool and two days on the reef. At about $300, Mike Ball's course is more expensive than those in Cairns, but better quality. Call 077-72-3583 for details and try to book in advance.

The **Adventurer's Resort** also offers dive courses. Day trips to the reef aren't worth it from Townsville because companies such as Reef Link go to a spot where the reef is nearly dead—which is why the Four Seasons floating hotel is allowed there. It takes two hours to get to the reef, and the price isn't good, either. Save your reef trip for the Whitsundays, Cairns, or Port Douglas.

The **Barrier Reef Wonderland** on the marina is an essential stop, even for those with a moderate interest in the reef and its complex ecosystem. It houses the world's largest living coral reef aquarium, a museum, and theater with a variety of multimedia shows. The aquarium has a great display on the evolution and corals of the reef, as well as a history of scientific research on the reef. Entrance cost is high (about $9) but well-spent, and the aquarium is open daily 9:30am-5:00pm.

Castle Hill looms 300 meters above Townsville and affords a great view of Magnetic Island and the city. There's a trail to the summit. The **Panorama Restaurant**, halfway up, has a balcony where you can enjoy a nibble while taking in the scenery (closed Mon-Tue). If you don't feel like walking, the Explorer Bus Company and Pioneer Express run tours up the mountain.

Sundays there's a craft market on the mall 8:30am-12:30pm, with local art, crafts, and food.

Billabong Sanctuary, 17 km south of the city, is a wildlife preserve full of crocodiles, kangaroos, wombats, and other Aussie animals (open 9:00am-5:00pm daily; admission $9). If you don't have a car, there are half-day tours to Billabong (W-Sat). Call the Explorer Bus on 71-5024 for reservations.

Food

Finding a decent breakfast or lunch in Townsville is easy enough, but dinners often hurt the budget. The best bargain in the city is **Fast Food Chinese**, a take-out joint on Flinders St. East, where a good meal runs about $7. Carry your meal to the mall, where there are concrete tables and chairs with umbrellas.

If you need a carbohydrate fix, head to **Luvit's Pancake Restaurant and Coffee Shop** (205 Flinders St. East). Run by a Dutchman-turned-Australian, they have all kinds of pancakes filled with fruit, cheese, and meat. It's open 6:00am-9:00pm daily. For lunch try the **Metro Eastside Cafe** (235 Flinders St.), for pizzas or a quiche with hearty salad. At **Josch's** (on Flinders St. Central), curry or a steak sandwich in their outdoor courtyard is your best bet.

Nightlife and Entertainment

Three recommendations for nightlife are the **Criterion Hotel** (the "Cri") for drinking and hanging out (corner King St. and Flinders St. East); the **Crown Hotel** (Tomlins St., across the river), which sometimes closes off the street for outdoor festivities and has a live band on Sunday; and the **Terrace Nightclub and Cabaret** (corner Flinders and Wickham Sts.), which has a disco and, like most other nightclubs in town, a "come as you are" night on Sunday, with no dress code or cover charge (open nightly until 3:00am). For more extravagant entertainment, there's a casino in the **Sheraton Hotel** on Sir Leslie Thiess Dr. (the continuation of Flinders St. East). It's open until 2:00am most nights, later on weekends.

Trips from Townsville

You'll notice in advertisements around town that a few tour operators offer rafting trips down the Tully River from Townsville. The same companies offer the trip from both Mission Beach and Cairns, and since it's more expensive from Townsville, we suggest you wait until you're further north.

Charter Towers

Tourist Information, 61 Gill St., phone 077-87-1280.

About 135 km southwest of Townsville on the Flinders Hwy., Charters Towers was Queensland's most populous city, with over 30,000 inhabitants at the turn of the century. They were drawn by the largest gold source ever found in the state, and their legacy lives on in the form of beautifully preserved buildings.

If you visit, don't miss the **Venus Gold Battery** or the former **Stock Exchange**. The **National Trust Information Centre** is in the Stock Exchange Arcade (phone 077-87-2374), and they'll provide an orientation to the town, now a humble pastoral center of about 9,000.

Getting There: Buses run daily from Townsville. Inquire at Townsville tourist information for departure points and schedules.

Accommodation: The **Charters Towers Hostel** at 58 York St. (phone 077-87-1028) closes mid-December to late January.

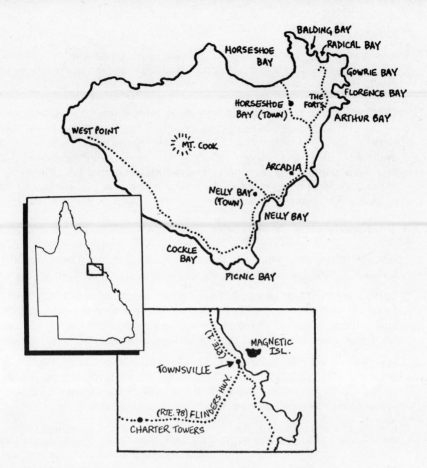

Magnetic Island

Just 8 km off the coast of Townsville, the suburb of Magnetic Island doubles as a mecca for hostellers. It's hard for backpackers to fathom that such a spectacular setting of rugged mountains and hidden bays is visited almost exclusively by budget travelers.

Getting There: Hayles Ferry departs 168-192 Flinders St. (cars) or the Breakwater Terminal on Sir Leslie Thiess Dr. (foot passengers). Call 71-7277 for information. It runs daily, and the last ferry over is in early evening. Most run to Picnic Bay, though some also go to Arcadia. The slow ferry takes 35 minutes. Westmark Ferry has extended evening service to Magnetic on Fri & Sat nights (phone 21-1913), departing from Reef Wonderland.

Orientation: Almost half of Magnetic Island is a national park, so all roads and other evidence of civilization are on the east and south coasts of the island. Picnic Bay, where the ferry arrives, is on the southernmost tip, and all hostels, stores, and activities are in Picnic Bay or the east coast settlements of Nelly Bay, Arcadia, and Horseshoe Bay. Keep in mind that distances on the island are too lengthy for walking, and, unless you're unusually fit, the mountains will present problems for bikers. Supplies are available in Picnic Bay and Arcadia.

Getting Around: Mokes are the preferred transport around Magnetic, and they're a must if you're on the island for only a day. Rent at the **Picnic Bay Jetty** (phone 78-5377) for about $35/day. Bicycles and motorcycles are also available. A bus meets Hayles and Westmark ferries in Picnic Bay all day Mon-Fri and until early afternoon on weekends (excluding the earliest boat of the day). Most buses cover all the island settlements, while a few go up to Radical Bay Resort (northeast tip of the island). Call 78-5130 for information.

Accommodation: Accommodation choices on Magnetic are plentiful and offer great value for money. A swimming pool is a big plus in summer, since box jellyfish prevent swimming in the ocean. All accommodations but the Camp Magnetic Hostel in Nelly Bay provide free pick-up from the jetty.

Backpacker's Centaur House, 27 Marina Pde., Arcadia (phone 077-78-5668). Dorms. Friendly atmosphere but a bit crowded. Free snorkeling equipment. Hilary, the manager, offers excursions to the local pub and the Forts at sunset; Frank gives fishing tours to backpackers. Central to hikes.

Magnetic Island YHA-Associate (Queensland Recreation Camp), Picnic Bay (phone 077-78-5280). $5.50/dorm bed, campsites available. Run by friendly family. Opossums eat from your hand and peek in the showers. $5 all-day island tour with excellent narration. Hostel open all day.

Geoff's Place, Horseshoe Bay (phone 077-78-5577). Campsites, cabins, chalets. On a large piece of land with woods and grass. Lots of travelers and somewhat impersonal. Swimming pool. Budget restaurant. Snorkel rental. A variety of freebies if you stay a few days. Every night there's an "Aussie Barbie" with steak, chicken, fish, and salads (about $7).

Magnetic Hideaway Hostel, 32 Picnic St., behind Picnic Bay Mall at jetty (phone 077-78-5110). Fans. TV.

Foresthaven, 11 Cook Rd., Arcadia (phone 077-78-5153). Dorms, 4- or 5-person units with kitchen. Bush setting. Units are generally intended for families or tour groups, but it's a good place to avoid the backpacking mob. Near public pool.

Camp Magnetic Hostel, Nelly Bay (phone 077-78-5151). Bush setting. Pool. Bike hire. All meals available.

Things to See and Do: Since much of Magnetic Island is inaccessible by motor vehicle, hiking is the only way to reach some of the best spots. There are 22 km of trails, leading through forests of eucalypt and hoop pine, up and down mountains, and to deserted beaches. Pick up hiking information at the kiosk near the ferry depot in Picnic Bay. Otherwise, the ranger station is on Hurst St. (end of Granite St.), and the office is open "whenever possible" on weekday afternoons.

For a great view and a chance to see koalas in the wild, hike to the **WWII command posts** from Horseshoe Bay Rd. The walk there and back takes 2 hours, and it's signposted from the road.

One fantastic way to see Magnetic is on horseback. **Horseshoe Ranch Trail Rides** (8 Gifford St., Horseshoe Bay; phone 78-5109 or 78-5439) offers guided rides (some overnight) for reasonable prices. Even the short rides go through a variety of terrain and end on a wide expanse of deserted beach where riders can take a swim with their horses. No riding experience is needed.

Radical Bay, Balding Bay, Florence Bay, Arthur Bay, and Nelly Bay are all fine for swimming, though not in summer. There's an enclosure at Picnic Bay to keep out the stingers. Florence Bay is the best place to surf, and Radical Bay has a low-key resort with hoards of rainbow lorikeets, a pleasant cafe, and a nice beach. Numerous water sports are available on the Horseshoe Bay beachfront at the boat ramp. You can also rent a 4-person power boat for fishing. For more information, call 78-5178 or 78-5169. Rent catamarans and sailboats at Nelly Bay on the beach next to Shark World (free lessons to beginners). **Shop 4** in Arcadia (phone 78-5799) offers diving trips and certification classes.

Townsville to Cairns

The 300 km coast between Townsville and Cairns is dotted with towns that provide access to rainforest, the reef, and beaches. Vast stretches of canefields intermingled with thick tropical forests give the coast a distinct, exotic flavor.

The former hippie colony Mission Beach is the primary destination in the area. Aside from being a wonderful little retreat in itself, Mission Beach gives access to national park forests, Tully, and Tully River rafting. Further south, Cardwell is the access point for Hinchinbrook Island, a must for anyone looking for a wilderness getaway.

Cardwell

A quiet seaside village, Cardwell hugs the shore opposite Hinchinbrook Island. While Cardwell is considered a departure point for the island, there are several interesting rainforest trips close by. The National Park Information Service in Cardwell (phone 070-66-8601) can help plan good bushwalks from the edge of town.

Cardwell is also convenient to **Edmund Kennedy National Park** (12 km north) where, in 1848, Edmund Kennedy organized an expedition to Cape York, during which 9 of the 12 explorers died. The park features mangroves, swamps, and pockets of rainforest. The park is inaccessible during the wet season.

The most important reason to stop in Cardwell is to get information, bookings, and permits for Hinchinbrook Island. The **Hinchinbrook Booking Office** is on 91 Bruce Hwy. across from the Seaview Cafe (phone 070-66-8539 or 66-8503).

Getting There: Cardwell is a regular stop on all Brisbane-Cairns bus services. Buses stop in front of the Seaview Cafe.

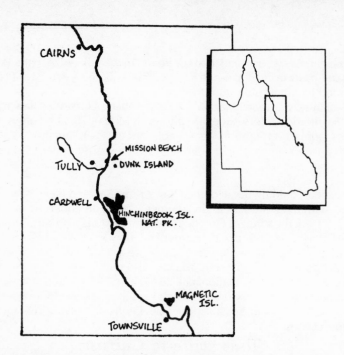

Accommodation: The **Backpackers Inn-Pacific Palms**, 186 Bruce Hwy. (phone 070-66-8671), is near the beach and has both twin and dorm rooms, plus tent sites and on-site vans. Rates start at $9/person for a dorm bed. Communal facilities include a kitchen, TV, BBQ, pool, and free bikes. Call from the bus stop for a ride.

There are 4 caravan parks in Cardwell, including the centrally located **Kookaburra Caravan Park** (phone 070-66-8648), which welcomes backpackers. All have on-site vans and self-contained units.

Hinchinbrook Island

Across a narrow channel from Cardwell, Hinchinbrook is the largest national park island in the world—374 square km of pristine beaches, towering mountains, and dense rainforests. Most of the island is undeveloped, with few roads and one resort on the northeast tip. The Barrier Reef is 15 km offshore, and fishing is excellent. There are several day tours to the island, but we recommend you camp overnight and really explore the reserve.

Hinchinbrook has several fantastic hikes. One leads to the 335 meter summit of **Granite Peak**, the highest point on the island. The eastern coast has a lovely trail down to **Zoe Bay**, where there's a waterfall. At **Ramsey Bay** you can see fossilized crabs, and at the **Mangrove Research Centre** there's a boardwalk over a sprawling entanglement of mangroves.

Getting There: The *Reef Venture* and the *Y-Not* depart every morning from the Cardwell jetty, and both offer ferry service or day cruises around the island. Make all bookings in Cardwell at the Hinchinbrook Booking Office.

Camping: Camping permits are available at the Hinchinbrook Booking Office in Cardwell. There are two campsites at the north end of the island. Get all information about the island in Cardwell before you leave, and *bring food and water!*

Tully

The small town of Tully, the rainiest spot in Australia, is surrounded by rainforest and sugar cane plantations. Although there aren't any good places to stay, the town is a destination for several trips from Mission Beach or Cairns—most notably rafting trips on the Tully River (see *Cairns* for further details). Other tours on the river take you fishing, canoeing, and rainforest-exploring, and they can be booked at the Mission Beach hostels or tourist office.

Mission Beach Coaches (phone 070-68-7273) runs a day trip from Mission Beach to the Tully Sugar Mill and a local cattle station. A day spent exploring these sites will help explain what's happening in those fields flanking the roads to Cairns and beyond. Don't miss these Tully-based activities, but stay in Mission Beach, which is better prepared for travelers.

Mission Beach
Tourist Information, phone 070-68-7187.

If you stop just once between Townsville and Cairns, stop here! Halfway between Townsville and Cairns, Mission Beach is a quiet community which began as an Aborigine mission and later became a center for 60's-style communes. The community now consists of "alternatives" and vacationers, but it's still not built up.

The town spreads along 8 km of undeveloped beach backed by lush rainforest, sugar cane fields, and fruit farms. The beach is almost deserted, and Dunk Island is only a hop away. Use Mission Beach as a base to explore Dunk Island, Edmund Kennedy National Park, and the rainforest around Tully. An added bonus is the fabulous YHA Treetops hostel.

Getting There and Getting Around: All major buslines stop in Mission Beach en route from Brisbane to Cairns. The Brisbane-Cairns train stops in Tully.

The only drawback to Mission Beach is that it's very spread out. The town is small, but accommodations are scattered all along the beach. Luckily, hitchhiking is common and it's easy to get a ride. The taxi phone is 68-8266, and you'll probably have to use it at some point.

Accommodation: There are two high quality hostels in the area, and the one you choose will depend on your priorities. Both are equally distant from town.

Treetops (YHA-Associate), North Mission Beach, Bingil Bay (phone 070-68-7137). $10/night. Small (24-bed) hostel. On 84 acres of rainforest. Built on stilts. A firm roof overhead, but most walls swing open for ocean breezes. Great ocean view from veranda, but a 15-minute walk to beach. Hostel provides bus service to the water taxi, The Hub, and the bus stop. Resident cassowary (rare bird, nearly the size of an emu). Horseback riding. Nature lovers should go out of their way to stay here.

Mission Beach Hostel, 28 Wongaling Beach Rd. (phone 070-68-8317). $10/night, dorm rooms. New, clean, and quiet. Across from Mission Beach resort, so you have a pub at night and can rent a tennis court or watersports equipment. 300 meters from beach and Dunk Island ferry, but no closer to town than Treetops. Setting is not nearly as impressive as Treetops.

Camping: There's a beautiful Town Council camping area on the beach just north of The Hub Shopping Centre in Mission Beach (100 meters from the bus stop). With your own tent, the cost for a site is $5/night. There are also cheap on-site vans.

Things to See and Do: Mission Beach has access to numerous inland and oceanside activities. First, some hiking suggestions: the **Kennedy Walking Track** in South Mission Beach follows Edmund Kennedy's route to Tam O'Shanter point. Another excellent rainforest walk begins across the road from the Mission Beach Hostel. (Ask the hostel manager to point you in the right direction.)

A variety of day trips could keep you occupied if you have the funds. **Floating Wilderness** (phone 68-6286) offers canoeing, fishing, and camping on the Tully River. Trips leave early, and there's pick-up in Mission Beach on request.

Cairns-based **Raging Thunder** and **Raft 'n Rainforest Co.** offer trips on the Tully River, and they pick up in Mission Beach (book at the hostels). Taking the trip from Mission Beach rather than Cairns saves about $10 (see *Cairns* for details).

On Friday, **Mission Beach Coaches** (phone 68-7273) has a trip to Murray Falls, a sugar mill, and a banana plantation. Clump Point (near the Hub and bus stop) is the departure point for boats to the reef and the resort island of Bedarra.

Dunk Island

Dunk Island is an easy and worthwhile day trip with plenty of hiking to keep you busy for a full day. The Aborigines called it "Coonanglebar" ("Isle of Peace and Plenty"), and, for the most part, the name still fits.

Aside from a resort complex on the southern tip, the island is a national park. 13 km of trails lead through eucalypt forest, secluded beaches, and the peak of **Mt. Koo-ta-loo**. The latter is an especially worthwhile hike, with a great view of the surrounding islands. The mountain hike takes two hours, while a hike including both Koo-ta-loo and beaches takes five.

Getting There: There are two major water taxi services. One departs from Wongaling (at Mission Beach Resort) five times a day, and the other from Clump Point Jetty, three times a day.

Accommodation: The resort is very nice, tucked away from the beach and camouflaged by pretty gardens. The resort is also very expensive. There is, however, camping at the southern tip of the island in a pine and eucalypt forest. It never gets too crowded because there are a limited number of permits, and the site is conveniently near the water taxi but hidden from crowds. Picnic tables and showers are a two-minute walk, at the resort waterfront complex. Obtain permits from the National Park Service at Mission Beach (phone 68-7183) or the Cardwell Information Center (phone 66-8601).

Cairns

Cairns, the unofficial capital of north Queensland, is a good-sized resort city on the verge of commercial explosion—but luckily for the budget traveler, it's not quite there yet. Cairns bustles with international travelers and offers loads of cheap accommodations and good deals, plus great partying for the hostel crowd.

The area is also renowned for world-class—and amazingly inexpensive—diving, and the game fishing, especially for black marlin, is also acclaimed. Just a few hours away lie the spectacular rainforests of the far north. In short, Cairns has so much to offer that travelers who get to Queensland would be crazy to miss it.

There isn't much to do in Cairns during the wet summer months from December to early April. The "wet" curtails several activities, including river rafting, swimming (because of stingers), and rainforest trips.

Getting There

All major bus companies run to Cairns from Brisbane (27 hours) and from Darwin/Mt. Isa. There's a special "Backpackers Int-X-Press" between Townsville and Cairns, offered through the Townsville International Backpackers. Call 077-72-4340 or 077-72-4366. Caper Fares are offered on the *Sunlander* and *Queenslander* trains from Brisbane.

Flights are available from all major Australian cities on Australian Airlines and Ansett. You can also fly to Cairns from the U.S. and from Port Moresby on Air Nuigini. For the Airport Bus, call 53-4722.

Orientation and Practical Information

Cairns is built in a simple grid, bounded by the Esplanade (along the waterfront) and the railroad lines at Water St. The Mall, at the intersection of Lake and Shield Sts., is two blocks from the water and, with the Esplanade, forms the center of activity in Cairns. Most boat launches depart from Wharf St.

You'll find that the most valuable source of information in Cairns is the local hostels, most of which provide bookings for excursions of all sorts. Since prices and offerings are constantly changing (sometimes daily), be alert to wharfside advertisements and ask advice from fellow travelers.

Important Addresses and Telephone Numbers (area code 070)

Cairns Convention and Visitors Bureau, 41 Shields St. (phone 51-7366). Tourist information, bookings, luggage storage, car and bike rentals.

Far North Queensland Promotion Bureau, corner Sheridan & Alpin Sts. (phone 51-3588). Tourist information.

General Post Office, corner Abbott & Spence Sts.

American Express, 91 Grafton St., P.O. Box 1625, Cairns, QLD, 4870 (phone 51-6472).

Queensland National Parks and Wildlife Service, 41 Esplanade (phone 53-4533 or 51-9811).

Railway Station, corner Shields & McLeod Sts. (phone 51-1111).

Coral Coaches, Tropical Paradise Travel, 25 Spence St. (phone 51-9533). Bus service to Port Douglas, Cape Tribulation, Mossman, Daintree, Bloomfield, and Cooktown.

Deluxe, Trinity Wharf (phone 31-2600), or "Welcome North Australia," City Place, 105 Lake St. (phone 50-5777).

Greyhound, City Arcade, 78 Grafton St. (phone 51-3131).

Pioneer Express, 58 Shield St. (phone 51-2411).

McCafferty's, Downunder Tours and Travel, 10E Shields St. (phone 51-5899).

Royal Automobile Club of Queensland (RAC), phone 51-6543.

Air Queensland, 60 Abbott St. (phone 50-4222).

Australian Airlines, corner Shield & Lake Sts. (phone 50-3777).

Ansett Airlines, 84 Lake St. (phone 50-2211).

Qantas, 13 Spence St. (phone 51-0100).

Transportation
Hostels, restaurants, nightclubs, and Marlin Jetty (the main dock) are all within easy walking distance of each other. Beach buses leave every hour from the mall (call 55-3709 for schedule information). **Wotan Moped Rental** is on Sheridan St. Taxis are available, but they're expensive and unnecessary.

Accommodation
There's more budget accommodation in Cairns than any other place in Queensland. It's literally stuffed with hostels. All those with Esplanade addresses will be rocking almost every night.

The Backpackers Inn, 255 Lake St. (phone 51-9166). Dorm beds and doubles. Free buses from town, or 15-minute walk. By far the quietest Backpackers hostel, but not much privacy. Gardens, swimming pool, large kitchen. Comprehensive booking office. Tours to Kuranda. Windsurfer and bike hire. The distance from town is the only drawback.

Action Backpackers, 93 The Esplanade (phone 31-1919). 6-8 person units with private bath and sink, doubles also. Very clean. Big communal kitchen. Comfortable common room with occasional movie nights. Weekly BBQ. Tour bookings. Highly recommended.

Jimmy's on the Esplanade, 83 The Esplanade (phone 51-5670). Dorms, doubles, and 4-bed rooms with private bathroom, kitchen. Outdoor picnic and lounge area. Swimming pool. Take-out food and travel service.

Cairns City International YHA, 85-87 The Esplanade (phone 51-2225). $12/dorm bed, $16/twin. Motel accommodation also available. Air conditioning or ceiling fans. Swimming pool. Travel agency.

Cairns YHA McLeod St., 20-24 McLeod St. (phone 51-0772). $10/dorm bed; $12/person double room; $16/single. Book ahead. Garden and pool. Excursion bookings.

International Youth Hostel, 67-69 The Esplanade (phone 31-1545). Swimming pool. TV lounge. Big kitchen. No rules or chores.

Caravella's Hostel, 77-81 and 149 The Esplanade (phone 51-2159 or 51-2431, respectively). Least friendly of area hostels, so avoid if possible. Swimming pool. Air conditioning available. Bike hire. Booking office.

The Reef Motel, 215 Abbott St. (phone 51-3540). Good option if you're fed up with the hostel scene. Very clean. Private bathroom in every room.

Things to See and Do

Cairns offers the cheapest rates and widest range of scuba diving courses to be found in Australia. Naturally, the Barrier Reef is where the action is for divers, and the best spots are on the outer reef, about three hours from Cairns by boat.

There are at least 7 dive operations in town. Beginners and certified divers have numerous options, and fierce competition keeps prices low. You can do a 5- or 6-day course for about $240 for 3 days in the classroom, then 2-3 days on the reef. Certified divers should be prepared to share any trip with a dive class, and beginners should know that there are so many people flooding the dive courses that safety standards may not be what they are in North America. Classes can run as large as 20 people.

Pro Dive (next to Marlin Jetty, phone 51-9915) is one of the best training schools, and their instructors are excellent and patient. They provide equipment and meals while you're on the boat. Pro Dive and others offer daily discounts, so keep your ears open.

There are also organized day trips for reef viewing, including snorkeling and glass-bottomed boat rides. The best trips are on the *Seastar* and *Quicksilver*; both can be booked through any hostel. If you plan to travel further north, however, save your reef viewing for Port Douglas, where more personalized trips are offered.

For beaches, head north. **Ellis Beach**, the nicest and most distant of the Cairns beaches, is 45 minutes away by bus (call 55-3709 for information).

The most accessible offshore islands are Fitzroy and Green, both full of tourists and not as nice as islands further south. We suggest going only if a stop is part of a package trip to the outer Barrier Reef. **Green Island** is a small coral cay with an underwater observatory, and if you don't plan to dive or snorkel during your stay, the observatory is interesting. Other tourist spots on the island, such as the **Marineland Melanesia** and **Barrier Reef Theatre**, aren't too thrilling. Snorkel rental is available and the beaches are nice.

Fitzroy Island has camping or 4-share cabins, plus cooking facilities, groceries, bush trails, a dive shop, and snorkel and canoe rental. For information, contact the **Fitzroy Island Resort** (at 51-0455 or 51-9588), Hayles Ferry, or any travel agent. **Hayles Ferry** (Wharf St., phone 51-0455) runs a few times daily to both Green and Fitzroy, and several of their launches stop on the way to the reef.

Further afield, two companies offer rafting trips down the Tully River. It's an excellent, hair-raising trip through dense rainforest—truly an adventure for the strong-hearted, especially when the river is swollen. Be prepared to fall out! Wait until the river is down if there's been considerable rain because, despite assurances of the guides, accidents do happen.

Raging Thunder (67 Grafton St., phone 51-4911) is the most popular company. It costs about $70 for a day of rafting, with transport, lunch, and dinner included. The **Raft 'n Rainforest Co.** (phone 51-4055, or after hours 55-1501) has a comparable trip, so look for the best price. Raft 'n Rainforest also offers extended rafting trips, trips to Barron River Falls, and rainforest camping in Palmerston National Park. About 30 km northwest of Cairns, Barron River Falls has mostly been diverted for a hydroelectric plant, but the 260-meter falls are nice anyway.

Mossman Gorge National Park/Daintree National Park is another popular destination, and trips leave both Cairns and Port Douglas (see *Port Douglas* section). Those planning an unguided trip north of Cairns should get all national park information in Cairns.

Keen fishermen should look into charter fishing off the shore of Cairns, reputed to have some of the best black marlin fishing in the world. Check the docks along Wharf St. and ask hostel agencies for charter options. The black marlin season is Sept-Dec.

Food

There's a variety of food in Cairns, everything from good fast-food to fancy seafood. Much of it is reasonably priced, so you won't be disappointed. Many of the take-out spots are on the Esplanade and they're pretty similar (fried foods, *dim sum*, pizza, etc.).

Backpacker's Restaurant, 25b Shield St. (in the Mall). Cheap all-you-can-fit-on-your-plate buffet, including of a variety of stews and pastas. Attractive and comfortable. Great value. Open 11:00am-midnight.

Lloyd's Corner Restaurant (BYO), Spence and Grafton Sts. (phone 51-2360). Indian/Italian (!) cuisine. Great use of local seafood, and superb pasta. Portions are so huge they feed two. Excellent pizza. Moderate to expensive.

Healthy Wealthy and Wise (no alcohol), Spence and Sheraton Sts. Hare Krishna's vegetarian chain. Special backpackers meal. Open daily 6:00pm-9:00pm. Cheap.

The Strand Bistro, half-block from Marlin Jetty, on the Esplanade. Has a veranda for sea breezes and a good view of The Esplanade. Good sandwiches. Open M-Sat 10:00am-10:00pm, Sun 11:00am-7:00pm.

Cockatoo's, Alpin St., off The Esplanade. Outside tables. Good jazz background music. Known for its large salads and quiches. No strict portion control, so you can serve yourself generously.

Nightlife

Nightclubs are where most of the "going out" action is in Cairns. Of the half-dozen clubs, most travelers go to either **The Playpen** (Lake & Hartley Sts.) or **The Nest** (82 McLeod St.). Dress codes are fairly strict, so don't wear sneakers or jeans. The Playpen has a casual, "come as you are" night on Sundays. Cover charge for most nightclubs is $7-$12.

There are a number of good pubs in town, but they're not frequented much by budget travelers. Travelers tend to drink at the Backpacker's Restaurant or in the hostels to save money for the nightclubs. However, if you're not into the nightclub scene, some of the pubs are quite good and popular with locals.

Oscar's Bar, in the Great Northern Hotel, 69 Abbott St. Live rock/jazz/blues 2-3 nights a week, and the crowd is fun.

The Strand Bistro, The Esplanade. Take your beer onto the veranda, which can accommodate large groups. Often filled with the scuba crowd from the Marlin Jetty.

Fitzgerald's Pub, Shield & Grafton Sts. Friendly atmosphere. Jazz Thurs, Aussie music Wed and Fri.

Trips from Cairns

Kuranda

The plateau northwest of Cairns, known as the **Atherton Tableland**, seems a world away from the heat and commercialization of the coast. Grazing pastures and fields of sugar cane, corn, and tobacco are nourished by rich, volcanic soil. The whole region was once covered by rainforest, only small pockets of which remain.

Kuranda, the main travelers' destination in the area, is 34 km northwest of Cairns. The trip there is worthwhile for the train ride alone. Ascending through thick rainforest and passing alongside the **Barron River Gorge**, the tourist train (which costs three times more than the regular train) stops for a view of the Barron River Falls. Usually, most of the water is diverted for hydroelectric power, but authorities channel it to the falls so tourists can enjoy it as the train chugs by. The Kuranda train station, built in 1915, seems more like a garden gazebo than a station.

A few minutes walk from the train station is the little town of Kuranda, worth an overnight stay. Try to be there for the market on Wed and Sun morning, when vendors sell exotic fruits, crazy t-shirts, Indonesian crafts, and jewelry.

Rainforest walks in the area are fantastic. (Beware of the directions in Mrs. Miller's hostel, which are inaccurate!) Walks to Jumrum Creek, Surprise Creek, and along Black Mountain Rd. are all nearby.

Two other Kuranda attractions are a Butterfly Sanctuary and a Noctarium. The **Butterfly Sanctuary** (Kennedy Hwy.) is expensive ($10; discount if you say you're from the hostel), but informative and beautiful. A huge glass and aluminum aviary is set amidst rainforest and gardens growing food for the butterflies. Guided tours run every hour from 10:00am-3:00pm daily. The **Noctarium** (8 Coondoo St.) features nocturnal animals indigenous to tropical Australia. It's open daily 10:00am-4:00pm and costs about $6.

Note: There are no banks in Kuranda.

Getting There: Make sure to take the local train rather than the tourist train. The local costs about $4; you'll spend $10 more to stop and take photos of Barron Falls. Sit on the right for the best views. Call 52-5222 in Cairns for schedules. The local doesn't run Sunday, but there's a bus that goes daily, departing from **Tropical Paradise Travel Centre** on 25 Spruce St. in Cairns.

Accommodation: Mrs. Miller's Hostel (6 Arara St.) announces itself on the approach to town with a huge billboard. While the setting for this YHA hostel is ideal, the establishment has degenerated lately. The men's dorm has no screens, so be prepared for mozzies, and the bunks are rickety. Plastered all over the buildings and grounds are little rules to abide by with the suffix "God Bless You, Love Mrs. Miller." Despite the quirks, the tropical garden setting couldn't be nicer, and there is a saltwater pool, TV and stereo, volleyball, and ping pong. Lights out at 10:00pm, though you can come in later. The hostel offers a mediocre dinner of salad, potatoes, and casserole or quiche. Call 070-93-7355 for bookings. Overnight cost is $11/person.

Cairns to Cooktown

The best part of Queensland lies north of Cairns, in the areas surrounding Port Douglas, Cape Tribulation, and Cooktown. Away from resorts and most of the trappings of civilization, these destinations offer a chance to experience jungle wilderness, unspoiled coast, and spectacular sections of the Great Barrier Reef.

Tourist season in the far north of Queensland is generally May-November (though flooding sometimes occurs on Cape York as late as May). Travel in December and April is possible for almost all destinations but uncomfortable because of extreme humidity and rain. January-March is very wet, and the most scenic territory is inaccessible. The far north, beyond Cooktown, is impossible to reach by road during the wet season.

You are now well into crocodile territory, so it's best not to wander off uninformed. Americans seem to have a real talent for stumbling across hungry crocs in the area. (A favorite local joke: *How do you separate two fighting*

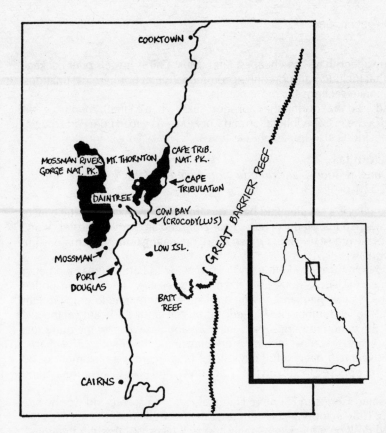

crocs? Throw 'em a Yank.) It's not as bad as it sounds, but pay attention to signs and local advice.

Getting There and Getting Around: If it's well into the dry season and you can afford it, rent a 4WD. The driving is exhilarating and unique, and the car gives you the flexibility to visit areas impossible to reach otherwise. There are a number of 4WD rental companies in Cairns charging as little as $70/day. Don't bother renting a regular car, because to get the most out of a trip you have to follow unpaved coastal routes, which are mostly for 4WD vehicles. (The exception is the Port Douglas-Cape Tribulation road in dry season.) A paved road goes inland directly to Cooktown, bypassing Cape Tribulation— but it skips the fun part.

If you can't afford a 4WD, **Coral Coaches** runs from Cairns to Port Douglas and Cape Tribulation, Mossman, Daintree, Bloomfield, and Cooktown on the scenic coastal route (except during the wet). They pick up at many hostels, and their Cairns depot is 25 Spence St. at Tropical Paradise Travel (phone 070-51-9533). **Pioneer Express** also has a daily service to Port Douglas and Cape Tribulation, with package deals that include accommodation at the Jungle Lodge in Cape Trib. They also take a direct inland route from Cairns to Cooktown.

It's easiest to book bus transport through your hostel in Cairns, and hostel booking agents have the cheapest fares. Most Cairns hostels offer package deals that include transport and accommodation at northern destinations. See separate sections for more details.

Be advised that during the monsoon season (Jan-March), road access is limited between Cape Tribulation and Cooktown. The road from Port Douglas to Cape Trib is also impassable at times.

Port Douglas
Port Douglas Tourist and Information Centre, 27 McRossan St. (phone 070-99-3211 or 99-3362).

Port Douglas is a smaller, laid-back version of Cairns, with a terrific beach, lots of watersports, plenty of pub socializing, and an excellent hostel. "Port" is one of the oldest towns in Queensland, pre-dating Cairns as a major shipping port.

The offerings for snorkeling and reef-viewing in Port Douglas are better than those in Cairns, though slightly more expensive. The reef is unspoiled and close to the mainland, giving day-trippers more time to enjoy it. Further, passenger numbers are limited, so you can enjoy the beauty of the reef with some tranquility. Trips leave the Port Douglas wharf to the outer reef and Low Isles, and most include snorkeling and coral-viewing. The charter boat *Wavelength* offers a full day on the outer reef for a maximum of 20 people (as opposed to 200 on the *Quicksilver*) and goes to an unfrequented area.

Mossman Gorge, in Daintree National Park, is a scenic and worthwhile day trip. Though tours are offered, you might as well hop the Coral Coaches bus and do it on your own. A rainforest trail takes you through the gorge, and at the end of the dry season you can climb the gorge walls from the riverbed.

Another hike near the Port Douglas hostel is the **Mowbray Falls** walk. Borrow a map from the hostel and rent a bike to reach the trail. The 6-hour walk takes you through rainforest to a swimming hole and, after a precarious climb over rocks, a lovely waterfall.

In addition to activities away from town, there are beautiful beaches in the region and an exotic Sunday morning market in the park, near the wharf museum.

Getting There: Coral Coaches goes from Cairns to Port Douglas a few times daily. Pioneer Express also has a daily service.

Accommodation: The **Port Douglas Traveler's Hostel** (111 Davidson St., phone 070-98-5200) is a 20-minute walk from town and certainly worth the effort. The common room/kitchen is a huge two-tiered, open air affair that allows a much-needed breeze to ventilate the building. The dorm rooms are immaculate, and the staff is eager to help.

If the hostel is full, there are a number of mid-priced motels in town. Try the **Port Douglas Motel** on Davidson St. (phone 070-98-5248).

Cape Tribulation

Once the most idyllic spot in Queensland, Cape Tribulation is fast becoming overrun with visitors. Nonetheless, the natural beauty of the Cape Trib area is overwhelming. It offers gorgeous beaches and adventurous hikes through the Daintree Rainforest, where several unique plants are among the most primitive on earth. The tropical rainforest grows to the edge of the beach— an unusual sight which should not be missed. Diving and snorkeling are also fabulous, especially around Undine and Mackay Cays. Be wary of stingers Nov-March (some years earlier or later), as well as crocs near the river mouths.

While the renowned **Jungle Lodge** hostel is near the township, we urge you to consider **Crocodylus Village**, about 30 km south in Cow Bay. Crocodylus offers the chance to see the area as it should be seen, in a completely untouched, natural setting. It's an absolute must for anyone venturing to northern Queensland.

Note: Cape Trib doesn't have a bank, but hostels accept credit cards and travelers checks.

The **Daintree Rainforest** spreads from the Thornton mountain range to the edge of the Coral Sea. In 1984, developers cleared a 4WD track through the forest from Cape Trib to Bloomfield, prompting enormous controversy. Conservationists believed the construction would upset the ecological balance of the Daintree, destroying one of the last rainforests of its kind. The developers got their way but, ironically, the road is barely passable much of the time because monsoons wash it out every wet season. While Cape Tribulation National Park is otherwise undeveloped, there are several walking trails through.

There's a daily rainforest/reef trip organized through the **Cape Trib Shop**, which provides a glimpse of each, emphasizing snorkeling. The tour leaves from Cape Trib Beach, in walking distance of Jungle Lodge. Crocodylus also offers superb snorkeling trips and rainforest walks, plus a 3-day climb to Mt. Thornton. Jungle Lodge has rainforest walks and a horseback trip. While you can do bushwalks on your own, horse-riding in the forests and along the beach is definitely worth the fee. Trips go daily. Scuba courses weren't available when we visited, but they would be worth checking out if offered, since nearby reefs are unspoiled.

Getting There: Coral Coaches runs two or three times daily to Cape Tribulation and drops off at Mason Store. Ask at Cairns hostels about package deals on a sailing excursion from Cairns to Cape Trib, with accommodation at a new hostel.

Cape Trib is accessible by conventional vehicle except during the wet (Jan-March), when the road between the Daintree ferry and Cape Trib is sometimes closed due to flooding. However, 4WD vehicles usually make it through. The ferry man at the Daintree river crossing will advise you. The 32 km of unpaved road between the ferry and Cape Trib is one of the most scenic in Australia, passing through thick rainforest.

Accommodation: Both the Jungle Lodge and Crocodylus (run by YHA) are 5-star hostels, and we think Crocodylus is the best hostel in Australia. Travelers often assume that the Jungle Lodge is for partiers and Crocodylus is for nature lovers, but Crocodylus has its share of great parties, too.

At **Crocodylus**, you stay in timber huts with fabric roofing, modeled after an African safari camp. The huts blend into surrounding jungle, where the noise of critters (everything from snakes to brush turkeys) is a constant background. Nearby is a beautiful beach, all around are trails through the forest, and there's a swimming pool. Dorm beds cost $12; self-contained units are a few more dollars. The hostel's restaurant serves excellent, cheap meals, but you can also cook yourself. Trips offered through the hostel are all good deals. Package deals that include all meals and transport from Cairns are available from Down Under Tours. Book at any Cairns hostel, or call 070-51-4911 or 070-98-9166. The hostel is about 30 km south of Cape Tribulation and 30 km north of the Daintree Ferry in Cow Bay (phone 070-31-2772). There's a shuttle twice daily from the Daintree Ferry (call ahead for times).

The **Jungle Lodge** (phone 070-53-6500 in Cairns) is about 3 km south of Cape Trib in a cleared forest, a short walk from Myall Beach. It has a rowdy, resortish atmosphere and, though the facilities couldn't be better, the place can become a zoo. There is a pool area and patio, and a great bar with late-night dancing and excellent music. The Lodge has its own power generator, which shuts down every night at 10:30pm, so bring a flashlight. It costs $12/night in dorms, and when it gets crowded there's a 3-night limit. They serve a great dinner, and fruit-tasting down the road is at 4:00pm every day but Sunday, featuring scrumptious tropical fruits. For package deals that include transport from Cairns and a few nights of accommodation, inquire at Cairns hostels or call 070-51-6135 in Cairns.

Since we visited, the increasing popularity of Cape Trib for hostellers has prompted the opening of another **YHA Hostel** with 150 beds. It's located at the corner of Avalon St. and Cape Tribulation Rd. (phone 070-51-2225 or 51-0772 in Cairns).

Cooktown

Sea Museum and Tourist Information Centre, Walker St., phone 070-69-5209.

Captain Cook beached the *Endeavour* for repairs on the coast near present-day Cooktown (hence the town's name). Nearly 100 years later, the discovery of gold at the head of the Palmer River put Cooktown on the map. Though it was once among the largest cities in Queensland, today it's a tiny, charming town, barely resembling its 19th-century roots.

The most northern outpost of civilization on the Cape, Cooktown is the access point for safaris into the tropical wilderness further north. Even if you're not planning a wilderness trek, it's great place to hang out for a few days. Cooktown offers scuba diving and fishing, museums, and a number of good walks through town and its outskirts. One main strip houses all the shops and eateries, as well as the bank and post office.

Getting There: Strikie's Feral Safaris (see below) offers the most exciting transport between Cape Trib and Cooktown, well worth the cost. Coral Coaches also runs the route three times a week. If you're driving yourself, try to take the coastal route between Cape Trib and Cooktown (4WD necessary). It's closed for months at a time due to muddy conditions, but when open it's a never-to-be- forgotten experience. During the wet and shoulder seasons, you must use a paved inland route from Port Douglas (you have to backtrack from Cape Trib). Pioneer Express and Greyhound use an inland route from Cairns.

Otherwise, hop a boat from Cairns or Port Douglas to Cooktown. The *Sundancer, M.V. Quicksilver,* and *2001* are advertised at most travel agents.

Accommodation: The **Backpackers Hostel** on Charlotte St. (phone 070-69-5166) is immaculate. Peter and Jan, the owners, are among the friendliest and most helpful hostel managers around (and Peter's pet kangaroo hops around the grounds as if he owns the place). The hostel also has the best swimming pool in all of hosteldom. Bugs are bad and Cooktown gets exceedingly hot, so sleeping isn't the best. Other possibilities:

Cooktown Motor Inn, Charlotte St. (phone 070-69-5357). All rooms have private bathrooms, some have air conditioning.

Hillcrest Holiday Lodge, Hope St., at foot of Grassy Hill (phone 070-69-5305). Common sitting room with exotic fish tanks and tropical decor. Swimming pool. Pool table.

Things to See and Do: The hike up **Mt. Cook** begins near the hostel. It's three hours roundtrip (fairly strenuous ascent), with superb views of the coast. If you have a car and want more views, the lookout at **Grassy Hill** is a 10-minute drive from town. From there you get a panorama of the coastline and sailboats dotting the shore of Cooktown. For an interesting glimpse into Cooktown's history, wander through the **cemetery**, and the **James Cook Historical Museum** has an excellent exhibit on Captain Cook's career.

Nearby **Cherry Hill Beach** is about as beautiful as a beach gets. Offshore trips from Cooktown include fishing and snorkeling expeditions, most of which are more expensive than those in Cape Trib. One laid-back but excellent operation is **Sharkey's Great Barrier Reef Adventures** (phone 51-0731). Lance (the owner, a Californian) will design whatever trip you want: scuba diving, snorkeling, or fishing.

The hostel can book a variety of 4WD tours and river trips. One of the best tour operators (and a genuine "Crocodile Dundee" character) is Bill Strikie of **Strikie's Feral Safaris**. Among his trips is a 4WD trek from Cooktown to Cape Trib. Book through the hostel or call 070-55-4700 in Cairns.

Food: Cooktown has quite a few cafe-style restaurants and markets on Charlotte St. For breakfast, try a fresh roll from the **Cooktown Bakery. The Galley** offers a good, cheap lunch (sandwiches, burgers, and chicken curry). The best dinner spot is the new section of the "middle" pub in the **West**

Coast Hotel. (There are only three pubs in Cooktown, known as the "top," "middle," and "lower.")

Cape York

The far northern tip of Queensland, a virtually untouched wilderness, is accessible only in the dry season, when deciduous vines shed their leaves and transform the rainforest into a wet desert.

Obtain all information on national parks and independent travel in the region in Cairns.

The trip to the tip of Cape York is forbidding to the average adventurer, as even the best 4WD vehicles can't get through much of the boggy terrain. Unless you have detailed knowledge of such climates, a guided 4WD safari is the only way to go. **Cape York Frontier Adventures** offers the best price (about $1,000 for a 15-day tour) and caters to the budget crowd. Their trips go all the way to the tip, with an optional Thursday Island visit. Tours run late May to early December, every 15 days. Inquire at Cairns hostels, the Jungle Lodge in Cape Trib, the Cairns Convention and Visitors Bureau, or write Cape York Frontier Adventures, PO Box 6883, Cairns Mail Centre, QLD 4871 (phone 070-57-7366).

Outback Queensland

Two-thirds of Queensland is covered by the **Western Plains**. Fed by an artesian water supply, the fertile plains become more arid as you travel inland, giving way to "channel country" and the **Simpson Desert** of the southwest, where temporary lakes and streams flow once a year, if that. Northwest Queensland is virtually deserted (except for Mt. Isa) and not too inviting for the inexperienced traveler.

If you're planning a trip from Queensland to the Northern Territory, there's no better way to sample outback life than to stop at a few settlements along the way. The highways from Brisbane and Rockhampton to the N.T. take you through Carnarvon Gorge, the gemfields around Emerald, and Longreach. All roads go through Mt. Isa. (See *Trips from Brisbane* for specifics about Carnarvon Gorge, and *Trips from Rockhampton* for specifics about Emerald.)

Birdsville, in the southwest corner of the state, is completely off the beaten track. The head of the Birdsville Track, it was once a crucial byway for cattle and supplies going between southwest Queensland and Marree, South Australia.

There are YHA and YHA-Associate hostels in Sapphire (near Emerald), Longreach, and Mt. Isa.

Mt. Isa

Tourist Information Centre, Centenary Park, phone 077-43-7966.

The town of Mt. Isa arises from nowhere, a land of seemingly endless red desert and rock outcrops. Some 26,000 people have chosen to civilize this small corner of nowhere because they're atop one of the richest stores of silver, lead, copper, and zinc in the world. **Mt. Isa Mines Ltd.** operates the largest single mine of silver and lead on the globe and is one of the world's top producers of copper and zinc.

Tours of the mines run twice each weekday. They last two hours and are certainly a must, but you have to book far in advance during tourist season (April-Sept), especially during school holidays. Contact Tourist Information.

Copper City Tours offers safaris to the outback from Mt. Isa; contact Campbell's Coaches at 43-2006 and Tourist Information. Mt. Isa is also home to Australia's largest annual **rodeo** (third largest in the world, locals claim), held in August.

Getting There: All major bus companies have service from Townsville. Greyhound also runs from Brisbane via Longreach three times a week. The *Inlander* train operates twice weekly from Townsville. Australian Airlines and Ansett fly into Mt. Isa.

To get to Mt. Isa on your own, take the Flinders Hwy. from Townsville (880 km) or the Landsborough Hwy. from Longreach (734 km).

Accommodation: The **YHA-Associate Hostel** in Mt. Isa is on Wellington Park Road opposite the Velodrome (phone 077-43-5557). It's open all day and costs $8/night. Another option is the **Silver City Lodge** (105 East St., phone 43-3297), a combination hostel/lodge that hosts local workers and travelers. Rooms have bunks, air conditioning, 'fridge, and TV, and they're all twins ($10/night). There are kitchen facilities and BBQs. They provide transport from the local bus and train terminals.

Longreach

The original Qantas hangar in Longreach, Australia's first aircraft factory, still functions. (Trivia buffs note: Qantas is an acronym for "Queensland and Northern Territory Aerial Services.") A big draw to this outback town is the **Stockman's Hall of Fame**, a bicentennial project glorifying the pioneers of the outback, with an art gallery, library, museum, and theater. The undertaking cost $11 million dollars, raised in a nationwide campaign. If cost and effort is any indication, it should be a great success.

Getting There: Greyhound goes to Longreach from Rockhampton three times a week, and a train runs almost daily from Rockhampton. Longreach is also accessible by car from Roma, 700 km southwest.

Accommodation: The **Longreach YHA Hostel** is at 120 Galah St. (phone 074-58-1529). Cost is $9/person. Overnight tours in the outback available.

Birdsville

Situated in the upper southwest corner of Queensland at the start of the famed Birdsville Track, amidst desert sand dunes and clumps of spinifex grass, the town of Birdsville has an old pub and a population of 30. It was established in the 1880's as a point for the collection of customs duties on goods from South Australia—a practice ended by federation in 1901.

See more on traveling the Birdsville Track in the *Outback South Australia* chapter.

Victoria

The most compact and urbanized Australian state, Victoria is the second smallest (about 3% of the country's total area) and the second most populous, with over 25% of the nation's population. Victorians, however, don't like to think of themselves as "second" on other scales, and Melbournians in particular view their part of the country as the center of action.

Their pride is well-founded historically. For much of the 19th century, Melbourne was Australia's most prominent city. It still vies with Sydney for dominance in finance and the arts. Victorians are known also for their adherence to Anglo traditions and old-fashioned notions of class. Old money and a proper education determine who belongs to the elite.

Nonetheless, Victoria's ethnic diversity is tremendous. Melbourne, in fact, has the largest Greek population outside Athens. The so-called "new" immigrants (Greeks, Italians, Indians, and Vietnamese, to name a few) are slowly but surely changing the face of Victorian society.

Victoria's countryside is some of the most lush and beautiful in Australia: small-scale farms and quaint farmhouses; several mountain ranges, including the Victorian Alps, the Dandenongs, the Mornington Peninsula, the Otway Ranges, and the Grampians; and prolific vegetation, with some of Australia's tallest forests. The most breathtaking scenery of all, however, is along the coast, where mountains and sea clash to form a rugged coastline of beaches backed by cliffs and other striking formations. It's a truly magnificent part of Australia which, happily, is not overwhelmed by tourism.

When to Go
Victoria is one of the best places to dodge Australia's summer heat. Victorian summers (Jan-Feb) are dry and clear. And while hot at times, cool changes bring the temperature down as much as 9°F every few days. Winter is chilly and often overcast or rainy, and snow buries the tops of the Great Dividing Range (Victorian Alps) for most of July and August.

Itinerary
Almost all of Victoria's best spots are in striking distance of Melbourne. Depending on where you're arriving from, make a special effort to see the Grampians (western Victoria), Beechworth (northeast Victoria), or the Great Ocean Road (southwest coast).

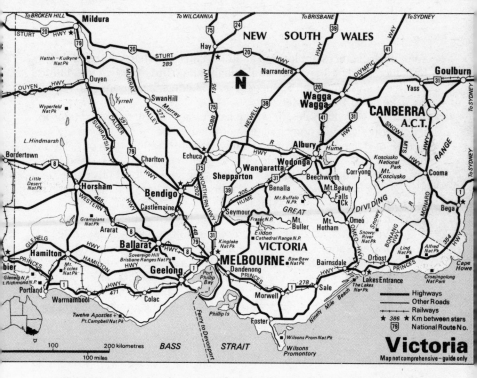

The Grampians mountain range is arguably the best place in the country to see kangaroos and koalas in the wild. Beechworth is a former gold boom-town with a fantastic YHA hostel and access to the Victorian Alps, the Rutherglen wine region, and the Murray River. The Great Ocean Road borders spectacular ocean cliffs and shoreline formations, the best of Victoria's "must sees."

Melbourne is known for historic architecture, stately gardens, and ethnic local color—gauge the amount of time you allot to Melbourne by your interest in these. You can't take all of the great trips from Melbourne in one visit. Our favorites are Healesville Sanctuary (a wildlife refuge in Healesville, an hour north of the city), Emerald (a village in the Dandenong hills with a memorable hostel), and Ballarat (one of Victoria's original gold towns, where a replica called Sovereign Hill recreates life at the height of the gold rush). Melbourne's beach retreats are plentiful and include Phillip Island, home of the fairy penguins, who attract more international visitors than anything else in the state.

Getting Around

Victoria is small and compact, making it much more manageable for travelers than other states.

Transport is provided primarily by **V/line**, the state-run rail service, which operates buses and trains, and you'll find yourself switching from one to the other for many destinations. V/line offers many deals worth investigating, including a two-week train pass, biking tours, and other excursions. V/line's central travel offices are located at 589 Collins St., where all schedules, information, and bookings are available (phone 03-619-1500, or 008-13-6109 toll-free within Victoria). Spencer St. and Flinders St. Stations also have information and booking services.

As in New South Wales, licensing laws protect the state-owned transportation system. At this point, using interstate buslines such as Deluxe, Greyhound, or Pioneer isn't an option unless you are traveling from out-of- state, have a bus pass, or are going to places where V/line doesn't go (and V/line goes almost everywhere buses go). There are several local bus companies that complement V/line services; if V/line doesn't have the information on them, YHA's travel service will.

When you're pondering how to get from one place to the next, don't bother asking Victour, the state-run tourist commission, for advice. Ask instead at **V/line Travel** (address above) or better yet, go to **YHA Travel** at 205 King St. in Melbourne (phone 03-670-7991). YHA's travel agents are knowledgeable and helpful. Hours are M-F 9:00am-5:00pm, Sat 9:00am-noon.

And don't overlook the tours offered by YHA Travel, which are inexpensive and well-organized. They also have some great camping trips under a program called "Portable Hostels."

Plane travel isn't necessary for a state as small as Victoria, but you can find good deals on flights from Melbourne or Phillip Island to Tasmania.

Attention drivers! In Victoria, cars turning left give way to those turning right (across the traffic). Driving in Melbourne entails maneuvering around tramlines. See below for special traffic laws.

Information

Tourist information resources aren't great but, luckily, there aren't too many tricks to traveling around Victoria.

Victour (230 Collins St., phone 619-9444), the government's tourist organization, is not very forthcoming with information on transportation, and the small Melbourne office is overcrowded and understaffed. Victour is, nonetheless, the best place to find information on various regions in the state.

YHA Travel has far more comprehensive transport information, plus an understanding of what it means to travel on a tight budget. It's a full-fledged travel agency, with booking services and information on travel throughout the country.

Local tourist offices tend to be part of retail stores, so weekend hours are limited to Sat morning.

Accommodation

Though a few Backpackers hostels have appeared in popular spots like Ballarat and Phillip Island, most hostels are run by YHA. There are about 20 YHA and YHA-Associates in the state, ranging from five-star quality to, er, rustic. Both YHA Travel and **YHA of Victoria** are at 205 King St. in Melbourne (phone 03-670-7991). Hours are weekdays 9:00am-5:00pm, Sat 9:00am-noon.

Officially, YHA of Victoria does not take phone bookings. They ask you to write ahead or pay and book from another YHA hostel, but if neither is possible, it won't hurt to phone. The hostels are promoted heavily locally, so during school and public holidays be sure to reserve. Baw Baw and Mt. Buller hostels need to be booked months ahead for ski season (June-Oct).

Caravan parks with on-site vans and camping areas are plentiful. Some Bed & Breakfasts on farms are inexpensive and a great way to meet locals. **Victorian Farm Holidays** publishes a directory, available at Victour, and you can book through Victour as well.

Hiking and Skiing

Victoria's numerous opportunities for hiking and skiing deserve clarification. First, your best resource is **Victoria's Dept. of Conservation, Forests, and Lands** (CFL) at 250 Victoria Pde. in East Melbourne. To help you decide where to go, **Information Victoria** at 318 Little Bourke St. has great picture books and information on all the scenic regions of the state. They also have topographical maps, as does the CFL bookstore.

Victorians love to hike, and they do it both on a casual basis in the state's many small reserves and more seriously in the Victorian Alps, the Grampians, the Otways, and Wilson's Promontory. The Mornington Peninsula, the Dandenongs, and the foothills of the Great Dividing Range (all a short distance from Melbourne) provide many opportunities for day hikes and strolling.

Victoria's best downhill skiing is found in the Victorian Alps, at Hotham or Falls Creek; closer to Melbourne in the southern Alps are Buller and Mansfield mountains. Cross-country skiing, possible at any of those resorts, is also good on Mt. Buffalo, Rawson, Baw Baw, and Mt. Donna Buang (outside Warburton in the Dividing Range foothills). Ski season is June-Oct, but mid-July through August is the most reliable time for snow.

History

Britain's original attempts to settle the area grew from fear that the French might capture Australia's southern coast first. The settlements—at Sorrento (Port Phillip Bay) in 1803 and at Corinell (Western Port Bay) in 1826—were both abandoned, and the idea of a convict outpost on the continent's southeast coast was all but forgotten.

As pastoralists from Van Dieman's Land began to look to the mainland for grazing, the first permanent settlement formed. Eventually, the British acknowledged these squatters and established a government in Melbourne. Convicts arrived in the late 1840's, and when gold was discovered in 1851, the population and the economy boomed. The gold rush brought an estimated 40,000 Chinese, among others. 1851 was also the year that the Port Phillip colony separated from New South Wales and became Victoria.

By the 1860's, Victoria's population leaped ahead of New South Wales. Melbourne was Australia's largest city and the center of most business activity through the 1880's, when many of today's architectural masterpieces were constructed. By the end of that decade, however, a depression hit Melbourne hard, and Sydney became Australia's top city.

Melbourne remains a major financial, manufacturing, and cultural center, while dairy and wool industries, fruit and vegetable cultivation, and coal mining form the basis of Victoria's economy.

Melbourne

According to some Aussies, Melbourne's mostly non-convict heritage makes it inherently snobby. (They forget that the first settlers were squatters from Tasmania.) The city does hold its head rather high. The annual Melbourne Cup (horse race) is a classy affair, and certain Melbournians don't let you forget that Prince Charles was graduated from Geelong Grammar, a nearby boarding school. With its English gardens, ornate Victorian facades, and intellectual pride, Melbourne is tenaciously upper-crust British in many respects.

But there's a flip side. Aussie-rules football originated in Melbourne, and the VFL (Victorian Football League) final is the state's most important day of the year. Further, the city's Asian and southern European populations have a growing influence on the city's culture and outlook.

You'll be pleasantly surprised by Melbourne if you visit in summer, especially if you've heard the snide comments of Sydneysiders. Victoria's summer is dry and clear, with regular "cool changes"—idyllic compared to Sydney's humidity. There's lots to see in the Melbourne area in summer, too, including gorgeous mountain areas and beaches (see *Trips from Melbourne* below). Winter is, true to reputation, cold and rainy. However, historic and architectural monuments in the city are a compelling reason to go, regardless of the season or circumstance.

Getting There

All major buslines service Melbourne. The trip is 10 hours from Adelaide, 13 hours from Sydney, 28 hours from Brisbane, and 45 hours from Perth.

Interstate trains from all major cities arrive at Spencer Street Station, and Caper Fares are available between Melbourne-Sydney and Melbourne-Adelaide. For interstate or Victorian train information in Melbourne, call V/line Travel at 03-619-1549 8:30am-5:00pm weekdays (after hours 03-619-1500). If you're calling long-distance within Victoria, the toll free number is 008-13-6109. V/line Travel is located at 589 Collins St.

You can fly into Melbourne from all over the world or any major Australian city. To get to the city from Tullamarine Airport, use **Skybus Coach Service** (phone 663-1400). The trip is about 30 minutes, so, if possible, avoid taxis.

Orientation and Practical Information

Downtown is defined by Victoria Pde. to the north, the Yarra River to the south, Spencer St. to the west, and Spring St. to the east. The section of Bourke St. that runs between Elizabeth and Swanston Sts. is a pedestrian mall, and **City Square** (Swanston St. between Collins and Flinders Sts.) serves as a focus of commercial and social activity. Most of Melbourne's smart boutiques and high-class hotels line **Collins St.** The western end of Collins St. is the financial center, with the stock exchange and major banks. An ornate arch across Little Bourke St. marks **Chinatown**.

The **University of Melbourne** is north of downtown, in the suburbs of Parkville and North Melbourne. **Carlton**, also immediately north, is an Italian neighborhood with the best street cafes in the city and frequent outdoor

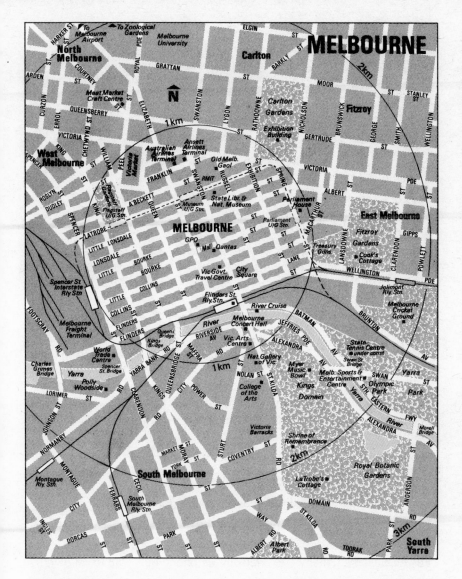

festivals. Southeast of downtown are the tony areas of **Toorak** and **South Yarra**, also good for eating and cafe-hopping. **South Melbourne**, predominantly Greek, is offbeat and artsy. **St. Kilda**, the hub of nightlife, borders Port Phillip Bay, where the palm-lined shore and ocean breeze is a welcome contrast to downtown.

Important Addresses and Telephone Numbers (area code 03)

Victorian Tourism Commission Travel Centre, 230 Collins St. (phone 619-9444). Information on Melbourne and Victorian destinations. No transport information. Tourist officers are hurried and impatient, and the place is cramped, but it has the best stock of brochures.

Victoria Information Centre, 318 Little Bourke St. Publications for sale on every aspect of Victoria, including beautiful picture books and topo maps. Information on camping and national parks.

General Post Office, corner Elizabeth St. and Bourke St. Mall.

U.S. Consulate, 24 Albert Rd., South Melbourne (phone 699-2244).

American Express, 105 Elizabeth St., GPO Box 5450, Melbourne, Vic., 3001 (phone 602-4666).

YHA of Victoria, 205 King St. (phone 670-7991). Memberships, travel agency, excellent information on getting around Victoria. Open M-F 9:00am-5:00pm, Sat 9:00am-noon.

Department of Conservation, Forests, and Lands (CFL), 250 Victoria Pde., East Melbourne (phone 412-4011). Victoria's National Parks department. Information on national parks and hiking in Victoria. Book shop at 240 Victoria Pde. sells topo maps.

STA Travel, 220 Faraday St. (phone 347-6911), Head Office. Or 1/F Union Bldg., University of Melbourne.

Royal Automobile Club of Victoria (RACV), 422 Little Collins St. (phone 607-2137 or 607-2211), or 550 Princes Hwy., Noble Park (phone 790-2211).

V/Line Travel (State Transit Authority, or STA), 589 Collins St. (phone 62-0771 for bookings, 62-3115 or 008-13-6109 for information). Information and bookings for all state-run train and bus services in Victoria, and interstate trains.

Suburban transport information: phone 619-0900.

Deluxe, 58 Franklin St. (phone 663-6144).

Greyhound, corner Franklin and Swanston Sts. (phone 668-2666).

Pioneer Express, corner Franklin and Swanston Sts. (phone 668-3144 or 668-2422).

Bus Australia/McCafferty's, 97 Franklin St. (phone 662-2788 or 63-9595).

Australian Airlines: phone 665-1333.

Ansett Airlines: phone 668-1211.

Air New Zealand: phone 654-3311.

Qantas: phone 602-6026.

United: phone 602-2544.

Taxis: phone 417-1111 or 347-5511.

Emergency: phone 000.

Transportation

Though it's the best way to get around downtown, walking in Melbourne can be a hazard to your health if you're not wary. Silent trams hum through the pedestrian mall, which can be quite a shock to tourists who assume they don't need to look before crossing. Also, there are no crosswalks that give pedestrians the right-of-way over cars, as in other Australian cities.

The "Met" (Metropolitan Transport Authority) runs all city and suburban transport, including trains, trams, and buses. Tram is the primary mode of transportation, and the Met distributes pamphlets with all specific tram routes, as well as publications on train and bus networks. They are available at a kiosk in the shopping complex behind Flinders St. Station (corner Flinders and Swanston Sts.), tram and bus depots, the Royal Arcade Kiosk, and an information office at 673 Bourke St. You can also call 619-0900 for general transport information. Suburban trains leave Flinders St. Station; most V/line country and interstate services depart Spencer St. Station.

A basic Met ticket allows two hours of travel on any kind of transport, priced according to distance zones. There are all kinds of tickets deals, from an all-day ticket to a "city saver" ticket for inner city travel. Fares range from $1-$6, and you buy tickets on trams and buses. Public transport runs to midnight M-Sat. The last trams and buses are slightly earlier on Sunday, stopping around 11:30pm. Even on Sundays there's never more than a 30-minute gap between services.

Driving: Driving in Melbourne is harrowing—especially if it's your first Australian driving experience—but if you learn the rules, you'll be much less confused:

1. Cars turning right (across oncoming traffic) have the right-of-way over cars turning left.

2. Because of tramlines, right-hand turns in the city center often require a special maneuver (indicated by traffic signs when applicable). This stunt is entirely counter-intuitive: Move left (in front of cars who are waiting for their red light to change) and wait until your own light turns red. Then, before the cars you are blocking get a chance to ram you, make your right turn.

3. Beware of designated bus lanes at prohibited times (usually rush hour). If you goof, hidden cameras will expose your blunder and make trouble.

For those drivers who plan to spend substantial time in Melbourne, the Melway's street directory is a must. Unfortunately, it costs over $20.

Accommodation

Our first choice for accommodation in Melbourne is the Backpackers hostel in St. Kilda. Not only is the hostel itself excellent, but St. Kilda is a cosmopolitan area with good nightlife and close proximity to the beach. Hostel rooms in Melbourne often get booked up, especially in the summer, so call ahead if you can. Any of the hostels will provide a list of alternate accommodation if they're full. YHA runs a special summer hostel at Queen's College, Melbourne University. Contact the head office for information.

Backpackers Hostel, 2 Enfield St., St. Kilda (phone 03-534-8159). Tram from Swanston St. Free pick-up from train and bus. Dorms and singles. Renovated building in excellent location. Clean and friendly. Family-owned and operated. A blackboard in the front hall has attractions and activity suggestions. Van takes guests on free trips to the market, movies, pubs, etc. If you're staying longer, get one of their furnished flats.

YHA, 500 Abbotsford St., North Melbourne (phone 03-328-2880). $13/night. Renovated terrace houses. Bunk rooms with 10-12 beds. Very clean, lots of character. 5-day limit. Near the Uni and Royal Park, close to downtown. Hostel open all day.

YHA, 76 Chapman St., North Melbourne (phone 03-328-3595). $14/night. Mostly twin rooms with single beds. Brick building. A variety of YHA tours to surrounding attractions, including a daily Melbourne tour, leave from this hostel. Around the corner from the Abbotsford YHA.

YHA, 118 Lonsdale St., City (phone 03-662-2366). $14/night. Central location, in city center. 10% discount for pre-booked stays of 5 or more nights.

Carlton Hotel, 197 Bourke St., City (phone 03-63-4379). $14/night. Fantastic location in the heart of the city, but that's its only virtue. Fairly dismal and not very clean. The first floor is a noisy bar and bistro. Small, unkempt kitchen. The "communal area" is the front hallway.

Miami Motor Inn, 13 Hawke St., West Melbourne (phone 03-329-8499). Typical motel. Next to the Victoria Market.

YWCA, 489 Elizabeth St. (phone 03- 329-5188). Motel prices. No kitchen facilities. There's also a building set aside for longer term guests called Richmond House at 353a Church St., Richmond (phone 03-428-1256).

West End Private Hotel, 76 Toorak Rd. West (phone 03-266-3135). About $28/single. A bit shabby, but nice parkside location. 20- minute walk from downtown, or take the tram.

Things to See and Do
Three pointers before you start exploring:

1. Many smaller museums and other establishments close during late December and January.

2. If you get tired of walking, there's an underground train that circles the city with stops at the Museum of Victoria, Parliament House, Flinders St., and Spencer St.

3. Finally, remember that much of Melbourne's character lies beyond the city center. Several neighborhoods retain ethnic traditions, so wander and partake of cafes and street-life.

Melbourne's construction heyday began at the height of Queen Victoria's reign, and you won't find a more thorough sampling of Victorian architecture in any former British colony. Downtown is cluttered with ornate, stately buildings that include examples of Edwardian and Art Deco architecture as well as the dominant Victorian motif. Collins St. and Spring St. display the best of these. A small museum in the bottom of the **ANZ Bank** (380 Collins St.) offers an orientation to Melbourne's financial district (open M-F 9:30am- 4:00pm). Or, if you're starting on Spring St., go to the **National Trust Bookshop** (Tasman Tce., 4 Parliament Pl.) and pick up a "heritage walk" (open M-F 10:00am-5:00pm).

The State Parliament House, the Treasury, the Windsor Hotel, and the Princess Theatre on Spring St. are all worth a look, and you'll probably want to check out the area anyway because the Fitzroy, Treasury, and Carlton Gardens are nearby. The **State Parliament House** was the seat of the federal government from 1901-1927, when it moved to Canberra. If Parliament isn't in session, you can get tours on weekdays.

The **Chinatown** area (Little Bourke St. and surrounds) is another historic downtown area to explore. A Chinese Australian History museum at 22 Cohen Pl. presents background on Chinese settlement in Victoria (open M, W, Th, F 10:00am-4:30pm, Sat & Sun noon-4:30pm; small admission fee).

Other interesting buildings just beyond downtown boundaries are the **Royal Exhibition Building** (Carlton Gardens), the **University of Melbourne**, and the **Queen Victoria Market** (corner Elizabeth and Victoria Sts.). The market, built in the 1880's, is still one of the most vibrant spots in the city, with lots of fresh produce and meats, ethnic foods, clothes, and knick-knacks. (Open T & Th 6:00am-2:00pm, F 6:00am-6:00pm, Sat 6:00am-noon, Sun 9:00am-4:00.)

The Uni (Parkville) is one of the more scenic Australian campuses. Check out specifically the law and arts buildings, also Trinity and Ormond colleges.

Luxurious gardens are another pleasant feature of Melbourne. Homesick settlers planted willow, pine, beech, birch, and poplar trees which now shade Melbourne parks and gardens in true English style. The oldest park is **Fitzroy Gardens**, where Captain Cook's childhood home sits, transported from England in 1934. The cottage, charming on the outside, is not worth paying to enter.

South of Fitzroy Gardens in Yarra Park is the **Melbourne Cricket Ground**, where the first England-Australia cricket match was held in 1877. The stadium was the main venue for the 1956 Summer Olympics. Both cricket and footy are now played there, and a museum in the cricket club displays sporting memorabilia (open W-Sun 10:00am-4:00pm; small admission charge). Call 654-6066 regarding tours of the complex.

Another beautiful parkland setting is the **Melbourne Zoo**, Australia's oldest (Elliot St. Parkville; take the tram or train). Many of the animals roam freely, and there is enormous variety. It's open 9:00am-5:00pm daily.

Of all the parks, however, the best place for a picnic or stroll among lush greenery, serene waterholes, and mammoth trees is the **Botanic Gardens** (between Alexandra and Domain Rd., South Yarra).

Melbourne's most striking example of architectural innovation is the **Arts Centre** (St. Kilda Rd.). You can't miss it, because a spire resembling the Eiffel Tower ("Awful Tower" to skeptical Melbournians) rises above the Concert Hall.

Three major buildings include a National Gallery, Concert Hall, several small theaters, and a Performing Arts museum. Tours of the complex run throughout the day M-Sat from 9:30am-4:30am, and backstage tours are once a week only (call 617-8211). The museum has temporary exhibits that usually involve a multimedia presentation, both informative and relaxing (open M-F 11:00am-5:00pm, Sat & Sun noon-5:00pm; admission charged). As for the National Gallery, it's the best in the country for Australian masters. Among the exhibits are present-day Aboriginal paintings and other 20th-century Australian art. (Open T-Sun 10:00am-5:00pm; small admission fee.)

Victoria's history is described in a dry but informative display at the **Museum of Victoria** (328 Swanston St.). A section devoted to horseracing in Melbourne is highlighted by the stuffed skin of a famous racehorse, Phar Lap. (Phar Lap's fame—and Phar Lap, for that matter—is spread far and wide: his heart is in Canberra and his skeleton is in Wellington, New Zealand.) There's also a science museum that's often cluttered with school kids, and a planetarium (open daily 10:00am-5:00pm; free admission).

Those with a taste for the morbid might venture one block north of the museum to the **Old Melbourne Gaol** where Ned Kelly, Australia's legendary "bushranger" (outlaw) was hanged. Plaster casts of criminals' faces decorate the old cells. (Open daily 10:00am-5:00pm; admission $5.)

Another landmark, a trading ship called the *Polly Woodside*, is the focus of an extensive **maritime museum** run by the National Trust (corner Normandy and Phayer Sts., South Melbourne; take the tram from Collins St. to Clarendon St.). Admission is $6, and the museum is open M-F 10:00am-4:00pm, Sat & Sun noon-5:00pm.

The historic home **Como**, in South Yarra, sits on a plot of land claimed in 1840, five years after first settlement in the Port Phillip area (Como Ave., South Yarra; take tram from Swanston St. along Toorak Rd). South Yarra itself is a chic, attractive suburb, and Como is worth checking out if you like elegant antiques (open daily 10:00am-5:00pm; admission $5).

As for activities, a bike/foot path follows the Yarra River, taking you by rowing clubhouses and parkland areas. It makes for great bike rides and good views of the city. City beaches are close by and nice (especially when it's very hot). Kerferd Rd. in Middle Park has the most fashionable of the city beaches; Sandringham and Black Rock are more laid back.

Food

Food is certainly one of Melbourne's greatest assets, and eating out is one of the best ways to acquaint yourself with the city. Its many immigrants are excellent restauranteurs, and "gourmet" Australian fare (that is, traditional Aussie with a *nouvelle* twist) is also good. Stiff competition keeps quality high and prices reasonable. *Melbourne's Cheap Eats* guide is not so cheap at $12, and *The Age's Good Food Guide* (with mid-priced and expensive restaurants) costs about the same, but those who plan an extended stay should invest in one.

The least expensive restaurants in Melbourne are Vietnamese; most are on Victoria Pde. in Richmond and Collingwood. Just north of the city in

Carlton, the Italian cafes of Lygon and Rathdowne Sts. are great for late-night snacking. Further north on Sydney Rd. in Brunswick you'll find very cheap, no nonsense Turkish food. Greek restaurants are everywhere, but there's a cluster on Swan St. in Richmond and a few good ones on Lygon St., Carlton. Go to Fitzroy for Thai and Indian food. Melbourne's Chinatown is in the city center, on Little Bourke St. and area, where you'll find mid-priced to expensive Chinese and Malaysian restaurants. For breakfast, walk down Brunswick St., Fitzroy; Lygon St., Carlton; and Toorak Rd. in South Yarra.

Whether or not you cook for yourself, a visit to the **Queen Victoria Market** is essential. Row after row of vegetable and fruits stalls fill the outdoor sheds, while inside are meats, cheeses, breads, and a huge variety of ethnic specialties. (Open T & Th 6:00am-2:00pm, F 6:00am-6:00pm, Sat 6:00am-noon, Sun 9:00am-4:00pm.)

Downtown Melbourne

Pellegrini's Espresso Bar (BYO), 66 Bourke St. (phone 662-1885). Bistro-style Italian. Reasonable. Always full of people, a dependable standby. Open M-Sat 8:00am-11:30pm. Moderate.

Ming Palace Restaurant (BYO), 76 Bourke St. (phone 662-3816). Cantonese and *yum cha*. Great service and food. Take-out available. Open M-W until 10:30pm, Th-Sat until 11:30pm, Sun 5:00pm-10:00pm. Moderate.

Rasa Sclangor (BYO), 7-9 Waratah Pl. (phone 663-2827). On second floor. Bamboo and other touches. Good Malaysian food. Serves lunch and dinner every night but Tues. Moderate.

Gopal's (no alcohol), 139 Swanston St. (phone 63-1578). Upstairs opposite the Town Hall. Hare Krishna vegetarian. 3-course special for $7. Take-out available.

Windsor Hotel, 103 Spring St. (phone 653- 0653). Best for afternoon tea in the Cricket Bar. Go in for a look, if nothing else. Open every day.

Carlton

Lygon and Rathdowne Sts. are lined with Italian cafes and restaurants. Many stay open late. For pizza, go to the north end of Rathdowne St. Just north of Carlton, in Brunswick, are some cheap Turkish restaurants. There's an **international food market** at 199 Faraday St. which offers food from eight nationalities. It's an uninspiring setting, but you can fill up cheaply. (Open M-Th noon-10:30pm, F & Sat noon-1:30am, Sun noon-10:00pm.)

Tiamo (BYO), 303 Lygon St. (phone 347-5759). One of the original cafes on Lygon St., and still the best. Go for any meal: breakfast and Sunday lunch are especially good. Open M-Sat 8:00am-11:00pm, Sun noon-8:45pm. Moderate.

L'Osteria Pizza and Pasta, 923 Rathdowne St., Carlton North (phone 387-5537). Best pizza in Melbourne. Dinner only, until 10:30pm. Closed Tues. Moderate.

Alasya (BYO), 555 Sydney Rd., Brunswick (phone 387-2679). Also Alasya 2 at 163 Sydney Rd. (phone 387-6914). Inexpensive and delicious Turkish food. Basic decor. Very popular. Open M-F noon-midnight, Sat 4:00pm-1:00am, Sun 6:00pm-midnight. Cheap to moderate.

L'Alba Coffee Lounge, 280 Lygon St. (phone 347-8607). Especially good in the morning. Very trendy. Always open. Moderate.

Genevieve's Restaurant (BYO), 233 Faraday (phone 347-3052). Uni hang-out. Serves all meals. Open Sun-Th 8:00am-midnight, F & Sat til 2:30am. Moderate.

Richmond and Fitzroy
Thai, Vietnamese, and Indian fare are specialties of Richmond and Fitzroy. Stroll down Brunswick St., Fitzroy, for Thai, and Victoria St., Richmond (or Victoria St., Abbotsford) for Vietnamese. **Potts Bread**, at 62 Gertrude St., Fitzroy, is a must for bread lovers and worth the steep prices.

Thai Thani (BYO), 293 Brunswick St., Fitzroy (phone 419-6463). Colorful umbrellas hanging from ceiling, and beautiful Thai food. Great value. Open nightly from 6:00pm. Moderate.

Soul Food (no alcohol), 273 Smith St., Fitzroy (phone 419-2949). Vegetarian. Great pizza. Open M & T 9:00am-5:00pm, W & F 9:00am-10:00pm, Sat 10:00am-3:00pm. Moderate.

Baker's Restaurant, 301 Brunswick St., Fitzroy (phone 419-7437). Good, cheap food. A hang-out for musicians and artists. Try the omelettes. Open 7:00am-10:00pm every day but Mon.

The Wholemeal Pizza (BYO), 302 Brunswick St., Fitzroy (phone 417-1996). Health food and, of course, pizza. Take-out available. Open 6:00pm-11:00pm every night. Moderate.

Rhumbaralla's Cafe, 342 Brunswick St. (phone 417-5652). An offbeat Fitzroy crowd. Best for breakfast and late-night snacking. Carrot cake and bran muffins recommended. Open M-Th 8:00am-midnight, F & Sat 8:00am-late. Moderate.

Phuong Huang (BYO), 371 Victoria St., Abbotsford (phone 428-2396). Simple Vietnamese food but cheap. Open 11:00am-midnight daily.

Charmaine's Ice Cream Like It Used to Be, 370 Brunswick St., Fitzroy (phone 417-5379). *The* ice cream store in Melbourne, despite the bad grammar. Open M-Th 10:00am-11:00pm, F-Sat 10:00am-midnight, Sun 11:00am-11:30pm.

Lord Newry Hotel, 543 Brunswick St., Fitzroy (phone 481-3931). Go upstairs (downstairs is formal) for quiet and casual and for grilled food. Good selection of beer and wine. Live music. Serves lunch and dinner every day but Sunday. Moderate.

St. Kilda

Leo's Spaghetti Bar, 55 Fitzroy St., St. Kilda (phone 334-5026). Faithful clientele after 30 years in business. Cafe and bistro. Omelettes, pasta, gelati, great minestrone (from $6). Open M-F 11:00am-midnight, Sat & Sun 11:00am-1:00am. Moderate.

Jean-Jacques Gourmet Takeaway and Bistro (BYO), 40 Jacka Blvd., St. Kilda (phone 534-8221). Upmarket gourmet: smoked fish platter, cheeses, sandwiches, etc. Open 11:00am-11:00pm daily. Moderate to expensive.

Nightlife

Melbourne nightlife centers around hotels, some with nightclubs and many with live bands. The cover charge for live music is usually around $8. For late outings try Fitzroy St. in St. Kilda (a seedy section of town with lots of nightclubs—don't walk around alone), Lygon St. in Carlton, and Fitzroy. Live music is listed on Friday in *The Age*, Melbourne's leading newspaper.

Pubs

Loaded Dog, 324 St. George's Rd., Fitzroy North (phone 489-8222). Renovated, attractive pub. Always popular, especially with younger crowd. Band every night. Large range of imported, Aussie, and home-brewed beers. Worth the wait to get in. Open M-Sat noon-midnight, Sun noon-8:00pm.

Tankerville Arms Hotel, 230 Nicholson St., Fitzroy (phone 417-3216). The best local bands play here. Open very late except Sunday, when closing time is midnight.

Cub Club (in Baden Powell Hotel), 61 Victoria Pde., Collingwood (phone 417-2626). Quiet and cozy. Good local bands (usually jazz and blues) every night. Open M-Sat until 3:00am, Sun until 2:00am. Music starts around 9:30pm.

Metropol Hotel, 50 Brunswick St., Fitzroy (phone 419-8703). Trendy and noisy. Great bands. Dancing. Pricey drinks but lots of fun. Open T-Sat until 11:00pm, M til 10:00pm.

Bouzy Rouge, Queensbury St., N. Melbourne (phone 328-1486). Go on Friday for excellent live music and dancing. Small, familiar atmosphere. Open until 1:00am Fri, other nights to 11:00pm.

Naughton's Hotel, 43 Royal Pde., Parkville (phone 347-2283). Uni hang-out. Jukebox and video screen. Open M-Sat til midnight, Sun til 8:00pm.

Lemon Tree Hotel, 10 Grattan St., Carlton (phone 347-7514). Beer garden and cocktail bar. Young professional crowd. Open M-Sat 11:00am-1:00am.

Limerick Arms Hotel, 364 Clarendon St., S. Melbourne (phone 690-2626). Live music M-Sat. Open Sun-Th until midnight, F-Sat til 1:30am.

The Ritz Hotel, 169 Fitzroy St., St. Kilda (phone 534-0527). Nightclub/disco. Cover charge about $12. Open very late every night.

Other Suggestions

Mietta's, 7 Alfred Pl. (phone 654-2366). Elegant setting with casual clientele. Reminiscent of old Vienna. For after the theater or any time. A great place to chat. Drinks are expensive, but selection is endless. Small meals always available. Open M-Sat 10:00am-3:00am, Sun noon-8:00pm.

ID's Nightspot, Greville Rd., Prahan (phone 529-6900). Go for good local bands. Small, awkward space but good performers keep it crowded. Open M-Sat until 2:00am.

Jazz After Dark, Melbourne Arts Centre Studio Foyer and Jazz Lounge (100 St. Kilda Rd.). Great live jazz Fri & Sat only, starting after shows (usually 11:00pm). Popular with all ages. Cocktails and light supper available. Cover charge.

Entertainment

The first place to search for entertainment is Friday's *Age*. A kiosk opposite Myers in Bourke St. Mall sells half-price tickets for musical and theatrical events on the day of performance (cash only). For **Half-tix** offerings, call 650-9420.

Aussie-rules football ("footy") began in Melbourne in 1858. If you plan to see a footy match in Australia (which you should), the most convenient stadium is the **Melbourne Cricket Ground** in Yarra Park (phone 63-9052). For general information on matches, call the **VFL House** (Victorian Football League) at 654-1244. Tickets are $9. The season lasts April-Sept, when the VFL final is played and the entire country closes to watch the championship.

A second Melbourne sports obsession, of a wholly different character, is horseracing. Victoria takes the day off for the Melbourne Cup, held the first Tuesday in November at the **Flemington Racecourse**. Australia's upper crust makes sure to be seen, in full Ascot-style regalia, at this affair. For information, call 267-6144.

The city's preoccupation with sports does not preclude excellence in the arts, particularly the theater. Melbourne traditionally has been the trend-setter for the visual arts. Several small theaters in the city have been overshadowed recently by the **Arts Centre**, which has three theaters and a concert hall (100 St. Kilda Rd.). Since 1984, when the Art Centre was finished, the Melbourne Theatre Company has made its home there. The Concert Hall is state-of-the-art, with a complex array of sound boards that ensure good sound for any seat in the auditorium. Free lunchtime concerts are held weekdays (call 240-9731). Call 617-8211 for all Arts Centre information.

In summer (Oct-April), the Melbourne city council sponsors free entertainment in various city parks, including the **Myer Music Bowl** in King's Domain and **City Square** (call 329-0737). The University of Melbourne's **Student Union** often sponsors free lunchtime entertainment, plus monthly "Union nights," which begin in late afternoon and are very popular (advertised in *The Age*). Call 344-5417 for information on Uni happenings, including the student theater and cinema.

Most city cinemas are clustered near the intersection of Bourke and Russell Sts. Alternative theaters, showing classic and unusual films, are **Valhalla** (216 Victoria St., Richmond, phone 428-6874) and the **Carlton Movie House** (235 Faraday, Carlton, phone 347-8909).

Trips from Melbourne

Most of the best things to visit in Victoria are within day-trip distance of Melbourne. The Dandenong Hills, the foothills of the Victorian Alps, and Wilson's Promontory are all mountainous and woodsy, wonderful for hiking and taking refuge from summer heat. And don't miss Healesville Sanctuary in the foothills, probably Australia's prettiest wildlife sanctuary.

Beaches, too, are plentiful. The best are on the Mornington and Bellarine Peninsulas; Phillip Island and Wilson's Prom also rate. Phillip Island, where fairy penguins waddle nightly to shoreline nests, is Australia's third biggest tourist attraction—or so say the promoters.

Finally, there's the former gold rush town Ballarat, a 1.5-hour drive northwest, where a replica of the original mining site makes for a interesting day, if you're interested in that sort of thing. Mt. Buller and Mt. Mansfield, ski areas in the Victorian Alps, are about three hours from the city. See the Victorian Alps section for details.

There's so much to see in each area that you'll probably choose to stay overnight in most places. YHA and Backpackers hostels operate in Emerald (Dandenongs), Warburton (Dividing Range foothills), Phillip Island, Ballarat, Sorrento (Mornington Peninsula), Geelong, and Portarlington (both on the Bellarine Peninsula).

Lack of public transport is an obstacle some places, and infrequent service in other places is a hassle. Many trips can be reached on suburban Met train lines from Flinders St. Station. V/line services depart from Spencer St. Station. YHA Travel's tours are worthwhile, especially with the transportation problem.

For information on hiking, cross-country skiing, and national parks or state forests, go to the **Dept. of Conservation, Forests, and Lands** (CFL) at 250 Victoria Pde., East Melbourne (phone 412-4011). Hiking maps are available in the shop next door.

The Dandenongs

Thick forests, fern-laden gullies, quaint villages, and sprawling flower farms comprise the Dandenongs, seemingly a world away from Melbourne but just 45 minutes from downtown. A great hostel in Emerald makes the trip especially worthwhile for budget travelers. The flower farms, which provide cut flowers to florists all over Australia, are at their peak Sept.-Nov.

The **Wombat Corner Holiday Farm** in Emerald, nestled in lush hills near Emerald Lake, is probably the most popular hostel in Victoria, thanks to the setting and to Koos, the friendly bloke who runs it. Work on nearby farms and nurseries is almost always available, even in winter and for periods as

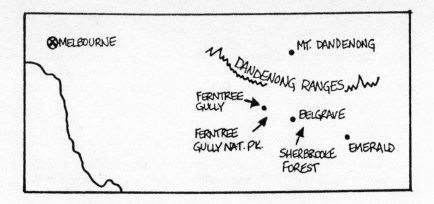

short as a week. As you can imagine, this makes for a hardcore hostel population. Though some hostellers stay for weeks, even months, the atmosphere is congenial. The hostel doubles during holidays and some weekends as a camp for school kids, which works to travelers' advantage in many respects: There's a trampoline, ping pong table, obstacle course, and farm animals on the property. The hostel buildings are cramped but in fine condition. Address is Emerald Lake Rd., Emerald (phone 059-68-4086 for manager's residence). Cost is $8.50/night. Call ahead if possible, since it's almost always full. The hostel is open all day.

Down the road at Emerald Lake you can rent paddle boats or use the waterslide. (Better yet, Koos might lend you a canoe.) **Sherbrooke Forest**, a car ride away (you can usually carpool with resident hostellers), is the best place to spot the lyrebird, an unusual species whose males proudly display their tail feathers. There are some nice day hikes through Sherbrooke Forest. For information, call 059-68-4893.

Several other state parks and reserves are scattered throughout the Dandenongs, including the popular **Ferntree Gully National Park** (off Mt. Dandenong Tourist Rd.). **Mt. Dandenong**, the highest peak of the range, has a tourist drive to the summit, for the best view around. Information on all state parks is available at the CFL Information Centre in Melbourne.

The biggest family tourist attraction in the Dandenongs is an authentic steam train called **Puffing Billy**, which runs from Belgrave to Emerald Lake on weekends and school holidays, stopping in Menzies Creek and Emerald. Call 03-870-8411 for schedule information. The whole trip costs $10, but for less you can, for instance, ride just from Emerald to Emerald Lake (which would leave you down the road from the hostel).

Getting There: Take the Belgrave line (Met) from Melbourne for Ferntree Gully or Belgrave. A local bus meets the train for the drive to Emerald and drops off at the top of the road to Emerald Lake, about a half-mile from the hostel.

Healesville and Other Mountain Refuges

The Dandenongs give way in the north and east to foothills of the Great Dividing Range. The "must see" of this scenic area is Healesville Sanctuary,

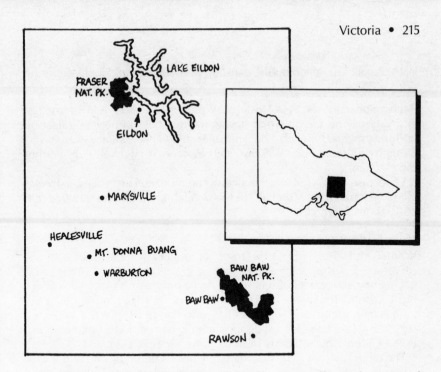

a great setting to view Aussie fauna. Healesville, Marysville, Warburton, and Lake Eildon are major destinations north of Melbourne, while Baw Baw and Rawson lie east of the city and are favored for skiing (mostly cross-country) in winter.

Healesville, Marysville, Warburton

Healesville Sanctuary is 4 km from Healesville on the Maroondah Hwy. (open daily 9:00am-5:00pm; admission $7). Koalas, lyrebirds, and wallabies roam free in a forested park surrounding an enclosed area that houses most of the wildlife, including some adorable duck-billed platypuses, Tasmanian devils, and wombats. Take a picnic.

Marysville, further in the mountains, is surrounded on all sides by stunning eucalypt forest, great for hiking. **Steavenson Falls**, Victoria's highest, are set in temperate rainforest close to town. Obtain national park information at the CFL offices in Melbourne.

Warburton, at the foot of Mt. Donna Buang, is populated and run mostly by Seventh Day Adventists. The Yarra River runs through town, and there's a path alongside. You can also take the 6 km hike up **Mt. Donna Buang** for a tremendous view of the area, but be warned that the path is overgrown with blackberry brambles. The trail begins across the river from town, east of the golf course, near the swing bridge. Cross-country skiing is the activity of choice on the mountain. Rent skis in Melbourne.

Getting There: The Lilydale train (Met) from Melbourne stops in Healesville and Healesville Sanctuary. To get to Warburton, take Martyn's bus from the corner of Swanston and Franklin Sts. in Melbourne (details available from

YHA Travel). There's no public transport between Emerald and Warburton, nor to Marysville.

Accommodation: The **YHA Hostel** in Warburton has a non-resident manager, and you may be the only one staying the night. It's impeccably neat but nothing special. Reach the manager between 9:00am-10:00am or 5:00pm-8:00pm (phone 059-66-2349). Address is Highfield Rd., Warburton ($7/night).

Otherwise, there's not much budget accommodation in the area. In Healesville, the **Park Drive Motel** at 316 Maroondah Hwy. (phone 059-62-5000) costs about $45/night.

Lake Eildon

While Lake Eildon and nearby **Fraser National Park** are popular with Aussie vacationers, they aren't of great interest to foreign visitors—unless you've got the funds to rent a houseboat and find a private arm of the lake. **Eildon Dam**, constructed in the 1950's, forms the major irrigation source for Victoria. It is enormous and surrounded by woodlands. Despite the wilderness setting, the lake and area are disappointingly barren. Tourist information is in the Eildon Library, across from the town shopping center.

The other key spot is the boat harbor, where waterskiing and windsurfers are available for rent. (Boat and equipment for skiing costs $30/hour; windsurfers cost $15/hour, $40/day.) There's also the *Lake Eildon Explorer* for scenic views by boat. The boat harbor is open 9:00am-5:00pm (10:00am-4:00pm in winter) daily (phone 057-74-2107).

Getting There: The drive from Melbourne takes about two hours. There is no public transport.

Accommodation: Eildon has numerous caravan parks with on-site vans and campgrounds. You can also camp at Fraser National Park.

Baw Baw and Rawson

If you've never seen a snow-covered gum tree, consider a cross-country skiing excursion at either Rawson or Baw Baw (in winter, of course). Baw Baw has a winter-only hostel, from which downhill skiing is also available. It's part of **Baw Baw Ski Village** in Baw Baw National Park (advance booking through Melbourne YHA office required; call 03-670-9611). There are no sleeping sheets for hire. Information on Baw Baw National Park is available from CFL in Melbourne.

There is no public transport to Baw Baw.

Wilson's Promontory

"The Prom" hangs on the continent by a narrow strip of land and resembles its southern neighbor Tasmania more than Victoria. Plant and animal life of the Prom is remarkably diverse, ranging from rainforest to eucalypt highlands. Its high peaks yield to secluded sandy inlets or plunge directly into the waves, making for dramatic scenery all around.

There are two drawbacks to this popular national park area: lack of public transport and large crowds. However, while crowds in the main camping and information area (**Tidal River**) are annoying, you can always find your own space on the trails through the park. If you have a way to get there, Wilson's Prom is a must, especially if you're not visiting Tasmania.

Getting There: The trip is about three hours by car from Melbourne. There is no public transport.

Information: The information center at Tidal River is open 8:30am-4:30pm daily (phone 056-80-8538). It's an excellent first stop, as there's a good museum, the National Park office, and an accommodation center. There's also information on guided bushwalks, including spotlight walks for animal viewing, and movies. You can also get information at Victour or CFL in Melbourne.

Accommodation: Tidal River is the main camping and accommodation area. There's also a grocery store and other facilities there, though shopping ahead of time will save money. Camping spots and cabins are heavily booked from the third Friday in December to the first Saturday after Easter, and during school holidays in June and September. Luckily, special camping sites are reserved for foreign visitors, but you must call ahead to get a space (phone 056-80-8538). Relatively cheap cabin accommodation is available off-season; book through Victour in Melbourne.

Hiking: The greatest thing about hiking at Wilson's Prom is that even on a short walk you can see a wide range of terrain. For day walks, bring a picnic and hike to one of the beaches. *Discovering the Prom on Foot* is a worthwhile purchase, available at Tidal River or at CFL in Melbourne.

Half- and full-day walks include Tongue Point, Lilly Pilly Gully, Oberon Bay, the hike up Mt. Oberon, and Sealers Cove (the least-frequented because of its length). Good short walks include Darby Beach, Picnic Bay, Whiskey Bay, Squeaky Beach, and Norman Bay.

You must have a permit for overnight camping, and overnight hikes are generally booked a month in advance. Fires aren't allowed at most campsites. You can hike all year, but it's nippy in winter. To book for overnight hikes, write to *The Ranger, Wilson's Promontory National Park, Tidal River, Vic., 3960* (phone 056- 80-8538). Otherwise, book at Tidal River, but don't always expect to get a place. Be forewarned about biting (and extremely annoying) sandflies; bring repellent!

Ballarat

Gold Centre Tourism, 202 Lydiard St., North Ballarat (phone 053-32-2694). Open M 9:00am-6:00pm, T-Sun 8:00am-6:00pm.

The main attraction in Ballarat is **Sovereign Hill**, in our opinion Australia's best historic replica. Using photographs and paintings, the designers created an excellent imitation of the makeshift settlement at the site of Victoria's first gold discovery in 1851. The result is an elaborate portrayal of life in the goldfields, on the actual site, complete with period costumes, working mines, stores, and craftspeople selling their wares.

Sovereign Hill makes a great day trip from Melbourne during non-vacation periods, but it's a zoo during school holidays. The adjacent **Gold Museum** has a mish-mash of displays, including an good chronology of the state's history (open 9:30am-5:20pm daily, except Friday). Sovereign Hill is on Bradshaw St., just south of town, and is open 9:30am-5:00pm daily. The $10 entrance fee isn't cheap, but you'll spend several hours there.

Ballarat itself is a prosperous country town, with Victorian-style buildings worth a look. There is a town gallery and museum, as well as a few private galleries.

Getting There: Ballarat is 113 km from Melbourne, about 1.5 hours by car. V/line trains serve Ballarat from most western Victoria destinations (call 03-62-0771 in Melbourne; 053-31-4983 in Ballarat; or 053-32-2657 for reservations only). All major buslines stop in Bailarat, but generally you can use them only if you're coming from another state.

Accommodation: The **YHA-Associate Hostel** is part of Sovereign Hill, in a replica of the 1857 government camp. It's open all day, and you should book ahead (call M-Sat 8:00am-8:00pm, or Sun 8:00am-noon, 4:00pm-8:00pm sometimes; phone 053-31-1944 or 33-3904). Cost is $11/night. The entrance is off Magpie St.

Werribee Park

About 45 minutes from Melbourne on the way to Geelong, Werribee Park includes a historic mansion, gardens, and animal park. The mansion is a graceless but impressive showpiece on the exterior, with some rooms open for viewing. The surrounding gardens and African animals are the real draw. The zoo is available only by tour on weekends and public holidays (call M-F 03-741-2444 for information).

Werribee Park grounds are open M-F 10:00am-4:00pm, weekends and public holidays 10:00am-5:00pm (and daily 10:00am-8:00pm in summer). Mansion hours are approximately the same, except it closes at 4:45pm in summer.

There is no public transport directly to Werribee Park, but the Werribee line on the Met stops in town.

Geelong and the Bellarine Peninsula
Geelong Tourist Bureau, 83 Ryrie St. (phone 052-97220). Open M-F 9:00am-5:00pm, Sat 9:00am-2:00pm, Sun 10:00am-2:00pm.

Geelong has been a major shipping port for wool and wheat since 1893, when the Hopetoun Channel was dredged across Corio Bay. The city's well-preserved history is largely overshadowed by industrial din, so avoid a disheartening visit and head straight for the refurbished harbor on Corio Bay. Or stroll along the Barwon River, which flows south of the town center and meets the sea at Barwon Heads.

There's a National Trust mansion called **Barwon Grange** on Fernleigh St. in Newtown, near the river (hours vary, so call first at 052-21-3906). Other significant addresses in Geelong are a trendy pub called the **Bush Inn** (58 Corio St.) and **Sawyers Arms** (2 Noble St., Newtown), a family pub with good meals.

Otherwise, don't linger too long in the city. Those with cars can visit a half-dozen wineries around Geelong, including **Idyll Vineyard** (phone 052-76-1280), the area's first 20th-century winery (opened in 1966) after the phylloxera decimation of the previous century. Vineyards are mostly open on weekends, or weekdays by appointment. Also within striking distance of Geelong are the seaside towns of Torquay and Bell's Beach (see below for details).

Most importantly, Geelong is the access point for the **Bellarine Peninsula**, where beaches and the historic seaside towns of Portarlington and Queenscliff surpass Geelong and its wheat silos by a long shot.

Just 35 km east of Geelong, **Portarlington** has a small, pretty beach on Port Phillip Bay that is sheltered from the surf. **Queenscliff**, an old naval town and fishing port on the southeast tip of the Bellarine, offers quaint terrace homes and Victorian hotels from the mid-19th century. Pick up a pamphlet on historic sights at the town hall (Learmonth St.; phone 052-52-1377). A few buildings of particular interest are **Queenscliff Fort**, built in the 1880's to defend southern Australia (and never used), and the **Black Lighthouse**, made of bluestone. Have a drink or counter meal at the **Ozone Hotel** (42 Gellibrand St.) on the Victorian balcony overlooking the sea. There are numerous crafts shops around town, as well as a fish market at the jetty. And be sure to take a ferry ride to Portsea (on the Mornington Peninsula) and the cliff walks for views of the Mornington Peninsula and Port Phillip Heads.

Getting There and Getting Around: Geelong is 75 km southwest of Melbourne, about a 1.5-hour drive with the inevitable traffic. V/line runs trains daily from Spencer St. Station in Melbourne to Geelong (phone 052-26-6491 in Geelong). The Geelong train station is close to the YHA hostel. Most buslines stop in Geelong, either on the Melbourne-Adelaide route or in a special feeder service from Melbourne. You can use these services if you're traveling interstate.

A local bus service from Geelong train station to Portarlington runs twice daily. It also leaves from Tattersalls, on Moorabool St. in Geelong. On school days, there's a limited bus service between Portarlington and Queenscliff.

The Bellarine Peninsula is flat and excellent for biking.

Portarlington is 35 km east of Geelong; Queenscliff is 30 km southeast.

Accommodation: The Geelong **YHA Hostel** is at 1 Lonsdale St. (phone 052-21-6583). Call 8:00am-10:00am, 5:00pm-10:00pm (manager is non-resident).

There's also a hostel run in conjunction with YHA about 6 km from Portarlington called **Shangri-La** (12 Grassy Point Rd., Portarlington; phone 052-59-2536). If you have trouble getting through to the managers, call 5:00pm-7:00pm.

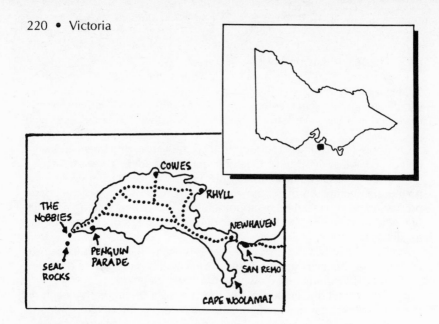

Phillip Island

Phillip Island Information Centre, Phillip Island Rd, Newhaven (phone 059-56-7447). Open daily, 9:00am-5:00pm.

Phillip Island is famous for the **fairy penguin parade**, an event that occurs at dusk on one of the southern beaches. Over 350,000 camera-laden tourists come each year to watch the procession of these tiny creatures. The island is also home to fur seals, mutton birds, and koalas, all of which are protected.

Despite hundreds of gawking visitors, the animals don't appear to be bothered—yet. But it's just a matter of time before the penguins decide to find some privacy. Unfortunately, the crowds and commercialization make it difficult to enjoy the natural beauty of Phillip Island.

Getting There and Getting Around: Although the ferry from Stony Point (on the east side of the Mornington Peninsula) is a tempting way to get to Phillip Island, the service is unreliable, running only weekends and certain times of the year. Half-day tours are available through AAT King, Pioneer Express, and Greyhound. However, the best deal is definitely YHA's tour, which goes once a week.

Otherwise, take V/line's bus/rail service from Spencer St. Station to Cowes, a trip that takes about three hours with transfers. Victour has schedule information (phone 619- 9444). Note that not all services make the correct connection.

Island public transport is non-existent, unfortunate since the island is 22 km long and 10 km wide, and the main attractions are a considerable distance from towns. However, the terrain is flat and cycling is easy. Rent bikes at 149 Thompson St., Cowes (phone 059-52-2982) or at the Backpackers hostel (slightly cheaper). Otherwise you'll need to call a taxi (phone 52-2712) or thumb a ride.

Orientation: Visitor Information is on Phillip Island Rd. just past Newhaven, the most eastern town on the island. If you're traveling by public transport from Melbourne, you won't be able to get to there easily because buses head straight for Cowes, 13 km northwest. Accommodation, restaurants, and stores are all in Cowes, where most of the island's permanent population of 4,000 lives.

The main tourist attractions are on the south side of the island, the focus being the penguin parade and the Nobbies in the southwest corner.

Accommodation: YHA and Backpackers hostels are in Cowes. The YHA-affiliated hostel is a small, two-bedroom building in a caravan park, which shares an amenities block with the other park residents. Though clean and adequately equipped, the cramped set-up is stifling. The congenial owner of the park has lived on the island for most of his life and knows the territory well. Contact **Anchor Belle Holiday Park**, 272 Church St. (phone 059-52-2258). Book ahead, especially in summer, and bring sheets. Cost is $9/night.

The **Phillip Island Backpackers** is closer to town, and its lay-out is much better than the YHA. Call for free pick-up from the bus or ferry. Address: 1-3 McKenzie Rd., phone 059-52-2167. Cost: $9/night.

Things to See and Do: The penguins do their thing on Summerland Beach, off Ventnor Rd., 8 km from Cowes on the south side of the island. Large grand-stands with spotlights provide easy viewing, and an enormous tourist complex lies in the nearby dunes. The penguins appear unaffected by all the attention, mainly because the area is carefully designed to protect them and their nests.

Tickets for the show ($6) go on sale a half-hour before dusk at the **Penguin Reserve**; otherwise, the beach is free. To avoid the line, buy a ticket from the Information Centre near San Remo (the east entrance to the island). Most of the tourists hurry off after the birds have waddled by, but if you stay around, the penguins will often join you on the beach. The parade is largest during chick-hatching season from Dec-Feb, when parents must come ashore to feed their young.

Other protected wildlife live on and around Phillip Island:

In the 1800's, the fur seal was hunted nearly to extinction, but since 1891 it has been protected. A fur seal sanctuary at **Seal Rocks** is accessible only by ferry tour from the Cowes jetty.

Mutton birds (a.k.a. "short-tailed shearwaters") return each September to their Phillip Island nests after a 17,000 km journey to the Bering Strait, returning via the Alaskan and American coastlines and New Zealand. Once hunted for food and oil, mutton birds are now protected. Their rookeries, on the southeast coast near **Cape Woolamai**, are used until their migration in late April.

Koalas were first introduced to Phillip Island in 1870. The population has declined in the last 15 years because of a disease that causes infertility in females. The koala reserves are south of Cowes near **Rhyll**. Koalas sleep during the day, so it's best to see them after sunset (with the help of a strong flashlight).

All along the southern coast are scenic cliffs, rocky inlets, and basalt formations, including the **Collonnades** at Woolamai Beach and **Pyramid Rock**, both products of ancient volcanic activity. The southwest tip of the island, known as the **Nobbies**, is a volcanic rock stack around which boardwalks have been built, providing very civilized viewing of the blowhole, coastal scenery, and Seal Rocks (through a coin-operated telescope). Cape Woolamai, the highest point on the island, has a trail to the top. Phillip Island also has dozens of sandy beaches; the most beautiful are on the north side around Cowes.

The Mornington Peninsula

Frankston Information Centre, 54 Playne St., Frankston (phone 03-781-5244). Open M-F 9:00am-5:00pm, Sat 9:00am-11:30am.

The beaches of the Mornington Peninsula are popular with Melbourne residents, since the city is only 100 km away. The dramatic coastline is both beautiful and historically important: from 1803-1808, Victoria's first settlers lived just east of modern-day Sorrento.

The southern peninsula became a fashionable resort area 100 years ago, and it continues to have an elegant, old-world flavor. Beaches are good for more than sunbathing—the "back beaches" get considerable surf. Major destinations include **Arthur's Seat** (spectacular views), historic resort towns of **Portsea** and **Sorrento**, and **Cape Schanck National Park**, with coastal cliffs and beaches for 25 km along the south side of the peninsula.

Although **Frankston**, 40 km south of Melbourne, is basically unappealing, it has an excellent information center with reams of material on the peninsula, Victoria, and even other parts of the country. There's also a tourist information office in Sorrento.

Getting There: You can make the Mornington Peninsula a day trip from Melbourne if you leave early, but you're better off relaxing in Sorrento for a night or two. Take the Frankston line to Frankston on the Met, then a bus to Portsea and Sorrento. The service runs several times daily. For schedule information call **Peninsula Bus Lines** at 03-786-7088 in Frankston or 059-86-5666 in Rosebud. Or, take interstate buslines to and from Rosebud or Mornington.

Accommodation: The YHA-Associate hostel, **The Bells Hostel**, is at 3 Miranda St. (phone 059-84-4323) and costs is $9/person.

Things to See and Do: For the best views of Port Phillip Bay, take a chairlift or walk up **Arthur's Seat**, the highest point on the peninsula. At the summit, there's a small picnic area with gum trees, a park, and a restaurant. Below the summit is **Matthew Flinders Lookout**, where Flinders surveyed the coastline in 1802. An expensive chairlift to the top operates only weekends and holidays (Sat noon-5:00pm, Sun 11:00am-6:00pm). Arthur's Seat is just off the Nepean Hwy. as you approach Rosebud. There's no public transport.

Sorrento and Portsea are nearly on the tip of the peninsula. In **Sorrento**,

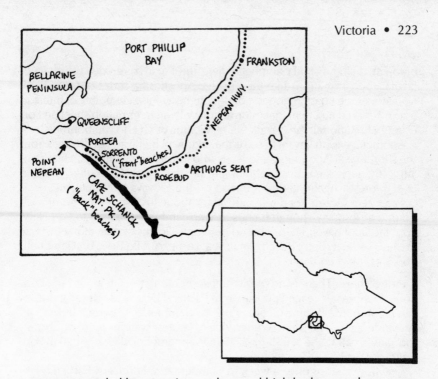

estates surrounded by sweeping gardens and high hedges are the summer homes of Melbourne's elite. The main street is lined with quaint shops and cafes. There's a great ferry ride from Sorrento to Portsea and onto Queenscliff, across Port Phillip Bay.

According to Victorians, a Portsea address is even more desirable. The **Portsea Hotel**, with its outdoor beer garden and Victorian splendor, is a must for the view and the riotous summer parties. It's on the Nepean Hwy.

The most important thing about the Mornington Peninsula is its beaches, and there are two kinds: the calm "front beaches," which face the bay, and the ocean-facing "back beaches," which get lots of surf and are part of Cape Schanck Coastal Park. **Portsea Back Beach**, the most popular, has striking rock formations and cliffs that make for beautiful walks. **Point Nepean** and the western end of the peninsula, once a quarantine area, is now part of the Cape Schanck Park.

The Southwest Coast and the Great Ocean Road

Bordered on one side by the steep, thickly forested Otway Ranges and on the other by a rugged coastline with many precarious views, the Great Ocean Road winds along Victoria's south coast for 300 km between Torquay and Warrnambool. Though it's the lengthiest route between Melbourne and South Australia, it's undoubtedly the best way to go.

The most striking section of the drive occurs between Princetown and Peterborough, including Port Campbell. There, the ocean has eroded weird, spectacular rock formations like the "Twelve Apostles," a series of rock stacks isolated off the coast. Signposts on the highway indicate points of interest, but you should augment that information with an information sheet on Port Campbell National Park, available at Victour or CFL in Melbourne.

Another area you'll want to see is the section of highway that diverges from the shoreline at Apollo Bay and leads into forests of the Otways. High rainfall in the ranges ensures prolific plant life, with grand mountain ash and beech forests. Again, get information on the Otways in Melbourne.

The Great Ocean Road officially starts about 100 km southwest of Melbourne at Torquay. Though it ends in Warrnambool, the road to Port Fairy, Portland, and beyond continues to be scenic. Towns of note along the way include Torquay, Bell's Beach, Anglesea, Lorne, Apollo Bay, Port Campbell, Port Fairy, and Portland.

Getting There: There is no public transport along the Great Ocean Road. You can, however, reach Port Fairy and Portland by way of V/line's train/bus service from Melbourne/Geelong or Mt. Gambier, S.A. (which links to an Adelaide train). The service runs twice a day, reservations required. For information, call V/line at 055-62-2725 in Warrnambool, 055-25-0020 in Portland, or 03-619-1500 in Melbourne.

Greyhound stops once a week in Campertown, Port Fairy, Portland, and Warrnambool on one of its Adelaide-Melbourne services.

Accommodation: There are numerous caravan parks along the coast, plus a few official campgrounds. CFL has two campgrounds in the **Port Campbell National Park** area.

On Cape Otway at Apollo Bay, the **Bimbi Caravan Park** on Cape Otway Lighthouse Rd. (phone 052-37-9246). Overnight cost for on-site tent or caravan ranges from $5-$15, including breakfast.

In Port Campbell, the **C.F.L. camping area** has showers and laundry. You won't need to book except during Easter and summer vacations. Call park information at 055-98-6382 to reserve a spot.

There's a stellar YHA hostel in Port Fairy, called **Emoh**, in a historic home. The managers are involved and enthusiastic. Cost is $8.50/night; the address is 8 Cox St. (phone 055-68-2468), in walking distance of the Greyhound depot.

Finally, about 40 km west of Portland on the Mt. Gambier Rd. in Mt. Richmond National Park, there's a YHA-affiliated home hostel at **Nioka Farm**. It's in the heart of fishing, canoeing, and hiking country. You must book ahead with Ruth and Terry Stanley (phone 055-20-2233), and they'll pick you up in Portland if you need. Cost is $15/night, breakfast and dinner included.

Torquay, Bell's Beach, Anglesea, & Lorne

These four towns are basically beach resorts, and all but Lorne are within day trip distance of Melbourne. Surfing is the main reason to visit Torquay or Bell's Beach (which hosts an international surfing competition annually at Easter). Tourists flock to Anglesea's golf course, where there are friendly

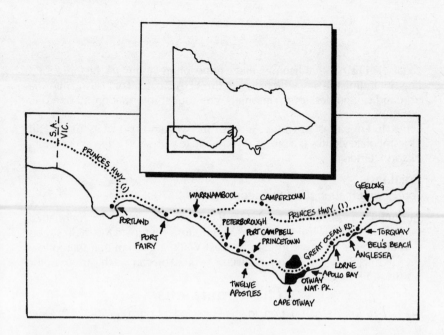

'roos by the dozen—a great photo opportunity.

Lorne, further south, is about two hours from Melbourne by car. Built on a mountainside, it's a lovely, old-style resort town with a nice beach and good fishing pier. The **Lorne Hotel** is a good lunch stop, if you're traveling in leisurely fashion.

Apollo Bay to Port Campbell

The Great Ocean Road turns inland to the Otway Ranges at Apollo Bay (190 km from Melbourne), so those who want to spend some time exploring the Otways will want to stay in the Apollo Bay area. Get information on the Otways in Melbourne, Apollo Bay, or Port Campbell.

For a brief look, take a short forest walk right from the road at **Maits Rest**. The road rejoins the coast 90 km later at Princetown, where the best scenery begins. Numerous coastal formations lie between Princetown and Port Campbell, the most famous being the **Twelve Apostles**, **Thunder Cave**, and **Loch Ard Gorge** (sight of a famous shipwreck). Beyond Port Campbell are **The Arch** and **London Bridge**.

Port Campbell is worth some time. There are various scenic walks in the area, including the precarious **Beacon Steps** (a chance to test your fear of heights) and the 1.5-hour **Port Campbell Discovery Walk**. The latter is signposted from the town beach and gives cliffside views and forest scenery. Information on **Port Campbell National Park**, which encompasses an extensive stretch of coast surrounding Port Campbell, is available in town at a terrific park information center (Tregea St., phone 055-98-6382).

Port Fairy

Skip Warrnambool and head straight to Port Fairy, where surfing, rich history, scenery, and a great youth hostel make it the best spot to stay on the south coast. Port Fairy has a fishing village atmosphere and many historic build-ings, including the one which houses the **YHA Hostel**. For historic informa-tion and self-guided tour pamphlets, call tourist information (phone 055-68-1002).

Just 16 km east of town there's an extinct volcano known as **Tower Hill**. Its immediate vicinity is a protected bird refuge with short walks and a natural history center.

Portland
Tourist Information, Cliff St. (phone 055-23-2671).

About 65 km west of Port Fairy is Portland, site of Victoria's first permanent settlement (1834). Historic bluestone buildings dominate the main streets. Portland gives access to the **South West Walk**, a 200 km trail that follows the Glenelg River and shores of Discovery Bay. You can reach various points on the walk by road.

The Grampians

Hall's Gap Tourist Information, town newsstand (phone 053-56-4247). Open daily.

To the delight of rock-climbers and thrill-seekers, the Grampians are even more rugged and severe than the Victorian Alps. **Hall's Gap**, on the eastern edge of the Grampians National Park, is the most accessible area in the coun-try for viewing kangaroos and koalas in their natural surrounds. Bird life is also prolific, and spring wildflowers cover the range with color between Au-gust and November.

There is a hostel in Hall's Gap, from which nature walks are accessible. Long-distance walkers will find many trails through the national park. Call the ranger in Hall's Gap for information (phone 053-56-4381). Better yet, visit CFL in Melbourne before leaving. Be sure to prepare for sudden changes in weather. You can bike on some roads through the park, and bus tours are also available.

Getting There: Hall's Gap, a 3-hr. drive from Melbourne (260 km), is on the way to Adelaide, 540 km further. The nearest public transport goes to Stawell West, 26 km northeast of Hall's Gap. Taxi (phone 053-58-1562) is the only sure means of transportation between the two. Greyhound, Pioneer Express, and a V/line train all go to Stawell. Also, check in the Chapman St. (Melbourne) YHA Hostel for tour opportunities.

Accommodation: The Halls Gap **YHA Hostel** is in a pleasant, woodsy set-ting on the corner of Buckler St. and Grampians Rd., 1 km before you reach Hall's Gap from Stawell (phone 053-56-4262 or 053-56-6221). The managers are not residents.

There are several campgrounds in the national park, as well as caravan parks in Hall's Gap. The **Hall's Gap Campground** is the best place in the Grampians to see wildlife up close.

The Murray River

The "mighty Murray" creates most of Victoria's northern border, twisting and turning over 2,000 km from Thredbo in the Snowy Mountains to Lake Alexandria, south of Adelaide. Houseboats with festive musical horns carry holidayers on the river, and commercial riverboats and paddle-steamers offer cruises of all shapes and sizes. There are two reasons to visit the Murray: its historical significance—in the late 1800's, riverboats were the primary means of transporting wool from the outback—and its prolific bird and plant life.

The best place to understand the Murray's history is the renovated port of Echuca. To enjoy its natural beauty, try camping along the river banks amidst the red gums. Most of the land along the river is public, maintained by the CFL. Camping is allowed in any place not designated a picnic area or posted "For Day Use Only," as long as you are 20 meters from the river and any lake, stream, or reservoir. Campfires must be strictly controlled, especially during the summer and early autumn. New South Wales fishing licenses are required, even for fishing on the Victoria side, and you can get them locally. For more information, contact the **CFL Work Centre** at 225 Pakenham St., Echuca (phone 054-82-4493) or the **State Public Offices**, Hargreaves St., Bendigo (phone 054-43-9000).

For more on the Murray, see the chapter on South Australia.

Echuca
Tourist Information Centre, 2 Leslie St. (phone 054-82-4525). Open M-F 9:00am-5:00pm, Sat & Sun 10:00am-4:00pm.

Echuca had its heyday from 1870-1895, when wool from outback stations was carried by riverboat to the railway terminus in town. A staggering 79 hotels appeased ever-thirsty boatmen in what became Australia's leading inland port. By the turn of the century, however, rail and road improvements made river transport obsolete. In 1969, the National Trust declared Echuca a historic area, and in 1974 the restored port opened to the public.

Though touristy, Echuca is interesting and worth a visit. A $4 ticket, purchased at the **Star Hotel**, gains admission to the entire complex. Among the attractions are the old wharf and a steam-driven barge called the *S.S. Pevensey*, used in the Australian movie *All the Rivers Run*. Also in the restored wharf area (but not included in the tour ticket), a movie theater shows old films on original projectors. The port is open 9:15am-5:00pm daily.

Riverboat cruises from Echuca are the least expensive on the Murray. The cheapest deal is on the *Pride of the Murray* paddlewheeler, which has daily one-hour trips and leaves from the riverbank by the port. There are a variety of other options, including lunch and dinner cruises. Reservations and tickets are available from the **Coach House** (57 Murray Esplanade, phone 054-82-5244), open daily 9:30am-4:00pm. Or, if you want to get on the river under your own steam, you can rent canoes, kayaks, and motor boats from the **Victoria Park Boat Ramp** at the end of High St. (phone 054-82-4063).

A walk along the banks of the Murray is a must. Short trails next to the old port lead to a pond stocked with fish and surrounded by shady gums and lawn. The bridge next to the pond leads to Moana, New South Wales, so you can step into another state if you're tired of Victoria.

Getting There: From Melbourne, there's a M-Sat V/line service to Echuca. The trip takes 3.5 hours.

Accommodation: Caravan parks along the Murray offer on-site vans and tent sites (check with Echuca's Tourist Information for details).

Mildura

Ron's Tourist Centre, 41 Deakin Ave. (phone 050-23-6160; after hours 23-6351). Open M-F 9:00am-5:00pm, Sat 9:00am-noon; holiday weekends 10:00am-2:00pm.

About 140 km east of the South Australia border, the region around Mildura is fondly called "Sunraysia" because it claims over 400 hours more sun each year than any spot in Queensland. Local industries take full advantage of this, and the area produces most of Victoria's dried and citrus fruits and over 25% of the country's grapes. There's a holiday, tropical feel to the town; locals seem to have perma-smiles.

Commercial paddlewheelers offer a variety of cruises on the Murray, different from those at Echuca because the trips go through the river's locking system. The *Melbourne* (phone 050-23-2200), restored in 1965 and still fired by wood, departs daily (except Saturday) from the **Mildura Wharf**. Many other boats offer lunch and dinner trips, cabaret and disco cruises, and overnight excursions. Details and tickets are available at Ron's Tourist Centre.

Just west of Mildura in Merebein, huge stainless-steel tanks owned by **Mildara Wines** (phone 25-2303) hold over 19,000 tons of local grapes. Mildara Wines also owns vineyards in the Coonawarra and Barossa regions of South Australia. They are best known for their fortified wines, especially dry sherries. Visitors can taste all the Mildara wines in their enormous tasting room (open M-F 9:00am-5:00pm, Sat 9:00am-1:00pm). A modern complex at **Lindeman's Karadoc Winery** in Red Cliffs (phone 24-0303) is also open for tastings (M-F 9:00am-5:00pm, Sat 10:00am-1:00pm), and guided tours are available on weekdays. You can also visit the dried fruit operation at **Sultana Sam Vineyards** (open daily 9:00am-5:00pm; Benetook Ave., phone 23-7562) or **Orange World**, a working citrus and avocado property (Silver City Hwy., Buronga, phone 23-5197).

110 km northeast of Mildura is **Lake Mungo National Park**, once part of the Gol Gol sheep station. Amidst the wind-eroded sand dunes (called "The Walls of China") by the dry bed of Lake Mungo, archaeologists have uncovered the earliest-known Aboriginal occupation site in Australia, dating back 38,000 years. Though the excavations are off-limits to the public, people venture out there to see the rugged landscape and geologic features. For more information, contact the Senior Ranger at the National Parks and Wildlife Service (81 Lime Ave., Mildura; phone 050-23-1278). The only way to get there without private transport is by bus tour through Ron's Tourist Centre in Mildura.

Ron's also runs trips to Broken Hill, Silverton, and White Cliffs, ranging from 1-3 days in length (see also Broken Hill chapter in New South Wales). Some of the major interstate bus lines run to Broken Hill from Mildura.

Getting There: Only Greyhound and Pioneer have interstate bus service to Mildura. V/line services stop in Mildura from other points in Victoria, and interstate trains stop on their Melbourne-Adelaide route.

Accommodation: Rosemont Holiday House, a YHA-Affiliate at 154 Madden St. (phone 050-23-1535), costs $15/person, but you get what you pay for: twin or single rooms with real beds, clean linen, and a cooked breakfast. There is a cheery common room, homey kitchen, and pool in the backyard. The owners are friendly and know the area well.

Beechworth and Surrounds

Tourist Information, The Rock Cavern, Ford St. (phone 057-28-1374). Open 9:00am-5:00pm every day.

You can't spend time in Australia without hearing about the "bushranger" (outlaw) **Ned Kelly**. Beechworth is in the heart of "Kelly country," where the criminal and his gang robbed banks and trains and made a habit of murdering police. In 1880, after years of guerrilla warfare against authorities, Kelly was caught and hung in Melbourne. Beechworth is still proud that Kelly and his cronies stood trial twice in its court and spent time in its jail.

The town's second claim to fame is a richly-preserved gold town heritage, which makes for genuine charm and historic significance.

Finally, hostellers flock to Beechworth for its top-notch **YHA Hostel**, housed in the former Star Hotel. This gorgeous, historic hostel is always buzzing and is a favorite with the Aussies themselves—largely because of Rosemary, the manager, who devotes her life to the well-being of travelers. Incidentally, she'll also help you find work.

Beechworth has scores of historic buildings, and town maps are available at the Rock Cavern Tourist Office near the hostel. The **Burke Museum**, a good place to start your exploration, recounts the gold boom, the era of Chinese settlement, and Ned Kelly's escapades (Loch St.; open daily 9:00am-4:30pm; admission $3). A not-so-obvious but also worthwhile stop is **M.B. Cellars Brewery Museum** on Last St., where antique brewery equipment and a great bottle collection are on display. Bottles, labels, and other paraphernalia are for sale. It's open 10:00am-4:00pm daily, and there's a small entrance fee for the display rooms. Rosemary will direct you to Gorge Rd. for walks and to **Murmungee Lookout** for an incredible view, if you have a car.

Beechworth is an excellent access point for the Victorian Alps, for those with their own transport. You can often get rides to the mountains from fellow hostellers, and hitching isn't too difficult.

Chiltern and **Rutherglen** are a short trip away, but again, there's no transport available. The former is a quaint town with a Historic Trust home called **Lakeview**, where Australian author Henry Handel (Florence Ethel) Richardson grew up.

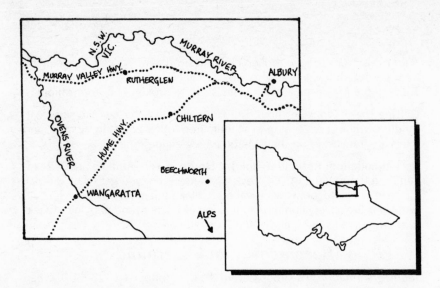

Rutherglen has 12 wineries, many of which are run by descendants of the original families who started them a century ago. Most wineries are close enough to Rutherglen for biking. Stop first in Tourist Information for maps and notes (open M-F until 5:00pm, Sat til 2:30pm). The Rutherglen wine district is especially known for ports and dessert wines. Inquire about bike rental at Tourist Information.

To reach Rutherglen, take the V/line train to Albury/Wodonga. The "Murray Express," a V/line bus service, links Albury and Rutherglen. For schedules and reservations, call V/line in Melbourne, or call the Rutherglen office at 060-32-9784 or 32-9663.

Getting There: Parkinson's Bus Service to Beechworth meets select Melbourne trains in the Wangaratta rail station every day but Saturday. Their depot in Beechworth is the Mobil Station on Main St. Call V/line in Wangaratta for information (phone 057-21- 5313).

If you're arriving from Sydney, most trains stop in Albury, and occasional local buses run from there to Beechworth (not Sundays). For information on the local bus, call **Golden Era Bus Lines** in Beechworth at 057-28-1272. Their Beechworth depot is the Caltex Station on Ford St. If you get stranded in Albury, Rosemary at the hostel will pick you up, but try first for local transport. Most interstate buslines also stop in Albury and Wangaratta.

Accommodation: The **Beechworth YHA** (33 Ford St., phone 057-28-1425) is beautiful, spacious, and friendly. Stay there! It's open all day and costs $9/night. In Rutherglen, the **Victorian Hotel** is about $22/single (90 Main St., phone 060-32-9610).

Victorian Alps

The film *A Man from Snowy River* publicized the spectacular scenery of the Bogong High Plains in the Victorian Alps. The real man from Snowy River, Jack Riley, actually lived in the Upper Murray River valley area around Corryong, way northeast of the Bogong High Plains. Regardless, the Alps are every bit as breathtaking as the movie depicts, with sweeping mountain plateaus and remarkable vistas.

The small villages of Myrtleford, Bright, Mt. Beauty, and Harrietville are valley access points, and during winter, ski resorts at Mt. Hotham, Falls Creek, and Mt. Buffalo buzz with vacationers. The **Ovens River** provides the best freshwater fishing in the state, and walks from the townships are a great way to appreciate area scenery for those who can't make it to the high country. There are several horse-riding outfits as well; it's an ideal area for trail rides. Two major national parks in the Alps are **Mt. Buffalo National Park** and **Bogong National Park**.

Getting There and Getting Around: From Melbourne, take a V/line train to Wangaratta. From Sydney, take a train or bus to Albury, where the transport is provided by Hoy's, with bus services from Albury through Wangaratta to Bright, Harrietville, Mt. Hotham, and Mt. Buffalo, and occasionally to Fall's Creek (on request). Hoy's also has some bus service from Melbourne. Services are limited in summer, though there's a special Saturday bus for hikers from Harrietville to Hotham Heights. You must book ahead for all rides.

In Harrietville, call **Hoy's Australian Alps Coach Travel**, Alpine Hwy. (phone 057-59-2622, after hours 057-59-2522). In Bright: **Jackaroo Blue**, 32 Ireland St. (phone 057-55-1084, after hours 057-59-2552). From Melbourne, call the Frankston office at 03-783-8100. If you're staying at the Mt. Buffalo Chalet, the chalet provides transport from Wangaratta 3 times a week.

Transportation between Falls Creek and Mt. Beauty is available during ski season from **Pyles** bus service. For schedule information, check with Falls Creek Accommodation and Information Centre at 057-58-3224.

Two tour companies have excursions to both Bogong and Mt. Buffalo National Parks: Jackaroo Blue and **Bright Alpine Tours** (22 Ireland St., Bright; phone 057-55-1093, after hours 057-55-1578).

Driving: Chains are required before ascending Mt. Hotham or Falls Creek in winter. The roads to each are unpaved and precarious at any time of year, with snow, ice, mud, and no guard rails. Take care!

One of the most scenic drives in Australia is the **Alpine Way**, built to access the Snowy River hydroelectric plant. It goes from Walhalla, Victoria to Mt. Kosciusco in N.S.W. and is the only road that crosses the Alps.

Tourist Information:

Bright: Pip's Place, 24 Ireland St. (phone 057-55-1335).

Harrietville: Old General Store, Alpine Rd. (phone 057-59-2553).

Mt. Beauty: Meg's Kitchen, Hollonds St. (phone 057-57-2512).

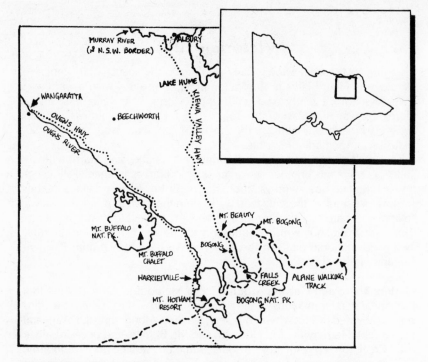

Mt. Hotham: Mt. Hotham Resort Office (phone 057-59-3550).

Falls Creek: Falls Creek Accommodation and Information Centre (phone 057-58-3224).

Accommodation: Bright and Harrietville are the most pleasant and convenient places to stay in the Alps, especially in non-ski season when the resorts don't have much going on. An excellent alternative to lodging in the mountains is the **Beechworth YHA Hostel** (see above), a half-hour drive north of most mountain destinations. You can often get rides to the Alps from fellow hostellers (a large proportion are Aussies), and hitching is pretty easy.

The **Aardvark Alpine Club** in Mt. Hotham Ski Village offers accommodation Oct-May for about $12/night. Be sure to call ahead (phone 057-59-3534). The **Hotham Chalet** on Mt. Hotham has the next cheapest accommodation for about $45/night (includes dinner, bed, and breakfast). Call them in advance as well (phone 057-59-2662).

Because of transportation restrictions and expense, you may do better staying in Harrietville or Bright, especially in summer. **Hoy's Bon Accord** in Harrietville has log bungalows which are mostly for groups, but they'll take individuals now and then. At about $27/night (including dinner and breakfast), it's worth a try (phone 057-59-2662). The **Alpine Hotel** in Bright costs $27/single (7 Anderson St., phone 057-55-1366).

Bright and Harrietville both have caravan parks with on-site vans: the **Harrietville Caravan Park** (phone 057-59-2523) and, in Bright, the **Alpine Caravan Park** (phone 057-55-1064). Check an RAC Guide or the Real Estate Office in Bright for other choices.

The only official campground in **Bogong National Park** is a small one at the foot of Mt. Bogong (end of Mountain Creek Rd.). Otherwise, you can camp anywhere in the park, provided you keep a good distance from water sources. There are cattleman's huts throughout the park, but don't rely on them. For information on the Mt. Bogong campground and camping in general, call CFL in Bright at 057-55-1577.

Staying at **Mt. Buffalo Lodge** isn't as expensive as you might think. In low season, it's $70/night with breakfast and dinner (1 or 2 people); high season rates (during long weekends and school holidays) are considerably higher. Tennis courts and a pool are some of the perks. Call 008-03-7038 (Victour) or 057-55-1500 for more information. The other accommodation on the mountain, **Tatra Inn**, is open only in winter and is exorbitant.

A more economic option is the national park campground on **Lake Catani**, open Nov-May for about $5/site. Bookings are difficult to obtain on weekends and holidays. Call the Park Office at 057-55-1466 on weekdays between 8:00am-4:30pm. Camping is not permitted elsewhere.

Myrtleford is the nearest town to Mt. Buffalo. If you can't get a place on the mountain, it's your best bet.

Bright and Harrietville
Bright and Harrietville are cheerful, pretty towns. Harrietville is the beginning of the **Mt. Feathertop Summit Walk**, and numerous short walks originate from Bright (especially along the Ovens River) and nearby Wandiligong. CFL trail notes for daytime walks are available in local stores and at the CFL office in Bright. You can rent tackle in Harrietville for fishing in the Ovens River.

Mt. Buffalo National Park
Mt. Buffalo National Park is ideal for scenic day hikes, most of which originate from the summit plateau. The historic mountain resort hotel, **Mt. Buffalo Lodge** ("The Chalet"), sits atop the mountain and is the hub of all activity. Rent walking boots, ski wear and equipment, and toboggans there. There's also a horse stable ($10/hour for rides), but you must call ahead.

In front of the Lodge, there's a hair-raising view of Buffalo Gorge at **Bents Lookout** and a worthwhile 2 km walk (look for "Gorge Nature Walk" signs). Among the other short hikes are **View Point Nature Walk** (4 km) from Lake Catani Dam Wall, **Dicksons Falls Walk** from Tatra Inn (4 km), and **The Horn Walk**, a steep, 1 km hike to the highest point on Mt. Buffalo (originates at the end of the Mt. Buffalo access road, which is unsealed). Information and maps for walking are available at the chalet and at the Park Office. (Park Office summer hours are M-F 8:00am-4:30, phone 057-55-1466. The winter office is at Cresta Valley; phone 55-1585.)

Cross-country skiing is quite scenic on Mt. Buffalo, and downhill is half as expensive as at Hotham, though not very extensive. **Dingo Dell** is for beginners; **Cresta Valley** has runs for all skiing levels. For a 24-hour snow report, call the National Parks Service at 057-55-1216.

Bogong National Park

The landscape of the Bogong High Plains is one of Australia's most renowned, and deservedly so. Within the national park are 11 of Victoria's 12 highest peaks, with Mt. Bogong the highest. Hiking (Nov-May) and cross-country skiing (July-Sept) are the best ways to appreciate the countryside; downhill ski resorts at **Hotham** and **Fall's Creek**, adjacent to the park, offer the best skiing in the state.

Direct access points to the park are Harrietville, Mt. Hotham Ski Resort, and Falls Creek Resort, all of which offer lots of hiking opportunities. Hotham and Falls Creek resorts sit on the high tableland. Both are mostly empty in non-skiing season, and the hostel at Hotham, while giving convenient access to trails, doesn't always hum with activity. On the other hand, Harrietville is in the river valley and can be reached by public transport any time of year.

There are numerous opportunities for day and overnight hiking in the park, including the 450 km **Alpine Walking Track**, which starts in Walhalla and crosses the Alps. If you're in shape, we suggest climbing **Mt. Feathertop** (Victoria's second-highest peak) from Harrietville, a full day's hike that leads to stunning views of the High Plains. The CFL has a free pamphlet on the walk. Tents are necessary for overnights, though campers may use former cattleman's huts scattered throughout the mountains. Maps are available at stores in Harrietville, Mt. Beauty, Bright, and the Mt. Hotham Alpine Resort Office. For advice over the phone, call the office at 057-59-3550 or the CFL office in Bright at 057-55-1577. Information on the area around Falls Creek is available at the information center in Falls Creek Village (phone 057-58-3224).

Beware of changing weather conditions! Fog is a particular problem, so don't wander too far off trails.

Skiing

Hotham and Falls Creek are the best downhill slopes in the area. Falls Creek is mainly for intermediate skiers, and Hotham has a range of slopes, with more expert skiing than Falls Creek. Lift tickets run about $40, plus $20 for equipment and extra for snow gear. Mt. Buffalo's areas, Dingo Dell and Cresta Valley, aren't large but they're half as expensive.

Other options in the Alps—and more accessible from Melbourne—are **Mt. Buller** and **Mt. Mansfield**. Mt. Buller is popular and crowded, but easy to reach. For information, contact the **Mt. Buller Accommodation and Information Centre** in Melbourne (77 Beach Rd., Sandringham; phone 03-598-3011) or the **Alpine Resort Accommodation Booking Service** (phone 057-77-6280).

Allaround Travel Services in Melbourne has many skiing package deals to Buller and Mansfield that include transport from Melbourne to the mountains (Mid City Arcade, 200 Bourke St.; phone 03-663-4485 or toll free 008-33-1238).

There's a beautiful, modern YHA hostel in **Mt. Buller Alpine Village**. From June-October, book through YHA in Melbourne (Mt. Buller Booking Officer,

YHA, 205 King St., Melbourne, Vic. 3000). Cost is about $30/night in peak season, but in summer (Nov-May), it's down to a regular hostel price ($8/night). In summer, book directly with the Mt. Buller Youth Hostel, Box 23, Mt. Buller, Vic. 3723 (phone 057-77-6181; call between 8:00am-10:00am or 5:00pm-10:00pm). Winter weekends and holidays tend to get booked up long before ski season.

Transport to Mt. Buller and Mt. Mansfield is available during ski season only by a three-company effort. Call any of the companies for information: V/line (phone 03-619-1500 or 008-13-6109), **Mee's Bus Lines** (phone 03-459-3000), or **Mansfield-Mt. Buller Bus Lines** (phone 057-75-2606). You can also book through Victour.

Cross-country skiing on **Dinner Plain** (Bogong National Park) is fantastic and cheaper than the downhill option. Cross-country is also very good on Mt. Buffalo. Equipment rental is available in Harrietville, Mt. Beauty, Falls Creek, and Mt. Hotham, as is trail information.

Horseback Riding

One of the best ways to see the Victorian Alps is atop a horse. There are three or four reputable stables offering trail rides by the hour or extended pack trips. Try **Bogong High Adventures** in Mt. Beauty (phone 057-57-2849) or **Nug Nug Trail Rides** in Myrtleford, a lovely area for riding (phone 057-54-2201).

Victorian Goldfields

Gold was first discovered in Victoria in 1851 in Clunes, about 40 km north of Ballarat. Within a year, thousands came to seek their fortunes in the creeks and hills near Ballarat, Castlemaine, and Bendigo.

Though touristy and often crowded with school groups, the best place for a full account of the gold rush is **Sovereign Hill**, a reconstructed mining town in Ballarat (see above). Bendigo, the richest of all the Victorian goldfields, today lacks the intrigue of Sovereign Hill. For rustic charm, Maldon and Castlemaine are smaller historic towns with lots of renovated buildings and museums.

Maldon, Castlemaine, and Daylesford

Maldon, 36 km south of Bendigo, was the first whole town to be classified by the National Trust. The Tourist Centre (High St.) distributes a historic-walk pamphlet that briefly covers the residential area.

A restored steam train travels along the original, 19th-century route between Maldon and Castlemaine, another gold rush town that once supported one of the busiest goldfields in the country. Originally known as the "Mt. Alexander Diggings," Castlemaine is more commercialized than Maldon. Besides visiting its restored houses and gardens, look for a bright yellow and red tin containing **Castlemaine Rock**, a hard candy brought in 1853 by an English confectioner named Barnes. It's still made with the original recipe by fourth-generation descendants.

Famous for mineral water rather than mineral wealth, **Hepburn Springs**

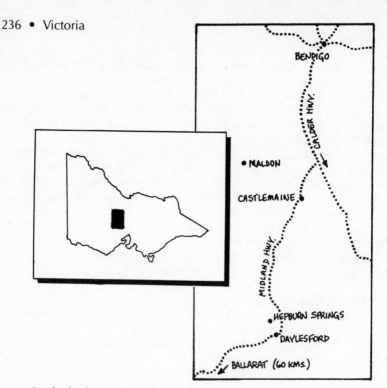

(near Daylesford) is a fun side-trip for the travel-weary. When the gold ran out, entrepreneurs saw potential in the bubbling springs, and for over 90 years they have been marketed to the health-conscious.

The **Hepburn Springs Spa Complex** (phone 053-48-2034) offers a variety of mineral water bathing options, from a large, heated pool to private bathrooms with bubble, mud, herbal, mineral, or electrical (!) baths. Massages and skin care programs are also available. Spa water, flavored by lime, iron, sulphur, or magnesium, flows free of charge from hand-operated pumps. The wooded reserve surrounding the spa complex has walking trails and is crowded on the weekends.

Getting There: V/line runs several trains daily to Castlemaine. You can get to Daylesford from Melbourne by both train and bus, but it's a few kilometers to Hepburn Springs. There is no public transport to Maldon.

Bendigo
Gold Centre Regional Tourist Authority, 182 High St., Calder Hwy., Kangaroo Flat (phone 054-47-7161).

Tourist information in town: Charing Cross, corner Pall Mall and View St. (opposite Alexandra Fountain).

Bendigo is a large country town with a few magnificent buildings, a beautiful public garden, and a bustling modern mall. Local active mining ceased in 1955, and now the area relies on its tourist trade—mostly Aussie travelers and school groups.

In the mid-1800's, the Bendigo district had a larger population than Melbourne, a high percentage of whom were Chinese miners. **Joss House**, the Chinese temple on Finn St., the **Dai Gum San Wax Museum**, and an annual Easter parade with a huge silk dragon are modern reminders of their influence. Local Chinese restaurants are terrific, as you might expect.

The **Central Deborah Goldmine** and **Talking Tram** tour are Bendigo's biggest tourist attractions. Open daily to visitors between 9:00am-5:00pm, Central Deborah Goldmine (phone 43-8070) operated between 1939-1954 and was the last mine to close on the Bendigo field. The steep $10 admission fee includes a guided tour of the above-ground buildings and equipment. Bendigo's Talking Tram goes on an 8 km loop through the city, with historical commentary. The mine and tram are next to each other on Calder Hwy., 2 km west of town and a 10-minute walk from the YHA hostel.

Renovated Victorian buildings house the Post Office, Law Courts, and School of Mines buildings on **Pall Mall** and are the highlight of the town center. Even more splendid is the **Shamrock Hotel** on the corner of Pall Mall and Williamson St., restored in 1981. Try a counter meal in the hotel's public bar (inexpensive). Upstairs is a pricier bistro.

Getting There: The train between Melbourne and Bendigo operates several times a day. The trip takes two hours. If you want to go up to the Murray, buy a ticket to Echuca. This service goes through Bendigo, and you can get off and spend as long as you want on the same ticket. The Bendigo train station is a five-minute walk from the center of town.

Accommodation: The YHA-Associate hostel is in the **Central City Caravan Park**, 362 High St., Golden Square (phone 054-43-6937), 3 km west of the town center. The accommodation is clean and acceptable, though impersonal and completely separate from the caravan park. Cost is $10/night.

The Southeast Coast

Gippsland

Gippsland is centered around the industrial Latrobe Valley, where coal deposits feed power stations in Morwell, Yallourn, and Loy Yang. While these State Electric Commission (SEC) stations are the most important source of electricity in the state, Gippsland is better known for its lush dairy country and timberlands. Mountainous northern Gippsland is dotted with old gold mining towns, and the Lake region is the largest inland water system in Australia and home of the country's largest commercial fishing port, Lakes Entrance.

Lakes Entrance has over 200 fishing boats and two huge fish-processing plants. The town's name is a reference to a man-made channel dug in 1889 to connect the area's vast coastal lakes with the sea. Lakes Victoria, King, and Wellington cover 400 square km along Victoria's southeast coast from Sale to Lakes Entrance.

If you're partial to beautiful, long, sandy beaches, Lakes Entrance is your place. **Ninety Mile Beach**, an impressive stretch of sand, can be reached

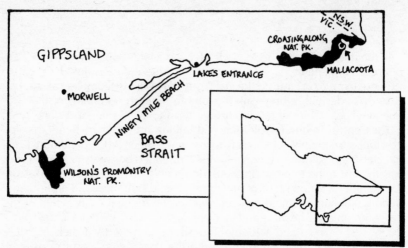

by crossing the Cunningham Arm footbridge from the center of town. Not surprisingly, watersports are the focus of local activity, including swimming, surfing, sailing, and fishing. Avoid visiting Dec-Jan unless you like crowds.

Getting There: From out of state, Greyhound, Pioneer, and Deluxe stop in Lakes Entrance (12 hours from Sydney). From Melbourne, take the V/line train to Bairnsdale and catch the bus to Lakes Entrance. (Call V/line first to make sure your train meets the connector service.)

Accommodation: The YHA hostel is in **Lakes Main Caravan Park** on 7 Willis St. (phone 051-55-2365), within walking distance (3 km) of the center of town and Ninety Mile Beach. It's small but clean, with a TV and common room. The owners are helpful and pleasant and own a pet rooster, who will introduce himself at the crack of dawn. Cost is $8/night.

Mallacoota

Located on a coastal inlet and surrounded by **Croajingalong National Park**, Mallacoota is a sleepy fishing and boating resort that leaps to life in the summer. The main reason to go to Mallacoota is to hike in the Park's woods and rainforest, explore its rocky outcrops, and enjoy miles of pristine beaches. For further information on Croajingalong National Park, contact its Park Office on Genoa Rd., Mallacoota (phone 051-58-0263). Fishing is a popular local activity, and you can catch prawns at night in the local estuaries.

Getting There: Take the V/line train from Melbourne to Bairnsdale, then a connecting bus (M-F only), which will drop you at the hostel. Interstate Greyhound, Pioneer, and Deluxe buses stop in Mallacoota. From Sydney, the bus trip is 9.5 hours.

Accommodation: The YHA hostel, located a few km from Mallacoota, is a cluster of depressing, rundown caravans in the **Shady Gully Caravan Park** (phone 051-58-0362). Cost is $8/night. There was a rumor of remodeling plans when we were there, so call for updated information. Otherwise, you can camp at designated areas in the park or stay in a guesthouse in town.

South Australia

"Town," anywhere in South Australia, refers to Adelaide. For example, the car mechanic on the Eyre Peninsula who says your car should be repaired "in town" probably means "in Adelaide"—650 km away. So sparsely populated is most of the state, and so comparatively modern and civilized is Adelaide and its immediate area, that this term shouldn't surprise. Though it's enormous in area, South Australia is small to the visitor: most sights are within 2 hours of Adelaide.

Adelaide and other population centers of South Australia are oases in a land literally dry as dust. Indeed, S.A. is the driest state in the driest inhabited continent on earth. Most visitors, however, remember rolling green hills and prosperous, attractive towns. South Australians seem to have built a protective fortress—grand buildings and gardens, and strongly-embedded English and German traditions—to protect them from a barren, harsh land.

There are many charming places to visit (most remarkably the wine valleys), but don't forget about the vast outback that is most characteristic of the state's geography.

When to Go
Since the climate within South Australia varies dramatically, it's difficult to recommend a best time to visit, but try to avoid summer (Jan-March), when temperatures in most of the state are often over 100°F (40°C) and inland regions are unremittingly hot. If you arrive in summer, stick to the coast and Kangaroo Island. Spring (Sept-Dec) and autumn (April-June) are the best months, while winter (June- Aug) is a good time to visit inland spots. (Winter in Adelaide and coastal areas is damp and chilly).

Itinerary
Allow plenty of time to enjoy Adelaide, a relaxing, lovely city. A visit to the Flinders Ranges is the best way to experience the desolate outback. Wine buffs should visit one of S.A.'s four wine valleys: the Barossa Valley, the Southern Vales, Clare Valley, or Coonawarra. The first three are easily accessible from Adelaide.

The long treks between Adelaide and both Perth and Alice Springs are classic Aussie trips, and you should try to take at least one, just for the experience. Adelaide to Perth by car follows the **Great Australian Bight**, the famous coastline where desert meets ocean. The train to Perth runs through

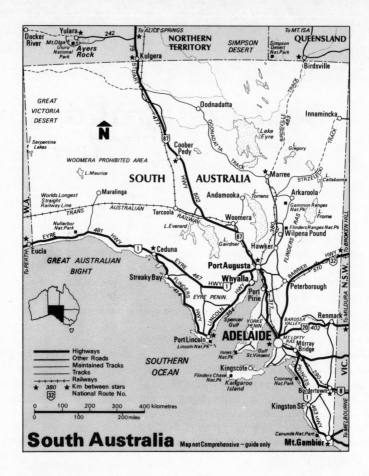

South Australia Map not Comprehensive – guide only

Highways
Other Roads
Maintained Tracks
Tracks
Railways
★ 380 Km between stars
[32] National Route No.

0   100   200   300   400 kilometres
0   100   200 miles

the **Nullarbor Plain**, where the longest stretch of straight railroad track in the world passes only herds of 'roos or emus and, every few hundred miles, a settlement of railroad workers. The Adelaide-Alice Springs stretch was pioneered in the 1850's, when camels made the legendary trek from Oodnadatta to Alice. That route, which can be traveled by train or bus, traverses desert and otherwise limited access areas. **Coober Pedy**, an opal mining town where inhabitants live underground to avoid the extreme heat, is on the way.

Note that many tourist sights in S.A. are open only on weekends and public holidays; several others close Mondays or both Monday and Tuesday.

Getting Around

The remoteness and isolation of most areas in S.A. makes having a car advantageous. However, for the same reasons, drivers must take extra care. Local buses service most on-the-beaten-track destinations from Adelaide, usually once a day, but sometimes only once or twice a week. Interstate buslines don't generally service tourist destinations (except, of course, Adelaide). Suburban Adelaide trains and a few historic local trains on the Fleurieu Peninsula are the only train services in the state, aside from interstate.

Information

S.A.'s government tourist bureau, **Tourism South Australia**, has an excellent information center in Adelaide, with details on transport and accommodation and good touring advice. Tourism South Australia also has offices in Melbourne and Sydney.

You'll usually find local tourist information in travel agencies or gas stations. People working there are usually friendly and helpful, but they don't have access to information on areas other than their own.

Accommodation

There are six YHA or YHA-Associate hostels in S.A., all of them in the southeast. Their Head Office is 38 Sturt St., Adelaide (phone 08-231-5583). Alternative hostel accommodation is offered only in Adelaide, the Barossa Valley, and Adelaide Hills. Those seeking to get off the beaten track will have to stay in local hotels and sometimes caravan parks.

Much of outback S.A. offers no accommodation at all, but camping along the road is no problem. Tourism South Australia publishes a series of pamphlets with comprehensive accommodation listings, including prices.

Bed & Breakfasts are common on the Fleurieu Peninsula and in the wine valleys. Tourism South Australia has a guide to these called *South Australia Homestyle Accommodation*, published by a B&B association. Most B&B's are on farms or in quaint, historic buildings, definitely worth considering if you're willing to spend a bit extra. Cost is about $25 per person per night, but it can be less.

Restricted Areas and Outback Features

Legal and climatic/geographical barriers render much of South Australia unnavigable. About a third of the state is Aborigine reserve or military testing zone. Entrance to the "defense zones" of Woomera and Maralinga is prohibited, while entrance to the reserves is highly restricted. (In 1957, the British detonated seven nuclear bombs for testing, killing an unknown number of Aborigines.)

Harsh desert conditions mean that access to most outback areas is limited regardless of legal restrictions. You will probably never see, for instance, S.A.'s mammoth system of salt lakes, the biggest of which, **Lake Eyre**, is the world's largest dry salt lake. On rare occasions when water accumulates, it becomes a virtual inland sea. The formidable **Simpson Desert**, which dominates northeast S.A. as well as parts of Queensland and the Northern Territory, is twice the area of Tasmania. Giant red sand dunes of the Simpson reach 30 meters and swell like ocean waves. Another feature: a 9,600 km **dog fence** stretching from Surfer's Paradise on the Queensland coast to the Great Australian Bight, just west of Ceduna, S.A. This gigantic barrier, the longest fence in the world, prevents wild dingoes from entering grazing areas.

Adelaide

About 70% of S.A.'s 1.3 million people live in Adelaide. Thanks to Adelaide-ans' respect for the past and emphasis on the aesthetic, you will be hard-pressed to find a part of the city that is unattractive. Its gracious, wide avenues and well-preserved stone buildings are a pleasure to contemplate, while the open skyline, ample parks, and lack of crowds create a soothing sense of space.

For the traveler, Adelaide is the ultimate walking city and an excellent place to learn something about Australia's colonial history. An equally important draw are the surrounding wine valleys and quaint mountain towns. The Barossa Valley, Southern Vales, and Adelaide Hills are all within a day's trip from the city.

In the rest of the country, Adelaideans are considered traditional and even high-handed, perhaps because theirs is the only colony that never took convicts. Or perhaps it's because the general S.A. public is adamantly church-going. Or perhaps it's because the population is noticeably older.

There is, however, an opposite opinion. Adelaide may be "traditional," but its tradition is founded on progressive legislation and religious tolerance. In fact, the first colonists in 1836 were middle-class liberals seeking freedom of religion and press. During the colony's formative years, settlers emphasized a representative government (representative, at least, by standards of the time) and a constitution protecting individual rights. In 1894, S.A. gave women the vote, the first Australian state and one of the first governments in the world to do so.

While it is true that Adelaide's original families still comprise something of an aristocracy, the city in most respects embraces the modern world. The **Festival Centre**, for one, puts Adelaide on the cutting edge of the performing arts. One of the fastest transportation systems in the world—the **O-bahn**, a combination train and bus—brings commuters to the city in a flash. Every October a race track is built through the streets of downtown for the **Australian Grand Prix**—an event that hardly reinforces the city's stodgy image.

Getting There

In addition to the major buslines (Deluxe, Greyhound, Pioneer, and Bus Australia), Stateliner and Premier Coaches service Adelaide from other areas of the state and outback New South Wales. Adelaide is 10.5 hours from Melbourne, 12 hrs. from Sydney, 28 hrs. from Brisbane, 32 hrs. from Perth, and 19 hrs. from Alice Springs.

The *Indian-Pacific* train from Sydney to Perth stops in Adelaide, which is the departure point for *The Ghan* to Alice Springs. Caper Fares are available from Melbourne on overnight trains and from Perth.

Australian Airlines and Ansett fly to Adelaide from all major Australian cities. Qantas flies from overseas. **Transit Regency Coaches** (phone 381-5311) picks up at major hotels and airline terminals every half hour, 7:00am-10:00pm. Cost is $4.

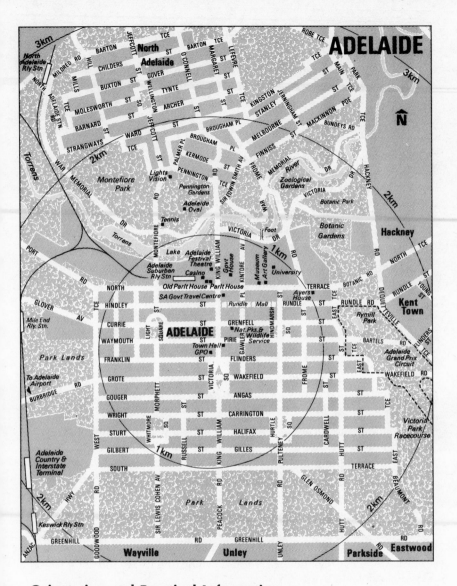

Orientation and Practical Information

Colonel William Light, the first Surveyor-General of the South Australian colony, began executing his plan for Adelaide in 1837. The city proper remains precisely as he envisioned it: Downtown is a simple grid, interrupted by five city squares and surrounded on all sides by park.

King William Street runs north-south through the center of the city, dividing the east and west sides evenly. Most east-west streets change names when they cross King William St. In the center of the grid, **Victoria Square**, designed to be the focal point of activity, is where you'll find civic buildings, the post office, and the Central Market.

The area most frequented by visitors is **North Terrace**, which forms the northern edge of the city. Museums, the University of Adelaide, and the Botanical Gardens border North Tce., which also happens to be the prettiest area to stroll. Most commercial activity occurs one block south of North Tce. on **Rundle Mall** and its extensions (Rundle St. and Hindley St.). The Torrens River meanders north of North Tce., dividing Adelaide from North Adelaide.

If you're ever disoriented, look for **Mt. Lofty**, southeast of downtown. Due west of the city are all the beach suburbs bordering Gulf St. Vincent.

An occasional red hue or gray smog in the atmosphere isn't human pollution. The red is dust blown from the outback during periods of dryness, and summer's gray haze is usually from bush fires.

Shopping hours are M-Th 9:00am-5:30pm, F 9:00am-9:00pm, and Sat 9:00am-noon. Evening shopping in the suburbs is Th until 9:00pm.

Important Addresses and Telephone Numbers (area code 08)

Tourism South Australia, 18 King William St. (phone 212-1644). All city tourist information, statewide information, bookings, and transportation. Open M-F 8:45am-5:30pm; Sat-Sun, public holidays 9:00am-2:00pm.

General Post Office, 141 King William St. (phone 216-2370).

American Express, 13 Grenfell St., Adelaide, S.A., 5000 (phone 212-7099).

YHA of South Australia, 38 Sturt St. (phone 231-5583). Hostel bookings, transportation bookings by bus and rail. Open M-F 9:30am-4:30pm, except public holidays. After hours, call the hostel at 223-6004 (until 9:30pm).

National Parks and Wildlife Service, 55 Grenfell St. General information on South Australian national parks. They'll give out telephone numbers for local rangers regarding information the office can't provide. For topographical maps, go to **Mapland** at 12 Pirie St. Both are open M-F 9:00am-5:00pm.

Wilderness Shop, 44 Grote St. (phone 231-0625). Information on hiking in South Australia and references for local bush-walking clubs. Shop sells books, calendars, etc. Open M-Th 10:00am-5:00pm, F 10:00am-9:00pm, Sat 9:00am-noon.

STA Travel, 55A O'Connell St., North Adelaide (phone 267-1855). Or Union House, Adelaide University.

Royal Automobile Association of South Australia (RAA), 41 Hindmarsh Square (phone 46-0321 for road service; 223-4555 general inquiries).

Keswick Railway Station, Burbridge Rd., immediately west of West Tce. (phone 217-4455 or 231-4366). All interstate and country trains. Pronounced "kess-ick."

Adelaide Railway Station, North Tce. (phone 210-1000). All suburban trains.

Central Bus Station, 101, 111 Franklin St. (phone 217-0777). Terminal for all interstate and country bus services. Deluxe (phone 212-2077), Greyhound (phone 212-1777), and Pioneer (phone 231-2076) have booking offices here.

Bus Australia, 101 Franklin St. (phone 212-7999)

Johnson's Bus Service, 101 Franklin St. (phone 231-5959)

Stateliner, 101 Franklin St. (phone 217-0777). Reservations for Stateliner and Mt. Gambier Motor Services.

Barossa Valley Bus Service, phone 085-65-6258

Yorke Passenger Bus Service (Briscoes), phone 212-7344

ABM Coaches, phone 349-5551

Yorke Peninsula Bus Service, phone 391-2977, or book through Bus Australia.

Australian Airlines, phone 217-3333

Ansett Airlines, phone 212-1111

Taxis, phone 223-3111, 211-8888, 223-3333

Emergencies, phone 000

Royal Adelaide Hospital, North Tce., corner Frome Rd. (phone 223-0230)

Transportation

The **State Transport Authority** (STA) is located at the corner of King William and Currie Sts. in the heart of town. All local bus/rail schedules and tickets are available there, as well as general directions and information. Avoid the STA office at lunch and rush hour. Otherwise, call 210-1000 for transport inquiries.

The bus is the major form of transport for travelers because, while the train system is extensive, it mainly serves commuter destinations. Should you need to use the train, the suburban rail station is on North Tce., west of King William St. Private bus companies service a few suburban destinations (listed above). Buses generally operate M-Sat until 11:30pm, Sun until 10:30pm.

Getting from suburb to suburb on the bus is annoying because you're usually forced to go into the city and transfer to get out again. The system operates within three zones and extends to some Adelaide Hills townships. Cost ranges from $1-$2. Most buses pass through the city at the Currie St./Grenfell St. intersection with King William St., and Victoria Square. All cash tickets allow two hours of unlimited transfers between bus, train, and tram zones. The rates go down during the "Interpeak" hours, M-F from 9:01am-3:00pm.

If you're going to use the bus frequently, look into some of the ticket specials like multi-trip passes and off-peak excursions. You must buy multi-trip tickets before you board a vehicle (get them at bus depots, railway stations, the STA office, and post offices).

The transport system's only surviving tram runs from Victoria Square to the beachside suburb of Glenelg. The Japanese-developed **O-bahn** is a commuter bus/train that transfers from the rail onto the road in one trip. Though it serves only commuter destinations, riding it may be worthwhile just for the experience.

Among the car rental options is **Half-Price Rent-a-Car** for around $30/day for the metro area (not including insurance). Call 231-3370 for their latest deals (open daily). 10-speed and mountain bikes are available at **Bike Moves** (phone 271-1854). For moped rental, call 211-7060. Be sure to ask about off-season discounts.

Accommodation

Hostels in Adelaide often get booked up, particularly the YHA hostel, by far the most attractive of the lot. You can always find a place somewhere (the hostels will help you), except during Adelaide's big events: the Grand Prix and the Adelaide Festival. Most hostel accommodations are about a mile southeast of Rundle Mall on Gilles St.

More central are the Backpacker's International on North Tce., the Backpacker's Inn on Carrington St., and the YMCA. None is within comfortable walking distance (with luggage) of train and bus stations. To reach the Gilles St. hostels, take the bus from King William St. to Pulteney or Hutt St.

Adelaide YHA Hostel, 290 Gilles St. (phone 223-6007). $10/dorm bed. Book by mailing ahead, through other hostels, or over the phone with a credit card. 4-night limit Dec-Jan. Excellent, modern facility with clean rooms and spacious common area. Very friendly managers. BBQ area. Luggage storage available at deli across the street for small fee. Office open 8:00am-9:30am, 1:00pm-10:00pm. Dorms closed 9:30am-1:00pm, late-night key until 1:00am. Annex space in St. Anne's College at Adelaide Univ. (great location). Book through YHA or call 267-1478.

Backpacker's Inn, 112 Carrington St. (phone 223-6635). Bus from downtown, or not a bad walk. Centrally located. Well-managed and secure. Office open 8:00am-noon, 5:00pm-10:00pm; 24-hour key for those staying.

Backpackers International, 307 North Tce. (phone 232-0823). Book at Gilles St. Backpackers (below). The most central of the hostels. Nice terrace house. Clean bathrooms and new kitchen. Less rowdy than the Gilles St. Backpackers.

Backpackers Hostel, 263 Gilles St. (phone 223-5680). Annex 253 Gilles St. Mostly dorm rooms, but couples rooms available. Not terribly attractive, but clean and organized. Very little kitchen space. Bicycle rental. Office closed 11:00am-3:00pm, dorms always open. Book here for North Tce. Backpackers.

Rucksacker's International, 257 Gilles St. (phone 232-0823). 4-person dorm room. Spacious dorms but small outdoor area. Reasonably clean. Pool table. Office closed 11:00am-5:30pm, but manager is in and out all day.

YMCA, Grenfell St. (phone 223-1611). Dorm beds, singles, doubles. Linen and towels included. Large and institutional. Very central location. No kitchen. Book from 10:30am; rooms available at 2:00pm, dorm rooms at 4:00pm.

Cotel, 57 North Tce., corner West Tce. (phone 211-7335). Great Victorian exterior and nice entryway, but needs upkeep on the inside. Not very secure. Crowded dorms with lots of semi-permanents. Dirty outdoor showers and toilets, kitchen unkempt. Cozy TV room. Dorms for couples with double-bed bunks (!).

Sportsman's Hotel, 185 Grote St. (phone 231-3250). Very cheap singles and doubles. Central location. Looks rough on the outside, but actually the pub is subdued and closes early. Pleasant, clean rooms with private sinks and coffee/tea-making facilities. Good meals in the pub downstairs.

Rumbalara Private Hotel and Hostel, 16 South Esplanade, Glenelg (phone 295-2390). Take tram from Victoria Square, about 20 min. ride. Dorms, singles, doubles. Linen provided. Magnificent, historic mansion that needs restoration. On the beach. Terrible beds, but they promised to replace them soon. Plenty of bathrooms, but they're not the cleanest. Fridge and TV in dorm rooms. Rustic kitchen facilities. Good meals available in the former ballroom, also licensed for wine and beer. Stay here if you want the beach, but don't bother otherwise.

Things to See and Do

City Center

Adelaide is a great walking town. Those with a special interest in architecture should start exploring the city at the **History Trust of South Australia** (Institute Building, North Tce. near Kintore Ave.), where you'll find self-guided tours with historic commentary (open M-F 10:00am-noon, 1:00pm-4:00pm).

The best historic introduction to Adelaide is a visit to the **Old Parliament House** (North Tce., west of King William Rd.) where, starting in 1843, S.A.'s first Legislative Council debated religious freedom and statehood and wrote a Constitution. There's an excellent commentary on the exploration and colonization of S.A., too. Take the 1.5 hour tour instead of the half-hour tour because the former includes simulated Council debates that bring the history alive. It's $2.50 either way. The long tour departs every 40 minutes starting at 10:00am (last tour at 3:20pm); the short tour departs every 40 minutes from 10:35am (last tour is 4:25pm). The museum is open M-F 10:00am-5:00pm, weekends noon-5:00pm.

Whatever questions you have left after the Old Parliament House can be answered at the **Migration Museum** (82 Kintore Ave.), which focuses on non-British immigration to S.A. Excellent displays depict what it was like to uproot one's life in the homeland and how Australia has treated its immigrants through the years. This museum is a great introduction for travelers who intend to explore the state, because many S.A. towns retain the ethnic character of their original settlers. The Migration Museum, housed in another landmark building, the old Destitute Asylum, is open M-F 10:00am-5:00pm, weekend and public holidays 1:00pm-5:00pm.

From the Migration Museum you can stroll the length of North Tce. and see the Univ. of Adelaide's buildings, the State Library, Natural History Museum, and Art Gallery. Don't miss the exhibit on Aborigines at the **Natural History Museum** (open 10:00am-5:00pm daily, admission free). The **Art**

Gallery of South Australia is nicely contained. Highlights are the Australian colonial paintings and turn-of-the-century Australian masters (open 10:00am-5:00pm daily, admission free).

Behind the Art Gallery and extending east to Kintore Ave., an area of restored buildings merge into the **University of Adelaide** campus—worth exploring, with several nice picnic spots. On the south side of North Tce., **Ayers House** has an elegant, overrated restaurant and hosts social affairs. If you decide to tour it, ask the attendant if you can go inside the upstairs rooms instead of viewing from behind ropes—they don't always offer automatically, but you paid for it! Ayers House is open T-F from 10:00am-4:00pm, weekends and public holidays from 2:00pm-4:00pm. Admission is about $3. Across the street from Ayers House, the **Adelaide Botanical Gardens**, another scenic picnic spot, are lush and pretty all year.

In the vicinity of Victoria Square, there's a free **Telecommunications Museum** (131 King William St.) with exhibits on telephone and radio technology. You can get hooked trying out all the old contraptions. Nearby is the **Central Market** (south side of Grote St., just west of Victoria Square), with the usual fruits and vegetables, plus fish and meat stalls and an area where craftspeople sell their wares. The handcrafted S.A. jewelry sold there, though displayed in small quantities, is some of the best in the country. The market is open T & Th 9:00am-6:00pm, F 9:00am-9:00pm, Sat 9:00am-1:00pm.

At the north end of King William St. by the shores of the Torrens River, the impressive **Festival Centre** is the centerpiece of the Adelaide Festival. Tours leave about five times a day (call 216-8729 or 216-8713 for schedule). The complex overlooks the Torrens, along which there's a lovely path. Following it east, you can walk behind the Uni to the zoo, across Frome Rd. The zoo has some fantastic birds and wallabies, among other animals. Call for feeding times. (Open 9:30am-5:00pm daily; $7, discount with student ID; phone 267-3255.)

Beyond the City Center

Definitely try to get out to Port Adelaide, and a visit to nearby North Adelaide is also worthwhile. Adelaide's favorite city suburb is Glenelg, with a somewhat polluted but picturesque beach. (None of the suburban beaches, like Brighton and Summerton, has surf.) The Adelaide Hills are especially beautiful in autumn, and people often take overnight trips or pass through on their way to the Southern Vales.

This section covers close-by trips to the Hills, while *Trips from Adelaide* covers the Hills extensively.

North Adelaide

North Adelaide was the first residential area of the city, and many original houses remain. It's now up-scale and chic, with fun shops and excellent, mid-priced restaurants. Take a bus or walk to Melbourne St., North Adelaide's main drag.

Glenelg

In 1836, Capt. John Hindmarsh set sail from England with 272 immigrants and crew aboard the *H.M.S. Buffalo*. They landed on the beach at Glenelg, where Hindmarsh proclaimed the colony of South Australia. Glenelg still holds a certain intrigue for Adelaideans. There are better beaches, but people nonetheless go there for Sunday afternoon walks or for **Magic Mountain**, a monstrous waterslide.

Aside from the beach, you can visit a replica of the *H.M.S. Buffalo* at **Patawalonga Boat Haven** (Anzac Hwy. and Adelphi Tce.). The bulk of the ship is now a restaurant, while the remaining rooms contain extracts from the log book, diaries of voyagers, etc. It costs $3, which is a lot for what you see (open M-F 9:00am-noon, 2:30pm-5:00pm, weekends and public holidays 10:00am-5:00pm).

The best visit in town is **Shelland** (corner Mary and Melbourne Sts.). It looks like a tacky souvenir store from the outside, but inside there's an amazing collection of shells gathered by one woman. The collection includes priceless cameos and other painstakingly crafted works from shells. The museum is free, and shell jewelry is sold in the store.

One of the best aspect of a trip to Glenelg is the **tram ride** there. You catch a little wooden tram in the center of Victoria Square, which runs every 15 minutes during the day, for about $1 each way. Get off at the terminus, a picturesque square flanked by an ornate Town Hall. Tourist Information is clearly marked, and you'll find town maps there as well as bike and water-sport equipment rental. It's open every day. There's also a hostel in Glenelg, on the beach (see *Accommodation*).

Port Adelaide

This historic seaport was established in 1840, four years after the founding of S.A. Although the suburb is largely industrial and appears uninviting, the History Trust of South Australia has put a lot of effort into renovating the old warehouses along the waterfront and a pocket of historic buildings in town. The result is attractive and interesting.

On Lipson St., the center of Port Adelaide's renovated area, you'll find an Information Centre in the former Sailmakers Building, and the **Maritime Museum**, the town's highlight. Buy your ticket for the Maritime Museum at the info center ($6.50, discount with student ID). Located inside renovated 1850's Bond Stores, the museum is filled with interesting memorabilia and displays, including a reconstructed penny arcade and models of the grimy ship holds used by the first immigrants to Australia. The ticket also gets you into the lighthouse and "No. 1 Boat Shed." (Open Sat-W and every day during school holidays, 10:00am-5:00pm.)

The bus to Port Adelaide departs the Ansett building on North Tce. and takes about 40 minutes. Ask the driver to drop you by the Maritime Museum.

The Adelaide Hills

South of the city, en route to the Adelaide Hills, the estate **Carrick Hill** (590 Fullarton Rd., Springfield) was built in 1939 in the style of an English manor house. While there is a collection of art and some nice furnishings, the real reason to go is the picturesque garden. (Open W-Sun and public holidays 10:00am-5:00pm, closed 12:30pm-1:30pm; closed all of July; admission $4, discount for students; $2.50 to get in the garden gates.) To get there, take the Springfield bus from King William Rd. and expect a long walk at the end (take a map).

There are two wildlife sanctuaries in the Adelaide Hills. Neither Cleland nor Warrawong sanctuaries is easy to reach without your own transport, but the hostels offer tours. **Cleland**, on the slopes of Mt. Lofty, has a natural bush setting where koalas, dingoes, 'roos, and emus roam (open 9:30am-5:00pm daily, except some fire-ban days; admission $4, discount with student ID). Cleland is accessible by the Summertown bus from Currie St. It's a half-hour walk from where you get off at Summit Rd. While you're there, drive or climb to the summit of Mt. Lofty for a great view of the city. The walk begins at the base of Waterfall Gully, on Waterfall Gully Rd. in Burnside.

Warrawong Sanctuary (Williams Rd., Mylor), more extensive than Cleland, is the better choice for those who have already been to the usual wildlife parks. Within its 35 acres, Warrawong aims to restore the ecosystem of the Hills to what it was before European habitation. Caretakers have saved several endangered animals, including the brush-tailed bettong, the rarest kangaroo alive. Half the entire bettong population of 500 live at Warrawong. Visitors generally see the sanctuary by guided walks during the day, at dawn, and at sunset, for $10. Most guided walks occur on the weekend; call 388-5380 for times. **Johnson's Bus Service** goes to the Warrawong (phone 231-5959).

Food

We must now discuss two S.A. specialties: the **pie floater** and the **Cornish pasty**. Consisting of a meat pie in a sea of thick pea soup, the pie floater is enough to staunch the heartiest appetite (and, perhaps, is better left for the South Australians). The pie floater truck is on Franklin St. next to the GPO. Pasties are advertised everywhere, but get the genuine Cornish product at **Perryman's Bakery** (54 Tynte St., North Adelaide). They pull piping hot trays of pasties and pies from the oven at noon, a cultural and culinary experience not to be missed.

Cooking for yourself? Then head to the **Central Market** (west of Victoria Square between Grote and Gouger Sts.), where you'll find fresh produce, Asian grocers, butchers, and fish stores (open T-Th 9:00am-6:00pm, F 9:00am-9:00pm, and Sat 9:00am-1:00pm). Go at noon on Sat for deep discounts on produce. Adjoining the market is an indoor shopping center with cheap restaurants and an International Food Hall with a bar in the center. It's open M-F 9:00am-5:30pm, Sat 9:00am-noon, and Sun 10:00am-4:00pm.

Although Adelaide has a small selection of inexpensive restaurants, the budget offerings are excellent and full of character. The cheapest are on Rundle St. (the eastern extension of the Mall) and Hindley St. (the western extension). Hutt St. is more sophisticated and slightly more expensive. Melbourne St. in North Adelaide has some exotic restaurants that would be a splurge for the budget traveler.

Adelaide also has numerous old hotels with hearty pub meals, and in the last few years many have added bistro sections with more expensive menus. Another way to fill up cheaply is to get Asian food at lunchtime. There are several choices in this category that offer good quality in a no-frills setting.

Breakfast, Lunch, and Snacks

Al Fresco Gelateria (BYO), 260 Rundle St. (phone 223-4589). Indoor/outdoor cafe-style. Italian breakfasts, all-day coffee, ice cream (gelati), and snacks. Open Sun-Th 8:00am-1:30pm, F-Sat 8:00am-3:00am, public holidays 9:00am-1:30am. Moderate.

Ruby's Cafe, 255b Rundle St. (phone 224-0365). 1950's decor. Renowned and imaginative breakfasts, from $6. Adventurous lunch/dinner menu (pesto souffle, Indian curry, and fish stew) that changes biweekly. $2 corkage fee. Breakfast W-F 7:00am-10:00am, Sun 9:00am-5:00pm. Lunch W-Sun from noon. Dinner daily from 6:30pm. Moderate to expensive.

Crossways (no alcohol), 79 Hindley St., first floor. Hare Krishna restaurant. All-you-can-eat vegetarian fare, and no harassment. Open M-F noon-3:00pm. Cheap, cheap, cheap!

Asian Gourmet (BYO), Central Market (phone 51-9657). Huge soup and noodle dishes, about $6. Open M-W 9:30am-3:00pm, T & Th 9:30am-5:00pm, F 9:30am-9:00pm. Cheap.

Penang Coffee House (no alcohol), Gilbert Place (alley off King William Rd.) (phone 231-2552). Noodle and rice dishes, none over $6. Open M-Sat 10:30am-11:00pm, Sun 4:30pm-11:00pm. Cheap.

Twains Malaysian Cafe, 184 Rundle St. (phone 223-3136). Hawker-style (soups filled with noodles and vegetables), about $6. Decor lacks character, but good value food. Open M-Th 11:30am-6:00pm, F 11:30am-9:00pm, Sat 11:00am-2:00pm. Cheap.

Clearlight Cafe (no alcohol), 201 Rundle St. (phone 223-5994). Health food restaurant at basement level, health food store above. Vegetarian dishes, soups, homemade bread, and fruit drinks. Most meals $6. Open M-Th 9:00am-4:00pm, F 9:00am-7:30pm. Cheap.

The Coffee Pot, 27 Rundle Mall (phone 212-1613). Freshly roasted coffee, $2/two cups. Scones, apple pie, desserts from $3. Newspapers provided. The perfect retreat on a rainy day. Open M-Th 8:30am-6:30pm, F 8:30am-10:30pm, Sat until noon.

Dinner

Fasta Pasta Bar, 131 Pirie St. (phone 224-0320). Semi-self serve. Excellent pasta and antipasto plates. Around $7, with bread included. Great value. Moderate.

Jerusalem Shishkebab House (BYO), 131b Hindley St. (phone 212-6185). Small and dark with burlap hanging from the ceiling. Great value Middle Eastern fare. Very popular and loud. $6/main. Open M-Sat 11:00am-11:00pm, Sun 4:00pm-11:00pm. Cheap.

The Abode of the Friendly Toad (no alcohol), 85 Henley Beach, Mile End (phone 43-5225). Catch bus #28 from Grenfell St. (about a 25-minute ride). Nonprofit restaurant run by volunteers—the best deal in town! Simple homestyle fare: soup, $1.50, $5/main with salad. Dinner T, W, F, Sat from 6:30pm, and lunch at 12:30pm on Th. Cheap.

Royal Admiral Hotel, 125 Hindley St. (phone 231-5929). Renovated pub. Counter meals with a South American accent on one side. Huge hamburgers ($3.50) and hot dogs ($3). On the other side is "Cafe de Pub," with innovative a la carte dishes (including rabbit and goat). About $10/main. Open M-Sat 11:00am on. Closed Sun.

Austral Hotel, 205 Rundle St. (phone 223-4660). Renovated, attractive pub with two options: counter meals (from $4) served noon-2:00pm and 7:00pm-9:00pm. A la carte bistro behind small front bar with veal, chicken, and fish dishes (from $9). Bistro open M-W 11:00am-midnight, Th-Sat 11:00am-3:00am, Sun 2:00pm-8:00pm.

Pluto Cafe, 28 Peel St., between Hindley and Currie Sts. (phone 231-4888). Modern and hot. Nouvelle cuisine. Buffet-style lunch, about $7. A la carte dinner, $14. Sinful, luscious (and pricey) desserts. A late night hangout. Open M-F noon-3:00pm, Th-Sat 6:30pm-4:00am.

Nightlife

Travelers assume Adelaide is void of nightlife until they walk down **Hindley St.** after 8:00pm. It's alive and hopping, with neon lights and crowds (and, believe it or not, a little sleaze), every night of week.

But aside from the hubbub on Hindley St., Adelaide nightlife doesn't offer much originality or choice. People tend to make a night of long, late dinners with groups of friends. Before setting off in search of good live music, check the entertainment section in Thursday's *Advertiser*, which lists band appearances for the week; or call SA.FM radio station (phone 272-1990).

Late night pubs tend to be a straight-laced, yuppie scene. **The Earl of Aberdeen** (316 Pulteney St.), **General Havelock** (162 Hutt St.), and the **Norwood Hotel** (The Parade, Norwood) are all attractively restored and filled with a 20-35 age crowd. For a more diverse group, go to the **Austral** (205 Rundle St.) or the **Exeter** (Rundle St.). Both have bands on weekends. The **Royal Admiral** (125 Hindley St.) is the only place in town where you can find free live music, but it's a bit small and crowded and can get rough. There's good food in the front bar. Remember that pubs tend to close at midnight most nights, and at 8:00pm on Sunday.

Sunday is a big night for night-clubbing, while Monday and Tuesday are quiet. Nightclubs in order of preference include:

The "Fez" Piano Bar (on Fridays), Festival Centre, King William Rd. in Elder Park. The best place to be on a Friday after 11:00pm. Live music is always good. Dancing. Very popular. About $6 to get in. Drinks are expensive. Open until 3:00am.

Cargo Club, 213 Hindley St. (phone 231-2327). The best place to hear live jazz. Uncramped, mellow atmosphere. Cover depends on the performers (free to $8). It's cheaper on week nights. Live jazz every night. Open W-Sun 10:00pm-5:30am.

Limbo's, 30 Fenn Place, just off Hindley St. (phone 211-7117). Local, original bands, interspersed with good DJ. Trendy crowd. The place to be seen. Cover usually $6. Open W-Sun 9:00pm-5:00am.

Le Rox, 9 Light Square, just off Hindley St. (phone 231-3234). In an old warehouse. Very crowded with young clientele. Good bands. Cover varies. Open Th 9:00pm-3:00am, F-Sun 9:00pm-5:00am.

The Adelaide Casino (North Tce., west of King William St.). The most attractive casino in Australia. In the old Adelaide train station, and the entrance area where you wait in line (sometimes for a half-hour or more) is the former lobby. Drinks are expensive (though the munchies are free). There are several bars to choose from. No sneakers or jeans, and men need collared shirts. Open M-F 10:00am-4:00am, weekends 24 hours.

Entertainment

For a town with a reputation for being old-fashioned, the **Adelaide Festival Centre** is a most sophisticated facility. In fact, Adelaide is something of a mecca for the arts, assisted by an illustrious biannual event called the **Adelaide Festival of the Arts**. The Festival Centre has several theaters and is the main venue for the State Theatre company, the Adelaide Symphony Orchestra, and the Australian Dance Theatre Company. For performance information, go to the theater or call the box office at 213-4788, M-Sat 9:30am-8:30pm. Buy tickets on the spot or through Bass ticketing agency (phone 213-4777, open M-Sat 9:00am-6:00pm). Student rush tickets are available for the theater company and the symphony (not for performances from out of town), a half-hour before show time. There's free live rock in the amphitheater on Sunday afternoon from 2:00pm-4:00pm.

For other performance information around town, see Thursday's *Advertiser* or the *Adelaide Review*, available free at most tourist sights and civic buildings. The *Review* covers art, live performances, architecture, restaurants, and literature.

Most of Adelaide's movie theaters are on Hindley St. and in arcades off Rundle Mall. On Tuesday, **Hoyt's Theatres** cuts ticket prices in half, as do most of the specialty movie houses. For unusual and classic films, try **The Trak** (375 Greenhill Rd., Toorak Gardens, phone 332-8020) and **The Classic** (128 Hindley St., phone 231-0752).

Adelaide is second only to Melbourne in Australian-rules football. There are several rival teams in the footy league, each representing an Adelaide suburb. The main ovals are **Football Park** in West Lakes and the **Adelaide**

Oval in town, where cricket is also played (footy season is April-Sept). For information, call the Recreation and Sport Administration Centre at 212-5855, or check the *Advertiser.*

Trips from Adelaide

Wine valleys, hiking, and beaches are all close to Adelaide. The Barossa Valley is about a 1.5-hour drive north of Adelaide, while 1-2 hours further north are the districts of Clare and Burra. Clare produces distinctive wines; Burra was S.A.'s first copper boom town. The Fleurieu Peninsula, south of Adelaide, has lots to explore in a compact area.

All peninsular destinations, including the Adelaide Hills, the Southern Vales wine region, the coastal retreat of Victor Harbor, and peninsula beaches, are within an hour's drive of one another. The only proximity problem on the Fleurieu is transport, which tends to be decent if the departure point is Adelaide but infrequent between various peninsula locations. A short boat ride off the Fleurieu's southern point, Kangaroo Island is a favorite with international visitors.

There are hostels in Nuriootpa (Barossa Valley) and Norton Summit (Adelaide Hills); in several other Hills destinations there are limited-access hostels along hiking trails. There are also YHA or YHA-affiliated hostels in Victor Harbour and the Inman Valley (both on the Fleurieu Peninsula), and Kangaroo Island.

The Barossa Valley
Tourist Information, Coulthard House, 66 Murray St., Nuriootpa, phone 085-62-1866. Open M-F 8:30am-5:30pm, weekends and public holidays 9:30am-4:30pm.

About 50 km north of Adelaide is Australia's largest wine region, the Barossa Valley, where 25% of Australia's wine grapes are crushed. Barossa wineries are larger and more commercial than those in the Southern Vales and Clare Valley, and therefore you get less personal attention. However, the big draw to the area for hostellers is the Bunkhaus in Nuriootpa, where you stay in the middle of a vineyard (literally!) in an atmosphere that is informative, fun, and homey.

The Barossa was first settled in 1842 by Germans and Brits. You'll appreciate the area's German origins when you try the local bakeries. Otherwise, the valley's main centers—Nuriootpa, Tanunda, and Angaston—are charming, Anglo-Australian. The Tanunda Hotel and other elaborate, Victorian buildings are popular with photographers.

Tanunda and Nuriootpa are closest to the vineyards. Before setting off, visit the **Nuriootpa Information Center** in Coulthard House. It has all sorts of good information, plus maps and details on vineyards. **Saltram's**, one of the largest and oldest wine producers in the valley, is a perfect first stop if you're tasting wines. The friendly owners make it a policy to explain their wine products to all tasters (inexperienced and connoisseurs alike).

There are more than just vineyards to see in the Barossa, especially in **An-**

gaston. At the top end of Angaston's main street is the oldest fruit-drying factory in Australia. **Collingrove** (6 km from town) was built in 1850 for the Angas family, the major underwriters for original settlement in the area. If you have yet to see a real Aussie homestead, take a look. (Open Oct-May: W-Sun and public holidays 10:00am-4:30pm; June-Sept: Sun 2:00pm-4:30pm. Admission $3.)

Getting There and Getting Around: Barossa Valley Bus Service (phone 085-65-6258) stops in Tanunda, Nuriootpa, and Angaston daily. It departs from the Central Bus Station in Adelaide and costs about $7/one-way. On return, make sure to buy a ticket in town so the driver knows to stop. Stops: Angaston, at Miles Newsagency; Nuriootpa, at Jet Fuels; Tanunda, at M. Clark Newsagent.

Renting a car with five people can be cheaper than renting a bike. Check the phone book for current deals (generally cheaper from Adelaide). Vineyards are mostly within biking distance of one another, and you can rent bikes from the Bunkhaus or Keils Gift Centre in Tanunda. **Valley Tours** (phone 62-1524) runs a day tour that includes a visit to Collingwood and some wineries. The tour costs about $24 (includes lunch).

Accommodation: For $10/night at the **Bunkhaus**, you not only stay in a great cottage in the middle of a working vineyard, you also get to know the Matthews, some of the friendliest hostel managers in Australia. They'll tell you about wines, serve big dinners (with plenty of wine, of course), and generally make the Barossa one of the most worthwhile destinations of your trip. They offer grape-picking jobs during picking season, too, if you're willing to stay a few weeks. The Bunkhaus is at the corner of the Barossa Valley Hwy. and Nuraip Rd., and the bus from Adelaide will drop you there on request. Call ahead to make sure they have room (phone 085-62-2260).

The cheapest alternative is the **Angaston Hotel** (phone 085-64-2428), for $18/single. In Nuriootpa, try the **Vine Inn Hotel Motel** (phone 085-62-2133).

The Adelaide Hills

The picturesque Adelaide Hills ring Adelaide to the south and east. It doesn't take much of a drive to find quaint mountain townships surrounded by sheep farms and woods. The Hills are especially worth checking out if you enjoy hiking. At the very least, pay a visit to Cleland Conservation Park on Mt. Lofty (see above). If you plan a trip to the Fleurieu Peninsula, make the effort to stop in the Hills first (all public transport passes through).

East and slightly north of Adelaide are Norton Summit, Morialta Falls, Black Hill Conservation Park, Gumeracha and Torrens Gorge, and Warren Conservation Park. South and southeast are Mt. Lofty, Belair, and Hahndorf.

Hiking: Obtain hiking information from the **Wilderness Shop** at 44 Grote St. (phone 231-0625, open M-Th 10:00am-5:00pm, F 10:00am- 9:00pm, and Sat 9:00am-noon) or the **Dept. of Sport and Recreation**, 25 Grenfell St., (phone 213-0556). The latter provides trail maps and free pamphlets with notes on the popular trails in the state, called **Jubilee Walks**. For in-depth advice, ask at the Wilderness Shop about **Adelaide Bushwalkers**. Members of the club are usually happy to talk about hiking in the area. The National Parks and Wildlife Service (55 Grenfell St.) or the YHA (38 Sturt St.) may also help.

The **Heyson Trail** begins near Cape Jervis and extends about 500 km north to the Flinders Ranges, directly through the Adelaide Hills. YHA has several limited-access hostels along the trail, and their Adelaide office has complete trail notes and good hiking advice. Note: the trail is closed Nov-April because of a fire threat.

The day hiker will find many beautiful walks in the Hills. Mt. Lofty (in Cleland Conservation Park) and Black Hill Conservation Park/Morialta Falls offer the closest getaways. The walk up **Mt. Lofty** begins at Waterfall Gully in Burnside and rewards you with a sweeping view of the city and surrounds. **Black Hill Conservation Park** has walks of varying lengths, and a day-long hike will take you from Black Hill to Morialta Falls (or vice versa). In winter and spring, overflowing waterfalls make the hike terrific, while in July and August wildflowers abound.

The best rock climbing in the vicinity is at **Morialta Falls**, which you can reach by suburban bus, with a 1.5 km walk from the stop. Maps and directions for Cleland, Morialta, and Black Hills Conservation Parks are available at Tourism South Australia in Adelaide.

Further afield, **Warren Conservation Park** offers an excellent day hike through woods and sheep pastures. From the fire station at the summit, there's an unforgettable view to the ocean. Trail notes are absolutely necessary. Unfortunately, there's no public transport out there.

Note: Due to the threat of bush fires, trails are often closed during high-risk periods in summer. There should be no problem hiking April-Oct, though.

Eastern Hills
In addition to all the walking opportunities in the eastern Hills, a few miles from the town of Norton Summit is a Historic Trust property known as **Marble Hill**, built in 1879 as the summer residence of the Governor. In 1955 a bush fire nearly destroyed the mansion, and the ruins are partially restored for visitors. You get a great view from the tower, and the grounds are perfect for picnicking (open W, Sat, and public holidays 1:00pm-5:00pm, Sun 10:00am-5:00pm; admission $3). A farm/hostel called Fuzzie's Farm is outside Norton Summit (see below). Make a detour to drive by Torrens Gorge if you're near Gumeracha.

Southeastern Hills
The **Recreation Park** in Belair is a stately setting for a picnic and walk, but avoid it on weekends and holidays, when there are tons of other people. If you do go on the weekend, look through the **Government House**, built in 1859 (open F-Sun and public holidays 12:30pm-4:00pm). Park maps are at the entrance kiosk. An STA bus goes by the park gates.

Southeast of Belair are the towns/suburbs of Stirling, Bridgewater, Mt. Barker, and Hahndorf. They all have tea rooms and shops, but if you're going to stop in just one place, make it **Hahndorf**, which still has an overwhelmingly German flavor, reflected in the buildings, customs, and even clothes. However, tourist crowds be annoying, so avoid the weekend or try to choose a rainy day. Hahndorf tourist info is in the petrol station at 76 Main St.

In this region of the Hills, private gardens are open to the public in March and April, when autumn foliage is at its best. Inquire at tourist information in Adelaide.

Getting There: If you're lucky enough to be driving, take the marked tourist roads rather than the main freeway. STA has daily bus service to Morialta Falls, Bridgewater, Stirling, Hahndorf, Mt. Barker, and Belair. **Johnson's Bus Service** (phone 231-5959, Central Bus Station, 101 Franklin St.) goes to Norton Summit (weekdays only). **E & K Mini-Tours** (phone 268-3743 or 337-8739) offers day and half-day tours through Adelaide hostels. Half-day trips go to Mt. Lofty, Cleland Conservation Park, Hahndorf, and Stirling (about $10). Full-day tours also include Gumeracha and Tea-Tree Gully (about $20).

Accommodation: YHA has limited-access hostels in Kersbrook (near the Barossa), Norton Summit, and Mt. Lofty, as well as further south along the Heyson Trail. To use them, you must visit the YHA Head Office in Adelaide and obtain directions and a key (one week in advance, if possible).

The other option for hostellers is one of the most unique hostels in Australia, known as **Fuzzie's Farm**. People generally stay for a week or two and learn some aspect of farming or carpentry. You pay a flat fee (around $30) for the entire visit, and the choice of apprenticeship is entirely up to the you. One visitor from Japan decided he wanted to learn how to weld, and since Fuzzie didn't know enough to teach him, he arranged for someone in town to do the training. An Australian woman we met made a beautiful jarrah wood table there. All nine hostellers live in a cabin made and furnished by the hands of apprentices—a cozy, unique setting. It's also possible to stay without working for about $20/night, including meals. The farm is in Norton Summit, but you must call first (phone 08-390-1464).

Licensed hotels are the least expensive non-hostel option. Cheapest are the **Gumeracha Hotel** (phone 08-389-1001) and the **Stirling Hotel** (phone 08-339-2045). There's also an inexpensive B&B called **Puddledock Farm**, 1 km from Warren Conservation Park on the Heyson Trail, past Kersbrook (phone 08-389-3189).

The Southern Vales
Tourist Information, Old Clarendon Winery Complex, Main St., Clarendon, phone 08-383-6166.

We highly recommend splurging on a rental car for a day of wining in the Southern Vales. (Premier Coachlines goes to McClaren Vale from Central Bus Station, but you need a car to visit vineyards.)

McClaren Vale, in the heart of the wine district, is an hour's drive south

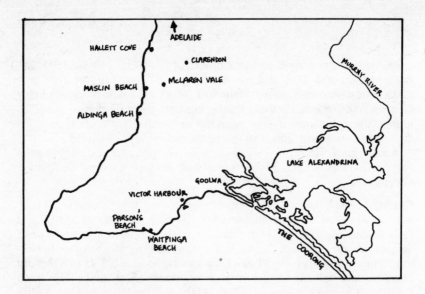

of Adelaide. The giant of wineries in the region is **Thomas Hardy's**, with **Seaview** a distant second. However, the great draw to the Southern Vales is dozens of small, family-owned vineyards. The winemakers often serve their wine themselves, and most of them enjoy explaining the product and chatting. Our personal favorites are **d'Arenberg** and **Coriole**, but don't trust our palates. Get a map with descriptions of the various wineries and follow your nose. Maps are available at Tourism South Australia in Adelaide.

While the village of McClaren Vale is most central to the vineyards, **Clarendon** is also a nice town for a pit stop. Unfortunately, there isn't a hostel in the area, and if you go on a weekend you'll be lucky to find a room anywhere. But assuming you're fit to drive, it's a great day trip or a convenient stop-off en route to Victor Harbour and Goolwa.

Fleurieu Peninsula Beaches
Suburban Adelaide beaches don't offer much surf or scenery, so beach-goers generally head south to the west coast of the Fleurieu Peninsula.

Hallett Cove is the closest of the good beach areas, where cliffs border small beaches, and there's a reef to snorkel on. Further south, **Maslin Beach** is nudist and also happens to be the best of the lot—white, wide, and sheltered from the wind. Snorkelers and divers should head for **Aldinga Reef**. On the southern side of the Fleurieu, **Waitpinga** and **Parson's Beaches** have the best surfing.

Victor Harbour
Tourist Information, 2 Stuart St., phone 52-1370 or 52-1200.

A casual, attractive beachside resort and traditional retreat for Adelaide's prominent families, Victor Harbour remains the favored getaway of city weekenders. Travelers have been known to stop on their way to Kangaroo Island and never continue, they like it so much. In summer, the hostel is popular and a party atmosphere pervades. The rugged coastal scenery is a big draw, as is the town's historic atmosphere.

Victor was the first place in S.A. known to white people. In 1802, explorers Matthew Flinders and Nicholas Baudin coincidentally met each other on the coast at Victor, and Flinders subsequently named the spot Encounter Bay. Soon after, sealers and whalers established S.A.'s first industry, whaling.

The first thing to see in Victor is **Granite Island**, attached to the shore by a pedestrian causeway. There's an antique, horse-drawn tram that goes across as well, for $1. Climb to the top (forget the little chairlift) for gorgeous views of the coast. You can practically touch the wild wallabies if you venture into the brush, and you'll see fairy penguins among the rocks during the day. Otherwise, you'll definitely glimpse them at dusk, when they waddle from the ocean to their nests. Short camel rides are available on the mainland beach next to the causeway.

For even better views and a break from the crowds, the former whaling station lookout on The Bluff at **Rosetta Head** is 1 km west of Granite Island. This walk is a bit more taxing, but well worth it. **Urimbirra Wildlife Park**, 5 km north of Victor has 'roos, crocs, and koala feeding in the early afternoon. It's located along the main highway from Adelaide (open daily 10:00am-5:00pm; admission $4).

A few km east of Victor is **Port Elliot**, where a historic guest house called **Thomas Henry's** serves an excellent meal, if you're willing to spend a bit extra. Main courses (such as rabbit, kangaroo, and fish) range from $12-$18.

Getting There: Premier Coachlines runs daily to Victor Harbour from Adelaide (Central Bus Station, phone 217-0777). It takes 1.5 hours and also goes to Port Elliot. For the return, the bus departs Southern Holden in Victor (phone 52-1200 for schedules) or the post office in Port Elliot (phone 54-2046).

The alternative is the *Southern Encounter*, an authentic steam train that chugs over the Adelaide Hills every Sunday (and on some public holidays). The scenic, unique trip takes 3.5 hours. Note that the train doesn't run if there's a fire ban, and in summer they can't use the old steam engine because of the fire hazard. The cost is $28 roundtrip, and you must book in advance, either at Tourism South Australia, the Adelaide railway station on North Tce., or Keswick Station.

Accommodation: The YHA-affiliated hostel in Victor is part of a guest house called **Warringa** (16 Flinders Pde., phone 085-52-1028). The hostel is on the ocean in two separate houses, each with full facilities and rooms for 4-8. The managers are very mellow, so drinking in the hostel is permitted and dorms are open all day. Dorms and doubles available.

Otherwise, there are a number of quaint B&B's and farmstays in the area, and the caravan parks in Port Elliot or Hindmarsh Island (near Goolwa) have nice beach locations. Pick up Tourism South Australia's *Fleurieu Peninsula Accommodation* guide for the latest prices.

20 km northwest of Victor Harbor is a **YHA Hostel** hidden away at Inman Valley. It's a nice retreat if you can get there (no public transport). Call 085-58-8277 for bookings and directions. Overnight cost is $6/person.

Goolwa

The 2,000 km Murray River, which once brought hundreds of paddle steamers through Victoria and S.A., empties into the ocean near Victor Harbour at Lakes Alexandrina and Albert. The Younghusband Peninsula forms an ocean barrier to the whole wetlands system of the Murray Mouth, creating a vast wildlife sanctuary. A narrow passage of water separating the peninsula from mainland is called the **Coorong**, famous as a bird sanctuary and for its rich marsh lands.

The former river port of Goolwa lies at the Murray's final bend. With the introduction of paddle steamers in 1853, Goolwa had a brief, illustrious stint as the trade-off point between boats that brought goods from inland and overseas export ships. Subsequent railway development altered trading routes, and Goolwa was a virtual ghost town by the 1880's. But it still has some charming old buildings and galleries, and the **Signal Point** complex has an extensive "interpretive centre" focusing on all aspects of the Murray River. The displays are imaginative, fun, and well worth your time and money (open 10:00am-5:00pm daily; museum costs $6). Tourist information and a cafeteria with huge windows overlooking the Murray are also part of the complex.

River cruises leave the wharf at Signal Point; the *M.V. Encounter* offers the best deals. Weekday prices are $10 for 2 hours, and cruises head either up the mouth of the river or to Lake Alexandrina and the Coorong. Most of them leave at 11:00am. Make sure to book a day ahead during school holidays and summer weekends.

Getting There: Unfortunately, getting to Goolwa from Victor Harbour is harder than getting there from Adelaide. **Johnson's Bus Service** (phone 08-231-5959) goes from Adelaide to Goolwa once each weekday (not public holidays). It takes 2 hours.

The *Cockle Train* runs along the coast between Goolwa and Victor Harbour during school holidays and some weekends. The train cars were built around 1915, and it's a scenic ride ($10). Call the Victor Harbour railway station at 085-52-2782 or reserve a place through Tourism South Australia. Otherwise ask at tourist information about the Goolwa taxi shuttle (runs twice weekly).

Kangaroo Island
K.I. Tourist Association, PO Box 244, Kingscote, phone 0848-22-540.

Kangaroo Island is probably the most renowned tourist destination in S.A., but unfortunately it's not well-suited for the traveler who is both on a tight budget and accustomed to exploring places without tour guides.

Getting to "K.I." costs a bundle, and no public transport exists on the island. Further, long distances and gravel roads eliminate the biking option. People who visit tend to take day tours (there are several good ones), but they are expensive and, of course, don't allow much freedom. The hostels now offer discount alternatives (try the Penneshaw hostel). We suggest calling hostels from the mainland before deciding to go, since the opportunity to get on an inexpensive tour would make or break a visit to the island.

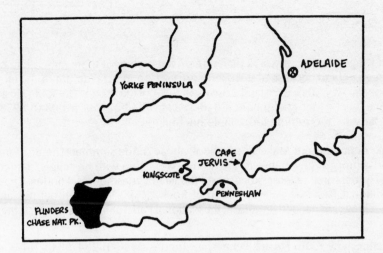

Despite these hassles, Kangaroo Island deserves its immense popularity. Tight controls have kept tourism from tarnishing one of the most unique areas in Australia. Because the island is isolated, several animal and plant species have evolved differently from those on the mainland. This, and the fact that Kangaroo Island has no major predators (including human), makes it a novel and prolific wildlife sanctuary.

The K.I. kangaroo is one such unique creature, with darker fur, shorter limbs, and stouter build than its mainland counterpart. The tammar wallaby, seen throughout the island, is probably extinct on the mainland. Other animals, such as the Australian sea lion, New Zealand fur seal, koala, platypus, and possum thrive in the protected environment.

Flinders discovered and named Kangaroo Island in 1802. Poor soil and isolation kept the population tiny until post-WWII farming efforts succeeded. Aside from spectacular coastal scenery and large tracts of protected bushland, the island is dotted with small farms and, here and there, an abandoned settler's house.

Getting There and Getting Around: The cheapest way to get to K.I. is on the *Philanderer III* auto ferry (phone 0848-31-122 or 008-01-3111), which departs Cape Jervis and arrives in Penneshaw three times a day. The trip takes over an hour and costs $26 each way. Cars cost $50 each way, and drivers should note that gas tanks must be more than half empty for the trip. You can book at tourist information in Adelaide or Victor Harbour. *Note:* Ferry does not operate mid-June to late August.

The K.I. Connection Bus (phone 08-272-6680) from Adelaide meets the ferry. It costs $10 one-way, and leaves the Bus Australia terminal at Central Bus Station. Flights from Adelaide are also available. Tourism South Australia in Adelaide will know the best airline deals.

Nearly 145 km long and 56 km wide, Kangaroo Island is no cinch to get around. The only thing resembling public transport is **Island Bus and Taxi** (phone 22-640), which runs a few times a day (dependent on bookings) between Kingscote, American River, and Penneshaw. Rental cars are available in Kingscote and, if you're planning on a rental, do it there rather than on the mainland because of steep ferry prices. Commercial day tours, the most popular way to see the island, cost about $70, but the Penneshaw Youth Hostel gives a cheaper tour (phone 0848-31-284, 0848-31-173, or 008-01-8258). Roads are too remote for reliable hitchhiking.

Accommodation: Make sure to book ahead in the summer. The first three accommodations in this list are dorm-style, set up with hostellers in mind; the others are the least expensive of the island guesthouses. Flinders Chase National Park has a campground at Rocky River, for which permits and bookings are needed. Inquire at the National Parks office, Dauncy St., Kingscote (phone 22-381).

Penneshaw Youth Hostel, Penneshaw (phone 0848-31-284, 0848-31-173, or 008-01-8258). 4-bed rooms and twins. Tours offered—be sure to book ahead. Stay here if there's room.

Tandarra Holiday Lodge (phone 0848-31-018). From $12/night. Book ahead.

Guestward Ho Cottages, Penneshaw (phone 0848-31-173). Hostel accommodation in cabins. Call ahead for bookings and directions.

Hill Farm Hostel, Kingscote (phone 0848-22-778). Call ahead for ride from Kingscote.

Hoey House, Island Beach, Penneshaw (phone 08-47-5837). $20 for 1-2 people.

Beachfront Cottages, Frenchman's Tce., Penneshaw (phone 08-332-1083). $30 for 1-2 people.

Things to See and Do: There are two "must sees" on K.I.:
First, **Flinders Chase National Park** encompasses the entire west side of the island and offers prolific wildlife and spectacular coastline. On the road into Rocky River, there's a campsite and information center, with maps and information on wildlife. Koalas and kangaroos live in the vicinity, and brief walks originate there. Binoculars are a great advantage. Dirt tracks from the station lead to awesome rock formations at **Admirals Arch** and **Remarkable Rocks**, on Cape du Couedic. Wave-eroded rock outcrops are often composed of deep red ironstone or covered by bright orange lichen, creating a vibrant array of colors, particularly in wildflower season (Aug-Nov). Note that fishing and swimming anywhere on the south coast is very dangerous. The park entrance is an hour's drive from Kingscote.
The second must, **Seal Bay Conservation Park** is 50 km south of Kingscote. A visit may be your only chance ever to get near a wild sea lion; members of this colony are unusually casual about humans. (However, don't touch or provoke them. As you will see, they have serious teeth.) Over 10% of the population of Australian sea lions lives there among the coastal dunes.
The American River and north coast of the island are popular fishing areas;

surf, rock, river, and deep sea fishing are all possible. For more information, inquire at the **Dept. of Fisheries** in Adelaide (135 Pirie St.) or call one of these numbers in Kingscote: 22-222, 22-571, or 22-498. Diving is especially good because of the abundance of water life, including dolphins, fur seals, and sea lions. Inquire in Penneshaw or Kingscote and at the hostels.

Burra and Clare

Burra and Clare are the last outposts of civilization on the trek north of Adelaide, before real outback towns take over. Each is about a 2.5-hour drive north of the city, within 30 km of one another. Burra was among the first mining towns in Australia, and Clare is a gentrified, historic town in the heart of a wine valley. Both are pastoral centers for area sheep stations. The most valuable rams in the world are bred at nearby Collinsville and Bungaree Stations, and you can stay at the Bungaree homestead, outside of Clare, in bunk accommodation.

An overnight trip to either town is possible from Adelaide, while both are on the way to Broken Hill (New South Wales), the Eyre Peninsula (west of Adelaide), or the Stuart Highway.

Burra

Tourist Information, Market Square, phone 088-92-2154. Open 10:00am-4:00pm daily.

Copper was discovered at Burra Creek in 1845, and, by the early 1850's there were extensive underground and open mines. The operation was soon overshadowed by mines elsewhere, but not before it had boosted S.A. out of an economic slump. Most of Burra's original buildings remain, and the mine site is nearly as it was in the 1850's.

In addition to two National Trust museums and the original mine site, a visit to **Redruth Gaol** in North Burra is essential. The jail was the setting of the film *Breaker Morant*, based on a true story of three Australians court-marshalled during the Boer War. You gain entrance to the jail, miner's dugouts, and powder magazine by buying a key from tourist information (pay $10 and get $5 back on return of the key). Also at tourist information is a self-guided historic tour.

Note: Museums are open in the afternoon only and closed Monday.

Getting There: ABM Coaches (phone 08-349-5551) runs from Adelaide to Burra three times a week. Bus Australia also goes to Burra once a day from Adelaide, though this route is tenuous.

Accommodation: Try either the **Burra Hotel** at 5 Market Square (phone 088-92-2389), the **Kooringa Hotel** at 4 Kingston St. (phone 088-92-2013), or the **Bon Accord Cottage** on Linkson St., North Burra (phone 088-92-2627).

Clare

The picturesque Clare Valley is an oasis in flat, dry station country. The 20-odd Clare Valley wineries are generally open for tasting W-Sun 10:00am-5:00pm, and a visit to some of these, as well as the nearby town of Mintaro, makes for a great day if you have a car. To get yourself on course, visit tourist information at the north end of Main St.

Wineries of the region are small and often family-run, so the reception is usually friendly and informative. The most unique is **Seven Hill Cellars**, begun by Jesuits in 1851 to make sacramental wine. They now make wine for commercial purposes, too, and, though the wine is nothing to rave about, the chapel and grounds are fun to explore (closed Sunday).

Mintaro, 19 km southeast of Clare, is a historic town with tea rooms, a gallery, vintage car museum, and an expensive B&B. Just beyond Mintaro is **Martindale Hall**, the setting for the film *Picnic at Hanging Rock*. The estate was built in 1880 by Edmund Bowman who, on request of the lady he loved, brought English craftsman and spent a fortune making the house as grand as her father's castle in Scotland. She ended up rejecting him, and he ended up bankrupt. The mansion is open for viewing daily from 1:00pm-4:00pm and offers dinner and accommodation Th-Sun, in case you're looking for an elegant (and expensive) evening.

Those without their own transport might find a trip to Clare worthwhile just to stay at **Bungaree**, a sheep station established in 1841 by the family who still runs it. Accommodation is available for a few people for $14/night or $16 with breakfast (cooking facilities are available). Rates are negotiable if you work. Bring your own linen and blankets. If you aren't interested in staying but want to see the old homestead, tours are available. Inquire at tourist information or call the station. Bungaree is 12 km north of Clare on the road to Port Pirie. Phone 088-42-2677 for information.

Getting There: Stateliner (phone 08-217-0779 in Adelaide) comes through Clare once daily on the Adelaide-Broken Hill route. Inquire also about a new Greyhound service, which may go through Clare.

Accommodation: In addition to **Bungaree**, try either **Bentley's Hotel Motel**, 191 Main North Rd. (phone 088-42-2815) or **Christison Caravan Park**, Main North Rd. (phone 088-42-2724), 4 km south of town, with on-site caravans and cabins.

The Southeast

Robe and Mt. Gambier are the major access points to an area that offers international travelers a chance to see summer vacation spots of local tourists. Rich in history and gourmet food, southeast S.A. has an unspoiled coastline and interesting inland destinations. The Coorong, Robe, and Beachport are the obvious coastal choices. From Mt. Gambier you can easily reach the Coonawarra wine region and limestone caves at Naracoorte.

There's only one hostel in the entire southeast, in Beachport. Pick up Tourism S.A.'s leaflet *Southeast South Australia Accommodation* in either Mt. Gambier or Adelaide for the latest lodges and prices. Some specific possibilities are suggested below.

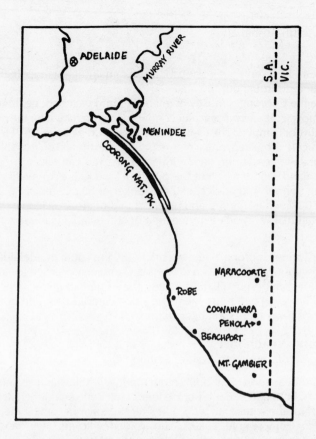

Getting There: Mt. Gambier Motor Service takes two routes between Adelaide and Mt. Gambier, one along the coast and one inland. The coastal service runs daily except Saturday, and the major stops are Meningie, Robe, Beachport, Millicent, and Mt. Gambier. The inland service stops four times a week in Padthaway, Naracoorte, Penola, and Mt. Gambier. Make reservations at Central Bus Station in Adelaide (phone 08-217-0777) or in Mt. Gambier at the Shell Station, 100 Commercial St. (phone 087-25-5037). The trip between Adelaide and Mt. Gambier costs $25 one-way.

The only service from Victoria to Mt. Gambier is Greyhound's once-a-week trip from Melbourne, which follows the Great Ocean Road along the Victorian coast.

You must pass through Mt. Gambier to get from the coast to inland areas like Naracoorte and Coonawarra.

The Coorong

The Coorong is a marshy, salty channel between the mainland and a 145 km strip of sand dunes called the **Younghusband Peninsula**. A protective peninsular barrier provides sanctuary for thousands of birds and flora. Breeding colonies of pelicans, sea gulls, and terns lie atop small islands in the channel; bird watchers gaze from afar with binoculars, and hunting is allowed seasonally. Aborigines have inhabited the Coorong for thousands of years, and a reserve is set aside for those remaining. Archaeological sites are scattered throughout the area.

While the Coorong is mostly of interest to bird watchers, geologists, and archaeologists, it offers a peaceful communion with nature for the traveler—especially for campers. The campground at **Salt Creek** (near Park Headquarters) is nicely protected, and a nature trail begins there. You're also allowed to camp anywhere in the park with a permit. You can take any car along the mainland sand tracks, but the peninsula tracks are for 4WD only. For camping permits and advice, call the ranger at Salt Creek at 085-75-7014 or 75-1200. For background and practical information, pick up a pamphlet at the National Parks office in Adelaide or at the Park Headquarters in Salt Creek.

Getting There: Coorong National Park is 180 km south of Adelaide. Those arriving without a car will need to take Mt. Gambier Motor Service to Meningie, 10 km from the park. Unfortunately, there's neither public transport nor tours to help you get there. Meningie has a caravan park and hotels, and just out of town there's a ranger station.

Robe and Beachport
Robe Tourist Information Centre, Smillie St.

Robe and Beachport were both frequented by whalers and sealers during the 1830's. In 1847, S.A. Governor Frederick Holt Robe established Robe Town as a port for the southeast; a decade later the town became a major point of entry for Chinese gold-seekers, who avoided Victoria's steep "landing tax" by disembarking at Robe and walking overland to Ballarat. In 1857 alone, 17,000 Chinese immigrants landed.

Robe is now a fishing port and vacation spot for the affluent. Its main street is endowed with charming buildings, nice restaurants, and expensive art galleries. The surrounding coast offers scenic spots to picnic and wander, and nearby Beachport has a **National Trust Museum** and a huge jetty for fishing.

The **YHA Hostel** in Beachport is on the ocean (Beach Rd., phone 087-35-8197). It costs $6/night and is closed for a month each year beginning around June 1.

Mt. Gambier
Tourist Information, Lady Nelson Park, Jubilee Hwy. East (phone 087-24-1730). Open 9:00am-5:00pm daily.

Built on the side of an extinct volcano, Mt. Gambier is an attractive city of 20,000 that serves as a commercial and administrative center for southeast S.A. and southwest Victoria. Its countryside is dominated by Australia's largest planted forests of Radiata pine, imported from California over a century ago. Wood-processing and wood products are a mainstay of Mt. Gambier's economy, as is cheese-making.

Among the museums and galleries, plan to give at least an hour to the

Lady Nelson Park Interpretive Centre, home of the local tourist information office. The Centre covers all aspects of area history, including geology, geography, and culture.

Mt. Gambier's best-known feature is its **Blue Lake**. From November or early December to late March, this 80 meter-deep volcanic lake changes from dull green to deep blue. Immediately south of Mt. Gambier is **Mt. Schank** (at Port MacDonnell), which offers expansive views of the coast after a steep climb. Also close, the underwater caverns at **Piccaninnie Ponds** attract divers from all over the world.

Mt. Gambier gives access to Coonawarra and Naracoorte, as well as south coast towns like Robe and Millicent.

For accommodation in Mt. Gambier try the **Lakeside Lodge**, 10 Gwendoline St. (phone 087-25-3460) or **Mac's Hotel** at 21 Bay Rd. (phone 087-25-2402).

Coonawarra and Penola
Penola Information Centre, Arthur St. (phone 087-37-2855).

The Coonawarra wine valley, about 50 km north of Mt. Gambier, is best known for producing high quality red wine. Coonawarra's 15 wineries are usually open for tastings M-Sat 9:00am-4:30pm. The **James Haselgrove Winery** and **Hollicks Winery** offer lunch, while the expensive **Chardonnay Lodge** has a gourmet menu and wines of the region. It's an excellent area for cycling, and several national parks are in the vicinity.

The oldest town in the southeast, **Penola** lies at the southern edge of the wine growing district. A guided walk around town is available through the Information Centre. Highlights of Penola are timber cottages built in the 1850's and **Yallum Park** estate, built by Coonawarra's original vintner, John Riddoch. (Ask tourist information about an appointment for viewing the estate.) Local crafts and pottery are available in galleries around town.

The **Log Cabin Hotel Motel** on 58 Church St. in Penola (phone 087-37-2402) is the cheapest accommodation option in the region.

Naracoorte
Tourist Information Centre, MacDonnell St.

Situated 50 km north of Penola and 85 km northeast of Kingston, Naracoorte is a center for sheep-raising and wool production. There are several opportunities to buy wool products around town, and the **Wool Gallery** on Rolland St. gives a synopsis of the industry's history.

However, the prime draw to Naracoorte is nearby limestone caves, of which there are at least 60. **Naracoorte Caves Conservation Park**, 12 km southeast of town, encompasses 17 caves, and three are open for inspection. If you have to choose, see **Victoria Cave**, where archaeologists are studying fossil remains of ancient marsupials. Of the 54 fossilized species found, 13 are now extinct. Blanche Cave and Alexandra Cave are also open for tours. **Alexandra Cave** is still active, while **Blanche Cave** is dry. The former owner of the land used to throw parties in Blanche Cave (from which there are also archaeological remains, of a sort). Tours of the caves are 9:30am-4:00pm, daily (phone 087-62-2340).

Camping is available in the campground at the Caves Conservation Park. Otherwise, try the **Naracoorte Hotel Motel** on 73 Omerod St. (phone 087-62-2400).

The Murray River in S.A.

Loxton Tourist and Travel Centre, East Terrace, Loxton (phone 085-84-7919). *Renmark Tourist Centre,* Murray Ave., Renmark (phone 085-86-6703).

Loxton, the logical stop for those traveling to and from Mildura and other Victorian Murray River destinations, has two advantages over better-known rivertowns in Victoria: the town remains unadulterated by tourism, and the hostel is in a wooded location on the river.

Though not too many people stay there, the **Loxton YHA-Affiliate Hostel** offers a fantastic base from which to experience the Murray River. The building itself was originally constructed to house soldiers testing nuclear bombs near Woomera. The kitchen and adjoining dining room/common room are huge, and picture windows take advantage of the river view. The hostel is owned and run by the **Riverfront Caravan Park**. Rent canoes and bikes at the caravan park office. Call 085-84-7862 for bookings.

Loxton Historical Village is the only touristy attraction in the area. Just up the road from the hostel, it consists of 25 restored buildings dating from 1900, depicting life in the early farming community.

The **Loxton Cooperative** crushes an enormous amount of grapes, and most of it goes into bulk wine-making. The giants in Aussie wine-making, including Orlando, Penfold, and Seppelts, all own (or buy from) area vineyards. **River cruises** are available in nearby Renmark, through the Renmark Tourist Centre.

Getting There: Stateliner (phone 08-217-0777 in Adelaide) runs from Adelaide to Renmark daily and to Loxton five days a week.

From Mildura, Vic. or New South Wales, Greyhound's Adelaide-Sydney or Adelaide-Brisbane service stops in Renmark and nearby Berri.

The Yorke Peninsula

Monotonous grainfields and quiet seaside villages of the Yorke Peninsula are boring to some, relaxing and pure to others. Visitors, mainly family holidayers and retirees, stick to the shore. The major destinations are Port Vincent, where the hostel overlooks a coast laden with harvestable seafood; Innes National Park, where cliff-lined beaches and coastal dunes are a great spot for camping; and the historic "copper triangle" towns of Moonta, Kadina, and Wallaroo.

Aside from one YHA-Associate in Port Vincent, the accommodation options are caravan parks, hotels, or camping. Caravan parks with on-site vans and campsites are available in most coastal towns on the peninsula. Hotel rooms cost $20-$30 a night for a single. The further south you get, the scarcer the accommodation. Pick up Tourism Australia's pamphlet for the latest lodging info.

Getting There: The **Yorke Peninsula Bus Service** (phone 08-391-2977, or book through Bus Australia at 08-212-7999) operates daily between Adelaide Central Bus Station and Point Turton. The route zigzags across the peninsula, including stops in Maitland, Port Vincent, and Edithburgh. It takes about three hours to reach Port Vincent from Adelaide and costs $28 roundtrip. The same company operates a service to Moonta M-Sat. Local public transport is non-existent.

Drivers should note that most roads aren't well-traveled and towns are infrequent, so go in a reliable vehicle. The south and west coasts are accessible only by dirt roads.

Port Vincent

A little seaside town, Port Vincent consists of a few grocery stores, the **Grainstore Gallery** (which sells paintings and local crafts), and a few other small businesses. Its coastline teems with clams, mussels, and oysters—ask the hostel manager to direct you.

The YHA-Associate hostel, **Tuckerway**, is near the beach (phone 088-53-7285 or 53-7030). It's a large cement building set up to accommodate school, church, and girl-guide groups. Weekends are usually busy, but weekdays you'll probably have the place to yourself unless it's a holiday. Bunks and twin rooms are available, and there's a huge kitchen and large dining and living area. Electricity is controlled by a coin-operated meter that eats up about 20 cents a night, and your bed costs $4.50/night. The bus drops off in town, and the hostel is about 1 km north, up an incline.

Innes National Park

Innes National Park covers 22,240 acres of deserted scrubland, coastal dunes, and beaches. The beaches are wide, virtually deserted, and backed by limestone cliffs. There's excellent surf, especially at **Pondalowie Bay** on the west side. The highest limestone cliffs are found at the most southern tip of the peninsula, around **Cape Spencer** and backing **Ethel Beach**. **Inneston**, a deserted gypsum mining town within the park's boundaries, has become a historic site, and you can explore its ruins.

Obtain permission to camp in the park from the ranger at **Stenhouse Bay** (phone 088-54-4040). Stenhouse Bay and Ethel Beach have open-air showers, and you'll find supplies at the store in Stenhouse Bay. Alternately, east of the park (16 km east of Marion Bay) is a privately-owned camping area called **Hillocks Drive**, an enormous area of uninhabited, rugged coastline and beaches. "Key hire" for an overnight site is $4, or $3 per vehicle for a day pass, collected at the homestead at **Butlers Beach**. No facilities, but the owner will let you use the homestead shower for a small charge. On-site vans are available. Call 088-54-4002 or ask for details at the Port Vincent YHA hostel.

The Copper Triangle

The Copper Triangle lies at the Yorke's northern extreme, where mining towns Kadina, Moonta, and Wallaroo were settled by Cornish miners in the mid-1800's. Australia's "Little Cornwall" is rich in history and virtually untouched since the original smelters and mines closed in 1923.

A shepherd discovered copper in 1859 at **Kadina**, and two years later a richer lode was discovered near present-day **Moonta**. The mining operations combined to create Wallaroo and **Moonta Mining and Smelting Co.**, managed by immigrants from Cornwall, England. Cornish traditions are still strong in the region: local shops sell Cornish and English-style foods, including pasties (a vegetable and meat turnover). In May of odd-numbered years, Moonta celebrates the world's only Cornish festival, **Kernewek Lowender**.

Most historic attractions are open only on Wednesday, weekends, and public holidays. Southeast of Moonta at the old mine site in the former Moonta Mines Model School, the National Trust runs a great **museum** depicting Moonta's history through colorful local characters (including one Joshua Skinner, Senior Surface Captain for decades, and great-great-grandfather of one of the authors of this book). The museum will help you understand the mine sites, which you can explore on your own. Admission is $2.50 (free to National Trust members); open W, Sat, Sun 1:30pm-4:00pm, and public holidays 11:00am-4:00pm.

In the mining area, there's an 1870's **miner's cottage** open the same hours as the museum ($1 admission). Instead of walking, you can take a narrated tourist train from the museum parking lot or a tourist tram from across the street.

Don't leave without trying a **Cornish pasty**. All the bakeries and restaurants serve them piping hot, with tomato sauce.

Accommodation: Local hotels are the only accommodation choice. The **Royal Hotel** (2 Ryan St.) and **Cornwall Hotel** (20 Ryan St.) have rooms for about $16/person. The Royal's nightly fee includes breakfast.

The Route to Western Australia

Edward John Eyre was the first explorer to go overland from the east to west coasts of Australia, a feat clinched in 1840 when he and an Aborigine companion named Wylie were the only survivors of an expedition from Fowler's Bay, S.A. to Albany, W.A. The only paved road from east Australia to Perth bears Eyre's name, as does S.A.'s largest peninsula. Starting in Adelaide, the 2,815 km drive to Perth on the Eyre Highway takes about 35 hours. A diversion down the Eyre Peninsula to Port Lincoln adds 300 km to the trip.

Local hotels are the cheapest accommodation, aside from camping and caravan parks. Pick up Tourism S.A.'s leaflet *Eyre Peninsula Accommodation* for current info.

Getting There: Stateliner goes from Adelaide to the Eyre Peninsula daily, stopping in most towns along the coast. It costs about $40 one-way to Port Lincoln (terminal is on Lewis St.).

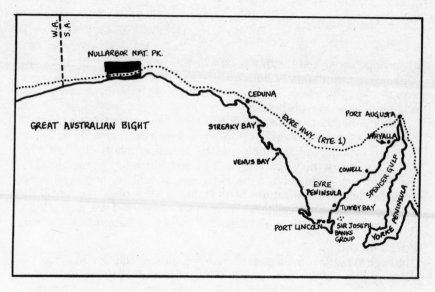

Deluxe, Pioneer, Greyhound, and Bus Australia cross the country on the Eyre Hwy. daily, bypassing the Eyre Peninsula. (They do stop in Ceduna.) The *Indian-Pacific* train also traverses the country, from Sydney and Adelaide. Unlike the road, the train passes directly through the Nullarbor Plain on the world's longest stretch of straight railway track.

The Eyre Peninsula

Eyre Travel/Port Lincoln Tourist Information, Tasman Tce., Port Lincoln (phone 086-82-4577 or 82-3255). Open M-F 9:00am-5:30pm, weekends and public holidays 9:00am-noon.

Whyalla Maritime and Tourist Complex, Lincoln Hwy., Whyalla (phone 086-45-7428). Open M-F 8:45am-5:10pm (hours vary).

Ceduna Gateway Tourist Centre, 58 Poynton St., Ceduna (phone 086-25-3155). Open M-F 8:40am-5:00pm.

Commercial and sport fishermen haul in fish all along the coast of the Eyre Peninsula: tuna, king prawns, rock lobster ("crayfish"), shark, whiting, snapper, garfish, Coffin Bay oyster, abalone, scallops, salmon, squid, and lots of stuff you've never heard of. Tumby Bay, Port Lincoln, Streaky Bay, and Ceduna all offer charter fishing, but you can drop a line anywhere along the peninsula and have a good chance of catching something. There is, of course, abundant seafood in local restaurants.

Small, unspoiled communities dot the coast of the Eyre, and you can stop in almost any and find friendly locals, refreshing ocean spray, and a place to fish. Towns along the Spencer Gulf (east coast) enjoy calm, protected waters, while the western side of the peninsula gets a beating from the Southern Ocean. Major towns and points of interest are, from east to west: **Whyalla**, a large industrial town that thrives on steelworks and iron quarries; **Cowell**, where jade from the nearby Minbrie Ranges is processed (one of the largest jade deposits in the world and Australia's only commercial jade-mining operation); and **Tumby Bay**, off which are the Sir Joseph Banks Group of islands, a marine conservation area where sea lions and Cape Barren geese live, also accessible from Port Lincoln. **Port Lincoln** is the major Eyre Peninsula destination (details below).

On the west coast, you can sometimes see whales off the shores of **Venus Bay**. **Streaky Bay** is renowned for its fishing and protected harbor. **Point Labatt** denizens include Australia's only mainland sea lion colony. Finally, **Ceduna** is located past the junction of the Eyre and Flinders Highways. In addition to fishing, Ceduna has a few museums, and 34 km northwest is the **Overseas Telecommunications Earth Station**, connecting Asia, Africa, Europe, and Australia by satellite. Visitors can see a video and take guided tours M-F starting from 10:00am and departing every hour (last tour at 3:00pm).

Port Lincoln

Although Whyalla is the largest town in S.A. after Adelaide, Port Lincoln is the focal point of the Eyre Peninsula. Established in 1839 on Boston Bay, Port Lincoln was the original choice for a state capital. The town has since regained notoriety as the home of Dean Lucan, fisherman/weightlifter who won a gold medal in the 1984 Olympics. The population is around 11,000; major industries are fishing and shipping. Grain, wool, lamb, and tuna are all exported from the port.

Boston Bay is sprinkled with islands to visit, and diving in the outer islands and reefs is excellent. Cruises on the *Investigator* leave the town jetty for destinations in the bay, depending on the day. They don't operate in winter.

About 30 km southwest of town is one of the most scenic drives in the country, **Whaler's Way**. An unsealed road that passes by coastal rock formations equivalent to those on the Great Ocean Road in Victoria, it's a treacherous and awesome route that leads to the southern tip of the peninsula. You need to get a permit and keys from tourist information to get on the road (deposit required).

There are a few historic buildings and museums in town. See especially the **Axel Stenross Maritime Museum**, where a Finnish boat builder set up shop in the 1920's. His ship-building workshop, a working blacksmith shop, and old photos depict Port Lincoln's maritime history (97 Lincoln Hwy; open T, Th, Sat, & Sun 1:00pm-5:00pm. Call first to confirm times at 82-3624).

The Eyre Highway and the Great Australian Bight

The Great Australian Bight includes the coastline between West Point, S.A. (tip of the Eyre Peninsula) and Cape Pasley, W.A. (west of Esperance). Part of the Bight borders the **Nullarbor Plain**, where desert meets ocean in fantastic and forbidding cliffs, and a maze of caves may be the largest cave system on earth. The coast is basically an uninhabited frontier. Signposts along the highway indicate scenic lookouts. Don't bypass them.

Drivers should pick up a magazine called *Across Australia by Eyre Highway*, available from Tourism S.A. in Adelaide. It describes each town along the highway, plus gives information such as petrol station hours. Roadhouses along the Eyre Highway are generally open daily 6:00am-11:00pm. Most stations accept Visa or Mastercard, but there are no full-fledged towns between Ceduna, S.A. and Norseman, W.A, so do your banking and shopping ahead of time! Tourism S.A. has all-inclusive accommodation listings. It's also helpful to consult the Royal Automobile Association of South Australia (R.A.A.) before departure.

Outback South Australia

Because large portions of outback S.A. have restricted access, tourist-oriented information on "the outback" is a reference to the northeast third of the state, bounded approximately by the Stuart Highway in the west and the eastern and northern state borders. The Flinders Range and the Stuart Hwy. route to Alice Springs (going through Coober Pedy) are fairly accessible. The huge expanse of land beyond these areas, including the Simpson and Sturt Stony Deserts, is for real adventurers with 4WD and a willingness to tackle the conditions of desert outback.

Desert weather is extreme. Summer (Jan-March) can get exceedingly hot, up to 50°C (120°F). In winter it often gets below freezing at night, even when days are warm.

Outback Roads

Four roads traverse the S.A. outback: The paved **Stuart Hwy.** (see *The Stuart Highway, Northern Territory* for travel suggestions. The N.T. section of the highway is more eventful than the S.A. section); the **Oodnadatta Track** from Marree to Oodnadatta, ending at the Stuart Hwy.; the **Birdsville Track**, from Marree to Birdsville, Queensland; and the **Strzelecki Track** from Lyndhurst to Birdsville.

The Birdsville Track was once the only link between cattle country in Queensland and the railroad at Marree, a notoriously difficult journey braved by cattle drovers for decades. It's possible to drive the Birdsville yourself, even without 4WD, if you have a very reliable and sturdy car. Go between May and October and allow at least two days. You must bring all supplies, spare parts, and enough food to last a week in case of flash flooding. Check with the police at either end of the track for road conditions and let them know your timetable. Ask Tourism S.A. for further information.

Oodnadatta is not as famous for its track as for its role in getting supplies from Adelaide to Alice Springs. Until 1929 the railroad from Adelaide ended in Oodnadatta, and camels carried goods the rest of the way to Alice Springs. Afghan cameleers first arrived in the mid-1800's, and many still live in Marree and Oodnadatta.

Property owners along outback routes generally don't mind if you camp by the roadside. It would be unusual for them to notice you anyway, since stations span thousands of acres. Don't camp near creeks if there are forecasts for rain because of flash flooding.

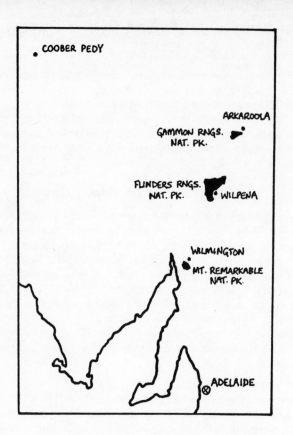

The Flinders Ranges

The Flinders Ranges are among the most ancient landforms on earth. Weathered and sunbaked for millennia, these red quartzite mountains form a landscape unique to Australia. A visit is especially worthwhile for those who have yet to experience the arid inland of the continent. Depending on the season, the Flinders Ranges are either hauntingly stark or vibrant with wildflowers. Always, the rock formations stun newcomers.

While a visit makes most sense for those who enjoy hiking, there are several other diversions: 4WD tours, scenic flights, and sightseeing are all possible from either Wilpena or Arkaroola. Hikers would be prudent to go between May and October, when temperatures are moderate. The best time is July-October, when wildflowers blanket the range.

Wilpena and Arkaroola are the major centers from which to explore the ranges. **Wilpena** is four hours closer to Adelaide but accommodation costs $70 and up, unless you're camping. **Arkaroola** is more remote but gives access to equally spectacular scenery. Bunkhouse accommodation is available in Arkaroola. Camping is an option in either place. Price of accommodation aside, if you are comfortable with well-beaten trails and more people, go to Wilpena. If your object is a rough 'n tough outback experience, choose Arkaroola.

A third option is **Mt. Remarkable National Park**, at the southern end of the ranges (access by Wirrabara or Wilmington). Though the mountains there don't have the arid character of the mid and north ranges, they are only 260 km north of Adelaide (as opposed to 430 km Adelaide-Wilpena, or 660 km Adelaide-Arkaroola).

Hikers should get supplies and topographical maps in Adelaide, because the towns have only essentials.

Getting There: Stateliner goes to Wilpena once a week from Central Bus Station, Adelaide (phone 08-217-0777). The trip takes 8 hours. The same bus also stops in Wirrabara and Wilmington (for Mt. Remarkable National Park). Stateliner runs to Arkaroola twice a week (12 hrs.). The road to Wilpena is sealed, but the Arkaroola route is unsealed, narrow, and sometimes rough, though passable in a conventional vehicle. Occasional flash floods in February and March render Arkaroola inaccessible for short periods.

Wilpena and Flinders Ranges National Park

The town of Wilpena consists of the **Wilpena Pound Resort** and a few stores. Tourist information is available at the motel office and store, and you can hire 4WD vehicles in town. Park information is available at either Wilpena ranger station (phone 086-48-0048) or Oraparina ranger station (phone 086-48-0017).

Wilpena Pound, in Flinders Ranges National Park, is the most awesome feature in the Flinders Ranges. It's like a giant rock bowl, ringed by jagged mountains that have resisted the weathering of the ages. Inside, gorges and valleys flourish with Red River gums and Cypress pine. All variety of kangaroo, wallaby, and birds flock to this sprawling oasis, where for a century cattle and sheep destroyed plant life, and non-native animals like cats and goats upset the ecosystem. The Pound is gradually reclaiming its original character—the only notable evidence of human interference is some homestead ruins, just off the trail from the main campground.

The best hike in the Pound (but not an easy one!) goes up **St. Mary's Peak**. There, from the highest point of the Pound, you can see the entire bowl. It's a strenuous 6-7 hours roundtrip. The **Heyson Trail**, which begins in the southern Fleurieu Peninsula and extends to Mt. Hopeless in the northern Flinders, passes through the Pound (trail is closed Nov-April because of a fire ban). Other features of the park are **Brachina Gorge** and ruins at **Aroona**.

Hikers should pick up the pamphlet *Bushwalking in the Flinders Ranges National Park*, which outlines the walks and includes general maps (available from park rangers and the National Park Service in Adelaide). It's easy to get disoriented if you deviate from the marked trails. If you intend to do so, be sure to buy a topo map in Adelaide.

Accommodation: The least expensive resort rooms are $70/single or $72/double, but there's camping in the national park. A designated campground lies near the Pound, or you can camp anywhere with ranger approval. Campfires are allowed, except Nov-March.

Arkaroola and Gammon Ranges National Park

The Gammon Ranges form the northern section of the Flinders Ranges, where you'll find the most arid, rugged, and remote country of all. The Gammons are extremely ancient, as old as any area studied by humans. The harsh landscape, interspersed with deep gorges that provide shelter and moisture for lush plant life, is studded with mineral and gemstone deposits that attract fortune-seekers and geologists alike.

Hiking trails through **Mt. Painter Sanctuary** are accessible from Arkaroola, and Gammon Ranges National Park is a short drive away. The visitor information center in town has general maps and trail notes for hiking in Mt. Painter Sanctuary. **Italowie Gorge**, within the Gammon Ranges National Park, is one of the better-known sites and can be hiked; **Weetootla Gorge** is accessible by 4WD track.

The Park, with no marked hiking trails, is for expert hikers only. However, 4WD tracks provide real thrills for drivers, and safari tours are available from town. Ask in the information center about the "Ridgetop" 4WD tour, which follows old mining tracks to terrific views. Only those who are thoroughly prepared should attempt to hike extensively in the park. Get camping permits and information at park headquarters at **Balcanoona Homestead**.

The site of Australia's only current volcanic activity, **Paralana Hot Springs**, is 27 km north of Arkaroola.

Accommodation: Book Arkaroola accommodation in Adelaide at the **Arkaroola Travel Centre**, 50 Pirie St. (phone 086-212-1366). A night in the bunkhouse costs about $5 (BYO bedding), or singles are $18/night. Two 6-person cottages are available for about $55/night, a good deal for a group. There's a campground in town as well. (Campfires are permitted there, but **not** in the national park). Note: There's no public telephone in town.

Mt. Remarkable National Park

The bus to Wilpena stops at Wirrabara and Wilmington, both of which provide access to hiking in the Lower Flinders. There's a **YHA Hostel** in Wirrabara. (Keyholder is at 086-68-4158 and keys must be picked up by 6:30pm. Cost is $6/night.) The hostel is 10 km from town but conveniently located adjacent to **Wirrabara Forest**, where an offshoot of the Heyson Trail makes for nice hiking. It starts from the picnic ground at the Forest Headquarters, next to the hostel.

Wirrabarra is 25 km south of Mt. Remarkable National Park, where **Alligator Gorge** and **Mambray Creek** are highlights. Well-marked trails range from two hours to two days long.

Coober Pedy

For those traveling between Adelaide and Alice Springs, Coober Pedy is the perfect stopover. This little mining town has one of Australia's most diverse and interesting populations: Greeks, Serbs, Yugoslavs, English, Aborigines, Germans—you name it, they're in Coober Pedy to make their fortunes in opal mining, and they live, generally, underground. Subterranean dugouts are Coober Pedy's solution to extreme desert temperatures. Even the hostel is underground.

Coober Pedy mines produce the most of the world's opal, but there is no centralized mining operation. Miners generally work for themselves, staking their own claims and individually mining their plots of land. People still actually strike it rich!

Tourist information is available at most accommodations and businesses. George Van Brugge's **Rainbow Bus Tour** is the best way to see the area and get the lowdown from a former miner and true local. Tours run twice daily most days (call 086-72-5338, after hours 72-5021). George goes to underground churches and out to opal fields, and he even gives you a shot at "noodling"—sifting through piles of discarded earth from mine shafts in search of overlooked pieces of opal. Authorities warn you not to wander around the opal fields on your own, as abandoned shafts can be a serious hazard.

Getting There: The trip from Adelaide to Coober Pedy takes 12 hours; from Alice Springs to Coober Pedy it's 9 hours. Drop-off times are often in the wee hours. Stateliner, Deluxe, Pioneer, Greyhound, and Bus Australia all make the trip at least daily. You can fly to Coober Pedy from Adelaide.

Accommodation: Radeka's Dugout, the local hostel, costs $10/night in the bunkroom. Motel rooms are available for considerably more. The hostel is on the main street at the Deluxe and Pioneer depot. Call 086-72-5223 to book.

The Northern Territory

When non-Australians try to imagine "Outback Australia," the Northern Territory is what they conjure. Pastoralists were the N.T.'s first settlers, and gigantic cattle stations still occupy most N.T. land, though few travelers see them. The places they do visit—Alice Springs, Ayers Rock, Darwin, and Kakadu National Park—must be shared with a lot of other tourists.

However, the colorful earth and open space of the "Red Centre" has a physical character and exuberance that can overcome the tourist hordes and their buses. Likewise the ancient human history and rare wildlife of the Top End. It's still easy to find places in the N.T. remote and free of people, if you make a little effort.

In other respects, the Territory lives up to its outback image. Though it occupies one-sixth of the continent, less than 1% of the country's population lives there (about 170,000 people), and one-fourth of those are Aborigines. Many children get their education from the School of the Air, a classroom broadcast on television. The Flying Doctor Service, which originated in Alice Springs, is crucial to people who live in remote areas.

Known as "the land of people with no last names," the N.T. has always been a place to escape past identities. An irreverence for high culture pervades, most amusingly illustrated in annual events such as the Beer Can Regatta in Darwin and the Henley-on-Todd Regatta on the dry Todd Riverbed in Alice. Neither is exactly in the genteel tradition of yachting.

When To Go

The Top End and Red Centre are two distinct weather districts, but prime visiting times are about the same. High tourist season for Darwin and the Top End is June to mid-September. When monsoonal rains arrive in December (they last through March or early April), transportation and communication can halt for days, making travel impossible.

When deciding on a time to visit the Top End, you should consider Kakadu National Park's accessibility. Monsoonal flooding blocks some of Kakadu's best destinations long after the rains stop, sometimes into May. It's safest to plan a trip from late May-October (see *Kakadu National Park* section for further information).

High tourist season in the Red Centre is April-November (bring warm clothes June-August for frosty nights). At other times it's too hot for most travelers, especially if they're planning to camp.

Also consider going to the N.T. between seasons (April-May or September-October) to avoid crowds.

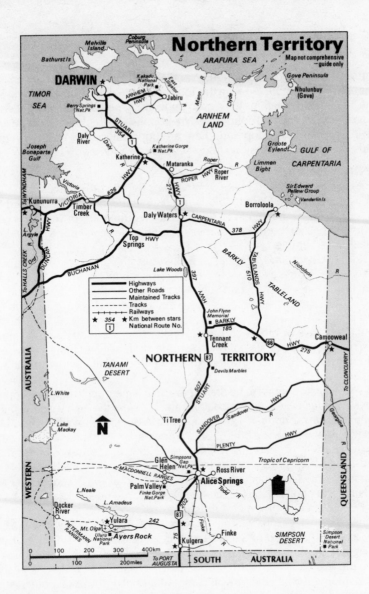

Itinerary

You'll definitely want to see **Ayers Rock**, a five-hour drive southwest of Alice Springs. You also don't want to miss **Kakadu National Park**, three hours east of Darwin. Consider the following additions:

The **MacDonnell Ranges** outside Alice offer quintessential Red Centre country—minus the thousands of people who deluge Alice and Ayers Rock. Especially if you enjoy camping, make some time for exploring the MacDonnells. Save just a day for Alice itself.

Second, the **northern section of the Stuart Hwy.** (Alice Springs to Darwin) is a classic Aussie trip. There's almost nothing along this route (a 20-hour drive) except a few settlements and roadhouses; it's a real outback experience that requires ample preparation, especially if you're in a private car.

Finally, there's more to see in the Top End than Kakadu National Park. Visitors have mixed reactions to **Darwin** depending, perhaps, on preconceived images—don't expect a sophisticated metropolis. We think it deserves at least two days. Also in the Top End, there are opportunities to visit Aboriginal lands and several excursions (mostly by tour) to the north coast.

Getting Around

Buses can get you to all major destinations, but the only places with local public transport are Darwin and Uluru National Park (Ayers Rock and the Olgas). All off-the-beaten-track destinations require tours or your own vehicle. In the best of worlds, all travelers should experience the N.T. in a four-wheel drive vehicle.

Deluxe, Greyhound, Pioneer, and Bus Australia all have interstate services to Alice Springs and Darwin, and some offer direct service to Ayers Rock. Each busline follows the Stuart Highway between Darwin and Alice Springs. Deluxe, Greyhound, and Pioneer have services from Darwin to Kakadu National Park.

An alternative way to reach Alice is on the *Ghan* from Adelaide, a famous train ride that more or less follows the route of Afghan and Indian cameleers who transported goods between Alice and Oodnadatta before the railway was completed.

If you're lucky enough to be driving yourself, remember to prepare properly (see *Stuart Highway* section for details) and consider the high gasoline prices when planning a budget. The **Automobile Association of the N.T.** in Darwin (79 Smith St., phone 089-81-3837) provides road maps and driving tips. Always check road conditions before embarking on adventures off the main roads. The Alice Springs hotline is 089-52-7111; in Darwin, it's 089-84-4455. Four-wheel drive is especially recommended in Kakadu National Park and certain destinations in the MacDonnell Ranges. You must book rental 4WDs well in advance during high tourist season.

There are two reasons why an organized tour in the N.T. might be the best way to see it. First, some great places are accessible by 4WD only, but if you're not comfortable operating a 4WD yourself, a tour is the only way to have the experience. Second, public transportation isn't usually available, and camping is often the only accommodation. For those without a car or camping equipment, budget tours are the cheapest way to get off the beaten track. See individual sections for tour operators, or consider tours that do the N.T. by coach, such as **Contiki** or **Camping Connection**.

Information

Obtain information and bookings for tours and some accommodation at Tourist Bureau offices in Alice Springs and Darwin. They have the most current information and are pretty efficient. It's worth paying for *Australia's Northern Territory Touring Map*, which includes highways, topography, and maps of the smaller cities.

Accommodation

Hostellers will find the N.T.'s YHA network comprehensive, including a hostel in Kakadu National Park. However, a tent is necessary for desirable remote destinations like King's Canyon or Jim Jim/Twin Falls in Kakadu. Book the hostel at Ayers Rock more than a week in advance, even in the hottest months (January and February). July school holidays present a problem at Ayers Rock, since the lodge gets booked up months in advance, but you can always camp instead. (Campers, remember that monsoonal conditions in the Top End make staying in a tent impossible during the summer.) Most N.T. towns have caravan parks with campsites and on-site caravans, and every town has a licensed hotel with a few rooms for rent. They've got character but are often noisy and cost about $30/single per night. The **N.T.'s YHA Head Office** is based in the Darwin hostel on Beaton Rd., Berrimah (phone 089-84-3902).

History

Aborigines have populated the area for at least 30,000 years. Sometime in the 15th century, Indonesian (and probably Chinese) fisherman began to frequent northern Australian shores in search of the trepang (sea slug).

The Dutch ship *Arnhem* made the first recorded European landing on Australia's northern coast in 1623. Many Dutch explorers examined the area but, finding nothing of economic interest, made no attempt at colonization. But after Matthew Flinders' exploratory voyage in 1803, the British saw a need to assert their hegemony over the area to thwart the French. Between 1824 and 1849, Brits made three unsuccessful attempts at settlement before establishing a permanent colony in 1869 at Port Darwin.

Soon after the Adelaide to Port Darwin Overland Telegraph was built in 1871, pastoralists began migrating west to utilize the plains for cattle grazing. The discovery of gold, silver, copper, and bismuth gave the Territory's economy a second basis. Tourism is now the third major industry.

Most foreigners don't know that the Japanese attacked Australia in World War II. They bombed across the entire north coast, from Broome to Cape Yorke; Darwin was hit the worst. Between February 1942 and November 1943, Japan bombed Darwin 64 times, killing 261 people. After Darwin was evacuated, inland N.T. towns of Adelaide River, Pine Creek, and Katherine became the focal points of Australian military activity for the duration of the war.

Government

N.T. politicians are notoriously corrupt and ineffective. Maybe because of a general disdain toward all authority, the Territory is still just that: a territory, not a state. Though a few concerned Territorians have been pushing for statehood since 1978, the major stumbling block is lack of population. Statehood would give the N.T. government control over all state functions (the federal government currently administers a few departments) and give Territorians federal representation equal to that of other states. The N.T. now has one member in the Australian House of Representatives and two Senators. (States have 12 Senators each.)

The Aborigines

Kakadu National Park, the most accessible place in Australia to learn about Aboriginal society and culture, is home to past and present Aborigines. Uluru National Park (Ayers Rock and the Olgas) is another good resource for this. The Darwin Museum and Art Gallery has a good Aboriginal art collection, while the public library in Darwin is the best literary resource.

It's possible to visit Aboriginal lands, mostly by tour. **Terra Safari** offers tours to Arnhem Land; a few operators go to Bathurst and Melville Islands, home of the Tiwi tribe (see those sections in *Trips from Darwin* for more information). Otherwise, individuals sometimes receive permission to enter Aboriginal reserves if their reasons are sound. Call the Land Councils before writing to find out what information they need to consider your request. See "Visiting Aboriginal Reserve Lands" in the *Appendix* for addresses.

About 1,000 people, mostly Aborigines, gather at Morrows Farm each year around Easter for the **Barunga Festival**, a celebration of Aboriginal heritage. This is a specialized event that will take some detective work to learn about. Start with the N.T. Tourist Bureau in Darwin, in the administrative offices.

Darwin

Aussies love to pick on Darwin. True, the town still bears scars from the 1974 cyclone, and it has a reputation for harboring misfits and drunks. Plus, Darwin suffers a wave of insufferable heat and humidity every spring. But this little city of 75,000 (no bigger than a large country town in New South Wales) has a distinct charisma.

As capital of the N.T. and Australia's gateway to Asia, Darwin has an ethnic diversity many Australian cities lack. The exotic ambiance, tropical friendliness, and casual lifestyle draw many from Melbourne and Perth—mostly young professionals doing time in regional offices or rebels looking to escape.

Kakadu National Park, a few hours away, is motivation enough to get to the Top End. Aside from harboring saltwater crocodiles and other tropical wildlife, Kakadu is important for understanding ancient Aboriginal culture. Darwin's proximity to Kakadu and the Aboriginal reserves of Arnhem Land and Gurig National Park cultivates an interchange and awareness between Aboriginal and European cultures rarely seen in other parts of Australia.

Darwin has been ravaged by three cyclones and World War II bombing raids in its 120-year history. The most recent and destructive cyclone occurred Christmas morning, 1974. "Tracy" flattened over half the town's houses and left 66 dead or missing. Vacant blocks and deserted buildings downtown still bear testimony to Tracy's devastation. The post-Tracy era has brought modern buildings and considerable civic development, as well as a renewed sense of pride and loyalty to the city among Darwinians who made it through the ordeal.

Darwin's wet season lasts from December to April, preceded by the "silly season" that begins in October and ends when the rains come in late December, relieving the city of miserable humidity. High tourist season is June through mid-September. Most tours to Kakadu and other areas end in Oc-

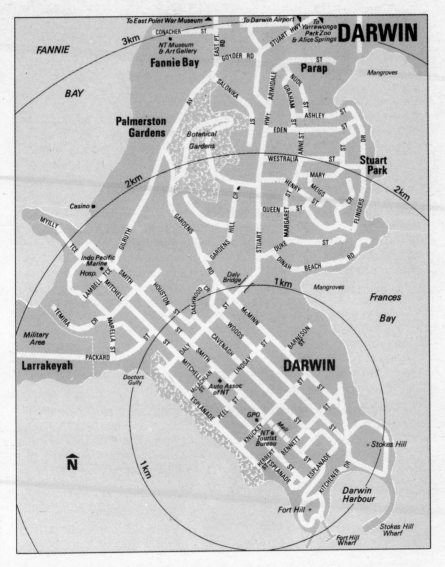

tober/November and start again in late May, depending on the weather. Check with the N.T. Tourist Bureau in any major Australian city for timely information.

If you happen to be in the Top End in early December, don't miss the annual **Beer Can Regatta**, where locals reinforce their deserved beer-swilling reputation while cheering a boat race with vessels made entirely of beer cans. It's a hilarious event.

Getting There

Bus Australia, Deluxe, Pioneer, and Greyhound run to Darwin direct from Alice Springs (19 hours) and Perth (57 hours). From Adelaide it takes 42 hours with a stopover in Alice; from Brisbane, 52 hours with stopover in Townsville; from Sydney, 67 hours with stopover in Adelaide and Alice or 72 hours via Brisbane. Buses are sometimes cancelled or delayed during the wet season due to flooding.

Airlines fly to Darwin from major Australian cities and from southeast Asia. **Darwin International Airport** looks like a giant converted hangar and maintains a level of efficiency that won't impress weary passengers one bit. Taxi service is practically non-existent, but bus #5 or #8 will get you to town (the bus doesn't run Saturday afternoons or Sunday). There is a private airport bus service which requires reservations (call 81-1102). The tourist information booth at the airport is helpful and has city maps.

Orientation and Practical Information

Greater Darwin is built on a small peninsula of land that juts into Beagle Gulf in the Timor Sea. The downtown area is surrounded on three sides by water: Frances Bay to the east, Fannie Bay to the northwest, and the Port Darwin area to the south. Smith St. Mall and Knuckey St. are the main shopping and business strips, with government and historic buildings in the southeast section of town. Suburbs expand to the north and east.

For those interested in anything from Aboriginal culture to the uranium mining issue, the **Darwin Library** on Cavenaugh St. has an extensive reference section on the Territory.

Hours of business are likely to be reduced considerably during the wet season. We've included telephone numbers wherever possible and suggest that you check before going.

Important Addresses and Telephone Numbers (area code 089)

Northern Territory Government Tourist Bureau, 31 Smith St. Mall (phone 81-6611). Everything you need to know about the city and the area is here. N.T. Conservation Commission has a booth in front with information on nearby parks and reserves. Open M-F 8:45am-5:00pm, Sat 9:00am-1:00pm.

General Post Office, corner Smith and Knuckey Sts. Open M-F 8:00am-5:00pm.

American Express, Travellers World Pty. Ltd., 18 Knuckey St. (phone 81-4699).

YHA Northern Territory Head Office, Beaton Rd., Berrimah (phone 84-3902). Mailing address: P.O. Box 39900, Winnellie, N.T. 0821.

National Parks and Wildlife Service, Commercial Union Building, Smith St. (phone 81-5299). Information on national parks, including detailed pamphlets on Kakadu National Park.

Conservation Commission of the N.T., Berrimah Farm, P.O. Box 38496, Winnellie, N.T. 5789 (phone 22-1211). Commission's information booth at front of the N.T. Tourist Bureau has pamphlets on all parks of the Top End.

Road conditions, phone 84-4455.

Automobile Association of N.T., MLC Building, 79 Smith St. (phone 81-3837).

Deluxe, 50 Mitchell St. (phone 81-8788).

Greyhound, 67-69 Mitchell St. (phone 81-8510).

Pioneer, 63 Smith St. (phone 81-6433).

Bus Australia, Darwin Motor Inn, 97 Mitchell St. (phone 81-1122).

Taxi, phone 81-8777.

Police, phone 22-3344.

Royal Darwin Hospital, phone 20-8477 or 20-8410.

Transportation

The sights in Darwin are spread out, but bicycle or public bus should suffice for seeing the central city and nearby areas. There's little public transport to places further afield. Without a tour, a car or your thumb is necessary.

The main public bus terminal in town is on Harry Chan Ave. between Smith and Cavenaugh Sts. (information line is 89-7513). The normal fare is $1, with weekly student passes available for about $3. (Depending on how nice the person behind the counter is, they may or may not accept a foreign student ID.) Buses depart regularly on weekdays and, on a limited basis, Saturday. There is no bus service on Sunday. Most runs end by 10:00pm. Free time-tables are available at the city terminal.

Car rentals include **Rent-a-Rocket** (phone 81- 6977 or 85-2049; they also have bikes), **Rent-a-Dent** (81-1411), and **Darwin Rent-a-Car** (81-9300 or 81-8332; rents mokes, too). **Avis** has 4WD vehicles (81-9922). Rent bicycles from **U-Rent** (41-1280) or **Tropical Bicycle Hire** (41- 0166).

Accommodation

Several good hostels have sprung up in Darwin, and the accommodation scene should continue to improve. If you have trouble finding room, the places listed below can refer you elsewhere. Unless noted, all hostels are downtown.

Darwin Rest House, 11 Houston St. (phone 089-81-1638). Swimming pool. Nightly BBQs. Manager takes people sailing and lends bikes.

Darwin Backpacker's, 88 Mitchell St. (phone 089-81-5385). Nice house with a pool. Large dorm rooms.

International Cotel, 99 Mitchell St. (phone 089-81-8266). Clean and newly-renovated. Air conditioning. Swimming pool. Can be crowded. BBQ every three nights or so.

Darwin City YHA Hostel, 69A Mitchell St. (phone 089-81-3995). $11/night. All twin rooms. Swimming pool. Open all day. Gorgeous facility and friendly management.

Temira Lodge, Kahlin Ave. (phone 089-41-1515). Fully serviced. Small kitchen in hallway. Swimming pool.

YWCA, 119 Mitchell St. (phone 089-81-8644). Discounted weekly rates. Swimming pool. TV room with VCR. No kitchen, but you can purchase cafeteria food for dinner. BBQ.

YMCA, The Esplanade at Doctor's Gully (phone 81-8377). Discounted weekly rates. Cement-block rooms and dull atmosphere. Videos available. Nice kitchen facilities. Clean.

Things to See and Do

Start with the **Fanny Bay Gaol Museum** (East Point Rd., Fannie Bay), a defunct, modern-day jail that has an excellent presentation on Cyclone Tracy, including stunning film of the storm (open 10:00am-5:00pm daily; free admission). Out in the same direction at the end of East Point is the **War Museum**, with two rooms of WWII relics (open 9:30am-5:00pm daily; admission $3.50). Because of its military base, Darwin was the only major Australian city bombed by the Japanese. Cannons and some of the old military installations still stand on East Point, and if you go at dusk there are always kangaroos hopping about. The area is bleak and run-down but has a beautiful view of Darwin Harbour.

Darwin's **Museum and Art Gallery** (Conacher St., Bullocky Point) has one of the best displays of modern and ancient Aboriginal art anywhere in the country. The natural history section concentrates on area wildlife and allows you to view spiders, snakes, and other nasties in graphic detail. The most popular exhibit is "Sweetheart," an infamous man-eating croc whose jaws are now forever poised for slaughter. The museum is free and open M-F 9:00am-5:00pm, Sat-Sun 10:00am-6:00pm.

Darwin is one of the few Australian cities without extensive parklands, but the **Botanic Gardens** off Gilruth Ave. are a good place to picnic (if you can avoid the sprinklers).

There are a few worthwhile visits in the town center. **Indo-Pacific Marina** (Smith St. West, corner of Gilruth Ave.), a fabulous aquarium with four reef communities, concentrates on marine life of the N.T. The aquarium is open 10:00am-4:30pm daily, April-October. Call 81-1294 for off-season hours. Admission is $8. At **Aquascene** (Doctor's Gully, west end of the Esplanade), you can feed the fish at certain hours, according to the tides (check times in the local tourist magazine or call 81-7837). Greedy fish come right up to fight for the grub. Unfortunately, you'll pay $3.50 for this privilege.

A walk around the historic part of Darwin provides a poignant understanding of war and cyclone devastation over the years. Start with the **Lyons Cottage** (corner of Knuckey & Esplanade Sts.). Erected in 1925, this house is one of the oldest buildings in town and has been converted to a small museum that details Top End history, including exploration by sailors in the 15th century and Chinese immigration in the 1870's. The display is open daily 10:00am-5:00pm (free). The **Government House** (southernmost tip of town, where the Esplanade makes a right angle turn), built in 1879, has suffered and recovered from Darwin's tragedies on numerous occasions. It still functions as a state building. Ruins of **Christ Church Cathedral** (corner of Esplanade & Smith Sts.) stand next to a new cathedral that replaced it after Tracy. There are more remains up Smith St. at the **Old Town Hall** (built 1883), once the most distinguished building in Darwin. It has not been repaired since the cyclone.

A complete historic walk through Darwin is published by the National Trust and is available at the Tourist Bureau in a pamphlet, or check the monthly tourist magazine *Top of Australia*.

The **Darwin Crocodile Farm** is 40 km south of Darwin on the Stuart Hwy., where among the featured brutes is an albino croc. Hours are 9:00am-5:00pm daily, but call first to find out feeding times (phone 88-1450). Admission is $7. **Yarrawonga Wildlife Park**, 20 km south of the city on the Stuart Hwy., is shabby, and the animals are packed into small areas.

Darwin is surrounded by beaches, not all of them great because huge tides create considerable mud flats. Sandy beaches include Mindil Beach, Fannie Bay, Lee Point, and Casuarina. The prettiest is the semi-nudist beach at **Casuarina**, which is vast and nearly deserted. Generally, you can't swim in Darwin from October-May because of the poisonous box jellyfish, but **Nightcliff Beach** has an enclosure to keep them out. On **Vestey's Beach** (between the Museum and the Sailing Club), there are windsurfers and sailboats for rent from 9:30am-7:00pm daily. Windsurfing lessons are given every day at 11:00am. Call 85-5040 for a reservation.

Daytime cruises in the harbor cost $20 (phone 81-6611 for information), but a cheaper alternative is to take the **Mandorah Ferry** ($16/roundtrip, from Stokes Hill Wharf). It departs Darwin about four times a day (call 81-3894 for schedule information).

The nearest forest wilderness is **Holmes Jungle Nature Park**, on Vanderlin Dr. in Karama. The park has a rainforest and swamp sanctuary with birds, palm trees, and tropical ferns, plus a number of trails. Pick up a map from the Conservation Commission booth in front of the Tourist Bureau.

The **Mindil Beach Market** (see *Entertainment*) and the **Parap Market** have the most colorful outdoor shopping. Parap Market runs Saturdays until about 1:00pm in the Parap shopping area and has fresh produce, jewelry, crafts, and Asian food. The Top End is a prime place for purchasing Aboriginal art, though the high quality art at the **Raintree Gallery** in town is expensive. Saturday's newspaper sometimes advertises art at cheaper prices. The best place to buy is at the outlying Aboriginal communities, where there is often a shop.

Food

Good, cheap food is hard to find in Darwin, and counter meals are scarce. When in doubt, go for Asian tucker. A couple of the hostels host frequent BBQ's. Also, the Mindil Beach Market on Thursday and the casino on Sunday offer some excellent, inexpensive dinners.

Asian Gateway (BYO), 58 Aralia St., Nightcliff (phone 85-1131). Best *satays* (meat kebab with peanut sauce) in the N.T. and a large selection of Thai food. Excellent value. Open daily 4:00pm-10:00pm.

Maharajah (BYO), 37 Knuckey St. (phone 81-6728). Wide range of moderately-priced Indian food. 10% less in front section, where curry and rice costs about $7. No shorts, sneakers, or thongs allowed in the main dining room, but there's no dress code for the front section. Open M-F noon-2:00pm, 6:00pm-late every night.

Uncle John's Cabin (BYO), 4 Gardiner St. (phone 81-3358). One of three restaurants run by an eccentric guy named John. A variety of gourmet meals; fresh fish is the specialty. Definitely worth the splurge. Open 7:30pm every night, March-November. Expensive.

Jessie's Bistro, three locations: Parap Hotel, 15 Parap Rd. (phone 81-2191); Casuarina City Centre (phone 27-9155); Berrimah Hotel, Stuart Hwy. (phone 84-3999). Steak and seafood. Extensive salad bar included in the price of main course (around $14). Open daily for lunch and dinner.

Nightlife

The people of Darwin consume huge amounts of alcohol, even compared to the rest of Australia. Though beer-brewing is Darwin's largest industry, they have to *import* beer from other states! It's great if you're into uninhibited drunkenness and wild partying. If not, there are places for more subdued entertainment.

The Victoria Hotel ("The Vic"), Smith St. Mall (phone 81-4011). No cover charge. Loud rock music. A rough local hangout. The steak house downstairs serves buffalo burgers at lunch. Open daily til 2:00am.

Fanny and Squires, 3 Edmund St. (phone 81-9761). Fanny's is a disco; Squires is a quiet, dark tavern with occasional solo musicians. Fannie's cover charge is $7 Wed-Sat, cheaper other nights. Both are open until 6:00am daily, starting 6:00pm at Squires, 8:00pm at Fanny's.

Beach Combers, corner Mitchell & Daly Sts. in the Top End Settler's Hotel (phone 81-6511). Bamboo booths and classic rock for dancing. No cover charge. Very popular. Open Wed-Sat 7:30pm-2:00am.

Darwin Hotel, corner Herbert St. & The Esplanade (phone 81-9211). Once the only "respectable" place for women to stay on their visits to the Top End. One of Darwin's original buildings, it attracts an older crowd. The Green Room, a lounge by the pool, is open 11:00am-11:00pm daily. The Kakadu bar is open M-Th noon-8:00pm, F noon-2:00am, and Sat 8:00pm-late.

Hot Gossip, 21 Cavenaugh St. (phone 41-1811). Flashy entertainment complex with a nightclub, cocktail lounge, bistro, and stage for live bands. Nightclub is open 8:30pm-wee hours nightly except Monday. Depending on the night, cover charges range from $7-$16.

Circles Bar, Mitchell St. in the Beaufort Hotel (phone 82-9761). Chic for Darwin. A yuppie hangout with expensive drinks. Open T-Sat 8:00pm-2:00am.

Diamond Beach Hotel Casino, Gilruth Ave. (phone 81-7755). 24-hour coffee lounge on weekends, piano bar, disco, and a cabaret with cover charges beginning at $10. No running shoes, thongs, or jeans allowed, and men must wear collared shirts. The best casino activity is free live jazz by the pool on Sunday 4:00pm-7:00pm, with a BBQ until 8:00pm. Gambling is open 1:00pm-3:00am daily.

Entertainment

From 5:00pm-9:00pm every Thursday, the **Mindil Beach Market** (on Mindil Beach) is the quintessential Darwin experience. All generations of locals flock there to dine on inexpensive Asian goodies as the sun sets, and entertainers serenade the crowd (BYO grog and picnic blankets). Jewelry and other crafts are for sale, too.

Darwin is famous for its pink sunsets. You can watch the sun's descent through palm trees while sipping tall drinks at the **Sailing Club** (East Point Rd. at Vestey's Beach). Since the Club is private, this is not an entirely legitimate activity for visitors, but they usually allow foreigners to sign in as guests. Hearty counter meals at the club begin at $8.

A much-promoted and touristy **evening cruise** from Fisherman's Wharf to Mandorah includes a seafood dinner of mud crabs and barramundi, plus a contrived Aboriginal *corroboree* for entertainment. It's a big, expensive bore—don't get sucked into this tourist trap.

Darwin's **Performing Arts Centre**, attached to the Beaufort Hotel at 93 Mitchell St., is one of the most handsome buildings in the city and hosts performances of all kinds. The box office opens at 10:00am. Student discounts are available and tickets are cheaper at the door (door sales begin 45 minutes before performances). Call 81-9022 for current shows or check the *Northern Territory News*. **Brown's Mart** at 12 Smith St., one of the few pre-20th century structures left in Darwin, occasionally holds performances (phone 81-5522), and big acts often play in the **Botanical Gardens** at the Gardens Amphitheater (phone 81-5294).

The **Darwin Cinema** (46 Mitchell St., phone 81-5999) is the lone movie theater downtown. Casuarina has the only other cinema in the area, on Trower Rd. next to Casuarina Village (phone 45-0174). Sunday afternoons at 2:00pm there's a free movie at the **Museum of Arts and Sciences** (phone 82-4211).

Trips from Darwin

The rugged outback and coastal wilderness of the Top End is almost no distance from Darwin. Fogg Dam, Kakadu National Park, and Arnhem Land lie to the east. To the south are the historic townships of Adelaide River and Pine Creek, plus Litchfield Park and Katherine (see *Stuart Highway* section). Trips north usually involve a short plane ride, either to the Cobourg Peninsula or Melville or Bathurst Islands.

Before leaving for the parks and reserves, check with the **Conservation Commission** booth at the N.T. Tourist Bureau or with **National Parks and Wildlife** in the Commercial Union Bldg. on Smith St. Both publish pamphlets with directions and descriptions of facilities and park flora and fauna. **The Department of Lands** in Moonta House (Mitchell St., between Knuckey & Herbert Sts.) provides detailed topographical maps for hikers.

For ocean-oriented people, fishing and diving are favorite Top End activities. Angling charters are available in Kakadu National Park, Arnhem Land, and the Mary and Daly Rivers. Diving among wrecks and coral reefs is popular and easy to arrange. Information and bookings are available from the N.T. Tourist Bureau.

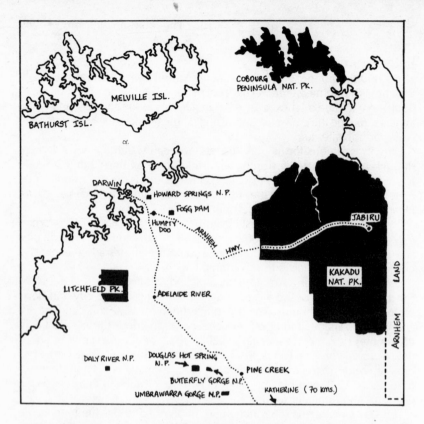

Out of Darwin, there are few hostels or cheap hotels aside from the YHA hostel in Kakadu National Park. Camping is the cheapest—and sometimes the only—way to go. The best place to rent camping gear is **U-Rent** at the corner of Knuckey and Mitchell Sts. (phone 41-1280).

Deluxe, Greyhound, and Pioneer run limited services east of Darwin to Jabiru (in Kakadu National Park), stopping at Humpty Doo, the Bark Hut Inn, South Alligator Motor Inn, and Cooinda. All major buslines travel south along the Stuart Hwy., stopping at Adelaide River and Pine Creek. If you decide to rent a car, remember that 4WD is often necessary in parks and reserves.

Along the Arnhem Highway

The Arnhem Highway, the only eastern route from Darwin, runs through Kakadu National Park and ends at Jabiru on the Arnhem Land border. Along the way, the little town of Humpty Doo boasts a local pub, the **Humpty Doo Hotel**, renowned for wild weekend parties, and all the poisonous snakes you've never cared to encounter at **Graeme Gow's Reptile World** (phone 88-1661), open 8:30am-6:00pm daily.

Just past Humpty Doo, 60 km southeast of Darwin, **Fogg Dam**, a wetlands area, serves as a dry season sanctuary for Top End birds like jabirus, ibises, darters, etc. It's a beautiful place to watch the sun rise. A bird book and binoculars are helpful, as there is no information on site.

A bit further down, the Arnhem Hwy. crosses the Adelaide River, where you can take a cruise on the **Adelaide River Queen**. The crocs in the river, billed as "World Famous Jumping Crocodiles," have learned to leap from the water for juicy bait, and though it's a tourist trap, you can snap some great photos.

Just before reaching Kakadu National Park, the Arnhem crosses the **Mary River**, a favorite spot of barramundi anglers. There's a campground and the **Bark Hut Inn**, which has fishing information.

Kakadu National Park

Though *Crocodile Dundee* put Kakadu National Park on the international tourist route, most people aren't aware of what the park offers aside from giant crocs with an insatiable appetite for ditsy blond women. In fact, the park is world-renowned for two reasons:

First, Kakadu's **sacred rock paintings**, some dated 30,000-years old, are among the most ancient paintings known. There are at least 5,000 rock painting sites within the park, most of them along the Arnhem Land escarpment. They range from thousands of years old to modern, the most recent painted in 1972. The art is the most spectacular example of Australian Aboriginal painting that's easily accessible to travelers.

Kakadu is equally famous for the **rare fauna and flora** it protects. Hundreds of bird species find sanctuary in the park's wetlands, while crocs, goannas, frill-neck lizards, and a score of other creatures are protected from human interference. Once a dying species, the saltwater crocodile population has been on the rise since legislation in the early 1970's protected it. Flora in Kakadu was saved by a campaign to eliminate mimosa, a nasty weed which buffalo have helped spread since their introduction to the N.T. in 1825. (Mimosa is still a huge problem in other parts of the N.T.) Scientists are studying many of Kakadu's rare tropical plant species—some of which have yet to be named.

Getting There and Getting Around: Most visitors don't realize how long it takes to get from Darwin to Kakadu, and they mistakenly think it's a convenient day trip. However, most destinations in the park are close to the eastern border—at least 100 km from the western entrance and 250 km from Darwin—and some attractions are off dirt roads. A regular car will be fine for reaching all the attractions except the waterfalls and canyons of the Arnhem Land escarpment, accessible by 4WD only. To get a real feel for the place, we suggest going by 4WD or taking an organized 4WD tour.

Greyhound and Deluxe run from Darwin to a few destinations in Kakadu: South Alligator Motor Inn, Cooinda, the YHA hostel, and Jabiru (via Nourlangie Rock). Pioneer runs daily to the South Alligator Motor Inn and Cooinda Motel.

Tour options are numerous and ever-changing. The time of year is a big factor; there are no 4WD tours December-April, and April-May access remains limited. If you have the option of a 4WD tour, don't pass it up. **World Expeditions**, for instance, runs a top-notch tour that includes four days in

Kakadu followed by sailing on the Cobourg Peninsula or canoeing on the Daly River. The personalized nature of the trip allows you to explore the park without feeling confined to a rigid itinerary. This option is on the expensive side but well worth it. Make bookings through the head office at 377 Sussex St., Sydney, N.S.W. 2000 (phone 02-264-3366).

For on-the-spot bookings, go to the N.T. Tourist Bureau in Darwin and compare prices. Tours from Darwin include **Terra Safari**, which has trips year-round and is highly recommended (phone 089-45-0863 or 27-0881, or book through the N.T. Tourist Bureau). Russell Willis, owner of **Willis' Walkabouts**, is filled with local knowledge and isn't tainted by commercialism, like many other tour operators (12 Carrington St., Millner, N.T. 5792; phone 089-85-2134).

The tours that operate within Kakadu aren't necessarily cheaper than those from Darwin. From the **Cooinda Four Seasons Hotel** (phone 79-0145 or 79-2545) or **Kakadu Holiday Village** (phone 79-0166), a day tour to Jim Jim Falls costs about $150. From Cooinda, **Wild Goose Tours** runs one-day wetlands tours July 1-November 31, and other day tours go to Nourlangie Rock and the uranium mine (call Cooinda number above).

Orientation and Practical Information: Kakadu National Park covers a huge area (12,500 square km) and encompasses a tremendous diversity of terrain: pink sandstone cliffs and waterfalls of the Arnhem Land escarpment, tidal flats of the seldom-visited coastline, monsoonal forests, and floodplains of the four rivers (East, South, West Alligator, and Wildman Rivers). The park was created in three stages: the first in 1979, the second in '84, and the third in '87. Negotiations over uranium mining rights are still in progress. Mining is now permitted in certain "conservation zones."

The government leases the park's land from the **Gagudju Association**, which represents all the local Aborigines. The Association and the National Parks and Wildlife Service jointly manage the park which, in addition to attracting tourists and scientists, is home to about 270 Aborigines from nine communities. Many of these people maintain their traditional lifestyles.

A word on **crocodiles**: Most visitors arrive in Kakadu with the idea that saltwater crocs are going to eat them up if they get within ten yards of a river. While you should exercise extreme caution in areas where there are crocs, some of the creeks and water holes are perfectly safe for swimming—and there's nothing you'll welcome more in Kakadu than a refreshing dip. Saltwater crocs can live in both salt- and freshwater. Warning signs are often posted, but do not swim unless you've asked an authority if it's safe, and beware of murky water in rivers like the South Alligator. Don't leave food near riverbanks, and don't harass salties from a boat, either—they've been known to sink dinghies when provoked. Most swimming areas have freshwater Johnston crocodiles, which are smaller than saltwater crocs and won't bother you unless you bother them.

Don't be alarmed if you see small fires in the bush areas of Kakadu. The rangers set these fires to maintain the rejuvenation cycle of the land and prevent destructive natural fires. Aborigines have practiced controlled burning for thousands of years and consider burned land to be clean land.

Information Centers: For advance information, write *Superintendent, Kakadu National Park, P.O. Box 71, Jabiru, N.T. 5796 (phone 089-79-2101)* or go to the **Australian National Parks and Wildlife Service** in Darwin (Commercial Union Building, Smith St., phone 81-5299), which distributes pamphlets on every aspect of the park. They also have information for hikers.

The **park headquarters**, 2 km off the Arnhem Hwy. on the road to Yellow Waters and Nourlangie Rock, has excellent practical and background information, including a handy map.

The **Jabiru Airport** has an information center where you can book cruises, flights, and tours into 4WD areas. Information, bookings, and maps are also available in Darwin at the N.T. Tourist Bureau.

When to Visit: The best time to visit is June to August, when the weather is dry and moderate. From December-early April, monsoonal conditions limit access, and none of the 4WD routes to the falls can be negotiated by car. Tours operate frequently June 1-September 30, and on a limited basis at other times. While the months between the dry and wet seasons (mid-April to May; October to early December) are extremely hot, they are a good time to avoid other tourists. Birdwatchers should come in October and November, when birds congregate in the few places where water is available.

What to Bring: Wear cool, comfortable clothing and bring a hat, sunglasses, and sunscreen. The heat can be searing, and flies and mosquitoes are ubiquitous. Insect repellent is a must (Rid is the best), and open-air campers should have a mosquito net. If you plan to do any hiking, bring a water bottle. Visitors to the falls should bring a bathing suit and, for Twin Falls, an air mattress. Binoculars come in handy.

Petrol and limited supplies are available at **Kakadu Holiday Village**, the **Cooinda Four Seasons Hotel**, and the border store near Ubirr. Jabiru township, on the eastern edge of the park, has groceries, petrol, and most other supplies.

Further Reading: Many excellent books about Kakadu and its Aborigines are available in Darwin. We especially recommend the following:

Kakadu: Our Land, Our Heritage by Lyn Allen and Chris Harris. The most comprehensive and updated overview of the park's history and ecology, with photographs.

Australia's Kakadu Man, Bill Neidjie by Bill Neidjie, Stephen Davis, and Allan Fox. Ruminations on the park and its native people through the eyes of one the tribal elders, Bill Neidjie.

Accommodation: The best way to get a feel for the park is to camp. The 12 campgrounds in the park, most of them near the major attractions, are detailed in the *Visitor Map to Kakadu*, and most are free. A permit is required to camp elsewhere. Camping is quite safe. There are few venomous snakes and no poison ivy or thistles—just crocs, biting green ants, and relentlessly persistent flies.

The **YHA Hostel** is in a former Aboriginal boarding school on the road to Ubirr, 50 meters past the border store on the left. The office is closed 10:00am-5:00pm, but the hostel is open all day. It closes from October/November to March/April depending on the rains (contact the head YHA office in Darwin for dates). It costs $7/night, and there are only 20 beds, so get there early or book ahead through other YHA hostels.

Kakadu Holiday Village on the Arnhem Hwy. (phone 089-79-0166) has camping, dorm bunks, singles, and doubles. It's a considerable distance from any of the park's sights.

Things to See and Do: Yellow Waters boat cruises depart several times daily from the Cooinda Four Seasons Hotel. They run two hours and cost $20. Rangers identify the myriad birds and reptiles that abound in this billabong, and there's always a croc or two sunning on the muddy banks. The cruise is a perfect introduction to the wildlife of Kakadu. Check at the Four Seasons or the Ranger Station for departure times. You can also rent boats and fishing tackle at the Four Seasons.

Cruises on the South Alligator River leave from Kakadu Holiday Village (limited operation during the wet season). Call 79-0166 for bookings and times. This cruise doesn't offer the bird life of the other, but there are plenty of giant crocs.

The paintings at **Nourlangie Rock**, estimated to be 30,000-years old, are spectacular examples of several styles of Aboriginal rock art. A wooden walkway guides you around the giant boulders where Gagudju Aborigines lived for thousands of generations. One shelter was inhabited until the mid-1970's. The ranger-guided tours are a must and depart daily from the parking lot at 9:00am and 2:00pm. The site is open from 8:30am-5:00pm.

Ubirr (open 8:30am-sunset) is equally impressive and has extensive examples of the more recent "X-ray" painting style. The bush at Ubirr is less thick than at Nourlangie, and a short climb yields a panoramic view of the entire area. Sunset tours by the rangers are the most popular. The two-hour tours leave from the parking lot at 9:00am and 5:00pm. Ubirr is 37 km off the Arnhem Hwy. on an unpaved but well-maintained road. At both Nourlangie and Ubirr you'll hear about two Aborigines: Najombolmi ("Barramundi Charlie"), a famous artist and tribal elder who restored many of the rock paintings before his death in the 1960's, and Bill Neidjie, who also worked on the restoration and wrote a book about Kakadu.

Not as frequently visited but definitely worth a look are the **Blue Paintings** (open 10:00am-5:00pm). Completed in 1964 by Najombolmi, the "X-ray" paintings (so called because they outline the skeleton and select internal organs of their subjects) are distinguished by the unusual use of blue pigment. Tours leave daily from the carpark at 11:15am and last 1.5 hours.

The **Arnhem Land escarpment** stretches 500 km along the eastern border of the park, with cliffs between 300-400 meters high. There is no hiking trail to guide you along the precipice, but a few places are accessible by 4WD, including Jim Jim Falls and Twin Falls. Both spots are like a tropical river paradise, and neither has the usual flock of tourists. **Jim Jim Falls** drops a sheer 200 meters and is a tiny trickle of water most of the time, but the pool at the bottom is lovely and cool for swimming, complete with a white sand beach. A marked trail starts at the first pool near the bottom of Jim Jim and leads to a gorgeous climb that takes a few hours round trip. The trail is poorly marked, but we found it easy to explore and discovered some off-the-beaten-track rock paintings in the process.

Twin Falls, a 350-meter drop in a series of falls, is accessible by water only. If you need provisions for the day, bring an air mattress and put your gear on top. To get there you have to swim briefly through three clear, blue-green pools with fine white sand. If you still have the energy, it takes about a half-hour to climb up the side (there's no marked trail).

Camping facilities are near both falls. If you don't have 4WD, a rough but passable road can get you to **Gunlom Falls**, also on the Arnhem Land escarpment, which were discovered in the 1950's by mining developers. There's a campground/caravan park.

Kakadu has few marked hiking trails; most are short walks around the publicized attractions. **Mamukala Nature Trail**, 7 km past Kakadu Holiday Village on the Arnhem Hwy., leads to spectacular wetlands teeming with bird life. Park rangers conduct short walks on this trail (contact park headquarters for details).

It may seem strange that there are tours of the **uranium mine** in Jabiru East. Despite the conflict of interest between park authorities and mining companies, the tour is well-publicized and popular, running three to five times daily in the dry season. For times, call 79-2031 or get a pamphlet at any of the information centers in hotels and stops along the road.

Scenic flights are available from the Jabiru Airport (phone 79-2031).

Arnhem Land

Bordering Kakadu National Park on the east, Arnhem Land was declared an Aboriginal reserve in 1931 and is one of the largest reserves (97,000 sq. km) in the country. Access to Arnhem Land is limited to those who hold permits. Apply by writing *Permits Officer, Northern Land Council, P.O. Box 3046, Darwin, N.T. (phone 089-81-7011)*. It takes about two weeks to obtain a permit, and visitors usually aren't allowed in without a tour group.

Terra Safari has a four-day tour into Arnhem Land that departs twice a week from the end of April through October and costs around $550. They join an Aborigine guide and emphasize the culture of the Mudteegarrdart tribe. Write *Terra Safari Tours, P.O. Box 39470, Winnellie, N.T. (or call 089-45-0863 or 27-0881)*.

South of Darwin

The **Stuart Highway** is the only southern route from Darwin. Along the road there are several remnants from the WWII activity in the Top End. Paved areas that parallel the road were wartime airstrips, and several roadside memorials honor war victims.

Historic Sights

A **WWII cemetery** at Adelaide River, 110 km from Darwin, commemorates victims of Japanese bombing raids on Darwin. The **railway station** at Adelaide River, built in 1888, is a typical outback train stop of the time and was a crucial depot during the war (phone 76-7040 for hours, which change according to whim). Pine Creek (231 km south of Darwin), once home to Chinese immigrants who came to work on the Overland Telegraph Line and seek their fortunes in the 1870's gold rush, has a **museum** that explains the Chinese influence and is cluttered with an eclectic collection of relics. The curators are true blue Territorians and love to chat (open 10:00am-11:00am, 2:00pm-3:00pm in April, May, Sept, and Oct; 10:00am-noon and 2:30pm-4:30pm in June, July, Aug; closed Nov-March). There's a **YHA Hostel** at Pine Creek (corner Main Tce. and Old Moline Rd.; phone 089-76-1254) in a historic building. Don't plan on a hot shower there, however.

Litchfield and Other National Parks

Two nature reserves and a substantial national park lie within 100 km south of Darwin. **Howard Springs Nature Park**, a rainforest setting alongside natural springs, has short walking trails and safe swimming. It's 26 km from Darwin off the Stuart Hwy. **Berry Springs** (turn off the Stuart 48 km south of Darwin, then another 14 km) is another good place to take a dip, and an open-range wildlife reserve is being developed by the Conservation Commission there. It wasn't open when we visited, but call the Commission at 22-0211 for information.

Litchfield Park has far fewer tourists than Kakadu and is at least as remote, with 4WD access only. The **Tabletop Range**, where the park is located, is a vast sandstone plateau that gives way to escarpment with plunging waterfalls and gorges among rainforests. The area is spectacular and virtually untouched, with possibly the largest termite mound in the world—6.9 meters high! No extensive hiking trails are marked, but if you have a compass and map, the area is certainly large enough for an overnight expedition. There are places to camp at the well-known natural sites. For more information on what to see and how to prepare, contact the Conservation Commission at 22-2311.

Getting to Litchfield Park, about a two-hour drive from Darwin, is nearly impossible without your own 4WD. There are one-day safaris to Tolmer Falls and Florence Falls in the park from Adelaide River, run by **Bushranger Tours** (phone 089-76-7047). The presently favored road into the park is the continuation of the Berry Springs road off the Stuart Hwy. A new road is being built from Bachelor, further south on the Stuart. Phone 84-4455 for road information, especially in the wet season.

Adelaide River is the jumping-off point for a few small nature reserves, including the **Daly River** (with excellent barramundi fishing), and **Douglas Hot Springs Nature Park** and **Butterfly Gorge National Park**, adjacent to one another. Further down the road towards Pine Creek is **Umbrawarra Gorge Nature Park**. All are good spots for picnics or relaxing in the shade. Camping is permitted at each.

Bathurst and Melville Islands

Directly north of Darwin, Bathurst and Melville Islands are inhabited by the **Tiwi**, a tribe that developed independently of Aborigines on the mainland and still maintains many of its traditional customs. The people produce ornate printed fabrics sold throughout Australia under the name "Tiwi Designs" or "Jilmarra." When the Pope came to Australia in 1986, Tiwi designers prepared his vestments. Another notable Tiwi art form are burial poles, featured in museums throughout Australia.

Fishing on the islands is excellent. The **Tiwi Land Council Office** issues fishing permits (in Darwin at 37 McMinn St., phone 81-4111; on Bathurst Island, phone 089-78-3991). **Tiwi Finz** offers fishing tours, and **Tiwi Tours** and **Australian Kakadu Tours** both offer expensive trips to the islands that emphasize understanding and meeting the Tiwi people. Book through the N.T. Tourist Bureau for all three operators.

To go independent of a tour, write for a permit (allow at least two weeks for processing) to *Permits Officer, Tiwi Land Council, P.O. Box 340, Darwin, N.T. (phone 089-81-4111)*. For information on flights from Darwin, contact the N.T. Tourist Bureau.

The Cobourg Peninsula

The Cobourg Peninsula, northeast of Darwin across Van Diemen Gulf, is a remote, fascinating place, where an Aboriginal reserve doubles as **Gurig National Park**. About 300 Aborigines live there.

On the north coast, the ruins of a failed British settlement at Port Essington are accessible only by water. The **Victoria Settlement**, as it came to be known, was the third attempt by England to secure the northern tip of the continent. The colony lasted from 1838-1849, when it failed from disease and harsh conditions. Stone foundations with crumbling walls and chimneys remain, and you can sometimes find bits of china and other artifacts.

Game hunters from around the world visit the Cobourg Peninsula to chase the *banteng* (a huge beast akin to the water buffalo) at thousands of dollars for a safari. The coast abounds in fish, crocs, giant sea turtles, mussels, and oysters, and the beaches of gorgeous, pearl-white sand and beautiful shells are irresistible. Best of all, the area is untouched and virtually uninhabited. The only drawback: the croc- and shark-infested waters aren't so good for swimming. There are also deadly poisonous cone shells and sea snakes, but locals know the safe swimming spots.

The easiest and least expensive way to the Cobourg Peninsula is by plane, but it is by no means cheap. **Wimray Safaris** and **Kakadu Air** have regular flights, and Wimray owns a few cabins on the shore (dinghy included). The best way to enjoy the place is aboard the *Zachariah*, a 13-meter sailboat run by **Cobourg Marine**. Peter and Rikki, the couple who run the operation, take you fishing, oystering, diving, and hiking through rainforests. They land at Port Essington for a narrated tour around the Victoria Settlement and go anywhere else you please. Tours last one to three days March-November.

Contact Cobourg Marine at G.P.O. Box 1529, Darwin, N.T. (phone 089-85-6923) or write **World Expeditions** about their Kakadu/Cobourg tour (includes sailing with Cobourg Marine) at 377 Sussex St., Sydney, N.S.W. 2000 (phone 02-264-3366).

If you plan to go without an organized tour, you must acquire your own entry permit into **Gurig National Park** from the Conservation Commission in Darwin (phone 22-0211). Allow at least two weeks. On arrival, check-in at the ranger station at Black Point. For further reading on the Victoria Settlement, try *Forsaken Settlement* by P.G. Spillet (Lansdowne Press).

Alice Springs

The only township in the area for hundreds of miles, Alice Springs is surrounded on all sides by brilliant red earth and ancient geologic formations. The MacDonnell Ranges and Ayers Rock are the main features of this innermost region of Australia, known as the "Red Centre." It's not to be missed.

"The Alice" today is a boom town of some 22,000. For its first hundred years, it was a rough little frontier town that served as an administrative center for the cattle industry, the Flying Doctor Service, and the Central Australian government. Since 1970, as tourist and mining industries have brought new interest in the area, the average annual rate of growth has been an impressive 7%.

Tourism has brought the biggest changes. Restaurants are likely to be licensed (and expensive), genuine "locals" are few and far between, and the service-related businesses have a blandness borne of the need to cater to all species of tourist.

However, no one who makes an effort to delve beneath the bland modern facades would say that Alice Springs lacks character. Have a look at the **Todd Tavern**, the local service/sports clubs, and the **Todd Riverbed** (where Aborigines gather), and you'll begin to see what Alice is all about. If you're still not convinced, attend the **Henley-on-Todd Regatta** in late September. The Todd River is completely dry, so the sailing crews challenge one another in bottomless boats amid much drinking and festivity.

An American satellite tracking station called **Pine Gap** has imported 300 American families to the area, easily identified by their left-driven cars. Seen from the air, the white domes of the station look extra-terrestrial. The existence of Pine Gap is an extremely controversial issue across the country. A clear account of its purpose has not been fully revealed to Australia, and there's fear that Pine Gap would be a prime target for nuclear attack. Don't bother trying to have a closer look; you won't get very far.

High tourist season for the Alice area is April-November. The winter months (June-August) are warm during the day (jeans and t-shirts) and often below freezing at night. While it is possible to travel through the area in summer, remember that temperatures regularly top 40 °C (105 °F) and that heat is sometimes prohibitive when exploring the outback. From September-November, the air is especially thick with flies.

Getting There

All major buslines service Alice Springs, including Greyhound, Pioneer, Deluxe, and Bus Australia. From Adelaide, the trip takes about 19 hours, from Darwin about 20. Each busline also has a connection or direct service to and from Ayers Rock.

The only rail service to Alice Springs, *The Ghan*, runs between Adelaide and Alice twice a week and takes 22 hours. Caper Fares are available for economy seats, costing slightly more than the bus.

Despite the thousands of tourists arriving in Alice by plane, the airport is modest—luggage still arrives on a hand-drawn trolley. An airport bus meets flights and goes to all hotel accommodations in town, including the Melanka Lodge and YHA hostel. Alice Springs taxis are on call at 52-1877 and probably won't be waiting at the airport.

Orientation and Practical Information

The Todd River, completely dry for 11 months of the year, runs through the middle of Alice Springs. **Todd Street** is Alice's main commercial drag and has a pedestrian mall. Most shopping and dining takes place within the grid of streets around Todd Mall. The **Alice Springs Regional Tourist Association** produces a map that includes greater Alice Springs, a detail of the town center, and a large map of the whole Red Centre with camping sites, petrol stations, and other important information.

Unlike the rest of Australia, Alice doesn't shut down on weekends. On Sunday, shopping centers are open all day, and pubs and nightclubs maintain their usual late hours.

In all seasons bring sunscreen and a hat, plus warm clothes for night.

Important Addresses and Phone Numbers (area code 089)

N.T. Government Tourist Bureau, corner Todd Mall and Parsons St. (phone 52-1299). Information on the town and surrounding area, including Uluru National Park (Ayers Rock and the Olgas).

G.P.O., 33 Hartley St.

Conservation Commission of the N.T., Gap Rd. (phone 50-8211). Information on national parks.

Area road information, phone 52-7111

Pioneer, Ford Plaza, Hartley St. (phone 52-2422)

Deluxe, Ford Plaza, Hartley St. (phone 52-4444)

Greyhound, Todd Mall (phone 52-7888)

Bus Australia, Melanka Lodge, 94 Todd St. (phone 52-2233)

Ansett Airlines, Todd Mall (phone 52-4455)

Australian Airlines, Todd Mall (phone 50-5211)

Alice Springs Taxis, (phone 52-1877, 24-hour service)

Police, Parsons St. (phone 50-1211)

Alice Springs Hospital, phone 50-2211

Transportation

There is no public transport in Alice. A bike, moped, or moke will do for getting around town, but since the best places to visit are further afield—and since the heat and sun in summer can be unbearable—a car is probably the best option. Some nearby destinations are accessible only with four-wheel drive. Hitching around town isn't difficult.

Almost all the car rental companies have a steep deposit fee (about $80) if you don't use a credit card. Mokes are about $25/day, plus $11 insurance, plus $.20 per km, plus 1.5% stamp duty. And, on top of all that, there's often a distance restriction of a 50 km radius. 4WD rentals run $70-$120/day, plus mileage. Make sure to book ahead in high tourist season. There several rental companies: **Cheapa Rent-A-Car** (94 Todd St., phone 52-9999), **EconoRent** (16 Kidman St., phone 52-8819), and **Centre Car Rentals** (Ford Plaza, Todd St., phone 52-1405), to name a few.

Rent bicycles from the YHA hostels or the Melanka Lodge/BP Station on Todd St. (phone 52-3717).

Tour prices are often equivalent to (or less expensive than) bus fares, rental fees, and other transport options. The YHA hostel operates the best local booking agency for budget-conscious travelers.

Accommodation

There's lots of cheap accommodation in Alice, but in high tourist season be sure to call ahead. Only the YHA hostels, Y.W.C.A., and Melanka Lodge are in the center of town, and several accommodations don't have kitchen facilities.

YHA Hostel, corner Todd St. and Stott Tce. (phone 52-5016). $9/night. Office closed 1:00pm-4:00pm. Common room with fireplace and pool table. Friendly atmosphere. Bike rental. Travel agency open daily during office hours.

YHA Hostel, corner Parsons St. and Leichhardt Tce. (phone 52-5016). $10/night. New hostel. Building is a remodeled open-air movie theater.

Melanka Lodge, 94 Todd St. (phone 52-2233). Stark, cement-block rooms. Can be noisy. Two swimming pools. Pool table. TV lounge. No kitchen facilities. We don't recommend the cooked breakfast. Open all day.

Arura Safari Lodge, corner Lindsay Ave. and Warburton St.; 15-min. walk from town (phone 52-3843 or 008-89-6118). Free transport from bus terminals. Very clean and pleasant. Only 16 dorm spaces, so call ahead. Outdoor common area with BBQ and pool.

Sandrifter Safari Lodge, 6 Kharlic St.; 15-min. walk from town (phone 52-8686). Cramped, with small kitchen. Outdoor common area. No noise after 10:00pm. No alcohol.

Campus Holidays, MacDonnell Range Tourist Park, 4.5 km south of town on Ross Hwy. (phone 52-6111). Standard-size tents are $22/one person, $18/two share, down to $10/six share. Large, airy, on-site tents with all cooking facilities. Swimming pool.

Stuart Lodge Y.W.C.A., corner Stuart Hwy. and Hartley St. (phone 52-1894). $30-$40/night. Linen included. Weekly 10% discount on application. All rooms serviced daily. Quiet. Lots of semi- permanents. TV lounge. BBQ. Open all day.

Mt. Nancy Motel, North Stuart Hwy., 7 km north of town (phone 52-9488). $18-$50/night, includes cooked breakfast. No kitchen facilities. Swimming pool. Lounge and bar. BBQ.

Alice Travellers Village, North Stuart Hwy., 8 km north of town (phone 52-8955). $16/night (four per room); $6/person camping; $12 for linen for length of stay. Huge new complex includes shopping mart, restaurant, bistro, pool, spa, game room. No kitchen facilities. Office open 6:30am-9:00pm.

Toddy's, Gap Rd., 2.5 km from town (phone 52-1322 or 008-89-6117). $14/bunk bed; $40/two-person cabin; $7 for linen. Reputation for being noisy, but facilities are clean. Swimming pool. Common room with fireplace. BBQ. Kitchen available, but crockery must be rented.

Things to See and Do
Alice Springs has far too many tacky, makeshift tourist attractions, prime examples of which are **Pitchi Ritchi Bird Sanctuary** and **Diorama Village**. Pitchi Ritchi is basically a junkyard of knickknacks that have rusted to near-disintegration over the years. Diorama Village uses model scenes to depict Aboriginal myths—definitely a tourist trap.

While the best things to do around Alice are in the surrounding wilderness, there are a few worthwhile visits in town. The **Old Telegraph Station** (3 km north of town center, on the Stuart Hwy.) is one of twelve original stations built from Adelaide to Darwin between 1870-72 to connect the Overland Telegraph Line. The cable linked Australia to the world telegraph network. Erected in 1871 after explorers found a pass through the MacDonnells at Heavitree Gap, the station was the first building in the district. They built it near some running springs on what is now the Todd River and named them for Alice Todd, wife of the superintendent for the telegraph project. The original "Alice Springs" are part of the reserve that adjoins the station, and there are picnic facilities and an enclosure with emus and kangaroos. The station is open 8:00am-9:00pm Oct-April; 10:00am- 6:00pm May-Sept. Admission is free.

Other notable buildings in the center of town provide a historic orientation to the area. **The Residency** (cnr. Parsons & Hartley Sts.) was built in 1927 for the Government Resident during Alice's short stint as capital of "Central Australia," a political entity from 1926-31. It is now a small museum and art gallery. Paintings inside by famous Australian artists Albert Namatjira and Sidney Nolan are worth a look. (Open M-F 9:00am-4:30pm, Sat-Sun

10:00am-4:00pm; free admission). **Adelaide House** on the Todd St. Mall was one of 15 hospitals established in the outback during the 1920's by missionary John Flynn (a.k.a. "Flynn of the Inland"). The hospital is open M-F 10:00am-4:00pm, Sat 10:00am-noon, and closed in summer. Behind Adelaide House is a stone hut where Flynn and Alfred Traeger succeeded in sending their first field radio signal in 1926, an extremely important development for Australians in the outback.

The **Royal Flying Doctor** on Stuart Tce. was another of Flynn's pet projects. At one time it serviced two-thirds of the continent. The base currently covers an 800 km radius and receives over 100,000 calls per year, and you can see how it operates by taking a guided tour. Tours are M-Sat 9:30am-3:30pm, with additional afternoon tours from Easter-October.

Southwest of the town center (cnr. of Memorial & Van Senden Aves.) is a barren **cemetery** with graves of Alice's important early denizens, including Harold Lasseter, a gold miner who swore he'd found an enormous reef of gold in the desert and died trying to relocate it. Albert Namatjira is also buried there, a famous watercolorist who, in 1957, became the first   Aborigine to receive full Australian citizenship. A few of his paintings are housed at The Residency, and photographs of him are in the front rooms at **Panorama Guth** (65 Hartley St.). The $3 admission to see Henk Guth's painted panorama landscape isn't worth it, but there's no charge to go in the front rooms (open M-F 9:00am-5:00pm, Sat 9:00am-noon, Sun 9:00am-2:00pm).

In the last century, hundreds of camels were imported to Australia to carry supplies for early explorers and settlers, and local camel farms provide a fine opportunity to experience the loping gait of these peculiar beasts. **Frontier Camel Farm** (8 km southeast of town on Ross Hwy.) is the best choice. Among their offerings are treks along the Todd Riverbed (about $18/half-hour), lunch or dinner trips to Chateau Hornsby Winery, and two-day safaris. The owner, Nick Smail, is a soft-spoken, informative guide, and great with his animals. He'll pick you up from wherever you're staying if you book ahead (call 53-0444 between 9:00am-5:00pm). The other local camel farm is **Camel Outback Safaris** (phone 56-0925).

The less patient may prefer seeing the MacDonnells on horseback. Try **Glenrowan** at 52-6447 (after hours) for trail rides.

The **Chateau Hornsby Winery** (15 km from Alice on Petrick Rd.) is intriguing in its own right. The wines range from average to awful, but every January it's the first winery on the globe to begin harvesting grapes. Wine tastings are $2, scrumptious beer bread $6, and chicken/cheese lunches $7. Chateau Hornsby is open daily 11:00am-4:00pm, and from March-Sept 6:00pm-11:00pm as well (with bush music and dinner). Call 52-5771 for more information.

Aboriginal arts and crafts and Akubra hats are the most popular tourist purchases in Alice. **Mbantua** (55 Gap Rd.) has quality Aboriginal handcrafts for excellent prices—don't mind the dusty items. It's nearly impossible to find a cheap Akubra, but any stock company that supplies hats for station hands will have the best deals, and you'll be guaranteed the real thing. Ask a local.

Food

Most of Alice's eateries are open every day. The options aren't too thrilling: either expensive, licensed restaurants or fast-food in and around the Mall. However, there are a few small health food cafes with wholesome meals and snacks, and the private service/sports clubs offer cheap, large counter meals. Cooking for yourself is certainly the least expensive option. Try **Coles Supermarket** on Todd Mall. For the cheapest fruit and vegetables go to **Head Street**, northwest of town.

La Casalinga, 105 Gregory Tce. (phone 52-4508). Pizza, pasta, and Italian fare. Open daily 6:00pm-10:00pm. Pizza available 5:00pm-1:00am. Moderate.

Melanka Steakhouse, 94 Todd St. (phone 52-2233). $12-$14/main. Pub-type food, fried and greasy. Chicken schnitzel, seafood, beef, huge buffalo steaks. All you can eat salad bar for $7. Open daily 6:00pm-9:00pm.

Cherry Tree Health Cafe (no alcohol), Shop 4, Fan Arcade, Todd St. Mall. Hearty vegetarian lunches. Salads, fruit and nut concoctions, fresh breads, pies, and scones. Open M-F 10:00am-3:00pm, Sat 10:00am-2:00pm. Moderate.

Jolly Swagman Cafe (no alcohol), Todd St. Mall. Homemade soup, damper, and percolated coffee. Open M-F 7:30am-5:00pm, Sat & Sun 9:00am-4:00pm. Moderate.

Nightlife and Entertainment

Nightclubs and hotels have strict dress requirements that prohibit jeans, pants with seams on the outside, sneakers, and thongs (flip-flops).

The **Todd Tavern** (cnr. Todd St. Mall and Wills Tce.), the oldest pub in town, is never empty. During the day, a few avid beer swillers hold up the bar, and at night they get lots of help. The Tavern's more recent additions include a piano bar and a disco.

Service and sports clubs offer a great chance to rub elbows with locals. Sign in as a foreign visitor and you'll count as a bonafide guest. The best ones to visit are the **Verdi Club** (Undoolya Rd., phone 52-3922) and the **"Memo" (Memorial) Club** (Todd St., phone 52-2166). They have bars, pool tables, poker machines, and good value counter meals. Most offer bands and dancing on weekends, and the crowd is all ages.

At **Lasseter's Casino** (93 Barrett Dr., phone 52-5066), gambling runs all day and night. The disco (about $7 cover) is open Sun-Wed from 11:00pm, Th-Sat from 9:00pm, and the piano bar begins at 8:00pm nightly. The **Sheraton** (Barrett Dr.) and **Gap Motor Hotel** (Gap Rd.) have pricey, exotic drinks and live entertainment most nights.

The **Alice Springs Film Society** (Totem Theater, Wills Tce., Anzac Oval) shows movies on the second and fourth Tuesday of each month. Check the Friday newspaper for listings or call 52-2372. There's also **Starline Drive-In** on South Stuart Hwy. (phone 52-2015). The **Araluen Arts Centre** (2.5 km from town on Lapinta Dr., phone 52-5022) features local and visiting performers, film screenings, and two art galleries.

Trips from Alice Springs

Don't leave the Red Centre without seeing Ayers Rock and taking a trip into the MacDonnell Ranges. The ancient, weathered MacDonnells form a 385 km arc around Alice. During their 500 million years of existence, water and wind have carved deep gullies, canyons, and unusual formations into the rock, making for some great day and overnight trips from town.

King's Canyon, on the unsealed route to Uluru National Park (Ayers Rock and the Olgas), is another worthy destination visitors tend to overlook because of its remoteness.

It's best to see the area surrounding Alice by car, preferably 4WD. Tour operators in town offer more unique forms of sightseeing, such as by horse, camel, and balloon. Check with the YHA travel agency or the N.T. Tourist Bureau regarding these and more conventional tours. The only available public transport goes to Uluru National Park.

There is accommodation at Glen Helen Gorge (western MacDonnells), Ross River Homestead (eastern MacDonnells), Wallara Ranch (en route to King's Canyon), and Uluru National Park. While these are within striking distance of most attractions, camping is the best option for those who want to see the more remote places.

If you plan to take overnight trips into the MacDonnells, visit the Conservation Commission on Gap Rd. for detailed information on camping, hiking trails, flora, fauna, and geology.

Western MacDonnell Ranges

The most prominent features in the MacDonnell Ranges lie west of Alice. Larapinta Drive leads due west and splits 47 km out of town, where there is a choice of going southwest in the direction of **Palm Valley** or west along Namatjira Dr., towards **Ellery Creek**, **Ormiston Gorge**, and **Glen Helen**. Glen Helen and Hermannsburg Mission, at the end of each road, are connected by a 4WD track, so it's possible to make a large loop. There's lodging at Glen Helen Gorge, and camping is permitted at Palm Valley, Ellery Creek, Ormiston Gorge, Glen Helen Gorge, and Redbank Gorge.

Simpson's Gap

Simpson's Gap, the closest national park to Alice Springs (23 km west), is usually overrun by tourists. Carved by a river that once flowed through the mountains, the narrow gap now has just a little pool at the bottom. Sometimes in the late afternoon you can spot rock wallabies and other wildlife among the boulders along the short path into the gap.

To get away from the crowds, try the unmarked walks starting at the entrance to the park. They lead to five other natural gaps. The Conservation Commission provides a pamphlet outlining the trails.

Standley Chasm

Standley Chasm (50 km west of Alice; $3 admission) is named after Ida Standley, a teacher who worked with area Aborigines. Apparently they led her to the chasm, which is so deep and narrow that the sun hits it fully only

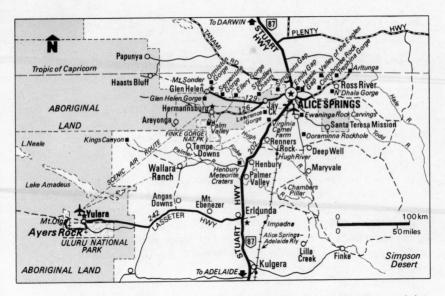

a few minutes each day at noon, when the red quartzite walls glow and the whole chasm glistens. Ida Standley, considered the first white person to witness this phenomenon, is buried in the vicinity.

The 15-minute walk to the chasm can be annoying if you're fighting the crowds, so go before or after the midday rush. There is a picnic area and kiosk.

Hermannsburg Mission and Palm Valley

Hermannsburg Mission (119 km west of Alice) is an Aborigine mission established in 1877 by the Lutheran church. Over 350 people still live there. Hermannsburg is best known for its "son," the painter Albert Namatjira. To visit, you need permission from the Aboriginal Land Council. Write at least four weeks prior to arrival to *Central Land Council, P.O. Box 3321, Alice Springs, N.T. (phone 52-3800).*

From Hermannsburg, a 17 km, 4WD-only road winds along the Finke River (billed as the oldest riverbed on earth) into **Finke Gorge National Park**, whose main feature is **Palm Valley**. Just before you reach Palm Valley from Hermannsburg, you can climb a lookout called **Initiation Rock**, site of initiation ceremonies for young Aborigine men of the Arunda tribe. At Palm Valley, the river walls shelter flora that existed throughout central Australia in a past, wetter age. The rarest of these specimens is the *Livistona mariae* palm, found only there. Cycads, the palm-like bushes that grow on the cliff faces, are among the most primitive plants in the world. A 7 km walking trail and driving track winds around Palm Valley.

The park has many other gorges (inaccessible by vehicle), and it's a great place for just wandering around. Camping is permitted but bring all your own supplies, including water. BBQs are provided. Make sure to call for road conditions if you're driving.

Sights along Namatjira Drive

Ormiston Gorge (132 km west of Alice) should be your primary destination on Namatjira Drive, but along the way are a couple of scenic picnic spots, including colorful waterholes at **Ellery Creek** and **Serpentine Gorge** (93 km and 104 km from Alice). The vivid geologic colorings of Ormiston Gorge make this one of the most impressive canyons in the MacDonnells. Once the outlet for a huge drainage basin, or "pound," Ormiston Creek carved a short path through the rock to form the gorge. The creek flows seasonally, but there's a permanent waterhole for swimming. **Mount Sonder**, the second highest peak in the MacDonnells and one of Namatjira's favorite painting subjects, looms above the gorge cliffs.

There is a marked, 2.5 km trail into Ormiston Gorge, and you can follow the creekbed beyond the end of the trail. An overnight hike to **Mount Giles** is also possible (contact the Conservation Commission for details).

Glen Helen Gorge, another ravine cut by the Finke River, is known for lovely reflections in its permanent pool of water. **Redbank Gorge**, 20 km west, is remote and, luckily, ignored by bus tours. The swim to its narrow upper end is quite an adventure.

The lodging at Glen Helen make it a popular jumping-off point for Palm Valley, Ormiston Gorge, and Redbank Gorge. **Mount Sonder Safari Lodge**, a YHA-Associate, costs $9/night, and you'll need to bring a sleeping bag in winter since blankets are in short supply. Reservations generally aren't needed. Phone is 089-56-7489. The second possibility is **Glen Helen Lodge** (phone 52-9732), which costs $30-$50/night. Camping is also available there, and they have a licensed restaurant and bistro.

Eastern MacDonnell Ranges

The natural features of the eastern MacDonnells don't quite equal the grandeur of those in the west, but **Ross River Homestead**, offering the only lodging facilities east of Alice, makes local sightseeing easily accessible. Camping is permitted at Corroboree Rock, Trephina Gorge, N'Dhala Gorge, Arltunga, and Ruby Gorge.

The only eastern route from Alice is the **Ross Highway**, which becomes unsealed 43 km out and ends at the Ross River Homestead, 82 km from Alice. Picnic spots along the way are **Emily Gap** (16 km east of Alice), **Jesse Gap** (23 km), and **Corroboree Rock** (49 km), an unusual pile of boulders in a columnar formation. You can visit **Trephina Gorge** (turnoff is 68 km from Alice, then another 13 km), **N'Dhala Gorge** (2 km beyond Ross River Homestead), and **Arltunga**, where there are ruins from an 1880's gold-rush town, on guided tours from the homestead. (Tours are considerably cheaper in the off-season.)

Though no longer a genuine station, Ross River Homestead is a pleasant and convenient base from which to see the surrounding gorges and sights. Built in 1898 as a depot for camel trains to the Arltunga goldfields, it later became a horse-breeding station. Now offering a ranch-style "outback experience" for tourists, Ross River has a quaint dining room and the only pub east of Alice, popular with local station hands. The Ross management offers day and overnight packages from Alice that include camel, horse, and hiking safaris, boomerang throwing, billy tea and damper making, etc. Bunkhouse accommodations are $14/night, camping is $4/person. Cabins, which hold up to six, cost about $70/night. Tour groups often stay there, so book ahead (booking office: 64 Hartley St. in Alice Springs, phone 52-7611). Ask about doing work around the homestead in exchange for room and board.

Getting There: A shuttle bus leaves Alice once a day. Call Ross River booking office at 52-7611 for details.

En Route to Uluru National Park

Southwest of Alice Springs are central Australia's most famous land formations, Ayers Rock and The Olgas. There are few very worthwhile stops on the way to Ayers Rock, though the major one, King's Canyon, is not on the direct bus route to Uluru National Park.

The two routes to Uluru both begin on the southern **Stuart Highway**. The bus route is fully paved, while the alternate route is exactly the same distance but follows **Ernest Giles Road** (the turnoff from Stuart Hwy. is 132 km south of Alice), which is unpaved and most of the time requires a 4WD (call Road Information in Alice). This second route is slower and inaccessible by public transport, but taking it is a fabulous way to see the brilliant red desert. It also gives you access to King's Canyon, the most spectacular gorge in the area.

Campgrounds on the Ernest Giles Rd. are at Henbury meteorite craters, Wallara Ranch, King's Creek campground, and King's Canyon. Wallara Ranch also provides lodging.

Henbury Meteorite Craters

Just after turning onto Ernest Giles Rd. you'll find the Henbury Meteorite Craters, three major craters and ten small ones. The largest is 210 meters across and 18 meters deep. The area also served as a practice site for the first Apollo moon landings.

Wallara Ranch

Wallara Ranch, 199 km west of the Stuart Hwy. on Ernest Giles Rd., is one of two stops for petrol and other facilities along the road. It is also a good place to spend the night, despite a few tour buses. Bunks run $14/night (linen is $5 extra), or you can camp. A pub and cafe at the ranch serves simple, inexpensive meals. Hot water is scarce and the showers are mildly revolting, but what do you expect in the middle of the desert? There are daily tours from Wallara to King's Canyon. For reservations and inquiries call 56-2901 in Alice Springs.

Perhaps the best tourist attraction in Wallara is its owner, **Jim Cotterill**. He loves to tell stories (mostly about himself), which he does every night with a slide presentation on the history of Wallara Ranch and tourism in the area. The Cotterill family came from England in 1952, when Alice had a mere 2,500 people, and Jim's parents started the first tour to Ayers Rock. They made headlines one week by taking 50 visitors there. (Today there are facilities for 5,000 a day!) Jim and his father built the 99 km road from Wallara to King's Canyon in the early 1960's.

King's Canyon

The walk through King's Canyon is definitely worth the effort. It's a half-day venture, more if you want to do some exploring. The trail isn't completely blazed, but the Conservation Commission's brochure has a good outline of the walk so you won't get lost. (The brochure may be available at Wallara Ranch, but try to get it before leaving Alice Springs.)

Begin at the end of the road from Wallara Ranch. The path leads to a plateau of unusual sandstone domes called the **Lost City**, weathered by windblown sand. Eventually you climb down into the ancient riverbed of King's Creek to an oasis of palms and ferns, and you follow the creek into the canyon. King's Canyon is vibrant with streaks of bright orange, white, red, and black, and a spectacular view of the valley lies beyond its enormous walls. It's possible, but rather treacherous, to climb up the side and regain the top of the plateau to view the surrounding countryside.

Camping is permitted in **King's Canyon National Park**. There's a campground 30 km east of the canyon, just after you enter the park ($4/campsite). Petrol is available, and there's an information kiosk.

Ayers Rock and The Olgas
(Uluru National Park)

Ayers Rock is probably the most unique natural landform in Australia, and certainly the most famous. The giant monolith juts abruptly 348 meters out of barren flat plains, rendering a most bizarre sight. Equally impressive but not as well-known, The Olgas, a group of gigantic stone domes, reach higher than Ayers Rock and have a similar intense red hue. These are the two main features of **Uluru National Park**, though the surrounding red desert is itself a draw to the area. Covered by mulga, spinifex grass, and desert oak, and inhabited by red kangaroos and many smaller animals, the area teems with life.

Situated in the middle of **Southwest Aboriginal Reserve**, the park has been a home and hunting ground to Aborigines for thousands of years. When the national park was created in 1950, Aborigines continued to live in the vicinity, though not without considerable upheaval. The tourist industry marred the landscape with buildings and invaded the privacy of resident Aborigines. But in 1985, the Commonwealth "gave back" the land to tribal leaders. The park is now owned by elders of the Pitjantjatjara tribe and managed by the Uluru Board, which has an Aborigine majority. The government pays the owners a small annual rent and has a 99-year lease on the land.

Getting There

Foreign visitors often don't know that Uluru National Park is 435 km southwest of Alice Springs, a good five-hour drive. Do not make the mistake of many tourists and put it on your list of day trips!

Innumerable tours from Alice Springs take visitors to Uluru National Park and back in two and three days. A word of warning: Tour operators from Alice are notorious for their inaccuracy, especially about Aboriginal culture.

All major buslines run regular services from Alice Springs to Ayers Rock. The bus trip takes about five hours. Buses run direct from Adelaide (20 hours). From Perth, Pioneer has direct service twice weekly that takes 32 hours. Services from Darwin (via Alice) take about 24 hours. Some buslines ask you to pay the $2 park entrance fee before leaving Alice Springs.

Most of the bus companies offer package deals that include transport to and from Alice Springs and tours of the park during the day, but they leave meals and accommodation up to you. This is a good way to avoid paying through the nose for unwanted luxuries, and it's especially convenient because distances within the park are considerable.

Ansett, East-West, and Kendell fly direct from major cities. The Airport-Yulara transport bus costs $7.

Of course, renting a car from Alice is a great idea, since it allows you to see some off-the-beaten-track sights en route to Ayers Rock.

Practical Information and Orientation

Yulara Resort, with the only facilities in the area, is near the park boundary and 20 km from Ayers Rock. The Olgas are about 30 km southwest of Yulara by unsealed road, and 35 km west of Ayers Rock. Maps are widely available, especially at the Yulara Visitors Centre and the park's Ranger Station. Vehicle entry fee into the park is $2.

To avoid the summer's searing heat, try to visit between April and November. In June and July (high tourist season), the temperature often drops below freezing at night but gets warm enough for short sleeves during the day. During in-between seasons, you'll need warm clothes in the evening. Bring a hat and sunglasses.

Accommodations are booked months in advance during school holidays in July, so plan accordingly.

Yulara

Before completion of the **Yulara Tourist Complex** in 1984, motels, shops, and other businesses surrounded Ayers Rock. In 1982, the government commissioned a complex to service tourists while conforming as much as possible to the contour and color of the surrounding land. The result cost $160 million and is a completely self-sufficient village, the only place within hundreds of kilometers to stay, eat, bank, or buy groceries. The buildings have many interesting features, especially the white canopies atop the Sheraton Hotel and the general shopping area. This unique (and costly) innovation ventilates the buildings and blocks ultraviolet rays. Most of the buildings have solar plates, which provide 70% of Yulara's power. Water comes from the largest desalination plant in the Southern Hemisphere.

Yulara offers accommodation for all budgets. There's both a Sheraton and Four Seasons Hotel, a bunkhouse, and a campground. Also included in the complex are a supermarket, liquor store, coffee shop, tavern, souvenir shop, newsstand, gym, tennis courts, pools, Aboriginal Art Centre (expensive), post office, ANZ bank, travel agency, and Visitors Centre. Most shops are open daily until 9:00pm, with a break from 6:00pm-7:30pm. The bank and post office are open only on weekdays.

There are daily guided tours of Yulara; inquire at Visitors Centre for times.

Information Centers

The **Yulara Visitors Centre** provides comprehensive information on everything in the area, while the **Ranger Station** has information specifically on the park and the local Aborigines. The Ranger Station (phone 56-2988; open 8:00am-4:00pm) is located 1 km before the Lasseter Highway intersects the loop around Ayers Rock. Maps of the area and pamphlets explaining the park's history, management, and environment are all available there. The station has books and souvenirs for sale and houses the **Maruku Arts and Crafts Centre**, with artwork of the Pitjantjatjara tribe. Local Aborigines own and supply the store, and they give frequent demonstrations of their tools and weapons. There's also a video every hour on the hour about the life and culture of the Pitjantjatjara. Ranger walks from the station cover topics concerning Aborigines, such as bush foods, burning of the land, and local stories. Call for schedule information.

The Yulara Visitors Centre (near the Four Seasons, phone 56-2122) is open daily 8:00am-10:00pm and has an in-depth display on geology, flora, fauna, and culture of the region, plus a small library. A number of excellent ranger tours are organized through the Centre, including a free stargazing walk at 8:00pm nightly and a daily two-hour trek through the dunes (about $5). Call the Centre to make reservations and ask about other tours, including day trips to Ayers Rock and the Olgas.

Getting Around

Distances around the park are too great for walking from place to place, so plan on using shuttle buses, guided tours, or your own vehicle.

A **shuttle bus** between Yulara accommodations and Ayers Rock departs a few times daily from Ayers Rock Lodge; check the Visitors Centre for schedule information. Roundtrip fare is $16, and the nightly sunset trip at 5:30pm costs $10. There's also a shuttle to the Olgas for about $25/roundtrip. A three-day bus pass is available. Various tours depart the Visitors Centre for a few hours at Ayers Rock or The Olgas. Call Ayers Rock Touring Company at 56-2066 for current details.

The Mobil petrol station has a **Thrifty Car Rental** (phone 56-2229) and moped rentals. **Hertz** is at the Ayers Rock News Agency (phone 56-2177), and **Budget** rents through the Ayers Rock Touring Company (phone 56-2066).

A free bus runs between all accommodations and the shopping area in Yulara Village.

Accommodation

Unless you are willing to pay over $100/night, Yulara has two choices for accommodation. **Ayers Rock Lodge** (56-2170) has bunkhouses (four per room) for about $16/night, plus $7 for linen. The rooms and bathroom blocks are clean and attractive, and there's a pool, BBQ area, and canteen (no kitchen facilities).

Ayers Rock Campground (phone 56-2055) charges $7/person for campsites and has on-site caravans for about $50/couple. There is a swimming pool and kiosk. Don't be scared by the howling dingoes! They sound vicious but don't attack humans who leave them alone.

Be sure to book ahead at least a week in advance, even during the lowest tourist times in mid-summer. It's very difficult to get a place during July school holidays. Note that camping is strictly prohibited inside Uluru National Park.

Ayers Rock (Uluru)

Ayers Rock is a monolith, a huge body of arkosic sandstone isolated amidst vast, flat plains. Geologists believe the sediments for Ayers Rock were laid approximately 500 million years ago. The monolith is 3.6 km long and 2.4 km wide, with a ground circumference of nearly 9 km. A close-up view of Ayers Rock reveals its smooth, red surface, blemished in places by dips and grooves made by water and wind. Rain has also caused black streaks on the cliff faces.

Four areas at the base of the Rock are closed to the general public because of their religious and cultural significance to the Aborigines. For the few thousand years that the people of the Pitjantjatjara tribe (or Anangu) have known the Rock, its use has been primarily practical. In seasons when the desert gets especially dry, they went to Uluru for food, water, and shelter. Some cave sites where young adult males are initiated into manhood are open to the public, the cave walls painted with animals and birds that illustrate Aboriginal legends.

Of course, you must climb the Rock. A marked trail begins at its western face. However, don't think the steep, 350-meter trek is an easy run-up, run-down walk. Nor is it entirely safe, as the plaques commemorating unfortunate ex-climbers will attest. The first 100 meters is so steep that there's a chain to grab for security and a tiny bit of help. The descent is even more harrowing (though much less painful). Sneakers are a must, bring a knapsack to carry a camera and water bottle (or champagne bottle, in our case!), and wear layers in winter. Most people start the climb in the freezing dawn, but during the ascent the heat can become exhausting. Summer's heat excludes anything but an early morning climb. The hike takes about two hours roundtrip. A walk around the base of Ayers Rock is approximately 9 km and also takes two hours.

Park rangers conduct daily hour-long walks (check at the Visitors Centre for times), starting at the base of the climb. They discuss local geology, flora, fauna, and Aboriginal beliefs about Uluru.

Despite hordes of people elbowing for the best vantage point, don't miss the sunset at Ayers Rock. As the sun descends, the Rock glows stunning shades of orange, deep red, and purple. The viewing area is just off the Lasseter Hwy., 14 km south of Yulara. Diehards should see the sunrise as well. In fact, sunrise is the best way to enjoy the Rock and avoid crowds.

The Olgas (Katatjuta)

Many tourists ignore The Olgas in favor of Ayers Rock, but those who see both often can't decide which they like better. The Olgas certainly rival Ayers Rock for uniqueness and mystique. This mountain range consists of 36 unusual rock domes made of boulder conglomerate, formed about the same time as Ayers Rock. Like Ayers, The Olgas are sheer and smooth, though some of the mountainsides sustain a little vegetation. The highest dome is **Mount Olga** (546 meters).

The Olgas are excellent for hiking, especially since there aren't millions of people. Walks range from easy to difficult, and each of the three marked trails takes one to two hours. The rangers also suggest some unmarked walking routes which require a detailed map. Consult a ranger before setting off on unmarked routes, and be sure to carry water with you.

As with Ayers Rock, sunrise and sunset are the best viewing times for the Olgas. There's a designated viewing area for sunset just west of the range.

Food and Entertainment

Ayers Rock Lodge provides breakfast, sandwiches, and simple dinners. Though barbecue packs with steak or lamb, bread, and utensils are about $8, the best option is to buy your own meat from the supermarket in Yulara, which has a good selection. Be prepared to rush to the barbecue grills as soon as the bus returns from the sunset viewing, or you'll get stuck in a huge line for the grill. There's a good liquor store in the shopping area, too.

The Old Oak Tree coffee shop in the main shopping area serves snacks and light meals and stays open until 3:00am on Monday and Thursday (otherwise hours are 7:30am-9:30pm). For pub meals, try the Four Seasons central bar or the Ernest Giles Tavern. The Ploughman's lunch at the **Four Seasons** is $7 for a hearty sandwich, salad, and air-conditioning. The **Ernest Giles** serves breakfast, lunch, and dinner. It also has a dance floor and DJ, with nightly parties (no cover charge) and the cheapest drinks in the area. For a splurge, try a traditional Aussie meal in the Stuart Room at the Four Seasons (phone 56-2100). For $25 you can have unlimited helpings, while the mid-priced regular menu includes buffalo and kangaroo steaks. Both the Sheraton and the Four Seasons have live entertainment most nights, mainly bush bands like the "Rock Wallabies." The **Mulgara Bar** at the Sheraton has happy hour from 5:30pm-7:00pm.

The **Community Hall**, next to the shopping square, hosts various nightly activities, including movies. There are many other diversions, including tennis (racquets are available for a small fee at Community Hall), aerobics, croquet, badminton, trampolines, and ballroom dancing (!). Inquire at the Visitors Centre.

The Stuart Highway

The Stuart Highway, also known as **The Track**, runs through the center of Australia for 3,070 dusty kilometers, from Darwin to Port Augusta. Most of it was a rough dirt road until 1987. Today, mostly buses and trucks use the

Stuart Hwy., Darwin's most direct landlink to the rest of the country. The following section covers the Northern Territory portion of the highway from north of Alice Springs to Katherine, 345 km south of Darwin. For sights near Darwin, see *Trips from Darwin*.

The road from Alice to Darwin goes through arid, remote country typical of the outback. The remains of several abandoned towns survive from the gold-rush era, but mostly the region consists of endless grazing plains for huge cattle stations and some homesteads along the highway. Make sure to have a beer at one of the hotels on the way. Though it will be a bit of a culture shock, there's no better way to gain an understanding of outback life.

The highway is named after **John McDouall Stuart**, a Scottish explorer who joined the search to find Australia's geographic center. Throughout the 1850's, Stuart took many trips into the interior of South Australia on expeditions suggested (and rewarded) by the government. His final coup was a coast-to-coast trek in 1861-62 on what became the route of the Overland Telegraph Line, now the Stuart Hwy. Most of the settlements, rivers, and monuments along the highway are named after explorers involved with Stuart's trek or workers on the telegraph. Stuart's journals, first published in 1864, are entitled *Explorations in Australia: The Journals of John McDouall Stuart*, edited by W. Hardman.

Weather

Seasonal conditions are extreme in this part of the country. The heat is no joke; every year people die of dehydration and over-exposure on the Stuart. Shade and water are rare, especially away from the main road. In the summer, it's common for the northern section of the highway to remain impassable for a week or two because of flooding.

Getting Around

Deluxe, Greyhound, and Pioneer operate daily bus service the length of the Stuart Hwy. Bus Australia does the route three times a week. Stops along the way include Wauchope, Tennant Creek, Daly Waters, Mataranka, and Katherine.

Driving: If you've got your own car, there are few things to know and do before you strike out. The information below comes from the pamphlet *Drive the Stuart*, compiled by Geo-Science Mapping Services and available at N.T. tourist bureaus:

1. Bring plenty of water. (This is *essential!*)

2. Outfit your car with a good tool kit and spare tire.

3. Find out where the gas stations are before you get underway, and always fill-up when you can. Stations are sometimes over 250 km apart.

4. Carry enough cash. Some places do not accept credit cards.

5. The road is long, straight, and mesmerizing. Travel with other drivers, if possible, and don't push yourself.

6. Watch out for animals on the road, especially at night. Kangaroos and

cattle are such a hazard that people in the outback attach large metal grids ('*roo bars*) to the front of their cars.

7. If you break down, stay with your car. Don't wander off to find help.

8. Large trucks, buses, and long road-trains that take the Stuart tend to drive fast and often take up more than half the road.

Accommodation

Assuming you'll take the trip in winter or in otherwise decent weather, camping is definitely the cheapest way to go. A licensed hotel (usually the town's oldest building), a roadhouse, and/or a motel exist in most every sizeable town along the Stuart. The hotels usually have 5-10 rooms and a common bathroom. Many of the roadhouses and motels have adjoining caravan parks with overnight vans, cabins, and campsites. Tennant Creek, Mataranka, and Katherine have YHA or YHA-Associate hostels.

Food and Supplies

The Stuart is not the place to look for gourmet fare, but you can certainly find adequate food along the route. Roadhouses have fast, simple meals and sometimes a small grocery. Licensed hotels serve counter meals.

Alice Springs to Tennant Creek

There are a few places to have a meal and rest along the 502 km between Alice and Tennant Creek. The first settlement you'll see is **Ti Tree**, 194 km north of Alice, with one of the N.T.'s first roadhouses, built in 1930. Barrow's Creek, 90 km further, is the site of a major Overland Telegraph station, and 110 km north is the town of **Wauchope**, known for a nearby rock formation called **Devil's Marbles**, a cluster of enormous, precariously-stacked granite boulders. One "marble" was removed to mark John Flynn's grave outside Alice. There are walkways with plaques describing the local flora and fauna around this peculiar formation, and camping is allowed on its eastern side. Accommodation is available in Wauchope at the **Wauchope Well Hotel** (phone 64-1963). A campground adjoins the hotel.

Tennant Creek

In the early 1930's, a wagon loaded with beer and materials for the construction of an outback hotel broke down 502 km north of Alice. Instead of repairing the wagon, all the gold miners simply shifted camp to the scene of the breakdown. Thus Tennant Creek was established (or so the story goes).

Tennant Creek was the last of the official gold-rush towns. Mining (gold, copper, silver, and bismuth) is still its main industry, although horse and cattle ranches and tourism run a close second and third. Tennant Creek has modern stores, hotels, motels, and a population of 3,200—a sizeable settlement for the Territory.

A few local attractions are worth a visit. The **Government Stamp Battery** (1.5 km east of town; open Mon-Fri) still crushes gold-bearing rock. You can walk around the old gold mines scattered about town. Fossicking for gemstones and gold is allowed in certain areas (inquire at the Dept. of Mines and Energy). **Mary Ann Dam**, 5 km north, is open for swimming, sailing, and picnics.

Accommodation:
YHA Tennant Creek, Leichhardt St. (phone 62-2719). $7/night. Left off the highway onto Windley St., follow to Leichhardt St. Ask hostel manager about discounts on area tours.

Tennant Creek Hotel, Paterson St., Tennant Creek (phone 62-2006). TV and fridge in room.

Outback Caravan Park, Peko Rd. (phone 62-2459). 1 km east of town. On-site vans and campsites. Swimming pool.

Tennant Creek to Katherine
Three Ways, the junction of the Barkly and Stuart Hwys., is 25 km north of Tennant Creek. There is basic accommodation, food, and fuel—and that's about it. On the southern side of the intersection is a John Flynn memorial, with a memorial to Stuart opposite. The **Barkly Tablelands** begin here, extending east to Burketown and northwest to Normantown. These arid grasslands are treeless, flat, and very Australian.

Approximately halfway between Alice and Darwin is the town of **Elliot**, established in World War II as a workshop area for the army. Elliot was going to become *the* stop-over between Alice and Darwin, but (obviously) it never happened. The **Elliot Hotel** (phone 62-2744) has four units (with private bathrooms and 'fridge). About 13 km west of Elliot, **Lake Woods**, the N.T.'s largest lake, is open for water sports and camping.

Daly Waters, 145 km north of Elliot, was established in 1861 and named after the Governor of South Australia. Originally it was an important campsite for telegraph workers and cattle-drivers. A large airstrip was built there during WWII, and after the war the town became an aircraft service center. The **Daly Waters Pub** (phone 75-9927) contains relics from the pioneering days plus modern accommodation.

80 km north of Daly Waters, **Larrimah** doesn't have much but a few ruined buildings left over from the rail center that carried supplies during WWII. The railway also serviced the region's copper and bauxite mining, which has been discontinued. Larrimah's hotel and the crocodiles at **Green Park Caravan Park** are local attractions. Accommodation is available at the **Larrimah Wayside Inn** (phone 75-9931). There's also the **Shell Station Roadhouse** (phone 75-9932) with three self-contained flats (private bathroom and kitchen facilities). The flats can hold six.

The **Old Mataranka Homestead**, a popular tourist spot because of its nearby thermal pool and rainforest, can be reached by a turnoff from the Stuart, 75 km north of Larrimah. The area was made famous by Jeannie Gunn's *We of the Never Never*, a book (and a movie) about her experience as the first European woman to settle in the region. Jeannie Gunn's home at Elsey Station is recreated in a display at Mataranka Homestead, and the **Old Elsey Cemetery** is worth a look. The **Mataranka Homestead and Thermal Spring**

Tourist Park (phone 75-4544), a YHA-Associate, charges $9/night. Call if you need a lift from town. In the caravan park, campsites are $6/person. All Homestead-operated tours offer a 10% discount to YHA card holders.

Cutta Cutta Caves, 27 km south of Katherine, are open April-October with daily tours ($5/person). A self-guided, above-ground walk passes through typical outback flora and eroded limestone formations.

Getting Around: In addition to regular interstate bus service at Daly Waters and Mataranka Homestead, a local company called **Travel North** (phone 72-1044) runs from Katherine to Mataranka and Cutta Cutta Caves. Their daily commuter bus runs from Katherine to the Homestead (only three times a week from Oct-March) and takes two hours. There's a transfer service from Mataranka to the YHA hostel for about $3 (phone on arrival). Travel North's daily bus tours to Cutta Cutta Caves run from Katherine in the dry season only (May-Oct).

Katherine and the Gorges
Katherine Tourist Information, corner Stuart Hwy. and Lindsay Ave., Katherine, phone 089-72-2650.

The **Katherine River Gorges** are a major destination for many travelers, especially from Darwin, 345 km north. Although it's possible to make the round trip from Darwin in one day, we suggest you stay overnight or not bother.

Stuart named the Katherine River after his benefactor's daughter. (Her name actually began with a C, but the spelling error was never corrected.) Katherine was a major support base for troops in World War II. During 1944, train service through town increased from one train every two weeks to 147 trains a week. The **Tindal R.A.A.F. Base** (just outside of town), built in 1942, is undergoing an expansion that may double Katherine's population of 4,500 in the next few years.

Getting There and Getting Around: All the major bus companies have daily service to Katherine, originating in either Darwin or Alice Springs. Most buses stop at the B.P. Service Station. Next door is **Travel North** (6 Katherine Tce., phone 72-1044), the local travel agent/tour company with a monopoly on all tours and transport to the attractions in the area: Cutta Cutta Caves, Mataranka, and Springvale Homestead. Travel North also operates daily commuter buses and tours to Katherine Gorge. Several commercial tours go to Katherine from Darwin.

Accommodation:
YHA Katherine, Victoria Hwy., 2 km south of Stuart Hwy. (phone 089-72-2942). $7/night. Next to river. Thermal pool. Tours to the gorges and other attractions. Strictly run; heed the curfew and alcohol ban.

Gorge Caravan Park, 29 km north of town, in Katherine Gorge National Park (phone 72-1253). Campsites $8.50/couple.

Riverview Motel and Caravan Park, 440 Victoria Hwy. (phone 72-1011). Motel costs around $45/night, with private facilities, 'fridge, and TV. Campsites $9/night.

Local Sights: The **School of the Air** on Giles St. teaches children on outback stations via television. Tours run Mon, Wed, Fri starting at 9:30am during the school year. Other sights are the local **hot springs** (open for swimming) and the **Katherine Museum** (Gorge Rd.; open seven days; admission $2.50). **Tillair** offers a scenic flight (contact Travel North for details).

Katherine Gorge National Park

About 32 km east of Katherine via Gorge Rd., the National Park features 13 steep, colorful gorges on the Katherine River. Visit between mid-May and late October to avoid monsoons. If you want to camp, obtain a permit by 3:30pm from the **Park Visitor Centre** (Gorge Rd., phone 72-1886).

The most popular way to see the gorges is on a ranger-guided **boat tour**. There are several options, including the standard two-hour cruise that goes through the first two gorges (about $15), a nine-hour cruise that reaches the fifth gorge and involves some walking ($60), and an eight-hour cruise/scenic flight ($120). Two-hour cruises depart several times daily. We recommend a longer cruise because the shorter one tends to be full of tour bus crowds. Book long cruises through Travel North. For the short cruises, just show up at the boat jetty and bring a swimsuit.

The best way to see the park is to canoe through as many gorges as you can. Contact **Canoe Hire**, next to the tour departure jetty (open daily 7:30am-5:30pm, phone 72-3301). Walking paths follow the gorges as well. For extensive hiking and canoe trips (it takes about five days to go through all 13 gorges), contact the Park Visitor Centre or Katherine's Tourist Office.

Western Australia

Larger in area than continental Europe and the British Isles combined, Western Australia's vastness and remoteness is almost inconceivable. To put things in perspective, two mid-sized phone books cover the entire state—one for Perth and one for the rest! Two-thirds of W.A.'s population of 1.5 million live in Perth, leaving just 500,000 people to fill out the remaining 2,527,600 square km. Large parts of the state, including most of the Gibson, Great Victoria, and Great Sandy Deserts, and the northern coast on the Timor Sea, are completely uninhabited.

Travelers in W.A. should keep two things in mind. First, you must be willing to rough it and make an extra, well-planned effort to reach places. Despite the difficulty of obtaining information before arrival in remote areas, it's absolutely necessary because supplies, transportation, and business hours are often random at best. Second, seeing W.A. could be the most uniquely Australian experience you have while you're in the country. It's truly one of the world's last frontiers—get there before it's discovered!

When to Go

Travel from Exmouth north is extremely tenuous during the summer (Dec-March) because of extreme heat, monsoonal rains, and cyclones. We suggest you wait until mid-April before going north because of flooding. There's no swimming in northern waters Oct-April because of box jellyfish. Inland destinations such as Kalgoorlie, the Hamersley Gorges, and the Gunbarrel Highway route are also uncomfortably (sometimes prohibitively) hot during the summer. Perth and the southwest corner of the state are nice all year, though winter (June-Aug) is chilly and rainy, and visiting hours for sights are limited. Christmas and Easter are popular in the southwest—book well ahead at these times.

The best time to visit W.A. is Sept-Oct, when spring wildflowers bring phenomenal color to the entire state. In the far north, wildflowers start blooming in late July/early August.

Itinerary

W.A. is as diverse geographically and climatically as it is large, and the season you go will, to a large degree, determine your itinerary. Make every effort to see the Hamersley Gorges and the Kimberley region (including Broome and the Bungle Bungle Range), for these are Australia's last frontiers. You

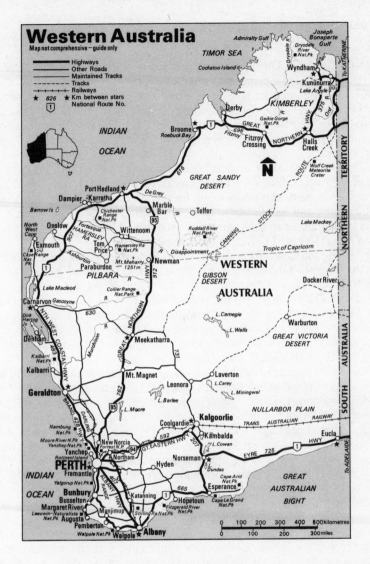

should also consider a four-wheel drive tour along the Gunbarrel Highway to Ayers Rock in the Northern Territory, which goes through rugged desert country. Kalgoorlie and the forested southwest corner of the state are worth seeing on your way to and from Adelaide; the lush southwest is welcome relief from the harsh landscape of most of the state.

Getting Around

Depending on your confidence with engine mechanics and willingness to spend big bucks on gas, W.A. is one place that, given a choice, you might decline to travel by car. On the other hand, bus and train service to many destinations is infrequent or non-existent, and the only towns with local public transportation are Perth, Albany, and Port Hedland.

Deluxe, Pioneer, Greyhound, and Bus Australia make a daily Perth-Darwin run that services most coastal destinations north of Perth. In addition, Greyhound goes inland through Cue, Meekatharra, Daydawn, and Newman. All buslines stop in Kalgoorlie on the Perth-Adelaide route, but not all can make drop-offs in the southwest due to licensing laws. Check with the bus companies regarding regulations. The southwest is accessible by Westrail trains and buses.

The Perth-Darwin bus run is a classic Australian travel experience, the longest uninterrupted bus route in the world: 60 hours long, with two drivers who switch every five hours or so. Be prepared to get dropped in places at all hours, and remember to book connecting buses ahead of time.

YHA members can get a variety of discounts on bus travel in W.A. Check with the YHA Head Office in Perth for the latest.

Interstate trains service Kalgoorlie and Perth from Adelaide and Sydney via the longest straight stretch of railroad track in the world, 478 km across the Nullarbor Plain. Westrail operates trains and buses to day trip destinations east of Perth and towns in the southwest. YHA members get a discount on Westrail tickets bought in Albany, Bunbury, Esperance, Kalgoorlie, Geraldton, and Perth. In addition, there are several reasonably-priced train/bus tours offered by Westrail that include transport but not lodging, allowing you to stay in affordable accommodation.

Tours are a popular way of seeing W.A. because of the vast distances and hardships involved in independent travel, and there are some excellent and affordable options. If you're going to spend money on a tour, do a 4WD trek, either in the Kimberley or along the Gunbarrel Route. Most tours of the Kimberley depart from Derby—take a good look at the Kimberley section of this chapter before traveling up there. YHA of W.A. offers a number of great tours, all of which get rave reviews, and their prices can't be beat. Go to the Head Office in Perth for the latest information. YHA tours generally need to be booked a week in advance.

Drivers, don't leave Perth without a dependable vehicle! Even on major routes like the Northwest Coastal Hwy., service stations are few and far between. Numerous abandoned cars along the road attest to the fact that the cost of towing a vehicle to the nearest mechanic exceeds the value of an average car. If you plan to travel on remote inland routes, always consult the locals first and bring plenty of extra water. If you're traveling through the Kimberley, consider renting a 4WD. Most scenic Kimberley destinations require 4WD, and the adventurous shouldn't miss the experience. Keep in mind that rentals from Perth are considerably cheaper than others.

The **Royal Automobile Club of W.A.** in Perth can supply you with all maps and information on hazards and safety precautions. The Perth breakdown number is 325-0333. Petrol stations are generally open M-F 7:00am-6:00pm, Sat 7:00am-1:00pm. At other times, stations work on roster schedules (posted at stations, or call 091-1573 in Perth).

Information

W.A. spreads so far and wide that no agency seems to have a grip on it all. The government-run **Western Australian Tourist Centre** provides most transport, accommodation, and tour bookings, and stocks general information on all destinations. Their offices are in Perth and all Australian capital cities. Information is also available in local tourist bureaus, although some literature, especially maps and national park information, is more easily obtained in Perth than elsewhere. Local tourist bureau hours are severely reduced in off-season.

Another major source of information is YHA. The Head Office (257 Adelaide Tce., Perth) acts as a travel agent, and they have the best knowledge of deals on everything from car rentals to tours and accommodation in remote areas.

The W.A. Tourist Centre publishes a tourist map of the state that indicates all roads, mileage, and physical characteristics, with commentary and advice. Ask for the *Western Australia Traveller's Guide*.

Accommodation

YHA has hostels throughout the southwest and in Coolgardie, Geraldton, and Kununurra. That leaves most of the state without hostels, but YHA's Head Office provides a useful list of budget accommodation in remote areas. Unfortunately, many places in W.A. have no budget accommodation at all. Camping equipment is extremely helpful, especially if you plan to travel in the Kimberley or see the Hamersley Gorges. See *Trips from Perth* for information on renting camping gear.

History

Surprisingly, this most sparsely populated part of the continent was the first to be explored by Europeans. Dirk Hartog made the first recorded landing in Australia at Shark Bay in 1616, and later his Dutch compatriots, aboard Dutch East India Company ships en route to Batavia, found themselves on the shores of what is now Western Australia. English exploration began when William Dampier explored the west coast (1688 and 1699). Like the others, he found it a harsh, uninviting land.

Settlement in W.A. began in 1826, when a small penal colony was established at the site of present-day Albany by the governor of New South Wales, to satisfy British desire for a military outpost. Soon after, Capt. James Stirling explored the Swan River estuary and convinced a group of investors and settlers to give the "Swan River Colony" (now Perth) a try. Settlers arrived in 1829 with promises of cheap, plentiful land, in the first attempt to colonize Australia without the help of convict labor.

By 1850 many of the original 4,000 settlers had left in search of better land and convict labor. The remaining colonists swallowed their pride and asked the British government for prisoners, and from that time the colony thrived.

Western Australia received statehood in 1890, around the time when gold rushes brought a major influx of people. Other factors have since drawn Australians west, including the availability of sheep-grazing land, soil suitable for wheat, pearls off the coast of Broome, and minerals in the Pilbara and Kimberley.

For an understanding of the human side of W.A. history, the best book to read is A.B. Facey's *A Fortunate Life*. A classic in Australian literature, it presents a vivid personal account of life in W.A. at the turn of the century.

Perth

The 1986-87 America's Cup yacht race put Perth on the world map. Despite recent fame, it remains one of the most isolated cities in the world, cut off from the rest of Australia by the empty outback and separated from foreign lands by the Indian Ocean. Adelaide, the nearest substantial city, is over 2,700 km east of Perth, connected by one lonely road across the vast Nullarbor Plain.

Progressive, dynamic, yet laid-back, Perth is the choice city of entrepreneurs who smirk at tradition. You'd never guess from its look and feel that Perth, founded in 1829, is almost the same age as Melbourne. Most of the original buildings have been replaced with modern highrises, and, after hours, locals spend their money and energy on outdoor activity rather than high culture. The city's location on the Swan River and Indian Ocean makes it an international meeting place for the most serious "yachties" and "surfies."

Although Perth is a glimmering, beautiful city, people don't usually visit to see city sights. The weather is too good for indoor activity, and the surfing and sailing draw everyone to the water. A trip to Perth would not be complete without enjoying its outlying areas, so get to the beach, spend a day at Rottnest Island, and save plenty of time for Fremantle, home of the Cup races and a major focus of Perth's social activity.

The best time to visit Perth is mid-September through November (depending on winter rainfall), when the area blooms with wildflowers. Summer weather is moderately hot and dry; winter weather is chilly but never freezing, with most rain falling June-August.

Getting There

Perth is serviced daily by all major buslines, from both Adelaide and Darwin. The Adelaide run takes 32 hours; the Darwin service (either coastal or inland) takes 57 hours.

The famous *Indian-Pacific* train runs three times a week from Sydney, with major stops in Adelaide and Kalgoorlie. Some services are exclusively first class and not all of them offer the sit-up option, but the train is certainly the most comfortable way to go and, with Caper Fares, prices for economy seats are better than the bus. Book trains well in advance for June, July, September, and October travel.

Many people get to Perth by plane, by far the most efficient (and expensive) way to go. Planes fly from all Australian cities and many cities around the world. The **Airporter Bus** to downtown costs $5, a taxi costs about $12.

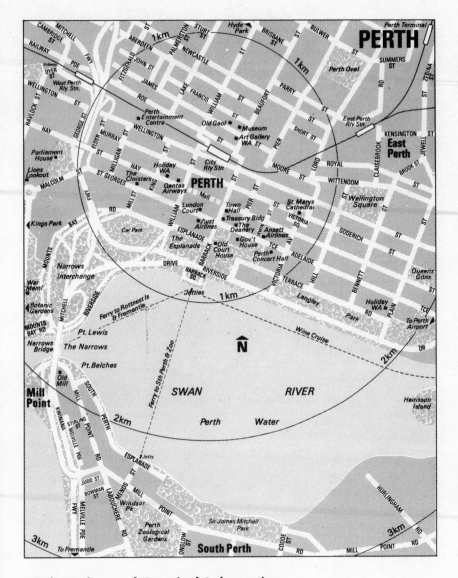

Orientation and Practical Information

Perth is extremely spread out, with the best nightspots and shopping in the suburbs and government departments scattered about the city. For the roving tourist, however, the city's center has all the essentials and is compact enough to explore on foot.

Major retail and office activity takes place in a concentrated downtown area around **Hay Street Mall**. Bordered to the south by St. George's Tce. and the north by Murray St., downtown is built on a hill that overlooks the Swan River. Primary shopping strips are Hay Street Mall and Murray St. The main civic and office buildings are also downtown, along St. George's Tce.

Most inner-city restaurants and nightclubs are in **Northbridge**. This suburb and neighboring **North Perth** also are the best places to find cheap accommodation. To get there, take the pedestrian crossing over the railroad tracks from the train station on Wellington St. (There are only a few ways to get across the railway line that separates the northern suburbs from downtown. Highways west and southwest of downtown create the same difficulty, so use a detailed map when walking.)

Suburbs of note include **Victoria Park**, with the Casino complex, **Subiaco**, a historic suburb with weekend markets and medium-priced shops, and **Nedlands** and **Claremont**, with up-scale boutiques, elegant homes, and the University of Western Australia. The millionaires live in Peppermint Grove and Dalkeith. Guildford and Mount Lawley are rich in history and have nicely restored buildings.

The **W.A. Tourist Centre** (772 Hay St.) has an excellent free guide called the *Perth/Fremantle Visitors Guide*, which includes downtown Perth, downtown Fremantle, and an overview of the suburbs.

Shops are generally open M-F 8:30am-5:30pm, Sat 8:30am-noon. They stay open until 9:00pm on Thurs in the city, and until 9:00pm Fri in the suburbs.

Important Addresses and Phone Numbers (area code 09)

Western Australian Tourist Centre, 772 Hay St. (phone 322-2999). City information center and center for travel in W.A. Open M-F 8:30am-5:30pm, Sat 8:30am-1:00pm.

General Post Office, 3 Forrest Pl. (phone 326-5211). Open M-F 8:00am-5:00pm.

U.S. Consulate, 246 St. George's Tce. (phone 322-4466).

American Express, 51 William St., Perth, W.A., 6000 (phone 233-1177).

Youth Hostel Association of W.A., 65 Francis St. (phone 227-5122). Office hours Mon 9:00am-5:00pm, T-F 8:30am-4:30pm, Sat 9:00am-1:00pm. YHA cards, hostel bookings, travel agency for budget travelers.

Department of Conservation and Land Management (C.A.L.M.), 50 Hayman Rd., Como (phone 367-0333). Information on all national parks and reserves in W.A.

Department of Sport and Recreation, Perry Lakes Stadium, Wembley (phone 387-9700). Information on all sporting activities, equipment rentals, and referral service.

Royal Automobile Club of W.A., 228 Adelaide Tce. (phone 325-0551 or 421-4444).

STA Travel, 426 Hay St., Subiaco (phone 382-3977). Or Hackett Hall, University of W.A.

Country and interstate train information and bookings: Westrail Travel Centre, City Rail Station, Wellington St. Information line: 326-2811; Westrail bookings: 326-2690; Interstate bookings: 326-2222.

Deluxe, 762 Hay St. (phone 322-7877).

Greyhound, 26 St. George's Tce. (phone 221-2700).

Pioneer, 26 St. George's Tce. (phone 325-8855).

Bus Australia, 30 Pier St. (phone 325-3288 or toll free 008-99-9098).

Australian Airlines, phone 323-3333.

Ansett, phone 323-1111.

Air New Zealand, phone 325-1099.

Qantas, phone 322-0222.

United, phone 008-230-322.

Police, 2 Adelaide Tce. (phone 222-1111).

Royal Perth Hospital, Wellington St. (phone 325-0111).

Transportation

Bus and rail services, as well as one of the ferry services, are run under the name **Transperth**. You can use the same ticket to transfer between bus, rail, or Transperth ferry services for up to two hours after first use. There are two Transperth information offices: 125 St. George's Tce. and the Wellington St. bus and railway station. For timetable information, call 221-1211.

The Transperth bus system consists of eight zones that radiate from the city center. All suburban buses depart from either the **Central Bus Station** (Wellington St.) or from numbered stands on **St. George's Tce.**, in the block between William and Barrack Sts. Before attempting to figure it out on your own, visit an information office and pick up a detailed timetable for your destination. (No comprehensive map of the system is available.) Most buses run daily until 1:00am. Beware—some services are infrequent, and we found ourselves stranded a few times.

Special deals include "Sightseer Tickets," which allow either unlimited all-day travel (after 8:00am) or five-day unlimited travel. There's also a "Multi Rider" pass (10 rides for the price of 9).

Transperth has a free "City Clipper" bus that operates four services (Red, Green, Blue, and Yellow) with five different routes in and around the city (M-F 7:00am-6:00pm; limited service Sat morning). Get a detailed guide of the Clipper service at the Transperth information offices, or call 325-8511.

The Transperth rail system (main terminal: City Station, Wellington St.) is not extensive. There are three suburban train lines which terminate in Fremantle, Armadale, and Midland and leave from City Station. Purchase tickets at the terminal or on board; the cost is comparable to bus fares.

Transperth operates a ferry service between the #1 Barrack St. Jetty (a five-minute walk from the city center) to the Mends St. and Coode St. Jetties in South Perth, an inexpensive way to see part of the river and enjoy a boat ride. Purchase tickets at the Barrack St. Jetty. From Sept-May, Transperth operates inexpensive cruises up the river (see *Things to See and Do* below).

A commercial tram runs from Kings Park to the Burswood Island Casino, departing 124 Murray St. and passing by the Barrack St. Jetty. It runs daily 9:30am-6:25pm (to 11:00pm Fri-Sat for the Casino run), every 1.5 hours.

There are many rental car companies throughout Perth and the suburbs. Most have competitive prices and include unlimited km. Before you jump into something, be sure to ask about the unspoken, wallet-draining extras: insurance, mileage, surcharges for short rentals, and a charge for "country driving" (anything that's out of the city limits—probably what you want the car for in the first place!). Also, if the company rents used cars, find out their size and age before you agree to anything.

Try **Bayswater Hire Cars** (160 Adelaide Tce., phone 325-1000), **Skipper Car Hire** (184 Albany Hwy., Victoria Park, phone 361-7644), **Thrifty** (126 Adelaide Tce., phone 325-4700), or **Rent-a-Dent** (27 Bishop St., Jolimont, phone 387-2044). Rent-a-Dent has cheap fares, but their used cars range from good to downright dangerous. Caveat renter!

Accommodation

Before booking into a Perth accommodation, consider staying in Fremantle. The YHA hostel there is excellent, and Fremantle itself has lots going on (see below).

YHA Hostel, 62 Newcastle St. (phone 328-1135). Bus 15 goes right to hostel, or a 15-minute walk from city center: walk across railway bridge, turn right on Newcastle St. $10/night. Basic wooden bunks. Bike and tent rental. Managers offer trips to the Pinnacles (at around $40/person) and anywhere else for which there's enough interest, such as the Swan River for paragliding.

YHA Hostel, 42-48 Francis St. (phone 328-7794). 5-minute walk from bus station: north on William St. (over railway bridge), left onto Francis St. $10/night. Cozy common room with fireplace. Bike hire. Trips offered at Newcastle YHA also apply here.

New Brittania YHA Hostel, 253 William St. (phone 328-6121). Three blocks from city center. From $12. Bunks, doubles, singles available. Linen and blankets supplied. Cots, no bunks. Very clean. TV rental. No kitchen facilities. Great location.

Travelmate Hostel, 496 Newcastle Street, West Perth (phone 328-6685). Bus 15 stops outside hostel. Rooms for couples, weekly rate available. $10 deposit with check-in. Cots, no bunks. Cement showers. No reservations taken.

Ladybird Lodge, 195 Oxford St., Leederville (phone 444-7395). Bus 15 from stand 7 (Barrack St.) to Leederville Technical College. $12/night, $65/week. Quiet, best for long-term.

Shoestring Travellers Hostel, 146 Carr St., North Perth (phone 227-8873). Take bus 250 to end of Carr St. Weekly rate available. 6 bedrooms in one house, 4-5 beds per room. Mildly chaotic, loud, cramped. Communal kitchen and living room, with TV and stereo. Free washing machine. A few free bikes for borrowing. Family-run. What it lacks in cleanliness it makes up for in character.

YMCA, 119 Murray St. (phone 325-2744), center of town. $16-$30/night. Linen and blankets provided. Check-out at 9:30am. No kitchen facilities.

YMCA Jewell House, 180 Goderich St. (phone 325-8488). Take the free City Clipper bus or walk. $26-$40/night. Upscale version of the Murray St. YMCA. Linen and blankets provided. No kitchen facilities.

The Grand Central Private Hotel, 379 Wellington St. (phone 325-5638). One block from GPO and main rail and bus terminals. From $20/night. All private rooms, shared bathrooms. Linen and blankets provided. TV, pool room. Launderette next door. No kitchen facilities.

Beatty Lodge, 235 Vincent St., North Perth (phone 328-1288). Take bus 250 to end of Carr St.; behind Shoestring Travellers Hostel. From $25/night. Shared bathroom facilities. Swimming pool. Cafeteria-style dining room. No kitchen facilities.

Mandarin Gardens Hostel, 20-28 Wheatcroft St., Scarborough (phone 341-5431). Bus 268 from Perth, also bus service from Fremantle. From $12. On the beach! Gorgeous location, modern facility, luxurious. Pool, TV in each room, etc. Stay here if you want to get out of town.

University of W.A.: Housing should be arranged well in advance. Both St. Catherine's and St. Columba's include three meals a day with the fee. St. George's has more luxurious accommodation, and its nightly fee includes breakfast only, since the room has a kitchen.

St. Catherine's College, phone 386-5847. About $25/night, including meals. Standard, single rooms. Shared showers.

St. Columba College, phone 386-7177. $120/week, with full board (weekly accommodation only). Linen included. Single rooms. Shared showers.

St. George's College, phone 382-5555. $30/night, with breakfast. Linen included. Private bathroom facilities, lounge, phone, TV. Kitchen available.

Things to See and Do

Start with **King's Park**, which covers a huge area of mostly untouched bushland minutes from downtown. Make sure to catch a spectacular view of the city from the east side, especially impressive at night. The park also houses some of the best botanical gardens in Australia, with greenhouses, free guided walks, and organized bushwalks. Call 321-5065 for information.

Perth's new **Cultural Centre**, north of the city center between James and Francis Sts., includes the **Art Gallery of W.A.**, the **State Library**, and the **W.A. Museum**, which houses "Mundrabilla 1," the largest meteorite ever found in Australia. Also don't miss an exhibit about the original Swan River Colony and social history of W.A., displayed in a renovated jail and courthouse from 1855. The Art Gallery of W.A. keeps a small collection of Australian paintings, including McCubbin's famous *Down on His Luck*, and usually has good exhibits (same hours as museum). For a rainy day, there are free videos available at the State Library and week-old copies of the New York and L.A. *Times*. All Cultural Centre sights are free.

History buffs will find some beautiful sandstone structures nestled among the modern highrises, though many aren't open to the public. Most of the original buildings date after 1850, when the arrival of convict labor marked the beginning of a flourishing colony.

For an orientation to Perth's architecture of the last century, begin on St. George's Tce. Just west of the King St. intersection, a red sandstone structure with gothic windows is the old Perth Boys' School, built in 1854, now W.A.'s **National Trust Headquarters**. Inside is a little shop with self-guided tours of historic buildings in the area.

Further east on St. George's Tce. are the **Central Government Offices** (built 1874-76), **St. George's Cathedral**, and the **Deanery**. Opposite are the **Government House Gardens** and **Supreme Court Gardens**, where you can peek over the wall and see the Government House, completed in 1863 for the Royal Governor. This and the Deanery are the only two original residences still standing on St. George's Tce. Further into the gardens are the **Old Court House** and the **Supreme Court**. You can tour the Old Court House, Perth's oldest remaining public building (built 1836), Tuesday mornings. At the west end of St. George's Tce. (opposite Mill St.), the **Cloisters** was W.A.'s first boys' home, completed in 1858.

Even if you don't intend to windsurf, socialize, or see a concert at **University of W.A.**, the lovely campus is worth a visit (Stirling Hwy., Nedlands). The clock tower of Winthrop Hall, visible from quite a distance, served as a navigational aide for us as we wandered, lost, through the wilds of King's Park. Get a campus map near the main entrance, in front of Winthrop Hall. In the same direction as the Uni is the suburb of Subiaco, one of the oldest residential areas of Perth. The *Pedal through the Past* pamphlet from the Tourist Centre outlines landmarks.

Free tours of the **Swan Brewery** are a must for fans of the black tinny (25 Baile Rd., Canning Vale). You must book ahead (call 350-0650). Another kind of swan is at the **Perth Zoo**, across the river at 20 Labouchere Rd., South Perth. It has an open area for wallabies and the usual range of native animals (open 10:00am-5:00pm daily). To get there, take the ferry from Barrack St. Jetty and walk 10 minutes from the drop-off; or take bus 36 or 38 from stand 40 in St. George's Tce.

Perth's open markets aren't as extensive or exotic as those in other Australian cities. The most accessible are the **Subiaco Markets** (Station St., open Th- Sat 9:00am-9:00pm, Sun 9:00am-6:00pm) and **Fremantle Markets** (corner South Tce. and Henderson St.), established in 1897, with good buys on fresh produce (open F 9:00am-9:00pm, Sat 9:00am-5:00pm, and Sun 11:00am-5:00pm).

Perth and Fremantle combined have more Australiana shops per block than any other place in the country, except perhaps The Rocks in Sydney. Here's the place to buy goodies for the folks back home, especially t-shirts (outrageously priced) and America's Cup paraphernalia (still!). Try the pedestrian malls in both Fremantle and downtown Perth, also the **London Court Arcade** (cnr. William St. & St. George's Tce. in the city). High quality Aboriginal art and crafts are available at the **Aboriginal Art Gallery**, 242 St. George's Tce.

Sports enthusiasts and beach lovers can't go wrong in Perth. Right in the city, the **Swan River** offers all kinds of water sports during summer. For windsurfers, sailboats, and catamarans, go to the south shore, where there are three rental companies. Windsurfers are also available on the shore behind the Uni at Crawley Beach. None of these businesses operates in winter. (See *Trips from Perth* for ocean beaches.)

Bike rental is available at the carpark behind the restaurant in King's Park (phone 405-3906) or on the shore next to the South Perth causeway (weekends only; phone 275-2320 or 364-8911). The YHA hostels in town also rent bikes cheaply. Many of the paths in King's Park are paved for bikers. Another great ride follows the river from the city past King's Park, the old Swan Brewery, the Uni, and some of the ritzy suburbs like Floreat and Peppermint Grove. You can cross the Swan at its mouth and end up in Fremantle.

Swan River cruises leave from Barrack St. Jetty. Prices range from $15-$50 for excursions around the harbor, lunch or dinner cruises, or day/night wine cruises (a great way to visit the Swan Valley vineyards). Fares are less in winter. Transperth has the cheapest deals, but their selection is limited, so check at the Jetty for the best offer.

Food

Cheap eats in Perth are not easy to find, but if in doubt go for the Vietnamese restaurants in Northbridge and on Oxford St. in Leederville. You won't pay over $9 for a substantial meal there. Also, both Subiaco and Fremantle Markets have a variety of cheap take-outs for lunch and dinner, as well as inexpensive produce.

Northbridge is Perth's main restaurant area, but the city proper has plenty of eateries for lunch, especially for health food lovers and vegetarians. **The Wholemeal** in the City Arcade (Hay St. Mall) is the best of these. Try also west Hay St. between downtown and Milligan St. for gourmet and healthy lunches.

Good pub meals include **Steve's** (171 Broadway, Nedlands), **Raffles** (Kintail Rd., Canning Bridge), and the **Sail & Anchor** (64 South Tce., Fremantle). In town, try the **Hyde Park Hotel** (331 Bulwer, North Perth), **Sassella's Tavern** in the City Arcade, and upstairs at the **Savoy** (636 Hay St.).

Keep in mind that many restaurants close Monday and Tuesday.

Downtown

Hawker's Paradise (BYO), William St., Northbridge (phone 227-9704). Excellent Chinese, Malay, Singaporian food. Very popular. Open for lunch and dinner, closed Tues. Moderate.

Mai Lan, cnr. Brisbane & Beaufort Sts., Northbridge (phone 328-1774). Best value Vietnamese food in Perth. Wine at bottle shop prices. Moderate.

Los Gallos Mexican Restaurant (BYO), 276 William St., Northbridge (phone 328-4728). Large meals. Discount to YHA members. Moderate to expensive.

l'Alba Cafe, 100 Lake St., Northbridge (phone 328-3750). Italian meals up to $12. Popular. Open 9:00am-2:00am daily.

Alberto's, 97 Francis St., Northbridge (phone 328-9136). Italian fare, including steak and seafood. Open 6:00pm-late nightly. Moderate to expensive.

The Fishy Affair, 132 James St., Northbridge (phone 328-3939). Consistently excellent seafood, worth a splurge. Whole crayfish sometimes on special. Open 6:00pm-11:00pm nightly. Expensive.

Fast Eddy's (BYO), 943 Hay St., Northbridge (phone 321-2552); 13 Essex, Fremantle (phone 336-1671). Burgers, steaks, sandwiches, desserts. Breakfast fare, too. Open 24 hours.

Noodle House (BYO), 67 Milligan St. (phone 327-7000). Vietnamese. Large servings. Lunch and dinner served daily. Open all afternoon Sunday. Cheap to moderate.

The Magic Apple (no alcohol), 138 Barrack, 447 Hay, and 115 Rokeby Rd., Subiaco. Hot and cold vegetarian health foods. Huge variety of salads. Open M-Sat 9:00am-8:00pm, Th till 9:00pm. Moderate.

Suburbs
El Gringo's (BYO), 13 Rokeby Rd., Subiaco (phone 381-9513). Mexican. Casual and fun. Dinner only, closed Mon. Moderate.

Cafe Arthur's (BYO), Stirling Hwy., Nedlands. Gourmet and *nouvelle* cuisine. Scrumptious desserts, late-night coffee. Popular with students. Open 10:00am-10:00pm daily. Moderate to expensive.

Nightlife
The day to socialize in Perth is Sunday, when many of the hotels put on **Sunday sessions** in the afternoon, including live music and outdoor BBQs. This Perth phenomenon takes place regularly in the summer, less often when it's cold. The beachside hotels in Cottesloe, Scarborough, and Fremantle, and Steve's in Nedlands, are renowned for their wild Sunday sessions.

As for nightlife: Northbridge was once the hub of Perth's nightlife and, though quiet on weeknights, it remains the best area to go at night if you can't get out of the inner city. There are a number of late-night cafes, nightclubs, discos, and restaurants there and on Murray St. in the city center. Northbridge nightclubs include **Rumours**, **Gobbles**, and **The Underground**. The hard-core discos are **Eagle One**, **Hannibals**, and **Jules**. All are open into the wee hours. They change hands frequently and fluctuate in popularity, so we have no firm recommendations. **Fast Eddy's** 24-hour cafe is a haunt for late-nighters.

Other popular places near downtown are the **Hyde Park Hotel** (see below), the **Queen's Tavern** (520 Beaufort St., Highgate) and the **Old Melbourne Hotel** (942 Hay St.), which has local bands downstairs.

The best of Perth's nightlife is out of town. Most local bands play in the suburbs, while Fremantle has a number of restored Victorian pubs with home-brewed beer and lots of character (see *Fremantle* for details). The Friday entertainment section of the *Daily News* discusses live music and is a good indicator of which places will be most popular. Radio station 96 FM also airs entertainment listings. The **Morley Park Hotel** in Morley, the **Herdsman Hotel** in Wembley, the **Raffles** in Canning Bridge, and the **Overflow Hotel** in Scarborough all book live bands regularly. For a peaceful evening with solo musicians, try the **Fairway Tavern** in Floreat Park.

Pubs usually close at 10:00pm M-W, 11:00pm Th, midnight on weekends, and 7:30pm or 8:30pm on Sun.

Pubs

Steve's Nedlands Park Hotel, 171 Broadway, Nedlands (phone 386-1340). Best on Thurs and Sun. Most popular nightspot for locals and students. Features a variety of live music, including classical on Saturday afternoons. When we were there, Steve's liquor license was in jeopardy due to neighborhood complaints about the Sunday session in the beer garden. It's a good party, but call to make sure they still have it. Open M-W 11:00am-11:00pm, Th-Sat 11:00am-midnight, Sun 11:30:00am-2:00pm, 4:30pm-8:00pm.

The Hyde Park Hotel, 331 Bulwer, North Perth (phone 328-6166). Live jazz Mon and Tues, cabaret-style bands other nights.

Burswood Island Resort/Casino, Great Eastern Hwy., Victoria Park (phone 362-7777). No sneakers, jeans, or t-shirts. Several bars, lounges and, of course, gambling. Open 24 hours, 361 days a year.

Cottesloe Hotel, 104 Marine Pde., Cottesloe (phone 384-2322). Beachside Sunday session 5:00pm-8:00pm. Live jazz Sat 3:00pm-6:00pm. Open M-Sat 10:00am-midnight, Sun 2:00pm-8:00pm.

Mundaring Weir Hotel, Mundaring Weir Rd., Mundaring (phone 295-1106). Traditional pub with Irish-style bush bands. The pig-on-a-spit party Sun afternoons is notorious. Open M-Th 11:00am-10:00pm, F-Sat 11:00am-11:00pm, Sun noon-6:00pm (band starts 2:00pm).

Entertainment

Fair weather and local enthusiasm make spectator sports the best form of entertainment in Perth. Sailing, cricket, footy, and equestrian events in particular are first rate.

Check sports sections in both daily papers or the *Western Mail* on Saturday for details on all spectator sports. *This Week in Perth*, a free tourist magazine available all over, also has sports information.

The main field for the W.A. Football League is the **Subiaco Oval**, where teams play Sat afternoon from March-Sept. There's an occasional Sunday or weeknight game (weeknights are usually at the W.A.C.A. cricket ground). Australian-rules football in W.A. is not quite up to the VFL (Victorian Football League) level, though fans would argue. There's at least one W.A. team in the VFL. On weekends from Oct-Feb, cricket is played all day at the **W.A.C.A. Ground** (Nelson Crescent, East Perth).

The **Perth and Fremantle Yacht Clubs** have sailing races every weekend in summer and at varying times throughout the winter.

Perth's horse shows attract international visitors from mid-Aug. through mid-Oct. **The Superdrome**, next to the Casino, and the stadium at **Brigadoon Country Estate**, Millendon (far northeastern suburb) are the prime locations.

The **Perth Concert Hall** (5 St. George's Tce., phone 325-9944) and **His Majesty's Theatre** (825 Hay St., phone 322-2929) are the city's major performance venues. Whether or not you plan to attend a show, His Majesty's Theatre is worth a look for its finely restored Edwardian design. Both have periodic free concerts and shows in the afternoon. The Perth Theatre Trust sometimes sponsors free concerts in these and other theaters, so keep an eye out. Outdoor concerts are held throughout the summer at the **Perth Music Shell** in the Stirling Gardens, and the Uni's theaters host non-university shows as well as student productions, particularly in the Octagon. There are a number of smaller theaters in town and nearby suburbs, with a variety of dramas, musicals, and concerts always playing. Big-time rock stars occasionally make it to the **Entertainment Centre** in Perth. For current information on jazz, call **Jazzline** at 271-2755. Look in the Friday *Daily News* and in *This Week in Perth* for what's happening in the performing arts.

Most movie theaters are in the center of town on Hay St. Three cinemas show foreign and unusual films: the **Windsor Theatre** in Nedlands (phone 386-3554), the **New Oxford** in Leederville (phone 444-4056), and the **Film and Television Institute** (FTI) in Fremantle, which is inexpensive and shows avant-garde as well as original Aussie films (phone 335-1055). The **Festival of Perth** in Feb/March includes a great film festival, with screenings in the Perth Concert Hall and the Octagon theater at the Uni.

Swan River **evening cruises** include the wine cruise to Rottnest Island (renowned as a pick-up scene), upriver jaunts featuring free booze and dancing, and, on the more subdued side, a seafood dinner run to **Lombardo's** in Fremantle. Shop for the best cruise rates at Barrack St. Jetty. If you need to make some extra cash, you can sometimes find waiter/waitress jobs on the booze cruises.

Trips from Perth

If you've come all the way to Perth, don't leave without a visit to Fremantle and Rottnest Island. Perth's northern beaches are another essential destination, world famous for surfing and windsurfing. Nearby trips into the Darling Ranges foothills include Cohunu Wildlife Park, Yanchep National Park, Kalamunda, Mundaring Weir, and John Forrest National Park. The Swan Valley (centered in Guildford) and the Avon Valley (including York, Northam, and Toodyay) intersect the Darlings. Destinations further afield are the Pinnacles, about 300 km north, and Wave Rock, 425 km southeast—both accessible from Perth. There are hostels in Fremantle, Kalamunda, Mundaring Weir, York, Toodyay, and Northam.

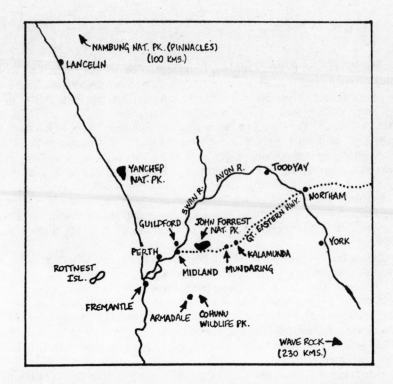

An abundance of theme parks and other tourist traps are scattered around Perth; among them are **El Caballo Blanco** (a Spanish wonderland), **Pioneer World** (a replica Aussie pioneer town), and **Elizabethan Village**. Although these places are highly publicized, you're better off spending your time and money elsewhere.

In the spring (Sept-Oct), wildflower tours go to country areas you might otherwise miss, and there are a variety of moderately-priced bus excursions. Check the *Sunday Times* for competitive tour operations, or ask in the W.A. Tourist Centre.

For the Intrepid

Hiking, canoeing, diving, fishing, and riding are all available within a short distance of Perth. The **Dept. of Sport and Recreation** (Perry Lakes Stadium, Wembley, phone 387-9700) is the best resource on all activities except horse riding. They will provide contact people in private organizations and clubs and locate needed equipment. Their detailed pamphlets on canoeing and cycling are available at the W.A. Tourist Centre. Another excellent resource for general outdoor activity is the YHA headquarters (257 Adelaide Tce.).

There is no definitive authority for hiking in W.A. The **Dept. of Conservation and Land Management**, or CALM (50 Hayman Rd., Como, phone 367-0333), has pamphlets on national parks, and the **Central Mapping Agency** (Cathedral Ave., just east of Barrack St.) has topographical maps, but none of their officers has much insight on where to go. For insider's advice, call one of the local clubs: **Bushwalkers of W.A.**, **Western Walking Club**, **Perth**

Bushwalkers, and **Action Outdoor** (the Dept. of Sport and Recreation will give you names of people to contact). Bushwalkers of W.A. offers a hike every Sunday and has occasional weekend-long walks, while Perth Bushwalkers tends to have weekend treks only. Both charge a nominal fee. The CALM publication on walks around Perth, *Beating about the Bush*, tends to discuss only well-marked, highly civilized treks. *Fifty Bushwalks in W.A.* by Richard Walne outlines one-day treks (8-32 km) for more serious hikers and includes about 20 walks in the Perth area. Either book should be available in local bookstores, and the Walne book is at the YHA office.

Diving Ventures (384 South Tce., S. Fremantle or 362 South St., O'Conner) runs daily trips to Rottnest Island in summer and leads tours up the coast as well. Their diving centers are full of information on diving throughout the state.

Riding has become increasingly popular in Perth, and whether you're a beginner, expert, or simply a spectator, there's lots going on in the local equestrian world. The staff at the **Equestrian Association** in Millendon (phone 296-1323) can recommend riding schools and guided trail rides. Two popular locations are John Forrest National Park, where trail rides are offered by **Swan View Equestrian Lodge** (cnr. Pechey & Taffe Rds., Swan View, phone 294-1476) and the Avon Valley, where horses can be rented in Northam (see *Avon Valley* below).

Don't despair if you haven't lugged outdoor equipment all the way to Perth; you can rent everything you need. Try **Carry On Camping Hire** (129 Burswood Rd., Victoria Park, phone 362-4455) and **Hire 'Em Holiday** (23 Harris St., Carlisle, phone 362-6996). Call first. The YHA hostel on Francis St. also rents tents and sleeping bags.

Beaches

Perth is famous for its beaches and excellent surf, the best of which are north of the city. **City Beach**, **Cottesloe**, and **Scarborough** are the best known, and Scarborough is the most commercialized, especially since the appearance of a luxury resort, Observation City. The new hostel there is fabulous. You can rent sailboats and windsurfers at Cottesloe in summer.

Other well-known local beaches include **Trigg Beach**, considered *the* place for serious surfers, and **Swanbourne**, for bathing *au naturel*. The windsurfing world championships are held 125 km north of Perth at **Lancelin**, which some swear has the country's best sailing. The W.A. Tourist Centre publishes *A Guide to Perth's Beaches*, with information on facilities and where to find the best swimming and surfing conditions.

Cohunu Wildlife Park and Armadale

Cohunu Wildlife Park is situated high up in the Darling ranges, 24 km southwest of Perth on the road to Albany, near Armadale. It houses Australian fauna in natural bush settings. Visitors are allowed to feed the animals, and koalas are sometimes available for cuddling and photos. (Open M-F 10:00am-5:00pm, weekends 10:00am-5:30pm.) Public transport is not terrific: take the bus to Gosnells, then catch a taxi to the park or make a trek up Canning Mills Rd., a left on Mills Rd., and a left through the park entrance.

Just south of Gosnells is **Armadale**, known for its host of tourist-related attractions like Pioneer World, Elizabethan Village, and Old Shantytown. Armadale also offers many good picnic areas, parks, and natural bushland at the Canning River and Dam, Mount Dale National Park, and Araluen Park. Take the Armadale train from City Station, or bus 219 from stand 23 on Pier St.

Yanchep National Park and Atlantis Marine Park

Located 55 km north of Perth, Yanchep National Park has some pretty, native bushland with a few enjoyable walks. Black swans nest in the park's lake, and there are hungry 'roos in the fauna reserve. Yanchep isn't the best place to see the W.A. countryside, but its proximity to the city makes it an easy day trip.

Next to the park, **Yanchep Sun City** is a complete tourist complex, with an 18-hole golf course, tennis courts, riding school, wildlife park, and holiday resort with beaches. The adjoining town is Two Rocks, where **Atlantis Marine Park** offers an excellent dolphin, sea lion, and seal show for about $12 (student discount available). Take bus 356 from stand 25 at the Central Bus Station to both Yanchep and Two Rocks (only one service a day).

The Pinnacles

The Pinnacles were formed by lime-rich rainwater that seeped through sand dunes to underlying plant roots. The roots eventually became fully coated with lime and the sand blew away, leaving limestone formations resembling tree stumps or up-ended logs. The Pinnacles, spread over 150 acres, are part of the **Nambung National Park**. The access road is rough, but 4WD isn't necessary. Sunset over the formation is especially beautiful.

The coastal town **Cervantes**, 245 km north of Perth, is the closest access to the Pinnacles. Beware: some tour companies don't make it clear that their "half-day trips" leave from Cervantes, not Perth. A trip to the Pinnacles from Perth is a full day. The **Pinnacles Caravan Park** in Cervantes has daily afternoon trips to the Pinnacles. **Pinnacles Tours** (phone 095-45-7041) leaves from Perth but also picks up in Cervantes at the Cervantes Service Station. YHA offers members a day tour from Perth.

Fremantle

Tourist information: phone 09-335-7652.

A visit to "Freo" (or better yet, a stay) should be first on your list of excursions from Perth. Established as a fishing port in 1829, Fremantle was a major WW II headquarters for both Australian and American naval forces. Now it's mostly known as the home of the 1986-87 America's Cup yacht races. It's hard to believe, but before the Cup, Fremantle was considered an industrial, run-down area. Today, ornate Victorian buildings are restored to their original grandeur, and the town has returned to affluence and buzzing activity. Freo's real estate owners have, no doubt, made out like bandits.

Although Australia lost the Cup, sailing is still the rage in Freo. International yachts and experienced sailors constantly wander through the port, and in summer the waterfront bustles with races and watersports. The added activity brings crowds, of course, so be sure to phone ahead for accommodation.

Getting There and Getting Around: Fremantle is a 30-minute train ride southwest of Perth from the Central Railway Station (M-Sat 6:00am-midnight, Sun 6:00am-8:00pm) or a bus ride on 103 or 106 from St. George's Tce. The train station is north of town on the Swan River.

Everything in Freo is in walking distance, and bike paths run beside the river and ocean. Rent bikes from the YHA hostel or **Bridge Cycle Hire** (phone 364-6077), near the Maritime Museum.

Accommodation:
YHA Fremantle, 96-98 Hampton Rd. (phone 09-335-3467). $9/night. From railway station, walk south along Market St., turn left on South Tce., then left again at Alma St. Follow to Hampton Rd. Very clean, spacious. Mostly quads. Bike rental. Extra space provided in summer, but it still gets booked up—call ahead. Long-term accommodation at 81 Solomon St. (phone 09-335-3537) and 100 Hampton Rd. (phone 09-336-2962).

'Roo on the Roof, 11 Pakenham St. (phone 09-335-1998). $12/night for singles and doubles. Linen included. TV room. Washer/dryer. Very clean.

Things to See and Do: There aren't many towns in Australia so beautifully restored as Fremantle. There are a series of free brochures at the W.A. Tourist Centre in Perth, plus information on Freo's history and things to see around town—perfect for conducting a self-guided walking tour.

Historic buildings and museums abound. The **Round House** (Cliff St.), built as a prison in 1830, is the oldest public building in W.A. The **Maritime Museum** (next to the Esplanade on Marine Tce.) houses remains of the earliest European mariners in the area. The **Fremantle Museum** (cnr. Finnerty & Ord Sts.) has more shipwrecks and pieces from the 17th century Dutch ship *Batavia*. The **America's Cup Museum** (43 Swan St., North Freo) displays models of all yachts that have competed for the Cup from 1851-1983. Entrance costs $5.

Within the renovated buildings are numerous tourist shops with hefty prices. The **Fremantle Markets** on South Tce., in operation since 1897, offer fresh produce and affordable clothing and crafts (open F 9:00am-9:00pm, Sat 9:00am-5:00pm, Sun 11:00am-5:00pm).

At the far end of **Fishing Boat Harbour**, boat sheds from the Cup race retain name plaques of the competing syndicates. Bond's old champion, *America II*, is discreetly housed in one of the local sheds (not open to the public). Next door is Success Harbour, home of the **Fremantle Sailing Club** (Marine Tce., phone 335-8800) and many mouth-watering yachts. Sailing races are held there on the weekends, and it's often possible to get on board as a crew member, even without experience. In the summer, windsurfers and sailboats are available for rent.

If you really want to sail and don't mind paying to crew, the *Leeuwin*, a model of an old clipper ship, takes week-long trips along the western coast from Freo to Carnarvon. They cater to less-experienced sailors and take people from high school age and up. For information, write *Sail Training Association of W.A., P.O. Box 1100, Fremantle, 6160* (phone 430-4105).

Food: There are plenty of cafes, restaurants and pubs in Freo, with the highest concentration on South Tce. *The* place to people-watch over a cappuccino is the renowned **Papa Luigi's** (33 South Tce.). Down the street, **Gino's Trattoria** (1 South Tce.) has better quality, cafe-style fare (cannelloni and pastries). **Food Affair** (Adelaide St.; Austrian-style), **Mexican Kitchen** (19 South Tce.), and **Vizzi's** (37 South Tce.; plentiful, cheap spaghetti) are all good value. The **Sail & Anchor** (64 South Tce.) offers BBQ lunches and German pub food on the outdoor terrace, and an expensive brasserie upstairs serves lunch and dinner.

The more expensive restaurants are along the Esplanade, where you pay for harbor views and fresh seafood. **Lombardo's** and **Cicerello's** are the best known. For yummy, cheap fish 'n chips, try a "lunch box" from **Kailis Brothers** on the Esplanade.

Nightlife and Entertainment: Pub hours in Fremantle are usually M-Sat 10:00am-midnight, Sun 11:30am-1:30pm & 4:30pm-7:30pm. Don't miss the **Sail & Anchor** (64 South Tce., phone 335-8433), a Freo institution, with its dark wood bar and brightly painted moldings. They brew their own beer, offer both informal and upscale meals, and have various forms of music nightly. Down the street is the **Norfolk** (47 South Tce., phone 335-5405), another renovated pub owned by the same brewing company, which also offers meals and has live, countrified rock 'n roll on Saturday. The **Newport Arms** (2 South Tce., phone 335-2428) has a live band nightly and a dance floor. **Clancey's Tavern** (Cantonment St., phone 335-1351) plays Irish folk music every night but Monday, and the **Esplanade Hotel** (45 Marine Tce., phone 430-4000) is great for a sunset drink. For live jazz, check ads in Perth's *Daily News*.

The **Film and Television Institute** (92 Adelaide St., phone 335-1055) shows mostly experimental and Australian films at cheap prices.

Rottnest Island

Rottnest Island Board, Rottnest Island (phone 09-292-5044). Open M-Fri 9:00am-5:00pm.

Situated 11 miles from Fremantle in the Indian Ocean, the island of Rottnest, fondly called "Rotto" by locals, is a nature reserve of secluded bays and deserted beaches. There are no motor vehicles (except a few public buses and police cars) and none of the noises or hassles of urban living. The only civilization on the island is at **Thompson Bay Settlement** on the east coast, with shops, hotels, restaurants, etc.

Rottnest's odd name comes from the rare, indigenous quokka, a relative of the wallaby resembling a rat. The European explorers who discovered the quokka appropriately dubbed the island "Rottnest" (Rat's Nest).

Rotto's beaches are beautiful and so plentiful you may have trouble deciding which to visit. Weather is the determining factor. Pick the side of the island unexposed to the wind and consider the less-frequented north shore. **The Basin** is a well-known beach north of Thompson Bay Settlement, and nudists hang out at **Pinky Beach** on the next bay east.

Island Marine Services (phone 292-5113) rents dinghies, dive gear, snorkeling gear, various boats, and windsurfers. Rottnest is the best place to dive near Perth, and many dive shops offer daily trips to Rotto. Try **Diving Ventures** in Perth (see above). There's also excellent deep sea fishing for sailfish and marlin, though you'll need your own equipment.

Just about everyone bikes around Rotto. Rent bikes for $8/day from **Rottnest Bike Hire** (phone 292-5043), but be prepared for hills. If you can't hack it, there's a two-hour bus tour for a few dollars.

Getting There: There are two ways to get to Rottnest. Several ferry companies offer rides from Perth (Barrack St. Jetty) and Fremantle, taking 1.5 hours. It's worth paying the extra fare from Perth to ride down the Swan River. **Rottnest Air Bus** leaves Perth's domestic terminal. The 12-minute flight costs $40 roundtrip.

Accommodation: You must book all island accommodation ahead of time. **Tentland** (phone 292-5033) has campsites for about $7/person (includes a mattress) and "safari cabins" ($22) with two twin beds, a refrigerator, and a stove. All showers are communal and cost $.20.

Swan Valley

Swan Valley Tourist Bureau, Midland Town Hall, 18 Great Northern Hwy. (phone 09-274-1522).

In 1827, Captain James Stirling led an expedition up the Swan River and enthusiastically decided it was a suitable site for a new British colony. Two years later the Swan River Colony was established, its main commercial area near the river's mouth (now Perth), with the fertile alluvial flats of the Upper Swan Valley providing farm land. **Guildford**, located at the junction of the Swan and Helena Rivers, became the main inland port and trade center for the region. Perth's gentry and wealthy pastoralists snapped up all property with river frontage and built impressive homesteads. Captain Stirling built his own farm and cottage there, which he named "Woodbridge House."

A number of Guildford's original sandstone buildings have been renovated. Dating from 1840-1900, they range from shops and dwellings to chapels and hotels and are mostly colonial Georgian style. Self-guided tours are easy with the help of brochures from the local tourist office. If you have a bicycle or energy for an extended walk, the Dept. of Sport and Recreation publishes a 7 km trek that covers the town's historic sites. Of note: the **Guildford Gaol** (1840) and the **Courthouse** (1866), both on Meadow St., and the **Rose and Crown Inn**, at 104 Swan St. Stirling's **Woodbridge House** now features an extensive Australiana museum called the Hall Collection.

In 1829, W.A.'s first vineyard was planted in Guildford at Olive Farm, with vine cuttings from South Africa. **Olive Farm Wines** (179 Great Eastern Hwy., South Guildford) is still in operation, and its original cellar, dug in the 1830's, is one of the oldest in the country. Today the valley's wine-making tradition continues to thrive. Regional grapes produce distinctive, fruity wines (especially good dessert wines and ports), which you can sample in many of the local wineries. Most operate M-Sat 10:00am-5:30pm, with shorter hours on Sunday. Tourist offices in Guildford and Perth provide maps of the valley with trading times and vineyard locations. Local public transport should get you to a few vineyards, although distances between them are considerable. There are seven wineries on the Great Northern Hwy., covered by bus 316, and bus 312 goes towards the Upper Swan, past Jane Brook Estate (with a short, involved walk). The largest and most affluent of the wineries is **Houghton Wines** (Dale Rd., Middle Swan), best known for its popular white Burgundy. **Sandalford Wines** is also good (West Swan Rd., Caversham). Both are destinations of the daily Swan River wine cruises from Barrack St. Jetty in Perth.

Getting There: Bus 306 from William St. and Transperth trains operate between Perth and Midland, east of Guildford. Also, Westrail's Perth-York daily bus service stops in Midland. Once there, take bus 312 or 316 into Guildford. The land is basically flat, but there are no bicycle paths or rentals. Bikes are allowed on the train, but not on the bus. Renting a car in Perth is the simplest way to go, and it certainly comes in handy if you make any wine purchases.

Mundaring and Kalamunda
Mundaring, at the foot of the Darling Ranges, is known for its dam ("weir"), which supplies water to towns as far as Kalgoorlie, 600 km away. There's a YHA hostel at the **Mundaring Weir** (Mundaring Rd., phone 09-295-1809), and its manager specializes in the area environment, offering an assortment of bushwalks and hikes through **John Forrest National Park**. Make an extra effort to get there during the wildflower season. The **Mundaring Weir Hotel** (near the hostel) throws a popular Sunday bash, with bush music and a pig roast. It's so worthwhile, some Perth-dwellers make the trip every week.

About 13 km west of Mundaring Weir, the small town of **Kalamunda**, also at the foot of the Darlings, is the start of the **Bibbulmun Track**, a 530 km hiking trail through the southwest section of the state. It's also known for its pottery and crafts. The **YHA Hostel**, 4 km south of town (Mundaring Weir Rd., phone 09-293-3869), offers bushwalks into John Forrest National Park and to the Mundaring Weir hostel.

Getting There: Westrail operates bus services from Perth to destinations further east (York, Hyden) and south (Albany), which stop in Mundaring. Bus 300 or 302 from stand 27 on Pier Street goes to Kalamunda and is known as the "Hills Service." There is no public transport for the extra 4 km to the hostel.

Avon Valley

York Tourist Bureau, 105 Avon Tce. (phone 096-41-1301).

Northam Tourist Bureau, Barbazon House, Beaver's Place (phone 096-22-2100).

The Avon Valley is in the Darling Ranges, 65 km east of the Swan Valley along the Great Eastern Hwy. When the Swan River Colony was first established, Governor Stirling sent 21-year old Ensign Dale in search of farmland to accommodate settlers. He found a fertile river valley that reminded him of the English countryside, and so he named the river Avon (pronounced "Ah-von") and the first town York (after Yorkshire). During the gold rush years of the late 1800's, York prospered as the main stopping point between the goldfields and Perth. But when the railway was constructed through Northam in 1894, York was cut off. Northam then took over as the main commercial area, and York mellowed into a quiet, pastoral town.

Although linked by location, the main towns of the Avon Valley are quite different in personality and interest. York and Toodyay are small and historically rich, while Northam is known as "Perth's inland playground," boasting golf, ballooning, gliding, and horse racing. Northam lacks character and charm, though it too has its share of history.

Getting There: Westrail operates daily bus service from City Station out the Great Eastern Hwy. and Route 120 to Northam and York. Westrail's Perth-Albany bus also stops in Beverley five days a week. The Dept. of Sport and Recreation has an Avon Valley cycling brochure which outlines exact routes and uses YHA hostels for accommodation.

Accommodation:

York YHA Hostel, cnr. South and Railway Sts. (phone 096-41-1372). Former convent that dates to 1876. Lovely garden. Charming and clean inside.

Northam YHA Hostel, Fitzgerald St. (phone 096-2-3323). In a historic railway station. Run-down and begging for repairs. Only if you're desperate.

Toodyay YHA-Associate Hostel, Stirling Tce. (phone 09-574-2435). Tiny hostel. Get key from Toodyay Tourist Centre across street or see notice on hostel door.

Things to See and Do: Settled in 1831, **York** is W.A.'s oldest inland town. The main street of old hotels, restaurants, and shops has been beautifully restored and retains the feel of pioneering days. (The YHA hostel counts among the landmarks.) The **Residency Museum** (Brook St.) was the home of York's magistrates until 1905 and now houses memorabilia of colonial York.

The town is nationally acclaimed for its **Vintage Car Museum** (Avon Tce.), and every September participants don period costumes and race antique cars in a classic known as the **York Flying Fifty**, throwing the sleepy town into pandemonium. Another well-known annual event is a **jazz festival** held in September, including a decorated umbrella competition, parade, and jazz in the street throughout the day. Every Saturday night from June-August, the **Settlers House** has a Christmas party—$30 buys a large meal and mulled wine, plus Christmas music and Santa. Walk-ins often can't get a place, but it's the perfect spot for tea or a sunset drink if dinner is booked up.

The best feature of **Northam** is the Avon River and its nesting colony of white swans, introduced by the early British colonists. There's a 1.5 km walking trail along the river from the town center to Mile Pool.

A few interesting old buildings are scattered about town, although Northam's commercial side puts a damper on historical spirit. **Morby Cottage**, the town's first farmhouse, the **Town Hall**, and **Clearview House** are among the oldest. Numerous activities are available for visitors, including treks on horseback with **Twin Pines Riding School** (594 Burlong Rd., phone 096-22-2164). The **Australian Sheepskin Products** tannery, also in Northam, runs free factory tours and sells quality sheepskin products.

Toodyay is a country town surrounded by bushland reserves, unspoiled by the typical tourist attractions. Just 9 km northeast of town, off Route 50 on Sandplain Rd., the **White Gum Company** (open W-Sun 10:00am-5:00pm March-Dec, phone 574-2284) has over 700 acres of white gum forest and sells a variety of dried and fresh wildflowers. Or try something different at **Hoddywell Archery Park** (Clackline Rd., phone 57-2410). It's open daily and has equipment rental and instruction, a natural bushland setting, and camping facilities.

Wave Rock

Hyden Tourist Information Centre, Lynch St. (phone 098-80-5089).

Wave Rock is one of the many bizarre geological formations that appear out of nowhere in the Australian outback. A massive, wave-like granite cliff created by erosion, Wave Rock is over 425 km southeast of Perth, accessible from either the Great Eastern or Albany Hwys. Westrail runs a bus service to Hyden from Perth once a week (5.5 hours). There's a caravan park and hotel in Hyden, and a caravan park at Wave Rock. Go to the Hyden Information Center for details.

North of Perth: Geraldton to Port Hedland

Northern W.A., the least populated area in Australia, is mostly desert wilderness, vast sheep and cattle stations, and a few enormous mining operations. There's simply not much to see along the 2,352 km trek from Perth to Broome: few towns, few people, few vehicles on the road.

Geraldton (population 21,000) and Port Hedland (population 11,000) are the only substantial communities along the way. The "must sees"—Kalbarri National Park, Monkey Mia, and the Hamersley Range—are impressive, but it's the singular experience of traveling in remote regions that makes the trip worth doing.

YHA has hostels and affiliates in Geraldton, Kalbarri, Monkey Mia, Carnarvon, and Wittenoom. Other budget accommodation is hard to find, so camping is an excellent option. Caravan parks are plentiful for campers, but there are few on-site vans.

A trip up the northwest coast is not advisable Dec-March, when heat is excruciating. Also, north of Exmouth, monsoonal rains and occasional cyclones make sightseeing difficult.

Getting There and Getting Around: Because gas prices are high, the bus is the cheapest mode of transport, even if you've got a car. Given the remoteness of the roads and the thousands of kangaroos that cause car accidents, it's also the safest way to travel.

However, bus connections often involve hours of waiting, and you inevitably get dropped off in the middle of the night when nothing is open and no one is around. Bring a blanket and pillow on board, even when it's hot outside (the air-conditioning gets chilly).

All the major companies have regular service up the North West Coastal Highway. The only other northern route, inland on the Great Northern Hwy., begins near Perth and joins the coastal route in Port Hedland. Greyhound is the only busline that services the Great Northern, through the outback towns of Cue, Meekatharra, and Daydawn, then up to Port Hedland via Newman on a dirt road.

Most places offer no means of getting around on your own, though organized tours are usually available. This is of particular concern when visiting the Hamersley Gorges, at least 100 km from the closest highway access. Car rentals in Perth are cheaper than local rentals, but not all Perth agencies are willing to rent for lengthy trips. **Budget Rent-a-Car** in Perth is about $400/week, including insurance and unlimited km (this price includes a discount with use of a credit card). Drivers are advised not to drive at night because of 'roos and cattle.

Geraldton

Geraldton Tourist Bureau, corner Chapman & Durlacher Sts. (phone 099-21-3999). Open daily, 9:00am-5:00pm.

Though there isn't much to see in Geraldton itself, this town on the western edge of the wheat belt is the access point for a number of excursions.

One of the best-kept secrets in Australia is the scuba diving around the **Abrolhos Islands** off the coast of Geraldton. Several well-known shipwrecks dot these waters, the most famous of which is the *Batavia*, a Dutch ship that crashed in 1629. Divers are permitted on the reefs and wrecks surrounding the Abrolhos with a chartered group only. **Diving Ventures** in Perth runs trips and provides information (see above).

Several tours operate from Geraldton, including one to Kalbarri National Park and a Westrail trip to Mt. Augustus (see below). There's also excellent fishing and a well-known museum that recounts the earliest exploration of Australia by the Dutch East India Company (Marine Tce., free admission). And Geraldton's a good place to try some Aussie lobster ("crayfish"). From mid-November to late June you can visit a lobster processing factory on the wharf.

Getting There: All major buses stop at the railway station, and the trip from Perth is 6 hours.

Accommodation: The Geraldton **YHA Hostel**, at 80 Francis St., costs $8 a night (office open before 10:00am and after 5:00pm; phone 099-21-2549). Bike rental is available, and the manager will tell you about scenic flights over the Abrolhos Islands and Kalbarri Gorges.

Other budget options include the **Palumbos Lodge** (311 Marine Tce., phone 099-21-4770), and **Sun City** (184 Marine Tce., phone 21-2205). There are also several licensed hotels ranging from $18-$36.

Kalbarri

Kalbarri Travel Service, Grey St. (phone 099-37-1104 or 37-1049). Open M-F 9:00am-5:00pm, Sat 9:00am-noon, Sun 10:00am-noon.

Nearly 600 km up the coast from Perth, **Kalbarri National Park** is known for its fantastic sandstone gorges, particularly worth visiting if you can't make it to the even more spectacular Hamersley Gorges. Between late July and November, the park's wildflowers are exquisite, making it a popular spring-time destination for weekenders from Perth and travelers from around the country.

Kalbarri National Park encompasses both river and coastal gorges. The **Murchison River** meanders through 80 km of banded cliff scenery, with walls up to 150 meters high. At one time the Murchison ran gently across the sandplains. When geologic movements changed its course, the river retained its original curves and carved new ones deep into the sandstone, creating unusually sharp twists and turns.

Of several lookouts, the most famous are **The Loop** and **Z Bend** gorges. Both are accessible by car off Ajana Kalbarri Rd. (The turn-off is 11 km east of town, then 23 km and 24 km on unsealed road.) Further east along Ajana Kalbarri Rd. are **Hawke's Head** and **Ross Graham Lookouts**.

There are trails into the river gorges from major lookout points, but contact the rangers in Kalbarri if you want to day-hike off the tracks (phone 37-1140, 37-1178, or 37-1192). Be sure to bring your own water.

The coastal gorges and cliffs are even more colorful than those on the river, and the surf has eroded an array of forms into the cliff face. They are reached by a rough road that leads due south of Kalbarri townsite. Lookouts accessible by vehicle include Red Bluff, Mushroom Rock, Rainbow Valley, Pot Alley Gorge, Eagle Gorge, and Goat Gulch.

At **Wittecarra Gully**, the closest lookout to Kalbarri, a plaque describes the sorry circumstances of Australia's first European settlement: In 1629, two sailors were left to survive or perish there by the captain of the *Batavia* for staging a mutiny. Other stories of disaster and exploration are associated with the area, the most notable of explorer George Grey, who was wrecked there in 1829 and had to trek back to the Perth colony by land. Kalbarri's streets are named after members of his party.

Camping isn't allowed in the park except with special permission from the ranger, and you need a group of at least 5 to stay overnight. Apply in writing to the *Ranger, Dept. of Conservation and Land Management, Greenough Regional Office, P.O. Box 72, Geraldton, W.A. 6530.* Hikes are generally two to four days, and there's a slim chance you could join a hike with one of the bushwalking clubs in Perth.

From the town of Kalbarri, you can fish off the bluffs or rent a boat. Horse riding is available at **Big River Ranch** (phone 37-1214), with day and overnight trail rides.

Getting There and Getting Around: All major buslines from Perth stop in Geraldton, then **Kalbarri Coachlines** takes you from Geraldton to Kalbarri (2 hours). Kalbarri Coachlines operates only Fri-Mon, and the delay for the connection is several hours. Make bookings through the W.A. Tourist Centre, the Westrail Travel Centre in Perth, or Kalbarri Travel Service.

Once you've made it to the booming metropolis of Kalbarri, transportation continues to be difficult. There are three options for seeing the gorges: rent a car in Geraldton or Perth, take a scenic flight (**Kalbarri Air Charter**, Grey St., phone 37-1130), or take a tour with **Kalbarri Travel Service** on Grey St. (phone 37-1104), which visits both the Murchison River and coastal gorges by bus. Family members who run the tours tell all sorts of entertaining anecdotes about the area. Their office has maps and tourist information.

Tours of Kalbarri National Park also leave Geraldton and Perth. Westrail operates 5-day tours from Perth that include coach travel and accommodation but leave you to your own devices for the rest of it. Holders of Austrail passes get a discount.

Accommodation: Averest Duplexes, corner of Carleton Cres. & Haselby St., has units with all facilities for $19/single, less as you get more people together ($11/per person with 4 people), linen extra. You must book in advance with Mrs. Crocos at 099-37-1101. All local caravan parks provide on-site vans. The cheapest are **Anchorage Caravan Park** (at the entrance to town, phone 099-37-1181), **Murchison Park Caravan Park** (Grey St., phone 099-37-1005), and **Lamb's Holiday Village Caravan Park** (Grey St. at the river's estuary, phone 099-37-1144).

Monkey Mia

Shark Bay Visitor and Travel Centre, Lot 8, Knight Tce., Denham (phone 099-48-1253). Open M-Sat 8:00am-5:00pm, Sun 9:00am-5:00pm. (Bank and post office, both in a store, are also open daily.)

Anyone in the rest of the country who hears you've been on the west coast will inevitably ask if you got a chance to pet the dolphins at Monkey Mia. No kidding—a school of dolphins arrives regularly to feed, and while you give them fish they'll let you pet them under the snout and belly (not, the authorities emphatically instruct, on their heads). They are always there in winter but leave periodically Nov-April. During these months, ask the tourist officers in Denham or Perth if they're around.

Shark Bay, the body of water on which Monkey Mia is situated, is the site of the first European landing on Australian ground. The big moment took place October 25, 1616 when Dutch Captain Dirk Hartog stepped ashore from the *Den Eendraght*. He left a plaque on the north shore of Dirk Hartog Island, in the bay.

The whole area around Monkey Mia is lovely. Most people bop in and out in a day—ample time to meet the dolphins—but for a rest from bus travel, hang out for an extra day, especially if you like fishing. Shark Bay is known for its snapper and whiting, and many other critters abound, including oysters, rock lobster, and turtle. Only those using nets or catching crayfish need a license, and a simple hand-line will catch some sizeable fish. **Denham**, 25 km across the peninsula from Monkey Mia, is the center of serious fishing.

Also nearby, **Shell Beach**, located on the road from Denham to Nanga, is covered with tiny shells that have accumulated up to 30 feet deep in places. Those with a biological bent will be fascinated by the ancient organic formations in **Hamelin Pool** called stromatolites, composed of calcium carbonate and algae. Thousands of algae layers create a soft, squishy surface, and they grow in both wide, mat-like patches and narrow columns. Stromatolites are one of the oldest living organisms on earth, found only in a few places along Australia's western coast and in North America. They are protected by law and should not be disturbed (i.e., don't walk on them!).

Getting There and Getting Around: Getting to Monkey Mia is a bit of a trick. Some Deluxe and Bus Australia services connect with a bus to Denham, but since the **Denham Seaside Coach** is a one-man operation, it runs only three times a week. Make the connection at the Overlander Roadhouse stop (9 hours from Perth). The Denham man picks you up there for the trip to Denham (1.5 hrs) and, if you're going on to see the dolphins, you wait 3 hours for the connection to Monkey Mia. Make the Overlander pick-up arrangements through Deluxe or Bus Australia ahead of time. Kalbarri Coachlines also operates a service from Kalbarri to Denham/Monkey Mia once a week, and you can hop on in Denham for the trip to Monkey Mia.

Make sure to check on the service out of Monkey Mia before getting stuck. The Denham Coach meets both north and southbound buses.

Denham Seaside Tours operates tours of Shark Bay and one- or two-day safaris. Book through the Visitor Centre.

Accommodation: Monkey Mia YHA Hostel, Bay Lodge, Denham (phone 099-48-1278). $11/night. Buses will drop you here. It's right on the shore, with spectacular sunsets.

The **Monkey Mia Caravan Park** (phone 099-48-1320) has on-site caravans.

Carnarvon
Carnarvon Tourist Bureau, 11 Robinson St. (phone 099-41-1146). Open daily 9:00am-5:00pm.

There isn't much to do in Carnarvon, the sleepy business center of the Gascoyne Region, except enjoy the sea air and tropical flowers. Situated at the mouth of the Gascoyne River, the land is extremely fertile and bears all sorts of tropical fruit and vegetables, most notably bananas.

Carnarvon was first settled in 1876 to service pastoralists. In the 1940's, NASA built a tracking station that later played a key role in the Apollo moon landings. (It's no longer in operation.) You can tour nearby fruit plantations, and the area is yet another excellent fishing center. The locals can tell you the best fishing spots, and there's a regular charter for deep-sea fishing.

Getting There: Buses drop you at the tourist bureau in town. The trip is 12 hours from Perth.

Accommodation: Carnarvon Accommodation Centre (YHA-Associate), 23 Wheelock Way (phone 099-41-2511). Mostly twins, $10/night. On-site caravans are available at the **Carnarvon Tourist Centre Caravan Park**, Robinson St. (phone 099-41-1438), 500 meters east of the Post Office. The **Port Hotel** on Robinson St. costs $25/single (phone 099-41-1704).

Exmouth

Exmouth Tourist Bureau, Maidstone Cres. (phone 099-49-1176). Open daily 9:00am-5:00pm.

Over 1,200 km north of Perth and situated on the remote North West Cape, Exmouth is off the beaten track of most backpackers. It is, however, a prime destination for serious fishers, divers, and marine biologists.

Reported to have the best game-fishing anywhere on the west coast, Exmouth waters are home to a huge variety of fish that hold several world records for size, including sailfish, Spanish mackerel, and marlin. Exmouth is also the easiest access point to **Ningaloo Reef**, the only living coral reef on the west side of a continent. Unlike the Barrier Reef, Ningaloo Reef is unspoiled and undamaged. Dolphins, hump-backed whales, and sharks abound.

It won't take you long to notice a high proportion of American accents and left-hand driven cars in Exmouth. One third of its population of 2,200 are American. A **U.S. Navy communications base**, built to keep contact with vessels throughout the western Pacific and Indian Ocean, moved into the area in 1967, and the town was built to accommodate people associated with it. Between April-Nov you can tour certain parts of the station. Book through the tourist bureau.

Nearby **Cape Range National Park** encompasses miles of deserted beaches, where giant greenback turtles lay their eggs in the summer. Limestone-composed Cape Range has explorable canyons and caves, with fossils of ancient sea life and Aboriginal paintings. The easiest access to the park is south of town from either Shothole Canyon Rd. or Charles Knife Rd., both narrow, winding vehicle tracks. An arduous and scenic 5 km trail to the top of **Shothole Canyon** connects the carparks at the end of each road. Alternatively, there's a 7 km loop from Charles Knife Rd. called the **Lightfoot Heritage Trail**. Be sure to bring water, and remember that the heat in these parts can kill.

To reach the park's 50 km of beach, take Yardie Rd. north from town. It follows the Indian Ocean shores to the southernmost boundary of the park, ending at the impressive **Yardie Creek Gorge**. There's an information center just after Yardie Rd. enters the park, 39 km from town, and the only available water in the park is at **Mangrove Creek**, 5 km after the entrance. Camping areas are scattered all along the beach. Cape Range National Park information pamphlets are available at CALM's office in town (745 Nimitz St.).

One of the best ways to see the endless beaches of North West Cape is by moke, available for rent in town. Also, don't miss the local prawns that come by the millions from Exmouth Gulf. The Kailis processing factory, south of town, sells them fresh.

Getting There: Bus Australia is the only coachline that goes all the way to Exmouth, a few times a week. Get off at Minilya Roadhouse (17 hrs from Perth) and transfer. Other buslines stop at Minilya Roadhouse, but unfortunately the wait for Bus Australia's feeder service to Exmouth (a 3 hr ride) can be nearly 24 hours. Ansett W.A. has a daily flight to Learmonth, and Cape Range Marine runs a shuttle from the airport to Exmouth.

Accommodation: Motels and licensed hotels in Exmouth are expensive. The **Exmouth Cape Tourist Village** at 968 Truscott (phone 099-49-1101) has on-site caravans for $32, as does the **Exmouth Caravan Park** on Lefroy St. (phone 099-49-1331). The latter also offers holiday units for $35/night.

The Monte Bello and Mackerel Islands
Tourist Information: Elaine's Variety Shop, Second Ave., Onslow (phone 091-84-6001). Open M-F 8:45am-noon, 1:00pm-4:30pm.

Not too many people know about these islands off the shores of Onslow and Dampier. Until recently, the Monte Bello Islands were under quarantine due to high levels of radiation from British atom bomb testing in the 1950's. They reportedly offer fantastic diving to the experienced. For information, go to Diving Ventures or the Dept. of Sport and Recreation in Perth. Get permission to visit by writing *Naval Officer Commanding W.A., PO Box 228, Rockingham, W.A. 6160.*

The Mackerel Islands have some cabins and an airstrip. With cabin rental ($70/night per person) comes transport from Onslow, food supplies, hot water, and a motored dinghy. Call 09-321-4797 or 09-384-3405 in Perth. It's a beautiful place for fishing and completely removed from anything civilized. From Onslow, you can take chartered fishing tours of both the Mackerel and Monte Bello Islands.

Getting There: The trip to the Onslow turn-off from Perth takes 17 hrs by bus. Onslow is 82 km from the drop-off, and no public transport is available from there.

Accommodation: The **Ocean View Caravan Park** (phone 091-84-6053) provides on-site vans.

Roebourne District
Roebourne Tourist Bureau, 173 Roe St. (phone 091-82-1060). Open M-F 9:00am-5:00pm.

The shire of Roebourne includes the towns of Roebourne, Cossack, Karratha, and Dampier, among others. Unless you're fascinated by company towns, mineral export, or off-shore petroleum development, the area doesn't offer a whole lot. You'll have to pass through if you're traveling by bus, and Karratha is a convenient access point for the Hamersley Range.

Dampier was the first company town in the area. Developed in the mid-1960's by Hamersley Iron, it serves as a port for shipment of iron ore and salt. **Karratha**, established in 1968 to house the overflow from Dampier, is now the largest town in the district. Nearby natural gas plants give the booming town a second industry.

The first delivery of supplies to early settlers came into the port of **Cossack**, a once-active town that now consists of abandoned stone buildings that are fun to explore. **Roebourne**, 8 miles up river from Cossack, dates to 1866 and is the oldest town in the region. Many of the original buildings are restored and still in use.

Getting There: All buses pass through the district, stopping in Dampier, Karratha, Wickham, and Roebourne. The trip is 20 hrs from Perth.

Accommodation: There's a YHA-Associate hostel in Dampier at the **King Bay Holiday Village**, The Esplanade (phone 091-83-1644 or 008-094-828). Singles are $12/night. Karratha and Roebourne both have caravan parks. On-site vans are available in Roebourne at the **Harding River Caravan Park** (phone 091-82-1063). The **Pennant Tourist Park** in Karratha (corner Mystery & Searipple Rds., 3 km from town, phone 091-85-1825) has some old tents for rent. Karratha also has a B&B called **Omar's Accommodation** on Mooligunn Rd. (phone 091-85-2868), for $32. There's no accommodation in Cossack.

It's easy to hitch a ride from the bus stops out to caravan parks, so don't waste money on a taxi.

Port Hedland
Port Hedland Tourist Bureau, 13 Wedge St. (phone 091-73-1650). Open M-F 9:00am-5:00pm, Sat and sometimes Sun 9:00am-11:00pm.

Port Hedland, by far the largest town in northwest W.A., is a convenient place for finding supplies and information on more remote destinations, especially Hamersley National Park. But the town is far from beautiful, and we suggest you skip it unless you need an overnight stop or an access point for greener pastures.

The most interesting thing about Port Hedland is the enormous boom it has experienced since the beginning of iron ore mining in the early 1960's. Prior to 1965, the town served as a port for pastoralists and small mining operations of the Pilbara region, exporting wool and livestock along with gold, tin, copper, and manganese. South Hedland, developed to support the population boom, consists of planned housing clusters that surround designated town centers.

Getting There: The bus from Perth to Port Hedland takes 23 hrs.

Accommodation: The **Wungalung Hostel** is at 159 Anderson St. (phone 091-73-1763) and costs $14/night. Other accommodation includes the **Esplanade Hotel**, Anderson St. (phone 091-73-1798) for $30/night and up.

Wittenoom and the Hamersley Gorges

Wittenoom Tourist Centre, Second Ave. (phone 091-89-7046). Open daily 7:30am-6:30pm March-Oct, 7:00am-1:00pm and 5:00pm-7:00pm Nov-April.

The town of Wittenoom services hikers and tourists in the **Hamersley Range National Park**, which encompasses the gigantic, mineral-rich gorges of the Hamersley Range. Aside from the nearly inaccessible gorges of the Bungle Bungle Range in the Kimberley region of W.A., these are the most spectacular canyons in Australia. If you stop nowhere else on the road between Perth and Broome, make the effort to get here, and plan for two or three days to see the gorges.

Wittenoom is an eerie, deserted place. When scientists discovered in the late 1970's that exposure to asbestos causes a fatal lung disease, the town was largely abandoned. A few stubborn locals remain, though the government has been trying to move the township elsewhere ever since their belated acknowledgment of the health hazard.

Getting There and Getting Around: Greyhound is the second best way to get to Wittenoom, after renting a car. One of their services stops at the Wittenoom turn-off, about 40 km from town. If there are three or more people, the hostel manager will pick up at the turn-off.

If you're driving, the quickest way to Wittenoom is from Newman on the Great Northern Hwy., 182 km east of Wittenoom. (A more direct route is under construction.) Access roads to Wittenoom from the coast originate near Nanutarra Roadhouse (377 km paved road), Karratha (288 km unpaved road), or Port Hedland (250 km mostly paved, but less scenic, road).

The area is too remote for successful hitchhiking, so your only other option for getting there (aside from tours) is to rent a car. Karratha has two car rental companies, while Port Hedland has several. You'll need a relatively large, dependable car (no need for 4WD) because roads around the gorges aren't sealed or well-traveled. Call 091-72-1976 for 24-hour road information.

Once you've gotten to Wittenoom, the major gorges are within hiking distance of town.

Practical Information: For specific hiking information and topographical maps, stop in Karratha at the CALM office (phone 091-86-8288) or make your way to the ranger station at Mt. Bruce in the Park (you'll have to hike to the summit, about a 2-hour walk; phone 89-8157). CALM in Perth also has the necessary maps. The Tourist Centre in town provides general maps of the gorges and roads in the area.

Dave Doust, the hostel manager in Wittenoom, has excellent hiking suggestions. He recommends a challenging 2-day hike through the gorges and accompanies his advice with important trail notes. The hike, through Wittenoom Gorge, Snell Gorge, Weano Gorge, Hancock Gorge, and Red Gorge, includes a few swims, using an air mattress to transport backpacks. Wear sturdy shoes and bring plenty of water for any hiking in the park. Dave doubles as Wittenoom's postmaster, so you'll find him in the post office during the day.

Temperatures sometimes get below freezing at night during high tourist season in winter, while days can be quite hot. The area is occasionally hit by cyclones from Dec-March, but the major deterrent from visiting at that time of year is the searing heat.

Accommodation: Camping is the cheapest way to go—about $5 a night in Wittenoom at the **Gorges Caravan Park**; free in the park (small surcharge if you have a car). Camping is allowed only in designated areas of the park, marked on park maps. There is a YHA-affiliated hostel called **Bungarra Bivouac** (74 Fifth Ave., phone 091-89-7026), and whether you're staying there or not, a stop for information on hiking is helpful. It's just $6/night, $35/week.

Things to See and Do: The rugged terrain of the **Hamersley Range** is typical of rough northwest country. Composed of layered sediments up to two billion years old, the Hamersleys rise gently out of sparse, rocky plains. However, several gorges in the range are anything but gentle. Sheer, multi-colored sandstone canyons cut sharply into the rock, and some are so narrow you can't see the sky from the bottom.

Most gorges are accessible by car on gravel roads, with trails to look-out points and into the chasms. There are more than 20 gorges in all. **Yampire Gorge** still has implements and machinery from the first asbestos mine in the area, and you can see blue asbestos in the rock, as well as jasperlite and iron ore. Afghan camel drivers used to stop at Yampire Gorge for water, and the old well is restored.

Fortesque Falls and **Circular Pool**, at the bottom of **Dales Gorge**, is an area with ferns and deep pools. Walk to your right from Fortesque Falls and you'll come to **Hidden Pool**, a good swimming spot with warm waterfalls.

Kalamina and Wittenoom Gorges, easily accessible by car, are long, wide gorges with excellent picnic spots, though the latter is bound to be thronged with visitors from commercial tours. Wittenoom Gorge was the primary asbestos mine of the area.

Be sure not to miss Joffre, Red, Hancock, Knox, and Weano Gorges, the steepest and most narrow of them all. Rugged climbing and dizzying heights are necessary to get the best views. **Weano Gorge** is especially beautiful. The most breathtaking view of all is at **Oxer's Lookout** at the junction of Joffre, Red, Hancock, and Weano gorges.

A number of **iron ore mines** in the Pilbara are open for free tours, including those at Newman, Mount Tom Price, and Paraburdoo. Check tourist offices in the district for current details, as tours vary according to season.

Food: Prepared food is available in Wittenoom at the **Fortesque Hotel** on Gregory St. at about $12 for a three-course meal, $5 for a huge order of "chips." Order before 6:30pm.

North of Perth: Inland

The immense inland area north of Perth consists of outback stations, Aborigine reserves, and uninhabited desert. The only paved road northeast of Perth is the **Great Northern Hwy.** (serviced by Greyhound), which goes through Cue, Meekatharra, and Daydawn. Each town serves as an administrative and supply center for sheep and cattle stations, and Meekatharra is a base from which to see Mt. Augustus, 343 km northwest (also accessible from Carnarvon). The **Gunbarrel Hwy.** traverses the Gibson Desert to central Australia, ending up at Ayers Rock in the Northern Territory.

Mt. Augustus

Mt. Augustus, a mountain that rises abruptly 713 meters from spinifex plains, is a monocline, a consolidation of sand and boulders that dips in one direction. Though 2.5 times the size of Ayers Rock, Mt. Augustus doesn't enjoy the same popularity because of its less distinctive appearance.

Mt. Augustus is 343 km northwest of Meekatharra and 460 km east of Carnarvon, accessible by regular vehicle except in the rain. Nearby **Mt. Augustus Station** provides all supplies, accommodation, and information. Call 099-11-6156 for bookings.

The Gunbarrel Highway

The Gunbarrel Hwy. traverses the Gibson Desert from Wiluna, W.A. (an old gold town east of Meekatharra) to the Ayers Rock area. You've probably figured out by now that a "highway" in W.A. is often a dirt road, and there's no better example than the Gunbarrel. 4WD is required to make the trip, and there are almost no supplies along the way. Thorough mechanical knowledge of your vehicle and extreme caution are essential.

If you're still undaunted, the following tips will be helpful. (However, don't leave without also consulting old-timers in Wiluna and getting a detailed map.) Carnegie and Docker River Settlements have food supplies, and Warburton and Docker River have gas; however, their supply is often low or empty so bring your own. While there are water wells along the way, they are inaccessible to those who don't know the land extremely well. You **must** bring your own water. Authorities advise two gallons per person per day, plus two gallons a day for your engine in case of radiator trouble. Do not drive off without a transistor radio. A 12-volt transistor will reach the **Royal Flying Doctor Service** on the following frequencies: Meekatharra at 4010 kHz and Alice Springs at 5410 kHz. The "common" frequency is 2020 kHz. Finally, you need permission to drive through the Aborigine reserves along the way. Find out whom to write at the tourist bureaus in either Perth or Alice Springs.

While trekking across the desert is perhaps better left to the experts, there's a way to experience it without risking your life. YHA of W.A. gets rave reviews for its 4WD tour from Perth to Alice Springs via the Gunbarrel and back to Perth via Kalgoorlie/Coolgardie. The 11-day tour costs about $600 (everything included), a price and quality that can't be beat.

The Kimberley: Broome to Kununurra

The Kimberley region (a.k.a. "The Kimberleys") is truly a last frontier. Three times the size of England, this vast and virtually untouched area conjures images of America's "wild west." The white people of the region are almost all men—working on the roads, mines, or cattle stations—and with them comes rough pubs and a feeling of lawlessness. The Aborigines of the Kimberley are an unhappy, dispossessed people caught between conflicting cultures. Nowhere in the country is their plight more obvious.

A series of ancient mountain ranges runs across the region, with several impressive gorges cut by monsoonal rivers that flood in the wet season. The Kimberley is extremely dry in the winter. Due to the weather conditions, it remained largely uninhabitable to all but the most dogged of settlers until the 1980's. The paving of the Great Northern Hwy., the damming of the Ord River, and most importantly, the recent discovery of great stores of minerals and natural gas—all have begun to "civilize" the Kimberley. But some civilization: Most places are still inaccessible without 4WD, and there are no roads of any sort along the coast, which still isn't fully explored.

Two exceptions to the rough 'n ready towns of the Kimberley are at opposite ends of the region: Broome on the west coast and Kununurra on the border of the Northern Territory. Each is a convenient access point for the rest of the region and each, in its own right, should be on the list of "must sees."

The best thing about traveling in the Kimberley is also what makes it annoying at times: the extreme remoteness means you have to plan ahead and spend extra money. Whether you take an organized safari (most leave from Derby) or rent a 4WD, the best destinations are costly but definitely worth saving for. Scenic flights are popular but expensive. Another thing to accept is a lack of cheap accommodation. Broome and Kununurra pose no problems, but in all other towns the choice is either a caravan park or an expensive hotel room. Limited banking is available, so if you need a specific bank, find out branch locations before traveling.

Most attractions are impossible to reach in the wet season Dec-March. Sometimes even the main road is impassable in these months, so plan accordingly.

Getting There and Getting Around: There are two ways to cross the Kimberley. The first is by bus or car along the Great Northern Hwy. All major buslines pass through the Kimberley on their Perth-Darwin route, stopping in Broome, Derby, Fitzroy Crossing, Hall's Creek, Turkey Creek, and Kununurra. The bus trip from one end to the other takes 14 hrs. Paving of the road between Broome and Kununurra was completed in 1986. It's a one-laner, and the buses zoom along, dodging 'roos, cows, and other vehicles all the way. The other option is the **Gibb River Beef Road** from Derby to Wyndham, formerly a route for cattle transport. Though very rough, it is the more scenic (see *Trips from Derby*).

Broome

Broome Tourist Bureau, corner Bagot Rd. and Great Northern Hwy. (phone 091-92-1176). Open M-F and Sun 9:00am-5:00pm, Sat 9:00am-noon (closed Sun from Nov-March).

The resort town of Broome is 2,500 km north of Perth, and thousands of km from any town nearly as civilized or populated. It doesn't look like much at first glance. But whether the lure is the remoteness, the pearls, the Polynesian flavor, or the famous Cable Beach, something about Broome has turned many a weekend visitor into a permanent resident.

Most of Broome's population of 3,600 are pretty well hidden away. Artists and "alternatives" give the place a sophisticated atmosphere, while the multiracial community adds a diversity and contrast rare for Australia.

Broome's proximity to Asia and the presence of pearls off its coast are the two most influential factors in its interesting history. Even before William Dampier visited in 1699 (Roebuck Bay is named for his ship), Malaysians probably came looking for pearls and fish. In the 1860's, pearling began at the Roebuck Bay settlement to provide mother-of-pearl for buttons. At first, Aborigines were forced to do the dangerous job of diving for shells, but before the start of the 20th century, Japanese, Filipinos, Malays, Indonesians, and Javanese had taken over the diving and crewing the luggers, at a considerable personal profit.

The Japanese were the most successful and numerous of the immigrants. During Broome's heyday in the early 1900's, it supplied 80% of the world market in mother-of-pearl, with 400 luggers (now there are two). The industry declined in WWII because of depressed wartime markets, and it never recovered after the Japanese were moved to prison camps. When plastic was developed as a cheap substitute for mother-of-pearl, the industry dwindled to almost nothing. In 1956, a pearl farm was established nearby, and many more have sprung up since. The cultured pearl industry has reclaimed Broome's reputation as a pearl center, though the town remains a remote spot.

Broome's annual festival is one of the best in the country. Over 20,000 people attend the *Shinju Matsuri* or **Festival of the Pearl**, with a float parade (led by the legendary Sammy the Dragon), sporting contests, etc. The events start with the full moon in late August and last 10 days.

Try to visit April-Oct, the most pleasant months. The "Green Season" (a euphemism for the wet season) from Nov-March is extremely hot and wet, with two or three cyclones each year.

Getting There: All major buslines stop in Broome, with terminals around the town. Deluxe runs a courtesy van to all accommodations. Ansett W.A. flies daily.

Practical Information: Business owners, hours, and prices are in constant flux in Broome, to the point where they're almost not worth printing. It's a good idea to call before making an effort to get anywhere, just to be sure the person on duty hasn't decided to spend the day at the beach.

Broome is the last outpost of civilization for those intending to travel through the Kimberley. As camping equipment won't be available elsewhere in the region, you may want to get it there. **Castaway's** (next to Deluxe on Napier Tce.) has good deals on tents and used fishing equipment.

Transportation: The only commercial transport in Broome is taxis, but renting a bike or moke is a perfect option since the land is flat and there's almost no traffic. **Trendy Rollers Cycle Hire** is in a truck on Napier Tce.; **Chinatown Bike and Moped Hire** (phone 92-1443) in Carnarvon St. rents bikes and mopeds. Also, a guy at Roebuck Bay Caravan Park rents bicycles early in the morning. At least three companies rent mokes and, like all the other businesses in Broome, the ownership is constantly changing. One of these numbers should get an answer: 92-1963, 92-1870, 92-1845. The four taxi companies are at 92-1772, 92-1445, 92-1870, and 92-1133. **Regional Rentals** offers 4WDs (phone 92-1006).

Regional Safari (1664 Farrell St., phone 92-1006) has tours to Winjana and Geikie Gorges and to the coast north of Broome. The tourist bureau books various fishing and 4WD safaris into the Kimberley, as well as tours around the area. No extensive tours of the Kimberley leave Broome.

Accommodation: You can camp at **Roebuck Bay Caravan Park** (phone 091-92-1823) for $10/night per tent. It's a nice beach location, south of town on Scott St. The **Bali Hai Caravan Park** by Cable Beach (phone 091-92-1375) is another, less desirable camping option—this place has a reputation for being dirty and noisy. A third option is **Broome Park** (phone 091-92-1776) on the Great Northern Hwy., which has on-site vans and camping. The **Goolarbooloo Hostel** on Paddy Court (off Dora St.) is a hostel for Aborigines, but anyone is welcome. The manager runs a tight ship, with an immaculately clean kitchen and bunk rooms (phone 091-92-1747, book ahead if possible). Rate is $14/night.

From there the rates jump dramatically, with the cheapest room in town at the **Roebuck Bay Hotel** (phone 091-92-1221) for $40 a single and $50 a double in the "old rooms," of which there are only a few. Rates at all the hotels and motels in town drop considerably in the wet season, when camping is a most uncomfortable option.

Things to See and Do: Cable Beach, 7 km northwest of town, is the first destination of most Broome visitors. The extreme tides daily wash all debris from the white, fine-grained sand of this seemingly endless beach. The only drawback is lack of shade, so be sure to bring sun protection. A mobile stand sells drinks and rents umbrellas, beach chairs, boogie boards, and jet skis (phone 92-1730). Rent ski boats and other recreational equipment from the **Roebuck Bay Resort** (phone 92-1898). Box jellyfish aren't too much of a problem, but don't swim in the wet season if there's an incoming tide and calm weather.

Across the road from the main beach entrance is **Lord McAlpine's Pearl Coast Zoological Gardens**, with exotic birds and native Kimberley animals (admission $6, open 9:00am-5:00pm daily). The sanctuary has spacious enclosures and lush surroundings. Down Cable Beach Rd. toward town is the **Malcolm Douglas Crocodile Farm** (admission $6, open 10:00am-noon, 2:30pm-5:00pm M-Sat). Living there are some giant man-eaters with heavy criminal records.

One of the best stops in Broome is the **Shell Museum** on Guy St., a one-room store cluttered with an incredible array of shells collected by the woman who runs it. She and her husband dive for the shells, and he etches them while she makes jewelry. Their handiwork is the best buy in town for shell products.

Not far from the Shell Museum is a **Japanese cemetery**, where headstones in the main section are inscribed in Japanese. Monuments in the graveyard memorialize divers who died from the bends or from cyclones that wrecked luggers at sea.

The **pearl sheds** in town on Dampier Tce. offer a range of pearl products, including natural pearls (worth thousands of dollars each), cultured pearls, and mother-of-pearl. While some of the pearls get processed locally, most refining and jewelry-making occurs where labor is cheaper. Pearls are sold in bulk to Japan, where they're shipped to various Asian nations for manufacturing, then sold back to retailers in Broome and other parts of Australia.

Don't expect any amazing deals on natural or cultured pearls. However, inexpensive mother-of-pearl products are available. The **Pearl Emporium** also has lovely antique displays—a must if you're serious about buying jewelry. **Lenny's**, the most expensive outlet, displays the largest pearls. For those interested in learning about the processing of pearls, there's a **pearl factory** on Hunter St. between Lucas and Gregory Sts. (open M-Sat 9:00am-1:00pm, with one tour a day for $5). Call 92-1865 for details.

Next to the pearl sheds on the corner of Dampier and Short Sts. is **Streeter's Jetty**, where pearl boats unloaded their treasures. Broome's two remaining luggers dock there, one of which is available for cruises (phone 92-1531 or 35-5736 for more info). Check the tourist bureau for other cruises.

There are a number of eccentric items around town that merit explanation, first and foremost being the remains of a **DC-3** sitting in the park across from the Tourist Bureau. In 1974, the plane crash-landed in Broome. Locals must have taken a liking to it, because the town bought the wreck and used its cabin to house the tourist bureau until 1980.

Contrary to what you might think at first glance, **Bedford Park** (at the junction of Hamersley, Anne, and Weld Sts.) is not a junkyard. Objects on the lawn include the town's first decompression chamber (used for treatment of the bends), a replica of Captain Dampier's sea chest, an old train coach, and an engine from one of the planes bombed in Roebuck Bay during WWII. Another interesting wartime remnant in Broome is the **Flying Boat wrecks** in Roebuck Bay, visible at low tide. They were bombed in WWII during a Japanese raid.

The **Historical Society Museum** on Robinson St. (admission $2) gives an explanation and history of the pearl industry and displays WWII newspaper clippings and relics.

The best sight of all in Broome occurs only a few times a year during the full moon. Through a rare optical illusion, the reflection of the moon at low tide gives viewers the momentary impression of a solid path of light up to the moon as it rises, called **"the golden staircase to the moon."** People come from all over with their tripods and fancy camera equipment to capture the sight. The best viewing spot is the beach at Roebuck Bay Caravan Park, or, if you're staying closer to town, from the shore by the Continental Hotel.

Food and Entertainment: Broome's so-called **Chinatown** on Carnarvon St. is the hub of entertainment and eating. Many of the buildings on the street originate from Broome's heyday in the early 1900's, when there were reportedly 30 brothels, 6 hotels, an opium den, and 8 casinos. **Sun Pictures**, an open-air theater built in 1916, recently re-opened for entertainment. There are a bunch of eateries along Carnarvon Street (none of them Chinese), our favorite being the **Tamarind Tree** (phone 92-2060). It's always open for lunch and sometimes dinner, and there are outside tables where you can sip a smoothie or eat your Lebanese/vegetarian sandwich under the shade of tropical plants.

The Chinese restaurants in town are good but expensive. They include **Tong's** (phone 92-2080) and **Wing's** (phone 92-1072), both on Napier Tce., and **Chin's** (phone 92-1466) on Hamersley St. You'll find a decent pub meal at the **Roebuck Bay Hotel** (built in 1883)—also the place to socialize on Friday night.

Derby
Derby Tourist Bureau, Derby Cultural Centre, Clarendon St. (phone 091-91-1426 or 91-1528).

While Derby is hardly a booming metropolis, the best tours of both coastal and inland areas of the Kimberley leave from there, and food, petrol, and other supplies are available at cheaper prices than elsewhere in the region. The most accessible and popular natural wonders are nearby **Winjana Gorge** and **Tunnel Creek**. The Gibb River Beef Road and the Mitchell Plateau are also reached via Derby (see *Trips from Derby* below).

Residents are very proud to have *three* grocery stores, a butcher, and a bakery. The town hosts such grand events as a **Frog Flying and Cockroach Crawl** on Boxing Day, a **Mud Crab Derby**, and, on a slightly more serious note, a **rodeo**. There's even a TV station, and, as of 1982, automated long-distance telephone service.

Derby has serviced the sheep and cattle stations of the west Kimberley since settlement in the 1880's. King Sound, on which the port is located, is difficult to navigate, and the lack of a jetty meant it wasn't used much until the gold rush near Hall's Creek in 1885, when Derby became a port of entry for hopeful gold-searchers. Today there are about 350,000 cattle on 39 stations in the western Kimberleys. Iron ore, diamond, silver, lead, and zinc are mined in the region, and plans call for massive mining of black granite and ilmenite. Derby has boomed since 1981, when oil was discovered nearby. Also, the Royal Australian Air Force has just completed a multi-million dollar base south of town.

Ask your bus driver to stop at the **Boab Prison Tree** on the way into Derby (they'll often stop anyway), a huge hollow tree reputedly used by police as an overnight cell for prisoners during the trek to Derby.

Getting There and Getting Around: All the major buslines stop in Derby, 216 km east of Broome and a 38-hr ride from Perth or a 21-hr ride from Darwin. Ansett W.A. flies daily from Perth and Darwin. There are taxis at the airport—and that's it for local public transport. Rental cars are expensive, and none of three companies guarantees that 4WDs will be available. The options are **Avis** (phone 91-1357), **Budget** (phone 91-1166), and **Hertz** (phone 91-1348). Roads are too remote for hitching, but desperate ride-seekers could talk to people in town about getting a lift.

Accommodation: Derby Caravan Park on Rowan St. (phone 091-91-1022) is $10/night per tent to camp, and they have a few on-site vans. Guest house accommodation with cooking facilities is also available at the **Coronway Lodge**, corner Sutherland and Stanwell Sts. (phone 091-91-1327).

Trips from Derby

Tours

Kimwest Tours has trips to Winjana Gorge and Tunnel Creek. Call 91-1647 or book with the Tourist Bureau. Charters are also available for fishing, watching cattle muster, and visiting the gorges (phone Ray McDonald at 91-1968). **Aerial Enterprises** conducts scenic flights over the rugged northern coastline (44 Villiers St., phone 91-1212 or 91-1132).

Sam Lovell runs safaris from Derby to such remote areas as the Prince Regent River, the Mitchell Plateau, and the Bungle Bungle Range. He is extremely knowledgeable about the region, and his tours are renowned as the best. They are expensive—about $850 for 6 days and $1800 for 14 days—but you won't find better value for your money, and there is almost no other way to get to the areas. Write or call *Sam and Rosita Lovell, 34 Knowsley St., P.O. Box 63, Derby, W.A. 6728* (phone 091-91-1084). Booking is also possible through the W.A. Tourist Centre and should be done well in advance. The Lovells can give information on Peter Lacey's 4WD/horse-trekking safaris into the Prince Regent River.

Winjana Gorge and Tunnel Creek

Winjana Gorge, Tunnel Creek, and Geikie Gorge are situated in the Oscar and Napier Ranges, southeast of Derby (see also *Fitzroy Crossing and Geikie Gorge* below). These limestone ranges are the fossilized remains of a coral reef of 350 million years ago, when the northwest portion of the continent was covered by ocean.

Winjana Gorge is 140 km east of Derby via the Gibb River Beef Rd., accessible only in the dry season. Cut by the Lennard River into the Napier Range, the canyon is narrow, with walls up to 90 meters high, and you can find fossils of ancient sea life in the rock. You'll spot a few small crocodiles in the riverbed pools, too. These are freshwater Johnston crocs, and they're harmless. Bird life abounds, including jabirus and cockatoos.

Winjana Gorge has a campground/caravan park with running (cold) water ($6/night per tent), open April-Nov. A 3.5 km marked trail beginning at the campsite is the best way to see the gorge. There are caves high in the canyon walls, and those who look carefully can see Aboriginal paintings. Of particular intrigue is **Pigeon's Cave** on the northwest cliff face. Very few Aborigines have been dubbed "outlaw" in white Australian folklore, but there was one called "Pigeon" in the Leopold Ranges during the 1890's, and this was his hideout. The remains of the police outpost, where Pigeon killed Constable Richardson to release a band of Aborigine prisoners, is 2 km down the road towards Tunnel Creek, marked by a signpost.

About 30 km south of Winjana Gorge, Tunnel Creek has carved a 750 meter tunnel into the limestone rock. You can walk its entire length with a strong flashlight, if you don't mind getting wet and chilly. Aboriginal cave paintings are near each entrance, and about halfway through is a bat-ridden cave.

CALM publishes a pamphlet called *The Devonian Reef National Parks*, which should be available at the Derby Tourist Bureau and at CALM offices in Perth or Kununurra. It provides general information on flora and fauna in the parks.

The Mitchell Plateau

The Mitchell Plateau in the far northern Kimberley is about as remote as you can get; some of the coastline is still unexplored. William Robert Eastman was the first European to traverse the plateau, in 1921. It wasn't until 1955 that John Morgan surveyed the route from Gibb River Station to Kalumburu Aboriginal Mission on the plateau, which is the route still used. Bauxite was discovered in the region in 1965, and since then a mining camp has operated in the area.

The W.A. Dept. of Sport and Recreation publishes a pamphlet on the Mitchell Plateau that includes information on 4WD tours and camping, with descriptions of local flora and fauna. Pick it up in Perth, because the tourist bureaus of the Kimberley only randomly distribute such information. The region is home to many rare plant and animal species, and the untouched tropical wilderness is a once-in-a-lifetime experience. There are walking trails at **Mitchell Falls** and **Surveyor's Pool**.

Don't attempt to find your way to the Mitchell Plateau without a detailed map and advice from someone who knows the area. In fact, if you aren't experienced with a 4WD or camping in the tropics, going without a tour leader is not advisable. There are signs and markers in some places, but the roads aren't marked with tourists in mind. Trekkers must be completely self-sufficient: **Drysdale River Station** is the last outpost for fuel and vehicle parts. Keep in mind that there are all sorts of "nasties" around: saltwater crocs, cone shells, taipans, and death adders.

The Gibb River Beef Road

Named for its original purpose—transportation of cattle to Derby and

Wyndham—the Gibb River Beef Road extends 646 km from Derby to south of Wyndham. It is now an access road for remote stations and is as "outback" as most people will ever get. Of the two roads across the Kimberley, it is by far the more scenic. Various gorges and stations are posted, and there's plenty of swimming and fishing along the way. The Derby and Kununurra tourist bureaus have indispensable road notes, though they aren't always available. Any W.A. Travel Centre office can also give you road notes.

Humble advice: 4WD is absolutely necessary to traverse the eastern section of the Beef Rd. and to gain access to all interesting sights. If you plan to do the entire length, you should have experience with 4WD and a basic knowledge of your engine. Bring along essential vehicle parts and a few spare tires. Water is available along the way, but carry some with you in case of breakdowns. Of course you'll be camping, so don't forget to stock up on all supplies before leaving. Supplies are available at **Home Valley Station**, **Mount Barnett Station**, and **Joe's Waterhole**; most other stations along the way also have supplies if you're desperate.

Don't expect a quick trip across. The Gibb River Rd. takes a good 12 hours to drive without stops. The road is sealed for the first 60 km from Derby, then turns to gravel and is relatively easy until **Mt. Elizabeth Station**, 330 km in. The remaining 316 km are extremely rough, with twists, turns, and sharp rocks. It would be a minor miracle to get through without puncturing at least one tire. Like anything that involves hardship and adventure, the difficulties are worthwhile if you're prepared and careful. Don't leave until you've gotten local advice and have a good map. The road is impassable during the wet season.

Fitzroy Crossing and Geikie Gorge

Fitzroy Crossing Roadhouse, Great Northern Hwy. (phone 091-91-5005). Open daily 6:00am-9:00pm. Does not provide tourist information.

Life in Fitzroy Crossing centers around the roadhouse, where groceries, supplies, prepared food, and gas are available. It's a rough, lonely little place that exists to serve mining camps, cattle stations, meatworks, and buses (all coachlines pass through, usually at some godawful hour).

There isn't much reason to stop except that "the Crossing" is the closest access to Geikie Gorge, 21 km northeast of town. Getting to the Gorge from town without private transport depends on your luck finding a ride.

Geikie Gorge (pronounced "geekee") is the most accessible and perhaps the most impressive of the three sights in the Devonian Reef National Parks. Like Winjana Gorge, Geikie Gorge's walls reveal fossils from a giant ocean reef that once existed there. Ranger-guided boat tours depart twice daily (April-Oct only) and last two hours.

The **Fitzroy River** is alive with critters of all sorts, including Johnston crocs, lizards, snakes, turtles, archer fish, and over 100 species of birds. Swimming is no problem (don't mind the crocs—they're harmless unless you harass them), but you can't step foot on the east bank, which is a wildlife sanctuary. The west bank, starting where the gorge wall begins, is also off-limits.

360 • Western Australia

Accommodation: In case you need to stay overnight in Fitzroy Crossing, the **Fitzroy Crossing Caravan Park** is about $8/night per tent or $38/two-person cabin (phone 091-91-5080). Camping at Geikie Gorge is a much nicer option. A tent site costs $8.50, and there are hot showers. No camping Dec-March.

Hall's Creek
Tourist Information, Main St. (Hair Fashion Bldg.) (phone 091-68-6087).

Progress has come slowly to Hall's Creek. The 301 km between Fitzroy Crossing and Hall's Creek wasn't paved until 1986, and locals rejoiced when automated long-distance phone service started a few years ago. Previously, they had to book calls with the operator and wait a few hours for their turn!

A few attractions make the town an interesting stop. Those traveling by car can visit **Wolfe's Creek Crater**, Australia's largest meteorite crater. It's an incredible 853 meters in diameter, located 146 km south of Hall's Creek on the Tanami Track.

Closer to town are the ruins of the original Hall's Creek post office and cemetery, about 20 km away. The settlement was built in the gold rush days when about 10,000 men swarmed to the Kimberley to mine the first substantial gold discovery in the country. The excitement was short-lived, and most gold-seekers soon left for Coolgardie and the Pilbara, but one gold mine called **Ruby Queen** operated until 1954 and remains intact.

Those with a strong interest in Aboriginal life should consider a visit to the **Balgo Community**, 250 km east of Hall's Creek. About 500 people from many tribes live there, and the community has a store and a service station. You must make arrangements ahead of time. Send a letter of inquiry with details on your proposed visit to *The Chairman, Balgo Hills Community Aboriginal Corporation, via Halls Creek, W.A., 6770.*

Those driving in the area should check with the police station for road conditions. Hall's Creek has the usual **Caravan Park** on Roberta Ave., with tent sites and on-site vans for $38 per couple (phone 091-68-6169).

The Bungle Bungle Range
The Bungle Bungles rank with Ayers Rock and the Great Barrier Reef for awe-inspiring natural beauty and originality. The range is a 235 square km area of giant ravines and beehive-like sandstone domes that are eerie, weird, and nothing short of amazing—something you will never forget.

Unlike Australia's other natural wonders, the Bungle Bungles are basically unexplored and undisturbed by commercialism or even campers. They have existed an estimated 350 million years and weren't known to white Australians until recently. The first scenic flights began in 1984, and 4WD safari operations are just now popping up. Even the CALM doesn't know much about the Bungle Bungles. Park officials have established a ranger station and campground, and there are two roads into the area, but they are so rough that authorities advise you to travel with at least one other vehicle. It takes a good 4 hours to reach the range from the main highway.

There aren't any established hiking trails in the Bungle Bungles; however, the ranger suggests a walk to **Piccaninny Creek** at the edge of the mountains, from the Piccaninny driving track. He warns that the rock face is fragile and dangerous for climbers. Campers need to bring all supplies, including food, fuel, emergency first aid, and water. (The last water is at **Bellburn Creek Crossing** on the road in.)

Getting There: The most popular way to view the Bungle Bungles is from the air from either Hall's Creek or Kununurra with **Slingair Charter** (Kununurra phone 091-68-2138, Hall's Creek phone 091-68-6155). Flights from Hall's Creek are about $30 cheaper than from Kununurra, but the flight from Kununurra includes spectacular views of Lake Argyle and the Argyle Diamond Mine. There are other flight operations from Kununurra; check with the tourist bureau for the latest. (Motion-sickness victims beware—there's often considerable turbulence.)

A number of 4WD safaris have been launched recently. There is one from Hall's Creek (150 km away), one from Turkey Creek (80 km away at the roadhouse Harry's Place, phone 091-68-7882), and a few from Kununurra (250 km away). Since most of the operators are new, we can't give recommendations or even estimate prices. Call the tourist information centers in each town to compare current offerings. Make sure to ask for prices, as brochures don't always include this crucial detail.

If you're going to Bungle Bungle National Park on your own, by all means talk with the CALM office in Kununurra before leaving (Coolibah Dr., phone 091-68-1177). They'll give you a pamphlet and tell you exactly where the campground is and how to find the ranger. You can obtain directions if you're approaching from Hall's Creek or Turkey Creek, but it's still a good idea to call for the other details. Remember, 4WD only!

Kununurra

Kununurra Visitors Centre, Coolibah Dr. (phone 091-68-1177). Open daily 8:00am-5:00pm.

Kununurra is the administrative center of Australia's most progressive irrigation project. The result of decades of research and work, the **Ord Irrigation Project** was intended primarily for rice and cotton cultivation. Though the original crops failed and the scheme was a financial disaster, irrigation has transformed the eastern Kimberley. Once arid and barren in the summer, the land is now lush, green, and productive year-round. The area's recent growth as an agricultural center is enormous, though limited by the cost of transporting produce and the lack of a nearby port.

The Ord River Valley is also notable for its history. It was there that the well-known Durack family established the Lissadell, Argyle, and Rosewood Stations in the 1880's. Mary Durack's account of the family's two-year trek from Queensland, *Kings in Grass Castles*, tells of the remote and wild country.

Close to Kununurra are some fabulous natural wonders, including the Bungle Bungles.

Getting There: All major coachlines stop in Kununurra on the Darwin-Perth route. The Perth trip takes 50 hours; from Darwin it's 9 hours. Ansett W.A. flies from Perth and Darwin daily.

Accommodation: There's a **YHA-Associate Hostel** (phone 091-68-1372) on Coolibah Dr. adjacent to the Uniting Church, 100 meters from where the bus drops you. It closes at 10:00pm and costs $9/night. On-site vans and campsites are available at **Kimberleyland Caravan Park**, 1 km from town on the Duncan Hwy. (phone 091-68-2021). Other recommended caravan parks for camping, further afield, are **Kona Park** (on Lake Kununurra, 4 km west of town off the Duncan Hwy., phone 091-68-1031) and **Hidden Valley Caravan Park** (phone 091-68-1790) on Weaber Plains Rd. The next cheapest option is the **Travellers Guest House**, 111 Nutwood Cres. (phone 091-68-1711) from $40/night. They'll pick you up when you get into town.

Transportation: Avis (phone 61-1258), **Budget** (phone 68-1680), and **Hertz** (phone 68-1257) all rent cars for as much as $90 a day. The best deal is a little Suzuki at Hertz for $40. 4WDs cost over $100 a day. Clearly, renting a car is not a cheap option. You'll do better hiring a bike and taking one of the excellent tours to get to remote places. **Two Wheel Freedom** (phone 68-2005) rents bikes from the Kimberleyland Caravan Park and from Messmate Way in town.

Kununurra is one of the few places where we highly recommend a tour. **Triangle Tours and Cruises** (phone 68-1272) is run by Gregor McQuie, who's been giving tours for 25 years. His Ord River wetlands cruise is especially good and includes personal memories about the building of Lake Argyle and Lake Kununurra, plus commentary on the surrounding wildlife. His pride and enthusiasm about the place is infectious, but don't take his facts and figures too literally. Triangle provides free pick-up at various points. Check the tourist bureau or **George's Kimberley Tours** (across the street) for these and other tours.

Scenic flights are an excellent way to see Lake Argyle and the Bungle Bungles—and the only way to see the Argyle Diamond Mine. Helicopter and plane rides are available through the tourist bureau. Fishing safaris and the like are also available.

Things to See and Do: The town of Kununurra was established in 1960 when farm plots were allocated for future irrigation by the Ord Irrigation Project. In 1963, the Kununurra Diversion Dam was completed, forming **Lake Kununurra** (a.k.a. "Ord River Wetlands") and transforming the mostly dry Ord riverbed into area teeming with birds, fish, and reptiles. Cruises through the wetlands are available, and it's possible to swim and fish off **Bandicoot Beach**, just below the Diversion Dam.

For the enterprising, the Dept. of Sport and Recreation has a detailed pamphlet on canoeing the Ord River between Lake Argyle and Lake Kununurra. It's a novice river course, and canoes are available at the **Kununurra Leisure Center**.

On the far side of Lake Kununurra off Packsaddle Rd., **Pandanus Palm**

Gallery sells zebra rock, an ancient claystone layered brown and white to form perfectly striped and dotted patterns (open daily 8:00am-6:00pm). Kununurra is the only place in the world where this curious stone occurs, and although most of it is now beneath the water of Lake Argyle, it's quite affordable.

While Lake Kununurra is the reservoir that directly feeds irrigation channels, **Lake Argyle** (50 km upstream) stores water permanently and releases it as needed. Dammed in 1972, Lake Argyle is massive, the largest man-made lake in the Southern Hemisphere. There is nothing on its shores but wilderness and a tourist complex, where you can camp in the caravan park (phone 091-68-1064). The Durack family's **Argyle Station Homestead** has been preserved and is now a pioneer museum.

Also in the Argyle Lake area is the **Argyle Diamond Mine**, which you can see only from the air. Industrial and gemstone diamonds were discovered on the site in 1979, and there's speculation that the mine is so rich it will last 100 years. Over 900 employees live in a huge complex and work two-week shifts for 12 hours a day, 7 days a week, then get flown home to Perth or elsewhere for two weeks. **Djaaru Gems** in town (across from the Post Office) sells some of the gemstone diamonds.

You can see agricultural plains fed by the irrigation scheme by going out Ivanhoe Rd. or Weber Plains Rd. Furrow, sprinkler, and overhead irrigation systems water the fields of peanuts, sorghum, beans, sunflowers, and other fruits and vegetables. Off Ivanhoe Rd. on Research Station Rd. is the former government research station, where crops were tested as part of a federal project beginning in 1945. In the same direction on Ivanhoe Rd. is **Ivanhoe Crossing**, where horse-drawn wagons once forded the Ord River en route to Wyndham. The dams cause strong currents year-round, and a number of people have drowned in the rapids, so be careful if you intend to fish. Swimming is not a good idea.

Nearer to town on Weber Plains Rd. is **Mirima Hidden Valley National Park**, where domes and ridges of aged sandstone make for great exploring and day hikes. Rock paintings and engravings of the Miriuwung Aborigines can be seen throughout the park. If you need detailed trail information, the CALM office in town (Konkerberry Dr.) can help out. Try to get to a lookout point either from the park or from **Kelly's Knob**, across Weaber Plains Rd. From a high vantage point, you can see an impressive distinction between fields that are irrigated and those that have yet to be cultivated. The **Carr-Boyd** Range rises in the distance, an ancient group of mountains under government control and leased to various mining companies and pastoralists.

If you find yourself in Kununurra during the wet season, **Black Rock Falls**, **Middle Springs**, and **Valentine's Pool** should be beautiful. They are on the old road to Wyndham, past Ivanhoe Crossing. Get there via Parry Creek Rd. (check locally to make sure it's passable).

Worthwhile day trips and overnights include Wyndham, the Bungle Bungle Range, and trips to various stations. **El Questro Station** (phone 091-68-2130), 32 km east of Kununurra on the Gibb River Beef Road, costs $10 a night to camp. From there you can bird-watch, fish (excellent for barramundi), and walk along the Pentecost River to Chamberlain Gorge. **Roy's Bush Camp** has pony rides, damper, and bush poetry. Yes it's contrived, but Roy Walker is a former Argyle stockman and makes his presentation with sincerity and humor. The camp is located 6 km from Spillway Bridge on Top Dam Rd., and the $14/night to camp includes the damper, etc. Book through the tourist bureau.

Finally, **Keep River National Park**, across the Northern Territory border from the Victoria Hwy., is like a small-scale version of the Bungle Bungles. Evidence of ancient glaciers and volcanoes lies among the sandstone formations along the Keep River, and there are several Aboriginal art sites. The tourist bureau has a helpful pamphlet on the geology and wildlife. A detailed hiking map may be difficult to find in Kununurra, as the park is managed by N.T. authorities, but try the tourist bureau. Bring your own water.

Food and Entertainment: The **Kununurra Leisure Center** pool offers relief on hot days. The rest of the center has squash, basketball, and other sports for a fee. For details call 68-2120. There's an outdoor cinema on Coolibah Dr.

The Lillyput Bar at **Gulliver's Tavern** (corner Konkerberry Dr. & Cottontree Ave.) is highly civilized for this part of the world. Their counter meals (lunch and dinner) cost around $12, and they have a happy hour Thurs at 5:00pm. It's open until 11:00pm M-Sat and until 1:30pm on Sun. The **Hotel Kununurra** (Messmate Dr.) is a bit rougher and packed most nights.

Wyndham

Tourist Information, O'Donnell St. (phone 091-61-1054). Hours vary.

The old port of Wyndham is 105 km north of Kununurra on the Great Northern Hwy. Early pastoralists shipped their belongings through Wyndham, and during the 1885-87 gold rush it was the point of entry for gold-seekers. Officially surveyed in 1886, Wyndham was the first big town in the East Kimberley, and it retained its prominence with the establishment of a meatworks in 1919. In its most active years, Kimberley cattle were shipped to international destinations through Wyndham. The port is still used on a limited basis for cattle transport, but the meat-processing industry has moved.

Make sure to get to **Five Rivers Lookout**, off Five Rivers Rd., for a spectacular view of Cambridge Gulf, including Wyndham and the old meatworks. The Forrest, Pentacost, King, Durack, and Ord Rivers are all in the distance.

Three Mile Valley (turn off Five Rivers Rd., 1 km from the hospital) has trails into little gorges and is a good picnic spot. The **Afghan Cemetery** memorializes Afghan camel drivers who carried supplies around the district. There are numerous picnic and walking spots in the area, such as **The Grotto** and a bird sanctuary at **Marlgu Billabong**. Tourist information will point you in the right direction.

Getting There: Greyhound and Pioneer go from Kununurra to the Wyndham Roadhouse.

Accommodation: The **Caravan Park** in Baker St., 1 km north of town (phone 091-61-1064), has a famous giant boab tree. It's the place to camp if you want to stay the night (no on-site vans).

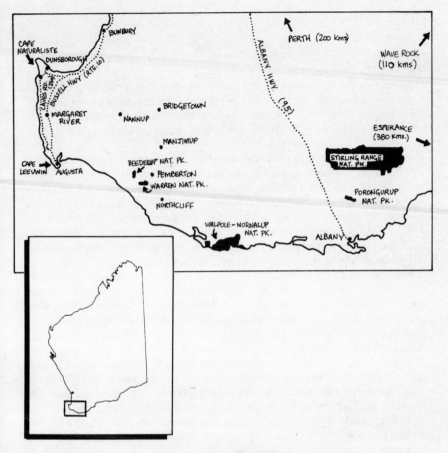

The Southwest

Unlike the barren, monotonous landscape that defines most of Western Australia, the southwest is both fertile and diverse. The coastal region from Cape Naturaliste down to Augusta is dotted with cattle farms, orchards, and vineyards. Forests of giant karri and jarrah trees dominate the region further east, while the rocky and remote southern coast boasts wild surf and excellent fishing.

Hiking in the southwest's numerous national parks and state forests is the best way to see and appreciate them. The Bibbulmun Track, a 530 km trail starting in Kalamunda (east of Perth) and finishing in Shannon on the south coast, has some fantastic sections. There are several coastal walks, and the Stirling Ranges, just north of Albany, has first-rate mountain climbing.

The Dept. of Sport and Recreation publishes two bicycle tour pamphlets. *Southwest Cycle Tour* describes a loop from Bunbury to Pemberton, and *South Coast Cycle Tour* includes an Albany-Stirling and Porongurup Ranges loop, and a coastal route from Albany to Pemberton. YHA of W.A. offers a 14-day 4WD tour from Perth through the southwest via Dunsborough, Pemberton, Albany, the Stirling Ranges, and Esperance, then north to Coolgardie, and back to Perth via Wave Rock. The tours depart the YHA hostel on New-castle St. in Perth and operate Oct-April.

Winter in the southwest is cold and often rainy, but it can be a beautiful time to visit because there are few people and the humidity brings out bril-liant colors. In summer, the days are hot, but it cools down at night. The choice time to visit is in spring wildflower season, Sept-Oct.

Getting There: Because distances are short, the southwest can be traveled comfortably, although public transport to most places is infrequent. West-rail's Perth-Bunbury rail service, *Australind*, runs M-Sat twice a day and once on Sundays. It takes 2.5 hrs; reservations are essential. (If you're carrying a bicycle or surfboard, space is limited so get there early.)

Westrail also operates four southwest bus services, either in combination with the train or directly from Perth. One service operates along the Bussell Highway (Route 10) between Bunbury and Augusta. To move eastward from there you must return to Bunbury. Two services run to Albany, one direct (Route 95), the other along the more scenic Route 10 via Pemberton and the forest region. The fourth service follows the Great Southern Hwy., then cuts over to Route 1 to reach Esperance. For schedules and reservations, call toll-free: Perth 008-326-2222; Bunbury 008-017-030; Albany 008-010-632. Greyhound bus passes are valid on Westrail services to Albany.

At the time of our research, Deluxe was the only interstate bus company permitted to drop off passengers from Perth in the southwest. Its daily Perth-Adelaide service follows the Southwest Hwy. (Route 1). Stops along the route include Bunbury, Manjimup, Denmark, Albany, and Esperance.

Hitching isn't always reliable. However, the Albany Hwy. (Route 95) be-tween Perth and Albany is well-traveled and shouldn't pose a problem. The Southwest Hwy. is also fairly busy.

Accommodation: Peak tourist times for the southwest are Easter and sum-mer school holidays (Dec-Jan) when accommodation is often fully booked. Also, the wildflower season is popular, especially with weekend travelers from Perth. Travel mid-week if possible.

YHA has 10 southwest hostels, most of which are good. The hostels at Dunsborough, Pemberton, and Albany are excellent. Camping is also a good way to go.

Perth to Margaret River

Although Mandurah, Pinjarra, Bunbury, and Busselton are sizeable cities and all on the tourist bureau's list of southwest vacation spots, they're not really worth the time or effort. The first two are basically resorts; **Bunbury** is an industrial shipping port and looks like it; and **Busselton** offers the usual touristy things without much that's unique. Margaret River is our suggested first stop for those using public transport.

Westrail's bus service along the Bussell Hwy. (Route 10) is the only public transport along the west coast. This is a good place to splurge and rent a car, because the scenic route is accessible only by private transport.

If you have your own wheels, take the coastal roads. From Busselton, go west on Route 10 and take the turn-off for Caves Rd. (Route 250) towards **Dunsborough** (a.k.a. Quindalup), a relaxing beachside hideaway. There's a resort-style **YHA Hostel** (285 Geographe Bay Rd., phone 097-55-3107; $9 per night) and **Greenacres Caravan Park** (phone 097-55-3087) on the beach at Geographe Bay, one km north of where John Bussell and his family set up the area's first permanent settlement in 1834, on the banks of the Vasse River. **Dunsborough Beach Cottages** (Gifford Rd., phone 097-55-3024) has beachside cottages for up to 10 people. They are fully equipped except for linen and blankets and cost $25/couple, $5 for each additional person.

To the west of Geographe Bay is the barren headland of **Cape Naturaliste**, covered with wind-lashed vegetation and sand dunes. One side faces the sheltered Geographe Bay; the other is exposed to the Indian Ocean, creating dramatic limestone cliffs. The cape's lighthouse, built in 1903, is open daily to visitors (closed Wed). Short walking trails to the lighthouse and cliff edges are provided.

Follow Caves Rd. south through Yallingup, where you can visit **Yallingup Cave** (1 km from the post office, open daily 9:30am-3:30pm). Just off the coastline south of Yallingup is a weathered rock outcrop called **Canal Rocks**, which creates a protected bay. About 5 km south is the **Canal Rocks Caravan Park** at Smiths Beach Rd., Yallingup (phone 097-55-2116), with on-site vans ($18) and campsites ($10/couple). It's next to **Smith's Beach**, known for its salmon run and good surf break. From Yallingup to Margaret River is wine country.

A series of protected areas along the 80 km of coast from Cape Naturaliste to Augusta, **Leeuwin-Naturaliste National Park** includes Yallingup, Cowaramup, Hamelin Bay, and Leeuwin. Any and all of them are worth a stop to see the rugged, wild coastline. Plans call for construction of a 5-day coastal walk from Cape to Cape, sections of which are already in place.

Margaret River

Augusta/Margaret River Tourist Bureau, corner Wallcliffe Rd. and Bussell Hwy. (phone 097-57-2147). Open M-F 9:00am-5:00pm, Sat-Sun 9:00am-3:00pm.

A haven for gentlemen farmers and summer vacationers from Perth, Margaret River is surrounded by dairy farms and wine-growing properties. Wines, excellent surfing (with waves up to 5 meters!), and fine crafts are the major draws to the area. Book your lodging in advance if you plan to go during summer holidays.

Getting There and Getting Around: A Westrail bus service between Bunbury and Augusta stops in Margaret River and connects with the Perth-Bunbury train. It operates 4 days a week. **Leeuwin Car Hire** (120 Bussell Hwy., phone 57-2671) is the only local car rental company, and they'll pick you up at your accommodation. Book tours through the tourist office.

Accommodation:

The Margaret River Lodge, 220 Railway Tce. (phone 57-2532). $12/bunk, doubles available. Rammed earth buildings. Clean and comfortable. Communal kitchen facilities and bathrooms. Bike and surfboard rental.

Margaret River Guest House, Valley Rd., off Turnbridge Rd. (phone 57-2349). $30-$50. Breakfast included.

Basildene Holiday Homestead, Wallcliffe Rd. (phone 57-2479). $30 and up/person. Breakfast included.

River View Gardens Caravan Park, Willmott Ave. (phone 57-2270). Close enough to walk to town. On-site vans $28; campsites $10/couple.

Prevelly Park Holiday Resort and Caravan Park, Mitchell Dr., Prevelly Park (phone 57-2374). About 10 km west of Margaret River, on the beach. On-site vans about $28, campsites $10/couple.

Things to See and Do: The wine industry of the southwest is confined to a small area from Yallingup to Margaret River. Most vineyards lie a few km from the latter. Although relatively new (the first vineyard, **Vasse Felix** on Miamup Rd., was established in 1967), the wine is excellent and internationally recognized. Take either a bike or car to visit the vineyards, because hitching isn't reliable, especially in winter.

About 20 wineries are open for tastings. Their summer hours (Sept-April) are 10:00am-4:30pm daily. May-August they're open only on weekends, 10:00am-4:30pm. The tourist office stocks a pamphlet called *The Vineyards of the South*, with descriptions of the local vineyards and a detailed map. The better-known wineries include **Sussex Vale** (Harman's Mill Rd., Willyabrup) and the **Leeuwin Estate** (Gnarawary Rd.), which hosts an enormous concert in Feb/March with international symphonies. (Inquire at the W.A. Tourist Centre or the local tourist office about tickets.) A few of the wineries also offer lunches: Try the plate of local cheese at **Cullen's Willyabrup Wines** (Caves Rd., Cowaramup) or hot soup and bread at the Leeuwin Estate.

Margaret River's second claim to fame is surfing. The coast is about 10 km west of town, with popular beaches at **Prevelly Park** (at the mouth of the Margaret River) and **Gnarabrup Beach**. It's safe to swim and surf year-round. In the summer, Margaret River buzzes with "surfies," especially during the two big surfing competitions in Nov. The **Margaret River Classic** has both professional and amateur surfers, while the **Margaret River Thriller** is for pros only.

Between 1922-27, a government settlement scheme lured about 100 people to the area. You can tour their relocated **Old Settlement** daily at Ellensbrook, near the town center. Built of jarrah and corrugated iron, the Settlement includes a house and farm buildings where local craftspeople demonstrate and sell their work.

Other buildings of note in Margaret River include the **St. Thomas More Catholic Church** (Mitchell St.), a beautiful example of construction with local products. The church is made of jarrah and karri timber and rammed earth. On a hill overlooking the town is the stately **Wallcliffe House**, built in 1865 out of local timber and stone by Alfred Bussell, one of the area's first settlers. The private home can be admired only from the outside. The **Margaret River Hotel** (Bussell Hwy., in town) is a refurbished hotel with a cozy bar and fireplace—nice for a glass of local wine or afternoon tea, especially in winter. The hotel also serves counter meals in its pub and pricey meals in a private dining room.

The **Margaret River Marron Farm** in Witchcliff offers cooked, whole marron (freshwater lobster) feasts for $9-$15. It costs $4 to enter the farm, but that includes a half-hour tour (operating every hour 10:30am-3:30pm), and you can stay all day to enjoy their swimming hole, small park area, and kiosk.

Margaret River to Augusta

Two roads cover the 45 km stretch between Margaret River and Augusta: the Bussell Hwy. (Route 10) and Caves Rd. (Route 250). If you've got your own transport, stick to the more scenic Caves Rd., which runs closer to the coast. There are over 300 limestone caves from Cape to Cape, but only four are set up for tourists, three of which are on Caves Rd.: **Mammoth Cave**, 21 km south of Margaret River (phone 57-2147); **Lake Cave**, 2 km south of Mammoth (phone 57-7543); and **Jewel Cave**, 8 km north of Augusta (phone 58-4541). All are open daily and have at least two tours a day. Entrance to each costs about $4.

Just south of Lake Cave is a turn-off from Caves Rd. onto Boranup Dr., a 14 km scenic loop through the **Boranup Karri Forest**. The forest's skinny, white karris are unlike the massive trees around Pemberton and quite spectacular. Toward the end of the drive, there's a coastal lookout and picnic area.

Augusta
Augusta Information Centre, Blackwood Ave. (phone 097-58-1695).

Located 35 km from Margaret River in the southwest corner of the continent, Augusta is the meeting place of the Indian and Southern Oceans. Founded by John Bussell in 1830, it is W.A.'s third oldest settlement.

A major draw to Augusta is the **Blackwood River cruise**. The *Miss Flinders* ferry runs cruises for either two hours ($14) or four hours ($17). Call 58-1474 or visit tourist information for details. Black swans, pelicans, and many other bird species live in the river's estuary. The famous **Cape Leeuwin Lighthouse**, 10 km south of town at the most southwestern point of the continent, was named for a Dutch ship that passed the point in 1622. The lighthouse is open for inspection T-Sun 9:30am-3:00pm ($2.50/person).

Another worthwhile visit in town is the **Historical Museum**, which outlines the area's history and the story of local timber exploitation (Blackwood Ave., open daily except Fri, 10:00am-noon & 2:00pm-4:00pm).

Getting There: Westrail runs a bus service between Margaret River and Augusta on Monday (40 minute trip) and another from Bunbury to Augusta via Busselton on Fri (3 hrs). Besides the stop in town, the bus also goes to Flinders Bay.

Accommodation: The YHA-Associate hostel, **Riverside Cottages** (cnr. Russell Hwy. and Blackwood Ave., phone 097-58-1433), is 1.5 km from town. There are only 13 beds, so book ahead in summer ($8/night).

Augusta to Pemberton

The area between Augusta and Pemberton is predominantly karri, jarrah, and pine forest. The karri is characterized by smooth, light-gray bark and great height, sometimes over 80 meters. The jarrah, only half as tall, can be identified by its dark, stringy bark. Jarrah is the most important commercial wood in W.A. Both trees are eucalypts.

Forests have always played an important role in local economics. Timber mills in the 1800's, originally worked by convicts, provided vital materials for ships and houses. Since then, W.A.'s timber industry has been centered in the southwest. Logging and regeneration are painstakingly controlled. In the karri forests, for example, it takes 100 years for a tree to be ready for cutting. The jarrah forests are often afflicted with *dieback*, a fungus that has damaged 20,000 square km of forest and bushland. Large quarantine areas have been designated to control its spread.

There is no public transport through the region. Those traveling on their own will take the Brockman Hwy. (Route 10) on a long, scenic route through Nannup. From there you can take two routes: the Brockman Hwy. (turns into Route 252), which goes east to Bridgetown and then south, or the preferable Nannup-Pemberton Rd. (Route 10) to Pemberton, which passes through **Beedelup National Park**, 20 km west of Pemberton.

All buses go through Manjimup, 30 km north of Pemberton, but not all continue to Pemberton. You may need to spend a night in Manjimup waiting for the Pemberton connection. **Manjimup Hotel** (Giblett St., phone 097-71-1322) is $24/single. **Manjimup Caravan Park** (Southwestern Hwy., phone 097-71-2093) has overnight vans ($24) and campsites ($9/couple).

Pemberton

Pemberton Northcliffe Tourist Bureau, Brockman St. (phone 097-76-1133). Open daily 9:00am-5:00pm.

Pemberton is the center from which to explore the most impressive national forests of the southwest. It's also a fisherman's heaven, with several stocked rivers brimming with trout.

The local tourist office is cozy and friendly. A wood-burning stove fills the room with a wonderful smell, and they'll let you leave your bags there all day. The office also has a small museum and free forestry videos, plus an excellent guide called *Big Tree Country* with the area's sights, fishing, and hiking in honest detail.

Note: Accommodation in Pemberton is completely filled during Easter and for a few weeks after Christmas.

Getting There: If you're relying on the Westrail bus, remember that it's easier to get to Pemberton than to leave if you're traveling east towards Albany. There's one "frequent" (once a day except Sunday) Bunbury-Northcliff service, and a more extensive but less frequent (once a week) Bunbury-Albany service, both of which stop in Manjimup and Pemberton. Deluxe stops daily in Manjimup and Walpole, but not Pemberton, on its Perth-Adelaide run.

For local transport, a car will come in handy, since most of the best parks and trees are a fair distance from town. Although the area is hilly, biking is a viable alternative for the fit. You can rent bikes from the YHA hostel if you stay there.

Accommodation:

YHA Pemberton, Pimelea Rd. (phone 097-761-153). $7/night. 8 km from town up a steep, winding incline. Wooden cabins amongst huge trees. Bike hire available. Office hours: 8:00am-10:00am, 5:00pm-10:00pm. Will pick up at Westrail bus with advance notice.

Warren Lodge, Brockman St., across from the tourist office (phone 76-1105). $10/bunk. Doubles available.

Pemberton Caravan Park, Stirling Rd. (phone 76-1300). On-site vans $19 and up.

Karri Valley Estate, 12 km southwest of town on the Pemberton-Nannup Rd., at Old Hop Gardens (phone 76-2020). $18/person for "lodge" room, with communal facilities and refrigerator.

Things to See and Do: The highlight of the Pemberton area is **Warren National Park** (12 km south of town), boasting the tallest virgin karri forest open to the public. **Maidenbush Trail**, a 9 km drive through the park, can also be walked (with caution). Vasse Rd. goes through the park and can be reached from either the Vasse Hwy. or Pemberton-Nannup Rd. The Bibbulmun Track follows the Warren River inside the park.

Also, don't miss the famous climb up **Gloucester Tree**, 3 km from town (unless you're afraid of heights, in which case you'll probably admire it from afar). The 61-meter lookout tree has 153 rungs hammered into its sturdy karri trunk.

Other forests are at **Beedelup National Park** (21 km from Pemberton on the Pemberton-Nannup Rd.), where the giant, hollow **Underwood Tree** is wide enough to stand in, and **Big Brook Lake** (a few km northwest of town and a 6 km walk from the YHA hostel). The 9 km **Rainbow Trail** at Big Brook Lake is a driving track through karri forest that follows a former railroad used for hauling timber. The lake itself is stocked with trout and marron. In summer, canoe and ski-boat rental is available.

River trout were first brought to Pemberton from Victoria in 1930. The Dept. of Fisheries now breeds up to one million fish a year and stocks the public fishing waters throughout the southwest with trout and marron. The Dept.'s **hatchery** off Stirling Rd. is open daily 9:00am-noon and 1:00pm-4:15pm (10:00am-2:00pm May-Aug), entrance $2.

Sept 1-April 30 is the official fishing season except in the Warren, Donnelly, and Blackwood Rivers, where fishing is allowed year-round. Marron season is Dec 15-April 30. You need a license only for marron (get it from the hatchery). The only place renting fishing gear is **Treenbrook Downs Trout Farm** (10 km south on Route 10, phone 76-1400), open 9:30am-5:30pm most days. For those who don't care about the sport but love the taste, **Jan's Diner** (on the main street) serves a whole, pan-fried trout with chips and salad— the best meal we had in the whole southwest.

Pemberton to Albany

As you head east toward Albany, take Route 1 along the coast via Walpole and Denmark (Westrail and Deluxe both follow this route). There are many relaxed spots for fishing, boating, and other water activities along the way, including **Denmark** on the Denmark River, one of the most popular towns. Also there, **Winniston Park** has an extensive collection of English antiques, some from the 16th century—a most unlikely setting for a display of British wealth and history!

Rivermouth Caravan Park (Inlet Dr., phone 098-48-1262), 1.5 km from Denmark at the mouth of the Wilson Inlet and Denmark River, has on-site vans ($25) and campsites ($9/two). The YHA hostel is 3.5 km from town at **Wilson Inlet Holiday Park** on Ocean Beach Rd. (phone 098-48-1267).

Walpole-Nornalup National Park covers 18,000 hectares of karri and red tingle eucalypt forests and includes 40 km of rugged coastline with wide beaches, dunes, and sheltered bays. Secluded walking trails and scenic drives through the forests and to the coast originate in Walpole. The local tourist office (in a craft shop on the main street) has detailed information and maps.

Albany

Albany Tourist Bureau, corner York St. and Peel Place (phone 098-41-1088). Open M-F 8:30am-5:30pm, Sat 9:00am-4:00pm, Sun 9:00am-1:00pm.

Established in 1826 as a military outpost for the British colony in New South Wales, Albany is the oldest settlement in Western Australia. Prior to settlement, Albany's coast had been a safe anchoring spot for whaling boats and exploration parties. Today, Albany is known for its deep harbor, spectacular scenery, and hiking in the Stirling and Porongurup Ranges.

Getting There and Getting Around: The Albany Hwy. runs 412 km between Perth and Albany, and the trip takes 4.5 hours. Westrail operates a daily bus service from Perth, as well as a weekly Bunbury-Albany service, via Pemberton and Denmark. Deluxe takes passengers between Perth and Albany, dropping off outside Albany's Tourist Bureau, down the street from the YHA hostel.

The only local public transport, **Love's Bus Service**, operates infrequent hours between town and Middleton Beach, weekdays and Sat morning, with an extension to Emu Point weekdays. There's also a service to the Albany Hwy. intersection. All the routes service shopping areas and the like, not tourist-related attractions.

Accommodation: Inexpensive B&Bs are plentiful in Albany, and there are a number of cottages available with full cooking facilities and good rates, as well as caravan parks which offer the usual on-site vans and camping sites. Cottages and caravan parks are on Albany's bays and beaches. Check at the Tourist Bureau for more listings.

YHA Albany, 49 Duke St. (phone 41-3949). $8/night. Close to town center. Large, with plenty of communal space. Clean. Doubles and quads. Bike hire. Friendly, knowledgeable manager offers hiking trips and tours.

Parkville Colonial Guest House, 136 Brunswick Rd. (phone 41-3704). $14-$35, B&B. Three-course dinners by arrangement.

Glen Affric Guest House, 138 Brunswick St. (phone 41-3757). $18-$35, B&B.

Willner Guest House, 9 Middleton Rd. (phone 41-3160). $15-$18, B&B.

Things to See and Do: Torndirrup National Park encompasses most of the southern peninsula that forms King George Sound. Giant granite boulders on the park's south coast have been shaped into magnificent, treacherous formations by the relentless Southern Ocean. Sights include the Blowhole, Natural Bridge, Gap, and Jimmy Newell's Harbour, and each can be reached by paved road. Another beautiful spot in the park is **Quaranup Reserve**, on the bay side, with sheltered, deserted beaches accessible by sand roads.

Whaleworld, at the east end of the park, was the area's last operational whaling station and still smells from the remains of its busy past (the station closed in 1978). All the original buildings are open to the public as well as one of the whaling vessels. There's also a museum display on whale anatomy and a gory video. It's open daily from 9:00am-5:00pm and is definitely worthwhile. A 40-minute tour is included in the $4 entrance fee.

Torndirrup National Park, a 20-minute drive from town, is reached via Frenchman's Bay Rd., but there is no public transport available. Biking is the best way to get out there, although it gets hilly around the park's border.

Sheltered beaches along Frenchman's Bay and Quaranup provide excellent swimming, snorkeling, and diving. **Southcoast Diving Supplies/Southern Ocean Charter** (Festing St., phone 41-5068) offers various diving excursions and fishing charters. **Middleton Bay**, east of town off Middleton Rd., is a convenient swimming beach where you'll sometimes see whales. **Two People's Bay**, 40 km east of town, is a nature reserve with a secluded beach and walking tracks. Surfing off the beaches to the east and west of town is also good. The weekly *Albany Advertiser* has up-to-date info on local fishing. Rent simple hand-lines from the YHA hostel.

Albany's historic atmosphere is a refreshing contrast to most of W.A. The National Trust's self-guided walk (available at the tourist office) outlines historic buildings, most of which are near the hostel. The **Residency Museum** on Residency Rd. describes early exploration and settlement—a story with an entirely different set of characters and circumstances than that of the west coast. It also has an extensive natural history collection. (Open M-Sat

10:00am-5:00pm, Sun 2:00pm-5:00pm; free.) About 1.5 km east of the town center, the **Old Farm at Strawberry Hill** (Middleton Rd., between Block and Seymour Sts.) was built for Albany's first Government Resident in 1831 and remains intact under National Trust care. Admission to the house is $3, and there's a beautiful English garden with a small tea room.

The Porongurup and Stirling National Parks are 35 km and 9 km north of Albany, respectively. The **Porongurups** consist of exposed granite peaks weathered into domes and unusual shapes. It's the perfect place for day hikes or rock-climbing, with three marked trails of 2-3 hours walking time. Beware of snakes in summer. No camping permitted. The Albany Tourist Bureau runs a half-day bus tour to the Porongurups for $20/person.

For more extensive hiking, go to the **Stirlings**. The range is ancient and weathered, but its summits are still impressive, with **Bluff Knoll** rising 1,170 meters and several others rivaling it. In winter, the mountains occasionally get a dusting of snow, rare indeed in this part of the country. Trails are numerous, and those who plan to camp overnight must tell the ranger. Bring water. The Visitor Center is at the Toolbrunup exit off Chester Pass Rd. (phone 27-9230 or 27-9218). There is no public transport to the Stirlings.

Albany's Tourist Bureau has brochures on trails in both parks, and the manager of Albany's hostel is an avid hiker as well as an authority on the mountains. He often takes hostellers on treks. There's a YHA-affiliate in the caravan park at the Stirling Ranges (phone 098-27-9229).

For hard-core rock climbers, **Cape West Howe National Park**, 30 km west of Albany, offers the best climbing challenges.

Food: There's good seafood at most of the pubs in town. Try a counter meal at **Weld Tavern** (Moir St.) or the **Amity Tavern** (corner Albany & South Coast Hwys., phone 41-4141). There are plenty of other small, decently-priced restaurants around town, as well as the usual pizza and fish 'n chip shops.

Esperance

Esperance Tourist Bureau, Dempster St. (phone 090-71-2330 or 71-2521). Open M-F 8:45am-5:00pm, Sat-Sun 9:00am-5:00pm.

Because of its distance from both Perth and Adelaide, Esperance is a remote destination. However, quite a few overseas travelers make it to the little seaside town, especially those on the Perth-Adelaide journey. Used initially as a shipping port for the Coolgardie goldfields back in 1893, Esperance now services nickel, wheat, and salt industries from southern W.A. The region was revitalized in the 1960's when American investors and Australian pastoralists developed area farmlands.

The ocean is surprisingly warm, and all kinds of water sports are popular, especially fishing. The local Surfcaster's Club publishes a guide with maps of the main fishing spots. Rent fishing and scuba gear from **Dempster Sporting Store** (65 Dempster St., opposite Museum Park).

Pink Lake, west of town, isn't always pink, but it's pretty anyway. The color is caused by high concentrations of salt-tolerant algae in the water. From the lookout point, you can see huge piles of nearly pure table salt heaped beside ponds at the east end of the lake.

Cape Le Grande National Park (48 km southeast of Esperance) offers a few easy walks through sandplains and hilly scrubland, all of which end at secluded bays or coves. A 15 km day hike along the Coastal Trail connects Le Grand Beach to Rossiter Beach. Campgrounds at **Le Grand Beach** and **Lucky Bay** cost $7.50/site. See the CALM pamphlet or the ranger at the park's entrance (phone 75-9022). No public transport is available to the park from Esperance, but there are numerous tours.

A two-hour cruise to **Woody Island** operates three times a week Jan-Feb and can be arranged other times. The island is a rugged, untouched wildlife haven where dolphins, seals, sea eagles, and other species are frequently in view. It's also possible to fish, snorkel, and dive there. If you want to spend a night or two communing with nature, there are tents on the island for rent (or bring your own), an amenities block, and hot showers.

Getting There: Westrail runs a Perth-Esperance bus service (10.5 hours) and a Kalgoorlie-Esperance service, via Coolgardie, which takes 5.5 hours. Both operate three times a week. Deluxe stops in Esperance on its daily Perth-Albany-Adelaide route. Most of the surrounding area, including the national park lands, is suitable only for 4WD. **Budget Rent-a-Car** is at Dempster Holden, Norseman Rd. (phone 71-2775). Bicycles are good in and around town but won't be helpful within Cape Le Grande National Park because of sandy roads. Rent bikes from the hostel or from Dempster Sporting Store. Local tour companies operate 4WD adventure trips into the bushland around Esperance.

Accommodation: The Esperance **YHA Hostel** is just off the beach, 2 km from the town center on Goldfields Rd. (phone 090-71-1040). It costs $8/night.

Kalgoorlie and Coolgardie

The Kalgoorlie region's first gold was discovered at Coolgardie in 1892. Alluvial (water-deposited) gold was everywhere, especially around Coolgardie, and the first arrivals literally picked their fortunes off the dusty ground. In 1893, Paddy Hannan and his small group of gold-seekers found nuggets near Kalgoorlie's **Mt. Charlotte**, and soon a square mile around Boulder became known as the "Golden Mile." The sub-surface wealth of this area, producing over 1,200 tons of gold to date, switched mining activity from Coolgardie to Kalgoorlie/Boulder. Hannan became a local legend, with streets, stores, and even a local beer named in his honor.

The Golden Mile boomed for a short and vibrant period, during which the Kalgoorlie-Perth railway was connected (in 1896). The population skyrocketed, businesses flourished, but living conditions were harsh and thousands died, mainly from lack of water. In 1903, a 350 mile-long pipeline was extended from the weir at Mundaring (east of Perth), bringing water to the Mt. Charlotte reservoir in Kalgoorlie—and with it, permanent settlement.

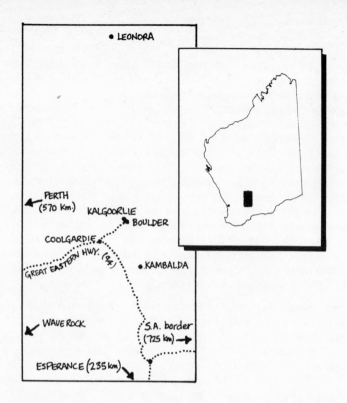

At the peak of the goldfields' prosperity, Kalgoorlie/Boulder's population reached 30,000. Today it's the largest township in the goldfield region, with over 20,000 inhabitants. Coolgardie's population once reached 15,000, but it is now a virtual ghost town except for the tourists who come to see its impressive old buildings.

The region continues to produce over half of Australia's gold. Modern prospectors search with metal detectors, hoping to find nuggets early gold-seekers missed. The largest find with a metal detector weighed 7.5 kilograms, and the Tourist Bureau says amateurs find a few nuggets each week. If you want to join the hunt, first obtain a "Miner's Right" from the Mines Dept. on Brookman St.

Getting There

All major buslines stop in either Kalgoorlie or Coolgardie (or both) on their daily Adelaide-Perth runs. From Adelaide, the trip is over 2,000 km and takes 25 hours. From Perth it is 770 km, 8 hours. Deluxe's Perth-Sydney service reaches Coolgardie in 7 hours from Perth.

Most interstate buses arrive and depart from the Kalgoorlie Tourist Bureau on Hannan St. In Coolgardie, they stop at service stations along Bayley St.

Railways of Australia operates a well-known coast-to-coast service that stops in Kalgoorlie. The *Trans-Australian* (Adelaide-Perth) takes 38 hours; the *Indian-Pacific* (Sydney-Perth) takes 65 hours. The *Prospector* operates only between Kalgoorlie and Perth, every day but Saturday. It takes 6.5 hours.

Ansett Airlines flies to Kalgoorlie from Perth. There is no air service from other cities.

Orientation and Practical Information

Hannan St., Kalgoorlie's main drag, houses most of the shops, the Post Office, the Town Hall, and the tourist bureau. Hannan becomes the Great Eastern Hwy. as it exits town.

There is no perceptible border between Kalgoorlie and Boulder (southeast of town), and very little that distinguishes one town from the other. **Burt St.** is Boulder's main street. Unfortunately, no tourist office publishes a decent free map of Kalgoorlie/Boulder, but the standard grid layout isn't too difficult to grasp. There is a pamphlet called *Gold Rush Country* available at the Kalgoorlie Tourist Bureau, with excellent background information and maps for the region, including outlying mining towns. It's quite out-of-date, so ignore the printed business hours.

Coolgardie, 40 km west of Kalgoorlie on the Great Eastern Hwy., is a tiny town with a main thoroughfare, **Bayley St.**, and a few secondary lanes. There is no bank or pharmacy in town.

Note: The annual Kalgoorlie horse races are held the last weekend in August, and all accommodation in the area is booked *a year* in advance!

Important Addresses and Telephone Numbers (area code 090)

Kalgoorlie Tourist Bureau, 250 Hannan St. (phone 21-1413). Open M-F, 8:30am-5:00pm, Sat 9:00am-noon.

Coolgardie Tourist Bureau, Bayley St. (phone 26-6090). Open daily 9:00am-5:00pm.

Boulder Tourist Bureau, 106 Burt St. (phone 21-3860). Open M-F 9:00am-4:30pm; Sat 9:00am-11:30pm.

General Post Office, 204 Hannan St., Kalgoorlie (phone 21-1413).

Pioneer Express, 34 Cassidy St. (phone 21-6765).

Greyhound, 34 Cassidy St. (phone 21-7100).

Police, phone 21-2822.

Hospital, phone 21-2222.

Transportation

Public transport between Kalgoorlie and Coolgardie is poor. A school bus runs weekdays between the towns, departing early in the morning from the Coolgardie shire office (Bailey St.) and returning mid-afternoon from the Kalgoorlie Tourist Bureau (Hannan St.). It costs $3 each way. Other than that, you'll have to fend for yourself. The local taxi service is 21-2177.

Goldenlines bus service operates between Kalgoorlie and Boulder approximately every 45 minutes, M-F 6:45am-6:00pm and Saturday 7:45am-12:35pm. Schedules are available from the Tourist Bureau.

In addition to the problem of distance between Kalgoorlie and Coolgardie, the lack of public transport to most Kalgoorlie/Boulder attractions can be annoying. Hitching is fairly safe and a popular mode of transport, even for the locals. Bicycling is another option, though the long, dusty stretches can be pretty gruesome in mid-day. Rent bikes at **Johnston Cycles** (78 Boulder Rd., Kalgoorlie, phone 21-1157 or 21-2483). None of the car rental companies in Kalgoorlie has great prices. Standard fees run $70/day, plus an insurance and km charge. The cheapest rate we could find was a manual Mitsubishi from Hertz (360 Hannan St., phone 21-4685) for $45/day plus insurance.

Tom Neacy's **Goldfield Adventure Tours**, run with YHA of W.A., is the least expensive tour and is probably the best way to get around and see everything, especially if you don't have private transport. His "Goldfields Highlight Tour" starts in Coolgardie and takes two days. For more information, ask at the tourist office or the YHA hostel. **Goldrush Tours** (Palace Chambers, Maritana St., Kalgoorlie, phone 21-2954) runs half-day tours every day for $20/person.

Accommodation

Dirt-cheap accommodation isn't available in Kalgoorlie, but there's a great YHA hostel in Coolgardie. Most licensed hotels in Kalgoorlie offer budget B&B accommodation for around $24/single and $40/double. There are plenty to choose from: **The Union** (1 Macdonald St., phone 21-1749), **The Grand** (Hannan St., phone 21-2353), **The Piccadilly** (164 Piccadilly St., phone 21-2109), **The Kalgoorlie** (319 Hannan St., phone 21-3046), and **The York Hotel** (the most civilized of the lot; 259 Hannan St., phone 21-2337).

Most of the caravan parks offer on-site vans or self-contained chalets and camping space, though many are already occupied by miners. Laundry facilities aren't provided in any of the hotels or the youth hostel, and only the hostel has private cooking facilities.

Surrey House, 9 Boulder Rd. (phone 21-1340). $25/single, $48/double. Very clean. Friendly management. Common room with TV. Breakfast available. Has many faithful clientele, so book ahead.

Goldminer Caravan Park, Great Eastern Hwy., Kalgoorlie (phone 21-3713). On-site caravans and vans, $30. Campsites $5/person.

Kalgoorlie Village Caravan Park, Burt St., Boulder (phone 21-4780). $20-$40/caravan. Campsites $5/person.

YHA Coolgardie, 56-60 Gnarlbine Rd., Coolgardie (phone 26-6051). Two blocks down Hunt Rd. from Bayley St., on the right. $8/night. Formerly the stationmaster's residence, now classified by the National Trust. Clean. Huge dining room and communal areas, with working fireplaces. Bathrooms in separate house at rear. Use washing machines at nearby caravan park. Book ahead Sept-Jan.

The Lodge, Bayley St., Coolgardie (phone 26-6166). $20/single, $30/double.

Things to See and Do

Your best introduction to Kalgoorlie is a walk down its wide, tree-lined streets. Poke your head into the restored stone hotels, and don't miss the **Town Hall** at the corner of Hannan & Wilson Sts., built in 1903. It has a Victorian-style auditorium with an intricate metal ceiling, a small art museum on the first floor, the original Paddy Hannan statue, and the Council Chamber upstairs. Check at the entrance for entertainment listings. (Open M-F, 9:00am-4:00pm.)

Ex-miners lead 90 minute tours through the **Hainault Gold Mine** in Boulder. Deep in its recesses, the mine is still in use, though the part you tour closed years ago. Tours run four times a day and cost $8 (call 93-1065 for tour times). To get there, take the bus to Boulder, then make the lengthy walk to the mine: Go east on Burt St., turn left at the end, and follow until the turn-off for the mine appears on the right.

The place to find a true slice of Kalgoorlie is out at the **Two-Up**, 5 km north on the road to Leonora (no public transport). Two Up, a gambling game which originated in the convict days, has been played in Kalgoorlie since the 1890's, although it wasn't legalized until 1983. A more civilized version is played in all the Aussie casinos. The game is simple: Two coins are tossed in the air and gamblers bet whether they'll land two heads or two tails. If it's a "split," the coins are thrown again. Participants sit inside a circular, roofless, iron shed watching the "spinner" toss the coins high into the sky, often betting hundreds of dollars. It's played daily 2:00pm- sunset except on miners' payday (every other Fri), when gambling is illegal.

Kalgoorlie's **Golden Mile Museum** (Outridge Tce.) is open daily 10:30am-4:00pm. Formerly the British Arms Hotel, it now houses a collection of mining artifacts and early 1900's relics. The School of Mines' **Geology Museum** (corner Egan & Cassidy Sts.) is open 9:00am-5:00pm M-F. It has an extensive mineral and gemstone display, with models of famous, locally-discovered nuggets. Fans of American Presidential trivia should note: Herbert Hoover caught gold fever in the late 1890's and came to Kalgoorlie to seek his fortune. His former residence on Elizabeth St. can be viewed only from the outside.

World War I had an enormous effect on the goldfields. Thousands of men left the mines to fight, and many mines closed for good. The **Goldfields War Museum** in the Boulder Tourist Bureau has an extensive display covering war history from the Boer War to Vietnam (open M-F 9:00am-4:15pm; Sat 9:00am-11:30am).

Coolgardie, 40 km west of Kalgoorlie, is the best place to experience the bygone era. The grand buildings along the main street remain almost exactly as they were in its most prosperous times. There are a few old-timers around who love to tell stories—the YHA manager can help you meet them. The **Goldfields Exhibition** (in the Tourist Bureau, Bayley St.; admission $3) is a comprehensive collection of the goldfields' history and the life of the miner. The BBC's 35-minute film *Gold Fever* usually runs three times daily. Commissioned by the Government in 1895, **Warden Finnerty's Residence** (McKenzie St., near the YHA hostel) is now owned by the National Trust (open M-Sat, except Th, 1:00pm-4:00pm; Sun 10:00am-4:00pm; $3 admission).

The **Coolgardie Camel Farm** (phone 26-6159; open daily 9:00am-5:00pm), 4 km west of Coolgardie on Hwy. 94, offers short camel rides ($3), plus day and overnight treks ($18/hour to $60-$90/day). The farm also holds an annual camel race on the nearest long weekend to Sept 17 (Coolgardie's birthday).

Much of the red semi-desert surrounding the gold towns is currently being mined, but nature lovers can visit **Burra Nature Reserve**, a water catchment area with dense vegetation, and **Victoria Park**, the site of an unusual rock outcrop. For information, contact the CALM on Hannan St., Kalgoorlie (phone 21-2095; open M-F 8:00am-4:30pm). They'll point you in the right direction for other hiking areas as well.

Food
Your best bet for eating out is to join the miners and locals in a counter meal. Almost all the old hotels offer a standard counter meal (steaks, chicken, schnitzel, with salad and chips) for a standard price ($8-$12) at the standard times (lunch noon-2:00pm, dinner 6:00pm-8:00pm). There's a handful of hotels near the intersection of Hannan & Maritana Sts., including **The Exchange** (Boulder Rd.), **The Grand** (90 Hannan St.), and **The Criterion Hotel** (Hannan St.). In Coolgardie, try the **Denver City Hotel** (Bayley St.). **The Tower** (corner Bourke & Maritana Sts.) and **The Palace** (Maritana St.) serve meals after hours. There are also a few Chinese restaurants, pizza places, and health food cafes.

Nightlife and Entertainment
Nightlife centers around the pubs, most of which are surprisingly subdued for the Australian outback. Beer-swilling night is Friday, especially on payday. The Tower and Palace Hotels have dancing until the wee hours (unlike the other pubs). The Denver City Hotel in Coolgardie has American country-western music on weekends.

Kalgoorlie has three movie theaters: **Cremorne Cinema** (Hannan St., phone 21-5577), **Twin City Drive-In** (Thermott St., phone 21-1110), and **Viewway Drive-In** (Oswald St., phone 21-2199).

For special entertainment listings, check the lobby of Kalgoorlie's town hall.

Trips from Kalgoorlie

Mining is the name of the game in the region surrounding Kalgoorlie. Extending north to Leonora and Laverton and south to Norseman, dusty soil conceals rich ore and mineral deposits. The land is flat, broken only by low outcrops of granite, dunes of windblown sand, and clumps of spinifex grass, sandalwood, eucalypt, and wattle trees. In the spring (Sept-Oct), wildflower displays are phenomenal, especially after a good rain.

While the mining towns aren't too thrilling, traveling through the desert frontier can be both exciting and memorable. **Wave Rock**, a unique granite formation weathered into an enormous wave-like shape, is 450 km south-west of Kalgoorlie by road. The only public transport is from Perth. (See *Trips from Perth* for more information.)

Getting There

Deluxe, Greyhound, and Pioneer service Norseman and Kambalda. Bus Australia goes to Norseman only. There's a bus twice a week from Kalgoorlie to Leonora on Trans-Continental Coachlines, which continues to Perth.

Those traveling by car should pick up *Gold Rush Country* at Tourist Information in Kalgoorlie before taking off. It includes maps and road details, such as where to expect cattle barriers and dead ends.

Accommodation

Plan to stay in Kalgoorlie. There is, however, an interesting option at **Sturt Meadows Station**, 45 km northwest of Leonora. It's a 300,000 hectare sheep station with several types of accommodation, including cheap lodging in the shearers' quarters (20 km from the homestead). Call 090-37-6186 for more information. Closed April-May (shearing season).

Things to See and Do

The two places to see mining activity are **Kambalda**, a modern nickel-mining town 60 km south of Kalgoorlie, and **Norseman**, 190 km south of Kalgoorlie. There are free tours of **Western Mining's** operation at Norseman, available weekdays at 9:30am. Norseman's Tourist Office (74 Roberts St., phone 091-39-1071) will provide more information. The Tourist Office at Kambalda is open weekdays 9:00am-5:00pm (phone 090-27-1446).

About 100 km north of Kalgoorlie, **Leonora** and the adjoining, nearly-abandoned town of **Gwalia** have interesting remnants from the gold rush days. The **Sons of Gwalia Gold Mine**, created in 1896 and closed in 1963, was the largest W.A. mine outside the Golden Mile, and it's been left basically untouched. Herbert Hoover built the mine's headframe in 1898. The local **Historical Gallery** (and tourist information) in the old mine office is filled with mining memorabilia (phone 090-37-6014).

Tasmania

Tasmania is a study in contrasts. While its Old World flavor is reminiscent of Great Britain 70 years ago, the rugged wilderness defies attempts to civilize it.

Taswegians are conservative and clannish. Small farms, many of them in the same family since first settlement, form the basis of the state's economy (though tourism now rivals agriculture for jobs and dollars). Quaint stone cottages and Georgian-style estates dot the countryside, and locals observe the tradition of Devonshire tea in the late afternoon. The dairy industry makes a variety of great cheeses and milk products (don't miss King Island brie and clotted cream). Other food specialties include muttonbird, fresh water trout, trevally, and myriad types of seafood.

But the trappings of civilization cannot hide the fact that more than half of Tasmania is too mountainous for habitation. Vast tracts of wilderness comprise some of the most remote country in the world. The southwester corner of the state doesn't have a single town or road, just a few hiking trails accessible only by plane. Intrepid travelers with a bent for hiking, rafting, and exploration will be in their element.

While most of "Tassie" is an ideal balance of rolling farm country and dramatic mountain peaks, there are exceptions. The northern towns of Devonport, Launceston, and Burnie are polluted and industrialized. Copper mining and exploitation of Huon pine forests (a tree unique to Tasmania) have devastated large wilderness areas. To combat such destruction, groups like the Wilderness Society, which originated in Tasmania, have become increasingly active and effective, in Tassie and throughout the country.

The best thing about Tasmania is that none of the picture-postcard setting is for show. It's entirely genuine, hence you need not fear tacky commercialism or price-gouging. And although tourism is big money for Tassie, you're rarely aware of many other travelers.

Two important points to remember: Tasmania virtually closes on weekends. Don't arrive on a weekend without information or a place to stay. (Go to the Tasbureau in any major Australian city first for maps and bookings.) Second, bring warm clothes and rain gear no matter what season. If you plan to do any hiking, bring warm woollies including a hat and mittens. (Seriously!)

Another tip: You'll likely visit many historic spots since Tassie is full of them. Most are run by the National Trust, and if you visit three or more Na-

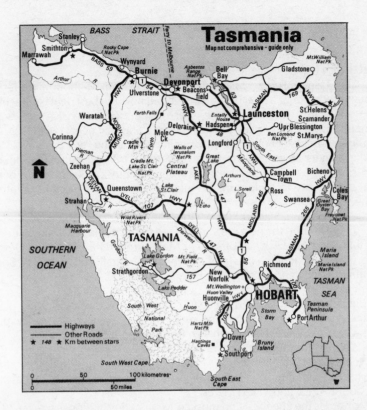

tional Trust homes and museums, you'll save money by buying a National Trust pass for Tasmania ($8). It's also cheaper to get a nationwide membership in Tassie than in other states (around $15).

When To Go
Weather is most reliable in February and March. Spring (Oct- Dec) and autumn (April-June) are beautiful times to visit—especially autumn because of the deciduous trees. Winter (June-Sept) is near freezing in most places. There's an occasional dusting of snow in Hobart and regular snow in the high mountains. Note that some hostels close in winter.

Itinerary
Tasmania is 300 km across at its widest, 290 km at its longest. You can get around the island in just a few days, though that would be skimping. Most hostellers stay two or three weeks and, if they take a hiking or rafting trip, a bit longer.

The best way to "do" Tassie is loop around the island with a few detours. If you stick to the outermost roads, the only section you'll miss is the inner midlands, an area with historic towns and small farms but not much in the way of things to do. Most people begin in the north (cheaper access than Hobart) and, depending on which town they start in (Devonport, Launceston, or Wynyard), head in a clockwise or counter-clockwise direction. This chapter is organized for a counter-clockwise loop.

Getting There

The **Abel Tasman Ferry** crosses the Bass Straight from Melbourne to Devonport. It used to offer a cheap sit-up ticket, but now the best deal is an economy berth. Fares vary according to season, the most expensive time being from mid-December to late January, when a one-way ticket costs $125. (It's considerably cheaper other times.) Bringing a car on the Ferry costs $90-$120. Students under 26 get 25% off with a university ID. Also, Deluxe, Greyhound, and the Ferry have cooperative deals when you buy a ticket from any mainland capital city to Melbourne on either busline and a Ferry ticket at the same time.

The Ferry leaves Station Pier, Melbourne three evenings a week and arrives in Devonport the next morning. Make reservations at Tasbureau or call the following Abel Tasman offices: in Melbourne, 03-645-2766; in Devonport, 004-27-9751; or toll-free from anywhere in Australia, 008-03-0344. Some Redline Coach services meet the Ferry en route to either Burnie/Wynyard, Launceston, or Hobart (check at Tasbureau before leaving).

Flights to Tasmania are dirt-cheap compared to other Australian plane routes. As long as the competition keeps up, flying will be the least expensive way to get there. Daily flights go from Melbourne to Wynyard, Devonport, Launceston, and Hobart; or from Sydney to Devonport, Launceston, or Hobart. East-West, Ansett, Air New South Wales, and Phillip Island Air Services are among the competitors. Consider going stand-by, and always ask about APEX and "Flexi" fares.

Wynyard is the cheapest and most convenient destination, since the YHA hostel is in walking distance of the airport. (Make sure to get Tasbureau's *Travelways* and a decent map before leaving, since there's not much information in Wynyard.) The cheapest flight currently is from Philip Island, Victoria, to Wynyard with Philip Island Air Services/Western Aviation.

You can also get to Hobart from New Zealand. Air New Zealand flies once a week from Christchurch; Qantas goes Auckland-Melbourne-Hobart, also once a week.

Getting Around

None of the big buslines operates in Tassie. **Redline Coaches** runs throughout most of the state; local bus companies service the east coast. It's all a very casual affair, with coaches doubling as school buses and mail trucks. Beware of weekends, when services are infrequent or non-existent.

The travel passes from Deluxe, Greyhound, and Pioneer include travel on Redline Coaches. You can buy a 14-day Tassie pass on Redline (which doesn't include the local buslines on the east coast), but unless you plan to backtrack or cover every inch of the state in a two-week period, the pass isn't worth it. Sector fares are cheap (the most expensive is about $30, from Queensown to Hobart) and it's easy to get rides with other travelers who have vehicles. Hitching is pretty good, but not as much of a cinch as everyone reports. One disadvantage to hitchhikers is frequent rain and cold.

Driving allows you to stop in all those quaint country towns ignored by the buses. Be prepared for lots of winding roads and hills and fewer safety barriers than you're probably used to. You'll need chains in the mountains in winter. Get maps and a touring guide from the **Royal Automobile Club of Tasmania**. In Hobart, corner Murray and Patrick Sts. (phone 002-38-2200); in Launceston, corner York and George Sts. (phone 003-31-3166); in Devonport, 5 Steele St. (phone 004-24-1806).

Information

The **Tasmanian Tourist Commission** ("**Tasbureau**") is the best of Australia's state tourist authorities. Knowledgeable and helpful, they're always aware of the budget traveler's needs. Pick up *Travelways*, their bimonthly newspaper that details everything, including bus schedules, hours, prices, and an exhaustive accommodation listing that even has some country pubs (only youth hostels aren't included).

Most Tassie towns have tourist information in local shops or town council offices, but YHA hostels usually have all the information you'll ever need. There's a *Let's Talk About...* pamphlet for every locale in the state, sometimes even a separate one for a specific sight within a town. Information inside includes a local map, comprehensive history, and sights, with no extra gloss or promotional jargon.

Accommodation

Backpackers Hostels have yet to infiltrate Tasmania, which leaves YHA the only hostel option (with one or two exceptions). Their network is comprehensive and for the most part good quality. Generally, hostels are closed from 10:00am-5:00pm, and there's supposedly a three-day limit, but the rule is rarely enforced. You'll find yourself hoarding 10-cent coins because their showers are coin-operated—annoying but necessary to ensure hot water for everyone. Hostel reservations aren't usually necessary. Note that some hostels close in winter (June-Sept).

Tasmania is the only Australian state that has Bed & Breakfasts everywhere, and they're a terrific deal. Some are hotels or inns, others are farm accommodation. A night at one is well worth the splurge if you pick your place carefully.

History

Founded in 1803 and declared a colony in 1825, Tasmania was settled just 15 years after the arrival of the First Fleet in Sydney Cove. Dutch explorer Abel Tasman discovered the island in 1642 and called it Van Dieman's Land in honor of the Governor General of the Dutch East Indies. It wasn't until 1772 that Europeans again visited Tasmania, and between then and 1803 several well-known explorers paid visits, most notably Cook (1777), Bligh (1788 and 1792), and the French explorers La Perouse and d'Entrecasteaux.

The Britiish instigated the settlement of Tasmania when they became anxious about possible French claims. In 1803, Lt. John Bowen sailed up the Derwent River with 49 others (35 of whom were convicts) and established a settlement which he named Hobart Town.

Between 1803-1853, over 69,000 convicts were transported from Britain to Van Dieman's Land, almost as many as to New South Wales. An equal number of free settlers arrived to take up pastoral leases for grain and sheep farms or to take advantage of sealing and whaling opportunities. In the early 1840's, the number of transported convicts increased, resulting in an over-abundance of labor. Subsequent unrest led to the anti-transportation movement, and in 1853 convict transportation to Tasmania ended.

Tasmanian Aborigines are almost certainly not of Melanesian origin as was once believed. Scientists postulate that the Tasmanian landmass separated from Australia 12,000 years ago, allowing the native people to evolve differently than the people of the mainland. European contact with the natives was brutal and, ultimately, fatal. Aborigines first were driven off their traditional hunting grounds and randomly killed. In 1828, full-fledged war began on them and by 1834, the 200 remaining natives were rounded up and taken to Flinders Island, where most died. They were eventually moved to Oyster Cove near Hobart, and the last native Tasmanian, Truganini (a.k.a. "Fanny Cochraine Smith"), died in 1876.

Among the atrocities committed during those years was the enslavement of Aborigine women by sealers; ironically, many of the part-Aborigines remaining—about 4,000 in all—are descendants of those forced unions.

There are two museums where you can learn about Tasmanian Aborigines. For a description of their traditional culture, visit **Tiagarra** in Devonport. A chronology and display about European contact is in the **Tasmanian Museum** in Hobart.

The Devil and the Tiger
The **Tasmanian Devil**, a rat-like marsupial carnivore distinguished by huge, vicious fangs, has become a symbol of Tasmania. You've most likely seen it before in a Bugs Bunny cartoon, but the real thing doesn't look or act at all like its cartoon version.

The **Tasmanian Tiger**, a wolf-like marsupial, is probably extinct. The last known Tiger in captivity died in 1936. A law protecting the animal was passed in 1938, probably not in time to save the few that remained. There are occasional unconfirmed sightings.

For the Intrepid

Spectacular wilderness areas are Tasmania's greatest draw, and it would be a travesty to visit without enjoying some kind of outdoor experience, whether it's a day's walk around the Tasman Peninsula or a two-week rafting adventure down the Franklin River.

This section is designed for those with special interests or expertise. Standard day-long excursions are covered by locale along with other things to see and do. Get all your information and equipment in Hobart, Launceston, or Devonport. Maps, transport, and supplies are rarely available in rural regions.

Hiking
There are day and overnight hikes wherever you go in Tasmania, the best time being December to late March. The most famous and most popular hike is the **Overland Track** from Cradle Mountain to Lake St. Clair. The walk

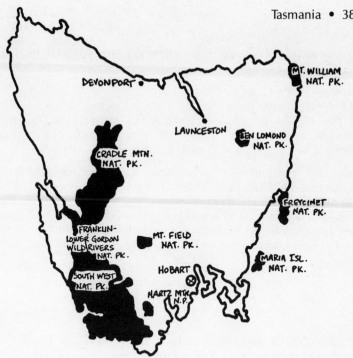

to **Frenchman's Cap** (Franklin-Lower Gordon Wild Rivers National Park) and the **Southwest Coastal trek** in Southwest National Park are other favorites. *100 Walks in Tasmania* by Tyrone Thomas is the bushwalkers' bible, available at sporting goods shops and newsstands.

Even for short walks, be wary of changing weather and deep mud. Snow sometimes falls in the mountains during mid-summer—often when you least expect it—so carry wool socks, pants, and top, thermal underwear, mittens, hat, and sturdy rain gear. Tasmania's mud requires about double the normal energy output of hikers, and a slip in the sludge is no joke with a heavy pack. Also, expect leeches! They're ugly but painless and easily removed with salt.

The following are essential hikers' resources:

The Wilderness Society, 130 Davey St., Hobart, Tas., 7000; phone 002-34-9366. They also have a shop in Hobart at the Galleria Arcade on Salamanca Place, an office in Launceston (76 Wellington St., phone 003-31-3999), and a shop in Devonport (31 Stewart St., phone 004-24-7393). The Society provides the best trail maps and trail notes, as well as guidebooks. Membership makes you eligible for their many treks, which last one to several days and are always great. Take a look at the Society's magazine *Wild* for an idea of the trips.

National Parks and Wildlife. In Hobart, 16 Magnet Court, Sandy Bay, Tas., 7005 (phone 002-30-2620); in Launceston, Prospect House, Bass Hwy., Prospect (phone 003-41-5312). Information on all National Parks, including how to prepare, how to get there, where to register, etc. Ask for their pamphlet *Safety in the Bush*.

Tasmap, Hobart Lands Bldg., 134 Macquarie St., Hobart (phone 002-30-3382); or Henty House, 1 Civic Square, Launceston (phone 003-32-2339). Tasmap produces topographical maps covering the entire state (about $6 each). The above addresses carry full stock. The most popular maps are also available at Tasmap in Devonport (64 Best St.).

Equipment rental/sales *in Hobart*: **Scout Outdoor Shop**, 107 Murray St. (phone 002-34-3885); **Paddy Pallin**, 32 Criterion St. (phone 31-0777); **The Jolly Swagman**, 107 Elizabeth St. (phone 34-3999). *In Devonport*: **Stafford's Bushwalkers Transport**, 12 Edward St. (phone 004-92-3167). *In Launceston*: **YHA Launceston**, 36 Thistle St., S. Launceston (phone 003-44-9779). It's a good idea to reserve equipment, especially in summer.

While there are huts on most major trails in Tassie, you'll always need a tent in case of over-crowding or emergencies. Wood is provided in some huts, but you must have a gas stove for camping because open fires are strictly prohibited. The three major hikes in Tassie are discussed below.

Cradle Mountain-Lake St. Clair: The Overland Track

This 80 km walk takes you through rugged mountain country, moors, and high mountain lakes with several optional side-trips. It's a minimum five-day trip, but allow seven. About 30 hikers start out each day in high season (Christmas-late January), most from the Cradle Mountain end. Maps are available from the ranger stations at either end or Tasmap, and trail registration costs about $10/person. For further information, call the ranger at Cradle Valley (phone 003-65-5187).

Access to the Cradle Mountain end is available from Devonport or Launceston. From Launceston there's a **Bushwalkers Transport** shuttle twice daily from Dec 1-Feb 28 for about $25. It leaves from 12 Edward St. (phone 004-92-3167) and will pick you up from the airport or Abel Tasman Ferry. From Launceston, **Mountain Stage Line** (10 Suffolk St., phone 003-34-0442) runs daily from Dec 1-March 30 for about the same price. Both companies will transport excess luggage to the other end, and both offer limited shuttle service during the off-season.

Some hikers begin at the Lake St. Clair end of the trail, best accessible from Hobart. **Bushwalkers Transport** at 28 Criterion St., Hobart (phone 002-34-2226) goes every other day in summer and costs around $25. The cheaper option is **Redline Coaches** from Hobart to Derwent Bridge (Lake St. Clair is a 5.5 km walk from there). The service runs between Hobart and Derwent Bridge once a day Mon-Sat.

Frenchman's Cap

At 1443 meters, Frenchman's Cap is the highest peak on the west coast and certainly the most distinctive. Its southeast face has a 300 meter vertical drop, while the summit always appears snow-covered because it's made of quartzite, which glimmers white in the sun. The 27 km walk takes you from the Lyell Highway at Collingwood River to the summit. You can make the trip in two days, but it usually takes longer. It's a tough, muddy, steep hike, and the area is subject to extreme temperature changes and heavy rainfall.

Register at **Collingwood River Station**, a three-hour drive northwest of Hobart. For transport, call Bushwalkers (above). Redline Coaches will sometimes drop you at Collingwood along the Hobart-Queenstown route, though there's no official stop. For further details on the hike, call the ranger at 004-71-1446.

Southwest National Park

Southwest National Park takes up a staggering 6% of the total area of Tasmania. One of the few large temperate-zone wilderness areas left in the world, most of it remains inaccessible to the casual traveler. You can get a glimpse at Lake Pedder, but only highly experienced outdoorspeople can see the rest of the park. Those who have the ability and who are eager to conquer new frontiers should get a hold of *Southwest Tasmania Bushwalker's Guide* by John Chapman. Maps are available at Tasmap only, no trail notes included.

The Park's **South Coast Track**—the third most popular walk in the state—is an arduous six-day hike through bogs and beaches, plus a tough section through the Ironbound Range. The 100 km trail begins at Cockle Creek (two-hour drive south of Hobart) and finishes at Melaleuca Inlet on Port Davey, where you either fly out or walk another eight days (!) to Scott's Peak near Lake Pedder. Par Avion or Tas Air can pick you up or fly supplies in. Contact **Bushwalkers Transport** for flight details. There is no resident ranger, so register at the local police station. Information is available from the **Mt. Field Ranger Station** (phone 002-88-1283).

Rafting

The **Franklin River**, Tassie's most famous whitewater rafting venue, is not a challenge most people take without a guide. Four days with a guide costs around $700, the full 16-day trip about $1600—not exactly affordable for most budget travelers, but an incredible experience nonetheless. Those interested should contact the following tour operators:

World Expeditions, 317 Sussex St., Sydney, NSW 2000 (phone 02-264-3366).

Tasmanian Rafters, PO Box 89, Huonville, Tas. 7109 (phone 002-95-1573).

Open Spaces, 28 Criterion St., Hobart, Tas. 7000 (phone 002-31-0977).

Collingwood, where the course begins, is a three-hour drive northwest of Hobart. Experienced rafters can get information on doing the trip unaided from the ranger at Collingwood, PO Box 21, Queenstown, Tas., 7467 (phone 004-71-1446). The ranger will also tell you current river conditions. The Wilderness Society has the best map and river notes, plus they rent equipment. It's not uncommon to get hot weather followed quickly by freezing conditions and snow, even in summer.

The **Picton River**, southwest of Hobart, is an excellent alternative to the Franklin, and its guided trips are a lot cheaper. Tasmanian Rafters offers special deals through the Cygnet YHA hostel, and they lead trips on both the Huon and Picton Rivers. Day trips cost $65, weekend trips $160. Open Spaces offers similar trips.

The rafting season in Tasmania starts around November and ends in April. Be sure to bring sturdy rain gear and woolens.

Biking

For trekkers with plenty of time and stamina, biking is a great way to see the state. The east coast is especially well-cycled because the terrain is gentler (though still mountainous) and the hostel system extensive. Not that cycling anywhere in Tassie is easy: between the hills, head winds, and mud, it takes determination to keep peddling. The best time to go is between early November and late March.

Doug Snare, the manager of Launceston's YHA hostel, rents bikes suited to Tasmanian conditions, with most equipment included in the price plus some instruction and travel advice (about $55/first week, $45/second week, $30/week thereafter; or $10/day, plus deposit). Whether you pass through Launceston or not, you could benefit from writing Doug with specific cycling questions. Write him care of **Rent-a-Cycle**, 36 Thistle St., South Launceston, Tas., 7249; phone 003-44-9779.

Cycle rental and some trekking equipment is also available in Devonport at **Hire-a-Bike**, 51 Raymon St. (phone 004-24-3889). A trip around the whole state takes 14-28 days; the east coast 10-14 days. Redline Coaches will send your bike ahead of you for a small fee. Biking enthusiasts who hesitate to jump into an adventure alone should look into cycle tours with **Brake Out**, based in Hobart (P.O. Box 275, Sandy Bay, Tas., 7005; phone 002-23-7020). Brochures are available from Tasbureau.

Skiing

Don't come to Tasmania just to ski, because adequate snow cover is never a given. Slopes range from beginner to intermediate, and downhill skiing is cheaper than in mainland Australia. There are two downhill locations: **Mt. Field National Park** (access from Hobart) and **Ben Lomond National Park** (access from Launceston). Ski rental is available at both.

Ben Lomond is the favored area, with seven tows but no mountain accommodation, and there's a daily bus in winter from Launceston. Direct questions to the Ben Lomond Park Ranger at 003-90-6279 or Tasbureau in Launceston. There's excellent cross-country skiing at **Cradle Mountain** June-October. Ben Lomond also has cross-country trails.

Fishing

Tassie is famous for trout fishing, especially at **Great Lake** and neighboring smaller lakes throughout the state's central plateau east of Cradle Mountain. Check Tasbureau in Launceston for information on renting equipment.

Several fishing guides are available in the Launceston area. In Hobart, the **Inland Fisheries Commission** (127 Davey St.) sells fishing licenses and can give you advice on sites. Fishing equipment and boats are available at **Lake Pedder** near Strathgordon (160 km northwest of Hobart). Contact the **Lake Pedder Motor Inn** at 002-80-1166.

Devonport

Tasbureau, corner Rooke and King Sts., phone 004-24-1526. Open M-F 8:45am-5:00pm, Sat 9:00am-11:00pm.

Devonport isn't worth more than a night's visit, and you might as well leave immediately if you arrive from the mainland in the morning. Passengers on the Abel Tasman Ferry can take Morses Coach into town for $1. There's no public transport from the airport; a cab costs about $10.

There is one worthwhile stop in Devonport: **Tiagarra**, on Mersey Bluff (a nice walk from town), houses the most extensive display in the state on Tasmanian Aboriginal culture, and though the sound effects and dioramas border on tacky, you can still learn a lot (admission $2.50). A map at the museum details rock engravings at various sites around Mersey Bluff, one of 13 places where Aboriginal art has been found in Tasmania.

Devonport is the best jumping-off point for Cradle Mountain. From Dec 1-Feb 28, **Cradle Mountain Coach Service** offers a daily hikers' shuttle for $25/one-way from 12 Edward St. (phone 24-3628). They'll provide transport at other times of the year on request. They'll also pick you up from the Ferry or airport. The other option for reaching Cradle Mountain is to rent a car. **Lo-Cost Car Rental** on King St. charges about $20/day plus insurance. Devonport is a good place to rent bicycles and equipment for cycle-touring. Try **Hire-a-Bike** at 52 Raymon St. (phone 24-3889). They have 10-speeds, with packs included.

Accommodation: Be sure to make accommodation and other arrangements ahead of time if you're arriving on a weekend.

The Devonport YHA hostel is called **MacWright House**, 115 Middle Rd. (phone 004-24-5696).

There are plenty of cheap guest houses, the least expensive being the **Trade Winds** (44 McFie St., phone 004-24-1719). It's not your typical quaint B&B (the place is covered with fake flowers and plastic trinkets), but the rooms are large and clean. The **River View Lodge** at 18 Victoria Pde. (phone 004-24-7357), with a view of the Mersey River, has friendly owners and is charming inside.

On-site caravans are available at the **Devonport Caravan Park** on Caroline St. (phone 004-27-8886) and the **Abel Tasman Caravan Park** at 6 Wright St. (phone 004-27-8794). Both are in East Devonport near the ferry terminal.

Getting There: The **Redline Coach** terminal is at 9 Edward St. (phone 24-2685). Buses arrive in Devonport from Hobart five times daily M-F and twice a day on weekends (a five-hour trip). Bus service from Wynyard takes about two hours and runs M-Sat (Sunday from Burnie only). There are services from Deloraine and Launceston every day. Some services to and from Hobart and Launceston (via Deloraine) meet the Abel Tasman Ferry.

Cradle Mountain

Even non-hikers should get up to Cradle Mountain for a view of the lake and heathland scenery. There are several walks of varying lengths around and near Lake Dove, at the foot of Cradle Mountain. Don't forget to bring warm clothes (in all seasons—it's been known to snow in January), sturdy shoes, and rain gear (it rains nearly every day). Be prepared for mud. Cross-country skiing is excellent there in winter.

The **Pencil Pine Lodge** is the first building you hit at the end of the 95 km road from Devonport. Once you've had your exercise, the lodge is a pleasant place to relax with a pricey Devonshire tea, consisting of a large pot of tea and two giant scones. There's a big open fireplace and an alpine lodge atmosphere. Three km up the road is the ranger station, campground, and beginning of several walks. Get a map from the ranger and be sure to sign in, even for day hikes.

Cradle Mountain is the beginning of the Overland Track (see *Hiking* above for more information), and Devonport is the best access point. Cabins at Cradle Mtn. are nearly impossible to get unless you book in advance, but a new facility is being built that should alleviate the problem. Call the park office in Sheffield at 003-63-5187.

Tasmania's Northwest

Tourist information available at Council Chambers, Saunders St., Wynyard; Tasbureau, 48 Cattley St., Burnie; Seaview Motel, Boat Harbour; and souvenir shops in Stanley.

The historic town of Stanley, the scenic coast, and the unusually warm and welcoming locals are all compelling reasons to visit this quiet farming district with hill after hill of cultivated fields that create a lush patchwork of chocolate-colored soil and verdant pastures. Wynyard should be your jumping-off point for the surrounding region of Burnie, Stanley, and coastal areas in between. (It's 72 km between Burnie and Stanley.)

Getting There and Getting Around: Redline Coaches has weekday service to Burnie, Wynyard, and Smithton from Hobart, Launceston, and Queenstown. Weekend services go to Burnie only. (Burnie terminal is at 117 Wilson St., phone 004-31-2660.) To get to Wynyard from the west coast, transfer in Burnie; to head west, get the first morning service from Wynyard to Burnie, then transfer. Wynyard is a 1.5 hour ride west of Devonport. There is no local public transport and hitching is possible, though not reliable.

Accommodation: The **Wynyard YHA hostel** (phone 004-42-2013) is at 36 Dodgin St., three blocks east of the airport, and costs $8/night. There's another YHA hostel in the **Stanley Caravan Park** (phone 58-1266). On-site vans are also available at the park (about $22/2 people).

A more expensive but great option (especially if you get a group together) is to stay in a cottage on Christine and Rodney Medwin's farm **Gateforth**, 12 km east of Stanley on Boyndey Rd., Black River (phone 58-3230). The

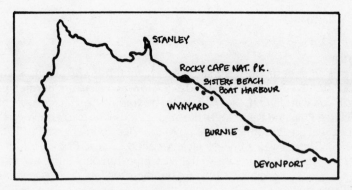

Medwins were among the first settlers in the area, and they're welcoming and informative. The cottage has all cooking needs, a trout-stocked pond, and a beautiful view of the rolling hills and ocean. Overnight cost is $50/couple, $10 each extra person (up to 6). No public transport is available to Gateforth.

The Coast West of Wynyard

Just 7 km from Wynyard is **Fossil Bluff**, named for the fossils of a giant wombat, giant kangaroo, and marsupial rhinoceros discovered in the limestone. Fossil Bluff is overshadowed by **Table Cape**, which gives a more commanding view of the coastline and has an old lighthouse at its tip.

About 14 km further west is the turnoff for **Boat Harbour** and **Sisters Beach**, with a gorgeous drive to the ocean along pastures bordering the water. Head straight for Sisters Beach, a beautiful white beach interrupted by craggy rock outcrops. Near the western end are two caves once inhabited by Aborigines. There's a bird sanctuary among the beachside cabins on Wattle Ave. (open Mon-Sat).

Those looking for good walks should head straight for **Rocky Cape National Park**, 31 km west of Wynyard on a hilly cape. The plant life in the park is tremendous, with native orchids and many wildflowers. On **Flagpole Hill** you can visit two former Aborigine caves. There are several walking trails in and around the **Sisters Hills**, all of them clearly marked (get recommendations first from locals or stop at the **Seaway Motel** in Boat Harbour).

Stanley

The historic port of Stanley sits on Circular Head at the foot of a distinctive mountain called **The Nut**, which looks like a giant square-headed whale from afar, with sheer cliff-faces all around. A trail up the western side makes a circuit around the top, or you can take a chairlift from the same place ($5/one-way, $7/roundtrip).

After serving as headquarters for the Van Dieman's Land Co., Stanley developed as a port for whalers and shippers of goods to the goldfields of Victoria. Most historic buildings can be viewed only from the exterior, but if you call ahead it's possible to get a tour through most of them. Call **Ruth Eslake** at 58-1309, or reach her at the Old Commercial Hotel, 28 Church St. (cost is about $4). Otherwise, take yourself around using *Let's Talk about Circular Head* as a reference. There are also some expensive craft shops to browse and quaint tea rooms for afternoon relaxation.

Burnie

Burnie is an undesirable destination except for those with an interest in local industry. The stench that pervades the town comes from Burnie's paper mills. If you can stand it, the mills might be your first visit. Free tours of the **Associated Pulp and Paper Mills**, the largest industry in town, run Mon-Thurs and begin at the Personnel Office on Marine Tce. (book by calling 31-1222, ext. 235). There's also a cheese factory called **Lactose Pty.** on Old Surrey Rd., a few km south of the Bass Highway. Tours run only once a week, and you must book ahead (call 31- 2566), but there are free tastings anytime on weekdays.

If you are stuck in town with nothing to do, go to the **Pioneer Village Museum** next to the Civic Plaza in High St. It has simulations of pioneer-era stores and businesses as well as old letters, photographs, and other documents that concern early Tasmania. (Open Mon-Fri 10:00am-5:00pm, Sat 1:30pm-5:00pm; admission $3.50.)

Strahan

The only town on Tasmania's western shores, Strahan provides the best access to the state's remote and mountainous "wild west" coast. The untamed splendor of this area is unique and formidable. Ironically, just 40 km inland, the mining operations at Queenstown and Zeehan have destroyed the ecological balance in surrounding regions, polluting rivers and creating an eyesore in the hills.

Most Aussies go to Strahan for a cruise on the **Gordon River** and find it disappointing "unless you're into seeing a lot of trees." However, conservationists covet the Huon pines you'll cruise past, since they are some of the last remaining large tracts of Huon forest.

There are several things to do besides the cruise in Strahan, and a short trip there is worthwhile if only to get a glimpse of the forest wilderness and pounding ocean, which flows unimpeded to South America.

Strahan is best known for its proximity to the worst penal colony in Australia, the **Sarah Island Settlement**, where the toughest criminals from Hobart were condemned. They were subjected to brutal treatment and in turn committed some horrific murders and violence. If you're curious, read *For the Term of His Natural Life* by Marcus Clarke (or see the silent movie at Port Arthur) or Richard Butler's *The Men That God Forgot*, based on a true story of mutiny aboard the *Frederick*.

There are two choices for exploring the area: river cruises and seaplane flights. If you've got the money, go for the plane. You'll fly over Queenstown, Sarah Island, and Hell's Gates, around Frenchman's Cap, and land on the Gordon River. Flights are 80 minutes and cost $90 (call **Wilderness Air** at 004-71- 7280).

Half-day **cruises** run up the Gordon River and around Macquarie Harbor for a look at Hell's Gates and Sarah Island. They depart the main dock at 9:00am, returning at 1:30pm. The advantage of a full-day cruise (9:00am-3:30pm) is that you also see Sir John Falls and stop at Sarah Island to walk among remains of the penal settlement ($30/half-day, $34/full-day;

10% discount for YHA members; call ahead at 004-71-7187). The cruise office sells a brochure on the settlement ruins and recounts sensational tales of attempted escapes. Another option for seeing Sarah Island is to get a fisherman to take you over.

The nearest ocean access is 6 km west of town, where you'll best get a sense of the rugged coastal isolation. A more popular spot on the shore is 12 km north of town, where huge sand dunes are especially stunning at sunset. The YHA hostel manager sometimes takes people there for a small fee. The manager will also drive you to the **King River**, where you'll see how pollution from the Queenstown mine has transformed life on the river.

Getting There: The limited schedule of buses to Strahan is such that if you're planning on a cruise or flight, you have to stay two nights (arrive in the afternoon, take tours the next day, leave early the following morning). Redline Coaches goes Mon-Sat mornings from Hobart to Queenstown (6 hrs.), where you transfer to their shuttle for the one hour ride to Strahan. They also go from the north coast (Burnie) to Queenstown Mon-Sat mornings (5 hour trip). Travelers from Smithton or Wynyard can hook up by taking the earliest morning service (Mon-Fri only). There's no direct transfer from Devonport.

Accommodation: Unfortunately, the **Strahan YHA-Associate hostel** on Harvey St. is cramped and run by a rather unpleasant man. Don't even think about having a glass of wine with dinner (absolutely no alcohol allowed on the premises) or going to bed after 11:00pm. Cost is $8/night, $10/non-YHA members, and you should definitely book ahead (phone 004-71-7255).

Alternatively, the **Strahan Lodge** on Ocean Beach Rd. (phone 004-71-7142) is about $25/night, $14 each extra person.

Queenstown to Hobart: Along the Lyell Highway

The most important things to see along this diverse stretch of road are two national parks, **Cradle Mountain-Lake St. Clair** and **Franklin-Lower Gordon Wild Rivers** National Parks, both accessible from the highway. Drivers should get the highway pamphlet from the Wilderness Society, with detailed notes about the sights and several short walks. (Pamphlet is also available at tourist information centers.)

Queenstown

You'll know when you've arrived at Queenstown because the surrounding mountains are various hues of pink and orange. According to legend, the exposed quarries were once a great tourist attraction because no vegetation would grow on the toxic soil. But when weeds and seedlings started to appear, the locals poisoned them to keep the tourist trade going!

Since 1893, the **Mt. Lyell Mining and Railway Corp.** has gutted the Queenstown hills for copper. Mining is the only purpose of this one-company town, and one gets the impression that residents' values have atrophied after a century of virtual isolation. You probably don't want to stay the night.

However, the tour of the mines will be of great interest to those with a metallurgic bent. The emphasis is historic, and you ride a bus around past and present mining sights. Tours cost $5, last 1.5 hours, and depart from **Farmers Carpark** twice daily Mon-Fri from Oct-May. You can drive yourself around the mines at 9:15am and 4:00pm any day ($4/person).

If you want to stay, go to the **Mountain View Holiday Lodge and Caravan Park** on Penganah Rd., where dorm rooms are $8.50/night and cabins are $30/couple (phone 004-71-1163 or 71-1332). (See *Strahan* for transport to Queenstown).

Franklin-Lower Gordon Wild Rivers National Park
The drive between Queenstown and Derwent Bridge takes you through Franklin-Lower Gordon Wild Rivers National Park. The park has two major attractions: the **Franklin River**, world famous for whitewater rafting, and **Frenchman's Cap**, distinguished by an awesome cliff on the east side of its summit.

The hike to Frenchman's Cap and back (two-five days) is the second most popular in Tasmania (see *For the Intrepid* above for more details on rafting and the Frenchman's Cap hike). For a short walk, look for **Donaghy's Hill Wilderness Lookout Walk**, posted from the road. The 20-minute walk reveals a spectacular panorama of the Franklin River Valley and Frenchman's Cap.

Lake St. Clair
Lake St. Clair, formed by a glacier and surrounded by craggy mountains, is famous for its beauty and great depth—it's so deep that the water temperature never gets above 5 °C (40 °F). The lake marks one end of the Cradle Mtn.-Lake St. Clair Overland Track, a walk that draws hikers from all over the world (see *Hiking* above). Just 5.5 km off the Lyell Hwy. from Derwent Bridge, it's an easy stop and well worth it, even if you just feed the brown wallabies and breathe the fresh mountain air. A taxi meets the Redline bus at Derwent Bridge ($5 fare to the Visitors Area).

There are a few walking trails from the Visitors Area, the longest being four hours. Ask the ranger in the main kiosk for information. Although there are no boat or water ski rentals, you can get onto the lake on the **bushwalkers launch** if there are enough people (it runs on demand). A 1.5-hour ride costs about $17/person.

Rustic log cabins amid lakeside woods fit the alpine atmosphere perfectly. It's nearly impossible to get a space on weekends and holidays, and advance bookings in summer are essential. But staying there at other times is possible and worthwhile. The most basic accommodation is the **bushwalkers cabin**—$7/night for a mattress and use of the showers and bathrooms. There are no utensils provided and cooking is done in the fireplace. (In summer, this option is available only to hikers on the Overland.) The other cabins cost about $10/person, and prices range from $20-$40 if you want a cabin to yourself. Book through Tasbureau or call the ranger in charge at 002-89-1115. There is also a campground.

Hamilton

A historic, quaint village in the heart of hops-growing and sheep-grazing country, Hamilton is a charming place to sip tea, eat scones, and browse through local craft shops. It is one of Tasmania's earliest towns, an offshoot of Hobart.

If you have your heart set on experiencing a Tassie B&B, Hamilton's the place. There are a few little inns and guest houses along the main road. Try the **Hamilton Inn** on Tarleton St. (phone 002-86-3204) or the **Old School House** on Lyell Hwy. (phone 86-3292).

Redline's Hobart-Queenstown service takes 1.5 hours from Hobart.

Hobart

At first glance, Hobart seems a world away from other Australian cities. Evidence of the past is everywhere, and although Sydney is a few years its senior, Hobart seems much older because there are few modern structures obstructing the historic originals. The population is rather old-fashioned, too. Generally, Hobart residents are staid and conservative, in keeping with their rural English roots.

A strong maritime tradition is integral to Hobart's ambiance, and the most important sailing event in Australia finishes at Sullivan's Cove in the city on New Year's Day each year. Aside from the crowds that gather for this event, known as the **Sydney-Hobart Regatta**, Hobart is surprisingly free of tourists and commercialism.

Getting There

Redline Coaches shuttles between Hobart and Launceston via the Midland Highway several times daily. The trip takes 2.5 hours express. The trip to Devonport takes 5 hours and runs on weekdays only; some Redline services pick up at the Abel Tasman Ferry in Devonport. Queenstown, on the west coast, is a 6-hour trip from Hobart. The service runs once a day, except Sunday.

Several domestic airlines fly to Hobart from Sydney and Melbourne. Air New Zealand and Qantas have direct service from New Zealand. Redline Coaches runs an airport shuttle to major hotels in town. If you need to get to the airport from town, the shuttle runs from the Redline Coaches terminal (call 34-4577 for information).

Orientation and Practical Information

Hobart lies on the western shore of the Derwent River, 20 km from its mouth. Bordered on the east by water and on the west by Mt. Wellington, the suburbs spread north in a narrow strip, as well as south and across to the Derwent's eastern shore. The downtown area lies behind Sullivan's Cove, with Elizabeth Street Mall and Franklin Square as the main areas of activity. Franklin Wharf is where all ships dock (and have for 150 years), and the main government buildings lie south of the wharf. The historic section of town, Battery Point, is on the south side of Sullivan's Cove.

It's nearly impossible to do any shopping or get anywhere during the

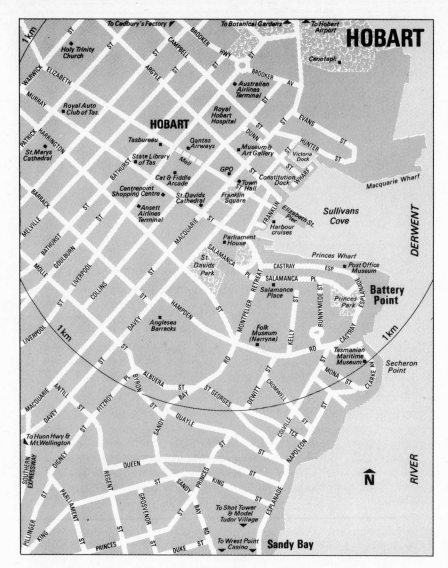

weekend in Hobart. Even on Saturday, few shops are open—though thankfully there's late-night shopping (until 9:00pm) Thursday and Friday and a large outdoor market Saturday morning at Salamanca Place.

Important Addresses and Phone Numbers (Area Code 002)

Tasbureau, 80 Elizabeth St. Mall (phone 30-0211). Information and bookings for city and Tasmania. Free city maps. Very helpful staff. Open M-F 8:45am-5:30pm, Sat-Sun 8:45am-11:00am.

General Post Office, corner Elizabeth & Macquarie Sts. (phone 34-6267).

American Express, Webster Travel, 60 Liverpool St., GPO Box 333D, Hobart, Tas., 7000 (phone 38-0200).

YHA of Tasmania, 28 Criterion St. (phone 34-9617). Bookings for all Tasmanian YHA hostels. Information on wilderness adventures. Open M-F 10:00am-5:00pm.

National Parks and Wildlife, 134 Macquarie St. (phone 30-8011).

Royal Automobile Club of Tasmania (R.A.C.), corner Murray and Patrick Sts. (phone 38-2200).

Redline Coaches, 96 Harrington St. (phone 34-4577). Timetables and bookings for state-wide coach travel. Airport shuttle service.

Glamorgan Coaches, phone 28-7530.

Hobart Coaches Pty. Ltd., 123 Murray St. (phone 34- 4077 or 43-8296). Service to Kettering (Bruny Island Ferry) and Dover (Huon Valley).

Tasmanian Motor Ways, 131 Collins St. (phone 23-8388). Service to Mt. Field National Park, New Norfolk, Port Arthur.

Australian Airlines, 4 Liverpool St. (phone 38-3511).

Ansett Airlines/Air New South Wales, 178 Liverpool St. (phone 38-0800).

East-West Airlines, 138 Collins St. (phone 38-0200).

Taxis, phone 34-3633, 23-7711, 34-8444.

Transportation
Hobart's comprehensive bus system will get you anywhere in the city and the suburbs, but beware of infrequent buses on the weekend. The Metropolitan Transport Trust of Tasmania sells a booklet with route details, including a city map with all departure points and a listing of tourist sites and how to reach them. Ask for *Hobart Bus Timetables* at the City Depot on the corner of Macquarie & Campbell Sts. All buses depart from the area around the General Post Office. In general, buses run M-Th 6:00am-midnight, F-Sat until 12:30am for inner suburbs, Sun 8:30am-9:30pm.

Get a "Day Rover" ticket if you plan to travel more than once by bus on a given day. This gives you unlimited travel between 9:00am-4:30pm and 6:00pm-12:30am weekdays, and all day on the weekend. Weekly passes are also available. Purchase passes and regular tickets from the bus driver.

A taxi may be necessary to get around on the weekend. Keep in mind that there's a small surcharge for phone bookings. Otherwise, rent a bike from **Graham McVilly Cycles** (phone 23-7284).

Accommodation
There are few budget accommodations in Hobart, and you're out of luck if you prefer a central location. However, finding somewhere to stay isn't a problem except late December-March, when you should call ahead. If you're in a bind, the University of Tasmania has two residential colleges that offer lodging during Uni holidays. **Christ College** costs $18/night (phone 23-5190), and **Jane Franklin Hall** is $24/night (phone 23-2000). Other possibilities:

YHA Bellerive Hostel, 52 King St., Bellerive (phone 44-2552). $8.00/dorm bed. Hostel is a historic school on a pleasant suburban street overlooking the Derwent River. Big wooden bunks. Fireplace. Friendly. Lights out 11:30pm (but you can come in later). Big drawback is scarcity of public transport on weekends. Hostel closed 10:00am-5:00pm; leave luggage in laundry area.

YHA New Town Hostel, 7 Woodlands Ave., New Town (phone 28-6720). $8.00/dorm bed. Old home in historic suburb, with nice yard. Lighter, cleaner, and more accessible than Bellerive, but the manager's sour-tempered reputation precedes her and most hostellers go to Bellerive if there's room. Essential food for sale. BBQ. Lights out at 10:00pm in winter, 11:00pm in summer, midnight on weekends; can get in later with combination. Hostel closed 10:00am-5:00pm.

Sandy Bay Caravan Park, 1 Peel St., Sandy Bay (phone 25-1264). On-site vans. Across from casino and next to the Uni. Great setup. Modern, clean, with tea and soap provided. Bike hire in summer.

Brooker Inn Hotel, 405 Brooker Ave., Moonah (phone 72-4722). If you're a student, the owner promises to work out a discount. Institutional but comfy. Singles and doubles with sink in room. TV lounge. Substantial distance from town.

Globe Hotel, 178 Davey St., cnr. Antill St. (phone 23-5800). 2 km from downtown. Pub downstairs closes early, so there's no noise problem.

Things to See and Do

Hobart began in 1804 as a settlement at Sullivan's Cove. Salamanca Place and Battery Point (both on the south side of Sullivan's Cove) should be your first visits. **Salamanca Place** is flanked by a series of warehouses built between 1835-1860 that now house antiques, clothing, and craft shops, mainly for tourists. While a bit pricey, you may find some treasures in these and other stores on the side streets of Battery Point. The wool products in particular are better and cheaper than those on the mainland, and Tasmania has some fair dinkum artists who sell their wares in this part of town. Stop at the **Wilderness Society shop** for beautiful books, cards, and posters of Tassie (in the Galleria Arcade off Salamanca Place). On Saturday morning, Salamanca Place comes alive with an open-air market. It has the usual jewelry, lots of second-hand clothes, wood carvings, inexpensive Huon pine products, and cheap souvenirs (9:00am-2:00pm).

The oldest building on **Battery Point** dates to 1818, and its narrow streets haven't changed much since the mid-1800's. Stop first at the **National Trust shop** in the Galleria Arcade (33 Salamanca Place) and pick up the pamphlet *Let's Talk about Battery Point and Salamanca Place*, with a map and details on history and architecture in the area.

There are a few "musts" at Battery Point. First is a museum at 103 Hampden Rd., housed in a Georgian mansion called **Narryna**, built in 1836 with stone from Scotland. This "folk" museum certainly doesn't depict the life of average folks. It is, rather, a collection of aristocratic implements and artifacts: beautiful furniture, china, paintings, scrimshaw, embroidery, and peri-od costumes. There are none of the usual glass casings and ropes, so you can wander freely. (Admission $3; open M-F 10:00am-5:00pm, Sat 11:00am-5:00pm, Sun 2:00pm-5:00pm; closed July.) The **Maritime Museum** is in another beautiful Georgian building called "Secheron House" at the end of Secheron Rd. It has an extensive collection of relics, paintings, and whaling implements. (Admission $2; open M-F & Sun 1:00pm-4:30pm, Sat 10:00am-4:30pm.)

A short walk southwest of Battery Point are the **Anglesea Barracks**, head-quarters of the military in Tasmania and the oldest military installation in Australia still in use. There are two entrances in Davey St.; take the main entrance (with the guard house) and go up the road to a map and a box with pamphlets (on the left, next to the parking lot). You're allowed to poke around anytime between 8:00am-10:00pm, though you can't go inside the buildings.

Begin your exploration of the city center down at **Franklin Wharf**, a great place to walk. There are no shops, just the smell of fish and several old schooners moored along the piers, including the *May Queen* and *Lady Nelson*. Brooke Street Pier and Ferry Pier are departure points for various harbor cruises and trips up the Derwent River. Cruise prices start at $10. A less expensive way to get onto the water is by **commuter ferry** to Bellerive, which has a bar on board resembling an old English pub. It runs M-F during com-muting hours (about 7:00am-8:00am and 4:00pm-5:00pm) and costs $1.50 (call 23-5893 for more information).

The **Tasmanian Museum and Art Gallery** at 5 Argyle St. has an impres-sive collection depicting natural history, Tasmanian Aboriginal history, con-vict history, and colonial art, mostly by the painter W.C. Piguenit (open 10:00am- 5:00pm daily). There's another collection of fine arts in town at the **Allport Library and Museum** in the State Library (cnr. Murray & Bathurst Sts.), with fine furniture, porcelain, and paintings that will intrigue those with a bent for antiques.

Two historic buildings on Campbell St. are worth a look. **Hobart's Theatre Royal** (29 Campbell St.) is the oldest theater in the country (circa 1834), and recent restorations are superb. The former **State Supreme Courthouse** and attached jail and chapel is another 1830's building; the chapel is one of the few Georgian churches found in Australia. Tours run three times a day for $3.

If you walk along Davey St. toward Battery Point, stop at the **Hobart Ten-nis Club** at 45 Davey St. and, with permission of the front desk, watch a game of Royal Tennis. Royal Tennis (or "court tennis") is tennis in its original form, a cross between the present-day game and squash, played with square racquets and a heavy ball in an indoor court. Royal Tennis is found only in Hobart, Melbourne, and a few exclusive places in England, France, and the U.S.

The **Hobart Botanic Gardens**, north of the city in the Queen's Domain, are spectacular in the spring. Rhododendrons, azaleas, and roses are among the hundreds of plant species represented in abundance, all in the shade of magnificent Northern Hemisphere trees. The setting is embellished by views of the stately Government House. Transport to the gardens is limited: bus #1 runs four times a day on weekdays, with an extra Sunday service during daylight savings. Otherwise, it's a 20-minute walk from the city center. Another scenic visit is **Mt. Wellington**, though unfortunately the summit is 20 km from the city and there's no public transport. Check Tasbureau for tours. Dress warmly if you're going up—in all seasons!

Suburbs to visit are **Sandy Bay** (for a taste of Hobart life in the present) and **New Town** (for a sense of the fashionable past). Sandy Bay is an area of young professionals and students, with the University of Tasmania on its southern border. 10 km south of Hobart in Taroona (past Sandy Bay on the Channel Hwy.) you can learn to make rifle shot at **Shot Tower**, where molten lead was dropped hundreds of feet into water to form bullets. It's worth going for the bus ride alone, which gives you a cliffside view of the bay and outer suburban homes. The panorama gets even better once you've climbed to the top of Tower. (Admission $3; open daily 9:00am-5:00pm; phone 27-8885.)

In New Town you can wander among old homes and visit **Runnymede**, a townhouse of the 1850's set in 5 acres of gardens (61 Bay Rd). Entrance costs $3.50, discount with student ID. (Open Tues-Sun 10:00am-4:30pm, phone 28-1269).

In keeping with Hobart's strong English associations, there's a **Cadbury's Chocolate factory** 12 km north of town on the Lyell Highway. The plant offers tours and samples. The most popular way to go is aboard a **cruise from Ferry Pier**, which runs three times a week ($22 fee includes the factory tour; the owner of cruise company, Paul Saunders, gives a 10% discount to YHA members). Call 34-9294 or 25-2794 for information and reservations. Tours last 1.5 hours, cost $6, and run three mornings a week (you must book ahead at Tasbureau).

Also north of the city is the **Risdon Cove Historic Site**, where Lt. John Bowen first arrived in 1803 with 49 soldiers, convicts, and tree settlers. After five months there, they decided a place across the river would be better. The site today consists of sprawling grounds where you are free to inspect the remains of the old settlement. It requires a strong imagination to appreciate the place, but bring along a picnic and enjoy the harbor views. The Visitors Centre there has a nice display that encapsulates the history of Tasmania. The Site is located off the East Derwent Hwy. on the river's eastern shore in Risdon Vale.

Food

Hobart is the seafood restaurant capital of Australia and, believe it or not, some seafood restaurants are even affordable! Be sure to try *trevalla*, a deep-sea fish unique to the area waters (not to be confused with the more common trevally). Scallops and squid are also good value. Try fresh takeaways for about $2 from the floating stalls on **Constitution Dock**, open daily until 7:00pm (unprepared fish available until 5:00pm).

Otherwise, food in Hobart is bland Anglo-Saxon, with little ethnic flair. Pubs meals are excellent, though you're generally limited to noon-2:00pm for lunch and 6:00pm-8:30pm for dinner. Make sure to have a Devonshire tea at one of the many cottages in Battery Point. The wharf area, Battery Point (particularly Salamanca Place), and Sandy Bay are the three places to find quality cheap eats.

Mure's, Victoria Dock (phone 31-2121). Reputedly the best seafood restaurant in Australia. Upstairs is fancy and expensive, downstairs is a casual counter-order restaurant and wine bar. Fried and grilled fish begins at $3.50. Helpings are small, so get two orders. Open daily 11:00am-8:30pm.

Skull Duggery Inn, 17 Old Wharf (phone 34-1903). Like a ship's interior, with seafaring relics on the walls. Seafood and meat with a Creole influence. Open M-Th 6:00pm-8:30pm, F 6:00pm-late; lunch M-F from noon. Moderate.

Mr. Wooby's, 65 Salamanca Pl, entrance is on a side street (phone 34-3466). Simple home-style cooking, in generous portions. Garlic bread, cheese platter, Lebanese dips, burgers, crepes, and quiche. Steak and chicken. Open til midnight T-Th, til 2:00am F-Sat, til 4:00pm Mon. Cheap to moderate.

The Parthenon (BYO), 51 Salamanca Pl (phone 23-4461). Outdoor tables. Very cheap takeaways for lunch. Souvlaki, dim sum, hamburgers (up to $4).

Knopwood's, 39 Salamanca Pl (phone 23-5808). Outdoor picnic tables. A popular daytime hang-out. Lunch about $7. Visiting writers and poets some nights.

Shippy's Bistro, 29 Trumpeter St., Battery Point, in Shipwright's Arms Hotel (phone 23-5551). Huge, excellent pub meals. Flounder appetizer is big enough to be a main course. Lamb is the specialty. Moderate.

Mummy's Cafe (BYO), Waterloo Crescent, Battery Point. Hidden away in a quaint sandstone cottage. Popular late-night hangout. Pies, quiche, lasagna, large desserts—nothing over $6.50. Toasted sandwiches are the specialty. Open M-Th 11:00am-midnight, F-Sat til 2:00am, Sun 11:00am-3:00pm.

Solo Pasta and Pizza (BYO), 50-B King St., Sandy Bay (phone 34-9898). Also located at Constitution Wharf. Sit-down or take-away. Very casual. Great homemade pasta dishes, pizza, and chicken. 20% discount for international students (ask for the owner, Saverio). Open M-Sat 5:30pm-late, Sun 5:30pm-9:30pm; lunch W-F noon-2:00pm. Cheap to moderate.

Mure's Fish Bar (BYO), 50 King St., Sandy Bay (phone 34-5961). (Same fishmongers as Mure's in town.) Counter order. Casual. A great deal. Mussels, raw oysters, fried fish—all below $6. Open M-Th 11:30am-8:00pm, F til 8:30pm, Sat 11:30-2:00pm & 5:00pm-8:30pm, Sun 5:00pm-8:00pm. Cheap.

Mayfair Tavern, 236 Sandy Bay Rd, Sandy Bay (phone 23-8200). Pub meals $7, including trevally, pepper steak, roast lamb, sausage, etc. Open M-W 11:00am-midnight, Th-Sat 11:00am-3:00am, Sun noon-8:00pm.

Fanny's Coffee Lounge, 172 Sandy Bay Rd., Sandy Bay (phone 34-8105). A late-night hang-out. Filled croissants, scones and crumpets, quiche, soup, and salad (all below $7). Open M-Th 11:00am-5:00pm & 7:00pm-midnight, F 11:00am-5:00pm & 7:00pm-3:00am, Sat noon- 4:00pm & 7:00pm-3:00am; closed Sunday.

Nightlife

Don't come to Hobart for raging nightlife. Weeknights are quiet, and Sunday night you can hear a pin drop.

Students are an exception to the subdued and conservative Hobart population. They keep the action going all week in Sandy Bay (the Uni suburb) and Murray St. in the city. While you're out on the town, be sure to try Cascade, Tassie's best-known beer (and one of the oldest brewers in the country).

The Dog House Hotel, 41 Barrack St. (phone 34-4090). Casual. Good mix of people. Cover varies, but usually $3. Live music six days a week, with some international bands. Guinness on tap. Open M-Sat 6:00pm-midnight.

Tattersall's Bar and Bistro, 112 Murray St. (phone 34-4172). Warm and comfy atmosphere. Conservative office crowd. Good bands, but not much dancing. $4 cover for jazz and blues, W-Sat nights. Open M til 10:00pm, T til midnight, W til 1:00am, Th-Sat til 2:00am.

Hadley's, 34 Murray St. (phone 23-4355). Go to the piano bar for a posh night out, and dress well. Open F-Sat til 2:00am.

Victoria Tavern, 30 Murray St. (phone 23-3424). Crowded but mellow. Live music Th & Sat. No cover. Open M-Sat until midnight.

Hotel St. Ives, 86 Sandy Bay Rd., Sandy Bay (phone 23-3655). City end of Sandy Bay Rd. Outdoor veranda. Live entertainment most nights. Home-brewed beer. Open til 11:00pm M-W, til 12:30am Th-Sat.

Nicholby's Wine Bar, 217 Sandy Bay Rd., Sandy Bay (phone 23-6030). Popular among young professionals, especially late at night. Expensive gourmet bistro and outdoor cafe (though affordable pate or cheese plate). Jazz quartets and vocalists. Open M-Sat 6:00pm-late, Sun jazz 4:00pm-8:00pm.

Wrest Point Casino, 410 Sandy Bay Rd., Sandy Bay (phone 25-0112). Australia's first casino. Variety of bars. "10 O'clock Club" has performers T-Sat from 10:00pm on ($4 cover). Free Sat afternoon jazz. "Neat casual dress" is the only requirement for entering. Open M-Th 1:00pm-3:00am, F-Sat 1:00pm-4:00am, Sun noon-3:00am.

Entertainment

Check advertisements in Hobart's daily newspaper, The Mercury, for what's up in entertainment, including free performance information.

The historic **Theatre Royal** (built in 1837) is Hobart's main stage, worth a look even if you don't plan to see a show (29 Campbell St., phone 34-6266; office open M-F 10:00am-5:30pm.) It has performances of every variety and student discounts apply with any university ID. The Backspace, in the back of the Theatre Royal, is a setting for experimental theater and late-night cabarets.

The **Tasmanian Symphony Orchestra** plays at the A.B.C. Odeon, 163 Liverpool St. (phone 35-3633) every two weeks except in January, and tickets cost about $17 (half-price if you're under 21). Free concerts, usually classical, are often held in the A.B.C. Hall. You can also hear classical music Saturday evening in **St. George's Church** at 28 Cromwell St. in Battery Point (phone 23-3393). Students and lecturers often give free performances from 1:00pm-2:00pm in the museum and town hall. For information, call the Conservatorium at 34-4285 or check the town hall publicity office. There's free jazz Saturday afternoon at the casino.

Movie buffs have limited options: there are only four city theaters. Check the newspaper. Aside from them, the **State Cinema** at 375 Elizabeth St., North Hobart shows alternative and documentary movies, some of them free. Call 34-6318 for an informational recording.

Trips from Hobart

A trip to the former convict colony Port Arthur is essential for any visitor to the Hobart area. Mt. Field National Park and the Lune and Huon River Valleys are great for outdoor activities, while Bruny Island, Richmond, or New Norfolk are scenic and historic. You can get to most day-trip destinations on Hobart Coaches or Tasmanian Motor Ways on a limited-schedule basis (Sundays are always bad). There are hostels in Cygnet (Huon River Valley), Lune River, New Norfolk, Port Arthur, Bruny Island, and Mt. Field National Park.

Lune River and the Huon Valley

The Huon Valley, south of Hobart, is a rich timber region and home of the native Huon pine. It's also the apple capital of the state, producing over half of Tasmania's apples and 25% of its pears. Though the European Common Market has all but killed the apple export industry, apples are still picked, eaten, and made into delights by local bakeries.

The farm **YHA Hostel** near Cygnet, on the eastern shore of the Huon River, offered deals on one- and two-day rafting trips on the Huon and Picton Rivers while we were there. Call for details. Guided bushwalks are also available. The hostel is at 340 Cradoc Rd., Cradoc, 4.5 km from Cygnet (phone 002-95-1551).

A highlight of the south, especially worthwhile in summer, is a trip to the **Lune River YHA Hostel**. Set in lush, rolling farm and forest country of the Lune River Valley, the hostel is one of the most inviting hostels you'll ever see, with a fireplace, veranda, and a flock of ducks in the backyard. The guitar is kept in tune (unlike most hostel-owned guitars), and you can hang out all day if you like. Bookings for the hostel aren't normally needed, but during summer call ahead (phone 002-98-3163). Make sure to bring warm gear in winter.

Several activities draw people to Lune River, including caving, hiking, and

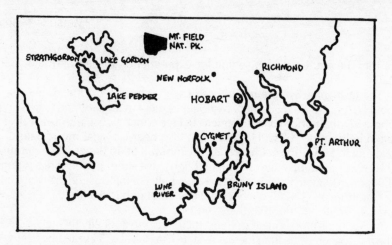

kayaking. **Hastings Caves** are a 45-minute walk from the hostel and cost $5. Tours run four times a day (call 98-3198 for schedule). There's a thermal pool on the way to the cave (not real warm in winter; $1). The more adventurous should explore the muddy glow worm caves at **Mystery Creek**, where you rent a helmet, light, and clothing for $4.50 (three-person minimum for tour).

Ask the hostel manager about kayaking; rental, including all safety gear, is $10/day, $6/half-day. There are a few falls in the area to hike to, and the beginning of the Southwest Coastal Walk is about 30 km south at Cockle Creek (see *Hiking* above for more information). Most hiking trails commence a good distance from the hostel, so a bike or some other form of transport is in order. (You can rent bikes from the hostel.)

Getting There: To get to Cygnet, take a two-hour ride on **Hobart Coaches** to Cygnet (runs five times daily, weekdays only). Unfortunately, getting to Lune River isn't so easy: Hobart Coaches goes to Dover, 20 km north of Lune River, and you must hitch from there. The hostel is on the main road, 3 km past a road to Hastings Caves. Buses run five times a day M-F, and the trip takes 1.5 hours. From December to mid-February, there's a shuttle that leaves from the YHA Head Office in Hobart three times a week.

Richmond and New Norfolk

Richmond and New Norfolk are both quaint, historic country towns. If you've got your own transport, choose Richmond, 26 km northeast of Hobart. Its quaint buildings were mostly built in the 1830's of sandstone from nearby Butcher's Hill. Even the local farmhouses are well-preserved and on a par with the restored main street.

There's little in the way of things to do in Richmond. The idea is to enjoy the picturesque setting, poke around the shops, and linger over a Devonshire tea. Pick up the *Let's Talk about Richmond* pamphlet at Tasbureau in Hobart or at a local store, and give yourself a walking tour.

You can't miss the distinctive **Richmond Arms Hotel**, with its impressive cast-iron balcony and dark wood bar. They serve meals from noon-2:00pm and 6:00pm-7:30pm daily. The oldest bridge in Australia, built in 1823, is still in use and (as you can infer from the tourist brochures) makes a lovely photograph. If you haven't already been to Port Arthur, the **Richmond Gaol** is worth a visit. (Otherwise it's redundant.) The Gaol has an extensive display on prison life (admission $3).

New Norfolk, 43 km northwest of Hobart on the Lyell Highway in the center of hops-growing country, is of similar historic importance as Richmond, though it's not quite as attractive. New Norfolk dates to 1807, when the convict colony at Norfolk Island moved there. Buildings of note are the **Bush Hotel** (Australia's oldest licensed hotel) and **St. Matthew's Church**, both built in 1825.

Getting There: Glamorgan's Hobart-Bicheno bus sometimes goes via Richmond, but services are extremely limited. Take **Tasmanian Motorways** from 131 Collins St. in Hobart to New Norfolk.

Accommodation: There's a small YHA hostel called **Bridge Toll House** on Boyer Rd. in New Norfolk. Go to the keyholder at 2 Rocks Rd. (no advance bookings).

Port Arthur

Port Arthur is a must. It's your best chance to understand Australia's convict past in graphic detail while enjoying the most distinctive (if not eerie) historic setting anywhere in the country.

Port Arthur is neither the earliest nor the most long-standing of Australia's convict settlements, but it's certainly the most famous. Begun in 1830 as a convict sawing station, Port Arthur was the third Tasmanian penal settlement and quickly gained a reputation as the harshest. However, rumors about brutality at Port Arthur were false mostly, spread by authorities as a deterrent. Although convicts at Port Arthur lived a difficult existence, the treatment of convicts at Macquarie Harbor and Norfolk Island was much worse.

In 1853, convict transportation from England ceased. The prison population diminished to those too sick or too old to leave, and Port Arthur officially closed in 1877. Most of the original buildings still exist, though bush fires in the 1890's destroyed several, and the sandstone has deteriorated due to moisture and salt. The result: you feel you're walking among ancient ruins rather than 150-year old buildings. Restoration has protected the sites from further weathering.

Spend half a day on the settlement grounds. Though the location of the youth hostel makes for a tempting back entrance to the site, the authorities will catch you for not having a badge. Pay the admission ($6) either at the Visitors Centre or the museum; passes are good for a week. Introductory tours run every hour on the half-hour beginning at 9:30am, with the final tour at 3:30pm (complex closes at 5:00pm). The tour is a good way to start if you don't mind being herded around with a bunch of people. Otherwise, begin at the museum (in the old Asylum/Town Hall) for an orientation and film at half-hour intervals. Maps and explanations are available there or at the Visitors Centre.

If you're not too tired after roaming the site, catch a ferry to the **Isle of the Dead**, the graveyard for free settlers at Port Arthur. Half-hour trips cost

$3, and 1- hour trips, including a look at Suicide Cliffs and Point Puer (where boys were confined), cost $5. Ferries depart at regular intervals through the day. (Boats don't run in mid-winter.) Don't overlook **Captain Cam's fish punt** at the Port Arthur dock, which has fresh fish (unprepared) at cheap prices.

Essential to any Port Arthur visit is a viewing of *For the Term of His Natural Life*, the 1926 silent film of Marcus Clarke's novel about the adventures of a young English convict wrongly transported to Australia. The film was mostly shot at Port Arthur. Nightly screenings take place in the Visitors Centre cafeteria at 8:00pm, and from October-May it also shows at 3:00pm. Just $6 buys you a fun flick, a wonderful talk from the man who shows the film, and all the tea and scones you can consume.

If you're looking for other things to do, the Tasman Peninsula is definitely worth exploring. **Remarkable Cave** is a scenic 5 km walk from the Port Arthur site. There's a stunning view of shoreline cliffs above the cave—more impressive than the cave itself. Alternately, a beachside walk on **Stewart's Bay Trail** from the historic site leads you to the local caravan park, where you can rent dinghies and fishing gear. The lookout on **Garden Point**, beyond the caravan park, is worth the extra walk. There's horse riding at **Seaview Ranch** in nearby Koonya (phone 50-3110). You may also want to check out the **Fox and Hounds Hotel** down the road from Port Arthur. It's another tourist-oriented replica, but the inside is dark and cozy and, most importantly, warm. Go for an early evening drink. (Open M-Th til 9:00pm, F-Sat til 10:00pm, Sun til 8:00pm.)

Getting There: The only access to Port Arthur is from Hobart (1.5-hour drive). Tasmanian Motorways leaves from 131 Collins St. in Hobart once a day weekdays. If you're arriving on your own steam, there are some interesting coastal formations along the way at **Eaglehawk Neck**, all of which are posted.

Accommodation: While there are a few B&Bs around, there's no reason not to stay at the **YHA Hostel**. It's drafty but otherwise fine. Call a day ahead to ensure a place in summer ($8/night; Champ St., phone 002-50-2311).

Bruny Island

Bruny Island has lots of rugged coastal scenery to explore if you have your own transport. Most don't realize it's 50 km long—not exactly convenient for walkers. If you can handle a few hills, bicycling is the perfect way to get around.

Truganini, the last native Tasmanian, was born on Bruny Island. Her father was the tribal chief and no doubt witnessed several visits by eminent explorers. Evidence of their landings is scattered about the island in the form of memorials and place names. European settlement began in earnest with the establishment of a whaling station in 1827 and a lighthouse in 1836. Apple farming, sheep and cattle raising, and timber and sandstone industries have been the basis of the economy ever since—but not to the detriment of the island's gorgeous physical setting. It remains untainted and, despite weekend tourists, the locals remain fiercely loyal to their rural life.

If you're intent on seeing it all, drive or bike around the island using *Let's*

Talk about Bruny Island as a reference, and give Adventure Bay, The Neck, and Labillardiere State Reserve plenty of time. **Adventure Bay** is the landing place of all the explorers (check out the **Bligh Museum** for details), and there are several marked walks in the vicinity. A sand bar that connects North and South Bruny, known as **The Neck**, has a long, pretty beach. In the evening, you can watch penguins waddling across the road there and home to bed. There's a 7.5-hour trail around the southwest peninsula in **Labillardiere State Reserve**, and south of the reserve's entrance is the oldest continually used lighthouse in Australia, the **Cape Bruny Lighthouse**, built in 1838.

Getting There: Ferries cross the D'Entrecasteaux Channel to Bruny several times daily from Kettering. Times are listed in *Tasmanian Travelways*. It's free for foot passengers and bicycles, $10/roundtrip for cars, M-F. After 1:00pm Fri and all weekend, the cost is $18. Take **Hobart Coaches** from 123 Murray St., Hobart to Kettering. The ride takes an hour and operates M-F only.

Accommodation: Hostellers go to Bruny just for the chance to stay at **House Sofia** on Dennes Point, where they get three meals a day and the warm hospitality of the owners (phone 002-60-6277). Be sure to phone ahead because there are often groups. If there's no room, try the **Channel View B&B** down the road (phone 002-60-6266). Dennes Point is unfortunately not the best location, especially if you've come over with no means of transport. There is, however, a **Backpacker's Hostel** in Adventure Bay situated in a historic guesthouse (Adventure Bay Rd. at Quiet Corner, phone 002-93-1265). It's a yellow house on the right. Overnight cost is $12.

Mt. Field National Park to Strathgordon

50 km northwest of Hobart, Mt. Field National Park offers some excellent day walks and a few overnight treks through rugged mountains and around beautiful lakes. You can get anywhere in the park and back overnight. If you're just passing through, take the short walk from the parking lot to **Russell Falls**, 15 minutes each way. Visitor Information and Park Headquarters both provide pamphlets and hiking information. There also are a few ski lifts for downhill skiing in winter, a half-hour walk from the parking lot.

Campers can stay at the campground near the park entrance; firewood is provided. Higher up in the Park there are rustic cabins starting at $12/night. Cabins have a pot-belly stove, heater, and cold water (book through the ranger at 88-1149). Otherwise, there's a **YHA Hostel** across from the park entrance. Dark wood and high ceilings give it a mountain-lodge ambiance, and there's a fireplace and guitar (Main Rd., phone 002-88-1369).

If you have a car, don't miss the drive to Strathgordon, along which there's an unforgettable view of Lake Gordon and Lake Pedder. This is the closest most people get to Southwest National Park, which spans the entire southwest corner of Tasmania and is largely inaccessible. **Lake Pedder** was a small lake until dams from the Gordon River hydroelectric plant flooded it in the early 1970's, causing massive environmental damage and transforming Scott's Peak and Mt. Solitary into mere islands in a giant reservoir. You can rent fishing equipment and boats at the **Lake Pedder Motor Inn**.

Getting There: To reach Mt. Field National Park, take **Tasmania Motorways** from Centerway in Collins St. (operates weekdays only). There is no public transport to Strathgordon.

Tasmania's East Coast

Whalers and sealers were the first to settle on Tassie's east coast, after which fishermen and farmers arrived to create the backbone of the area economy. Timber and tin, especially around St. Helens, were also important to the region's growth. Today, the east coast is a summer vacation spot for native Taswegians and mainlanders drawn by the beautiful beaches and mild temperatures.

An evenly-spaced string of YHA hostels along the coast makes the region especially good for bikers (see *Biking* above). For the backpacking crowd, several hostels provide attractive places to hang out and enjoy the peaceful setting. You can explore Maria Island from Triabunna, relax on the beach in Bicheno and St. Helens, experience farm life at St. Marys and Winneleah, and walk over granite mountains to gorgeous white beaches at Coles Bay. There are hostels in Triabunna, Swansea, Coles Bay, Bicheno, St. Mary's, St. Helen's, Winneleah, and the Merlikei Farm Hostel near Winneleah.

Be sure to do your banking in Launceston or Hobart before embarking on an east coast excursion. There are no automatic bank tellers along the way, and Visa and Mastercard generally aren't accepted.

Getting There and Getting Around: Several local buslines service the Tasman Highway, which runs along the entire east coast. **Glamorgan Coaches** (phone 002-28-7530) runs M-F from Hobart to Triabunna, Swansea, and Bicheno. **Peakes Bus Service** operates M-Sat between Swansea and St. Mary's via Bicheno. **Suncoast Bus Service** operates in conjunction with Redline Coaches and goes daily between St. Mary's and St. Helen's, and from St. Helen's to Derby and Winneleah. There's a school bus between Bicheno and Coles Bay (phone 003-75-1233). Glamorgan runs from Launceston (45 Brisbane St., next to the Caltex station, or Launceston airport, on request) southeast through St. Helen's, Swansea, and Bicheno.

Maria Island and Triabunna

About 90 km northeast of Hobart, Triabunna is the most convenient access point for **Maria Island**, a tiny place that was a convict detention center in 1826 and is now a haven for campers, who explore the penal colony ruins in **Darlington** (where the ferry lands), hike along the cliffs, and enjoy the beaches. Don't miss the spectacular **Painted Cliffs**, an easy walk from Darlington. Maps are available at a small Visitors Center (Commissariat Store) in Darlington.

Getting There: The ferry to Maria Island leaves from Louisville, 5 km from Triabunna, and the Triabunna hostel manager will gladly give you a lift to

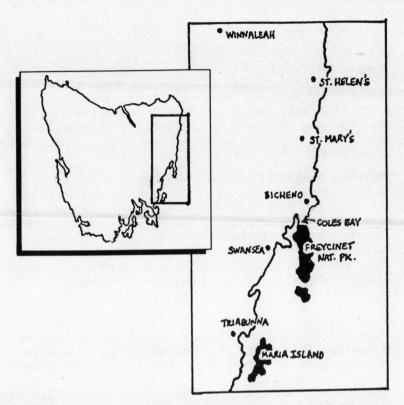

the pier. Daily ferries leave Louisville at 10:30am and depart from Maria Island around 2:30pm, so if you're a day-tripper you won't have much time there. The roundtrip is $12/day trip or $14/overnight (10% discount for YHA members).

To reach Triabunna, take Hobart Coaches from Hobart on weekdays. East Coast Bus operates Sat-Sun in January and February.

Accommodation: On Maria Island, there is spartan accommodation in the **Penitentiary** at Darlington, with mattresses and a wood-burning stove, for $6/night. Bring a sleeping bag and all supplies. Most visitors choose one of the three campgrounds. Make reservations through the ranger at 002-57-1420 during office hours.

The Triabunna **YHA Hostel** (Spencer St., phone 002-57-3439; $7/night) is a small farm run by a pleasant couple who grows and sells vegetables. The hostel, separate from the manager's house, has a large kitchen and common room area with a working fireplace. Don't miss their homemade chocolate cake! The hostel is closed June 1-Sept 30. The bus from Hobart drops off on the highway, about 2 km from the hostel.

Swansea
50 km north of Triabunna and 50 km south of Bicheno, Swansea is a bright coastal town with a cozy seaside **YHA Hostel** (5 Franklin St., phone 002-57-8367; $7/night). You can fish off its pier (literally out the back door) and collect shells on its quiet beach. Windsurfers, jet skis, and bicycles can

be rented next door.

First settled in 1821, Swansea was developed by sheep and cattle farmers, and area forests supplied lumber for local saw mill and woodchip industries. The **Bark Mill** (Tasman Hwy.) offers an interesting look at the district's history. The owner, Peter Lewis, is friendly and full of information. YHA members get a discount, making the admission fee about $3. Pick up a leaflet on historic buildings around Swansea at the mill.

Freycinet National Park and Coles Bay

Approximately 60 km northeast of Swansea and 40 km south of Bicheno is a coastal reserve known as Freycinet National Park. Red granite formations, white sand beaches, and the green ocean are the hallmarks of the park, a must for enthusiastic hikers and beach lovers. You may find ancient Aboriginal shell middens in the dunes. Walks ranging from a few hours to a few days wind through granite formations to sheltered bays, the most famous being **Wineglass Bay**. The park ranger station is at the northern border, with maps and good advice.

Accommodation: Coles Bay, a small township consisting of a general store, accommodation, and a post office, is the best place to stay near Freycinet National Park. There's a rustic **YHA Hostel** with two rooms and no hot water or showers. To stay at the hostel, you must book in advance through the YHA Head Office in Hobart (002-34-9617).

Other accommodation available is less rough. Built in 1932 as a health resort, **The Chateau** is a family holiday village with B&B accommodation. The food's not great (cold toast and cereal) and the rooms are marginal, but the staff is friendly (phone 002-57-0101). On-site vans and self-contained units are available at **Pine Lodge** (phone 002-57-0113), and at **Iluka Holiday Centre** (phone 002-57-0115), which also has campsites.

Bicheno

One of Tassie's most popular beachside resorts is Bicheno, 45 km northeast of Swansea. Settled as a coal mining port in 1854, Bicheno faded into obscurity until WWII, when it blossomed as a fishing village and tourist resort. Local history revolves around two heroines: an Aborigine woman named Waubedebar and Mary Harvey, both of whom performed life-saving feats off the coast.

The **Bicheno Dive Centre** (phone 003-75-1138) has day trips to Coles Bay for $70 and charges $20 for dives off the Bicheno coast. Mosquitoes and flies love the Bicheno beach life, too, so carry repellent.

Bicheno is an excellent place for seafood, and we recommend **Waub's Bay Bistro** (116 Tasman Hwy.). Though a little expensive (main courses around $12), they'll cook fish any way you want, and each plate comes with salad and fries. It also has a take-out shop, which, in addition to fish 'n chips, sells fresh fish and crayfish if you want to cook.

Accommodation: The Bicheno **YHA Hostel** (phone 003-75-1293) doesn't have much room, but it's clean, pleasant, and right on the beach—a good place to lounge and relax. A few fairy penguins come ashore near the hostel at twilight, and during the night you can hear their low cries. Ask your bus driver to drop you at the hostel, 3 km north of town on the Tasman Hwy. Bring food.

St. Mary's

St. Mary's is 55 km north of Bicheno and 45 km south of St. Helen's. Set amid 400 acres of farmland, with brilliant views of the Scamander coast, the YHA hostel **Seaview Farm** is ideal for those who want to relax and get away from everything (German Town Rd., phone 003-72-2341; $6/night). Self-motivation is the secret of success here, and you'll need it just to reach the hostel—it's a steep 8 km climb from town up a gravel road. Jeff Weston (the hostel owner) only comes down once a day to get his mail; he'll give hostellers a lift then, if you call ahead. Jeff is very friendly, enthusiastic, and devoted to giving his guests a taste of Tasmanian country life. The hostel is part of his home, and the atmosphere is familial and warm. No alcohol is permitted. Walks around the farm and into the surrounding mountains, and donkey rides, are the main activities.

Just south of St. Mary's is **Mt. Elephant Pass**, an extremely steep road with 180° switchbacks through dense forest. It's a challenge to drive (especially if you meet an oncoming bus) and an acrobatic miracle for a bicyclist, but certainly a rewarding experience.

St. Helens and Winnaleah

The largest town on the east coast, St. Helen's is 160 km east of Launceston. The **YHA Hostel** is a clean, new suburban house at 5 Cameron St. (phone 003-76-1661; $8/night). Outside the front door is a bay with black swans and a small jetty with fishing boats. The biggest attraction is **Binnilong Bay**, one of the best beaches in the state. It's 11 km from town, and hitching is usually no problem. Rent bicycles from **St. Helen's Suncoast Motors** (Cecilia St.).

Janice and Mervyn Chilcott own the **Merlikei Farm Hostel** (phone 003-54-2152; $7/night), 3 km from Winneleah and 4 km off the Tasman Highway. Don't miss this rare opportunity to participate in the operation of a dairy farm and get to know some friendly locals. Janice will supply an inexpensive (and good) breakfast, lunch, and/or dinner with advance warning. Call ahead to arrange a lift from Winneleah.

Buses operate daily between Launceston and St. Helens.

Launceston

Founded in 1806, Launceston was settled just after Hobart and has a similar convict colony/military outpost *raison d'etre*. Despite equal historical prowess, Launceston has nowhere near the beauty or charm of Hobart. It is noisier, dirtier, and less friendly than Tasmania's capital and, in an effort to attract conferences and other visitors, its tourist industry has marred its original charm.

Launceston is, however, a convenient access point for Deloraine and the lake area of Tassie's central plateau, especially if you're arriving directly from the mainland (otherwise, stay in Deloraine). It's also the best point of entry for bicyclers, who can rent all necessary equipment from the YHA manager and solicit his sound advice.

Getting There
Redline Coaches passes through Launceston daily from Hobart and Devonport. **Glamorgan Coachlines** services the east coast on weekdays. For those arriving by plane, Redline has an airport shuttle for $4. Call 31-9177 to arrange for pick-up when you depart.

Orientation and Practical Information
The Tamar River runs alongside the city center to form its northern border, while Elizabeth Street approximately marks the southern border of downtown. There's an uninteresting pedestrian mall on Brisbane Street and another pedestrian area called **The Quadrant** that links Brisbane and St. John Streets. The Quadrant has a few eateries and outdoor cafes. **Civic Square**, two blocks north of the Brisbane Street Mall, is a historic, pleasant area that includes government buildings and the public library. **Princes' Square** (St. John and Elizabeth Sts.) is a lovely park surrounded by restored buildings. It's probably the nicest spot in the city, along with **City Park**, west of downtown on Tamar St. Both have pretty gardens and good picnic spots.

Information:
Tasbureau, corner St. John and Paterson Sts. (phone 003-32-2101). Open M-F 8:45am-5:30pm; weekends and public holidays 9:00am-11:30pm.

Town Hall, Civic Square. Self-guided historic walking brochure and tourist information. Open weekdays 9:00am-5:00pm.

Information Kiosk, Brisbane Mall. Tourist information.

Transportation
Metropolitan Transport Bus schedules are available free at Tasbureau and the information kiosk in the mall. Most buses depart from various points along St. John's Street and routes are identified by the name of the terminus. Fares vary (up to $2), and you buy tickets from the driver. An all-day, off-peak pass costs $2.50 (good 9:00am-4:30pm and after 6:00pm weekdays, all day weekends and public holidays). As with all transport in Tasmania on Sundays, there's not much! In case you get stuck, taxis are available (try calling 31-3555 or 31-4466).

Accommodation
YHA Hostel, 36 Thistle St., South Launceston (phone 003-44-9779). $9/night. Huge converted warehouse. Impersonal. TV monopolized by the managing family. Midnight curfew. Bike hire. Advice and outfitting for cyclists (don't mind the manager's gruff manner—he has lots of useful pointers). Camping equipment and wet weather gear available for rent. Hostel closed 10:00am-5:00pm.

Enfield Hotel, 169 Charles St. (phone 003-31-4040). Nice management. Subdued crowd in downstairs bar, which closes early. Rooms have private sinks. TV lounge. The best budget hotel available.

Things to See and Do

There are three or four worthwhile sites in Launceston, first being **Cataract Gorge**, a 15-minute walk from the hostel at the end of Basin Rd. It's hard to believe that a reserve of this size and grandeur exists within the city limits. The gorge is formed in a tributary of the Tamar River and extends southwest to **Duck Reach** where, with patience, you'll see platypuses in the pool. Duck Reach is a 40-minute walk along a well-marked path. There are other trails all around the reserve's beautiful gardens. You can also ride a chairlift over the gorge for $3. Every night, floodlights illuminate the park for about an hour (usually around 9:00pm).

Next, go to **Town Hall** in Civic Square and get a copy of their historic walk through Launceston. Before you set off, visit **Macquarie House** (also in Civic Square), an 1830's warehouse with a small display on Launceston and its architecture. Included in the historic walk is the **Queen Victoria Museum and Art Gallery** (Wellington St.), notable for its colonial paintings and an exhibition on the history of Chinese in Tasmania. (Open M-Sat 9:00am-5:00pm, Sun 2:00pm-5:00pm).

There are three well-known houses in the countryside, the best of which is **Entally House** in Hadspen on the Bass Hwy., along Redline's route to Deloraine and Devonport. Determined sightseers can get dropped off by a Redline bus and, for the return trip, wave down an incoming bus. Built in 1819, Entally House has a good collection of period furniture (unidentified unless you buy a pamphlet). The best thing about the home is the grounds, on which there are several out-buildings and a display of old carriages. Go on a nice day and take a picnic. (Open daily 10:00am-5:00pm; admission $4.)

The other houses are Franklin House and Clarendon. The virtue of **Franklin House** is that it's readily accessible from town (take the Franklin Village line via Wellington St. and get off at the terminus). A Georgian mansion dating to 1838, Franklin House is noted for its cedar interior. (Open daily, 9:00am-5:00pm, til 4:00pm in winter; admission $4.) **Clarendon** is 27 km south of Launceston on the Midlands Hwy. in the historic town of Evandale, and unfortunately there's no public transport. Another Georgian mansion, Clarendon has extensive gardens, but its restoration is only partially complete. (Open daily 10:00am-12:30pm & 1:30pm-5:00pm, til 4:00pm in winter; admission $4.)

The **Waverley Woolen Mills**, 4 km from Launceston on the Northeast Hwy., are the oldest mills in Australia, and their ancient machinery is still in use. Tours take you through the entire complex, and the $3 admission fee is refunded if you buy any of their products—excellent deals on slightly defective items, too. Take the Waverley line (via Elphin Rd.) from St. John St. opposite Quadrant Mall. (Tours daily 9:00am-4:00pm; shop open daily 9:00am-5:00pm.)

Further afield, the **Tamar Valley**, rich in history, has gained recent fame as a wine center. It produces both reds and whites and caters to the gourmet market. **St. Mathias Vineyard** in Rosvears, 15 minutes from town by car on the West Tamar Hwy., provides samples of several area wines. (Open 11:00am-5:00pm; limited hours April-Nov, so call first at 30-1700). The Tamar Valley is spectacular in January, when lavender is in bloom.

Also accessible from Launceston are Tasmania's central highlands, a vast plateau with mountain lakes that are an angler's delight. **Great Lake** reportedly has the best trout fishing in the state. Though Deloraine is closer to the highlands, serious fishermen should get information and equipment in Launceston.

Nightlife and Entertainment

Launceston's **Casino** is popular with flashy Melbourne businessmen who fly in to gamble away the weekend. To get there, take the casino line from St. John Street in front of the Launceston Bank for Savings, and don't forget that the last bus returns at 11:30pm weekdays.

Owned by Boags, the local brewing company, the **Newstead Hotel** (160 Elphin Rd., Newstead) has the highest beer sales in northern Tasmania. To reach it, take the Norwood or S. Norwood lines from St. John Street opposite the Quadrant.

Deloraine

Deloraine is a National Trust-classified town set among small pastoral properties in the hilly farm district of the Great Western Tiers. In addition to cattle and sheep, race horses are bred in the area, and the Deloraine race course is one of the oldest in Australia. Deloraine is one of the gems of Tasmania, and the YHA-Associate hostel there only enhances its desirability—it's open all day, and every third night is free.

Be sure to have a look around town. (You'll receive a pamphlet about Deloraine's buildings on arrival at the hostel.) There are several old buildings dating to the 1830's, most of them still in use as inns and hotels. 2 km east of town on the Bass Hwy., the **Bowerbank Mill Gallery**, an old flour mill, is now a respected gallery for Tasmanian artists (open daily 10:00am-5:30pm). Try a Devonshire tea at **Bonney's Inn** or a counter meal at the **Bush Inn**.

The hostel's manager/owner, John, leads hikes every day in summer, mostly to Cradle Mountain but also to Liffey Falls, Meander Falls, and Glow Worm Caves. Trips are an average of $25/day, occasional overnight trips cost more. If you decide on the Cradle Mountain trek, remember that the drive there is two hours, leaving only four hours to walk. A better option is to hike nearby and join a longer Cradle Mountain trip.

If you have a car or bike, consider **Meander Falls** (30 km south, past Meander), the highest in Tassie (100 meters). The hike is beautiful, but do take the timing estimate seriously! While it's under two hours to reach the falls, the optional circular route back leads up a steep mountain. The trip really does take seven hours. And don't miss the short **Split Rock Falls** detour.

Liffey Falls is 30 km southeast of town, and there are plenty of walking trails around the falls and through surrounding rainforest.

Other nearby visits (not accessible by public transport) are the **Tasmanian Wildlife Park** (20 km west on Mole Creek Rd., past Chudleigh), and **Marakoopa** and **King Solomon Caves** (30 km west of Deloraine past Mole Creek). The Wildlife Park has tame Tasmanian Devils, wombats (which you can pet), and other native Tassie species, most of which wander freely. (Open 9:00am-5:00pm daily, admission $5.) The two Mole Creek caves are worth a visit if you've never seen a glow worm cave before, or if you miss John's personalized tour. Tours through Marakoopa and King Solomon run five times daily, less often in winter (call 003-63-5181 or 63-5182 for tour schedules). Admission for each is $5.

Deloraine is 66 km north of Great Lake. Fishing tours to Great Lake are available through **Bonney's Host Farm** (call 62-2122).

Getting There: Deloraine is 40 minutes west of Launceston, and Redline stops a few times daily.

Accommodation: The **Deloraine Hostel** is at 8 Blake St. (phone 003-62-2996), and coaches will drop you at the town's service station. Walk up the hill a few blocks from there and follow the signs. It's $8/night, every third night free. Bikes available for rent. (Hostel closed June-Sept.)

Appendix

Working Down Under

The key to finding work overseas is flexibility. If you've got time, an adventurous spirit, and the desire to work hard, opportunities await.

Keep in mind that room, board, and transportation will take a chunk out of your earnings unless you land a job that includes them (so, an all-inclusive job like ranch work can net more money than waitressing). Also, think about location and climate. The heat can often be brutal. Consider your priorities: Are you willing to be uncomfortable picking fruit for two weeks (sunburn, aching back, and strained eyes) to make money fast, or would you rather take a less strenuous job that will be kinder to your body (and, perhaps, your psyche) and earn money more slowly? Weigh all factors before jumping into something. The bottom line is to enjoy yourself, at least to some extent.

If you want to have a working experience Down Under and don't care about making money, look into C.I.E.E.'s volunteer work programs. There are both short- and long-term opportunities with agencies seeking skilled and unskilled volunteers, and often the programs provide room and board. For more information look at *Volunteer! The Comprehensive Guide to Voluntary Service in the U.S. and Abroad,* published C.I.E.E. If you're already in Australia and want to find out about volunteering, contact The Australian Trust for Conservation Volunteers, P.O. Box 423, Ballarat, Vic., 3350 (phone 053-32-7490).

The only way for U.S. citizens to work legally in Australia is with a resident visa (i.e. emigrate) or with a company willing to spend hours filing papers proving your job could not be filled by an Australian. We met several people who tried unsuccessfully to get working papers, and no one who actually got them. Canadians, Brits, Irish, and Japanese travelers between 18-30 can apply for an Australian working holiday visa while in their home countries. See the local Australian High Commission, Embassy, or Consulate.

The casual work opportunities in Australia are endless, especially if you're willing to do manual labor. The only time obtaining casual work may be difficult is during university summer holidays (January and February). And women, be forewarned: you may find discrimination when applying for outdoor work.

The best source for finding casual jobs are hostel bulletin boards, hostel managers, and fellow travelers. Jobs are often available at hostels in exchange for free room. Another source is private employment agencies, found in the

418

phone book. Or try the government's employment agency, the Common-wealth Employment Service (C.E.S.), though they can't help if you don't have working papers. The C.E.S. Casual Labor section has Sydney offices at 818 George St. (phone 02-219-7200) or 110 Darlinghurst Rd. (phone 02-332-1122). C.E.S. publishes a useful booklet on where and when to find agricultural work across the country (i.e. fruit-picking and grain-harvesting).

Fruit- and vegetable-picking jobs are abundant and ever-changing, varying according to the season and locale. Working as a "jackaroo" or "jillaroo" on a station (ranch) is another option, though often less glamorous than you might envision. The hours are long, and stations can be quite remote. Ex-perience in horse-riding and sheep-shearing for jackaroos is often required. Jillaroos usually work around the homestead. Cooking and house-keeping jobs on stations tend to appear during planting time. Men can find work mining, which can be incredibly lucrative. You'll need a local driver's license to work the machinery, for insurance purposes.

Finding pub work and waitressing is fairly easy because the turnover rate is high. Remember, you'll be paid by the hour, not by the tips. The blossoming tourist industry has opened up lots of jobs in hotels and resorts. Look to the Great Barrier Reef and ski resorts in both Australia and New Zealand for op-portunities.

Crewing for private yachts is a very popular and often attainable job, with a bit of persistence and luck. No sailing experience is necessary (though it is helpful), but those who've never sailed before should try out their sea legs before embarking on any major voyage. To look for a crewing position, hang around harbors in Cairns, Townsville, Fremantle, Sydney, and Darwin, and look trustworthy. In New Zealand, head to the Bay of Islands or the Westhaven port in Auckland. Yachts normally head Down Under in July-August, then flee before the monsoons hit (Oct-Nov). If you plan correctly, you may be able to sail your way around the continent, then head off on a global adventure—for free.

Working in New Zealand

C.I.E.E.'s "Work Abroad" program opens doors for students to work in tem-porary jobs in New Zealand between April 1-Oct 31. To qualify, you must be a degree-seeking student, U.S. citizen (or permanent U.S. resident), and at least 18 years old. For information, write C.I.E.E., Work Abroad, 205 East 42nd St., New York, NY 10017.

Canadian students will have no problem getting permission to work in New Zealand. They should contact C.U.T.S. (Canadian Universities Travel Service).

Studying Down Under

Study programs in Australia and New Zealand are open only to degree-seeking students and are highly competitive. We have heard only good reports from American students on study exchanges to Australia. Most say the work-load is, on the whole, easier than in U.S. schools because Australia's independent study system allows students to choose the amount of effort they want to expend. Participating students say that the programs are well-organized and that the experience is one of the best ways to get to know the country.

Australia and New Zealand follow the British academic system. At the end of their high school years, all students take matriculation ("matric") exams. Their futures depend heavily on the scores, and university education is usually specialized—first-year students start immediately with law, medicine, etc. "Arts and sciences" is the closest equivalent to America's liberal arts, for which a bachelor's degree takes three years plus an extra year for "honors." (Each discipline has its own time schedule.)

Although the academic year in the Southern Hemisphere (early March-Dec) doesn't correspond with the U.S. academic calendar, those Australian and New Zealand institutions involved in exchanges have a term from August-December.

The primary sources for study programs in Australia and New Zealand are the C.I.E.E.'s *Work, Study, Travel Abroad: The Whole World Handbook* and the Institute of International Education's (I.I.E.) *Academic Year Abroad*. Both books have comprehensive lists of institutions with study programs to Australia for both American university students (graduate and undergraduate) and high school students. Among the largest are the Experiment in International Living/School for International Training and the International Christian Youth Exchange. Check your library for more information on studies abroad.

Some American universities offer overseas study programs, either independently or through a larger organization like International Student Exchange Program (I.S.E.P.). If you're in school and want to spend a semester or year abroad, find out if your school is part of a program and, if not, ask about applying through a school that is. I.S.E.P. has over 200 U.S. and 100 foreign member institutions. For information, contact: International Student Exchange Program, 1242 35th St. N.W., Washington, D.C. 20057 (phone 202-687-6956).

To find out about Australian government-sponsored programs for international students, write Australia Development Assistance Bureau, Dept. of Foreign Affairs, P.O. Box 887, Canberra, A.C.T., 2601.

Buying a Car

If you're staying in Australia for an extended period of time, buying a car is a great idea. But remember that buying and maintaining a car is time-consuming, and be sure to allow ample time at the end of your travels to sell the car. Cars in Australia cost about twice as much as cars on the U.S. market. (You will, of course, be selling it at an equally inflated rate.) Gasoline ("petrol") costs 2-3 times the U.S. rate.

You'll need a dependable vehicle, not only because you don't want to waste time and money getting your car repaired, but also because many Australian roads are so remote that service stations can be over 100 miles apart. You obviously want to avoid breaking down at all costs. Especially keep this in mind if you plan to drive in the western and far northern parts of the country. Cars get a lot of wear and tear because several of Australia's "highways" are unpaved, and the intense heat is also a factor.

Car dealers in Australia are no different than car dealers anywhere else in the world. It's easy to get ripped-off. A few bogus outfits in Sydney sell cars and steal them right back. We met one hosteller who bought a car, left it overnight in front of his hostel, and awoke the following day to find it had disappeared. According to the hostel manager, this was just one in a series of cars stolen from hostellers, probably taken by the original sellers.

There are simple precautions you can take to avoid buying a stolen car or getting stuck with expensive repairs. Get the state's Automobile Association to inspect the car. This costs about $60, but if you're on the verge of buying, it's worth it. Membership in the Association is required, but if you're going to be driving around Australia you'll want to join anyway. In addition to pre-purchase inspection, ask the Association about state regulations regarding sale and purchase of vehicles and get one of their pamphlets on buying a car. (Ask specifically about government inspection slips, warranty requirements, and general laws regarding buyers' and sellers' obligations.) When you're buying, make sure the seller is fulfilling all his legal obligations to you.

To be sure the car is not stolen or does not have money owed on it (you are liable in both cases), check the registration to see if the stated owner is the person selling you the car. Also, in some states there is an agency you can call which has stolen car records (in NSW it's called the Register of Encumbered Vehicles). Tell them the car's registration number and engine serial number.

See *Getting Around* in the Introduction for Automobile Association membership details and other information.

Where to Buy
Assuming you'll be buying on the east coast, our advice is to buy in NSW or Victoria rather than Queensland. Everything is a bit more lax in Queensland—both the regulations and enforcement of them.

How to Buy
There are three ways to buy: through a dealer, through an auction, or privately. Which you choose depends on your mechanical knowledge and willingness to take a risk. Dealers are the least risky because of the regulations they must abide by. Most states, for instance, require dealers to give you some sort of warranty for cars costing more than a certain price (usually $3,000). Given the strong possibility of hidden problems in a second-hand vehicle, this may be worth it. Remember that the added security of buying through a dealer is no good unless you check out local laws and confirm for yourself that all the paperwork is legitimate.

Buying a car privately or through an auction is much less expensive, but also more risky. First, the car won't have a warranty; second, it could be stolen. You can't road-test or get a mechanic to inspect an auctioned vehicle, so a practiced eye is needed. Keep in mind that in an auction you'll be bidding against dealers.

Ask hostel managers in Sydney for advice on buying a car. They are used to referring travelers and can often lead you in the best direction. There is at least one reputable dealer in Sydney who sells cars to international hostellers with a guaranteed buy-back price.

Registration and Papers

Most cars come with a registration ("rego") which won't need renewal until the printed expiration date. Since registration is expensive (about $300) and involves an inspection, a recent registration adds to a car's value. Regos are renewed annually.

Dealers take care of ownership transfer papers and stamp duty payments (not included in the sticker price). Otherwise, contact the state's department for motor transport to find out requirements for official transfer of ownership.

Insurance

Be skeptical of insurance policies offered through car dealers, who get commissions and deals from insurance companies. Shop around for the best insurance (the best place to start is state Automobile Associations). Third party insurance (not including damage to third party property) is compulsory and paid with vehicle registration. We suggest that you also buy insurance that covers damage to third party property and, depending on your health insurance policy at home, personal accident coverage. Other policies cover theft, fire, and other damage to the car, but assuming your car won't be particularly valuable, you might not bother. Some insurance companies won't cover foreigners.

Visiting Aboriginal Reserve Lands

If you are interested in visiting Aboriginal reserve lands, you must first contact local Land Councils. We suggest calling first to determine what they need to consider your request (usually, some sort of statement of purpose and anticipated visit dates). Some Councils are strict, others more lenient. Your best bet is to try in the Northern Territory. Allow 3-4 weeks for your application to be processed, and address your letter to the Permits Officer.

The following list includes contact addresses for reserves mentioned in individual chapters:

Hermannsburg Mission, Central Land Council, P.O. Box 3321, Alice Springs, N.T., 5750 (phone 089-52-3800).

Arnhem Land (tours available through **Terra Safari** in Darwin), Northern Land Council, P.O. Box 3046, Darwin, N.T., 5794 (phone 089-81-7011 or 82-4511).

Bathurst and Melville Islands, Tiwi Land Council, P.O. Box 340, Darwin, N.T., 5794 (phone 089-81-4111).

Balgo Hills Community, Balgo Hills Community Aboriginal Corporation, via Halls Creek, W.A., 6770 (no phone).

State Land Council Offices

New South Wales, P.O. Box 1241, North Sydney, N.S.W., 2059 (phone 02-922-4611)

Northern Territory, see above addresses for Northern Land Council, Central Land Council, and Tiwi Land Council.

Queensland, G.P.O. Box 2453, Brisbane, QLD, 4001 (phone 07-229-5988).

South Australia, G.P.O. Box 1065, Adelaide, S.A., 5001 (phone 08-218-0211).

Victoria and Tasmania, 8th floor, 399 Lonsdale St., Melbourne, Vic., 3000 (phone 03-604-4400).

Western Australia, Box 6117, Hay St. East, Perth, W.A., 6000 (phone 09-220-3211).

Australian State Tourist Commissions

Tourism Commission of New South Wales, c/o Tobin Associates, 2121 Avenue of the Stars, Suite 1280, Los Angeles, CA 90067 (phone 213-277-7008).

Northern Territory Tourist Commission, 2121 Avenue of the Stars, Suite 1230, Los Angeles, CA 90067 (phone 213-277-7877) or 645 Fifth Ave., 9th floor, New York, N.Y. 10022 (phone 212-759-3306).

Queensland Tourist and Travel Corporation, 611 N. Larchmont Blvd., Los Angeles, CA 90004 (phone 213-465-8418) or 645 Fifth Ave., 9th floor, New York, N.Y. 10022 (phone 212-308-5520).

Tourism South Australia, 2121 Avenue of the Stars, Suite 1210, Los Angeles, CA 90067 (phone 213-552-2821).

Tourism Tasmania, 2121 Avenue of the Stars, Suite 1200 T, Los Angeles, CA 90067 (phone 213-552-3010).

Victorian Tourism Commission, 2121 Avenue of the Stars, Suite 1270, Los Angeles, CA 90067 (phone 213-553-6352).

Western Australian Tourism Commission, 2121 Avenue of the Stars, Suite 1210, Los Angeles, CA 90067 (phone 213-557-1987).

Australian Visa-Issuing Offices

In the U.S.:
1. Australian Consulate-General, 636 Fifth Ave., New York, NY 10111 (phone 212-245-4000). *For residents of Connecticut, Delaware, Florida, Georgia, Kentucky, Maine, Massachusetts, New Hampshire, New Jersey, New York, North Carolina, Pennsylvania, Rhode Island, South Carolina, Vermont, West Virginia, Puerto Rico, and Bermuda.*

2. Australian Consulate-General, Suite 2930, Quaker Tower, 321 N. Clark St., Chicago, IL 60610 (phone 312-645-9444). *For residents of Illinois, Indiana, Iowa, Kansas, Michigan, Minnesota, Missouri, Nebraska, North Dakota, Ohio, South Dakota, and Wisconsin.*

3. Australian-Consulate General, 360 Post St., San Francisco, CA 94108-4979 (phone 415-362-6160). *For residents of Alaska, Northern California, Colorado, Idaho, Montana, Nevada, Oregon, Utah, Washington, and Wyoming.*

4. Australian Consulate-General, 611 N. Larchmont Blvd., Los Angeles, CA 90004-9998 (phone 213-469-4300). *For residents of Arizona, New Mexico, and Southern California.*

5. Australian Embassy, 1601 Massachusetts Ave. NW, Washington DC 20036-2273 (phone 202-797-3222). *For residents of Maryland, Virginia, and Washington D.C.*

6. Australian Consulate-General, 1990 Post Oak Blvd., Suite 800, Houston, TX 77056-9998 (phone 713-629-9140). *For residents of Alabama, Arkansas, Louisiana, Mississippi, Oklahoma, Tennessee, and Texas.*

7. Australian Consulate, Penthouse Suite, 1000 Bishop St., Honolulu, HI 96813-4299 (phone 808-524-5050). *For residents of Hawaii.*

In Canada:

1. Australian High Commission, The National Building, 13th floor, 130 Slater St., Ottawa, ONT, K1P 5H6 (phone 613-236-0841). *For residents of Quebec and the Maritime Provinces east of and including Kingston in Ontario.*

2. Australian Consulate-General, P.O. Box 12519, Oceanic Plaza, Suite 800, 1066 West Hastings St., Vancouver, B.C., V6E 3X1 (phone 604-684-1177). *For residents of area west of and including Manitoba.*

3. Australian Consulate-General, Commerce Court North, Suite 2200, King & Bay Sts., Ccmmerce Court Postal Station, Box 69, Toronto, ONT, M5L 1B9 (phone 416-367-0783). *For residents of Ontario west of Kingston to Manitoba.*

Index to Locations

About the Authors

In 1986, **Lauren Goodyear** and **Thalassa ("Lassa") Skinner** toured Australia for six weeks with their singing group from Yale University. They both fell in love with the country and decided to return after graduating from Yale. This book is the product of their second, year-long trip.

Lauren now lives in Washington, D.C., where she teaches high school English and hosts visiting Aussie friends. On the side, she sings, hikes, skis, and schemes her return Down Under.

Also in D.C., Lassa conducts surveys for the Smithsonian Institution and spends summers in East Africa, digging up million-year-old fossils and artifacts. She devotes her spare time and energy to writing, tasting wine, and planning future travels.

More Great Travel Books from Mustang Publishing

Let's Blow thru Europe by Neenan & Hancock. The essential guide for the "15-cities-in-14-days" traveler, *Let's Blow thru Europe* is hilarious, irreverent, and probably the most honest guide to Europe ever written. Minor medieval cathedrals and boring museums? Blow 'em off! Instead, *Let's Blow* describes the key sites and how to see them as quickly as possible. Then, it takes you to the great bars, nightclubs, and restaurants that other guidebooks miss. Don't go to Europe without it! *"Absolutely hilarious!"—Booklist.* **$10.95**

Europe on 10 Salads a Day by Mary Jane & Greg Edwards. A must for the health-conscious traveler! From gourmet Indian cuisine in Spain to terrific take-out pizza in Italy, this book details over 200 health-food/vegetarian restaurants throughout Europe. *"Don't go to Europe without it"—Vegetarian Times.* **$9.95**

Europe for Free by Brian Butler. If you think a trip to Europe will be a long exercise in cashing traveler's checks, then this is the book for you. **Europe for Free** describes *thousands* of fun things to see and do all over Europe—and nothing costs one single lira, franc, or pfennig. *"A valuable resource"* — *U.P.I.* **$8.95**

DC for Free by Brian Butler. The author of *Europe for Free* has turned his talent for finding freebies on America's capital, and the result is a money-saving guide to hundreds of free things to do and see all over Washington, DC and its suburbs. *"Packed with valuable information"—Senior Times.* **$6.95**

The Nepal Trekker's Handbook by Amy R. Kaplan. A trek through the magnificent mountains and villages of Nepal is one of the world's most exotic—yet relatively accessible—adventures. This book informs would-be trekkers about every aspect of planning and enjoying a healthy, fun trek. From what medicines to carry to cultural *faux-pas*, it's an essential guide. *"A must"—Midwest Book Review.* **$9.95**

Hawaii for Free by Frances Carter. How could anyone improve on Hawaii, America's paradise? Simple. Make a vacation there a whole lot cheaper! From free pineapple to free camping to a free brewery tour, this book describes hundreds of fun things to do throughout Hawaii—and nothing costs one penny. *"Invaluable"* —*Aloha Magazine.* **$6.95**

Mustang books should be available at your local bookstore. If not, order directly from us. Send a check or money order for the price of the book—plus $1.50 for postage *per book* —to Mustang Publishing, P. O. Box 3004, Memphis, TN 38173. Allow three weeks for delivery. For rush, one-week delivery, add $3.50 postage. Foreign orders: U.S. funds only, please, and add $5.00 postage per book.